ENCYCLOPEDIA OF RAILWAYS

GENERAL EDITOR : O.S. NOCK

ENCYCLOPEDIA OF RAILWAYS

GENERAL EDITOR: O.S. NOCK

**Foreword by John Coiley, Keeper
British National Railway Museum**

OCTOPUS

International Editorial Consultants

Europe
Dr J N Westwood
Research fellow in history at the University of Birmingham, England.
Lately Senior History Lecturer, Sydney University, Australia.

USA
John H White Jnr
Curator, Division of Transportation, Smithsonian Institution, Washington DC USA

Canada
Raymond F Corley
Omer Lavallee
Authors of many railway books and directors of Railfare Enterprise Ltd.

Australia
John L Buckland
Author and photographer, Life member of the Australian Railway Historical Society.
Lately publications officer of the Australian Conservation Foundation.

New Zealand
Tom McGavin
Honorary Editor, The New Zealand Railway Observer; lately Publicity and Advertising
Manager, New Zealand Railways.

First published 1977 by Octopus Books Limited,
59 Grosvenor Street, London W1

© 1977 Octopus Books Limited
ISBN 0 7064 0604 4
Produced by Mandarin Publishers Limited
22a Westlands Road, Quarry Bay, Hong Kong

Printed in Hong Kong

CONTENTS

Endpapers: The cab of a British Midland Railway express locomotive No 158A.

Half title page: A SNCF diesel railcar on the Nice-Breil sur Roys line in the south of France.

Title page: Two South African Railways Class 25NC 4-8-4s at De Aar Junction, No 3428 *Ezette* and No 3465 *Carol*.

Contents page: Two 2-8-2s at Ojos de Agua on the Esquel branch line of the General Roca Railway in Patagonia, Argentina.

This page: A diesel-hauled Lima to Huancayo train at Meiggs, 4,270 m (14,000 ft) high in the Andes on the Central Railway of Peru.

FOREWORD

This encyclopedia relates the story of railways through-out the world so that their overall significance is better appreciated. In doing this the romance and fascination will become apparent and the wide interest understood.

Despite the compelling nature of the story it is difficult to explain the general sympathy engendered by railways. To some the answer will lie in the obvious appeal of the steam locomotive which many still regard as synonymous with railways. For a complete answer however a wider appreciation is required. It is necessary to go back prior to 1800, before the steam locomotive, to the beginning of the Industrial Revolution. Travel between towns and cities was relatively limited for most people and for all was a hard and often hazardous undertaking. The rapid development of railways from 1830 onwards led to immense social and economic changes. The railway offered a speed and flexibility for passengers and goods which the stagecoach and canals had never provided. Industry flourished, new towns appeared and gradually for many a new way of life opened up – especially town dwellers – the opportunity to live in or nearer the country, the chance of a day excursion into the country, to the races or the sea-side.

Today railways face very strong competition from road and air transport, nevertheless railways still have much to offer in the movement of heavy freight over long distances and passengers over short to medium distances, espe-cially commuter traffic. Furthermore, environmental and energy conservation considerations are currently tending to support future railway expansion in these directions. The most urgent requirement, however, is probably for the development of a greater flexibility in integrating with, rather than competing against, road and air trans-port both in practical terms and accountability.

I hope these few words about the railway story and the present position will put this volume in context and encourage the comparison between old and new to the benefit of the future. Fortunately, much of railway history can still be seen in museums and on privately preserved working steam lines from rural England to Colorado. In view of the impact of railways on society over the past 150 years it is not surprising there is a considerable enthusiast following for all aspects of railways. Much of this enthusiasm understandably centres round the steam locomotive now steadily disappearing even from Asia and Africa. It is to be hoped that this encyclopedia will widen still further the appeal of railways for their enthusiasts as well as those who simply wish to be well informed on all aspects of a very important mode of transport with an exciting future as well as an historic past.

John Coiley
Keeper
British National Railway Museum

HISTORY

GREAT BRITAIN

Railways before Stephenson

Wooden railways, guiding wooden waggons running on flanged wooden wheels, were probably first used in England in the early 16th century, the idea having arrived from Germany. These short lines were used inside mining enterprises and during the 18th century some were extended to carry coal to nearby wharves. The first iron rails were probably those used in Cumberland in 1728, and they soon became popular. The coal-mining area of Northumberland was served by as many as 20 lines in the 18th century, using gravity or horses as the motive force.

The first public railway, a line not purely for the use of a given industry, was the Surrey Iron Railway, opened from Wandsworth to Croydon in 1803. The first line to carry fare-paying passengers was the Oystermouth Railway, from Swansea to Oystermouth, in 1807.

Although Trevithick had shown in 1804 that a steam locomotive could pull a heavier load than a horse, it was not until 1812 that steam traction was shown to be a commercial proposition. In that year the railway from Middleton to Leeds,

Below: Richard Trevithick's *Catch-Me-Who-Can* of 1808. This was Trevithick's third locomotive. Its demonstration in London failed to attract financial backing and Trevithick, the 'father of the steam locomotive', built no further locomotives.

which had been authorized by a 1758 act of parliament as a coal-carrying line, was relaid to take steam locomotives working on Blenkinsop's rack system. The price of horse fodder having risen during the Napoleonic wars, steam traction was shown here to be an economic as well as a technical success. The Middleton Railway, though, was only a private industrial line.

The mine owners of Northumberland were not slow to imitate the Leeds example. One of their collieries, at Wylam, had tried a Trevithick locomotive as early as 1805, but found it too heavy for the track. In 1808, however, the wooden rails at Wylam were replaced by a cast-iron plateway, enabling locomotives to be used from 1813. These dispensed with the rack system, relying on the natural adhesion of wheel on rail. The success of *Puffing Billy* and its three consorts at Wylam colliery prompted a rival concern to introduce steam traction at nearby Killingworth colliery. It was George Stephenson who was entrusted with this new project, and his first locomotive appeared in 1814. This was similar to the Middleton locomotives, but without the rack. It was successful, and Stephenson proceeded to apply steam traction to several other local collieries. In 1817 he also built a locomotive for Scotland's first steam railway, the Kilmarnock and Troon plateway.

The age of Stephenson. 1820–1850

Stephenson's significance lies less perhaps in his locomotive work than in his railway-building. Like few others, he grasped the concept of a Britain criss-crossed by a network of steam railways. Like no other, he succeeded in arousing popular enthusiasm for this idea. Shrewd tactics, as well as a good product, enabled him to assert the claims of the locomotive over the equally plausible claims of steam-powered cable haulage. The first step from the short mining railway to the main lines of today was taken when, in 1821, he was appointed engineer of the Stockton & Darlington Railway.

This railway was built to cheapen transport of Durham coal to the coast. An earlier improvement had been effected by cutting a canal, and in 1820 there was a dispute as to whether a new canal or a tramroad should be the next step. The tramroad group won, headed by the Quaker Edward Pease, and obtained parliamentary powers in 1821. Two years later, convinced by Stephenson, Pease obtained an amending act permitting the use of locomotives. The line, surveyed mainly by Stephenson's son Robert, opened with great ceremony in 1825, being the first public steam railway. By this time edge rails rather than plate rails had been adopted, so it was indeed a true railway rather than a tramroad. Stephenson had also fixed the gauge at 4 ft 8 in to conform to the Killingworth gauge (half-an-inch was added later to reduce friction).

Although cable traction was used at the hilly inland end of the line, the coal trains were hauled over 20 miles of track by Stephenson's steam engines, horses being used for the passenger service. It could be said that the new railway was

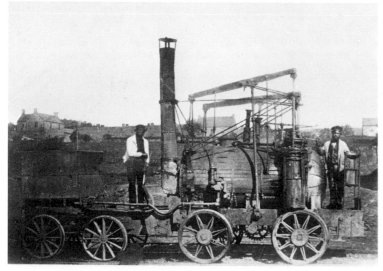

only an enlarged colliery line, but this is misleading, for it was a public undertaking; capital had been obtained from the public, and landowners who objected to the passage of the line over their land had been circumvented, placated, or overcome by parliamentary process. Over its metals the steam locomotive showed that it was potentially capable of long hauls.

It is the Liverpool & Manchester Railway, opened in 1830, which is regarded as the start of the Railway Age. Unlike the Stockton & Darlington, whose traffic was assured, the L&M was built to wrest traffic from canal and highway competitors. It used steam locomotives for both passenger and freight trains after the Rainhill locomotive trials, which it staged in 1829; it even entrusted to locomotive traction some steeply-graded line originally intended for cable haulage. Using locomotives of the Stephenson *Rocket* type, it carried in its first months much more traffic than had been anticipated, and its dividends were usually above ten per cent. It showed the potential profitability and usefulness of inter-city railways and was the inspiration of other railway projects in the 1830s.

The Lancastrians who had invested in the

Above left: Puffing Billy, the best-known of the Wylam colliery locomotives. It was built in 1814 and was still at work, slightly altered, in 1859.

Above: The Stephenson locomotive *Northumbrian*, an improved *Rocket*. The artist has included a suitably symbolic background in this scene of the L&MR.

Below: Early railway prints have left a useful record of how passengers and freight were carried.

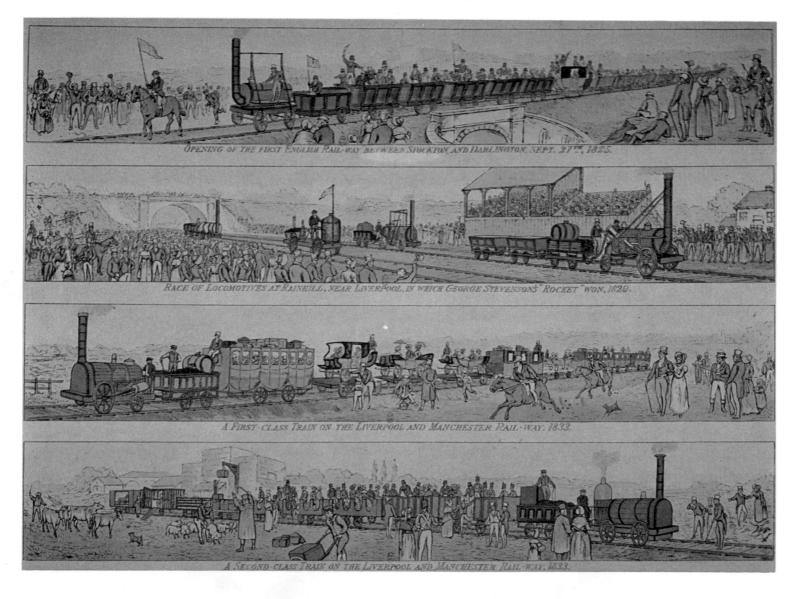

OPENING OF THE FIRST ENGLISH RAIL-WAY BETWEEN STOCKTON AND DARLINGTON, SEPT. 27TH, 1825.

RACE OF LOCOMOTIVES AT RAINHILL, NEAR LIVERPOOL, IN WHICH GEORGE STEVENSON'S "ROCKET" WON, 1829.

A FIRST-CLASS TRAIN ON THE LIVERPOOL AND MANCHESTER RAIL-WAY, 1833.

A SECOND-CLASS TRAIN ON THE LIVERPOOL AND MANCHESTER RAIL-WAY, 1833.

L&M were also prominent shareholders in the companies which followed it. Britain's first trunk railways, the Grand Junction, linking the L&M with Birmingham, and the London & Birmingham Railway, opened in 1837 and 1838, were among these. Many other companies were formed in the late 1830s, usually by local interests desiring to boost trade in their own locality, but increasingly by promoters seeking an outlet for the private capital which by this time was seeking railway shares.

From 1825 to 1840, inclusive, 2,420 km (1,500 miles) of railway were opened, of which about 1,770 km (1,100 miles) was in 1835 and after. By 1841 London was connected to Bristol by the Great Western Railway and to Southampton by the London & South Western Railway, while other main lines were extending towards Brighton, Dover, and Norwich. The shape of the future Midland Railway was already discernible in the lines, still unamalgamated, linking Gloucester, Birmingham, Derby and Leicester with York. The Newcastle & Carlisle Railway was almost finished, and so was the Edinburgh & Glasgow. In Ireland both Belfast and Dublin had short lines. Other short lines included the London & Greenwich, built on a viaduct, and the beginnings of the subsequently dense network in South Wales.

By 1840, the railways were a much-sought-after haven for private savings, and also for speculative funds. Most newly-promoted companies expected to pay dividends of more than 15 per cent, and their shares could be acquired for only a small deposit. Some investors accordingly signed up for blocks of shares for which they did not have the resources to pay in full, expecting to resell them at a profit almost immediately. For some years, therefore, new railways had little difficulty in raising capital. However, this 'Railway Mania' came to an end when general economic difficulties caused confidence to falter. The resulting crash of 1847 ruined many investors, but at least the boom of 1835 to 1846 had given Britain's railways a flying start. Without this inflow of capital the high but expensive standard of construction maintained by British engineers would have been put in question.

The new railways were soon seeking to defend their own territorial monopolies and to invade those of other lines. One railway would ally with another to buy off, purchase, or win control of a third line which seemed to threaten their joint interests. Some of the older and larger companies tended to restrict new investment to such defensive and offensive operations, rather than extending their lines into virgin territory. In these conflicts there emerged the 'railway king' who might control several lines and seek to win others. George Hudson, a York draper enabled by a legacy to buy his first railway shares, was the most famous of these. His bullying, wheedling, and dishonest tactics, combined with an intelligent lack of scruple, eventually gained him control of a fifth of Britain's mileage, with a particular strangle-hold on the Midlands and north-east, as well as a safe Tory seat in Parliament. But he was eventually outmanoeuvred, and fell from grace when it was revealed that he had paid dividends from capital, and had enriched himself at the expense of his shareholders. All the same, his activities had virtually created, from a collection of small lines, two of Britain's most prosperous companies, the North Eastern and Midland Railways.

Because of its pioneering role in railways, Britain's position of leadership in the industrial and technological revolution was maintained almost up to the end of the century. An obvious beneficiary was the engineering industry, which would supply much of the world's demand for railway equipment. However, railway transport as an industry paid heavy penalties for its early birth. In effect, the Railway Age came to Britain (and America) before there was a railway policy; the Railway Mania was perhaps one consequence of this, and so was the unplanned and often wasteful process of railway building. Too many companies were promoted and failed, too many built lines which could not pay or which were superfluous. It is true that new railway companies had to pass a private bill through Parliament in order to start work, but although this gave an opportunity for opponents to argue the case against each line, there was no guarantee that the railways most useful to the national interest would be those which were the most readily accepted.

In 1844 what became known as Gladstone's Railway Act attempted to bring more government supervision into railway affairs. Best known for its requirement that each company should run a daily 'parliamentary' train offering third-class passengers a reasonably comfortable ride at reasonably low fares, the act also tried to regulate construction of new railways. But while the 'par-

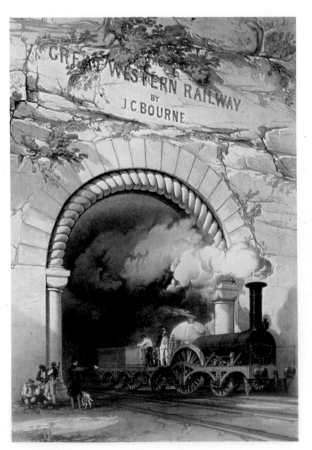

Right: An early Great Western train emerging from one of Brunel's tunnels, near Bath. The lofty portal (which narrows to a less extravagant bore a few yards inside) was intended to reassure apprehensive passengers.

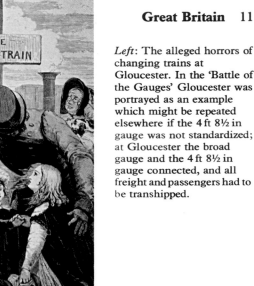

Left: The alleged horrors of changing trains at Gloucester. In the 'Battle of the Gauges' Gloucester was portrayed as an example which might be repeated elsewhere if the 4 ft 8½ in gauge was not standardized; at Gloucester the broad gauge and the 4 ft 8½ in gauge connected, and all freight and passengers had to be transhipped.

liamentary' trains, accepted reluctantly by many companies, were a great step towards the railways' eventual role as carriers of the masses, the attempt to limit new schemes was less successful, partly because the very fact of government intervention made investors even more confident in the security and value of railway shares.

As for railways in general, Queen Victoria had set all doubts at rest in 1842, when she was persuaded by Prince Albert to make her first train trip from Slough (near Windsor) over the Great Western Railway to the latter's London terminus at Paddington.

A company which was early in realizing that third-class passengers could be the most lucrative was the Midland Railway, one of whose constituent companies in 1840 carried 2,400 cheap-rate passengers in what was called an excursion train; the following year Thomas Cook founded his fame and fortune by organizing his own first excursion.

The Midland Railway was also one of the main protagonists in the 'Battle of the Gauges'. When George Stephenson perpetuated the 1,435 mm (4 ft 8½ in) gauge on the railways he engineered,

it was because he foresaw that one day Britain's railways would link up in a national network. However, there was no scientific reasoning behind that gauge. Naturally some engineers favoured others; a broader gauge promised better stability and lower costs per ton-mile, a narrower gauge was cheaper to build, especially in hilly terrain. The 'Battle of the Gauges' was fought mainly over the majestic 2,140 mm (7 ft 0¼ in) chosen by the Great Western's engineer, Brunel. Probably motivated by the desire to strike a damaging blow at Great Western finances, but arguing on the very real grounds that the difference in gauge required transhipment of passengers and freight at break-of-gauge stations, other companies demanded that the GWR conform to the 1,435 mm gauge. Parliament appointed a gauge commission, trials were held (in which the

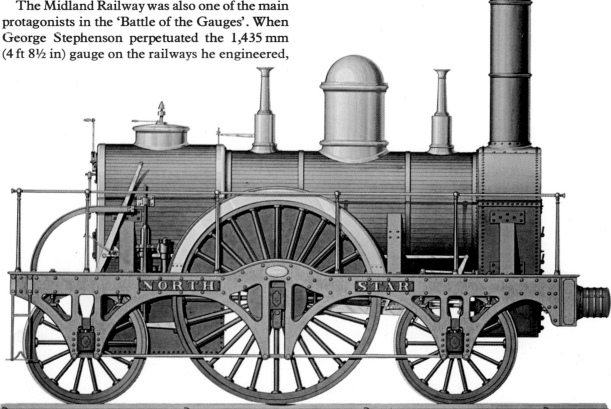

Left: One of the earliest and most successful of the Great Western Railway's locomotives, *North Star*. Built by Robert Stephenson in 1837, it hauled the first train from the Great Western's Paddington terminus on the Railway's opening day in 1838.

Right: A group of railway construction labourers (known as 'navvies' in Britain). Such men were hired by contractors, and their picks and shovels were the basic tools of railway-building. However, for moving materials and spoil, some contractors had their own locomotives; *Annie*, in this picture, was one such contractor's locomotive.

broad gauge triumphed), but in the end the greater mileage of the narrower-gauge companies prevailed. The Gauge Act of 1846 standardised 1,435 mm (4 ft 8½ in) and the GWR gradually reduced its broad-gauge mileage. The last GWR broad-gauge train ran in 1892. In Ireland, however, 1,600 mm (5 ft 3 in) was retained as the standard gauge.

Completion of the network. 1850–1880

On average, dividends paid by the early railways were much lower than expected, but because of low interest rates generally, railway shares remained attractive. The older companies tried to limit new construction, thereby restraining growth of the capital over which they would have to spread their dividends. The newer companies, often building lines which would obviously threaten the traffic of the older companies, in the expectation of being bought up, found that a greater share of capital had now to be raised by preference shares and loans.

By this time there were several big railway contractors in the business, men like Thomas Brassey and Samuel Peto, who had progressed from building the railways to actually financing them. They did this by accepting shares in the new railways as payment for building them. It was often contractors who were behind the various schemes for building lines to pressurize the older companies. A very successful contractor like Brassey, who built about 2,720 km (1,700 miles) of railway in Britain as well as nearly 4,800 km (3,000 miles) abroad, would seem to have had little need of such irresponsible strategies, but it was he who inspired and built the direct Portsmouth line which he then offered to the three companies which were already fighting each other for the Portsmouth traffic.

Because the successful opening of one new line was followed by construction of new feeder lines to it, because many localities were without railways and wanted them badly, and because the larger companies found that for one reason or another they needed new lines, mileage grew fast. There was a flurry of new projects just before and just after the Crimean war, and a minor railway boom in the 1860s. With government encouragement, railways began to co-operate rather than conflict. One company might secure, by negotiation or by parliamentary action, 'running powers' – the right to run its trains over a neighbouring railway. Thus for a time the Midland Railway gained valuable access to London by running its trains over part of the Great Northern. It soon found this was inadequate and built its own extension into the capital, but this kind of arrangement was quite common, and there were

Below: The *Flying Dutchman* of the Great Western Railway. The photograph was made in 1891, just as the broad-gauge era was coming to an end, and this broad-gauge train is passing over mixed-gauge track.

also agreements to end rate wars. Through running, especially of freight waggons, was facilitated in 1842 by the railways' establishment of the Railway Clearing House. Modelled on the great clearing banks, this office divided and allocated the revenue received from traffic running over several railways, levied agreed rentals when rolling stock was used over 'foreign' lines, and performed similar tasks.

Despite growing co-operation, there was occasional conflict in territory where two companies still struggled for dominance. The more extreme examples in the early stages involved brief struggles between opposing armies of workmen, and the placing of locomotives to block.

Traffic grew rapidly, as the railways both created and benefitted from economic growth. Until 1852 passenger revenue exceeded freight, for it was easier to attract new travellers, and to draw existing travellers from the road coaches, than it was to win traffic from the canals which had provided a reliable and cheap service, and well into the railway age paid better dividends than did the railways. So strong was their competition that the railways either bought them up, or made agreements with them.

In 1865 the railways carried 252 million passengers, not including commuters; travel was now within the reach of all but the very poorest. The new middle classes, and indeed the skilled working class, began to take their annual holidays at the seaside. Businessmen could travel as a matter of course. Workers could move to new jobs without feeling cut-off entirely from their families. Regular contact between scattered relatives was possible through the Penny Post, itself made practicable by the railways; the first travelling post office, in which mail was sorted en route, and which could pick up and set down mailbags at speed, appeared on the London to Liverpool route as early as 1838.

Meanwhile, railway freight services enabled industries to expand, and not necessarily be sited at the source of their bulkiest raw material. The

inland coalfields could compete more effectively, and indeed cheaper transport widened the market for all coal; by the 1860s more coal was carried to London by rail than by sea. Moreover, as traffic grew, so did efficiency; once track was laid, relatively little extra expense was incurred in passing heavier or more frequent trains over it. This enabled rates to be kept low. Most railways were not run simply as profit-making enterprises; their managers, like their promoters, felt a responsibility towards the areas they served. Their main aim was to increase traffic. Rate wars between railways were ended by agreement in the 1850s; henceforth competition, where it existed, would be maintained by service rather than by price.

Nevertheless, the railways were not held high in public esteem. Partly this was because of a general anxiety that they were undermining the accepted concepts of competition. Ostensibly the railways were competing against each other, but tended to act like a monopoly. Competition in the matter of fares and rates had been eliminated by mutual agreement coupled with government intervention. Where genuine competition did exist, as in Kent, where the South Eastern and London, Chatham & Dover railways provided competing services and duplicated stations for almost every town, the result was seen to be wasteful expenditure on a few prestige services and economies elsewhere.

Above: Construction of a British main line. This watercolour of 1841 shows the expensive earthworks required to satisfy the engineers' preference for going through, rather than around or over, the natural obstacles which they encountered.

Left: One of the earliest of the large freight sheds. This example was built by the Great Western Railway at Bristol.

Below: A fee-paid stamp used for letters sent by passenger trains of the Lancashire, Derbyshire and East Coast Railway.

A long-standing influence was the publicity accorded by the press to railway accidents. The first railways had a much better safety record than the road coaches which they displaced, but rare railway collisions were much more spectacular than overturnings of coaches. As trains became longer and faster, accidents became more serious even though they became rarer. In 1868 the *Irish Mail*'s collision with an oil train at Abergele, and the resulting deaths of over 30 people, made a lasting impression on the public mind. The South Eastern Railway was doubly unfortunate in the derailment of its continental boat train in 1865, because Charles Dickens was among the passengers, and he lived to tell the tale. In 1879 came the most horrific accident of all, when the pride of the North British Railway, the new 80-span bridge over the river Tay, collapsed in a storm, taking a train and 73 people with it. As with air accidents a century later, inquiries often blamed 'human error' as the cause of these catastrophes. The press was more just when it pointed out that perhaps 'human error' would be less frequent if operating men were not required to work 12 hours or more at a stretch, and if managers tried to anticipate where accidents were most likely to occur.

When the first railways were built, there was little managerial talent on which to draw. The only business with any resemblance at all to that of the railways was the business of war, so just as ex-soldiers made up a large part of those who built the railways, so did ex-officers make up a large part of the managing staff. An officer, after all, knew something about handling large bodies of men, not all of whom would be actually under his eye. An exception was the virtual creator of the London & North Western Railway, Mark Huish.

Top: An 0–4–0, nicknamed 'Coppernob', of the Furness Railway. Edward Bury, its designer, favoured bar frames and the so-called 'haycock' firebox.

Above: The heraldic crest of the Lancashire and Yorkshire Railway.

Below: Broad-gauge locomotives awaiting scrap or conversion to standard gauge at the Swindon Works of the Great Western Railway.

A very able, very unscrupulous, and very successful administrator, he had begun his career with the East India Company. The master-and-coolie relationships which he established were perpetuated by his successor, Moon. Despite the uncompromising nature of such managers, railwaymen took great pride in their jobs and were loyal to their companies.

By 1873 the railways employed 275,000 men, and although there had been sporadic attempts to form 'combinations', each man was still on his own when dealing with management. Most managements tried to maintain the 'just but strict' ideal of paternalism, and harsh discipline certainly did not diminish the loyalty which individual workers felt for their particular company. Working for the railway brought prestige, and in the early decades railways trained and disciplined men who came straight from the land without any marketable skill. Railwaymen believed that they had good job security, and by and large they did. But in times of depression railways could best economise by shedding labour, as they could not temporarily reduce their track or rolling stock. Also, men could be more easily dismissed for

misconduct than in other industries. This was justifiable, because incompetence, and especially drunkenness, put lives at risk. That railwaymen were a special case had been implied by legislation in 1840 and 1842 which allowed a railway management to hand over to a Justice of the Peace any worker found drunk or negligent.

One of the problems of management was the need to supervise men who might be working miles away from any senior manager. In the early days, and after, the temptation of station staff to steal money was sometimes irresistible. An exceptional theft was that of the registrar of the Great Northern Railway, who in 1857 was transported to Australia after defrauding the company of almost £250,000. More important than financial honesty, however, was safety, and there was a very real problem involved in ensuring that locomen and guards would discipline themselves to observe all the regulations, even when out of sight of a superior. The problem was largely sol-

ved by making signalmen responsible for reporting irregularities.

A Golden Age (1880–1919)

By 1880 the British railway network was virtually complete, with well over 24,000 km (15,000 miles) of mainly double-track route in operation. This was three-quarters of the ultimate mileage; the only important lines remaining to be built in the next 40 years were the last main line to London, that of the Great Central Railway, in 1899, the coal-carrying Hull & Barnsley Railway, some long lines in the north of Scotland, some alternative routes built by large companies, and a number of cut-off routes. Cut-offs were built to reduce the distance between traffic centres, and were undertaken especially by the Great Western. The GWR's cut-offs included a direct South Wales line avoiding Bristol and using the 7.2 km (4½ mile) Severn tunnel, which had been completed with great difficulty in 1886;

Above: A landslip on the Bristol and Exeter Railway near Dawlish. This line was engineered by Brunel, and later became part of the Great Western Railway. The picturesque section along the sea front has always been subject to landslips and storm damage.

Bottom left: *Peel*, one of the sixty *Problem* class passenger locomotives of the London and North Western Railway. These machines were built in the early 1860s, and had driving wheels of 2,311.4 mm (7 ft 7 in) diameter.

Below: Comparatively few narrow-gauge lines were built in Britain. This is an early photograph of one of the best-known, the Talyllyn Railway in Wales.

a London to Devon route shorter than that via Bristol; and a direct line to Banbury and the Midlands. There was also a brief blossoming of narrow-gauge railways and, after the Light Railways Act of 1896, of light railways built to lower technical standards to serve rural localities.

When the railways fell under government control in 1914 the route mileage of approximately 32,000 km (20,000 miles) was divided between a multiplicity of companies, each with its own style of architecture, locomotives, and uniforms. Certain technical norms were standardized between companies, however. Almost from the very first years couplings had been made uniform, to permit through running. Passenger vehicles were linked by the screw coupling, first applied on the Liverpool & Manchester Railway to eliminate slackness of the chains which jolted passengers from their seats when the train started. However, British railways, unlike those of Europe, never applied this coupling to freight trains and the loose chain and hook method continued, causing wear-and-tear and breakage of goods in transit.

Lever-operated handbrakes were applied to most freight vehicles. Before downward inclines trains had to stop while brakemen walked along to pin down these brakes. The need for a brake which could be operated along the full length of the train, and which would be automatic ('fail safe') particularly if a coupling should part, was recognised by press and public long before the railways did anything about it. The best brake was the American Westinghouse system, using compressed air. A British alternative, slightly less effective, was the vacuum brake. But the railways did not wish to spend the large sums of money involved; many passengers died before parliament forced the railways to act.

Some railways (the Midland for example, which staged the Newark brake trials of 1875) acted creditably, but most did not. Especially

nefarious was the LNWR. Its chief mechanical engineer, Webb, extracted great royalties from successive versions of his own non-automatic so-called continuous brake before an act of parliament put a stop to this income. The act, inspired by a Royal Commission set up after 80 Irish holiday makers had been killed in the 1889 Armagh accident, compelled the fitting of continuous and automatic brakes. The LNWR then proceeded, in the name of railway politics, to organize the so-called 'Euston block' of railways around the use of the vacuum brake, at a time when several rivals were inclining to the Westinghouse air brake. This tactic contributed to the situation where two kinds of brake were (and still are) used in Britain; through passenger vehicles running over the lines of companies using different systems had to be expensively dual-fitted.

Around the turn of the century it seemed that the competitive system, subject to government supervision, really did work. The government had stepped in to impose reliable brakes, and also to compel interlocking of signals on main lines, so that one signal could not conflict with another or with a point (switch). It is true that competition's effect on the standard of service seemed to be concentrated on a few prestige items; the 'Race to the North' in which the two rival groups of companies of the east and west coast routes tried to outpace each other on the run to Aberdeen, was one famous instance. Another was the struggle of the London & South Western and Great Western for the traffic from transatlantic liners calling at Plymouth.

Apart from direct competition, whose benefits were doubtful, there was the example-setting made possible by existence of many companies; a successful innovation by one would be followed by the others. This was especially marked when, in the mid-1870s, the Midland Railway began to provide the hitherto somewhat despised third-

Above left: The ceremonial banner of a branch of the locomotive men's trade union, nowadays well-known as ASLEF.

Above: A lounge car, one of several luxury vehicles included by the LMS Railway in its best trains. Such accommodation was designed to attract public attention rather than public patronage, and was never expected to yield a profit.

Right: A suburban passenger train guard of 1907. Although the term had yet to be invented, the 'corporate image' was very much emphasised by the British railway companies through distinctive uniforms, locomotives and decor.

Below: Interior of a LNWR boat train before the first world war. The LNWR took great pride in these trains, which ran from London to Liverpool.

COFFEE & CIGARS.
L. & N.W. AMERICAN SPECIAL.

class passenger with padded seats, and dropped the custom of confining such passengers to the slower trains. This was very much resented by most of the other companies, but they gradually followed suit and discovered that third-class traffic, because there were many more passengers per vehicle, could be highly profitable. Second class was then gradually eliminated. Other benefits received by passengers in this period were the increasing use of bogie vehicles, and of coaches lit with gas (later electricity). The GWR was the first, in 1891, to introduce a gangwayed all-corridor train.

The lower-paid also benefitted by the Cheap Trains Act of 1883. This, while reducing the statutory requirement of a daily 'parliamentary' train to the requirement to provide sufficient accommodation at one penny per mile, also required suburban lines to operate workmens' services in the early morning and early evening at very low fares. The first such trains had been introduced voluntarily years earlier by the London, Chatham & Dover and other railways, and did much to encourage the growth of city suburbs.

A technical advance with which a few companies experimented variously, while gaining encouragement from each others' successes, was electrification. The NER electrified 53 km (33 miles) from 1904 to 1906 at 600 volts; the Lancashire & Yorkshire converted several suburban lines, experimenting with a different system on each, while the LBSC and Midland went as high as 6,500 and 6,600 volts. All these lines were short, but the London & South Western Railway had a scheme for extensive conversion at 650 volts dc of its London suburban network. Part of this scheme, the London (Waterloo) to Wimbledon conversion, was completed in 1915.

Many improvements, especially those of comfort or safety, brought higher costs but not higher revenues. This was one cause of the railways' declining profitability. Probably more serious, around the turn of the century, were price increases in the railways' two most important inputs, labour and coal. Railwaymen had succeeded in forming credible trade unions and launching strikes which achieved at least part of their aims. In the 1890s, in particular, the General Railway Workers Union (mainly for the lower paid, and rather militant), the Amalgamated Society of Railway Servants, and the somewhat superior Associated Society of Locomotive Engineers & Firemen emerged as real forces.

Although a six-week strike in Scotland was superficially unsuccessful, it prompted parliament, in 1893, for the first time to regulate the working hours of adult males, in this case of railwaymen. A setback to trades unionism was the Taff Vale strike of 1900, in which management successfully sued the union for damages. In 1911 there was a widespread strike; its main achievement was that government pressure forced the companies for the first time to sit down and talk with the unions; hitherto only the North Eastern Railway had shown readiness to recog-

nise them. In 1913 there was a realignment of the various railway unions. The ASRS, the GRWU and the Signalmen joined to form the National Union of Railwaymen, but the grander clerks and locomen maintained their own separate and not especially fraternal unions.

On the outbreak of war in 1914 the government took control, but not ownership, of the companies. They were operated as a co-ordinated network by the Railway Executive Committee, which consisted of nine leading company managers and had been established, as a precaution, in 1912. The railways were given a financial guarantee, based on their 1913 dividends, and wage increases paid because of rising living costs were also financed by the government. However, the government's undertaking to pay compensation for deferred and increased maintenance costs was denied immediately the war ended. The Treasury and Board of Trade refused to pay the companies until one railway took them expensively to court.

In exchange, government traffic was carried free. Much of this was over the South Eastern & Chatham and the London & South Western Railways, which served the Channel ports. Carriage of the British Expeditionary Force to France was rapid and trouble-free; even Kitchener praised the railways. The North British and Highland railways were the two most affected by increased traffic flows, due to the heavy coal and personnel movements to Thurso for the Grand Fleet; the latter company, single-track and never prosperous, borrowed equipment from others to solve its crisis. Other locomotives and vehicles were sent to France. Railway workshops turned to war production, while many skilled workers joined the army (and in due course many were returned to railway service, when they were more needed). In 1917 passenger services were greatly reduced, and fares correspondingly raised.

Amalgamation and Nationalization 1920–1947

The Railway Executive made such a good job of organizing the railways in wartime that, to many, a return to the uncoordinated competition of the old companies was unthinkable. After the war the railways were not handed back by the government until 1921, and in those last three years there was much discussion about nationalization.

In 1920 the government published a White Paper which rejected nationalization but recommended amalgamation of the old companies into seven big new railways (Western, Southern, North Western, Eastern, North Eastern, London, Scotland). An advanced feature of this plan was inclusion of railway-worker representatives on the boards of the new companies. However, opposition to this plan led to a slightly different amalgamation plan being adopted in the Railways Act of 1921. This omitted all mention of worker representation, although it did contain what for the time was an almost equally radical provision, an obligation of the new companies to undertake collective bargaining with the trades unions.

The Railways Act came into force on January

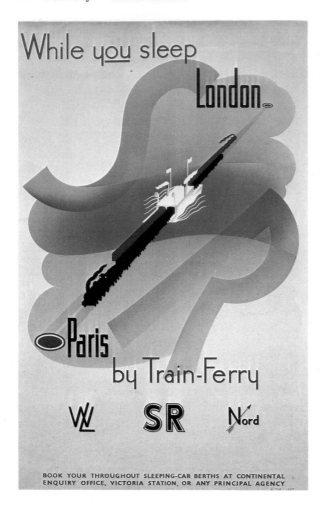

While you sleep

London.

Paris

by Train-Ferry

W̌ L̆   SR   N̂ord

BOOK YOUR THROUGHOUT SLEEPING-CAR BERTHS AT CONTINENTAL
ENQUIRY OFFICE, VICTORIA STATION, OR ANY PRINCIPAL AGENCY

1, 1923, and established just four new companies, each having, in the main, a territorial monopoly. The Great Western Railway was the only old name to survive this amalgamation; it combined with the central and southern Welsh railways to become the company responsible for the western part of England, possessing 6,000 km (3,700 miles) of route. In the inter-war period it remained the most prestigious of the new companies. It installed automatic train control on all its main lines, something which the other companies failed to do, and thereby drastically reduced the frequency of collision.

The new Southern Railway became the most enterprising of the new companies. It was the smallest of the new groups, possessing only 3,500 km (2,200 miles) of route. It was formed largely by the joining of the old London & South Western, London, Brighton & South Coast, and South Eastern & Chatham railways. Most of its revenue came from passengers, even though the port of Southampton, which it owned and managed, originated considerable freight. Its principal preoccupation was electrification, and it extended the 650 volt third-rail electrification system of the old London & South Western Railway to cover not only London's southern suburbs but also a new outer suburban zone which extended as far south as Brighton and Portsmouth (119 km or 74 miles).

Second in size of the new companies was the London & North Eastern, with 10,600 km (6,600 miles). This covered eastern England and eastern and central Scotland, being essentially an amalgamation of the old Great Northern, Great Eastern, Great Central, North Eastern, North

British, and Great North of Scotland railways. It would win renown in the thirties with its streamlined trains, hauled by the locomotives of Nigel Gresley; *Mallard*, which broke a world record at 203 km/h (126 mph), was an LNER locomotive. This railway also experimented with steam railcars and towards the end of its life had undertaken Britain's first real main line electrification, from Manchester over the Pennines to Sheffield, on the 1,500 volt overhead system.

Biggest of the new companies was the London, Midland & Scottish. This was of 12,500 km (7,800 miles), and served the Midlands, the north-west, and much of Scotland. It was really too big for efficient management, and the senior staff of its main constituent companies (the Midland, London & North Western, Lancashire & Yorkshire, Caledonian, Glasgow & South Western and Highland railways) had difficulty in working amicably together.

The LMS later led the other companies in adoption of diesel locomotives for shunting, and in mass production of rolling stock. Like its ostensible rival, the LNER, it derived much valuable publicity from its streamlined locomotives and trains. Shortly before nationalization, it ordered two diesel-electric main line locomotives which were the progenitors of one of the best British Railway diesels, the Class 40. Its staff relations were fairly good, but various economy drives, sometimes mean-spirited, meant that its employees did not feel much affection for it.

The main problem faced by the British railways was loss of traffic to the rapidly-growing road-haulage industry. This competition had been accelerated by the first world war, the aftermath of which saw the release to civilian life of second-hand army trucks and army-trained truck drivers. The traffic lost was high-value merchandise, which traditionally paid high freight rates.

Above: One of the special bulk trains which, in the 1970s, were regarded by British Rail as the most promising source of freight revenue; a type 40 diesel-electric locomotive at Edinburgh with a train of bulk cement vehicles.

Top left: A Southern Railway poster of the 1930s. Although in many respects conservative, the inter-war companies were leading patrons of advanced styles in art, architecture and decor.

Below: A London-bound electric multiple unit train near Dover in 1975. The third rail system of electrification begun before the first world war by the L & SWR was extended by the Southern Railway, and later by British Rail, to cover most of south-east England.

Countermeasures by the railways included political action, which helped to secure the Road Traffic Act of 1931. This, to a small degree, made it more difficult for road hauliers to start new services, and more expensive (through license fees) to run any service. However, the continued requirement that railways, unlike road operators, should reveal the rates they charged, weakened their competitive position.

The second world war brought relief from road competition, but presented new problems. Air bombardment, though it caused less than 1,000 fatalities, disrupted operations which were already complicated by the blackout, changing traffic flows, and under-manned maintenance services. Passenger services were somewhat restricted, and an advertising campaign was launched with the slogan 'Is your journey really necessary?' As in the first world war, the railways were taken over by the government, working through the Ministry of Transport and its Railway Executive Committee.

Modern Times (1948–1976)

Nationalization of major public service industries was prominent in the manifesto of the Labour Party, which gained power in 1945, and on January 1, 1948 the four railway companies became British Railways. The jibe that on that date the British stopped operating railways and began to play at trains is unfair, but nevertheless is not without a measure of justification. A successful organizational structure was never devised, and repeated organizational changes only introduced uncertainty and discontinuity. Such changes included abolition of the initial Railway Executive and British Transport Commission, and introduction of the British Railways Board (BRB) as the top policy-making body. The operating regions which replaced the old companies were frequently trimmed or extended, and the North Eastern Region was eventually absorbed by the Eastern (the other regions are the Scottish, Western, Southern, and London Midland).

In its early years BR coped with general post-war economic difficulties, a savage press campaign designed to show that nationalization could not work, a maintenance backlog, and internal animosities. One of its first acts was to construct an unnecessary new range of standard steam locomotives. In 1955 it decided to eliminate steam traction, and the last steam locomotive was built only seven years before the running of

the last steam train in 1967. An equally unwise diesel policy followed the modernization plan of 1955. Although six designs of diesel locomotive would have sufficed, by 1967 BR had bought well over 40 different types from various makers, usually in small lots and with little compatibility between the different designs. Moreover, the most experienced and successful builder of diesel locomotives, General Motors in the United States, was excluded from this flood of orders.

With diesel multiple-unit trains the situation was even less rational – over 200 different types and sub-types were built when three would have been sufficient. Some of these acquisitions were unsatisfactory, and many had very short lives. At the same time, a much more urgent improvement was postponed because of lack of funds. This was the equipment of British wagons with the air brake, as used on most other railways. Failure to make this change meant that Britain would remain alone among the advanced nations in operating unbraked freight trains.

Meanwhile, with the re-emergence of highway transport and the spread of the family car, traffic dropped at a time when labour and fuel costs were rising. The appointment of a successful industrialist, Beeching, to take charge of BR, marked the beginning of a new climate of opinion. His two reports of 1963 and 1965 recommended, in particular, elimination of loss-making services so that the railways could devote all their resources to handling the bulk longer-distance traffic for which they were most suited. There followed in the mid-1960s withdrawal of many branch and secondary services, so that route-mileage fell to about 18,500 km (11,500 miles). Despite the inevitable loss of jobs, the trade unions in general acquiesced in this policy, with the result that from 1963 to 1969 traffic per employee increased by almost a half. After that, however, productivity improvements tailed off and in 1976 BR still employed an excessive labour force, especially in its administrative grades.

Meanwhile, however defective the organizational structure, there was a high level of technical competence in BR which, when not discouraged, could produce good results. Electrification schemes were successfully carried out, resulting in increased traffic. Fast container trains (Freightliners) won back some high-value traffic from the highways, while unit trains carried bulk commodities efficiently and with high utilization of equipment. Centralised Train Control has eliminated the majority of signal boxes on principal routes and reduced train delays. The high speed train (HST), first introduced in 1976, brought top speeds of 200 km/h (125 mph) to passenger services. The tilting-body advanced passenger train (APT), expected in 1978, would bring even higher speeds without realignment of curved track. Although a plausible case could be made that BR was investing capital in glamorous trains rather than in less spectacular fields which would give a greater return (automatic fare collection, for example), the new passenger trains have had a very positive impact on the British public's opinion of its railways.

Below: The prototype APT (Advanced Passenger Train) of British Rail. A tilting body and applied research into wheel-rail interaction will enable these trains to move at 150 mph (250 km/h) with little re-alignment of existing curves.

HISTORY

FRANCE

Although in 1769 Nicholas Cugnot had demonstrated his steam carriage on the streets of Paris, it was not until the 1830s that the first French steam railways appeared. Early lines were built in the mining area of St Etienne, linking the coalfield with the Rhône and Loire rivers. The first of these lines had been operational from 1827, using 40 horses, each pulling four wagons, to link Pont-de-l'Ane with Andrézieux.

In 1830, the first section of another line, destined to link St Etienne with Lyon, was opened. When complete in 1832, this double-track railway was 58 km (36 miles), and marked a notable advance. Its engineer was Marc Seguin, who was prepared to spend capital on tunnels, earthworks and viaducts in order to obtain a shorter and easily-graded route. Seguin had visited England, was acquainted with Stephenson, and able to make his own contribution to steam locomotive technology. His railway had ordered two Stephenson locomotives as models, after which Seguin built two locomotives of his own design. These were fitted with multi-tubular

boilers, in which Seguin was a pioneer, and with axle-driven fans to provide a good draught. In 1831, this line gained further distinction by providing a passenger service. A third line, from Andrézieux to Roanne, was opened in 1833.

Knowledge of events in Britain and America, and the successful operation of the St Etienne lines, aroused the enthusiasm of the Saint-Simonite social philosophers. The railway seemed to fit admirably into their scheme for an ideal society based on free industrial activity; one of them, Michel Chevalier, started a ten-year public discussion in 1832 with a newspaper article proposing a Mediterranean railway. France was then an agricultural nation with good roads and canals, but the Saint-Simonites held that France could and should have railways too; it was simply necessary to devote to railway construction the funds which were habitually spent on making war. Lively discussion of the railway question was a major preoccupation of the press and the National Assembly for a decade. In this debate, which at least made Frenchmen very conscious of railway problems, even if it did little to bring railways into existence, was a strong ideological current which would persist for decades. Opponents of private companies, in their advocacy of state railways, claimed in the 1830s that railways were inherently aristocratic, in the 1840s that they were essentially royalist, and during the Third Republic that they were undoubtedly anti-republican. It was this ideological trend that explains the viciousness of the abuse to which the railways were subject right up to their nationalization in 1938.

While the public arguments were raging, the government granted a few concessions to companies seeking to build lines which would obviously be a part of any future railway plan; from Paris to Rouen and Le Havre, Lille to Dunkerque, Strasbourg to Basle, and a few others. Public opinion had begun to swing in favour of railways after the Pereire brothers had built the Paris–St Germain line in 1837. As they had calculated, to

Right: Nicholas Cugnot's steam carriage of 1769.

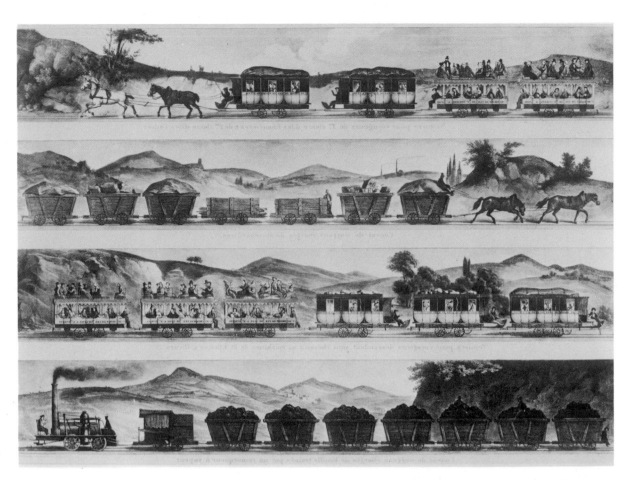

Top: The railway from Lyon to St Etienne, the first to use steam traction in France. These views show the line as it was in the early 1830s, when horses were still used to haul the passenger trains. The third picture shows the first and second class passenger cars moving by gravity between St Etienne and Givors.

win France it was necessary to win Paris, and Paris was won by building a steam railway which conveyed Parisians to their weekend promenades in the woods of St Germain. But most of the other companies soon exhausted their capital and the state in 1840 took a significant step by agreeing to guarantee the interest on the Paris–Orléans Railway's shares, making it easier for that company to raise fresh capital.

The growing realization that the state-versus-private enterprise debate was ignoring the main issue, which was how to find the money to build trunk railways, persuaded the Assembly to pass the compromise Railway Law of 1842, which envisaged both state and private participation. By that year only 580 km (360 miles) of line had been opened, but the 1842 railway plan envisaged lines radiating from Paris to the Belgian frontier, the Channel ports, to Marseille via Lyon, to the Spanish frontier via Toulouse and via Tours and Bordeaux, to Rouen and Le Havre, and to Brest via Nantes. There were also to be two cross-country lines from Marseilles to Bordeaux and from Dijon to Mulhouse. The government, helped by local authorities, was to provide the land, roadbed, and engineering works, and to this infrastructure the companies would bring their superstructure: track, rolling stock, buildings, and personnel. This law did not work quite as had been intended; local authorities soon escaped their share of the burden while the private companies, many of which were soon bankrupt, obtained more favourable financial conditions. But some important principles remained: state cooperation and intervention, the state's right to claim ownership after a period of company ownership (99 years became the accepted period, but the state had the right of earlier purchase), the

Centre: Doubledeck passenger vehicles could be found in France almost from the beginning of the railway age. This picture shows one of the earliest varieties in use on a holiday suburban train.

Below: Marc Seguin's pioneer locomotive for the St Etienne line. His fan arrangement for stimulating the fire is immediately behind the locomotive.

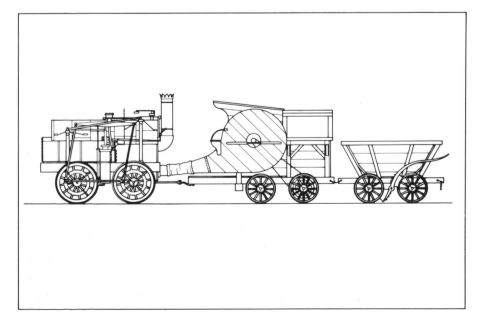

Above: Inside a locomotive workshop towards the end of the 19th century: In reality, activity was usually less frenetic than this picture suggests, the artist having compressed several operations into one moment of time.

failed to complete their concessions and the state had to step in to finish the work. But capital was more easily obtained after 1851, when the practice of financing the companies by bonds as well as shares began.

Initially subject to British influence, French railway engineering soon evolved a style of its own. The British-designed and -built structures of the Paris–Le Havre line, expensively built in order to provide a cheaply-operated and long-lasting route, were matched elsewhere by French engineers. Tunnels and long high viaducts became a mark of French railways as much as of British. Indeed, the Nerthe tunnel near Marseille, opened in 1848 and with a length of 4,639 m (5,155 yards), was well in advance of its time and showed what could be achieved in difficult terrain. French signalling, too, soon took a distinctive form, tending to indicate maximum speeds rather than the route to be followed, and with a predilection for chequerboard and disc indications. Three early French engineers who influenced world locomotive design were Giffard, who invented the cone feedwater injector in 1859, Le Chatelier, who as early as the 1840s showed the importance of correct locomotive balancing, and de Pambour, who designed the first practical steam pressure gauge. Later in the century, Flaman of the Est Railway invented the locomotive speed recorder, which provided a documentary statement of the speeds reached during a run; this was called the *mouchard* by resentful locomotive crews, who were punished if the machine revealed infringements of speed limits. The French school of locomotive design really had its beginnings with Polonceau of the PO Railway, who from 1850 introduced a range of truly French locomotives. Hitherto, the British tradition had prevailed, Robert Stephenson being the main influence, with designs by the Englishmen Buddicom and Crampton also having widespread popularity. Polonceau's successor, Forquenot, was notable for imposing a wholesale standardization both of designs and components, and his 2–4–2 passenger locomotives were so efficient that they survived until after the second world war.

Under the Second Empire, in which modern technology was admired and public criticism suppressed, the railways seemed destined for a period of prosperity and expansion. But general financial difficulties in France stifled many expectations. Meanwhile, the multiplicity of small companies was becoming a hindrance. At the end of 1851, the 3,800 km (2,360 miles) of route were divided between 28 companies, but in the following years there was a series of mergers so that by 1858 the network was divided between six companies, each with a territorial monopoly.

Of these the oldest was the Nord Railway, whose origins went back to 1842. This connected Paris with Calais, the Belgian frontier, and the mining areas centred on Lille. Owned by the Rothschilds, who were struggling with the Pereires' Crédit Mobilier for control of the French railway system, it was a prosperous company with heavy traffic and easy terrain. The sec-

state's right to enforce its plan of the network, to supervise tariffs and safety standards, and to have its representatives on company boards. Also, the plan ensured that Paris would be the hub of the railway system, a promise that many Frenchmen criticized for favouring one part of the country over the others.

By 1848 France had built about 2,000 km (1,250 miles) of railway, compared to about 6,000 km (3,750 miles) in Britain and more than 5,000 km (3,100 miles) in Germany. The 1848 Revolution was damaging for the railways, which were sabotaged in several localities; stations were demolished and bridges burned. Railway workers demanded not only wage increases but the expulsion of foreign railwaymen; apart from well-known British engineers like Locke (who engineered the Paris–Le Havre line) and Buddicom (who built British-type locomotives in French workshops), many lesser British mechanics had been hired by French railways, and this had aroused great resentment. These difficulties, and concurrent financial troubles, together with revolutionary politics, almost led to nationalization. Even with the installation of the Cavaignac government, which did not favour nationalization, the companies continued to encounter financial problems despite the restoration of traffic and confidence. Many companies

ond company, the Paris–Orléans, originated in the Paris–Orléans Railway of 1843 and owned the Paris–Bordeaux main line; a feature of the latter was that it did not enter the two major intermediate cities, Orléans and Tours, because of the initial hostility of their citizens. The second main line of this company, from Orléans to Toulouse, would be opened later in the century. The Paris–Lyon–Méditerranée Railway was an amalgamation of the Paris–Lyon, Lyon–Méditerranée, Lyon – Genève, Dauphine, and Grand Central railways. The Grand Central, the 'Bourbonnais' line, had been a vital bone of contention in the struggle between the Pereires and Rothchilds, having been intended to provide a second route from Paris to the Mediterranean through the Massif Central. With its long and busy main line, serving the three great French cities of Paris, Lyon and Marseille, the PLM could be regarded as the biggest of the French railways; in 1867 it would additionally absorb the Savoy lines formerly belonging to the Italian state of Piedmont.

The Est Railway was distinct because it was regarded as a strategic railway, and for that reason had more double track than was commercially necessary. Serving the area adjacent to the German frontiers, it had its origins in the former Strasbourg Railway, and included the Paris–Strasbourg, Paris–Mulhouse main lines to which in 1860 it would add the new Paris–Reims–Charleville line. The Ouest Railway was a merger of companies which already shared the terminus at St Lazare in Paris. These were the Normandie, St Germain, and Bretagne companies, and the main lines of the Ouest were from Paris to Le Havre, to Cherbourg, to Granville, and to Brest. Finally, there was the Midi Company, very much the creation of the Pereires (who were natives of Bordeaux). Still incomplete in

1914, it had a main line from Bordeaux to Toulouse and Sète inaugurated in 1857, and also undertook the Bordeaux–Bayonne and Narbonne–Perpignan lines. It did much to promote the tourist attractions of southern France, and was the only big company without access to Paris.

In return for its support and protection, the imperial government expected the companies to co-operate in extending railways to localities which were now demanding them. Largely for political reasons, the creation of what was, after 1859, termed the 'new network' began. The companies had no government subsidy in building these light-traffic lines which they did not really want; but under the Franqueville Convention of 1859 they did have a government guarantee of interest on capital invested in the new lines (in return for which they agreed to let the government share in profits above a certain level made

Top: The impressive opening ceremony at Dijon in 1851 of the Lyon to Dijon line. This line later became part of the Paris–Lyon–Méditerranée Railway, France's greatest trunk railway.

Above: Cable traction on the heavily-graded suburban line from Lyon to Croix-Rousse.

by either the 'old network' or the 'new network'.)
Even with the 'new network' complete there were
many areas still without a railway, but after 1865
departments and communes were encouraged to
build their own 'local-interest' lines. The example had been set by the Bas–Rhin department,
which had successfully financed the construction
of three short lines in the Strasbourg area. The
1865 concept envisaged lines of up to about
40 km (25 miles), usually metre-gauge, not competing with the big companies, and without expensive engineering features. However, it was
not long before the local-interest lines became
too ambitious. Often preferring standard gauge,
they began to form end-on links with each other,
thus threatening to create new main lines. In the
1870s this prompted the government to persuade
the big companies to take over several of them.

That the Germans made far better use of rail
transport in the Franco-Prussian war was more a
reflection on the French army staff than on the
railways. The latter provided the required trains,
but the military authorities too often failed to load
them properly or even to send them in the right
direction. Confused railway transport was a key
factor in the French defeat, and for a time the
railways were a convenient scapegoat, with
renewed demands for nationalization. During the
Third Republic, the railways were once more
subject to savage criticism, and in 1872 they felt
obliged to organize their own joint public information department to dispense what they frankly
termed *publicité-doctrinale*.

A first step towards nationalization came in
1878, when a state organization, the Etat Railway, was formed to take over 2,615 km
(1,625 miles) belonging to overgrown but
unprofitable local lines in the south-west. The
Etat was soon in difficulties, but improved its
position by gaining access to Paris by means of
running powers over its two neighbours, the
Ouest and PO railways. Meanwhile the government itself was in trouble. In the aftermath of
defeat, in 1879, it had adopted the Freycinet Plan,
authorizing the creation of a 'third network', but
soon found that the cost of building these
thousands of kilometres of unprofitable line was
an insupportable burden. It escaped this self-
imposed problem with the conventions of 1883,
under which the big companies took over the new
lines.

Despite political and ideological assaults, and
constant complaints about tariff levels, the
decades before 1914 were good years for the railways. A profitable future seemed likely, engineering standards were high (the PLM was using rail
as heavy as 60 kg/metre [132 lb/yd] before 1914),
and services were improving. The most celebrated of the Wagons-Lits trains, the *Orient
Express*, left Paris for the first time in 1883, usher-
ing in the epoch of the great international trains,
which brought great prestige if little profit. Internal passenger services were less frequent than in
Britain or Germany, but the one or two heavy
daily trains which were operated over the main
lines steadily became faster and more comfortable. Although six-wheeled passenger stock would

survive until well after the second world war,
bogie stock was built for the better trains from
about the turn of the century. The PLM's bogie
stock of 1900 was remarkable for its length (20 m
or 64 ft) and, as was usual, was confined to first-
class passengers.

French locomotive design was studied, and
sometimes imitated, in other countries. In particular, it was in France that the principle of
compounding, or dual expansion, was most per-
sistently and carefully pursued. Anatole Mallet
who, though a Swiss, spent his working life in
France, introduced his two-cylinder compound
on the Bayonne–Biarritz Railway in 1877, and
later demonstrated his articulated four-cylinder
compound at the Paris Exhibition. Sauvage of the
Nord Railway made a success of the three-
cylinder compound, and du Bousquet, one of the
greatest locomotive designers of the 20th century,
evolved with his associate de Glehn a four-
cylinder system of compounding which had a
long reign in France and elsewhere. In general,
the French four-cylinder compound, especially
after it had been improved by André Chapelon in
the inter-war years, was the most effective pattern
of locomotive in terms of power output per ton of
engine or per ton of coal, even though because of
its complexity it was more expensive to build and
maintain, and required very skilled crews.

New forms of traction were not ignored. Internal combustion railcars were tried, and French
engineers were especially interested in electrification. At the end of the century the Ouest
Railway was operating in regular service three
steam-electric locomotives, in which steam drove
generators powering electric traction motors.
This idea, a forerunner of the diesel-electric
locomotive, was not pursued, but in the early
years of the century a number of lines were electrified. The heavily graded metre-gauge St
George de Comiers to La Mure line was converted at 2,400 volts in 1903. The Midi Railway
not only electrified its Bourg Madame and Ville-
franche lines, but experimented with six different
designs of locomotive on the latter. The
Paris–Versailles Rive Gauche suburban line was
electrified on the third-rail 650 volt system in

Below: The last days of steam
traction on the former Nord
Railway main line from Paris
to Calais. An American-built
locomotive, No 141R 881,
leans to the curve at Etaples.

1902, and in the Alps the metre-gauge St Gervais–Vallorcine line was also converted before 1914. As for the main lines, in 1900 the PO Railway began to electrify its Paris-Orléans line at 1,500 volts with overhead current collection.

But in 1900 the PO, Est, Midi, and Ouest railways were still drawing on the government's guarantee of interest. Least likely to extricate itself from its deficit was the Ouest, the standards of whose services sometimes reflected its general poverty. In France the public generally tolerates a poor service or a taxpayer-financed service, but rarely both, and the unpopular Ouest was nationalized in 1909, becoming part of the Etat Railway. By 1914 only the PO and Midi railways were still in deficit, even though the railways' financial prospects had been further clouded by labour troubles. Trade unions had been recognized in France since 1884, and in 1909 the right to strike was extended to railwaymen. France's first national railway strike followed in 1910, and was brought to an end only by a government

Above: A former PLM Railway 4-6-2, modified by Chapelon and transferred to the Northern Region, waits to leave Boulogne Maritime with a Paris boat train.

Below: By many standards the S.N.C.F. 141P was the most efficient locomotive type ever built. This picture shows one of these 2-8-2 machines, built in the 1940s, being serviced at Le Mans.

mobilization order served on the railwaymen.

Railway route-length was 39,450 km (24,500 miles) in 1913, despite the loss of the Alsace and Lorraine lines in 1872. The performance of the railways in the first world war was commendable. Even the confusion caused by the unexpected German advance on Paris in 1914 was short-lived, although the consequent loss of Nord rolling stock was serious. The Est and Nord railways carried the main burden, dispatching hundreds of special trains daily and being helped by the loan of rolling stock and locomotives from other French and British railways. But tariffs fell behind the rise of prices, and much maintenance was deferred; when the war ended the railways were once again in a threatening financial situation. The introduction of the 8-hour working day in 1919 was an additional burden, since it obliged the railways to hire an extra 100,000 workers. There was a railway strike in 1920 to back a demand for higher wages and nationalization. This failed, partly because railwaymen in the re-

gions most affected by the war were very reluctant to stop work.

The government tried during the first post-war years to operate a scheme whereby the railways would have a common fund which would receive excess profits from prosperous companies and pay out money to those which were unprofitable. This naturally discouraged the quest for efficiency, even though bonuses for good management were provided. Railway deficits grew alarmingly during the depression. One third of the loss was accountable to the Etat Railway, but all the railways were now in deficit. The smallest deficit was that of the smallest company, the Alsace–Lorraine Railways, which had been established as a separate organization, under the supervision of the Est Railway, after the recovery of the territory lost in 1872. In 1934 the PO and Midi railways amalgamated in the hope of realizing worthwhile economies. The introduction by the Popular Front government of the 40-hour week meant that an extra 90,000 railwaymen were needed. The same government tried to negotiate with the companies an agreed plan of nationalization, but failed and lost power in 1937. The Centrist government which followed succeeded, after long discussion, in nationalizing the railways by organizing the Société Nationale des Chemins de Fer (SNCF).

The SNCF began its life in January 1938; 51 per cent of its capital was held by the state, and 49 per cent by the companies. It was managed by its *Conseil d'Administration*, but for most matters was divided into six administrative regions (Nord, Est, Ouest, Sud-Ouest, Sud-Est, and Méditerranée). It had the status of a limited company, but with certain privileges, and came within the responsibilities of the ministry of public works. Although there were hopes that the network would eventually become profitable, and indeed there were some good years, the SNCF is today still in deficit.

In 1939 French railways performed their mobilization tasks as well as they had in 1914. In 1940, just as the German break-through was imminent, they were planning a return to the pre-war timetables. In the disastrous weeks of the German advance, much French and Belgian rolling stock was evacuated southwards. After the 1940 armistice the railways of the occupied zone were placed at the disposition of the Germans. By 1944 the initial German railway controllers had been supplemented by about 25,000 German technical staff, needed to cope with the difficulties caused by the Resistance movement. The latter, on the railways, had small beginnings (deliberate delays and intentional errors) but grew to massive and well-planned acts of sabotage and espionage. During the war 4,000 railwaymen were killed by the Germans or by Allied bombing, 1,200 were wounded, and 20,000 deported.

At the end of the war the railways were in a very damaged and run-down condition, but in the 1950s SNCF, with massive financial support, began a reconstruction based on the newest technology, and in particular on electrification. The intention was that the SNCF would become financially self-supporting, and although this was not realized, the French taxpayer had at least the satisfaction of knowing that his railways set standards of service and technical progress which were envied and imitated in other countries.

In the inter-war years, electrification had continued. Having electrified its Paris-Orléans line, the PO converted its two main lines from Orléans, to Bordeaux via Tours and to the eastern Pyrenees via Toulouse. The new Ouest Region of the SNCF electrified from Paris to Le Mans, and other lines were converted in the south. On non-electrified lines there was great use of diesel railcars. These took many forms, ranging from what were virtually buses on flanged wheels to streamlined Bugatti railcars and high-speed multiple units. At the time of its formation the SNCF operated about 650 railcars, which produced almost one quarter of the passenger-train mileage.

After the second world war the first big electrification project was the step-by-step conversion of the former PLM main line from Paris to Marseille. Simultaneously a start was made with the

Above: The latest SNCF design of doubledeck outer-suburban rolling stock, a traditional French solution to the problem of carrying more commuters without increasing the number or the length of trains.

Left: Since the 1930s French railways have made great use of railcars for cross-country and branch-line services. In this picture a modern *autorail* is passing through the Picardy countryside.

Near right: A pair of SNCF secondary service diesel locomotives at work on a heavily-graded line.

Far right: No 2D2 9119 brings a Paris to Marseilles *rapide* into Dijon in 1967. This class of 36 locomotives appeared in 1950.

introduction of new fast trains with stainless-steel rolling stock; the *Mistral*, from Paris to the Mediterranean, became a record-breaker and a symbol of the post-war railway renaissance. Before completion of the Marseille electrification it was decided, after successful experimentation, that future major electrification schemes would be with the more efficient industrial frequency 25,000 volt ac system. France took a world lead in this system, with the result that many overseas railways placed orders for French equipment.

The first major electrification at 25,000 volts was of heavy-traffic routes of the Est Region around Metz, followed by the Est and Nord main lines. Meanwhile, using locomotives designed for the Marseille electrification, but running over a straight stretch of the former PO main line, French electric locomotives broke the world record with a speed of 329.9 km/h (205 mph). However, with existing alignments, such speeds could not be realized in ordinary service. A step towards ultra-fast passenger services came in 1974 with authorization of the entirely new Paris Sud-Est line, which will parallel the existing Paris-Lyon main line and be designed for speeds well in excess of 250 km/h (155 mph) for a new generation of turbo-trains.

On non-electrified lines, the SNCF policy was to use steam traction, with diesel main-line locomotives being introduced unhurriedly. This enabled the French to dieselize without an excessive number of designs for locomotives. In recent years, to accelerate passenger services on non-electrified lines, gas turbine multiple-unit trains have been introduced. The fuel consumption of these is quite high, but their performance and popularity has been very satisfying; some have been exported to the USA and Iran. Meanwhile, freight traffic levels have been maintained by means of new special trains, such as the fast *Provence Express* operated in the fruit season to Paris, containerization, a successful campaign to induce all factories to possess and use their own private sidings, and the new SNCF charter of 1971, giving the railways somewhat more commercial freedom than was orginally envisaged.

History of German Railways

Although Germany pursued the 19th century technological revolution with a fervour unmatched elsewhere, the first step on that road, the construction of railways, was taken hesitantly and only because of persistent efforts by enthusiasts like Friedrich List and King Ludwig of Bavaria. List had returned from exile in America full of enthusiasm for railway transport. He realized that a planned railway network would have political as well as economic benefits, for it would facilitate the creation of a united Germany centred on Prussia. At that time, more and more German states were joining the customs union (*Zollverein*) sponsored by Prussia, and a railway system centred on Berlin would confirm Prussian leadership. List's plan for a railway network, published in 1833, did anticipate the main lines which were eventually built: for the most part, these radiated from Berlin, although the German network was never so strongly centred on Berlin as French railways were centred on Paris.

But Germany's first public steam railway, from Nüremberg to Fürth, was largely the achievement of Ludwig of Bavaria, who had been attracted by the possibilities of steam traction, and had sent Bavarian engineers to study foreign practice. He followed the advice of George Stephenson, and it was a Stephenson locomotive, *Der Adler (The Eagle)* which hauled the first train when this 8 kilometre (5 mile) line was opened in 1835.

In 1837 the first section of the Leipzig–Dresden Railway in Saxony was built. This railway was open throughout in 1839, carrying no fewer than 412,000 passengers in its first year and amply justifying the claims of its most fervent advocate, List. In Prussia, the short Berlin–Potsdam line was opened in 1838, and the same year saw the appearance of Germany's first state railway, from Brunswick to Wolfenbüttel. The first sections of the important main lines were opened in 1839: the Frankfurt Main to Hattersheim section of the Taunusbahn, the Magdeburg to Kalbe section of the Magdeburg to Leipzig railway, the Cologne to Müngersdorf section of the

Rheinischer Bahn, and the Munich to Maisach section of the Maximiliensbahn. In the following year the Frankfurt Main to Wiesbaden and the Magdeburg to Leipzig lines were completed, and the first sections opened of the Baden State Railway (from Mannheim to Heidelberg) and of the Berlin–Anhalter Bahn's line towards Wittenberg.

From 1840, construction went forward rapidly yet steadily. The Prussian railway law of 1838 was perhaps the crucial step forward; it promised no assistance for private railway companies and did not envisage any immediate state railway construction; but because it did not actually forbid railway-building, it allowed those with sufficient enthusiasm and capital to obtain official approval for their projects. Among the early lines allowed under this law were the routes from Düsseldorf to Elberfeld, Berlin to Stettin, and Berlin to Köthen. Moreover, despite its initial mistrust of railways, the Prussian government soon decided to give financial support, either by buying shares or by guaranteeing the interest on the companies' capital. After about 1842, the Prussian government, with a full treasury and a general staff increasingly disposed to regard railways as a military asset, began to actively promote a planned railway network.

In 1842 there were 578 km (363 miles) of line in Germany, but this increased rapidly thanks to the new Prussian enthusiasm. The new lines were usually commercially attractive, like the key Minden to Cologne line, but an exception was the Ostbahn. This connected Berlin with Königsberg and the Russian frontier, and was undertaken largely for strategic reasons and at the expense of the Prussian taxpayer. From 1849 to 1879 the co-existence of state and private railway-building, introduced at the time of the Ostbahn project, was the foundation of Prussian railway policy.

In non-Prussian Germany, state construction came earlier. In 1842, the Hanover government began to build railways to retain the transit traffic moving towards Hamburg and the Rhineland. In 1850, Württemberg, rather late to enter the railway age, opened its first line, a state railway serving Esslingen. In Baden, which also opted for

Below: The beginning of German steam railways. The Stephenson locomotive *Der Adler* hauls the first train from Nüremberg in 1835.

Above: An impression of German railways in the 1830s. As on all early railways, breakdowns did occur. However, the artist has preferred caricature to realism, as is exemplified by the 'reins' held by the locomotive driver.

Above right: An early print of the Leipzig-Dresden Railway. The lower picture shows the Leipzig terminus.

Below: The erecting shop of the pioneer locomotive workshop established by Ernst Borsig at Berlin in 1841.

state railways, the Rhine Valley line from Heidelberg reached the Swiss frontier at Basle in 1846. The free city of Frankfurt, already becoming a centre of private railways, shared with Hesse-Kassel the ownership of the key Main-Weser Railway that linked the city with Hanover and the north.

Compared with Britain, German railway construction was cheap. Little capital was lost on no-hope lines, tunnels and viaducts were avoided wherever possible, station platforms were low or non-existent, and level crossings were preferred to bridges. At the end of the century it was calculated that the Prussian State Railways had cost £21,469 per mile to build, compared to the £56,000 of the British railways.

By 1850, the German railways had clearly developed further than the French. About 4,800 km (3,000 miles) were open, and it was possible to travel from Munich via Nüremberg, Leipzig, and Berlin to Hamburg, Stettin, the Rhineland or Silesia. From the start, the Germans began to make their own contributions to railway practice and technology. And not only in Germany itself; the Dresdener Karl Beyer, for example, anglicized himself and founded a great British locomotive works. Another Dresdener was Johann Schubert, who, with Beyer had visited England in the mid-1830s. In 1839 he com-

pleted the first German-built locomotive, *Saxonia*, which made its first run on the Leipzig–Dresden Railway. His pupil, Max von Weber, son of the musician, became an engineer of the same railway, for which he designed some notable iron bridges, developed a locomotive speedometer, and provided locomotive crews with unusually ample protection against the weather. In 1848 the chief engineer of the Taunusbahn, Heusinger, independently developed a valve gear similar to that simultaneously invented by the Belgian Walschaert. Another innovative engineer was Joseph Trick of the Esslingen locomotive works, whose *Alb* of 1849 was a pioneer hill-climbing locomotive, and who also invented the Trick port, a supplementary channel for steam passing into the cylinder.

The German locomotive industry, which would blossom into many firms scattered all over the country, and which would later develop a substantial export business based on reliability, prompt delivery, and keen pricing, was founded in 1841 when three great firms had their beginning: Maffei in Munich, Kessler in Karlsruhe, and Borsig in Berlin. The larger German states had their own locomotive building works by the end of the 1840s, among them being the well-known Hanover works, founded in 1846 when George Egestorff built his first locomotive, *Ernst August*, for the Hanover State Railway.

The Prussian army general staff under von Moltke had a sound appreciation of what railways could achieve in war. More railways were built towards and along the frontiers even though, in the east, they were not commercially justified. Moreover, a military railway, carrying civilian traffic, was opened near Berlin to train the new railway battalions. In the Franco-Prussian war, the speed with which German reserves were moved by rail was a key factor in the French defeat. When Prussian forces entered France their advance was well supported by the railway battalions, which quickly brought the local railways back into operation.

The victorious conclusion of the war and the establishment of the German Empire marked a new stage in railway development. Von Moltke and Bismarck had long wanted a unified all-German state railway system; only by this means,

Above: A dining car of the *Mitropa* organization, the company which operated railway catering and sleeping cars throughout Germany until 1945. The photograph was made in the inter-war period, although the vehicle dates from an earlier era.

they thought, could the Berlin government exercise the centralized control and co-ordination necessitated by the important commercial and military role of the railways. German public opinion began to move in the same direction, and from 1879 the Prussian government began to nationalize the big railway companies.

In 1879 the Prussian State Railways totalled 5,300 km (3,290 miles), and these were partly state lines taken over when Hanover was annexed in 1866. Prussian private lines totalled about 9,400 km (5,830 miles), and there were also 3,900 km (2,420 miles) of private lines operated by the state. In 1909, after 30 years of nationalization and state railway construction, there were 37,400 km (23,190 miles) of state line, only 2,900 km (1,800 miles) of private, and with no state-operated private mileage.

However, a unified system for the whole Empire was beyond Bismarck's grasp. Bavaria, in particular, resisted any Prussian attempt to gain control of its railways, and nationalized several private lines to prevent the Prussian government quietly buying them up. Some other German states were also jealous of their railway systems. However, Prussia was able to join with Hesse-Darmstadt in 1896 to purchase the largest

Below: The derailment of a Berlin to Cologne night train at Lehrte, near Hanover, in 1926. Twenty deaths made this one of the *Reichsbahn*'s worst accidents.

remaining German private line, the Hessian Ludwigsbahn, to which it soon added other Hessian lines. Meanwhile, Bismarck had established, as a neighbour of the Prussian State Railway administration in Berlin, the Imperial Railway Office. This co-ordinated the standards and policies of the various German railways. Although Bavaria usually resisted Prussian proposals initially, in general the Prussian government got its way on most important railway issues. Prussian innovations were frequently imitated in the other states – in 1892, for example, Prussia introduced trains of vestibuled corridor vehicles (*Durchgangswagen*, hence the term 'D-train'), for which it levied a supplementary fare, and this D-train concept was soon standardized throughout Germany. But the adventurous yet premature acquisition by the Prussian railways in 1912 of a Swiss-engined diesel locomotive was not imitated.

Of the empire's main lines, about two-thirds eventually came under the railway department of the Prussian government. Under the department's guidance, a good service was offered, aided perhaps by the military-style discipline imposed on railwaymen (who did not join trade unions and who stood at attention when spoken to by a superior). The railways became highly profitable, which was gratifying for the government because it provided a regular source of income that was not subject to a vote in the Reichstag. The chaotic freight rate system was simplified after the establishment of the empire, but then became progressively more complex as the authorities introduced more and more 'exceptional rates' to maximize profits and influence the direction of economic development. Some exceptional rates aroused great resentment; among these were the special low rates granted to foreign freight moving towards German ports. The aim was to capture traffic from the Dutch and Russian ports, but Prussian landowners began to complain that these rates allowed Russian grain to compete unfairly with their own. But such complaints had little effect; contrary to what had once been expected, state-owned railways did not use their profits to lower charges or improve services. They aimed to maximize the income of their owners, just like private railways.

In 1914, Germany possessed a total of almost 59,000 km (36,500 miles) of state railways, of which 23,300 km (14,480 miles) were double-track. Private main line railways totalled only 4,700 km (2,910 miles). Of the state mileage, more than 39,000 km (24,180 miles) belonged to the Prussian State Railways, nearly 8,500 km (5,270 miles) to Bavaria, and nearly 3,400 km (2,100 miles) to the Saxon State Railways. Other large systems were the 2,100 km (1,300 miles) of the Imperial Railways (the lines of Alsace and Lorraine, acquired in 1872), the Württemberg State Railways (2,100 km or 1,300 miles), the Mecklenburg State Railway (1,100 km or 680 miles), the Baden State Railway (1,800 km or 1,120 miles), and the Oldenburg State Railway (675 km or 420 miles). Most of these systems included some narrow-gauge trackage, totalling

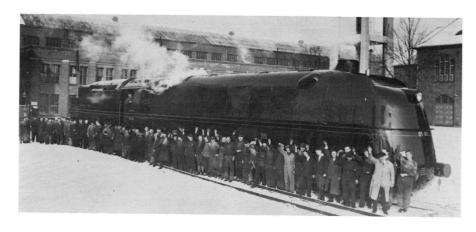

Above: A high-speed experimental 4–6–4 locomotive built by Borsig for the *Reichsbahn* in 1935. Designed to haul 250-ton trains at over 160 km/h (100 mph), this locomotive was streamlined down to rail level, access to the wheels and valve gear being through roller-blind side doors.

Above right: A double-deck commuter train of the Prussian State Railways at Tempelhof in 1912.

Below: The exhibition celebrating the centenary of the German railways at Nürnberg in 1935, with new electric stock on the right-hand track and experimental streamlined locomotive in the centre.

Bottom: The so-called 'rail-Zeppelin' at Hanover in 1931. The 1930s were a period of intense experimentation for German designers, with emphasis on high-speed steam and internal-combustion machines.

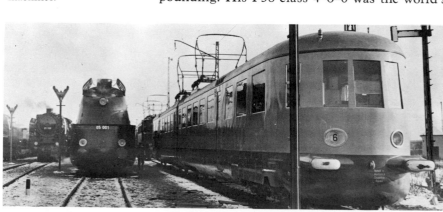

1,078 km (670 miles), of which almost half was in Saxony, where a number of rural or mountainous areas were (and still are) served by 750 mm (2 ft 5½ in) gauge lines. Train services, for speed and frequency, were superior to most European railways. Eleven pairs of passenger trains served the Berlin–Hamburg route daily in 1910, and Munich was only ten hours from Berlin.

Prussian State Railways could boast of several influential locomotive engineers. In 1880 the chief mechanical engineer of their Hanover division, von Borries, introduced a two-cylinder compound system which was adopted by several Central and East European railways. Even more important was the work of Wilhelm Schmidt, who at the turn of the century succeeded in designing a really practicable superheater. This achievement was the most significant advance in locomotive technology since the age of Stephenson, as it enabled steam to be used much more economically. Robert Garbe, responsible for locomotive design from 1895 to 1917, confirmed the Prussian school of locomotive construction, designing machines for reliability and ease of maintenance more than for high power output or low fuel consumption. He preferred low boiler pressures and avoided the complications of compounding. His P38 class 4–6–0 was the world's

most numerous passenger locomotive. The Bavarian State Railway represented a completely different design philosophy. Perhaps because coal was dearer in the south, the BSR favoured compound locomotives, built in the local workshops of Maffei at Munich. This firm designed for the Bavarian and the Baden state railways a handsome and efficient type of four-cylinder compound 4–6–2 which would remain in service until after the second world war.

During the first world war, the German railways performed well their long-studied function of rapidly carrying reserve troops to the frontiers and, later, shifting troops between the eastern and western fronts. Contrary to what might have been expected, freight traffic actually fell during the war years, while the number of railwaymen increased from 764,000 in 1914 to 925,000 in 1918. The subsequent peace treaties reduced the network by 8,000 km (4,960 miles) with the Alsace and Lorraine lines returning to France and 4,000 km (2,480 miles) of line in east Prussia, Posen, and Silesia going to the new state of Poland. Additional mileage was lost to the railways of the Saar, Belgium, Czechoslovakia, Lithuania, and Denmark. Moreover, 5,000 locomotives were demanded by the victors as reparations.

Paradoxically, it was only the end of the German Empire which enabled the realization of Bismarck's dream of a truly centralized railway system. The new constitution of 1919 transferred the state railway systems and the significant private lines to a new organization, the Deutsche Reichsbahn (DR). This was a state enterprise, responsible to the minister of transport but having financial autonomy. However, in 1924 the victorious powers imposed through the Dawes Plan the reorganization of the DR, which was to become a mixed rather than a purely state enterprise, with half of its management board nominated by the western powers and with a western official as watchdog. This regime lasted until 1930, when the semi-private, semi-state nature was retained but the western official withdrawn. The centenary of German railways was celebrated at Nuremberg in 1935, by which time Hitler was describing DR as Germany's 'biggest socialist enterprise'.

In 1939, now again under exclusive government control, DR possessed 60,000 km (37,200 miles) of route, and supervised another 14,000 km (8,690 miles) of local or private lines.

Punctuality, regularity, precision, and discipline were still in evidence. Track and engineering features were rather more substantial than purely economic considerations would have warranted. Services were good, but capital investment had not kept pace with new technology. Automatic signalling, for example, lagged behind that of other countries. Under the leadership of Richard Wagner, the Prussian tradition of locomotive design had been embodied in a new series of standard locomotives for DR. These were built for a long trouble-free life, and in fact Wagner's Pacifics of the mid-1920s were still hauling inter-city trains from Berlin in the mid-1970s. In the late 1930s, German railways were noted for their high-speed diesel multiple-unit trains, and especially for the *Flying Hamburger*, which averaged 125 km/h (78 mph) over the 288 km (179 miles) from Berlin to Hamburg. But lengthy experiments with ultra-high-pressure and ultra-high-speed steam locomotives actually bore little fruit.

Although as early as 1879 von Siemens demonstrated his rudimentary electric locomotive at the Berlin Exhibition, it was not until 1905 that the first short sections of railway were electrified. Pre-1914 schemes, completed after the war, included the Hamburg and Berlin third-rail suburban lines, and main-line electrification at 15,000 volts around Breslau and Gorlitz, and in Bavaria and Württemberg. Completion of these schemes made up most of the inter-war electrifications, although a scheme to link Rome and Berlin by an all-electric route was started, with work continuing even during the second world war.

During that war, the German railways suffered severely from bombing, although the rather excessive track capacity usually offered alternative routes when lines were cut. Damaged bridges were quickly rebuilt by laying steel beams, up to one metre deep, to support the track. Most damaging were hits on train control installations, which could not be replaced quickly. Material shortages meant that, for example, zinc chloride replaced creosote as a sleeper preservative, and sleepers were made of smaller cross-section to save wood (laminated sleepers were tried, but their glue failed within a year). Oil shortage compelled withdrawal of hundreds of diesel railcars. Coal shortage meant that 25 per cent coke was added to locomotive fuel. This dilution, or the use of brown coal briquettes, necessitated two firemen per locomotive and reduced power output. Despite a quite lavish use of labour, by 1945 the track was under-maintained; only the high pre-war standards and the imposition of a general 80 km/h (50 mph) speed limit enabled the railways to carry on. The standard wartime locomotive, of which thousands were built, was a Wagner 2–10–0 modified to economize in scarce metals and skilled labour, and fitted with a commodious cab suited for tender-first running and for accommodating sleeping bunks for the crew.

Conditions were grim in the late 1940s. Apart from wartime destruction, decay, and disruption, the railways had to recover from the progressive division of Germany into two republics. This division cut across previous traffic flows so that once-important main lines like Berlin-Hamburg and Magdeburg-Hanover lost most of their traffic. In West Germany, the key routes ran from north to south – from Hamburg through Hanover to Munich, and from Hamburg through Münster to Cologne and down the Rhine. In East Germany, scarce funds were used to build diversionary routes to enable East German trains to avoid West Berlin. The Berlin-Rostock line became vital; Rostock was the nation's only major seaport.

The railways of West Germany, which took the name of Deutsche Bundesbahn (DB), established their headquarters at Frankfurt. In the early years, coal and material shortages meant that services were kept to an uncomfortable minimum, and reconstruction did not start until the 1950s.

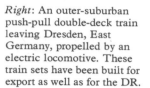

Right: An outer-suburban push-pull double-deck train leaving Dresden, East Germany, propelled by an electric locomotive. These train sets have been built for export as well as for the DR.

Above: German Federal Railways electric locomotive. No 218-103-0 pulls out of a busy station.

Far left: A diesel multiple unit train of the DB enters the Petersberg Tunnel, amid Moselle vineyards. This line, from Koblenz to Trier, is now electrified.

Left: A diesel-hydraulic locomotive of the DB. This class V 200 four-axle design was introduced in the 1950s and exemplified the German preference for diesel-hydraulic, rather than diesel-electric, locomotives.

Below: E 103 type electric locomotive of the DB. In 1965 Henschel built the first of this class, which was followed by a production batch acquired for high-speed services.

However, as the German 'economic miracle' progressed it was possible to make big investments to handle the ever-growing traffic. Electrification of the main lines and dieselization of other lines was undertaken. Diesel-hydraulic locomotives were initially favoured, using the Voith transmission developed before the war. On branch lines the railbus became popular. The D-train was supplemented by the Trans-Europ Express trains on international services and, later, by the Inter-City internally; the latter is a first-class-only TEE-style train running at regular intervals between important cities. Automatic signalling, neglected before the war, was widely applied. However, DB required government grants and government investment to maintain its services. In the mid-1970s it seemed that public opinion was turning against this financial burden. There was obvious scope for reducing mileage, for nine-tenths of the traffic was carried over only one half of the mileage.

DB was rather larger than the railway system of East Germany, DR. In 1975 DB possessed nearly 29,500 km (18,300 miles) of route, of which 8,600 km (5,330 miles) were electrified at 15,000 volts. About 380 million tons of freight and 1,500 million passengers were carried. In East Germany the DR possessed nearly 14,500 km (9,000 miles), of which 1,385 km (860 miles) were electrified (mainly at 15,000 volts but including a short stretch at 25,000 volts and some third-rail suburban mileage). Some 264 million tons of

freight and 633 million passengers were carried. In 1945 many main lines in the eastern zone were singled, so that rails could be sent to the USSR. There is still a considerable mileage of this single-track main line, although re-double-tracking continues. It is only since 1966 that DR has been substantially modernized; in fact from 1955 to 1965 passenger traffic actually fell, due to the poor facilities. DR mileage (like DB) has declined slightly, with the closing of some branch lines.

In both Germanies steam locomotive construction recommenced in the early 1950s, the designs being mainly inherited from Wagner's pre-war design office. But steam construction lasted only a few years, and DB was expected to end steam traction in 1977. DR steam locomotives will probably last longer, especially on the narrow-gauge lines, where Mallet and Saxon –Meyer articulated locomotives are still at work.

The German locomotive industry, because of the Depression, had been virtually reduced to four major builders by 1939: Krauss-Maffei, Krupp (crippled by bombing in 1943), Henschel, and Borsig. The last is now the Hans Beimler works in East Germany, with a sizable home and export business in electric and diesel locomotives. A works at Babelsberg also builds locomotives for DR; this turned out the Class V118 diesel-hydraulic main-line locomotive, but in recent years main-line diesel acquisitions have been Russian-built diesel electrics of 2,000 and 3,000 hp. The carriage works at Görlitz has built fast inter-city multiple units, and also large numbers of double-deck locomotive-hauled push–pull trains.

In West Germany, high-speed passenger services have received great attention. The Class 103 electric locomotive, capable of 200 km/h (125 mph) running, has been in service for some years, but track alignments prevent it fully exploiting its speed potential. Probably the new ET420 diesel multiple unit will be the interim solution for high-speed travel by IC (Inter-City) trains. In the longer term, new high-speed railways are projected. These will relieve existing lines already operating at full capacity, and will have alignments suitable for speeds of perhaps 300 km/h (190 mph). Work has already started on sections of the Hanover–Würzburg and Mannheim–Stuttgardt high-speed lines.

HISTORY

EUROPE

AUSTRIA AND EASTERN CENTRAL EUROPE

Austria

Austria's first public railway was opened in stages from 1827. At the beginning, this railway linked Linz with Budweiss, was of 1,106 mm gauge, horse-powered, and operated on a toll system. The first steam railway, and the real start of the railway age for Austria, was the Kaiser-Ferdinands Nordbahn from Vienna to Brno in Bohemia, whose first section was opened in 1837. Cunningly named to associate the royal title with the enterprise, the Nordbahn was undertaken by the Rothschilds as one more part of their railway empire. When private investment seemed unlikely to finance further railways, the government formed the State Railway, whose most notable achievement was the sinuous and heavily-graded line over the Semmering pass towards the Adriatic.

In 1851 trials were held to choose a locomotive design for the Semmering section. Although none of the competing designs was accepted, the unusual entries by distinguished locomotive builders did much to influence central European locomotive design. Most notable was the work of

Below: An old electric locomotive and a modern 4–6–4 tank locomotive at Linz in 1967. The type 1073 electric, dating from the mid-1920s, is distinguished by the provision of only one driving cab.

the Scotsman, Haswell, who managed the workshops of another railway (the Vienna-Raab) and had been building American-style locomotives for Austrian railways. He used the occasion to introduce to Europe the heavy eight-wheeled freight locomotive. Later, Haswell built a locomotive with four outside cylinders; Austrian locomotive design, because the unusual combination of weight restrictions, gradients, curves, poor coal and the need for competitive scheduling of international transit trains would always be distinctive.

Soon after the completion of the Semmering railway, the state withdrew from the railway business, its funds exhausted. At this time two French banking families, the Rothschilds and Pereires, were struggling for domination of the European railway networks. The Pereires' Crédit Mobilier took over much of the former Austrian state railways, establishing what it called the Austrian State Railway Company, which, in fact, was a private concern managed in Paris. This was re-nationalized only in 1909, and until Hitler annexed Austria, there was always a Pereire on its board. Meanwhile, in the 1850s, the Rothschilds had made their own gains; their Südbahn included the Semmering Pass line from Vienna to Trieste, and their Franz Josef Railway linked Vienna with Budapest and Belgrade. Other companies included the Kaiserin Elisabeth Bahn from Vienna to Salzburg and Passau, and the North Western into Slovakia. Some confident companies embarked on spectacular mountainous main lines; the Arlberg route, finished in 1889, had a 10,250 metre (6.3 miles) tunnel, among others, and linked Innsbruck with Feldkirch. Another mountainous line, the Tauernbahn in Carinthia, was finished in 1909.

The state began to reassert itself in the 1880s. Its new State Railway progressively bought up the old companies; in 1914 Austria had about 19,300 km (12,000 miles) of railway (excluding Hungary) and only 4,000 km (2,500 miles) of these were still privately owned. World War 1 resulted in the dismemberment of the Austrian Empire, which not only reduced the mileage but also meant that many main lines were truncated and lost their significance. After the peace treaties Austria was left with only about 6,300 km (3,900 miles) of railway; its territory lay lengthways from east to west, which meant that its main lines could be divided into the longer and more easily graded east-west routes, and the shorter north to south routes. It was these latter, passing through difficult terrain, which carried heavy international traffic towards the Mediterranean.

In 1924 the Südbahn, last of the big railway companies, was finally nationalized; its financial position had been fairly hopeless in the reduced Austria, as its main lines to the Mediterranean had been cut short at Graz and Brenner. In that year the Federal Austrian Railways (ÖBB) organization was founded to own and administer the national network. After Hitler annexed Austria, the Austrian railways formed part of the *Deutsche Reichsbahn*. Then, after 1945, there were adjustments following the division of the country into

occupation zones. However, despite a change of name to Austrian Federal Railways (ÖBB) in 1947, the state railway organization still functions as formerly, with responsibility for all non-local lines. In 1975 the ÖBB controlled 5,864 km (3,650 miles) of route (of which about 450 km [280 miles] was 750 mm or metre gauge), and of those 5,864 km, 2,610 km (1,620 miles) were electrified. There were also one or two short lines independent of the ÖBB. These included the coal-carrying GKB from Graz to Köflach, and the local railways of the Styrian province.

Although steam traction still lingers on the GKB and certain narrow-gauge short lines, diesel and electric locomotives and multiple units handle all ÖBB standard-gauge traffic. Austria was among the pioneers of electrification, with its 92 km (57 mile) St. Polten to Gusswerk line being converted at 5,000 volts in 1911. Sub-

Above left: Class E94 electric locomotive, acquired from Germany by the Austrian Federal Railways as war reparations. These very successful locomotives were built for the German *Reichsbahn* from 1940 to 1945.

Above right: One of the well-known interwar class 1670 electric locomotives of Austrian Federal Railways leaving the Arlberg Tunnel with the *Vorarlberg Express* in 1967.

Below: A German war-built 2–10–0 at work on the privately-owned Graz-Köflacher Bahn (GKB) in Austria.

sequent electrification was at 15,000 volts in accordance with an early standardization agreement reached with the neighbouring railways of Switzerland and Germany. Modern equipment is made in Austria and some is exported. Inter-city electric multiple units serve the main cities, with the heavier locomotive-hauled trains found largely on international services. In recent years great efforts have been made to attract passengers. The *Konfort* de-luxe rolling stock is probably the most comfortable passenger accommodation to be found anywhere. Double-tracking and electrification continues; in 1976 electrification of the Ostbahn from Vienna to the Hungarian frontier was finished, and work is in progress on converting the Linz-Graz section of the north-south main line.

Czechoslovakia

The Czechoslovak State Railways (ČSD) were formed to administer most of the lines within the new state which was established after World War 1. Czechoslovakia comprised principally Bohemia and Moravia, hitherto under Austrian rule, and Slovakia, which was formerly part of the kingdom of Hungary. Railway technique was largely Austrian in origin, while the layout of the network had been determined by the needs of the Austro-Hungarian Empire. Bohemia had possessed a fairly dense network, as well as a top-grade main line, part of the former Vienna-Krakow route. But lines between Bohemia and Slovakia were insufficient for the new state. Therefore, in the inter-war period, new railway construction and upgrading was concentrated on this link between the two key constituents of the republic.

Czechoslovakia inherited two locomotive works, which were soon amalgamated to form the ČKO Works at Prague. The Skoda armaments works turned to locomotive production in 1919. It was not long before a distinctively Czech school

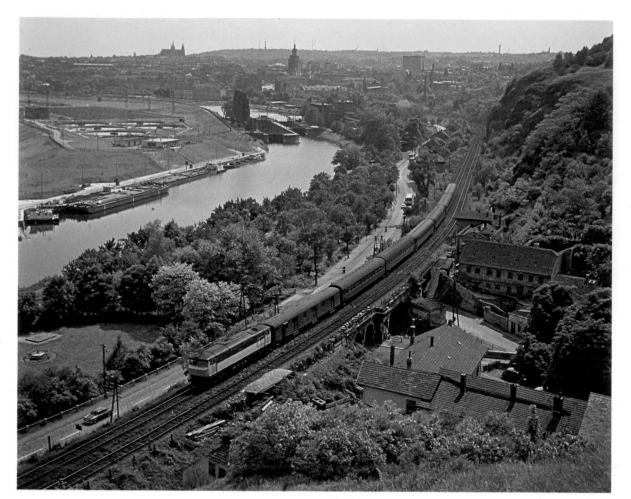

Left: A Czech type T478 diesel-electric locomotive leaving Prague with a train to Decin.

Below: An East German type VT18 diesel multiple unit, forming the Berlin-Vienna *Vindabona* train, on Czechoslovak track near Tabor.

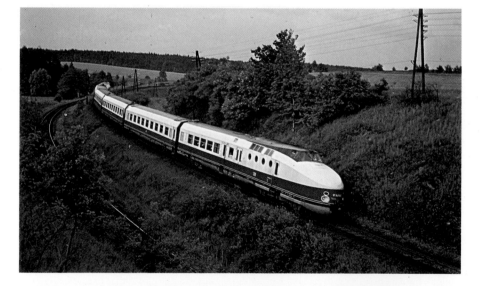

of locomotive design made its appearance. In the immediate post-1945 years, this absorbed French influence, and produced a range of locomotives which were far more French than Austrian in inspiration.

There was considerable war damage in the final years of the war, but railway modernization resulted, by 1975, in the electrification at 3,000 volts of nearly 2,400 km (1,500 miles) of the total 13,000 km (8,100 miles). Several new lines have been built, including a 101 km (63 mile) 1,524 mm (5 ft) gauge line to transport iron ore across the Russo-Czech frontier (some narrow-gauge mileage also still exists). Another fruit of Russo-Czech co-operation is the supply by Skoda of the passenger electric locomotives used by Soviet railways, while Soviet-built diesel-electric mainline locomotives are used by the ČSD.

Hungary

Hungary's first steam-operated public railway was from Budapest to Vác (34 km or 21 miles), opened in 1846. This was part of the Hungarian Central Railway, which eventually linked Budapest with Vienna. After the 1848 revolution, the Hungarian Central, in common with Austrian companies, was taken over by the state until the government in Vienna decided to revert to private ownership. When the Pereires established their private Austrian State Railway, the Hungarian Central was included in the deal. In 1867, the Kingdom of Hungary was re-created. Railway administration was one of the matters, henceforth, handled in Budapest rather than Vienna. By that time, a fairly dense network of lines had been added to the original Hungarian

Central, and these were progressively taken over by the Royal Hungarian State Railways (MÁV), which was formed in 1867 as the state railway administration. After World War 1, MÁV lost its lines in Transylvania (to Roumania) and in Croatia (to Yugoslavia); this reduction had one benefit, however, for it took the most difficult mountain routes out of the system.

Hungarian locomotives had been strongly influenced by Austrian practice and were often designed by Austrians. However, the Brotan boiler was a home-grown feature, designed to cope with the impure water found in Hungary. After a slow start, Hungarian railway engineering developed rapidly; Ganz is a well-known exporter of diesel and electric locomotives and railcars, and it was a Hungarian, Kando, who evolved the early three-phase electrification system, which he

Above: A Hungarian push-pull suburban train.

Below left: A 324 class 2–6–2 of MAV in secondary passenger service. Several hundred of these useful locomotives were built from 1910 onwards. Some, like this example, had Brotan boilers.

Below right: A V43 type electric locomotive, built in Hungary for the MAV from 1964, to designs supplied by a West European consortium.

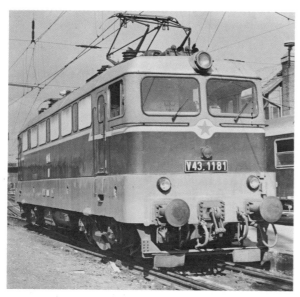

2,500 km (1,550 miles) of route had been opened, all railways were nationalized. By 1914 there were 3,600 km (2,240 miles) of route, including the main international artery connecting Vienna with Constantinople. New construction and territorial acquisitions brought the mileage to about 11,000 km (6,830 miles) by 1975, of which nearly 600 km (370 miles) were narrow gauge.

Locomotives were traditionally imported, usually from Germany, but many Hungarian types were absorbed when Transylvania was acquired. In the 1930s, two domestic locomotive works came into production at Malaxa and Resita. Steam traction is expected to survive for several more years, despite the import of Russian diesel-electrics, and the steady electrification of key routes; electrified mileage totalled 1,296 km (805 miles) in 1975.

THE BALKANS

Albania

Albania's first public railway was opened only in 1947, although at least two narrow-gauge mineral lines had existed previously. The first post-war line, from the port of Durres to Peqin and then to Elbasan, had been begun by the occupying Italian forces during the war. This line was short, like all Albanian lines, being 76 km (47 miles). A line from the capital Tirana to Durres (38 km or 24 miles) was opened in 1949. Several other lines have since been built, much of the constructional work being undertaken as volunteer projects by organizations like the Young Communists. Polish tank locomotives appear to have been used in the early years, but these were followed by Czech diesels. Some Chinese equipment may also be in service. Colour-light signalling is the rule, and some lines, which run through mountainous and unstable terrain, have demanded considerable engineering competence in their construction. Both passenger and freight services are operated; passenger trains are quite frequent, because Durres, which is the pivot of the network, is also a holiday resort.

Bulgaria

Bulgaria's first railway was from Ruse (where it connected by ferry with the Bucharest-Giurgiu line in Roumania) to the port of Varna. This was built in 1866, when the Ottoman Empire still held sway in Bulgaria. The Turks withdrew in several stages, after which the various lines were taken over by the Bulgarian State Railway. This organization (BDZ) by 1975 owned 4,050 km (2,515 miles) of route, of which 245 km (152 miles) were narrow gauge and 1,330 km (826 miles) electrified. The main lines run from the capital Sofia eastwards to the Black Sea ports and towards Turkey. Traversing country which is primarily agricultural and mountainous, the BDZ has always preferred the more powerful types of locomotive; steam locomotives usually had eight, ten, or twelve driving wheels, and were of Austrian and German design. Three main lines (Sofia-Ruse, Sofia-Varna, and Sofia-Plovdiv) have been electrified, and work is in

began to apply in northern Italy in 1902. Kando later applied an ingenious split-phase system to Hungarian railways, although this was superseded by the conventional 25,000 volt system after 1962.

Mileage in 1975 was about 7,600 km (4,700 miles), of which 1,200 km (745 miles) were electrified. There were 330 km (205 miles) of 750 mm gauge line scattered about the country, as well as 35 km (22 miles) of 5 ft gauge, connecting with Russian lines. The current five-year plan (1976 to 1980) envisages further electrification, so that by 1980 electric and diesel traction should account for 93 per cent of all trains.

Roumania

Roumania's frontiers have changed many times during the railway era, and the present Roumanian State Railways (CFR) operate lines which were once part of the Austro-Hungarian and Ottoman empires as well as lines built in independent Roumania. The first line, from Tchernavoda to Constanza, was an Ottoman enterprise although built by British engineers. The first line in Roumania proper was from the capital Bucharest to the Danube at Giurgiu (69 km or 43 miles), opened in 1869. In 1888, when about

progress on converting the line to the Greek frontier. Diesel locomotives are obtained from Russia, Roumania and Austria, while electrics come from Czechoslovakia, although some have also been built at Sofia. Under the current five-year plan it is expected that the network will be 53 per cent electrified by 1980, while the number of freight stations is to be halved.

Above: A scene on the Bulgarian narrow gauge. After 1945 Polish and East German builders supplied 2–10–2 tank locomotives for the 760 mm gauge lines; the last two digits of the locomotive number indicate the gauge.

Greece

The present organization of the Hellenic State Railway (SEK) dates from 1920, when the state took over three private companies. In 1955 the Thessaly and the Franco-Hellenic railways were nationalized, followed by the Peloponnesian Railways and Railways of Northern Greece in 1962. Since 1971 SEK has had the status of a limited company. Although present plans envisage the conversion of some narrow-gauge track to standard gauge, Greece is a country where the narrow gauge still has considerable importance. Standard-gauge mileage in 1975 was 1,560 km (970 miles) and narrow gauge 1,010 km (630 miles). Most of the narrow-gauge mileage was accounted for by two systems, the metre-gauge Thessaly railways with a 162 km (100 mile) main line from Volos to Kalampaka,

Below left: A massive 2–12–4 tank locomotive of the Bulgarian State Railway. Twenty of these units were built in the 1930s to handle coal trains to Sofia.

Below right: On the Yugoslav State Railways at Ljubljana. The Austro-Hungarian influence is exemplified in this picture, which shows an ex-Hungarian 2–6–2 tank locomotive in the foreground, and an ex-Austrian 2–8–2 tank locomotive.

and the metre-gauge Peloponnesian Railway, with over 800 km (500 miles) of track. The first state line built as such was from Piraeus to Papapouli between 1904 and 1909, but there had been several private railways built previously. The standard-gauge 10 km (6 mile) Athens-Piraeus Railway was opened in 1869, and later in the century the Thessaly and Peloponnesus metre-gauge systems were built. The SEK's first line was a venture designed to connect with the Turkish and Serbian systems and for that reason it was built to standard gauge. Although that line never achieved its object of winning international traffic from Brindisi for Piraeus, the line did connect Athens with Salonika by 1916. The latter city already had rail connections built by the Turks, linking it with Constantinople and with Serbia.

Steam traction is virtually extinct in Greece, being superseded by diesel power. The SEK acquired Alco diesels for its main-line services, and the narrow-gauge railways were early users of railcars. Electrification of the Athens-Domokos line is under discussion.

Yugoslavia

Yugoslavia was created after World War 1 from Serbia and various parts of the Austro-Hungarian Empire. Thus Yugoslav State Railways (JZ) inherited a collection of truncated main lines which had lost their original purpose and a collection of locomotives reflecting mainly Austrian and Hungarian practice. During World War 2 many German locomotives were acquired. Soon after the war a part of Italy around Fiume was added to Yugoslavia, bringing with it some Italian railway track and equipment.

The oldest line in Yugoslavia is that from Ljubljana to Maribor, opened in 1849 and later extended to Trieste, forming, with its Vienna connection, an important trading and political artery of the Austrian Empire. In Serbia, there was an important main line from Belgrade to Nis, and a few branches of standard or 750 mm gauge. 750 mm lines also formed a network in Bosnia and Herzegovina. After the formation of the new state, some narrow-gauge lines were converted to standard gauge and a few new lines needed by the

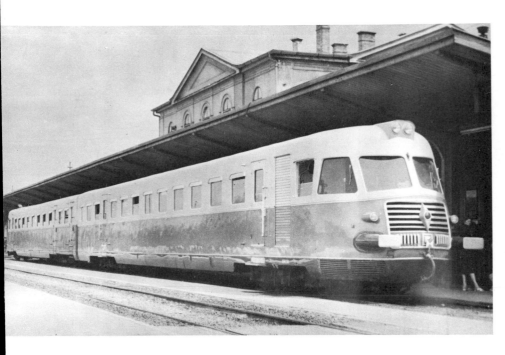

changed circumstances were also undertaken. Notable among the latter was a new main line between Belgrade and Zagreb, and a heavily graded line from the port of Split to Zagreb. More recently, a new line has been built from Belgrade to Bar on the Adriatic. This latter line also runs through forbidding country; it is 476 km (295 miles) long, and is being electrified at 25 kV. The acquisition of Fiume introduced electric traction to Yugoslavia, and the Italian 3,000 volt system was used for the first conversions. The JZ main line is accordingly electrified at 3,000 volts west of Zagreb and at 25kV from Zagreb eastwards to Belgrade and Skopje. By 1974, of the total railway mileage of 10,398 km (6,460 miles), 2,310 km (1,435 miles) was electrified. Total mileage has been reduced slightly over the last two decades because some lines have been closed; the narrow-gauge routes were particularly subject to closure, and were down to 1,045 km (650 miles) by 1974, and since then have declined even further.

BELGIUM AND LUXEMBURG

Belgium

Despite its small size, Belgium made an early mark in railway history with its many innovating engineers and because it was first to treat railway construction as a matter to be organized and planned by the state. The coming of the steam railway coincided with the winning of Belgian independence in 1831, and the desire of the new nation to make its mark was reflected in the eagerness with which it embraced the new technology. Belgian public opinion was additionally attracted by the possibility of capturing trade from the Dutch ports by building railways through Belgium which would bring Central Europe closer to France and Britain. The government accordingly undertook two main lines. The necessary law was passed in May 1834, and a year later the first section (Malines to Brussels) was opened in the presence of George Stephenson, its technical adviser, and of the royal family, its most influential support. By 1844, the two railways had

Above: A two-car diesel set at Ljubljana in 1960. The Yugoslav State Railways used these trains on the Belgrade-Zagreb-Ljubljana main line until electrification.

Below: A type 212 diesel locomotive leaves Antwerp with a stopping train.

been completed: there was a north-south line from Antwerp through Brussels to the French frontier, and an east-west line from Ostend to Germany via Louvain (Leuven). The two lines crossed at Malines (Mechelen), where the state railway established its workshops.

However, the state railway, having achieved much, gradually withdrew from new construction, so that by 1870, of a total network of more than 3,000 km (1,850 miles) the state owned less than 900 km (560 miles). A variety of companies had been organized, often strongly influenced by British practice, even though a Belgian railway equipment industry was quick to develop. One railway company owned no track, but earned its living by hiring locomotives to companies which had laid their track and then discovered they had insufficient funds to buy engines.

In time, the financial difficulties besetting the companies together with political trends brought state ownership back into popularity, so that by 1914 private companies owned less than 300 km (186 miles) of the total 5,000 km (3,100 miles). The state railway was reorganized in 1926, becoming Belgian National Railways (SNCB). In 1975 it owned about 4,000 km (2,485 miles) of route, of which 1,300 km (810 miles) were electrified.

Meanwhile, towards the end of the nineteenth century, a network of local light railways had

been set up under a separate corporation, the SNCV. The first SNCV line was from Ostend to Nieuport (221 km or 137 miles), opened in 1885. Although these metre-gauge light railways could not offer the fast through services of the mainline organization it was possible to meander along SNCV tracks between all the main Belgian centres.

Walschaert, who invented a most successful locomotive valve gear, Belpaire, who devised a new kind of firebox, and Nagelmackers, who introduced the Wagon-Lit concept to European railways, are only three of the many Belgians who made important innovations in railway technology and operation. Locomotive policy was influenced by the coexistence within Belgium of flat lowlands and difficult hilly country on the route to Namur and Luxembourg. Belgian electric and diesel locomotives are home-built, usually in cooperation with foreign builders. Surrounded by countries with differing systems of electrification, Belgium has a special interest in multi-current electric locomotives, and possesses a stock of locomotives capable of working on four different systems in Belgium, Holland, France and Germany.

Luxemburg

In neighbouring Luxemburg, there were in 1975 271 km (168 miles) of railway, of which half was electrified. Since 1947 these lines have been owned by the Luxemburg National Railways (SNCFL) in which 51 per cent of the capital is held by Luxemburg and 24½ per cent each by Belgium and France.

EUROPEAN RUSSIA

In the nineteenth century, railway building and operation in Russia was characterized by the frequently changing balance between private companies and state railways. Railways were badly needed to develop industry, to promote grain exports, to move soldiers to meet internal disturbances and external threats. But the treasury lacked the resources to build all the railways which the government wanted, Russian entrepreneurs were much less venturesome than western capitalists, and because of the difficulties of dealing with a militarized bureaucracy, foreign capitalists were reluctant to invest in Russia except on very favourable terms.

The first public railway was from St Petersburg to Tsarskoye Selo, a popular village resort close to the Tsar's summer palace. This 6 ft (1,828 mm) gauge line was of 25 km (15 miles), and was built by an Austrian citizen using mainly British equipment. This line did have the intended effect of interesting influential opinion in railway building; Nicholas I, very aware of the military significance of railways, decided to start building key main lines. The St Petersburg to Moscow Railway was built by army engineers under the supervision of the American engineer, Whistler. The 5 ft (1,524 mm) gauge was chosen, and this became the Russian standard. However, another

Above left: An SNCB type 122 electric locomotive at Brussels.

Above: The new Soviet Railways' station at Cheliabinsk, in the Urals, with a Czech-built electric locomotive heading a long-distance train.

Below: One of the 0 class compound 0–8–0 locomotives on light duties at a Moscow terminus in 1959. Many thousand units of this tsarist Russian standard freight locomotive were built.

early main line, the Polish section of the Warsaw-Vienna Railway, was built to standard gauge in order to connect with the Austrian system. The third of Nicholas' lines was the long St Petersburg-Warsaw Railway. Of these, the expensively engineered St Petersburg-Moscow Railway was opened in 1851, and the Warsaw-Vienna and the St Petersburg-Warsaw lines were finished in 1848 and 1862, both having been taken over by the state after their private managements had faltered. In subsequent years, many other lines were started both by the state and by companies, so that by 1883 there were 23,700 km (14,700 miles) in operation. After the 1880s attention was increasingly turned to railways in Asiatic Russia, even though a number of new significant lines were built in European Russia. Indeed, the strategically important Archangel and Murmansk lines were completed only in 1899 and 1916 respectively. The former was originally narrow gauge; 750 mm, 3 ft 6 in (1,067 mm) and 3 ft (915 mm) gauge lines accounted in 1913 for 2,900 km (1,800 miles) of the Empire's total of 70,500 km (43,900 miles).

State railways usually bought standard government locomotive designs, as did the private lines very often. The government, through its technical commissions, encouraged standardization of rolling stock and equipment. This meant that production runs of some items were unsurpassed elsewhere. The standard 0 Class freight locomotive introduced in the 1890s was built in about 8,000 units, which was of great help in World War 1, when the rear railways were required to transfer locomotives to the railways nearer the front. By that time Russia was self-sufficient in railway equipment production, through the system of generous government subsidies to manufacturers.

Seven years of war, revolutions, and civil war left the railways in a sad state. Not until 1929 were they restored to their 1913 condition. Fuel crises, rail shortages, and locomotive shortages were the main problems. One thousand 0–10–0 freight locomotives were bought from Sweden and Germany. In the 1930s, massive industrialization brought greatly increased traffic at a time when little investment was being made available to the railways; this brought successive transport crises which the execution for 'sabotage' of railway workers and officials did nothing to alleviate. In the mid-1930s, therefore, extra funds were granted which were devoted to upgrading a few key routes. A dieselization drive in waterless central Asia failed and large orders were then placed for 2–10–0 steam locomotives fitted with condensing apparatus.

Despite all kinds of difficulties, the capability of the railways did improve during the 1930s, and they performed surprisingly well during the difficult days of World War 2. But only in the 1950s, after the death of Stalin, could railway modernization start in earnest. Since then, electrification and dieselisation have almost eliminated the steam locomotive and on the old St Petersburg to Moscow Railway, now the electrified October Railway, high-speed passenger

trains are running their trials. Thanks to a deliberate neglect of road transport, and the failure of the inland waterways to justify the considerable funds invested in them, the railways are still by far the USSR's most important carriers, carrying far more traffic than any other railway system. By the 1950s Soviet economists could claim that with only one tenth of the world's railway mileage, Soviet railways were carrying almost half the world's freight traffic. Mileage (Europe and Asia) in 1975 was 138,250 km (85,870 miles), of which 39,000 km (24,200 miles) was electrified at 3,000 or 25,000 volts. There were also 3,000 km (1,600 miles) of narrow-gauge line, and the mileages just quoted do not include the lengthy non-public lines owned by the industrial ministries, notably the colliery and forestry lines.

Above: A Soviet railway poster of 1954, carrying the slogan, 'The USSR – a Great Railway Power'.

Below: An SU type 2–6–2 locomotive leaving Leningrad with a local train. This was the standard passenger locomotive of the Soviet Railways for several decades, being an enlargement of a 1910 design.

HOLLAND

As in Russia and Bavaria, in Holland it was the reigning monarch who pushed a reluctant nation into the railway age. The Dutch had several reasons for rejecting the railways; they were already investing heavily in steamboats to exploit more fully the potentialities of their internal and international waterways, they knew that because they had little industry railway equipment orders would be placed with foreign companies and, after all, the Netherlands was a small country in which no place was more than two days' journey from the capital. When the first railway was proposed, Dutch capital came forward only after the king had given his personal guarantee that, even if the line was unprofitable, he would ensure that a dividend was always paid. In 1839 the inaugural train was hauled over the Amsterdam to Haarlem railway by a Stephenson locomotive, the *Arendt*. Its gauge was the unusual 1,945 mm (6 ft 4½ in) but this was later changed. Other railways followed, but only slowly. French and British capital played a large role, which meant that French and British technicians were often employed. They, in turn, ordered the necessary equipment from their own countries. The Netherlands, very different from Belgium, was almost entirely lacking in an engineering industry; the most notable engineering feature of Dutch railways, the 1,040 metre (1,137 yd) Moerdyck Bridge, was the work of the French Gouin Company. The Dutch Rhenish Railway derived two thirds of its capital from Britain, although this did not prevent the Dutch authorities stipulating a 2 metre gauge. Since the purpose of this line was to provide a connection between Amsterdam and Cologne, connecting with a standard-gauge German line on the frontier at Emmerich, the line was, not surprisingly, unprofitable until the government reluctantly granted a subsidy for re-gauging.

One reason for the slow development of railways was the dense network of waterways capable of carrying freight more cheaply, although somewhat more slowly, than the railways. Freight revenue therefore, has always taken second place to passenger revenue in Holland. Indeed, the first railway did not consider the provision of freight cars worthwhile. Only when Amsterdam was connected with Arnhem did freight begin to figure in railway traffic. The unprofitable Franco-Belgian enterprise, the Netherlands Central, whose main line from Utrecht to Zwolle was opened in 1864, never possessed a freight locomotive. In modern times, the relative scarcity of freight traffic is even more apparent, for most of the freight traffic moves at night, utilizing locomotives which work passenger services during the daytime.

By 1880 there were ten companies, of which three were dominant: the Netherlands Railway, whose main line was from Amsterdam through The Hague to Rotterdam; the Dutch Rhenish Railway; and the State Railway Operating Company. Competition between these lines was ruinous. Consequently, in 1890, the state imposed a new grouping. From the existing railways were created two large enterprises of approximately equal size, the State Railway and the Netherlands Railway. The former lay mainly in the south and bought its locomotives from England; because these locomotives had a left-hand driving position the Railway positioned its signals on the left of the track, even though its trains ran on the right-hand track.

The difficulties which began to beset the railways after World War 1 prompted the two companies to cooperate more closely. In 1938, the dual system came to an end when both were united to form the new Netherlands Railway Company (NS) in which all shares were held by the state. Much damage was suffered during World War 2, in 1940 through invasion, during the war through deferred maintenance, and in 1944 through invasion again, flooding, non-cooperation by Dutch railwaymen with the Ger-

Above left: The new post-war station at Rotterdam, with a standard e.m.u. train on the centre track.

Top: The *Sprinter*, a prototype of the e.m.u. train with which the Netherlands Railways expect to replace the older post-war electric trains.

Above: Restaurant service in one of the Netherlands Railways longer-distance trains.

Below: One of the few Spanish standard-gauge lines, the Langreo Railway, outside the RENFE system.

man authorities, demolition, sabotage, and removal of railway property by the retreating Germans. When the war ended there were only 144 serviceable locomotives and less than 500 freight cars.

Wartime destruction gave an opportunity for complete reconstruction, out of which emerged one of the most modern railway systems in Europe. Electrification and the widespread use of diesel railcars had been the policy before the war, and this was continued after 1945. In 1967 the government began to plan for a coordinated passenger transport system in which the railways would play a leading part; it was thought that mass use of the automobile for daily travel would be impossible in a country like Holland and, if not impossible, certainly unpleasant. To this end subsidies were considered justifiable to enable NS to provide a standard of service which would be of overall national benefit, even though unprofitable in commercial accounting terms. The emphasis has been on rapid, frequent, interconnecting and regular-interval passenger services. These are mainly provided by electric multiple-unit trains, locomotive-hauled trains being used primarily on international services, with diesel multiple-units on secondary lines. New station designs have succeeded better than in most countries in combining modern materials and methods with forms which are not merely fashionable but pleasing too. Some new railways

are still being built, notably the Amsterdam-Schiphol link (which may be extended to Leiden to provide a shorter route between Amsterdam and The Hague) and, in the near future a new railway in connection with the *Deltaplan* land reclamation scheme. Mileage in 1975 was about 2,800 km (1,740 miles), of which 1,700 km (1,060 miles) was electrified at 1,500 volts. A new generation of fast electric multiple-unit trains, the 'Sprinters', is coming into service.

THE IBERIAN PENINSULA

Spain

Spain entered the railway age in 1848 when the 28 km (17 mile) line from Barcelona to Mataró was opened. Poor, thinly populated, and largely mountainous, Spain was not promising railway territory, and some years elapsed before the first main lines were built: Madrid-Alicante in 1858 and Madrid-Barcelona in 1860. British technical assistance was important in these early years, and so was foreign capital. From about 1855, an influx of French capital resulted in the formation of four large companies which dominated the network until nationalization. These were the Northern, whose main lines were from Madrid to Irun and from Barcelona to Zaragoza and Pamplona, and which absorbed the Central Aragon Railway in 1926; the Madrid-Zaragoza-Alicante; the Madrid, Caceres & Portugal (after 1928 the

Right: One of the French-built electric locomotives which handle the bulk of Dutch locomotive-hauled trains, both passenger and freight. No 1312 is standing at Hook of Holland with the *Holland-Scandinavia Express*.

Above: One of the RENFE's many heavily-graded lines. Because of the mountainous terrain, the inter-war Spanish designers favoured locomotives with four or five driving axles.

main constituent of the Western Railway); and the Andalusian Railway. World War 1 brought financial problems, and the destructive Spanish civil war made reorganization essential. In 1943 the state bought up the companies and Spanish National Railways (RENFE) took over the 1,676 mm (5 ft 6 in) gauge lines; that gauge was standard in Spain, although there was a considerable mileage of narrower gauge route (mainly metre-gauge) which was not taken over by RENFE.

Until the 1960s RENFE operated a variegated and antiquated stock of steam locomotives; in recent years, however, there has been considerable electrification and dieselization; steam traction ended in 1975. In 1975, of the RENFE's 13,430 km (8,340 miles) of route, 3,450 km

(2,140 miles) were electrified. Electrification, at 3,000 volts, has been based on French practice, and the main routes converted have been the north-south trunk line from Irun to Seville (and later Cadiz) via Madrid, main lines in the north west, and the coastal line from Cerbere to Tarragona via Barcelona. In 1976, the latter electrification was linked with the other electrified lines by conversion of the line through Zaragoza.

Steam locomotives in the twentieth century were built largely in Spanish workshops, but much modern equipment is imported, or built under license. However, in the Talgo trains, with their unique suspension, and in the development of variable-gauge rolling stock for international services, Spain has made a distinctive contribution to railway technology.

Below: 4–8–0 locomotives at Ronda in 1966. This wheel arrangement was popular in Spain, thanks to its good traction characteristics.

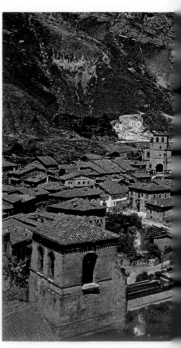

Above: The Portuguese Railway's metre-gauge suburban service at Oporto. A German-built 2–6–0 tank locomotive enters Senhora da Hora in 1968.

Below: An Irun-Madrid train passes Pancorbo. The train is of the 'Talgo' type, offering low centre of gravity and the possibility of maintaining high speed over winding track.

Portugal

Railways made an inauspicious start in Portugal, for in 1856 the inaugural train of the first railway, from Lisbon to Cintra, broke down and the King was obliged to disembark. Later, railway construction was accompanied by a more than normal amount of financial skullduggery. Nevertheless, by 1866 it was possible to travel by rail from Lisbon through Spain into the rest of Europe. However, the Portuguese adoption of the Spanish 1,676 mm (5 ft 6 in) gauge had far-reaching consequences; by making rail freight transits to the rest of Europe so inconvenient that the British were helped in maintaining their seaborne hold on Portuguese trade. By increasing construction costs, that decision encouraged the subsequent introduction of the metre gauge for lines serving the less prosperous inland areas.

The Portuguese Railway Company (CP) operates almost all the Portuguese railways, through the granting of a concession valid until the year 2000. In 1975 there were 2,835 km (1,760 miles) of broad gauge route and 760 km (470 miles) of metre-gauge. Until the 1970s line closures were rare, but it is anticipated that perhaps 900 km (560 miles) of the 1975 mileage may be closed. The main Lisbon-Oporto line carries a heavy traffic, and so do certain of the other coastal lines, but in the agricultural and depopulating areas of the interior, and especially in the north where the metre gauge predominates, prospects are not bright.

There has been considerable modernization; steam traction has been virtually eliminated except on some sections of the metre gauge. Electrified mileage in 1975 was 406 km (252 miles) this being accounted for by the Lisbon-Oporto line, converted on the 25,000 volt system under French guidance.

IRELAND

Ireland's first railway was the Dublin & Kingstown, opened in 1834. This 1,435 mm (4 ft 8½ in) gauge line connected Dublin with its mailboat quay, thereby improving the connection with London. Later part of the Dublin & South Eastern Railway, this short line made locomotive history as the first public railway to make regular use of tank locomotives. In 1839, the Ulster Railway, from Belfast to Armagh, was built to a gauge of 1,880 mm (6 ft 2 in), followed by the Dublin & Drogheda's 1,600 mm (5 ft 3 in) gauge line. However, in 1846 a railway commission decided to standardize the 5 ft 3 in gauge. That same year marks the end of the era of optimism for Irish railways, for the potato famine of the mid-1850s reduced the population and dampened economic development. Ireland's continuing situation as a sparsely populated agricultural territory (Belfast was the only industrial city) meant that Irish railways could rarely afford new equipment and led a precarious life until, in recent decades, most of them were closed.

Over the years, Irish railways coalesced into five large companies and a host of small lines. The five large were the Great Southern & Western, which had its Dublin-Cork main line and also served Limerick and Killarney; the Great Northern, second largest and often regarded as the best, linking Belfast with Dublin and providing one of the two routes (via Portadown) from Belfast to Londonderry; the Midland Great Western, from Dublin to the west coast; the Dublin & South Eastern, whose main line was from Dublin to Wexford; and the Northern Counties Committee, which as the Belfast & Northern Counties had been taken over by England's Midland Railway in 1903 and had a main line from Belfast to Larne and another from Belfast to Londonderry via Coleraine.

As with so many other railway systems, World War 1 marked the end of an era for Irish railways. Higher labour costs, higher fuel costs, and the rise of the internal combustion engine were threats which in Ireland were compounded by political factors, beginning with the Dublin Rising of 1916. When the country was partitioned in 1921, the frontier separating the six northern counties from newly independent Southern Ireland cut the lines of five railways; four of these were small but the fifth was the Great Northern, whose lines crossed the frontier at 14 points. At about the same time, the wartime government control of the railways was ended, the strengthened trade unions began to agitate for more pay and better conditions, and the Irish civil war started. During this war the railways were a prime target of the rebels. Armed attacks and sabotage were a daily occurrence. In eighteen months the GS & WR had its track damaged in almost 400 places, and the Dublin & South Eastern suffered damage to a third of its locomotive stock. The railways, never very prosperous, began to accumulate deficits and the possibility of the bankruptcy of the GS & WR, a major Irish undertaking, was very real.

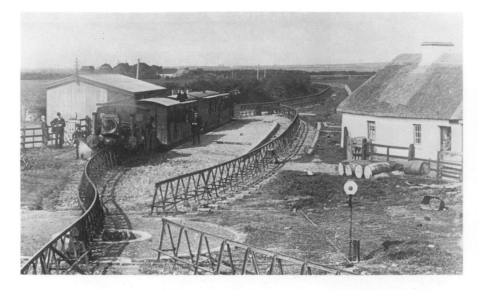

From 1925, 26 southern Irish railways, with the GS & WR predominating, were amalgamated into one company, the Great Southern Railways. Among the 26 were many 914 mm (3 ft) gauge lines which served rural areas – mostly built towards the end of the nineteenth century. The Great Northern was left out of this merger, because it was largely a Northern Irish line. In Northern Ireland the NCC continued to function as before and was able to acquire new standard locomotives and rolling stock. The Great Northern did its best in an attempt to compete with the NCC for public esteem, and reduced its schedules on the Belfast-Dublin run to 155 minutes for the 181 km (112.5 miles) run.

The second world war brought more traffic to the railways of both parts of Ireland, rescuing them from a situation in which costs were again threatening to overwhelm receipts. However, reduction and interruption of coal imports meant that many southern Irish railways could not carry the traffic which was offered. At one point in 1942 the GSR could run passenger trains on only two days per week. The meagre supply of coal which did reach the railways was of such poor quality that trains were sometimes marooned when locomotive fireboxes could no longer cope.

In 1944 a general election was fought over the issue of whether Southern Ireland's transport system should be reorganized. The government won this election, and in 1945 the Great South-

Above: The continental Lartigue monorail system, which had little to recommend it apart from its ingenuity, had its most extensive application in Ireland, where it was adopted for the short Listowel and Ballybunion Railway (1888-1924) pictured here.

Above right: Irish short lines were often enthusiastic pioneers of the rural rail car, like the County Donegal example shown here.

Below: Freight practice on the Irish Railways (Coras Iompair Eireann) has recently moved from the predominant use of general user open or covered wagons to specified types for train-load working and mechanized handling. The special fertilizer train of uniform palletized fertilizer wagons typifies the new development.

ern Railways was duly amalgamated with a Dublin bus company (DUTC) to form the Irish Transport Company (CIE). The CIE's first business was dealing with another coal crisis in the winter between 1946 and 1947, which it did by cancelling all passenger trains except the night mails to Cork, Wexford and Athlone. Meanwhile, in Northern Ireland, the local Parliament in 1948 passed a bill which established the Ulster Transport Authority (UTA), combining the NCC, the 80-mile (129-km) Belfast & County Down Railway, and the Northern Ireland Road Transport Board. In general, the Northern government was less sympathetic to railways than the Southern and in particular it wished to close most of the Great Northern mileage which lay in its territory. In 1958 the Great Northern was dissolved, with its northern sections going to the UTA and its southern becoming part of CIE. Within ten years another reorganization eliminated the UTA, the northern railways becoming Northern Ireland Railways. Northern Irish route length is now very reduced; it was about 1,200 km (720 miles) in 1937 and 357 km (221 miles) in 1975, the surviving lines being those from Belfast to the border, to Larne, to Bangor, and to Portrush and Londonderry. However, there have been various improvements designed to make these lines important passenger routes. On the Belfast-Dublin line, new eight-coach trains with a diesel-electric locomotive at each end went into service in 1970. In Belfast itself a new station, Belfast Central, is intended largely to bring together the modernized inner and outer suburban services.

In the south, the CIE was facing unprecedented financial problems by 1976. It, too, in recent decades has closed many lines and stations so that route length in 1975 was down to 2,189 km (1,360 miles) compared to about 4,265 km (2,650 miles) in 1937. It closed its narrow gauge sections as soon as it could, and then turned to branch and secondary lines. Unlike the Northern Ireland Railways, it remained interested in freight traffic and modernized its services where it could. It was one of the first railways to change over entirely to diesel traction, this being achieved in 1963. There was a carefully-thought out dieselization plan, and this gave fairly gener-

ous security to locomotive men displaced by the new technology. The dieselization programme was supervised by the celebrated locomotive engineer Bulleid, who went to the CIE after leaving British Railways. Bulleid, in an endeavour to utilise Ireland's only plentiful fuel, and to further his own ideas about locomotive design, built a novel peat-burning steam locomotive which, however, did not progress beyond prototype form because diesels seemed more promising. Peat-burning locomotives were not new to Ireland and, with the exception of the patented Drumm battery railcars of pre-war years, were Ireland's main innovation in traction development, although the Irish railways were among the pioneers in the large-scale use of petrol- and diesel-engined railcars.

ITALY

Political fragmentation delayed the creation of an all-Italian railway network; independent states made their own plans with scant reference to their neighbours. The first line was opened by the King of Naples in 1839, a short line from Naples to Portici. Then came the 13 km (8 mile) Milan-Monza line in 1840. Pope Pius IX was one of the first to envisage a national network; apart from interesting himself in the Papal States railways, he dreamed of main lines bringing pilgrims from all parts of Italy. By 1865, after political unification, the already considerable route length was divided between four companies: the Southern, Roman, Northern, and Calabria & Sicily railways. However, after several decades of discussion the Italian State Railway (FS) was established in 1905.

Above: Two of the three diesel railcars used by the Circumetnea Railway in Sicily. This 950 mm (3 ft 1½ in) gauge line of 114 km (71 miles) is a small independent railway.

Below: An E645 class electric locomotive descends from the Brenner Pass with the Alps express from Copenhagen to Rome.

Below right: An Italian State Railway 2-6-0 with a secondary passenger service. This locomotive, with its distinctive combination of outside steam chests and valve gear with inside cylinders has survived into the last days of the steam era.

In 1975 the FS possessed about 16,075 km (9,985 miles) of route, with minor railways operating an additional 3,850 km (2,390 miles). Due to political pressures, there has been very little closing of lines, with the result that one third of the FS route length carries two per cent of the traffic. Although having an undistinguished record in steam locomotive design, the Italians were very advanced in railway electrification. From 1901 a three-phase system (now superseded by the conventional 3,000 volt system) was introduced in northern Italy, and by 1939 Italy led the world in the proportion of her mileage under catenary. All main lines are now electrified. Such main lines include the Milan-Bologna-Florence-Rome-Naples trunk route, and the (formerly Austrian) Milan-Venice-Trieste line. In 1975 nearly 8,000 km (5,000 miles) of the FS were electrified. On non-electrified lines, diesel locomotives, especially diesel railcars, predominate, although steam traction still survives. Like most European railways, the FS makes a financial loss, but state subsidies permit continued improvements. Current projects include the new Rome-Florence high-speed *Direttissima* route, intended to relieve pressure on the existing main line.

POLAND

The Polish State Railways (PKP) were established in 1919 by the government of the new state of Poland. Poland's railways had been built by the former rulers of Polish territory: Russia, Prussia, and Austria. There was accordingly a wide variety of practice and technique and in the inter-war period the PKP concentrated on standardizing the most essential items. In particular, the wide Russian-gauge railways and their equipment were converted to European standard gauge, and the number of locomotive classes reduced. New locomotives and equipment were to a large extent built in Poland.

World War 2 began with the virtual disappearance of Poland, the railways being divided between the Russian and German systems. Later the ebb and flow of the Russo-German front was accompanied by re-gauging and re-regauging as each side imposed its own standards. The new Poland which emerged after 1945 had lost much of its eastern, former Russian, territory and extended its western frontier to contain more former Prussian territory. This had a corresponding effect on the PKP, which acquired additional ex-German equipment and stayed with the Euro-

Above: A Polish Ok22 class locomotive at Choszczno in 1975. This was one of the first classes to be introduced by the PKP, in 1922, and was a Polish version of the well-known Prussian P8, of which several hundred units worked on Polish lines.

Below: A PKP electric locomotive at Lublin. Present plans envisage that 40 per cent of the Polish network will be electrified by 1985.

pean standard gauge. Because of the acquisition of Silesia, Poland's heavy industry could expand rapidly, which is why PKP now carries more freight than any of the other European railways, excepting Soviet railways. Steam traction is still used, although electric, and later diesel, locomotives have taken a growing proportion of the traffic. Electrification at 3,000 volts began before the war, with a Warsaw suburban scheme. After the war the first main-line conversion was of the 320 km (200 mile) Warsaw-Katowice line in 1957. Of the 23,600 km (14,660 miles) of route in 1975, 5,120 km (3,180 miles) were electrified. New lines are still being built, including a new main line, intended for heavy freight trains (up to 5,000 tonnes), from Silesia to the Baltic ports.

SCANDINAVIA

Denmark

Unlike her Scandinavian neighbours, Denmark was faced more with water than with mountain barriers when constructing her railway network. The gaps separating the islands and the Jutland peninsula were a serious obstacle to railway movement, even when train ferries were provided, and it is only since 1930 that a handful of long bridges like the Storstrom (3,200 metres or 3,500 yards) and the Little Belt (1,178 metres or 1,289 yards) have alleviated, but not eliminated, this problem.

Mileage in 1975 was about 2,000 km (1,240 miles). The first railway was built by the Zealand Railway Company in 1847, linking Copenhagen with Roskilde (30 km or 19 miles). The Danish State Railways (DSB) was formed in 1885 to unite the railways which the state had either bought or built itself; the first state railway was built in 1862 from Aarhus to Randers in Jutland. Most of the railway mileage is now owned by the DSB. Electrification has made little headway, with only suburban lines at Copenhagen being converted, a process which began in 1933 and is still not complete. However, Denmark was an early adherent of dieselization. In the 1930s the 'Lyntog' fast diesel trains were introduced between main centres, while Danish builders exported successful diesel-electric locomotives. In the early days British, and later German, influence was strong, but at the end of the nineteenth century there came an urge to make the railways truly Danish. Otto Busse was appointed to design a distinctive range of locomotives; this he did, producing a succession of under-boilered and rather old-fashioned designs until finally he produced his masterpiece, an Atlantic which outlasted all other European designs of that wheel arrangement. After Busse's death, the DSB returned to German models for its locomotives, although its most successful subsequent design was the compound Pacific built in Sweden for both Swedish and Danish railways. The terminus at Copenhagen, red brick and with a timber arched roof, was also built during the 'neo-Danish' period, and resembles a folk museum. In recent years there has been an effort to attract passenger traffic with faster and

more comfortable trains. A regular-interval service with new equipment has now replaced the '*Lyntogs*' on the key Copenhagen to Fredericia and Aarhus route.

Finland

Being part of the Russian Empire until 1918, Finland standardized the Russian 5 ft (1,524 mm) gauge right from the start. Her first railway was opened in 1862, from Helsinki to Hämeenlinna (108 km or 67 miles). Soon afterwards, in 1870, a link with Russia was opened, from Riihimäki to St Petersburg. Apart from certain technical features, there was little uniformity with the Russian system, and the distinctiveness of Finnish equipment is still a feature of Finnish National Railways (VR). Locomotives of Finnish design were built from 1874, by Tampella and Lokomo. Mileage reached a peak in the early 1940s, exceeding 6,000 km (3,725 miles) but declined when much of eastern Finland was ceded to Russia. Mileage by 1975 had climbed back to 5,975 km (3,710 miles), of which 395 km (245 miles) was electrified. Although steam traction ceased in 1975, electrification came late to Finland, partly because Finnish diesel locomotives and diesel multiple-unit trains had been very successful. However, in the 1960s the first main line electrification, from Helsinki to Riihimäki and Seinäjoki, was undertaken. For this 25,000 volt scheme Finland imported the locomotives, from the USSR. New lines are still being built, and a current project is another link with the Russian railways, mainly for freight.

Norway

More mountainous than Sweden, with less population and industry, Norway has not yet developed a railway system comparable with those of her neighbours. The line from Christiania (now Oslo) to Eidsvoll was opened in 1854. 43 miles (69 km) long, it was undertaken by

Robert Stephenson, thereby bringing early Norwegian railways into the British orbit; even the rule book of this pioneer line was printed in English as well as Norwegian. This was a private line at first, but subsequent main lines were state railways. Three main lines were built, from Oslo across the mountains to Bergen, from Oslo to Stavanger, and from Oslo to Trondheim. The Trondheim line was originally by a route completed in 1880 via Røros, which suffered from a break of gauge. To save construction costs, the state had decided at one stage to encourage the 3 ft 6 in (1,067 mm) gauge rather than Stephenson's standard gauge, and there are still a few lines of the narrower gauge still functioning, although most have been re-gauged. A direct line to Trondheim via Dovre was opened in the 1930s, this being the occasion for the introduction by the Norwegian State Railways (NSB) of its most notable locomotive type, the 2–8–4, 4-cylinder compound fast passenger locomotive.

Above: A Danish State Railways diesel-hauled train. The locomotive, like so many Scandinavian diesel units, was built by the Swedish firm NOHAB under licence from General Motors.

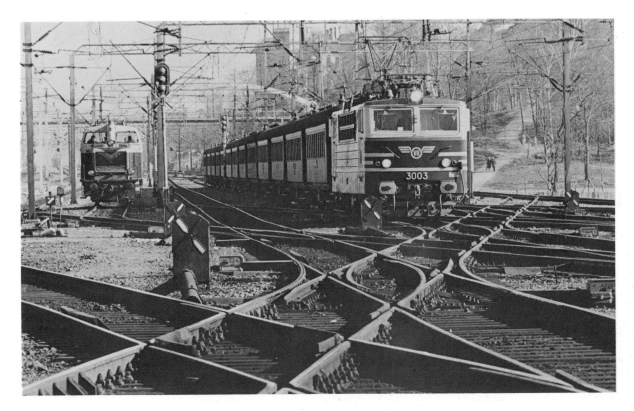

Left: One of the twenty-seven electric locomotives built in the USSR for the first Finnish mainline electrification out of Helsinki.

Extension of Norway's railways into the mountainous and under-populated north has been quite recent. Narvik, which was joined to the Swedish system in 1902, was only a farm before the railway came, and is still not linked to the Norwegian network. However, the Arctic harbour of Bodø was reached by a line from Trondheim in 1962. More recently, a line from Narvik into the far north as far as Tromso has been projected. This 220 km (136 mile) line would facilitate the development of off-shore oilfields. Mileage in 1975 was about 4,250 km (2,640 miles), of which 2,450 km (1,520 miles) was electrified. Most electrification has been achieved since the war, although the first conversion dates from 1911, and electrified mileage in 1945 was 605 km (376 miles). As in Sweden, the 15,000 volt system was chosen, and much of the equipment is imported from Swedish builders.

Sweden

Sweden's first public steam railway was a privately-built line of 18 km (11 miles) opened in 1856 from Nora to Ervalla. Two short state-built lines serving Malmö and Gothenburg were opened later the same year. Sweden's first main line, from Stockholm to Gothenburg, was not finished until 1862. Between 1860 and 1880 there was considerable construction in the centre and south, the mountainous north being served later. There were about 8,000 km (4,970 miles) of route in 1890, and almost 17,000 km (10,560 miles) by 1930. 1975 mileage was 11,360 km (7,060 miles), of which 182 km (113 miles) was narrow gauge.

As early as 1853 the Swedish parliament decided that main lines would be state-built and operated, but only about a third of the present network was built by the state. The private lines, secondary and often narrow gauge, have been progressively acquired by the state railway (SJ), although this process is not yet complete. Narrow-gauge lines were usually of 3 ft 6 in (1,067 mm) or 891 mm (three Swedish feet) standard.

One of the best-known Swedish lines is the Lapland Railway, beyond the Arctic Circle. This was completed in 1902 and exploits the rich iron ore resources around Kiruna; it transports ore to the Gulf of Bothnia and also to the ice-free port of Narvik, in Norway. The Swedish part of the line was electrified in 1915, and the short (40 km or 25 mile) section into Norway in 1923; the Norwegian section is the steepest, with a drop of 518 metres (1,700 ft) in 39 km (24 miles) but the grade is in favour of loaded trains.

Electrification in Sweden started early; the first section of the private Stockholm-Roslagen railway was converted at 700 volts in 1894. The Stockholm-Gothenburg main line was electrified in 1926, the Stockholm-Malmö line in 1933, and the Gothenburg-Malmö line in 1936. By 1945 Sweden had the world's second largest electrified mileage (5,400 km or 3,350 miles), being surpassed only by Italy. 7,520 km (4,670 miles) of Swedish railways were electrified by 1975, 6,960 km (4,322 miles) being SJ lines. About 90 per cent of the traffic is now electrically hauled, with diesel power handling the rest; however, some steam locomotives are kept in reserve.

A number of lines have been built solely as pioneer routes, with little expectation of breaking even financially. The most notable of these is the 'Inland Railway' which runs from the Arctic Circle southwards down the centre of Sweden. This is lightly trafficked, but nevertheless essential for the sparse population which it serves. It is diesel operated, and train services are modern and rapid. Many halt-type stations are self-service, with intending passengers operating signals to halt the train at the platform. Because of such labour-saving techniques, the number of railway employees per unit of traffic carried is lower in Sweden than elsewhere in Europe. Other labour-saving devices (which enabled SJ to claim a figure of only 3.6 workers per track kilometre in 1974) are the wide use of centralized train control; what was claimed in 1973 to be the world's longest continuous stretch of CTC runs from Narvik through Sweden to Norrköping (south of Stockholm) a distance of 1,700 km (1,050 miles).

Although British rolling stock was imported in the early years, it was not long before Sweden was producing, and exporting, railway equipment. Locomotives were built at Motala and by Nydquist and Holm (NOHAB); the latter company still makes the mechanical parts for electric

Above: A St Moritz to Chur train on the Rhaetian Railway in Switzerland. This metre-gauge line serves the best-known winter resorts.

Below left: The Söderhams Railway, opened in 1861 and one of Sweden's pioneer lines. The locomotive in this early photograph is *Finnveden*, built in Manchester by Beyer, Peacock.

Above right: The Sitter Viaduct on the Bodensee-Toggenburg Railway, an independent Swiss short line. The train is hauled by an electric motor-coach.

Below: This 4-cylinder compound 2–10–0 was built for the St Gotthard line, but is now preserved outside the SLM works at Winterthur, Switzerland, where it was built in 1917.

locomotives and builds main-line diesel-electrics under licence from General Motors. In the inter-war years, the Ljungstrom brothers designed what was perhaps the world's most successful type of steam turbine locomotive. Three of these ran for many years on the private Grängesberg-Oxelösund coal railway. Sweden was also a pioneer in diesel traction. Diesel locomotives, and a diesel-electric railcar, were in service before World War 1. The Swedish company ASEA builds the electrical parts for both diesel and electric locomotives and in recent years has produced and exported successful thyristor-controlled electric locomotives. In 1975 an experimental tilt-body train broke the Scandinavian speed record by reaching 238 kph (148 mph). Regular-interval passenger services were introduced in 1973 on the first 149 miles (240 km) of the Stockholm-Malmö line. Recently a special effort has been made to design attractive second class coaches, and SJ in 1973 became a pioneer in the use of closed-system train toilets.

SWITZERLAND

Switzerland's first railway was opened in 1847, from Baden to Zurich (23 km or 15 miles). Other lines followed, despite the difficulties experienced by companies in raising capital. A dense network was created over the years, and when the great Alpine tunnels were built a lucrative international transit traffic developed. The Gotthard tunnel was finished in 1882, followed by the Simplon in 1906 and the Lötschberg (connecting eastern France with the Simplon) in 1913. Having no fossil fuels but a potential abundance of hydro-electricity, Swiss railways early adopted large-scale electrification; a metre-gauge electrification was undertaken as early as 1893. Later the 15,000 volt system was standardized, facilitat-

ing interchanges with the Bavarian and Austrian railways.

After a referendum in 1898 the main Swiss railway companies were nationalized, the Swiss Federal Railways (SBB or CFF) assuming their management. Nationalization was a gradual process and is still not complete – more than a hundred minor and two major independent railways still exist. One of the latter is the Berne-Lötschberg-Simplon, opened in 1913 to connect with the Simplon tunnel. Electrified from the start, this 115 km (71 mile) line carries a dense traffic and is very profitable. The other major independent railway is the metre-gauge Rhaetian Railway, built by local initiative to serve mainly the winter sports areas of the Grisons Canton. All-electric, with 363 km (225 miles) of route, its first section was opened in 1890.

Switzerland's pace-setting role in electrification was supported by a very active engineering industry. The Winterthur Works, builders of steam locomotives, changed to the production of mechanical parts for electric and diesel locomotives, while Oerlikon and Brown-Boveri not only supplied the Swiss railways with very advanced electrical equipment but also developed a strong export business whose products introduced many innovations into railway technology. The inter-war development of a truly high-speed electric locomotive was largely a Swiss achievement.

New tunnels, track-doubling, station reconstruction and new rolling stock are all featured in current work. In relation to her area, Switzerland leads Europe in frequency of train service, provided largely by electric push-pull train sets. Of the SBB's 2,860 km (1,776 miles) of route in 1975, all but about 20 km (12 miles) were electrified.

HISTORY

USA

Above: The celebrated race on the Baltimore and Ohio Railroad, between Cooper's *Tom Thumb* and a horse. The horse won.

The United States was not the birthplace of the railway, but few nations have had their history and development so decisively shaped by a new mode of transport. Both in Britain, birthplace of the railway, and in Europe, the new railways usually served cities already well established. In America, still a largely unpopulated continent of vast distances, many railways were themselves to create new centres of population.

First rails

The first American railways naturally leaned upon the pioneer work of such English inventor–engineers as William Murdock, Richard Trevithick, and the father and son team of George and Robert Stephenson. America's first railways came as the climax to a generation of change in the field of internal improvements. The success of the Lancaster Turnpike, completed in 1794, had created an urgent demand for more improved roads, including the National Road, built to Wheeling, Virginia, and further west early in the 19th century. Robert Fulton's *Clermont* on the Hudson in 1807, and the *New Orleans* on the Mississippi a few years later, had introduced the practical and romantic steamboat

to the rivers of the nation, while the celebration in November 1825 marking completion of New York's Erie canal had started a canal mania from the Hudson river to the states of the old northwest.

Railways appeared along the Atlantic seaboard at several places during the 1820s. In 1825 Col. John Stevens had transported hardy house guests in his 'steam waggon' around a circular track on the grounds of his Hoboken, New Jersey, estate. Gridley Bryant a year later opened his broad-gauge Granite Railway at Quincy, Massachusetts, to haul stone on its way to the Bunker Hill monument. In Pennsylvania in 1829 the resident engineer of the Delaware & Hudson Canal and Railroad, Horatio Allen, decided that the English-built locomotive, *Stourbridge Lion*, was too rigid and heavy for American track. On July 4, 1828, ground was broken on the Baltimore & Ohio Railroad, and in 1830 Peter Cooper's small experimental locomotive, *Tom Thumb*, made its first run on the 21 km (13 miles) of completed B&O line. Later that same year, on Christmas Day 1830, the *Best Friend of Charleston* pulled a short passenger train out of Charleston, South Carolina, providing the first scheduled steam railway service in America.

In 1830 there were only 37 km (23 miles) of completed line in the United States. But growth came quickly, and more than 1,610 km (1,000 miles) were in operation by 1835. All the New England and Mid-Atlantic states, except Vermont, had some trackage by 1838. In the late 1830s even such western states as Ohio, Indiana and Kentucky were projecting several railways. By 1840 the nation could claim 4,500 km (2,800 miles) in operation, and nine states – Massachusetts, Connecticut, New York, New Jersey, Pennsylvania, Maryland, Virginia, South Carolina, and Georgia – each had more than 160 km (100 miles) of completed route. Pennsylvania, with 1,213 km (754 miles), was first in the nation. Much of the early trackage was built from important eastern sea ports westwards towards Lake Erie or the Ohio river. Boston, New York City, Philadelphia, Baltimore, Charleston, and Savannah were all competing for western mar-

Below left: 'Old Ironsides,' Matthias Baldwin's first full-size locomotive, hauling the first train of the Philadelphia, Germantown and Norristown Railroad in 1832.

Below: An early lithograph of a typical mid-century American train.

Right: A poster of an early American railroad, later part of the New York Central. As elsewhere in the world, posters served both as advertisements and as timetables in the early days.

kets by the 1840s. In 1850 three-fifths of the 14,480 km (9,000 miles) of railway in operation were located in the 11 Mid-Atlantic and New England states. At mid-century New York, with 2,189 km (1,361 miles) of route, had replaced Pennsylvania as the leading railway state.

Partly because of the novelty of rail travel, passenger traffic was greater than freight in the early years. The first passenger coaches were little more than stage coaches with flanged wheels, as illustrated in 1831 by the three-car train pulled by the *DeWitt Clinton* on the Mohawk & Hudson Railroad in New York. By the time Fanny Kemble, the English actress who toured America, was calling her coach 'a long greenhouse on wheels', passenger coaches had lost their stage coach design. The early American locomotive typically had four driving wheels, and within a dozen years was equipped with a bell, whistle, headlight and a pilot or cowcatcher at the front. The absence of fences along much of the early right-of-way made such warning and safety devices necessary.

By mid-century many locomotives had a leading swivelled bogie or truck under the smokebox, making them 4-4-0s; they were known as American-type locomotives. At mid-century all locomotives, regardless of wheel arrangement, were woodburners. Accidents were frequent. Coaches and wagons could derail, axles did break, couplers could unfasten, and faulty or loose iron strap rails could cause unbelievable injury and havoc in piercing a coach floor.

In the first years there was some opposition to the new mode of rapid transport. Some doctors warned of the excessive speed, a few divines preached against the iron horse, and nearly all canal owners and road or coaching companies were in opposition. But the railway quickly proved superior to earlier forms of transport. Rail freight, while not as cheap as water-borne traffic, was cheaper than road haulage. Merchants welcomed the railway because it ran 12 months of the year and was not affected by vagaries of season or weather. Certainly train schedules were much faster than those of the stagecoach, the Conestoga wagon, the canal packet, or the white and stately river paddle steamers.

Below: Motive power units of an American horse-drawn service are detached for watering. Horse-drawn trains survived on short lines well into the steam age.

Early maturity

Already by 1850 American railways had nearly tripled the mileage of canals, and were carrying far more freight than was moved over the decaying roads of the nation. At mid-century many projected railways were being built to towns and small cities far from any navigable river. But the decade after 1850 was probably the most important in the history of American railways. What had been a scattering of short lines from Georgia to Maine in 1850 became by 1860 an iron network serving adequately all the states east of the Mississippi. As the only 'big business' then on the American scene, the expanding railways participated fully in the prosperity and optimism which appeared with the discovery of gold in California. Few other economic institutions in the nation at that time did business on so vast a scale, financed themselves from such a variety of sources, or employed such numbers of men of varied skills.

In the 1850s the railways expanded from 14,480 km (9,000 miles) to well over 48,280 km (30,000 miles) of line. The network more than tripled during the ten years, and achieved a rate of increase higher than for any other decade save that of the 1830s. During the 1850s the United States was building railways about as rapidly as all other nations combined, and by 1857 had nearly half of the total world mileage. As the iron network expanded during this period total railway investment grew from $300 million to more than $1,100 million. With such a huge investment, railway securities dominated stock market activity by the middle decades of the century. Already, US railways had achieved a certain maturity.

Construction in the north-east – where most of the system was already built – was much slower than in the rest of the country, and the route-

length there did not quite double during the 1850s. Even so, early in the decade four important trunk lines were completed westwards: the New York Central and the Erie to Lake Erie, and the Pennsylvania and Baltimore & Ohio to the upper Ohio river. At mid-century far fewer railways were to be found in the states south of the Potomac and Ohio rivers, but, during the next decade the South expanded its rail network from 3,218 km (2,000 miles) to about 15,285 km (9,500 miles). Three southern states, Virginia, Georgia, and Tennessee, each had well over 1,600 km (1,000 miles) of line on the eve of the Civil war. Even with this increased rate of construction, the typical southern railway lagged well behind its northern counterpart at the end of the decade. In quality of construction, availability of traffic, numbers of employees, and standard of equipment and maintenance facilities, the South was much inferior to the North. In 1860 the southern railways were ill-prepared for the armed conflict which lay ahead.

The most significant construction in the decade before the Civil war occurred in the west and the upper Mississippi valley. In this area the network grew from about 2,011 km (1,250 miles) in 1850 to 17,700 km (11,000 miles) by 1860. Construction in just three western states,

Illinois, Ohio, and Indiana totalled nearly 11,265 km (7,000 miles), or about one-third of all construction in the country during the 1850s. Several of the new lines in these three states connected with one of the four trunk lines in New York, Pennsylvania, and Maryland. A major consequence of construction north of the Ohio river was a shift in the total flow of commerce from a north–south axis of the Ohio and Mississippi rivers to an east–west axis of trunk lines serving such eastern seaports as New York, Philadelphia, and Baltimore. Western river steamboat traffic grew modestly in the 1850s, but railway traffic in the west doubled and doubled again.

An indication of the economic importance of western railways could be seen in the rapid growth of Chicago. In 1850 it was a lake port with a population of 29,000 and a single short rail line. By 1860 Chicago was served by 11 different railways, had 70 trains a day arriving or departing, and a population of 109,000. One of the most important railways serving Chicago was the Illinois Central, a north–south line which, upon its 1856 completion, was said to be the longest railway in the world. Its construction, along with several shorter lines in Iowa and Missouri, had been hastened by the new federal land grants.

The Civil war (1861 to 1865) was the first

Left: West Point station on the New York and Hudson River Railroad, photographed in 1859. This line later became part of Vanderbilt's New York Central.

Right: A scene of the mid-1870s, showing the New York Central's line through the New York inner suburb of Harlem.

Far left: A well-known picture of a well-known event; the official photograph of the last-spike ceremony at Promontory, Utah, on May 10, 1869.

Left: The suspension bridge over the River Niagara, an impressive example of early American railway engineering. The photograph dates from 1859.

Right: A rather grand artist's impression of the parlor car accommodation offered to the American first-class passenger in the 1870s, and not only on Sundays.

Below: Railway construction in the USA. This is a typical scene of the era of railroad expansion after 1850.

American war in which railways played an important role. Both the North and the South were greatly dependent upon river and coastal transport, but the rail systems of each were used extensively. Heavy movements of excited volunteers and their ordnance were common on both fronts in the summer of 1861. But massive troop movements were also occasionally made. In midsummer 1862, Gen Braxton Bragg's army of some 30,000 men was moved 1,247 km (775 miles) by Confederate railway over an indirect route from north-eastern Mississippi to Chattanooga, Tennessee. Even longer was the Union troop movement in the autumn of 1863, when Edwin Stanton, Lincoln's Secretary of War, directed the movement of 30,000 soldiers from Virginia to Tennessee to relieve the Confederate siege of Chattanooga. The 25,000 blue-clad troops, plus all their equipment, were moved about 1,930 km (1,200 miles) in 30 trains of 600 coaches in less than 12 days.

Both Union and Confederate railways suffered destruction during the war, but the tough foot soldiers under Gen William T Sherman made destruction a fine art as they moved through Georgia and the Carolinas in 1864 and 1865. By the end of the war the railways of the South were in a chaotic state. When Salmon P Chase, chief justice of the US Supreme Court, toured North Carolina not long after Appomattox, the best train the military could find for him was described by a press correspondent as 'a wheezy little locomotive and an old mail agent's car, with all the windows smashed out and half the seats gone'.

Western railways

In the three decades before the Civil war, American railways had grown into a system which served the eastern half of the nation quite well. In the year of Appomattox the western fingers of this iron network reached nearly to the edge of the frontier in Wisconsin, Iowa, Missouri, Arkansas, and Texas. West of the frontier of 1865 stretched the Great Plains, or the 'Great American Desert'. Such public figures as Horace Greeley and Abraham Lincoln believed it might take a century to settle this last frontier. They were proved very wrong in the generation after the Civil war, as rapid railway construction in those years moved well ahead of the frontier line and drew millions of Americans into the western territory. Only half-a-century would be needed to see the admission of the last of the continental 48 states.

The 50 years after the Civil war were in fact a Golden Age for railways in the United States. In those years no new modes of transport seriously challenged them. As lines were projected to, and reached, the Pacific, new mileage records became routine. The same years saw significant advances in revenue, equipment, employment, and operational efficiency.

During the pre-war 1850s, because of the growing sectional struggle, the proposed railway to the Pacific had been fully discussed but never started. Finally in 1862 a Pacific Railway bill was passed by Congress and signed by President Lincoln.

Two companies were created to build the line: the Union Pacific to build westward from the Missouri river, and the Central Pacific eastward from Sacramento, California. Both companies were to receive ten sections (raised to 20 sections in 1864) of federal land for each mile of completed track, and to be given 30-year federal loans, the amount to vary with the difficulty of the terrain.

The Union Pacific was started late in 1863, but most of the construction was delayed until later in the decade. Important figures in the management of UP were Dr Thomas Durant, a man more interested in manipulation of railway securities than in medicine, and Gen Grenville Dodge, a veteran of the Civil war. In the same years the Central Pacific was being pushed eastwards under the direction of four practical Sacramento businessmen: Leland Stanford, Collis P Huntington, Mark Hopkins and Charles Crocker. The Chinese working for Charley Crocker had drilled Summit tunnel, made giant earth fills with hand barrows, and learned to lay track with a speed which even impressed the Irish track gangs working for the Union Pacific contractors, Jack and Dan Casement. Together the two railways had laid 2,864 km (1,780 miles) of track, and the merging lines met in a barren valley north of the Great Salt Lake in Utah. On May 10, 1869 the Golden Spike ceremony took place between the cowcatchers of two locomotives, Central Pacific's wood-burning *Jupiter* and Union Pacific's coal-burning No 119.

In the next 25 years four other railways were built west to the Pacific. To the south the Southern Pacific built a line from southern California to New Orleans, while the Atchison, Topeka & Santa Fe built from Kansas westwards to southern California. In the north, the Northern Pacific

Left: A Union Pacific Railroad poster of the 1860s. This was issued before the completion of the transcontinental railroad, when trains connected with Wells, Fargo coaches for onward destinations.

a generation. But the record for route-length was gained by Texas in 1910.

Construction of many of the railways west of the Mississippi was helped by land grants provided by the federal government. The land grant programme had started in 1850 when legislation sponsored by senators Stephen Douglas and William King had provided grants for the Illinois Central-Mobile & Ohio route from the Great Lakes to the Gulf of Mexico. In later years grants were offered to about 80 different lines. The great bulk of the 131 million acres eventually granted went to lines in the west. About 40 per cent of the 1880 rail track in western states had been constructed with the aid of land grants. Shorter lines received modest grants, while larger grants (of 20 or 40 sections per mile of line) were given to four of the first five Pacific railroads. Several 'Granger' railways located in the northern central plains also received grants.

All railways receiving land grants were required to charge reduced rates of about 50 per cent for all federal or national government traffic. A Congressional report in 1945 estimated these savings to the government to be nearly $900 million. A fair estimate of the value of the total land granted (at the time the grants were made) would be $500 million.

Below: An artist's impression of the 1880s, showing a typical American train making an unscheduled halt while the locomotive crew carry out repairs.

was built from Minnesota to Seattle by 1883, and within a decade James J Hill had completed his almost parallel route, the Great Northern.

During the half-century after the Civil war the rail network increased sevenfold, expanding from 56,320 km (35,000 miles) in 1865 to 85,275 km (53,000 miles) in 1870, 149,640 km (93,000 miles) in 1880, 263,932 km (164,000 miles) in 1890, 310,540 km (193,000 miles) in 1900, and an all-time record of 408,700 km (254,000 miles) in 1916. The decade of record construction was easily the prosperous 1880s, when over 112,650 km (70,000) miles of line were added to the nation's network. More than 19,300 km (12,000 miles) were constructed in the single year 1886 to 1887. Some of the construction in the half-century was in the east, more of it was in the south, but most was in the trans-Mississippi west. Certainly a major fraction of all the new railways created in the late 19th century had the word 'Pacific' or 'Western' included in their corporate title. By 1870 Illinois had the greatest route-length of all the states, an honour it was to hold for more than

Above: The elevated railway in New York in steam days, in the 1880s. Raising the tracks above street level was the cheapest method of providing a right-of-way in city centres for inner suburban trains.

Left: A Union Pacific Railroad train of the 1870s. The 4–4–0 ('American') type locomotive with spark-arresting smokestack was the basic motive power of US railroads at this period.

Four important 'Granger' railways, the Chicago & North Western; Chicago, Milwaukee & St Paul; Chicago, Rock Island & Pacific ; and Chicago, Burlington & Quincy, all received federal land grants. The Granger area of mid-America might be described as the nine grain-growing states from Kansas, Missouri, and Illinois north to Canada. This area was also a region in which the National Grange, a farmer's organization often critical of the railways, was strong and well-established. The nine-state area was subservient in an economic way to Chicago and to a lesser degree to such satellite cities as St Louis, Kansas City, Omaha, Minneapolis and St Paul. However, Chicago was the main eastern terminal for each of the Granger lines. The four railways brought prosperity to that city, and themselves, in carrying grain, beef, and pork from the prairie states to the storage silos and stock-yards of Chicago.

In the same years some of the western mountain states were beginning to experiment with narrow-gauge lines. The narrow-gauge mania appeared in the United States, as in Britain, shortly after a paper, 'The Gauge for the Railways of the Future', was read by Robert F Farlie before a meeting of the British Railway Association in 1870. It was soon suggested that the sharper curves and lighter locomotives and rolling stock typical of narrow-gauge lines would be excellent for western mountain mining areas where it was expected that traffic would never be heavy. Some of the new narrow-gauge lines were built in eastern states, but more were found in the west. Typical would be Gen William Jackson Palmer's 914 mm (3 ft) gauge Denver & Rio Grande, which was projected and built into the Colorado mountains during the 1870s and 1880s. Much narrow-

gauge track was also built in California and Nevada. In the 11 western mountain and coastal states nearly one-sixth of all route-length was narrow-gauge.

However the narrow-gauge roads were never economical, and could not exchange cars with standard-gauge lines.

In the post-Civil war years builders such as Grenville Dodge, James J Hill, William J Palmer, and William B Strong were adding hundreds of miles of new line to the railway network. By the early years of the 20th century most Americans lived within 40 km (25 miles) of a railway. Nearly all of the 100 million population were literally within the sound of a locomotive whistle.

Corruption, discrimination and regulation

As the record railway expansion developed in the half-century after the Civil war, America shifted from being an agrarian people to become an industrial nation. But these same decades were in other ways a period of retrogression, brought on by extensive corruption and discrimination within the railway industry. Causes of the corruption include the pronounced *laissez-faire* economic theories then in vogue, the near monopoly conditions enjoyed by most railways, and the low post-war tone of public and private morality. Many, perhaps most, of the post-Civil war railways suffered from the evils of inflated construction costs, fraudulent stock market manipulations, and incompetent management. Concurrently, widespread discrimination in freight rates between individuals, localities, and articles forced merchants, farmers, and communities to agitate for government regulation of the railways. By 1914 this regulation had become increasingly rigorous. Corruption and chicanery found in some of the north-eastern trunk lines after the Civil war was especially bad. Such financial pirates as Daniel Drew, Jim Fisk, and Jay Gould were expert manipulators of both the Erie Railroad and the stock market, as they endeavoured to fleece Cornelius Vanderbilt. Commodore Vanderbilt, himself an expert at watering the stock of his New York Central during the late 1860s, was remembered by the general public for his probably apocryphal remark: 'Law! What do I care about law? Hain't I got the power?' Vanderbilt insisted that all his locomotives be painted a sombre black, without any bright colour or brass, and some of his employees started to call the locos 'Black Crooks'.

Certainly both the Commodore and his son, William H Vanderbilt, were very effective in their lobbying efforts with the New York legislature in Albany. The Vanderbilts and their fellow railway presidents were also experts at rate wars, and construction, or threatened building, of duplicate lines in their competitor's area. One such competition between the Pennsylvania and the New York Central in the mid-1880s grew so bitter that it was ended only by the strong-handed intervention of the country's top banker, John Pierpont Morgan.

During the early post-Civil war years there was also much corruption in the southern states as businessmen from the north – many of them dishonest – moved into the defeated region. Most of the activity of these 'carpetbaggers' was in the six-state area from Virginia to Alabama. These greedy visitors from the north built few railways in the south. They were more eager to raid state or railway treasuries than they were to construct new trackage. In North Carolina more than $17 million of state bond money produced construction of only 150 km (93 miles) of line. Much of this bond money went into the pockets of a ring headed by a smooth and genial gentleman from Illinois, Milton S Littlefield. In Georgia a former carriage maker from Connecticut, Hannibal I Kimball, was equally corrupt.

Corruption was present in the false-front construction companies and inflated costs associated with building of many of the western railways. One of the worst instances was the Crédit Mobilier, the construction company which had won contracts for building much of the Union Pacific. Crédit Mobilier made an extra illicit profit for such men as Dr Durant, Sidney Dillon, and the Ames brothers, Oakes and Oliver. When this scandal broke in 1872, it was estimated that Union Pacific 'insiders' may have reaped total dishonest profits of as much as $23 million. Other western lines, such as the Central Pacific, also profited from separate construction companies, but many of them escaped the publicity present in the Crédit Mobilier affair.

In the post-Civil war decades the railways had some difficulty with their expanding labour force. The number of workers increased from 163,000 in 1870 to 1,701,000 in 1916 and on the eve of the first world war one worker out of every 25 was a railway employee. Workers had a pay scale perhaps a quarter higher than the national average, with average annual pay increasing from $465 in 1880 to $886 in 1916. The somewhat

higher wages paid to train crews – drivers, firemen, conductors and brakemen – was no doubt the result of the establishment of their brotherhoods, or unions, in the years just after the Civil war. By 1900 some 20 different unions served the interests of thousands of employees.

The moderately favourable position of railway labour in the early 20th century had not been achieved without occasional disputes and even some violence. Baltimore & Ohio workers went on strike in 1877 over a wage dispute. The strike quickly spread across the nation with violence and riots in Pittsburgh, Buffalo, St Louis, Chicago, and St Paul. The militia was called out in Pittsburgh where property worth $5 million was destroyed. Later in the depressed 1890s a second major disturbance occurred when hundreds of trains in the mid-west were stopped in sympathy with the 1894 strike of Pullman Company employees. Many of the strikers belonged to the American Railway Union formed a year earlier by Eugene Debs. When federal troops were brought in the strike was broken, Debs was jailed, and the workers slowly returned to their jobs. Some of the workers were blacklisted – barred from future railway employment – while others could return to work only upon their promise to resign their union membership.

Railway customers, both in the east and the west, frequently complained about freight rates. In the trunk-line region rate wars were often so frequent that rates might be changed nearly every week. Bargain rates often were followed by excessively high rates of new railway pools or combinations of competing lines. Freight shippers also complained about the practice of rate rebates, made very effective by John D Rockefeller and his Standard Oil Company, and a form of discrimination which favoured the big producer at the expense of the small independent shipper.

Some of the most outspoken railway critics were western farmers, who had to have rail transport, but who lived in areas often served by only a single railway. Western farmers were unhappy about discriminatory long and short-haul rates, pools, and the whole practice of charging 'what the traffic will bear'. They also complained about downgrading of their grain at local silos, often owned or controlled by the railway, and the universal railway practice of issuing free passes to members of the press and local, county, and state officials.

The unhappy farmers sought relief through a new organization founded in 1867, the National Grange of the Patrons of Husbandry. The Grange grew rapidly and 800,000 farmers had joined by 1875. The early Granges were intended to be social and educational in nature, but soon the angry farmers were using them as political vehicles to obtain relief from railway abuses. Granger laws regulating railway freight rates were passed by the legislatures of Illinois, Minnesota, Wisconsin, and Iowa between 1871 and 1874. Other states did likewise, and western farmers were encouraged when early decisions of the US Supreme Court upheld the Granger legislation.

Below: Building the Northern Pacific Railroad. A construction train at Green River, in the Cascade Mountains, in the 1880s.

Above: Building the Santa Fe Railroad in the late 1880s. A construction train is dumping spoil for a fill at Fort Madison, Iowa.

Below: The yards of the Central Pacific Railroad at Sacramento, California. The photograph was made about 1875 and shows, among other typical railroading items, a gangers' trolley to the left of the woodburning locomotive.

Below right: A day train at Burlingame, in the early years of the Santa Fe Railroad.

However, in the Wabash case of 1886, the US Supreme Court held that a state could not regulate any rates on goods going outside the state. Thus, since only the federal government could regulate interstate commerce, some form of federal regulation was inevitable. In February 1887 Congress passed, and President Grover Cleveland signed, the Interstate Commerce Act. This law created a five-man Interstate Commerce Commission with the power to require that all interstate freight rates be 'reasonable and just'. Railway abuses such as pools, rebates, and long- and short-haul discriminations were also prohibited. However the railway industry and its lawyers soon proved that this first regulation was rather nominal – of the 16 rate cases going to the Supreme Court between 1887 and 1905 only one went against the railways. A much stiffer form of federal regulation would appear early in the 20th century.

Uniformity and consolidation

One of the major developments in the Golden Age of American railroading after the Civil war was the integration and uniformity of operation. This was achieved through a host of innovations and technical advances. More powerful motive power plus larger and more varied types of rolling stock permitted longer trains, faster service, and lower rates. New efficiency was gained by introduction of the air brake, automatic couplers, and standard time. All of these helped to achieve an integrated, efficient rail service, which in turn promoted further industrialization, expansion of urban population, a shift from regional to national markets, and the growth of an interdependent economy typical of the 20th century. In addition, widespread adoption of standard gauge speeded up all rail service.

At the end of the Civil war scarcely half of the rail network was built to the 1,435 mm (4 ft 8½ in) standard gauge. The Erie was 1,829 mm (6 ft) gauge and many of the lines in Ohio used 1,473 mm (4 ft 10 in) gauge. But most of the variation was the 1,524 mm (5 ft) gauge common in the south. By 1881 some uniformity of gauge had been achieved, and on June 1, 1886, the remaining southern lines converted to standard gauge. With this new track uniformity a greater interchange of rolling stock was possible, and soon a system of wagon rental by the day (*per diem*) was worked out among all the railways.

The first steel rails in the nation were imported from England in 1863 for use by the Pennsylvania

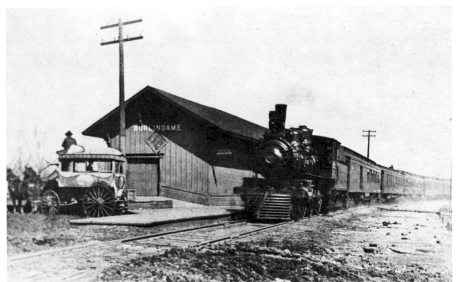

Left: A track gang at Ponca City, a Santa Fe Railroad station in Oklahoma. The photograph was made towards the end of the nineteenth century.

Right: A Currier and Ives print of an American junction at the period when the 2–6–0 locomotive (at left) was threatening the virtual monopoly of the 4–4–0.

Below: An engraving of a typical American passenger terminal; Philadelphia in the late 1880s.

Railroad. American-manufactured steel rail was soon available, but general acceptance of the harder-wearing rail was achieved only in the 1880s and 1890s. Improved service also resulted from bridging of major rivers and replacement of existing wooden bridges with stronger iron and steel spans. A reduction in the accident rate resulted from the improved train control possible with block signals and later interlocked signals.

In the early 1860s the typical locomotive was the American type (4–4–0), a loco which had a name rather than a number, probably cost $8,000 to $10,000, and was still using wood for fuel. The New England locomotive builder, William Mason, tried to merge beauty with strength in his engines, claiming that locomotives ought to 'look somewhat better than cookstoves on wheels'. At about the same time that coal replaced cord wood, the emphasis shifted from beauty to bulk and greater tractive power. Adding extra pairs of driv-

ing wheels resulted in such new types as Ten-Wheelers (4–6–0), Moguls (2–6–0), and Consolidations (2–8–0). A larger and broader firebox placed behind the driving wheels, and supported by a trailing bogie, gave increased power to such types as Atlantics (4–4–2) and Pacifics (4–6–2). By the early 20th century several railways were introducing articulated locomotives with two complete sets of driving wheels. Such changes in design greatly increased the tractive force of locomotives. Between 1869 and 1919 the tractive power of typical Pennsylvania engines rose from 5,443 kg (12,000 lb) to 38,182 kg (84,000 lb). This half-century of improvement permitted heavier and faster passenger and freight trains.

Many changes in freight and passenger stock appeared in the same years. New types of freight equipment were developed shortly after the Civil war: refrigerated wagons for meat and fruit in 1867, horizontal tank wagons in 1868, and

Right: A timber trestle bridge on the Northern Pacific Railroad in Idaho. The photograph was made in 1910; a steel structure later replaced this bridge.

noon on Sunday, November 18, 1883. Public opinion was generally favourable, but a few complained that they preferred 'God's time – not Vanderbilt's'.

In the 1860s the brakeman's work of coupling wagons and stopping trains was slow and dangerous. In operating 'link-and-pin' couplers, many brakemen suffered crippling accidents, and on dark and icy nights the best of trainmen found it difficult to set hand brakes on a line of moving wagons. Major Eli H Janney, a Confederate veteran, patented an automatic coupler in 1873, but it was slow in being accepted. A campaign for greater railway safety finally brought about federal legislation in 1893, and soon all trains were equipped with automatic couplers. In the late 1860s George Westinghouse invented an automatic air brake which was operated from the locomotive. The new brakes were quite effective and not difficult to operate, but too expensive to be widely used. The new couplers and brakes were generally used on passenger equipment before being adopted for freight service. Again, the safety legislation of 1893 eventually made such brakes standard equipment on all trains.

After the Civil war the capitalization of the rail network increased eightfold from $2,500 million in 1870 to $21,000 million by 1916. By the early 20th century most of these securities were owned by Americans, with a declining portion held abroad. But, as total investment grew, there was a decline in the number of individual railways because of a growing trend toward consolidation and mergers. This was very marked in the years following the panic-depression of the mid-1890s. By 1906 nearly two-thirds of total route-length was under the control of one or other of seven huge systems. These seven combinations, with the major lines controlled, were: Vanderbilt (New York Central, Chicago & North Western); Pennsylvania (B&O, Chesapeake & Ohio); Morgan (Southern, Erie); Gould (Missouri Pacific); Rock Island system; Hill (Great Northern, Northern Pacific, Burlington); and Harriman (Union Pacific, Southern Pacific, Illinois Central).

The many technical improvements in the half-century up to 1916 brought about a fall in freight rates from something over 2 cents per ton-mile in the late 1860s to 0.75 cents per ton-mile in the early 20th century. At these low rates cattle from Texas, meat packed in Chicago, steel from Pittsburgh, shoes made in New England, and ploughs manufactured in Moline could all be moved economically over greater and greater distances. Rapid industrialization of the nation was accompanied by a pronounced growth of freight traffic, from 10,000 million ton-miles in 1865 to 366,000 million in 1916. Growth of freight traffic was much greater than passenger, and soon total freight revenue was three to four times as high as that from passengers. In 1916 the Interstate Commerce Commission reported that railways were carrying 77 per cent of all inter-city freight traffic and 98 per cent of all commercial inter-city passengers. On the eve of the first world war railways had a clear monopoly of transport.

improved cattle wagons with water troughs and feedbins by the 1880s. Coal wagons of iron were found on some lines before the Civil war, but they were very common in the 1870s and 1880s, and their size had increased to 50-ton capacity. All wagons increased in capacity, from 10 tons per wagon in the 1860s to about 40 tons half-a-century later. Between 1870 and 1915 average payload of Illinois Central freight trains increased from 100 tons to well above 500 tons.

Changes also came in passenger equipment. Crude sleeping cars had been available on a few lines in the 1850s, but it was left to George Pullman in the late 1860s to improve upon these earlier efforts. In the 1870s and 1880s dining cars, many of them built by Pullman, became quite common on first-class trains. Hot water or steam heat replaced the corner coal stove by the 1880s, and in the 1890s electric lights were beginning to replace the earlier kerosene or gas lamps. Corridor connections between coaches were also found on newer stock before 1890.

By the 1870s most of the larger lines belonged to one or more of the co-operative fast freight lines running between major cities, known by such names as Star Union, Empire, and Great Western Dispatch. The public also demanded more rapid travel, and new 'Fast Mail', 'Express', and 'Limited' passenger trains were soon the vogue. In 1893 an American-type New York Central locomotive, No 999, reached a record speed of 180.2 km/h (112 mph). A dozen years later 'Death Valley Scotty', a rich California miner, had paid the Santa Fe $5,500 to run a special train east to Chicago, covering the 3,647 km (2,265 miles) in a record-breaking 45 hours.

Even with all the technical innovations, railways were still operating in a patchwork of hundreds of different time zones, with each major city using its own local time. A Chicago newspaper claimed there were over two dozen different times in Illinois alone. An 1870 proposal of the *Railroad Gazette* for a single national time zone gained little support. A decade later William F Allen, editor of the *Official Guide of Railways*, made the railways accept four standard time zones based on the 75th, 90th, 105th, and 120th meridians of longitude. The change occurred at

American railways at war

Twice in the 20th century the railways of America have faced the rigours of a world war, and twice they have helped the nation to victory. In the years after 1914 the railways were not too well prepared to meet the crush of war traffic which quickly appeared.

In the years prior to the first world war, railways had lost several contests with labour and the federal government. Regulation of railways by the national government had become much more extensive early in the 20th century, years in which railways still had a monopoly both in freight and passenger service. The Elkins Act (1903) and the Hepburn Act (1906) together had ended the practices of rebates and free passes, and had also strengthened the ICC, giving the Commission the right to establish 'just and reasonable' maximum rates. A still greater control of rates by the ICC came with the Mann-Elkins Act (1910).

Since the ICC in these years had consistently refused rate increase requests to meet higher operating costs, many railway managers on the eve of the war found themselves short of motive

Above left: A Santa Fe Railroad poster issued in 1947, just as the railroads were beginning the long post-war struggle to hold their passengers against air and highway competition.

Above right: The *Denver Zephyr* (Chicago to Colorado Springs) on the Denver and Rio Grande Western Railroad. Stainless steel equipment with 'vista dome' observation cars was a post-war development adopted by many railway companies in the competitive struggle against the airlines.

Below: A Baldwin-built 2–10–2 of 1912 hauling a freight extra in Cajon Pass on the Santa Fe Railroad. Cajon Pass, through the Rockies, was one of the most difficult sections of this railroad.

power, rolling stock, and properly maintained track. Nearly one-sixth of all railway mileage was in, or close to, receivership. Finally the Adamson Act (1916), which gave the four operating unions an eight-hour day without any reduction in pay, was upheld by the Supreme Court in March 1917. This action increased labour costs, placing a further financial strain on the industry.

After the United States entered the first world war, a glut of war traffic was moved toward eastern seaports. Many wagons were not unloaded at their destination, and wagon shortages grew, reaching a record 158,000 by November 1917. Faced with this crisis, and the coldest winter weather in several years, President Woodrow Wilson placed the railways under government control on December 28, 1917 – a federal control that would last for 26 months. William G. McAdoo, director-general of the federal rail system, was empowered to use the 408,690 km (254,000 mile) network as a single system, to reduce wagon shortages, eliminate surplus services, and to raise wages, fares and rates as might be necessary. Given the transport crisis in the deepening winter of 1917, federal operation of the railways was both necessary and inevitable.

But owners and managers were unhappy with the rental paid to them during federal control, the lack of maintenance carried out during the McAdoo years, and the high cost of labour inherited from federal operation. Average yearly wages for rail workers climbed from $1,004 in 1917 to $1,820 in 1920. Managers had learned important lessons between 1917 and 1919 and they resolved that, should another war crisis appear, they would prefer a wholehearted, unstinting co-operative effort rather than government direction and compulsion.

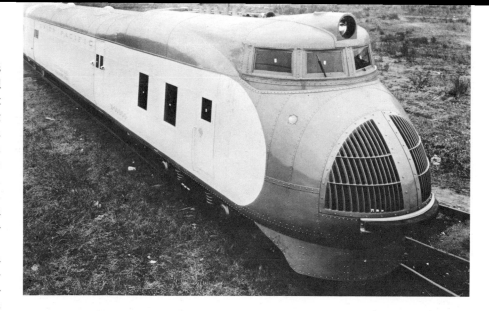

During the 1920s and 1930s the railways enjoyed first a period of moderate prosperity, and then suffered through years of depression, deficit operation, and numerous receiverships. During the 20 years there were modest declines in mileage and equipment, and a marked decline in numbers employed. But in the decades prior to Pearl Harbor the industry made marked gains in wagon capacity, daily usage of wagons, train speed, and general operating efficiency. Between 1921 and 1941, annual ton-miles of freight service per employee had more than doubled.

As the nation entered the second world war in December 1941, a primary objective of the railways was to avoid the extent of government control they had experienced during the previous conflict. While the co-operative efforts of the railways succeeded in avoiding federal operation, some overall direction was clearly required. On December 18, 1941, President Roosevelt created the Office of Defense Transportation, with Joseph Eastman as director, to co-ordinate all the transport facilities of the nation.

Using a quarter to a third fewer locomotives, wagons, and employees than were available in the first world war, American railways fully met the war traffic challenge facing them. In each of the four war years (1942 to 1945) rail freight hauled was at least 50 per cent greater than that of 1918. Shortages of petrol and rubber during the war years also caused much civilian and commercial traffic to be shifted from road and air transport to the railways. However, the second world war, unlike the first, was a two-front conflict. Since traffic moved both east and west, there were few empty wagons from 1941 to 1945.

Both railroad labour and the industry itself made gains during the war. Between 1941 and 1945 wages climbed by one-third while consumer prices rose only by one-fifth. The flood of war traffic brought general prosperity to the industry, and many lines, in or near receivership during the depression, were able to put their financial houses in order. Some $2,000 million of bonds, or nearly one-fifth of the railways' funded debt, was soon redeemed. In the decades since the second world war the railways have continued to play a vital role in the security of the nation.

Railways in decline

In the 60 years since the record route-length was achieved in 1916, freight traffic has increased modestly, while passenger traffic has steadily declined. In the same years much traffic was lost to new modes of transport. In 1916 about 77 per cent of all inter-city freight in the nation moved by rail, but this had dropped to 74 per cent in 1930, 67 per cent in 1945, 43 per cent in 1960, and only 37 per cent in 1975. Commercial inter-city passenger traffic fell even faster, from 98 per cent in 1916 to 47 per cent in 1950, and only 6 per cent by 1975. Since the early 20th century the railways in turn have had to compete with the electric interurban tramway, thousands and then millions of private cars, inter-city buses, larger and larger lorries, aeroplanes, and a growing network of pipelines of greater size and capacity. In the same

Above: The Union Pacific Railroad's *City of Salina* of 1934, which marked the beginning of the streamline era in America.

Below: A timetable folder of the Pennsylvania Railroad, issued at a time when World War One railroad congestion was bringing an enforced reduction of passenger services.

years, improved and more efficient water transport appeared on the nation's lakes and rivers. Some of this new competition has been transitory in nature, but much has been stubbornly permanent.

At the turn of the century the vast nature of rail traffic had justified such fine new stations as those at St Louis (1894), Washington Union (1907), and Pennsylvania station (1910) and Grand Central Terminal (1913) both in New York City. But the station most Americans knew best was the depot down at the end of 'Main Street'. Thousands of small depots served rural and small-town America and were the focal point of communication with the outside world. In those years the nation really seemed to need each new line built, and every little valley could afford a branch line.

In the years after the first world war road vans began to carry furniture once moved in rail wagons, farmer's lorries carried livestock to market, and pipelines replaced the railway tank wagon. During the 1920s millions of American families purchased their first motor car, and on the eve of the Great Depression 23 million cars were on the nation's roads. Railway timetables

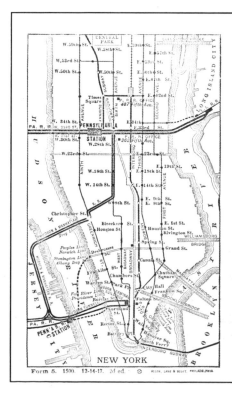

grew thinner and thinner as passenger trains were discontinued because patrons were shifting to the car, bus, and aeroplane. Soon there were significant declines both in mileage and in employment. Total length declined from 408,690 km (254,000 miles) in 1916 to 374,900 km (233,000 miles) in 1940, 354,000 km (220,000 miles) in 1955, and 321,800 km (200,000 miles) in 1975. The number of employees dropped from 1,650,000 in 1916 to 1,025,000 in 1940, 780,000 in 1960, and only 490,000 in 1975. By the mid-1970s mileage was less than that of 1902, and the level of employment was similar to that of the early 1880s.

Since the first world war the government has favoured the competitors of the railway industry with far less stringent regulation and with more generous subsidies. In these years there was no decrease in federal regulation of railways. The Transportation Act of 1920 increased the Inter-state Commerce Commission from 9 to 11 members, with new powers of regulation over both rates and the issue of new railway securities. The rate-setting policy of the Commission during the 1920s sought to assure the railways a 'fair rate of return' on their investment. When most railways were faced with deficits in the early depression years of the 1930s the Emergency Railroad Transportation Act of 1933 tried, without suc-

cess, to achieve a reduction in rail operating expenses. In 1940 another Transportation Act made few specific changes, but did establish the general principle that all competing modes of transport should be treated alike. Greater freedom in rate fixing plus a new flexibility in reduction of passenger service was given under the Transportation Act of 1958.

Though recent years have seen the industry in decline, numerous technical innovations and improvements have been made in the middle decades of the 20th century. Perhaps the major technical change was the introduction, and full acceptance, of a new form of motive power – the diesel locomotive – in the years between the mid-1930s and the late 1950s. Diesel locomotives were not cheap, and the original cost might be two or three times the cost of a steam engine, but the very low operating costs and ease of maintenance made them very attractive. In the decade after the second world war the industry spent more than $3,000 million on 20,000 diesel locomotives. By 1955 some 50 railways had no steam locomotives at all. In 1957 diesels were moving 93 per cent of all passengers and 92 per cent of all freight. By the mid-1960s, the best chance of seeing a steam locomotive was to visit a museum.

There were other technical advances too. In

Above: A narrow-gauge train of the Denver and Rio Grande Railroad. This railroad once possessed, in addition to its standard-gauge main lines, several hundred miles of 914 mm (3 ft) gauge track, mainly in Colorado. One 72 km (45 mile) section still remains as a tourist line.

Below: The Santa Fe Railroad's roundhouse at Los Angeles. The three-unit FP 7 type diesel locomotive in the centre has just arrived from Chicago with the Railroad's first dieselized transcontinental passenger train.

passenger service, air-conditioning, dozens of new stainless-steel streamliners built after the war, slumbercoaches and vista-domes slowed, but did not halt, the decline in passenger traffic. Welded rail, new track maintenance equipment, hot-axlebox detectors, computers, microwave communication, mobile office units to replace depots, and Centralized Traffic Control all combined to improve operating efficiency. Piggyback service, container freight, unit coal trains, multi-level automobile wagons, cushion underframes, roller bearings, and high-capacity box wagons all worked to improve freight service. In fact, annual ton-mileage of freight per rail employee more than tripled in the 25-year period, climbing from 358,000 ton-miles per worker in 1940 to 1,092,000 ton-miles by 1965.

American railways today

The relatively good financial health enjoyed by the railways during the wartime 1940s has not been maintained in recent years. Strong federal regulation, high taxes, and continued labour problems, along with loss of traffic to competitors, have resulted in a low rate of return on investment. Even during the five war years (1941 to 1945), average rate of return was only 5 per cent. In the late 1940s it averaged on 3.5 per cent, and since 1950 has been only about 3 per cent, well below that of competing modes. In the recent past (1971 to 1975), this figure has dropped to just over 2 per cent. The financial health of railways varies from region to region, with western and southern lines being much stronger. In the last five years western lines have achieved an average return of 3.3 per cent while southern lines earned nearly 4.5 per cent. In the same period north-eastern lines had deficits for two years out of five, and the rate of return in the best year was only 0.5 per cent.

As railway employment declined in the years after 1945, the unions became stubbornly reluctant to change any work rules – rules which, in management's view, limited productivity and caused 'featherbedding' – over-provision of staff. In one area of dispute, elimination of firemen on freight trains, management made modest gains during the 1960s. Certainly labour received generous pay in the post-war years. Average annual wages increased from $2,720 in 1945 to $4,719 in 1955, $7,490 in 1965, and $15,324 in 1975. In the 1960s and 1970s, the uncompromising attitude of the unions to pay scales and work rules have reduced the scale of economies contemplated in several consolidations and mergers, and made possible by technical innovation.

As the railways suffered a decline both in traffic and financial health in the mid-20th century, many lines looked toward the possible advantages available through consolidation or merger. In the years after 1960 such mergers as the Erie-Lackawanna, Chesapeake & Ohio-Baltimore & Ohio, Seaboard Coast Line, and Burlington Northern were planned and eventually completed. Most important was the Penn Central, a 33,770 km (21,000 mile) system formed in 1968 by consolidation of two north-eastern lines, the

New York Central and the Pennsylvania. Not all of the mergers achieved the economies hoped for, as illustrated by the bankruptcy of the new Penn Central in 1970.

Even though passenger train deficits grew in the years after 1945, the Interstate Commerce Commission was slow in permitting major reductions in service. Finally, in 1971, the government established the National Railroad Passenger Corporation, generally known as Amtrak. Amtrak provides a federally-subsidized, and much reduced, passenger service over about one-tenth of the national network, and has greatly diminished the annual passenger deficits of individual railways.

In the early 1970s several north-eastern railways, including the bankrupt Penn Central, faced serious financial problems and were collectively losing money at the rate of more than $1 million a day. Early in 1976 the Consolidated Rail Corporation, generally known as ConRail, was established by federal law to take over the operations of six bankrupt north-eastern railroads, the largest of which was Penn Central. The federally-financed ConRail consists of some 27,350 km (17,000 miles) of line in 16 states and employs about 95,000 workers. A major advantage of ConRail is the chance to eliminate duplicate facilities and provide improved service through consolidated operations over preferred routes. Federal money has been made available for track rehabilitation and improvement and replacement of equipment. However, creation of ConRail has raised serious questions concerning the future of private-versus-public ownership of the nation's railway system.

While American railways have suffered a serious decline in recent decades, they are still a vital part of the nation's economic life. The inherent economy of the flanged wheel running on a steel rail – the essence of railway – is not likely to become obsolete. Railways still have much to offer a nation concerned about its environment, and wishing to conserve its resources of energy.

Above: A Santa Fe diesel road-switcher locomotive, specially painted for the 1976 Centennial, stands behind a preserved steam locomotive.

Contrasted with the neighbouring United States, the railway era came late to British North America. An inhospitable climate, a sparse population settled almost entirely along or adjacent to seacoasts or navigable waterways, and introduction of commercial steamboats in 1809, were factors which delayed construction of trunk railways in what is now Canada until the 1850s.

The earliest recorded use of the railway principle in Canada was in 1823 when the Royal Engineers constructed a 150 m (164 yd) double-track inclined plane at Quebec to carry materials from a wharf to the Citadel on the escarpment. Animal-powered tramroads were introduced at other locations in the 1820s. The first public railway, the 'Company of the Proprietors of the Champlain & Saint Lawrence Rail-road', chartered in 1832 by the Legislature of Lower Canada, was opened for public service with a Stephenson-built locomotive on July 21, 1836. Really a portage line, it connected Laprairie, on the opposite shore of the St Lawrence river from Montreal, with St Johns, 25 km (15½ miles) distant on the navigable Richelieu river. From St Johns, passengers and goods were carried southward into the United States on board steamers.

When the rivers and lakes became frozen in the winter season, railway and steamers ceased operations until spring.

Canada's first railway did not become a year-round operation until 1851 when its standard-gauge line was extended southward to Rouses Point, New York state. This extension, the first international railway connection between Canada and the United States, joined with recently-completed US lines through to the New England coast, an event celebrated by a 'Railroad Jubilee' in Boston the same year.

In 1849, legislation was introduced in the Province of Canada to encourage construction of trunk railways by private capital, by guaranteeing interest on investment under certain conditions. An ill-conceived provision added in 1851 had the effect of forcing the use of 1,676 mm (5 ft 6 in) gauge, on the Canadian trunk system. Eventually, this provision was repealed and the network was narrowed to standard gauge (1,435 mm) at great expense in the 1870s.

By the end of 1851, Canada possessed less than 145 km (90 miles) of public railway in operation. In contrast the United States boasted nearly 17,000 km (10,500 miles) of route, concentrated

Above: One of the best-known photographs of Canada's history. The last spike (allegedly golden, but actually iron) of the Canadian Pacific's transcontinental line is driven in, near Craigellachie in the Rockies.

Below: A specially decorated train inaugurates a new Canadian Pacific line. The late 19th century witnessed the opening of numerous lines in Canada, and each was expected to bring new prosperity to the district it served.

around and linking centres in the industrial states. The first Canadian trunk line was a railway linking Montreal with Portland, Maine, begun in 1847 and completed in 1853 to be integrated into the newly-formed Grand Trunk Railway of Canada. GTR extensions linked Montreal with Quebec in 1854, and with Toronto in 1856. Subsequent extensions westward to Port Huron on the St Clair river, and to Rivière-du-Loup on the lower St Lawrence, gave the GTR a main line more than 1,300 km (800 miles) in length by 1860, the longest railway under one management in the world at that time. Its engineering embellishment was the Victoria tubular bridge at Montreal, 3.1 km (1.89 miles) in length, crossing the St Lawrence river, which was designed by Robert Stephenson and opened in 1860 by the Prince of Wales.

The 1850s witnessed construction of the first railways in the sister colonial provinces of New Brunswick and Nova Scotia. The railways in the maritime provinces were constructed and operated as public works. By the end of 1860, there were 3,440 km (2,138 miles) of public railways in the three provinces, all but 120 km (75 miles) of which were constructed to broad gauge. At the same time, the USA had almost attained 50,000 km (31,000 miles) of railways.

Under the terms of the British North America Act of 1867 the provinces of Canada (split into two new provinces, Ontario and Quebec), New Brunswick and Nova Scotia joined to form the Dominion of Canada. The provincially-owned railway systems of the two maritime provinces were entrusted to the new Dominion government, which assumed responsibility to extend them, connecting them with one another and with the railway network of Ontario and Quebec. This system, the Intercolonial Railway, was completed on July 1, 1876 and formed the nucleus of what is today Canadian National Railways.

Confederation of British Columbia, the colonial province on the Pacific coast, which took place in 1871, contained a stipulation influenced by the completion of the United States transcontinental in 1869. This was that a railway would be

completed across Canada within ten years. The intervening territory had been acquired by Canada from the Hudson's Bay Company in 1869. The Dominion government, then committed to the Intercolonial Railway, had no resources to devote to the Pacific Railway. Though a desultory start was made in 1876, the impetus to complete the transcontinental did not come until 1880 when the federal government signed a contract with a syndicate of Montreal businessmen. This was embodied in legislation passed in February 1881 incorporating the Canadian Pacific Railway. For certain land and cash concessions, the new company agreed to complete the railway by 1891 and operate it, efficiently, forever. Under unprecedented difficulties, the railway was completed in less than half the stipulated time, the last rail linking the east with the Pacific coast being laid in the British Columbia mountains on November 7, 1885. Scheduled transcontinental service was inaugurated in the following summer.

The ensuing three decades saw an unprecedented expansion of the Canadian railway network. A route-length of 17,100 km (10,200 miles) in 1886, doubled by the end of 1905 and tripled before the end of 1914. After completion of its transcontinental line, CPR's expansion in the east by the acquisition of existing local railways was matched by similar expansionist policies pursued by the Grand Trunk. Partly by new construction and partly by absorption of existing railways, CPR completed a through international railway linking Montreal with Saint John, New Brunswick, across the State of Maine, in 1889. Concurrently, the GTR strengthened its connections through to Chicago, to maintain its position as the main line of central Canada.

Opening-up of the prairie to settlement, initiated by construction of the CPR and acknowledged by creation of the new provinces of Saskatchewan and Alberta in 1905, brought about the third great privately-owned railway system, the Canadian Northern (CNoR). Beginning as a small local railway in western Manitoba in the late 1890s, this system expanded its lines eastward and westward, reaching Port Arthur at the

Below: Another Canadian Pacific switcher marshals a passenger train in a city terminal.

Below right: A Canadian Pacific switching locomotive assembles a freight train. As in the USA, the eight-wheeled box-car was the basic item of freight rolling stock in Canada.

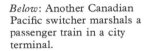

head of the Great Lakes in 1902, and Edmonton in 1905. Concurrent purchase of local railways in Ontario, Quebec and the maritime provinces, many of which remained physically-isolated from the body of the Canadian Northern system until its demise, made clear its pretensions to become the second transcontinental.

The Grand Trunk Railway, in the midst of one of its rare periods of prosperity, also had aspirations in the west. The Federal government tried to bring the GTR and the CNoR together in a common transcontinental endeavour in 1902 and early 1903, but without success. Later in 1903, however, an arrangement was entered into between the federal government and the Grand Trunk to create a National Transcontinental Railway. This would consist of an 'eastern division' from Moncton, New Brunswick, via Quebec city and northern Ontario to Winnipeg, 2,880 km (1,790 miles), to be built by the federal government under the GTR's supervision and turned over to the GTR for operation, under lease, upon completion. At its own expense, the GTR would construct the 'western division' as the separately-incorporated Grand Trunk Pacific Railway, to extend from Winnipeg, via Edmonton and Yellowhead Pass to a new port on the Pacific, Prince Rupert, a distance of almost 2,800 km (1,740 miles). As time progressed 'NTR' was used solely to describe the eastern sections as distinct from the GTP in the west.

Work on this project began in 1905, and the GTP was completed through to Prince Rupert in April 1914. With the exception of the Quebec bridge, the NTR east of Winnipeg was also completed by the end of that year, but as the GTR was in financial difficulties it was unable to implement its projected lease. The NTR was thereupon entrusted to Canadian Government Railways (formerly the Intercolonial Railway) for operation.

The Canadian Northern completed its own Pacific extension to Vancouver in the autumn of 1915, its route paralleling that of the GTP through Yellowhead Pass. Capital shortages arising as a result of the outbreak of war in 1914 resulted in bankruptcy of the Canadian Northern and its takeover by the federal government. In 1918, the title 'Canadian National Railways' was introduced to designate all railway lines operated by the government of Canada, including the CGR, the CNR and the NTR. Further financial reverses resulted in government takeover of the GTP in 1919, followed in 1920 by its parent, the Grand Trunk, both being amalgamated into the Canadian National system in 1923.

While these events were taking place, a number of noteworthy engineering works were achieved. Just prior to its assimilation into Canadian National, the Canadian Northern completed an electrified approach to Montreal through the 5.1 km (3.2 mile) Mount Royal tunnel, the second longest railway tunnel in Canada. A suburban passenger service in Montreal still in operation at time of writing is Canada's only main-line electrification. In 1917, after two major setbacks, the Quebec bridge, carrying the National Transcontinental over the St Lawrence, was opened to traffic.

Along the main line of Canadian Pacific, North America's only spiral tunnels were opened in the Kicking Horse Pass in the autumn of 1909. The winding main line over Rogers Pass in the Selkirk mountains was eliminated in 1916 with completion of the 8.08 km (5 mile) Connaught tunnel, Canada's longest. The tallest railway bridge in Canada, the CPR viaduct at Lethbridge, 95.7 m (314 ft) in height and 1.6 km (1 mile) long, was completed in 1909.

During the 1920s, both major railways were occupied by construction of a dense network of grain-collecting lines in the prairie provinces, unaware of the economic menace appearing on the horizon in the form of the motor car. A third coastline was added to the railway map of Canada in March 1929, when the CN-sponsored Hudson Bay Railway reached Churchill. A second connection to the Arctic watershed was effected in 1932, when the Temiskaming & Northern Ontario Railway, one of several provincially-owned railways, reached Moosonee, on James Bay. Unfortunately, attainment of these northern ports has been largely symbolic, and not marked by substantial traffic achievements.

Advent of the depression of the 1930s was marked by heavy traffic decline on Canadian railways, whose route length reached 67,000 km (41,630 miles) in 1933. CPR management put

Left: A Canadian Pacific 2-8-2 hauls an eastbound freight across the Ship Pond Stream Viaduct, near Onawa.

Upper right: General Motors diesel locomotives haul a Canadian National Railways' freight train through Toronto, 1952.

Upper far right: A Canadian Pacific passenger train at Dorval, near Montreal. The track on the right is the Canadian National main line.

Lower right: An early diesel-electric locomotive of the Canadian Pacific Railway, No 7000, a switcher.

Lower far right: A freight locomotive assists diesels with a Canadian National train at Toronto.

Below: A Canadian Pacific 2-10-4, a type built especially for the steep grades of the Rockies, passes beneath a ventilator fan-house as it leaves the Connaught Tunnel.

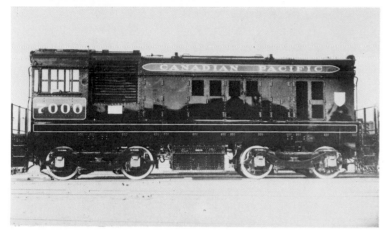

forward arguments favouring integration of CN into a unified system managed by CP, a proposition which was politically unacceptable. However, the Canadian National-Canadian Pacific Act of 1933 ushered in a period of abandonment of some parallel lines, joint use of some facilities and the pooling of passenger services between major centres in Ontario and Quebec.

Attention was also being given to the economies implicit in conversion from steam to diesel motive power. CN had experimented with diesel-electric railcars, and shunting and main line diesels, in the 1920s, while CPR's first experimental diesel locomotive appeared in 1937. Though both railways started to acquire production batches of diesel shunters during the second world war, a programme of total conversion was not begun until the late 1940s. Phasing-out of steam locomotives on both of Canada's major systems and most of its minor ones was completed by the end of 1960, effecting economies and increasing efficiency, availability and capacity.

Confederation of the colony of Newfoundland with Canada in 1949 added to CN over 1,100 km (700 miles) of 1,067 mm (3 ft 6 in) gauge, formerly operated by the government of Newfoundland. In the 1950s and 1960s a spate of new construction associated with natural resource development in northern Quebec, Alberta, British Columbia and the North West Territories, had the effect of increasing the route length of the Canadian network to 74,000 km (46,000 miles) by 1973. The unprecedented prosperity of the 1950s and 1960s brought the motor car within easy reach of the whole population and this factor, aided by the completion of the Trans-Canada highway system supplemented by new arterial roads in densely-populated areas, resulted in a marked decline in

passenger train patronage and consequent withdrawal of many trains. Services on the transcontinental routes of both railways, as well as those between principal cities, were sustained, after 1967, by payment of 80 per cent of specified losses on such services by the federal government under the National Transportation Act of that year. On the other hand, freight tonnages soared to record highs, thanks to the development of the 'unit' or block-train concept in the late 1960s.

In the late 1970s, the railways continue to play a crucial role in Canada, constrained by the limited resources of a nation possessing large land areas but inhabited by a small population. Despite apprehensions about long-term supplies of natural resources which were once thought to be limitless, the potential for long-haul unit trains of minerals and agricultural products is good, and performance will be aided by probable electrification of main lines when the cost of capital borrowing diminishes. During the writing of this article in late 1976, the government is formulating a basic passenger train network policy, to be fully supported financially; CN and CP are studying participation in providing this service.

To concentrate on developing a high-capacity network of main lines between major-producing communities, thousands of miles of under-utilized branch lines are proposed for abandonment by the railways, particularly in western Canada. However, an artificial economic situation, fuelled by statutory grain-hauling rates set at 1897 levels and strong regional refusal to accept technological change, has prevented any effective action. On the whole, however, the future of the Canadian rail network is promising, provided that those in whose hands policy decisions rest choose to use this investment wisely.

HISTORY

SOUTH AMERICA

In general, South America is populated most thickly around its coastline and sparsely in its interior. Railways developed there rather late owing to political uncertainty in the republics formed after Independence in 1825, the low state of their finances, and the lack of confidence in them shown by the banker countries of Europe. The vast area of the continental interior, the difficulties of travel, the obstacles to coastal sea communication posed by Cape Horn and the Humboldt current on the west coast, the wealth of raw materials in demand for export on which badly-needed loans might be arranged in Europe, and the need to weld isolated rural populations into nations, combined to make construction of railways a political necessity. Men with the acumen to promote them and the technical experience to construct them were fortunately on hand at the right time.

The pioneer among these was the true father of the steam locomotive, Richard Trevithick, who was in Peru between 1816 and 1824. On his heels came the North American, William Wheelwright, who introduced commercial steam navigation in the Pacific, and subsequently built railways in Chile and Argentina. Another 'giant',

Upper right: A Fiat diesel railcar set at Tucuman, on the General Belgrano Railway.

Right: Plaza Constitucion Terminus in Buenos Aires. The heavy commuter service from this station was for decades handled by British-built tank locomotives. This picture was made when diesel locomotives were beginning to take over these duties.

Bottom right: A British-built 4-6-0 of 1914, named *Churrinche*, takes a Quequen train through the Buenos Aires suburbs at Temperley on the General Roca Railway.

Below: A metre-gauge 2-10-2, built in 1937 by Henschel in Germany, halts at Diego de Almagro on the Salta-Socompá transandine line of the General Belgrano Railway. This nine-car train ran once weekly when this picture was made in 1972.

whose railway construction career began before Wheelwright's death, was Henry Meiggs, also an American. Foreign capital built most of the railways.

Bulk traffic is of major importance on South America's 105,000 km (62,100 miles) of railways, generally moving towards the ports from sources of supply in the interior. In Argentina this traffic was originally cattle, in Brazil coffee, and on the west coast minerals and nitrate. Before the oil era, traffic from the ports to the interior was considerably lighter, but there is now far less non-revenue movement than formerly.

Argentina

An Argentine commission was formed in 1856 to purchase material for a short line projected between Buenos Aires and Floresta, later part of the Buenos Aires Western Railway. At the close of the Crimean war rail material used by the Allies was sold off. Advantage was taken of this to acquire among other things two locomotives of 1,676 mm (5 ft 6 in) gauge originally intended for India. No gauge had yet been specified for the Buenos Aires line, and the locomotives purchased decided the issue. Opened to traffic in 1857, this little railway was the first in the country.

Pioneer railway engineer in Argentina was an American, Allen Campbell, whom William Wheelwright had contracted in 1850 to survey the Caldera-Copiapó line in Chile. Campbell made the alignment for the projected Rosario-Córdoba line which was brought to fruition by Wheelwright. His object, never achieved, was to extend the Caldera-Copiapó line over the Andes and across to Rosario, then being considered for development as the principal port for export to Europe of minerals from Chile and produce from Argentina. The line became part of the Central Argentine Railway.

The 'Big Four' British-owned railways were, in order of route-length: the Buenos Aires Great Southern, Central Argentine, Buenos Aires Pacific and Buenos Aires Western. Besides these systems there were five lesser British-owned lines. All these British properties were bought up and taken over by the Argentine government under General Perón in 1948. Mergers took place, and the ex-British lines lost their old identity under new names, the main systems becoming the General Belgrano Railway (the ex-Argentine State system of 14,848 km [9,220 miles] of metre gauge), Bartolomé Mitre (ex-Central Argentine), General Roca (largely the ex-Great Southern), General San Martín (including the BAP), and Domingo Faustino Sarmiento (with the ex-BA Western).

Heavy suburban commuter traffic in and around Buenos Aires is no new development; electrification started in 1909. Much of it is handled by the Domingo Faustino Sarmiento system, but the heaviest traffic is on the Bartolomé Mitre.

Argentina's share of South America's total rail mileage amounts to some 42 per cent, broad gauge predominating. Besides the metre and some narrower gauges, there are more than 3,000 km (1,864 miles) of standard-gauge line.

Brazil

Brazil's 1975 total route length of 30,430 km (18,962 miles) includes four gauges: 1,600 mm (5 ft 3 in) confined to the Central regions, ubiquitous metre gauge, and small amounts of 1,435 mm (4 ft 8½ in) and 762 mm (2 ft 6 in). Not only the most industrialized country in South America, Brazil is also the largest.

Birth of the rail network was due mainly to the energies of the Imperial statesman Baron Mauá, who was responsible for the first line in Brazil opened in 1852, 14.5 km (9 miles) of track in the Rio de Janeiro district. This was the beginning of the old Dom Pedro II Railway, which later became the Central of Brazil, and was of 1,600 mm gauge. So too was the São Paulo Railway opened in 1867, linking São Paulo city with the port of Santos. This was originally a coffee export route with a unique set of cable-operated inclines, the inspiration of a young British engineer named Daniel Fox, for the steep ascent of 760 m (2,530 ft) up the Serra do Mar. Farther north, for example on the Leopoldina Railway,

Far left: Chilean State Railway's 2-6-0 locomotives leave Lota with a freight train. Steam traction in Chile has been progressively limited to the southern extremities of the system.

Left: A Bolivian Railways 2-8-2 No 671 at Vila-Vila.

Right: Passengers occupy themselves with photography during a servicing stop on the Chilean Trans-Andean Railway before electrification.

Far left: A steam railcar in the Bolivian Andes. Steam railcars have had a short reign in South America.

Left: A Swiss built electric locomotive of 1958 on the Chilean section of the Trans-Andes Railway.

Right: A passenger train on the Oroya in Peru. The photograph dates from the 1870s and shows a Rogers 2-6-0 locomotive hauling rolling stock.

Below: On the 914 mm (3 ft) gauge Huantayo-Huantavelica Railway in Peru. Locomotive No 107 arrives at Huantayo.

another British enterprise, rack systems were used on the steep inclines of the Serra do Mar.

Road and air competition, combined with an inherent Brazilian dislike of anything old-fashioned, caused a serious decline in rail traffic after the second world war, though a few systems such as the broad-gauge Paulista and metre-gauge Sorocabana remained viable. Latterly, the vast haematite deposits of Minas Gerais, the steel industry of Volta Redonda and the enormous manufacturing potential of São Paulo, fastest-growing city in the world, have created freight movement in bulk to renew the lease of life of railways in Brazil. Construction of several heavy-duty freight routes for export traffic is in progress (1976), and extensive track upgrading, gauge conversion and electrification are planned under a ten-year development programme begun in 1974.

Chile

Chile's claim to the first railway in South America is not justified, although William Wheelwright's Caldera-Copiapó Railway, a standard-gauge copper carrier, was opened in 1852. The difficult line from the port of Val-paraiso to the capital Santiago – 185 km (115 miles) – begun in 1852 and suspended with only four miles built, was completed in under the contract time by Henry Meiggs and opened in 1863. A 1,676 mm (5 ft 6 in) gauge State Railways network had been inaugurated in 1859, and Meiggs began his construction operations in South America with works on the southern section of the system. The brothers Juan and Mateo Clark, who had built the Buenos Aires Pacific line to Mendoza, played a major part in construction of the metre-gauge Chilean and Argentine Transandine railways across the Cordilleras between Mendoza and Santiago, a high rack-assisted line which reached an altitude of 3,136 m (10,452 ft).

The nitrate boom in the last quarter of the 19th century inspired construction of a number of railways, the most notable being the 762 mm (2 ft 6 in) gauge Antofagasta Railway (converted to metre gauge in 1928), and the standard-gauge Nitrate Railways of Iquique, both British-owned. The 1,067 mm (3 ft 6 in) gauge Tocopilla Rail-way first used the articulated Kitson-Meyer double-engine steam locomotive in 1898, subsequently adopted widely elsewhere. Bulk traffic in Chile today is mostly copper.

Chile's route-length of 9,536 km (5,922 miles) includes 2,948 km (1,830 miles) of 1,676 mm (5 ft 6 in) gauge in the Southern network. Elsewhere, metre gauge predominates. The network is laid out in the form of a longitudinal spine, from which feeder lines branch off to the ports and sources of traffic.

Peru

Peru planned a similar rail network to Chile's, but prodded by the ambitious Meiggs, who transferred his activities there in 1868, the government under President Balta overspent available resources. Loans were raised in Britain and France on the security of guano; but the foreign debt could not be serviced on account of the declining reserves of this fertilizer. The situation became desperate when Peru was conquered in the Pacific war of 1879 to 1882 and lost to Chile the valuable nitrate territories which might have saved her from ruin. Before he died in 1877, Meiggs built several standard-gauge railways not interconnected, only one of which – the Oroya line (later the Central of Peru crossing the Cordillera at a maximum altitude of 4,742 m or 15,806 ft, – was at the time economically justified.

Richard Trevithick came to Peru in 1816 with a number of his Cornish pumping engines for the mines of Cerro de Pasco, and mooted a rail link between the capital, Lima, and the port of Callao, 14.5 km (9 miles) distant. The upheavals of the Wars of Independence prior to 1825 prevented construction of the railway, which might have been the world's first public carrier but was not built and put in service until May 1851, a few months before Wheelwright's Copiapó Railway.

The Peruvian Corporation, formed in 1890 to take over Peru's foreign debt in exchange for the principal railways and other assets, relinquished possession of these to the government in 1972. Stiff road competition and soaring operating costs made them a financial liability, even the once secure Central with its assured bulk traffic of minerals and petroleum to and from the central mining region. Although Peruvian rails have the highest summits in the Andes, no racks are used on the steep grades, which are climbed by adhesion only.

Bolivia

Though the first railway operating in what is now Bolivia was the short Huanchaca narrow-gauge line between Uyuni and Pulacayo, the country's railway history really commences with extension of the 762 mm (2 ft 6 in) gauge Antofagasta line from Chile into Bolivia as far as Uyuni in 1889 and to Oruro in 1892, all of which was finally converted to metre gauge in 1928. The Antofagasta (Chile) & Bolivia Railway (FCAB) was formed by a lease of The Bolivia Railway Company's lines, all metre gauge, from Oruro to Viacha, San Pedro to Cochabamba, Rio Mulato to Potosí, and Uyuni to Atocha. Until 1917 the company operated into La Paz over the track of the electrified Guaqui-La Paz Railway, built in 1906 as an adhesion line on a gradient of 1 in 14.3.

State lines included the Bolivian section of the Arica-La Paz Railway (rack-assisted) (1913), the Atocha-Villazón (a link in the *Diagonal de Hierro* international route between Mollendo in Peru and Buenos Aires), the Potosí-Sucre, and the Yacuiba-Santa Cruz. Railways are vital to landlocked Bolivia as a medium for transport of tin and other minerals; but a prestige line of 680 km

Other countries

Uruguayan State Railways, created in 1952, took over the 1,568 km (974 mile) Central Uruguay Railway, which had its beginnings in 1872 and handled considerable cattle traffic. This and the 512 km (319 mile), Midland, both originally British-operated, were the principal Uruguayan systems, and both are standard gauge.

Paraguay's first railway dates from 1859 and was built to 1,676 mm (5 ft 6 in) gauge. This was extended to the Parana river in 1911 and converted to standard gauge to permit wagons to be run from the Argentine North-Eastern Railway through to Asunción on the Paraguay river. Since the state takeover, the 438 km (272 mile) British-operated Paraguay Central Railway has been known as the President Carlos Antonio Lopez Railway. Timber and fruit are the principal traffics handled.

Although no less a man than Robert Stephenson was in Colombia on a mining venture during 1824 and 1825, he was in no way concerned with railway construction. Before nationalization, five British companies operated there, but the physical nature of the country does not favour private enterprise, and state control of all railways was opted for in 1922. Today's Colombian National Railways have a route length of 3,436 km (2,135 miles) in five divisions, of which the 914 mm (3 ft) gauge Pacific division is the most important. Longest is the Central division with 1,368 km (850 miles). Four new lines were under study in 1976. Andean mountain conditions prevail in much of Colombia, though altitudes are not comparable with those to the south.

Ecuador's rail history commenced in 1871 when the Guayaquil & Quito Railway was begun. This was a 450 km (280 mile) 1,067 mm (3 ft 6 in) gauge line completed in 1908 with joint US and British capital. Besides this principal railway, which has in its time plunged from comparative prosperity into penury and is presently holding its head just above water as part of the Ecuadorian State Railways, there is a 372 km (231 mile) line from Quito to San Lorenzo operated as a separate entity, two other 1,067 mm gauge short lines, and two of 750 mm gauge. The mountainous G&Q is a spectacular line with adhesion grades of up to 1 in 18, and a summit of 3,552 m (11,841 ft).

Venezuela is a country hitherto not endowed with any major rail system, but a project has started for construction of 3,700 km (2,290 miles) of new line by 1990, 1,160 km (721 miles) of which are to be ready by 1979. Some 177 km (110 miles) are already in operation. Venezuela's first railway was a 610 mm (2 ft) gauge line built in 1877 to serve the Aroa copper mines. A 137 km (85 mile) line from the port of La Guayra to Caracas (no longer in use) was built in 1883 by a British company and electrified in 1927. Venezuela's railway system of today uses standard (1,435 mm) gauge.

The 29 km (18 miles) of the Guyana Government Railways are the remains of a 96 km (60 mile) standard-gauge line, the beginnings of which date back to 1848. Surinam has 85 km (53 miles) of metre-gauge line.

(423 miles) opened in 1954 between Puerto Suarez, facing the Brazilian frontier at Corumbá, and Santa Cruz has little traffic potential, though it is currently being extended to Trinidad Beni for development purposes. High altitudes characterize Bolivian railways, the highest summit being at Condor, on the Potosí line, where it reaches 4,710 m (15,705 ft).

Heavy financial losses in its Bolivian section obliged FCAB to suspend operations there in 1954, and the government nominated a State Railways board to take over. At present, Bolivian National Railways operates two unconnected rail systems – the 2,101 km (1,306 mile) Western and the 1,222 km (760 mile) Eastern. Studies began in 1975 for a 300 km line in central Bolivia as a link in a projected railway between the Brazilian port of Santos and the Chilean port of Arica; this would also connect the two national networks across the continent.

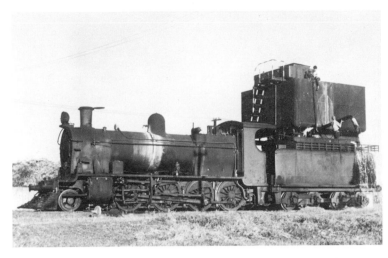

Above: No 129, a Uruguayan State Railway 2–8–0, takes water at the important junction of Paso de los Toros. The locomotive was built in Britain in 1914.

Above right: No 11 of the Guayaquil-Quito Railway in Ecuador. This 1,067 mm (3 ft 6 in) gauge locomotive was built in the USA by Baldwin in 1900.

Right: A train of nitrate empties on the Tocopilla Railway in Chile. The 1,067 mm (3 ft 6 in) gauge box-cab electric locomotive was built by GEC and works on the 1,500-volt system.

Above left: The daily through passenger train on the Cuzco to Santa Ana railway in the Peruvian Andes. The American (Baldwin) oil-burning 4–6–0 is about to leave the station at Macchu Pichu.

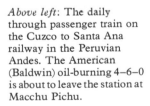

Below left: A British-built 2–6–0 of the Paraguay Central Railway. The smokebox plaque commemorates the nationalization of this railway in 1961.

The FCAB in Chile remains (1976) the only surviving major British railway enterprise still operating in South America. Britain in the 19th century, as the world's banker and the most experienced nation in rail transport, held a dominant position in the operation of South America's rail network. Latterly, Japanese influence has appeared, and rolling stock has been supplied by Communist-bloc countries, as well as from previous sources. Britain's influence today is mostly as a consultant.

Reversion to state ownership and administration was not at all unwelcome to many of the foreign private companies, whose losses were no longer tolerable due to dramatic increases in all costs. Moreover, freight traffic, other than movements in bulk, was sorely eroded by road transport, much of which lacked adequate control; and passenger traffic had been creamed off by the airlines, which in many cases were favoured by the huge distances involved and their highly competitive tariffs.

But state administration has allowed too much say in technical matters by politicians who knew nothing about them, and senior posts were often filled by unqualified people. The standardization so cherished by the private companies suffered greatly as motive power, rolling stock and other equipment was acquired from countries wherever loans could be arranged, with little regard for adequate provision of spares. Diesel-electric traction began to replace steam once it had proved itself in North America and Europe, but steam is found in Paraguay, Ecuador and parts of Brazil.

Plans for new construction indicate a chance for survival of the railway system in many countries of South America, and where sources of bulk traffic exist it may long remain the only practicable means of moving raw materials in quantity from the interior to the ports for export.

HISTORY

ASIA

Railway development in Asia has been uneven, and only India and Japan have adequate networks. In these two countries much investment has been devoted to the improvement of existing facilities, whereas in China, Siberia, and parts of the Middle East new lines are currently being built to districts hitherto without a railway.

The Indian Sub-continent

India was well placed to benefit from the railway age of the mid–19th century. Britain, the colonial power, was eager to promote both economic development and the spread of western culture, and it had access to the rich British capital market. To attract British investors, the guarantee system was put forward by Lord Dalhousie, the governor general, and adopted in 1854. This provided for government supervision of routes and standards, while guaranteeing to the new London-based Indian railway companies

Below: A 762mm (2 ft 6 in) gauge 0-6-2 on the turntable at Nadiad, on the Indian Western Railway's extensive narrow-gauge system. The locomotive, of class W, was built in Britain in 1913.

that in bad years, when receipts were insufficient to pay a 5 per cent dividend, the government would pay the difference. Thus investors were given the possibility of great profits, and the certainty that the government would protect them from great losses. This was expensive, but nevertheless was an excellent way of having railways built where the government wanted them. India was the first Asian territory to receive an extensive and well-planned network, and its railways were very solidly built.

India's first public steam railways were opened in 1854 to a gauge of 1,676 mm (5 ft 6 in). These were the first short sections of the Great Indian Peninsula Railway from Bombay and of the East Indian Railway from Calcutta. Other lines soon followed. Despite the availability of capital and government support, railway-building was beset with problems. The steep-sided plateau of central India entailed difficult sections of railway out of Bombay and elsewhere, where the line zig-zagged uphill with trains changing direction at successive reversing stations. The sudden floods of India's wide rivers scoured out the foundations of early bridges, and also caused rivers to change their course, so that a long bridge might be left high and dry far from the river it was intended to span. Although labour was plentiful and cheap, it was subject to fatal disease, as was the British supervisory staff. There was an underlying contest between railways and Hindu culture. Railways required precision, punctuality, and literacy, and did not tolerate cultural traditions like the caste system; when ordinary Indians uncomplainingly sat down with lower-caste passengers in the early trains it was evident that the new technological culture would be in opposition to the old religious culture. This cultural impact, together with the railways' creation of a pool of skilled Indian labour, prepared the country for modern industrial life.

The guarantee system fell into disfavour in 1869 and for some years most lines were government-built, while the policy of acquiring existing companies was progressively expanded and continued up to 1947. But by 1880 it was clear that the state alone could not achieve the rate of construction necessary for the needs of a developing country, so modified guarantee terms were introduced to stimulate further building. However, the decision taken by the state at this time that it should, as far as possible, be responsible for future construction led directly to adoption of a second gauge. The government was particularly interested in building lines to stimulate development in less prosperous areas, and to relieve famine. However, to build a greater mileage with the same investment, it was decided to introduce the cheaper metre gauge as an alternative to the existing 1,676 mm (5 ft 6 in) gauge. This saddled India with the expense and delay of break-of-gauge transhipment, a problem which was intensified with the construction of some 762 mm (2 ft 6 in) and 610 mm (2 ft) gauge lines in later years. When India became independent in 1947, of her 65,000 km (40,500 miles) of railway routes half, including the inter-city trunk routes,

was of 1,676 mm (5 ft 6 in) gauge, 25,600 km (16,000 miles) was metre gauge, and 6,400 km (4,000 miles) was narrow gauge.

In general the Indian railway companies, both private and state, provided reasonably cheap and fast transport for the population and the economy, both of which were growing rapidly. By 1947 all except a few short lines were under state ownership and management; an intermediate stage of organization by which certain of the old London-based companies had sold their fixed structures to the government but continued to operate their trains under contract, came to an end during the second world war. The railways had long been India's biggest employer; in 1903 they employed 400,000 workers on 48,000 km (30,000 miles) of line, in 1915 600,000 (of whom 8,000 were European), and they now employ over 1,500,000 (all Indians).

After the bloodshed and turmoil on the railways in early 1947, when the Empire of India was divided into independent India and Pakistan, new zonal railway organizations were set up to replace the old company administrations. Several of the former railways had been split between the two new nations, and their main lines truncated. The new railway zones, forming the Indian Government Railways, had some operational autonomy, but were under the general supervision of the Ministry of Railways and its Railway Board.

The main achievement of Indian Railways has been the provision of cheap transport for an economy rapidly growing under the guidance of

Top: The Indian metre gauge at Agra Fort. YG and YP class locomotives wait as their train is watered.

Left: Red-turbanned baggage porters await the next train at Ahmedabad.

Below: A train of the heavily graded narrow-gauge Darjeeling-Himalaya Railway curves around the celebrated Ghun loop. Like India's three other mountain railways, this line does not pay its way but is regarded as an asset for the tourist industry.

successive five-year plans. Its second achievement, in most years, has been to make a profit. Being the largest industry and the largest employer, as well as part of the public sector, it has also been required to take a lead in certain social objectives; hence the introduction of *Janata* trains (fast long-distance services for third-class passengers), the opening of all jobs to members of any caste, and the cultivation of Hindi as an all-Indian language.

Although some important connecting lines have been built, a few single-track lines doubled, and some metre-gauge track converted to broad-gauge, the vastly increased traffic has been accommodated mainly by the existing infrastructure. Passenger traffic in 1975–76 was about double the 1,284 million paid journeys registered in the 1950–51 accounting year, while freight traffic grew from 93 million tonnes in 1950–51 to 122 million tonnes in 1974–75. During the first five-year plan increased capacity was obtained by the mass application of new improved steam locomotives (the WP 4–6–2 and WG 2–8–2 classes on the broad gauge, and the YP 4–6–2 and YG 2–8–2 classes on the metre gauge), the introduction of block trains running from a single origin to a single destination, and the widespread use of four-axle freight wagons. Electrification at 25,000 volts ac is now relieving the pressure on the busy Calcutta-Delhi, Calcutta-Bombay, and Bombay-Ahmedabad routes. Dieselization has had a smaller but useful impact.

Electric locomotives are built at the Chittaranjan works, formerly a steam locomotive works

established with British assistance in the late 1940s. Main line diesel units, essentially of US (Alco) design, are built at a works near Varanasi. In 1976 there were about 11,000 locomotives available, of which over 8,000 were steam. Annual production of locomotives approached 150 units; none are imported and steam locomotive construction ceased in 1972. All passenger stock is built at the Integral Coach Factory at Perambur, and IR has gradually become self-sufficient in production of much equipment which formerly had a high content of imported components. Recently, IR workshops have begun to win small export orders.

Top: The erecting shop of the locomotive works at Moghulpura. This photograph was made before Independence, when the works belonged to the North Western Railway; on the formation of Pakistan they became part of the Pakistan Western Railway.

Below: A line of newly-built 2-8-2 locomotives turned out by the Tangshan Works in 1976, just before production was interrupted by the great Chinese earthquake of that year.

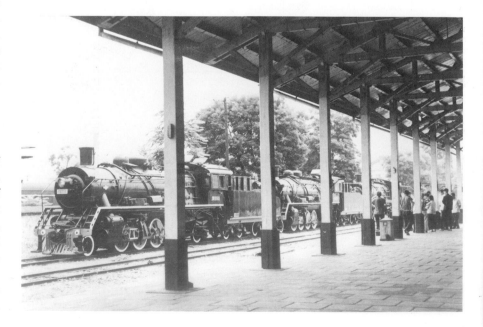

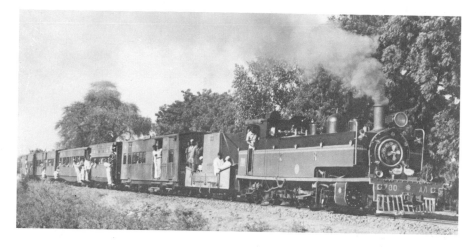

Peculiarly Indian difficulties in recent years have been the refusal of large numbers of passengers to buy tickets, the reckless pulling of 'alarm chains' (communication cords), sabotage, theft of live catenary wire on electrified lines, signalling equipment, and of goods in transit. Bribe-taking, several coal crises, a proliferation of competing railway trade unions, and a chronic apathy among lower officials at times has led to high accident rates, long ticket queues, and other unpleasantness. The 'national emergency' declared in 1975 quelled the strike-prone unions and persuaded officials to work more conscientiously, but its long-term effects are questionable.

In Pakistan the former North Western Railway was renamed the Pakistan Western Railway after Independence, and achieved a steady traffic growth, especially on its main line from Karachi to Lahore and Rawalpindi; parts of this line have been electrified by a British consortium. US diesels have been imported, although steam traction still works some services, including the once-weekly train on the celebrated Khyber Pass line. In former East Pakistan, now Bangladesh, the mixed metre and 1,676 mm (5 ft 6 in) gauge system is run-down because of the 1971 war, but still functioning. The Burmese Railways, once administered from India, are in a grave situation after decades of war, civil war, and revolution. In Sri Lanka, on the other hand, the (5 ft 6 in) gauge railways, built by the British independently of the Indian system, are dieselized and flourishing.

China

Railways came late to China and, despite extensive new construction during the last two decades, large areas of the country are still awaiting rail transport. An obstacle to early development was a weak government, usually opposed both to modernization and foreigners. A cultural difficulty was the impossibility of laying a track without disturbing somebody's ancestors, because the Chinese dead were buried and worshipped in innumerable family plots. After several British proposals had been refused by the government, subterfuge was employed. In 1876 the Woosung light railway was built, near Shanghai. The British promoters of this line had secured permission for a road to be built, upon which they then laid tracks and operated steam trains. But when the train killed a local man, either by accident or conspiracy, the line was dismantled.

Meanwhile, 160 km (100 miles) from Peking, a coal-mining mule tramway had been allowed. The British engineer of this mine company, quietly encouraged by the local governor, built a locomotive from scrap iron. In 1891 this unusual machine, named *Rocket of China*, went into service despite government hostility. It was the first locomotive built in China and, equally significant for the future, was of 1,435 mm (4 ft 8½ in) gauge. This line, the Kaiping Tramway, later became the Chinese Railway Company, part of the future Peking-Mukden main line of the Imperial Railways of North China.

The military superiority of the western powers, from time to time brought into action against the Chinese, opened the country to western commercial influence, and in the competition for 'spheres of influence' railway-building concessions were a main weapon and a main object. This scramble for concessions was especially lively after Japan's defeat of China in 1895, which caused forward-looking officials to appreciate the military value of railways. British, Russian, Belgian, French and German interests predominated, but there was also some American participation. Tsarist Russia invested great military and financial resources in building the Chinese Eastern Railway from west to east through Manchuria and then on to Russian Vladivostok, thus completing the eastern section of the Trans-Siberian Railway.

After China had been weakened by the war

Above left: No 700, a 2-8-4T built in Britain in 1912 for the Great Indian Peninsula Railway, still at work on a narrow-gauge branch line in 1975.

Above: A modern 4-6-2 of the RM class stands in the new station at Peking in 1976.

Below: An American-built lightweight 2-6-2 of the inter-war period pulls out of Peking.

against Japan, Russia obtained the right to build the South Manchurian Railway. This was a southerly branch of the Chinese Eastern Railway from a junction at Kharbin (virtually a Russian town on Chinese territory, with railway workshops and railway troops) to Port Arthur, a strategic port leased by Russia from the Chinese. The Russo-Japanese war of 1904 to 1905 (caused partly by Russian railway expansionism) ended with the South Manchurian Railway in Japanese hands, although the Chinese Eastern remained Russian. Thus Manchuria was divided into Japanese 1,067 mm (3 ft 6 in) gauge and Russian 1,524 mm (5 ft) gauge territory, according to the prevailing sphere of influence. Similar gauge diversity occurred elsewhere in China. The Chinese Eastern Railway was taken over by the Japanese in the 1930s, was returned to Russia in 1945, and was transferred back to China in 1952. Standard gauge (1,435 mm) is now prevalent in China, including Manchuria where the original Russian lines are now serving the Republic's most heavily-industrialized region.

Apart from railways built as foreign concessions, a number of lines were built by the Chinese with the aid of foreign capital. These were collectively known as the Chinese Government Railways. A milestone was the 210 km (130 mile) Peking-Kalgan Railway, finished in 1909, which was built without the aid of a single foreigner. Meanwhile, popular opposition to foreign influence and control, which had briefly manifested itself in bombardment of the Chinese Eastern Railway during the Boxer Rebellion, led to calls for nationalization. The conflict between the provinces (which wished to build their own lines, without foreign help), the Peking government (which wanted to bring all railways under its control to strengthen its internal political and military position), and interests opposed to foreign influence, led directly to the Chinese Revolution and the overthrow of the dynasty. So-called railway protection societies were a leading revolutionary force in this upheaval. The new Republican government chose a policy of gradual nationalization, combined with a pro-

Above: Chinese-built diesel locomotives still have an external similarity to Russian designs.

Above right: One of the best-known Japanese locomotive types, the C62, hauls a fast Sapporo to Hakodate train.

Centre right: A Japanese National Railways 485 type electric multiple unit for the 1,067mm (3ft 6in) gauge lines. This train is designed for dual ac/dc operation.

Bottom right: Another of the Japanese independent lines, the Keihan Electric Railways (serving Kyoto and Osaka) uses this all-aluminium electric multiple unit.

Below left: A 2000 class electric multiple unit train of the Nishi-Nippon Railway. This line is one of the many short lines which remain outside the Japanese National Railways. It is of standard gauge, and electrified at 1,500 volts.

gramme of new government railways. However, the troubled state of the country, culminating in civil war and Japanese occupation, brought the railways to a distressing condition.

In 1949 a strong communist government was installed which, following the Russian example, opted for rapid industrial development, with emphasis on basic heavy industries. Railway transport was an essential part of this growth, and over the last two decades there has been extensive rebuilding and re-equipment, as well as construction of new lines. There had been about 16,000 km (10,000 miles) of railway in 1935, perhaps 22,000 km (14,000 miles) in 1949 (of which half was unusable), but thanks to new construction (largely in the hitherto neglected western areas) there were about 35,000 km (21,750 miles) in 1971.

In the 1950s Russian technical assistance was important, the Soviet-operated Chinese Eastern Railway serving as a training ground for Chinese railwaymen. Chinese-built rolling stock had pronounced Russian features. After withdrawal of Russian aid the Chinese were able to build on that foundation and are now producing their own steam, diesel, and electric locomotives. Steam traction still dominates, but many passenger trains, as well as all services on a few lines, are diesel-hauled. There are great hopes for electrification, and selective imports of French and German electric locomotives suggest that a careful study is being made of foreign experience. Electrified mileage is as yet small, but the policy is to electrify mountainous main lines while leaving the eastern plains to steam and diesel traction. One standard steam locomotive, still being built in 1976, is a 2–10–2 freight machine based on a Russian design. Also still in the Russian tradition is the division of passenger facilities into 'hard' and 'soft' classes.

Japan

Railway development could not begin in Japan until after the Meiji Restoration, when an anti-foreign, anti-industrial and feudalistic regime was replaced by rulers who believed that only by imitating Western progress could Japan

become strong. That other island power, Britain, became a model to be admired and Japanese railways, like the new Japanese navy, were created with British help. In 1869, one year after the Restoration, the British ambassador recommended railway construction and the Japanese cabinet agreed. However, there was a conflict between the cabinet's desire for state-owned railways and the shortage of government funds. Thereupon the ambassador introduced one Horatio Nelson Lay, who presented a scheme for a 9 per cent loan on the London market. Believing this financial entrepreneur to be a relative of the much-respected Lord Nelson, the Ministry of Finance agreed.

Despite opposition from those who thought that foreign indebtedness was a snare, from highway hotelkeepers and from coolies, the first line was opened in 1872. The Emperor himself graced the opening of this 29 km (18 mile) Tokyo to Yokohama line, the beginning of Japanese Imperial State Railways. Two more government lines, from Kyoto to Osaka and Kobe to Osaka, were opened in 1873 and 1874. More lines followed later; the 1877 Kyoto-Otsu line was noteworthy in that it was planned entirely by Japanese, although construction was supervised by Europeans. Construction and operation were complicated by Japan's geography. Most of the population and economic activity was in the narrow coastal strips of the several islands, the interior being mountainous, volcanic, and crisscrossed with rivers subject to sudden floods. Japan's geography also meant that coastal shipping could handle much of the freight traffic more cheaply than the railways; hence the greater relative importance, compared to other countries, of passenger traffic.

Due to shortage of funds, from about 1890 the government encouraged private companies to build lines. Each company tended to serve a particular part of the country, so there was little competition. Despite the existence of a government plan for railway construction, there was a Railway Mania in 1896, with many unnecessary lines being built. This was followed by a depression, in which several of the new companies became bankrupt. The private railways began to merge; by 1905 there were 39 companies operating 5,150 km (3,200 miles), but the six largest accounted for 3,780 km (2,350 miles) of these. Private mileage was considerably greater than that of the state railways; indeed, some of the latter had been sold off by the government to raise funds.

On average the private lines were more profitable, and probably more efficient, than the state lines. Nevertheless, after the victorious Russo-Japanese war had brought a spirit of assertive nationalism, the proponents of nationalization won the day. By 1912 there were 8,000 km (5,000 miles) of state railway, and only 965 km (600 miles) of private, and this preponderance of the state railways over short private lines has continued to this day. One of the arguments in favour of nationalization was that it would bring an end to the 'narrow gauge' 1,067 mm (3 ft 6 in) which had been standardized in Japan, and its replacement by 1,435 mm (4 ft 8½ in). This faith in the transforming effect of an extra 368 mm (14½ in) between the rails would, 60 years later, be tested by the construction of new lines to the broader gauge.

Nationalization was also intended to prevent foreign investors influencing railway policy. However, it was not until the 1920s that Japan finally became independent of foreign locomotive builders, even though the first locomotive built in Japan appeared as early as 1892. During the inter-war years, aided by the country's commercial and military expansion, the railway supply industry developed rapidly on the basis of exports to other Asian territories. After the second world war, the loss of Asian markets was compensated by sales to other areas; steam locomotives were exported to South America as late as the 1960s. With the spectacular high-speed New Tokaido

Above: An engine shed on the Trans-Siberian railway. The photograph was taken in 1911.

Line from Tokyo to Osaka serving as a potent advertisement from 1964, Japan has since secured large export orders for more modern equipment, including electric and diesel locomotives.

The 515 km (320 mile) New Tokaido Line marked the end of the post-1945 reconstruction period, during which the Japanese National Railway was transformed into one of the world's most modern, though unprofitable, systems. The steam locomotive was finally retired in 1976. The New Tokaido Line was also the first stage in creation of a proposed new separate railway system of electrified high-speed trunk lines of 1,435 mm (4 ft 8½ in) gauge, known as *Shinkansen*, laid on gently-graded and gently-curved alignments. The frequent 'bullet train' service of the new line attracted many new passengers, and on one memorable day in 1969 more than half-a-million were carried. But although an extension to Hakata has been added and two more routes are under construction, it is not certain that other planned lines will be built. Track

Below: A double headed mixed train with woodburning locomotives crosses a newly completed bridge on the Trans-Siberian line in 1911.

Above: Locomotive No. 564.32, beautifully maintained, steams through the palm groves on the Malaysian West Coast main line from Singapore.

Above right: A Japanese built woodburning 4–6–2 crosses a timber viaduct near Haadyai in Thailand.

maintenance costs have been higher than expected, and airline competition will be stiff on the longer and less densely-populated routes. Critics claim that capital would be better spent on Tokyo's commuter services, where there is severe overcrowding. Nevertheless, on existing *Shinkansen* routes in 1975 revenue exceeded all costs by 62 per cent.

Asiatic Russia

Apart from the Trans-Siberian Railway, built in the final decades of the Tsarist empire, the Russians built many lines in central Asia. Among these railways, which caused great alarm in London because they seemed to point towards India, were the Trans-Caspian, linking the Caspian Sea with Tashkent, and the Turkestan-Siberia line, which ran southwards to Alma Ata from a junction with the Trans-Siberian. The Turkestan-Siberia was finished by the Soviet government, which has built many more railways both in central Asia and in Siberia. The Baikal-Amur Railway, now being built, is a heavy-duty freight line running parallel to, and north of, the Trans-Siberian to the Pacific. Traversing spectacularly difficult country, subject to earthquake and permafrost, the line's main task will be exploitation of new oilfields; interestingly, a railway was

chosen in preference to a pipeline for purely economic reasons.

South-East Asia

The Royal State Railways of Thailand comprise about 3,800 km (2,360 miles) of metre-gauge route. The first line was built in 1897, northwards from Bangkok. In general, German influence predominated in the north, where 1,435 mm (4 ft 8½ in) gauge prevailed, while the southern lines were British influenced. The latter were of metre gauge, as the British intended to link the Thai system with their own metre-gauge system in Malaya. Until 1917 there were therefore two separate systems, but when a new river bridge at Bangkok made a physical connection possible it was decided to convert the northern lines to metre gauge. In due course connections were made with Malayan railways, and also with nearby Cambodian railways. But, despite the Japanese extension of the River Kwai line during the second world war (since abandoned), a link with the Burmese Railway has not yet been achieved.

Coal and oil are imported, so Thai steam locomotives usually burned local wood, often high-quality teak. Since wood supplies were not inexhaustible, the Royal State Railways were one of the first to experiment with diesel traction. Swiss and Danish diesel locomotives were imported, and six of the Danish batch, built in 1931, were still at work in the 1960s. After the second world war the railways were in a run-down state, and new steam and diesel locomotives were imported. The last series of steam imports were 4–6–2 and 2–8–2 woodburners from Japan. In recent years steam traction has been pushed to the southern extremities of the system by diesel-electrics and diesel-hydraulics from Europe, Japan, and the U.S.A.

The link with the Malayan railways was useful to both countries (as well as to the Japanese in 1941); through passenger services still run between Singapore and Bangkok. The Federated Malay States Railway (later, after Independence,

Right: The *Shinkansen* speeds over a viaduct on Japan's New Tokaido Line.

the Malayan Railway Administration or PKTM) was one of the smartest and most advanced of the many British colonial railways. Among its features were the imposing station at Kuala Lumpur, built in Islamic style, and a highly-standardized locomotive stock, with successive generations of British-built Pacifics handling the bulk of the traffic. During a modernization plan, carried out with foreign financial help from 1971 to 1975, complete dieselization was achieved (but only temporarily, for some of the Pacifics were returned to traffic during a loco shortage in 1976). Present extent of the network is 1,665 km (1,035 miles), but an additional main line, crossing the peninsula from east to west, may be built.

Indonesian State Railways are of 1,067 mm (3 ft 6 in) gauge, although this has not always been so. The first line of the private Netherlands Indies Railways, opened in 1864, was of 1,435 mm (4 ft 8½ in) gauge. However, a second system, the State Railway, adopted 1,067 mm gauge, and until the second world war these two gauges co-existed. At one period the main route connecting the capital Batavia (now Djakarta) with the second city, Surabaya, was 1,067 mm gauge at both ends, with a 1,435 mm gauge section in the middle. Eventually this difficulty was alleviated by laying a third rail in the middle section, transforming it into a dual-gauge line. When the Japanese occupied the Dutch East Indies in 1941 they sent all the 1,435 mm gauge equipment to China, thereby permanently solving this gauge problem.

Although there are three isolated lines in Sumatra, most of the Indonesian mileage is in Java. Despite the 1969–74 rehabilitation plan, during which many of the main lines were upgraded, old equipment is still used and services on branch and secondary lines are poor and unreliable. Apart from a short length of line electrified between Djakarta and Bogor during the Dutch regime, steam and diesel traction prevail. The latter comprises US diesel-electrics and German diesel-hydraulics, and these haul the better long-distance passenger trains. The steam stock includes modern Krupp-built 2–8–2s, as well as big Mallet-type machines. Many are very old, and the popularity of roadside tramways is reflected in the large number of steam tram locomotives. Steam locomotives came from a variety of countries; the Dutch East Indian railways gave no preference to Dutch locomotive exports. The present network is about 6,400 km (4,000 miles), plus about 500 km (310 miles) of 750 mm (2 ft 6 in) and 600 mm (2 ft) gauge track.

The Middle East
The most highly developed of the Middle East railway networks in recent times is that of Turkey, thanks to a burst of construction and modernization between the wars. After the formation of Ataturk's republic mileage almost doubled and the hitherto unco-ordinated administration of the previously scattered railways was centralized in a new organization, Turkish State Railways (TCDD). Despite the mountainous character of

Above left: A 2-8-8-0 Mallet type locomotive, built in Germany in the 1920s, working on a Javanese branch line of the Indonesian State Railways.

Above centre: No B5308, a 4-4-0 built in the Netherlands in 1914, hauls a mixed train on the Madiun-Slahung branch of the Indonesian State Railways.

Above right: A modern diesel multiple unit train of the Turkish State Railways near Istanbul.

Below: A British-built 2-8-2 on a Turkish State Railways local train at Izmir.

most of the country, it is now crossed by about 9,869 km (6,133 miles) of 1,435 mm (4 ft 8½ in) gauge routes covering a territory considerably smaller than the old Ottoman Empire. Steam traction is still widely used; this is mainly of German origin or inspiration, although after the second world war some 2–10–0 locomotives were built in TCDD workshops. On the 196 km (122 miles) of electrified route, French locomotives are working. Diesel locomotives are mostly German and American, although some are built in Turkey.

The close connection between railways and diplomacy and strategy in the area, was well illustrated in 1903, when the first sections of the Baghdad Railway were started. This was a German-financed and German-engineered line from Constantinople to Baghdad, and caused great alarm in London and Paris because it introduced German influence into this uneasy region. This 1,435 mm gauge line was finished in 1918, and after the end of the Ottoman Empire the northern part remained in Turkey.

Another highly political line was the Hedjaz

Railway, from Damascus to the holy city of Medina. Its aimlessly unique gauge of 1,050 mm (3 ft 5¼ in) is variously alleged to be the result of French bureaucratic logic or of a clerical error. This was the line which suffered the attacks of Lawrence of Arabia in the first world war. after which it fell into disuse. However, in 1963 a beginning was made in restoring this 1,302 km (809 mile) line, which now lies in Syria, Saudi Arabia, and Jordan. The Jordanian section is now largely operational, including a 116 km (72 mile) extension to Aqaba Port completed in 1975.

One consequence of the Baghdad Railway was the introduction of 1,435 mm (4 ft 8½ in) gauge to Iraq. Of Iraq's approximately 2,530 km (1,570 miles) of railway, 1,235 km (767 miles) are 1,435 mm gauge and the remainder metre gauge. The metre-gauge sections still reflect British influence; indeed, during the First world war campaign against the Ottoman Empire the British brought metre-gauge rails, locomotives and rolling stock from India, and much of this is still in use. New 1,435 mm gauge main lines are now being built, financed by increased oil revenues, and diesel locomotives have been imported from Canada and France. In neighbouring Syria, the existing 585 km (364 miles) of 1,435 mm gauge railway is to be supplemented by about 1,500 km (930 miles) of new main lines. One of these, from Latakia to Kamyshly, opened in 1976, is Russian-financed and operated by Soviet diesel locomotives. Israel, whose lines were originally the British Palestine Railways, is also building a new line, southwards to Eilat on the Red Sea. The present network is 595 km (370 miles) of 1,435 mm gauge, with entirely diesel traction.

The most spectacular Middle East development is in Iran, where the present network owes much to Russian and British engineering. The line southwards from the Caspian was a rare example of Tsarist Russian railway enterprise abroad. Further development took place under British and Soviet occupation during the second world war. Now, a new 20-year development plan envisages construction of several main lines, as well as doubling and electrification of existing routes. Dieselization was completed several years ago, and some fast French gas-turbine multiple-units are now in service. One of the new lines will join with Pakistan Railways at Zahedan, where there will be a bogie-changing installation to permit through running between the Iranian 1,435 mm (4 ft 8½ in) gauge and the Pakistani broad gauge. This will be a further link in the United Nations-financed Trans-Asian railway; another section, between Iran and Turkey, is already complete.

HISTORY

AFRICA

Development of railways in the African continent was at first closely bound up with the colonizing activities of European powers, and a study of the railway map shows how small lines, quite independent of each other, were driven into the interior to tap natural resources. This kind of activity was most marked about the turn of the century on the west coast. Development on the south shores of the Mediterranean, under French influence in Algeria and Tunis, and in Egypt and the Sudan under British influence began much earlier, and in the latter case was hastened by strategic needs. In southern Africa the development could have been much the same but for the momentous discovery of gold in the Transvaal, which turned a leisurely colonizing movement into a mighty industrial project, and led to the great unfulfilled conception by Cecil Rhodes of a 'Cape-to-Cairo' railway – all under British control. The constituents of the present South African Railways – the Cape Government, Natal Government, Central South African – were rapidly developed as major transcontinental links, assuming a character quite unlike the small separate colonizing railways in the north-west, and the lines bordering on the Mediterranean coast. The tables at the back show the dates of origin of all of the railways of Africa, with their present extent, and diversity of rail gauges.

The first railway in Africa was built, under strong British influence, to improve the lines of communication between England and India. It was not until 1868 that the Suez Canal was opened, so the first section of Egyptian railways ran between Alexandria, Cairo and Suez, conveying passengers between one steamer port and the other. It was opened throughout in 1858, but after completion of the canal the section between Cairo and Suez was dismantled. But from the important Alexandria-Cairo link the present Egyptian Railways developed, and a lengthy line was constructed beside the Nile as far south as Luxor-High Dam. It became much favoured by tourists, and express trains with dining and sleeping cars were introduced connecting with the Sudan river boats. It was this rapid development that led to Rhodes' conception of the Cape-to-Cairo Railway. Farther west, the somewhat shaky start of the Algerian Railway Company, from 1860, led to its absorption by the Paris, Lyon & Mediterranean Railway, and it was developed into an efficient and prosperous undertaking, running high-speed passenger trains comparable with those on the parent railway in France. In Tunisia the bulk of the railway system is metre gauge, with a section in the north of 1,435 mm (4 ft 8½ in) gauge. Operation is now entirely by diesel traction.

In 1880 Cecil Rhodes reached two great milestones in his career. He founded the world famous de Beers Mining Company, in Kimberley, and he became a Member of Parliament, in Cape Colony. His interest in diamond mining was allied with the advance of the Cape Government Railway northwards towards the Orange river, and in prospecting further into Stellaland the idea was born of a railway that would eventually

Above: Wood-burning Garratts lie idle on Angola's Benguela Railway, closed by the war following independence in 1976.

Left: A South African Railways Class 25 NC 4–8–4 No. 3452 *Maria.* The Class 25 non-condensers were among the finest main line steam locomotives in use on South African Railways, along with the Class 25 C condensers.

run the entire length of Africa, linking up with the Egyptian system. But beyond the Orange river were the two Boer republics, and of these the northerly one, then known as the South African Republic, was definitely hostile to Great Britain. So under Rhodes' direction the line to the north was surveyed on a westerly course, through Bechuanaland, which was under British influence, skirting the Boer republics, and heading for Matabeleland. Then, in 1886, came the sensational discovery of gold on the Witwatersrand, in the heart of the Transvaal, and there ensued a dramatic railway building race, northward from Kimberley by the British-sponsored Cape Government Railway, and westwards from Lourenço Marques, urgently desired by the South African Republic, but financed largely by Dutch investors. In a complicated game of politics and railway building Rhodes won the day, and the first train from the south entered Pretoria on New Year's Day 1893, 2½ years before its Dutch-financed rival.

In the meantime Rhodes was urging his contractors to press on through Bechuanaland towards what is now Rhodesia, though all railway constructional activity was delayed by the South African war. It was after conditions had returned to normal, and the Zuid Afrikaansche Spoorweg

Right: On the narrow gauge in South Africa. A freight train, with accommodation for lower-fare passengers in the brake van, being hauled by a 2–8–2 locomotive.

Below: Steam power at a South African colliery. Industrial railways, especially in mining, operate many steam locomotives, including former South African Railways units.

Bottom: A 58th Class Garratt locomotive of East African Railways crossing a viaduct on the Kisumu branch in Kenya.

Maatschappij (ZASM from Delagoa bay to Pretoria) had become the Central South African Railway that real progress began towards its amalgamation with the British-owned Cape Government Railway, and Natal Government, to form the unified South African Railways in 1910. This network had already extended far beyond the two original lines converging upon Pretoria, from the Cape and Delagoa Bay respectively. There was also the Natal main line from Durban, which provided connections to the cities of the Transvaal and southwards into Cape Province, while another of the original lines rivalling that from Cape Town in the constructional race to the winning areas, that from Port Elizabeth, became a secondary main line of considerable importance.

It was, however, development of Johannesburg as the centre of gold mining activities that gradually changed the whole operating strategy of South African Railways. Originally, while Johannesburg and Pretoria were the goals of business travellers, the focal point of SAR was Cape Town and the connections made there with the

mail steamers from England. The luxury express trains that ran the 1,000 mile (1610 km) length of SAR main line were the very lifelines of the service. To no lesser extent were those that took the 'Cape-to-Cairo' line northwards from Kimberley, heading for the cities of Rhodesia. Now, Johannesburg is the focal point of all South African railway activity. Most of the lines radiating from the Reef area are electrified, operating an intensive commuter service, and there are long-distance express trains heading for Durban, Port Elizabeth and Cape Town. An important northern line is that leading to Mafeking to join the 'Cape-to-Cairo' line, and over it are operated through passenger and freight trains between Johannesburg and Bulawayo.

South African Railways still operate a large fleet of modern steam locomotives. The motive power policy, arising from electrification on the Reef and from Cape Town, has been to concentrate steam in the areas between, maintaining huge 4–8–2, 4–8–4, and Beyer-Garratt locomotives at a high standard of efficiency. Some lines, particularly the desert sections where water is scarce, are being changed over to diesel traction; but there are such ample supplies of good

locomotive coal in the Transvaal that it is logical to maintain steam traction wherever it is still economically practicable. The main-line centres of Kimberley and De Aar are still great strongholds of steam. SAR has a small mileage of 610 mm (2 ft) gauge. This is in the coastal districts of Natal and eastern Cape Province, where services in the country districts are operated by recently-acquired 2–8–2 and Beyer-Garratt steam locomotives.

The Rhodesia Railways of today constitute a rather truncated version of the original extent because of the separation of that part now forming Zambia. The opening up of railway communication in what is now Rhodesia began with a two-pronged drive, one from the port of Beira in Mozambique, heading westwards towards Salisbury, and the second was of course the projected Cape-to-Cairo line. This latter, having reached Bulawayo, then turned north-westwards for a while to make a crossing of the Zambesi at Victoria Falls, and then to proceed north into the Congo. The present international frontier between Rhodesia and Zambia is in the middle of the great steel arched bridge overlooking Victoria Falls.

Above: Garratt locomotives of the British-owned Benguela Railway on shed at Nova Lisboa.

Left: A 58th Class Garratt 4–8–4 + 4–8–4 working on East African Railways. This unit has been fitted with a Giesl chimney to aid combustion efficiency.

Right: On the 2 ft gauge of the Angola Railways. Like the nearby Benguela Railway, this railway has suffered from the recent war in Angola.

Below: A block mineral train of the Rhodesia Railway. Heavy mineral traffic is the mainstay of several railways in Southern Africa.

Rhodes stipulated that the line should be carried not only near enough for passengers to see this great spectacle, but near enough for the carriages to be wetted by the huge curtain of spray that is always rising. Rhodesia, being a completely land-locked country, now has four rail outlets: the line to Beira, entering Mozambique territory soon after passing Umtali; the line into Zambia, over the Victoria Falls bridge; the original 'Cape-to-Cairo' line, which goes to the south through Botswana (formerly the Bechuanaland Protectorate), and a new line opened in 1973 linking with South African Railways at Beitbridge. For many years now Rhodesia Railways has operated all traffic, passenger and freight, on the line southwards through Botswana, locomotives and train crews working on the caboose system between Bulawayo and Mafeking.

Six other African railways, each with its own particular significance, can be distinguished by their several functions as colonizers, strategic desiderata, and belt conveyors of heavy minerals in bulk. The Uganda Railway, begun in 1896, was a colonizing route, hacked through virgin jungle to make connection between Mombasa and Lake Victoria. Its main line was completed in 1901, and formed the parent stem of the present East African Railways. The Benguela Railway pioneered by Robert Williams, with a concession from the Portuguese government, set out in 1902 to build a line from Lobito Bay, Angola, to the frontier of the Belgian Congo 1,335 km (830 miles) inland. But progress was slow, though hastened by strategic necessities in the first world war. The frontier was eventually reached in 1928. One of the earliest ore-carrying railways was the 224 km (139 mile) line in Swaziland, opened in 1964, connecting with the Lourenço Marques Railway. This is operated by steam locomotives obtained secondhand from Rhodesia Railways. By contrast, an ultra-modern set up is that of the LAMCO Railroad in Liberia, built by the Liberian American-Swedish Minerals Company. This operates 12,000-tonne ore trains, hauled by three diesel-electric locomotives over a 267 km (166 mile) line between Nimba and Buchanan. Even heavier trains will run on the 864 km (540 mile) line built by the South African Iron & Steel Corporation from Sishen to Saldanha bay, north of Cape Town. When electrification is completed, the three daily trains will load to 20,200 tonnes hauled by three locomotives each of 5,000 hp.

In April 1968 an agreement was signed between the governments of Tanzania and Zambia, and the Peoples' Republic of China, whereby the latter undertook to supply finance and technical services for the Great Uhuru (Freedom) Railway from Dar-es-Salaam to Kapiri Mposhi in Zambia, 1,860 km (1,150 miles). Construction was carried out by Chinese engineers and work teams with headquarters in Tanzania. The gauge is 1,067 mm (3 ft 6 in) to connect with the existing railway in Zambia, and motive power is German-type diesel-hydraulic locomotives. The line was opened in 1975 but will not be operational at full capacity until 1978.

HISTORY
AUSTRALIA

The route length of railways in Australia is over 44,000 km (27,000 miles) of which 40,250 km (25,000 miles) are owned and operated by seven government railway authorities. These public railways handle approximately 100 million tonnes of freight and over 400 million passengers per year. In addition, railways owned and operated by private companies move more than 100 million tonnes of freight, more than half of which is iron ore for export.

The first steam railway in Australia, opened on September 12, 1854 between Melbourne and Sandridge (now Port Melbourne), was only 5 km (2¼ miles) long and built to 1,600 mm (5 ft 3 in) gauge by the Melbourne & Hobsons Bay Railway.

On September 26, 1855 the first railway in New South Wales, from Sydney to Parramatta, 22.5 km (14½ miles) of 1,435 mm (4 ft 8½ in) gauge was opened, thereby creating a break-of-gauge problem that has persisted for over a century. Like the pioneer Hobsons Bay railway, the Sydney railway was promoted by a private company, but fell into financial difficulties, was taken over by the New South Wales government, and became the first government-owned railway in the British Commonwealth.

Between 1854 and 1875 lines began to radiate from the major seaboard centres to tap the resources of the hinterland, but expansion was slow because the private companies which had initiated railway construction in Victoria and New South Wales soon found the task beyond their resources. So despite lack of public finance, the several colonial governments either took over, or initiated construction.

Gauge problem

Attempts were made by the governments of Victoria, South Australia and New South Wales, on the advice of the British government, to settle on a uniform gauge before construction commenced; 1,435 mm (4 ft 8½ in) gauge being recommended and adopted. However, on the advice of the Sydney Railway's engineer, Francis Shields, New South Wales decided to opt for 1,600 mm (5 ft 3 in) gauge and the other colonies were duly informed and accepted the broad gauge. Both Victoria and South Australia ordered locomotives and rolling stock from Britain for that gauge in 1852 and 1853.

Following the unexpected resignation of Shields over a reduction in salary, his successor, James Wallace, an Englishman, succeeded in persuading his employers of the superiority of Stephenson's standard gauge. The NSW government allowed the Sydney company to revert to standard gauge. Despite strong protests to the Colonial Secretary in London by Victoria, the British government assented in 1854 to an act fixing the gauge in New South Wales at 1,435 mm (4 ft 8½ in). The other two colonies

Above: Coward Spring, a wayside station in the arid territory served by the Central Australia Railway.

Below: Locomotive No 1 and her three sisters were the first locomotives to run in New South Wales in March 1855. They were built by Robert Stephenson in 1854 and were 0-4-2 versions of the standard 0-6-0 design of the British LNWR.

Below left: A masonry viaduct at Picton, near Sydney, on the southern main line of the NSW Railway in the 1870s.

Above: Kuranda Station in North Queensland. The British tradition of decorating stations with flowers and shrubs has been taken a long stage further in Australia where the climate gives every encouragement to amateur railway horticulturists.

Below right: One of the early locomotives of the Melbourne and Hobsons Bay Railway. No 5, an 0-4-0 well tank locomotive, was built by Robert Stephenson in 1858.

Below far right: Tarradale Viaduct on the Melbourne to Fanhurst line in Victoria.

claimed that another change would be too costly for them as rolling stock was being built for 1,600 mm (5 ft 3 in) gauge – and so the muddle began!

South Australia, after preliminary skirmishing with private companies and government-appointed boards, finally opened the Adelaide City & Port Railway 11.9 km (7½ miles) long from North Terrace, Adelaide to Port Adelaide Dock station (which had all the hallmarks of a Brunel structure) on April 21, 1856. This was not, however, the first railway opened in South Australia, but was preceded by a horse tramway, 10.6 km (6.19 miles) in length and built to the same 1,600 mm (5 ft 3 in) gauge and opened for traffic on May 18, 1854. This antedated the Hobsons Bay line in Victoria, which was the first steam-operated railway in Australia.

The three other Australian colonial railways all began with steam power. On July 31, 1865 Queensland opened a line linking Ipswich to Grandchester (33.6 km; 21½ miles) built to very light standards on 1,067 mm (3 ft 6 in) gauge; Tasmania opened its first railway – privately owned and constructed to 1,600 mm (5 ft 3 in gauge) – between Launceston and Deloraine, 72 km (45 miles) on February 10, 1871; and Western Australia opened a 54.7 km line also of 1,067 mm (3 ft 6 in) gauge, linking the port of Geraldton with Northampton on July 26, 1879.

Both Queensland, Western Australia and later Tasmania and South Australia accepted the proposition advanced by another Irish railway engineer, Abraham Fitzgibbon, Queensland's Engineer-in-chief, that narrow gauge (1,067 mm, 3 ft 6 in) railways were cheaper to operate as well as to construct, and built (and in Tasmania's case converted) all or some of their railways to this gauge. They were of light construction, steeply graded and sharply curved. Thus was Australia's gauge problem compounded.

Development and expansion

The great construction period of Australia's railways extended from the early 1870s to the mid-1920s following initial extensions in Victoria and New South Wales to link provincial centres inland with the capital or a port. In Victoria, the initiative was provided by private companies which invariably failed, either before construction commenced, or soon afterwards. One exception was the Geelong & Melbourne Railway, a 1,600 mm (3 ft 6 in) gauge line linking the port of Geelong, on Corio Bay with a government line at Greenwich (now Newport) 61.6 km (38½ miles) opened for traffic on June 25, 1857.

This was followed by government lines linking Geelong with Ballarat 86.4 km (54 miles) opened April 11, 1862 and Melbourne with Sandhurst (now Bendigo) 162 km (100¾ miles) opened in stages and finally throughout on October 21, 1862 and extended two years later to tap the river Murray trade at the port of Echuca a further 90 km (56¼ miles). Both the Geelong-Ballarat and Melbourne-Bendigo lines were lavishly built with double tracks, heavy earthworks and large viaducts. These were certainly the most elaborate main lines of railway constructed in Australia in the 19th century, costing £8½ million.

The failing Geelong company was acquired by the government on September 3, 1860.

Meanwhile private companies built extensions of Melbourne suburban railways and all were absorbed into the Hobsons Bay Company by 1865. This in turn was acquired by the government on July 1, 1878 to gain access for its Gippsland line.

In New South Wales lines were extended inland from both Sydney and Newcastle, but it was not until the completion of the first bridge across the Hawkesbury river on May 1, 1889 that the two cities were linked by rail, without the interruption of a ferry.

Completion of this major bridge marked the retirement of John Whitton, engineer-in-chief of the NSW Railways for 32 years after his arrival from England in 1857. To him must go the credit for superbly engineered and constructed main lines radiating from Sydney – north to the Hawkesbury river, south to Goulburn, west to Bathurst, including the remarkable ascents and descents of the Blue mountains by means of the Lapstone zig-zag and the Great zig-zag at Lithgow, and the Illawarra line to the south coast.

Tasmania, after its initial flirtation with broad gauge, authorized the Tasmanian Main Line Railway Company to build a line of 1,067 mm (3 ft 6 in) gauge northwards from Hobart, the capital, to Evandale (196 km; 122 miles). Thence by means of a third rail and running powers over the broad gauge line which had been taken over by the government in July 1872 from the defunct Launceston & Western, a further 17.6 km (11 miles) to Launceston was opened for traffic on November 1, 1876.

Meanwhile, on the mainland, construction continued apace as settlements sprang up in the wake of the 'gold rush' era of the 1850s and 1860s in New South Wales, and Victoria, and in South Australia in the early 1870s. The latter colony initiated a project for constructing a railway across the continent, from Port Augusta on Spencer gulf to Palmerston (Port Darwin) in the Northern Territory. This line of 1,067 mm (3 ft 6 in) gauge which crossed and recrossed the rugged Flinders ranges was opened in sections between 1880 and January 1, 1890 when it finally reached Oodnadatta (764.2 km; 477.5 miles). This was the terminus 1,100 km (688 miles) from Adelaide until after transfer on January 1, 1911, under the terms of the Northern Territory Acceptance Act 1910, of the railway and territory from South Australia to the Commonwealth Government.

Under the terms of the act, the Commonwealth undertook to complete the north-south railway, though no time was specified. The line was leased to South Australia and worked as part of SAR until January 1, 1926 when Commonwealth Railways assumed control and took over working of the Central Australia Railway. This was extended a further 473 km (294 miles) from Oodnadatta to Alice Springs, opening for traffic on August 2, 1929. There remains a gap of some 960 km (600 miles) between the southern terminal of the North Australia Railway (also initiated by the South Australian government and extended by the Commonwealth) at Birdum 505 km (316 miles) south of Darwin. In 1976, while a new standard-gauge line from Tarcoola to Alice Springs was under construction, the North Australia Railway was closed.

Inter-Colonial connections

The first direct link on 1,435 mm (4ft 8½ in) gauge between Sydney and Brisbane (986 km, 613 miles) was established on September 27, 1930. However, a ferry crossing – Australia's only train ferry – of the Clarence River at Grafton, NSW, remained until completion of a combined rail road high-level bridge opened on May 8, 1932.

In Western Australia the necessity of connecting the capital city, Perth, with the port of Fremantle, was soon recognized. On April 21, 1879 tenders were received for the first section of what was to become the Eastern Railway from Fremantle to Guildford, east of Perth (32 km, 20 miles), opened for traffic on March 1, 1881. This was extended gradually over the Darling range to Beverley 177 km (110 miles) from Fremantle. The discovery of gold at Coolgardie and subsequently at Kalgoorlie at the end of the 19th century spurred construction by the government of the Eastern Goldfields Railway from Northam

Right: Local freight service at Gowra on the New South Wales Railways in 1970. The locomotive is a 4-6-0 rebuilt from a 4-6-4 tank unit made redundant by electrification.

Below: The special train *Western Endeavour* crosses the Great Dividing Range near Bathurst hauled by Pacific No 3801 and her sister locomotive, No 3813 in 1970.

Below left: The last regular steam-hauled train in Australia. British built 4-6-0 No 3246 takes the evening train to Singleton, out of Newcastle, New South Wales, in 1970.

Below: A standard gauge New South Wales Railway's Pacific No 3801 hauls the special *Western Endeavour* train over mixed gauge track in Western Australia. Extra water tanks behind the tender compensate for the lack of watering facilities on the normally fully dieselized section.

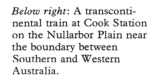

Below right: A transcontinental train at Cook Station on the Nullarbor Plain near the boundary between Southern and Western Australia.

(105.6 km from Perth) for 273 km (170 miles) to Southern Cross, opened in 1894 and extended to Kalgoorlie, 612 km (380¼ miles) east of Perth, on January 1, 1897.

From the Golden Mile (Kalgoorlie) railways were extended to Menzies (128 km; 80 miles) on March 22, 1898 and finally to Laverton (960 km; 600 miles from Fremantle) in 1905. From Coolgardie another line extending for 375 km (233¼ miles) south was built to the port of Esperance, on the Great Australian Bight, and opened in 1908. Both the Esperance and Menzies lines have recently been converted to standard gauge.

Western Australia with an area of 975,920 square miles – almost half the total of Australia – and small population and resources prior to the gold discoveries, adopted proposals for building private railways under the land grant system in 1882. This provided for a line from the port of Albany, on King George sound, for 391 km (243 miles) to Beverley of 1,067 mm gauge by the West Australian Land Company in return for grants of land along the route. This line, known as the Great Southern Railway, opened on June 1, 1889 and was taken over by the Government on December 1, 1896.

In all the other mainland colonies, construction was initiated from the capital cities, but Queensland pursued a different policy of building railways inland from the principal ports, Rockhampton, Townsville, Cairns, and later Bundaberg, Bowen and Maryborough. This began with the Central Railway (at first known as the Great Northern) from Rockhampton to Westwood 53 km (33 miles) in 1867 and the Great Northern Railway from Townsville to Charters Towers 132 km (83 miles) opened in 1880.

Construction of the lifeline of Queensland Railways – the long North Coast line linking all of the formerly isolated lines to Cairns with Brisbane, the capital, commenced in 1910. The final gaps were closed in 1924, giving a 1,678 km (1,043 mile) main line of 1,067 mm (3 ft 6 in) gauge which is among the busiest in Australia.

Narrow gauge for economy

South Australia, seeking a more economical means of extending its railways, chose the narrow gauge for the important line linking Port Pirie, site of the silver-lead-zinc smelters, with Broken Hill, in far western NSW, where the ores are mined – a distance of 406 km (254 miles).

Other long-distance routes in New South Wales were lines to Bourke on the Darling River (820 km; 513 miles) reached in September, 1885 – including the second longest dead straight track between Nyngan and Bourke (185 km; 115 miles) – and Hay on the Murrumbidgee River (748 km; 467 miles) reached in July, 1882.

Queensland's railways were extended further inland from their coastal starting points until the system reached a peak of 10,397 (6,498 miles) in 1932, the largest individual system in Australia, closely followed by New South Wales with over 9,600 route-km (6,000 miles).

Victoria, although the smallest mainland state possessed the largest network of main and secon-

dary lines and branches for its size, peaking at around 7,500 km (4,700 route-miles) in 1936, including some lines extending into the Riverina district of southern NSW built to 1,600 mm (5 ft 3 in) gauge and worked by VR under the Border Railway Agreement Act of 1922, NSW providing the land and stations.

Linking east and west

The period of most intensive railway construction in Australia was the decade from 1910 to 1920, when 12,500 km (7,768 miles) of new line were opened. With the involvement of the Australian Federal government following federation of the former colonies on January 1, 1901, a new body, Commonwealth Railways, took over progressively, by agreement with the state of South Australia, the existing sections of the then proposed north-south transcontinental link between Port Augusta and Darwin. In addition, CR was responsible for constructing the east-west transcontinental link of 1,690 km (1,051 miles) through largely uninhabited near-desert between Port Augusta, SA and Kalgoorlie, WA. This was agreed prior to federation and was built to 1,435 mm (4 ft 8½ in) gauge and opened for traffic in October 1917, after four years' arduous work.

This line, known as the Trans-Australian Railway, was an epic achievement against great odds, as throughout its length it does not cross a single permanent surface watercourse and crosses the Nullarbor plain with the world's longest straight track – 478 km (297 miles) – between Ooldea, SA and Nurina, WA.

By further agreement with South Australia, the Trans-Australian was extended by 89 km (56 miles) from Port Augusta to Port Pirie, SA to shorten the circuitous 1,067 mm (3 ft 6 in) gauge route via Terowie and Quorn. This was replaced by an extension of SAR's 1,600 mm (5 ft 3 in) gauge line from Redhill to Port Pirie, which became unique in having railways of three gauges – 1,600 mm, 1,435 mm and 1,067 mm. As a result of this extension, the TAR route was 1,782 km (1,108 miles) and, from September 1937 the transcontinental timetables were appreciably improved, assisted by the introduction of more powerful locomotives.

Quite a dramatic change followed the introduction of diesel-electric traction on the TAR in October 1951, transforming the economics of operating this railway. Diesel-electric traction spread rapidly on all state systems as well and was virtually completed in little more than a decade. Australia has a long tradition of indigenous motive power and rolling stock construction, and most, but not all, the diesel locomotives were built in Australia under licence from the major US manufacturers, General Motors (EMD) and Alco, and the British firm, English Electric.

Electrification

Electrification in Australia was pioneered by Victoria Railways which converted its entire Melbourne commuter system of 276 route-km (172 miles) to 1,500 volts dc overhead operation between 1919 and 1928. The system has since expanded appreciably, as has the 232 route-km (145 mile) Sydney metropolitan system, electrified at the same voltage between 1926 and 1932. Sydney operates double-deck commuter trains, first introduced in NSW in 1964.

Subsequent expansion of both systems' commuter operations has tied in with extension of main-line electrification in both states on the same 1,500 volts dc system, but using locomotives of 2,400 hp in Victoria and 3,780 in NSW. The NSW system also uses both single- and double-deck electric multiple-units for outer-suburban services on the Western line over the Blue mountains to Katoomba and Mount Victoria (about 120 km; 76 miles), and on the so-called 'Short North' main line to Gosford (80 km; 50 miles) from Sydney. Both systems are currently replacing their original e.m.u. stock with sophisticated stainless steel equipment, of double-deck design in the case of Sydney.

Gauge standardization progress

Minor steps towards achieving a uniform gauge were taken in 1930 with extension of the NSW line 162 km (95 miles) from Kyogle, NSW to South Brisbane, Queensland, in 1937 with the connection of the 1,435 mm and 1,600 mm gauges at Port Pirie, SA, and conversion to 1,600 km gauge of the Mt Combier line in 1955.

Above: A re-gauging ceremony in Australia.

Right: Part of a mural at Spencer Street Station in Melbourne.

Centre: A new train service (1962) between Melbourne and Sydney.

Bottom left: The Victoria Railway yard at Flinders Street, Melbourne.

Bottom right: A train arrives at the new Inter-state Railway Terminus at Perth.

Work started in 1955, the first section being an extension of the standard gauge as an independent line from Wodonga (near Albury) to Melbourne 316 km (198 miles) completed in 1962.

Next was construction of a new standard gauge line linking Perth, the industrial area of Kwinana and the port of Fremantle, with the western end of the Trans-Australian at Kalgoorlie in Western Australia. This was a much more complex and formidable undertaking, involving construction of a new route from Midland to Northam avoiding the steep grades of the original line through the Darling range and built as dual-gauge double-track for trains of either 1,435 or 1,067 mm gauge. This 115 km (72 mile) section which included some of the biggest cuttings in Australia and five major bridges, was commissioned on February 15, 1966 and extended to Merriden on November 11, 1966.

Further progress enabled operation of iron ore trains from Koolyanobbing to Kwinana 496 km (310 miles) to start in April 1967. Completion of the final 200 km (125 miles) to Kalgoorlie ahead of schedule on August 3, 1968 to connect with the Trans-Australian, eliminated a break-of-gauge bottleneck which had existed for half a century.

The final link in the chain providing a standard-gauge railway from east to west was forged at Broken Hill, NSW on November 29, 1969. This marked completion of standardization of the former SAR, 1,067 mm (3 ft 6 in) gauge line from Port Pirie and its extension via a more direct route to Broken Hill, a distance of 397 km (247 miles). Now only one link remains uncompleted – between Port Pirie and Adelaide in South Australia – to connect all the mainland capitals by standard gauge. This last section of some 250 km (155 miles) is now in the final planning stages and is expected to be completed before 1980. Meanwhile, remaining breaks-of-gauge between 1,435 and 1,600 mm lines are being bridged effectively by a system of bogie exchange, pioneered by Victoria Railways in 1962, at Dynon Yard (Melbourne), in Peterborough and Port Pirie SA to permit through running of freight wagons without transhipment.

A number of official inquiries and royal commissions followed but it was not until a Federal government members' committee under the chairmanship of Mr W C Wentworth MP presented its report to the Commonwealth government in 1953 that a compromise plan was found acceptable and financially practicable. Under this plan the gauge between Australia's mainland capitals would be standardized at 1,435 mm (4 ft 8½ in) by new construction and conversion and upgrading of existing lines, with exception of the 1,600 mm gauge Melbourne and Adelaide line.

HISTORY
NEW ZEALAND

The 4,670 km New Zealand railway system (about 2,900 route miles) serves some three million people. It is a progressive undertaking with a distinctive blend of British and North American features. Although it had its origins in British colonial practice of the mid-19th century, American influence was strong, especially during the 1880s and 1890s, and from 1900 New Zealand's 1,067 mm (3 ft 6 in) system developed its own individual characteristics in both equipment and operating methods.

Within 20 years of the beginnings of organized European settlement in New Zealand, where British sovereignty was proclaimed in 1840, preparations were being made to build the first railways. By the late 1850s new settlers arriving from Britain were thoroughly familiar with the benefits that railway transport could bring. Because the settlements were small and scattered, inter-settlement communication at first was mainly by coastal vessel, and the first railways were built to link ports with the hinterland or to bring coal or ore from mines to the ports.

The first railway in New Zealand was a short line of 914 mm (3 ft) gauge opened in February 1862 to bring chrome ore down from Dun Mountain to the port of Nelson. Small wagons were hauled by horses. The Dun Mountain Railway lasted barely ten years because demand for the ore dried up.

The next railway to be opened, on December 1, 1863, was a 7 km (4¼ mile) section from Christchurch to Ferrymead of the Lyttelton & Christchurch Railway financed by the Canterbury Provincial Government. This proved to be the first section of the present NZR system to be opened, and the first in New Zealand to use steam locomotives for motive power. Laid to a gauge of 1,600 mm (5 ft 3 in), it was completed through a 2,595 m (2,838 yd) tunnel to Lyttelton in November 1867.

Meanwhile construction to a track gauge of 1,435 mm (4 ft 8½ in) had started at Invercargill and Auckland, and other promoters were contemplating a gauge of 1,067 mm (3 ft 6 in). It was not until Julius Vogel, the colonial treasurer, and

the General Government stepped in at the close of the 1860s that a measure of uniformity was introduced, and railway construction was seen as a matter of national rather than provincial interest. Vogel's immigration and public works policy, adopted by the General Government in 1870, resulted in a flurry of railway construction. A gauge of 1,067 mm (3 ft 6 in) was adopted throughout New Zealand and all wider-gauge lines had been converted by the end of 1877. The provincial governments were abolished in 1876 and New Zealand's first main line was completed in 1879. This was from Christchurch to Invercargill, 594 km (369 miles).

New Zealand's first express trains – so-called to distinguish them from the usual mixed trains calling at all stations – were introduced on this route, from Christchurch to Dunedin in September 1878, travelling 370 km (230 miles) in 10 hr 55 min, and from Dunedin to Invercargill in January 1879, 224 km (139 miles) in 6 hr 30 min. Through passengers to Invercargill had to stop overnight at Dunedin. Today the diesel-hauled *Southerner* covers the entire distance from Invercargill to Christchurch, now 591 km (367 miles), in less than ten hours, even though top speeds are limited to 90 km/h (56 mph).

After 1880 construction continued at a less hectic pace, and by 1900 more than 3,300 km (2,000 miles) of government-owned railways in ten separate sections were in use. Almost all railway development in New Zealand has been undertaken by the General Government, but in the 1880s some encouragement was given to private enterprise, and, out of several companies formed at that time, two were of special importance. The Wellington & Manawatu Railway in 1886 completed a 134 km (83 mile) line linking Wellington with a junction at Longburn on NZR's Foxton-New Plymouth railway, and worked it with conspicuous success until 1908 when it was purchased by the government to form part of the Wellington-Auckland main trunk railway. The New Zealand Midland Railway Company, financed in London, undertook the much more ambitious task of linking Greymouth

Left: Wellington harbour, showing the network of freight facilities which provide the New Zealand Railway with much of its revenue.

Far left: The Wellington to Auckland daytime train, the diesel multiple unit *Silver Fern*, crosses Waitet Viaduct.

Below: The famous Rimutaka line in New Zealand as it was in steam days, with several rack locomotives working each train over the pass.

Below left: The NZR's *Endeavour*, with modernized rolling stock, hauled by an American-type Da class diesel locomotive.

with Nelson via Reefton, and with Christchurch across the formidable Southern Alps. Some sections of line were built and opened west of the Alps, but the major task proved too much for the company and by 1900 it was left to the government to complete the railway via Arthur's Pass to Canterbury. This was accomplished eventually in 1923 when the 8,566 m (9,368 yd) Otira Tunnel was opened for traffic. The Greymouth-Nelson line was never completed.

A major work finished in 1908 was the North Island main trunk line linking the Auckland and Wellington sections of railway to provide through rail communication for the first time between what are now New Zealand's two largest centres of population. Subsequent construction programmes were interrupted by the first world war (1914–18), the great economic depression of 1930–35, and the second world war (1939–45), but the last main line was completed in December 1945. This was the Picton-Christchurch link in the South Island.

In 1953 the NZR system reached its maximum extent of about 5,690 route-km (3,535 route-miles), but the closing of a number of rural branch lines that had outlived their usefulness has reduced its aggregate length to 4,672 km (2,903 miles) by mid-1976. In 1962 a rail ferry service (for passengers, motorcars, and freight wagons) was inaugurated between Wellington and Picton with one vessel to link the North Island and South Island railway systems. Today four rail ferries are in use on this service.

Railway engineers have never had an easy time in New Zealand. Major engineering works in the form of long bridges, high viaducts, long tunnels, steep gradients, and massive earthworks have characterized railway building from the beginning, and even then sharp curvature has been unavoidable in following the valleys and climbing over or through the hills. The earliest railways, because of the sparse population and their developmental character, were of light construction suitable for axleloads of only 8 or 9 tonnes and for speeds of about 30 to 40 km/h (18 to 25 mph). The subsequent history of the system accordingly has been one of almost continual renewal, strengthening, and rebuilding to equip it to cope with expanding traffic, especially on the main lines. Today NZR main-line track is suitable for axleloads in the region of 16 tonnes and for speeds up to 100 km/h (62 mph) with suitable rolling stock. Extensive use is now made of mechanized equipment for track maintenance.

Major reconstruction projects have included the Wellington-Tawa Flat deviation through two long double-track tunnels (1937) and the 24 km (15 mile) Rimutaka deviation and its 8,800 m (9,624 yd) tunnel opened in 1955 between Upper Hutt and Featherston to by-pass and replace the original longer tortuous line with its 1 in 15 Fell-worked incline. Another tunnel about 8,830 m (9,657 yd) long was expected to be open for traffic in 1977. It is on a new 25 km (15½ mile) rail link through the Kaimai Range designed to shorten the rail distance between Hamilton and Tauranga by as much as 52 km (32 miles).

Most railways in New Zealand are single track, but several sections in the vicinity of the four major cities have been duplicated. The electric train tablet system of train working on single lines was introduced in 1901 and became standardized with two-position balanced-arm semaphore signals and mechanical interlocking. Automatic signalling and power interlockings were introduced from the 1920s, with centralized traffic control (CTC) added in stages from 1938 on the busier single-track sections.

Electric traction was first introduced on the NZR in 1923 for hauling trains through the long Otira Tunnel on a gradient of 1 in 33. Later installations were in 1929, Lyttelton-Christchurch; 1938, Wellington-Johnsonville; 1940, Wellington-Paekakariki; and 1953 to 1955, Wellington-Upper Hutt. The Lyttelton-Christchurch electrification was removed in 1969 following the introduction of diesel-electric locomotives. The route length of electrified sections of the NZR, all on the 1,500 volts dc overhead-contact system, is now about 99 km (61 miles), mainly at Wellington where suburban electric multiple units carry some 50,000 passengers every working day and smaller numbers on Saturdays, Sundays, and holidays.

The pattern of train service established by the 1920s provided for a network of mixed trains to and from country towns and provincial centres,

Left: A Ja class 4-8-2 waits in a loop as the Greymouth-Christchurch railcar passes by after leaving the Otira Tunnel in New Zealand's Southern Alps.

with local passenger trains to and from the major cities, supplemented by at least one through express or passenger train each way daily on all main routes, and additional freight trains wherever the volume of goods traffic made them necessary. With the advent of motor transport and improved roads, however, a start was made in the 1920s on the substitution of buses for lightly patronized trains, a process that was very much accelerated between about 1945 and 1950.

Coal shortage from 1944 through to the early 1950s resulted in severe restrictions in train service, and on many provincial routes the daily passenger train was reduced to a frequency of only two or three trains a week. To alleviate the situation many steam locomotives in the North Island were converted to burn oil instead of coal, but it was not until the wholesale introduction of diesel traction from 1955 onwards that passenger services began to improve.

The use of diesel railcars was inaugurated in a small way in 1936 after earlier inconclusive trials with petrol-engined, battery-electric, and steam cars, and was considerably expanded from the mid-1950s. The present administration, however, appears to be disillusioned with the economics of railcar operation, and many such services lately have been replaced either by passenger trains or by road coach services.

Since 1968 the standard of most surviving inter-city passenger trains has been markedly improved by the introduction of new equipment for the *Silver Fern* daytime and *Silver Star* overnight services between Wellington and Auckland, and by the upgrading of older equipment for other trains such as the *Southerner, Endeavour,*

Right: Two British-built 200 hp diesel shunting locomotives at work in Lyttleton harbour.

Below: A Wellington to Auckland fast freight hauled by a class Ew electric locomotive up the stiff grade from Pukerua Bay in 1965.

Blue Streak, and *Northerner.* Patronage of non-suburban trains had recovered from a low of about 1.5 million journeys a year to about 1.9 million by 1976.

Whereas in 1925 some 33 per cent of the NZR's total revenue was derived from passenger traffic, and about 63 per cent from goods and parcels, by 1975 the proportion contributed by rail passengers was a mere 5 per cent of the total. Freight and parcels contributed 75 per cent, and the balance came mainly from road services, the Cook Strait rail ferries, and catering services. The primary function of New Zealand Railways in the 1970s is undoubtedly that of a freight carrier. During the financial year from April 1975 to March 1976, 88 per cent of total traffic was represented by goods trains. Averaging 566 tonnes each in gross weight, excluding locomotive, and carrying an average load of 249 tonnes, these trains ran a total of 15,261,851 km (9,483,272 miles) at a statistical average speed of 26.7 km/h (16.6 mph) between terminals. Since 1953, the last year of virtually all-steam working, the average net load carried on each train has almost doubled, and the average speed of goods trains has risen by 37 per cent from 19.5 km/h (12.7 mph). The total weight of goods carried each year is now well over 13 million tonnes, compared with less than 10 million tonnes in 1950 and about 7 million tonnes in 1925.

Traditionally the character of freight traffic has been predominantly rural, associated with the farming and extractive industries, but in recent years manufactured products have become a much more important component. Nevertheless the products of primary industry, and supplies for that industry, remain important. In the early 1970s, the NZR was quick to adapt to the introduction of containers into import and export traffic, and has encouraged their use by freight consolidators for internal traffic as well. Recent years have also seen the introduction of many new types of wagon specially designed or adapted to meet the needs of users by simplifying loading and unloading processes. The conveyance of suitable goods in bulk instead of in small individual packages, and the use of pallets to facilitate mechanical handling, have been encouraged.

A vigorous commercial organization maintains constant contact with rail users and with possible sources of worthwhile traffic, and specialist working parties have been set up to work with local authorities in developing railway facilities in urban and industrial centres to suit future needs. Similar groups have been established to examine methods of freight handling and train operation to ensure that these aspects too are developed in the most effective, useful, and economical manner.

PASSENGER TRAVEL

Most people who have encountered railways at all probably made their first direct contact with the iron road at the door to a railway carriage. Indeed, for many, rail transport is synonymous with passenger travel and they probably give little thought to the fact that, at first, railways were never seen as a means for improving communication between members of the human race. Yet such was the case. The builders of the medieval mining railways in Central Europe or the 18th century mineral tramways and waggonways of Britain were most certainly not thinking of carrying *people* in their new-fangled vehicles.

It is not known when the first passenger journeyed on the railway – it was probably an illicit ride anyway – but history does record that the first public passenger railway (horse-drawn) was opened between Swansea and Mumbles in South Wales in 1807 and that Richard Trevithick carried the world's first steam-hauled fare-paying passengers by way of a private demonstration railway at Euston Square, London, in 1809. Both seem to have been a little ahead of their time and arguably the new order did not really become established for almost another generation. Controversy rages over the first true passenger railway in the accepted modern sense of the word. There are three prime contenders, two English and one American.

In September 1825, the Stockton & Darlington Railway opened for business with a steam-hauled train carrying passengers. This was the first occasion on which passengers had ridden behind steam on a public railway. However, after opening day, passenger haulage reverted to the horse-drawn mode until 1833, the new steam engines being far too precious to haul people rather than the really valuable cargo – coal. The two other rivals were the Baltimore & Ohio and the Liverpool & Manchester railways. Of these two, the Americans were first in the field in 1827, but they, like the S & D, favoured horses. It was a few years before steam came into its own. The Liverpool & Manchester on the other hand was designed from the outset as an inter-city route using mechanical means of propulsion and when it was opened in

1830 the modern concept of a true main-line railway was realized for the first time.

Another essential difference was that the L & M owned its own carriages as well as the right-of-way. Some early companies, including the S & D, regarded the railway, like the canals and roads of earlier years, simply as a right-of-way along which private hauliers could ply for hire. The L & M realized that the technological nature of a railway would pose problems for such an approach and from the outset held that the railway should be a complete transport system within itself – so was born the modern railway idea.

Early days

The first locomotives were small and not very powerful and the potential ability of the steam locomotive to haul heavy loads was not fully realized, if even anticipated. There was little realization that vehicles of a size vastly bigger than road transport could be hauled on rails. Early trains drew heavily from earlier technology.

Most early railway development took place in Europe and North America. On both sides of the Atlantic, the original carriage builders drew their inspiration from other contemporary forms of land transport. What might be termed the 'stage coach' style rapidly became dominant. Interestingly, this type of vehicle became a familiar sight in many parts of the world and most were recognizably of the same species. However, an early clue to the later dominance of rail can probably be traced to the very first horse-drawn vehicles on rails By fitting a stage coach with railway wheels it was discovered that one horse could pull on rail a weight which would demand four or six animals by road. Before long, someone in the railway business realized that this ability to pull heavier loads per unit of power made possible the building of bigger vehicles. The favourite solution was the building of carriages which, effectively, consisted of several stage coach bodies fastened together on one rigid railway chassis.

Problems, however, were encountered. On the old road coaches, passengers had been allowed to ride at lower fares outside the coach on bench seats fitted to the roof and to the front and rear of the coach. This, risky and dangerous enough on a 16 km/h (10 mph) horse-drawn stage coach over a

Below: A typical European 19th century carriage, inspired by stage coach building. This beautifully restored Chemin de Fer du Nord 1st Class carriage is preserved at the French Railway Museum, Mulhouse.

Coaches &c. employed on the Railway.

No 1, The Northumbrian, Steam-Engine, &c.   2, 3, 5, Carriages for Passengers.   4, Private Carriage.   6, 7, Carriages for Cattle.

London, Published Feb.ᵈ 1833, by Ackermann & C.º 96 Strand.

bad road was a potentially lethal recipe on a 48 km/h (30 mph) steam-hauled train with limited bridge and structure clearances. The attempt was, of course, made but was soon abandoned. Yet demand for economic travel, which the cheaper 'outside' coach seats had created, could not be ignored. Some form of economy railway vehicle was urgently needed. Regrettably, most European railways responded grudgingly with a variety of open-top four-wheelers scarcely better than coal waggons. Perhaps the one redeeming feature was the difficulty of falling out; often no seats were provided at all and protection against bad weather was frequently confined to provision of holes in the floor for the escape of rainwater. All this contrasted poorly with the often elaborately-furnished covered coaches provided for the wealthier passengers – yet people in increasing numbers travelled in these harsh economy conditions.

Between these two extremes of comfort, an intermediate standard also developed which essentially married the roofed-in quality of the upholstered coach with the accommodation of the open-top vehicles. This development established the beginnings of a three-class system of

travel which remained the standard in Britain and Europe for many years. Nevertheless, there were many regional variations as well as considerable differences in quality between different railways systems.

The stage coach type of vehicle remained the most dominant form of carriage for many generations throughout Britain and Europe and in those

Above: A contemporary engraving of coaches used on the Liverpool & Manchester Railway during the 1830s.

Below: Open topped third class carriages are shown in this contemporary engraving of London's first main line terminus – Euston 1837.

Top right: An early engraving of pioneer horse-drawn transport on the Baltimore & Ohio Railroad.

parts of the world where European nations were responsible for railway development. However, in North America a distinctive and new approach was rapidly established.

The first railways in North America were constructed when the USA was barely fifty years old and when large tracts of land were still under separate and often colonial administrations; a contrast to the situation in Europe where most countries (with the notable exception of Germany) were already well-established political units. In Europe, the early railways were built to reinforce existing economic patterns in an already partially-industrialized region. The railways were well engineered, built at considerable expense and exhibited remarkable feats of civil engineering to maintain good alignment. In a phrase, European railways were built tolerably straight and level. Thus the rigid four-wheel vehicle, and its later derivative with six wheels, gave no problems on the well-engineered and well-drained lines characteristic of most early routes in West and Central Europe.

This was not the case in North America. Some of the early lines on the Eastern seaboard did clearly show their European ancestry. Very soon, however, the railway was seen as a major instrument for 'opening up' the new lands across the

Appalachian mountains. The sheer speed of railway travel made the railroads a vital, unifying factor in the rapidly-developing USA and, later, in Canada. Lines were needed quickly over what, by European standards, were vast distances. Compromise with the rigid civil engineering standards established by European builders offered the only possible way. Lines of a more contorted nature were laid down – with heavier gradients and sharper curves to minimize construction costs. Many of these lines were later upgraded to carry heavier modern traffic but, in the fledgling years, this very different approach had a profound effect upon vehicle design.

The characteristic rigid-frame European-style coach performed badly on the sharply-curving and unconsolidated early American railroads. In consequence, from the 1830s, the Americans had developed what became global standard for a railway coach – a long vehicle running on two independent bogies, or trucks. The bogies permitted the building of a much larger coach since each bogie could pivot and move independently of its partner.

Allied to this mechanical difference was the equally rapid adoption of a totally different concept of interior layout. The traditional compartment-style coach found limited acceptance in North America. The open 'saloon' with centre gangway rapidly became standard. The 'saloon' was more neighbourly and, across the great distances, afforded an opportunity for passengers to stretch their legs from time to time – an impossibility in the contemporary European train. Early American trains, moreover, did not generally provide as many different classes or categories of accommodation as those in Europe.

From a very early stage, these separate lines of development emerged and continued their own independent evolution for over a century. There was a certain amount of cross-fertilization to and fro across the Atlantic but, even in the second half

Below right: In America, as in Europe, some early locomotive hauled coaches clearly showed their road vehicle ancestry – Baltimore & Ohio train of the 1830s.

of the 20th century, coaches can still be regarded as either American or European in basic inspiration for this distinction is not confined to these two areas of the world.

Railways spread rapidly throughout the globe from the mid-19th century onwards. The newly-developing systems in Latin America, Africa, Asia and Australasia not unnaturally drew on the experience (and mistakes) of the early European and American pioneers. Naturally enough – for in many cases the new systems were financed and built by capital from the older industrial nations – railways in the developing continents tended to exhibit many of the characteristics of the parent country. This was as true of passenger vehicles as of any other aspect. Throughout the Americas, North American concepts gained the ascendancy, despite a considerable infusion of European capital, ideas and equipment. In India, railways tended to be British in style of operation but, in response to the particular nature of that subcontinent, the coaches quickly developed their own characteristics; in Australia and New Zealand, although coaches frequently exhibited both American and European features, they were usually recognizably one or the other.

In Africa and in many parts of Asia, the railway was often built to narrow gauge (for economy), but with vehicles scarcely distinguishable from their standard-gauge contemporaries in terms of physical size.

So much for the origins of the passenger train – what of its later ramifications? Early trains were all very similar and the majority stopped at almost every station. In time, different categories of traveller emerged, each category with individual needs. Railway designers were but a short step from the realization that coach design ought to reflect changing circumstances and needs. The era of specialization began in this way – a period of specialization which is still with us. Over the years, this has presented an astonishingly variable, yet historically accurate, reflection of changing ideas and social customs. At the top of the list, inevitably, comes the long-distance, inter-city express.

The inter-city train

The phrase 'inter-city' is relatively modern, a part of the contemporary jargon seemingly indispensable to our modern civilization – yet the reality behind the expression is rooted in railway history. The Liverpool & Manchester Railway pioneered easier communications between large centres of population and the long-distance main-line train has been at the heart of passenger operation since that time.

At first, all passenger trains stopped frequently, wherever and whenever travellers might be expected to board. As railways expanded and the distances involved increased, so did the number of stops. Before long, management realized that division of its basic service was a possibility. A large number and wide distribution of stations offered a greater passenger potential. Gradually, certain trains were able to omit some intermediate stops (at the smaller settlements) yet still

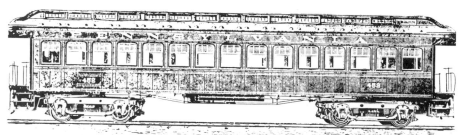

retain adequate fare-paying passenger loads from the larger centres. This was the beginning of the concept of the express train for long and medium distances and of the stopping train to cater for smaller stations over shorter stretches of line. The omission of certain stops on some journeys had the advantage of reducing end-to-end times of the journey – from time immemorial a certain way of increasing the attractiveness of the service.

Nevertheless, journey times were lengthy and, even in the small countries of Europe, it became necessary to consider what might most delicately be described as the 'bodily needs' of the passenger. This sensitive matter was almost an unmentionable subject in Victorian Britain and certain worthy citizens probably recoiled in hor-

Top: The early use of the four wheel bogie on a North American coach of 1834.

Above: Classic 19th century American coach 'architecture' on the Pennsylvania Railroad (1880s).

Left: Some early American coaches were no larger than their European counterparts – a grounded body originally used on the Western Railroad of Massachusetts.

Below: A somewhat stylized engraving of the arrival at Jamestown of the first train of the Atlantic & Great Western Railroad from New York.

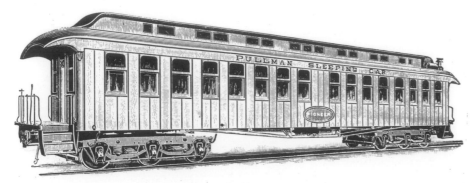

Above: Pioneer, the first complete Pullman sleeping car.

ror at the thought of a lavatory in a train. Progress was, however, inevitable and lavatory-equipped coaches gradually made their appearance. Some companies went to extraordinary lengths to disguise the presence of such essential conveniences.

Lavatories, of course, occupied floor space and this space was not, in the strictest sense, revenue earning. The railways were consequently reluctant to provide more than minimum facilities and, often for first-class passengers only. Even when lavatory facilities were available for all classes of travel, not all compartments could gain access to lavatories. It became for the passengers a test of their knowledge of carriage construction in selecting an adequately equipped compartment. The obvious solution was some form of continuous passageway throughout the length of the coach, but despite the American example of the centre-gangway open saloon, European railways were slow to follow suit. After all, corridors implied even more non-revenue space, larger and heavier coaches and larger locomotives to pull the trains – and this would demand new capital investment. Shareholders would, naturally, expect to see a healthy return on their investment.

It is hard to pin-point accurately the precise moment when improved passenger amenities began to create the forerunner of today's inter-city express. Neither is it possible to pin down with certainty the reasons which impelled the railways to begin to mend their ways. What is certain is that, by the 1870s, railway administrations throughout the world were responding to pressures for improvement. Whatever the precise reasons, the last quarter of the 19th century saw

Below: Mantua Junction, West Philadelphia – a typical North American railroad scene of the period.

rapid improvements. These tended to appear first in the countries of origin of the early railway systems. This was distinctly fortunate for later-developing countries (in the railway sense). Latecomers to railways were spared many of the miseries which had beset early travellers in Europe and North America.

As was common in the Victorian period, improvement was a combination of private entrepreneurial activity and corporate shrewdness. Space precludes mention of all the activities which took place, but three noteworthy personalities merit special mention.

Chronologically, the first was the American, George Mortimer Pullman who during the recovery from the American Civil War in the 1860s, had quarried a rich vein of 'railway gold' by the introduction of a fleet of luxurious parlor cars and sleeping cars. He persuaded the companies of the USA to operate these luxury cars across their various railway 'frontiers'. Built on the American pattern, large, spacious and more agreeable than their railway-owned contemporaries, the Pullman 'Palace' cars became the symbols of the best in American railroading. The very early Pullman cars were not always comfortable and some were distinctly basic. They were marketed with considerable vigour, however, and, as the 19th century progressed, their amenities and comfort improved in giant steps forward. The companies reacted to Pullman competition by providing comparable stock of their own – often purchasing the coaches from Pullman's own works.

Pullman himself was neither innovator nor inventor. Many others were operating sleeping and parlor cars long before he seriously entered the trade. Although Pullman eventually dominated the North American scene, other operators, such as Woodruff and Wagner, should not be forgotten. They too operated some very agreeable vehicles, some even better than Pullman's own cars, but the Pullman organization proved to have the better staying power.

In continental Europe, the frontiers were not only boundaries between railway companies, but often international borders as well. It was just as difficult for the various national railway companies to agree as it was for their political masters. The prospect of international through-services, desirable as they were to the traveller, seemed increasingly remote. One visionary – a Belgian entrepreneur called Georges Nagelmackers of Liège – refused to be discouraged. He had visited North America in the 1860s and was highly impressed with Pullman's activities. He was less impressed with the quality of the early Pullman cars than he was with the service the Pullman cars provided. Consequently, in 1869, Nagelmackers began a similar development in Europe. At first, his cars were small, but, from the beginning, were designed to give greater comfort and privacy than the Pullman cars of his original inspiration. His were, initially, all sleeping cars (convertible for day use) and available only by payment of a supplementary charge.

Unlike Pullman, Nagelmackers had more than railways with which to contend. Customs barriers, politicians and the chaos of the Franco-Prussian war must have complicated matters hugely. Nagelmackers had his rivals including those who wished ill of his endeavours. His main rival was the American, William D'Alton Mann. Mann was also trying to establish a similar European service. Mann was arguably less of a visionary than Nagelmackers and in 1876 the two effectively resolved their differences by amalgamation. Nagelmackers took full control of a newly-constituted International Sleeping Car Company, better known as the 'Compagnie Internationale des Wagons-Lits et des Grands Express Européens' or just 'Wagons-Lits' as the public knew them.

To the names of Pullman and Nagelmackers must be added a third – James Allport of England. If his name is internationally less well-known than the other two, his influence was no less significant. Although he served only one British company, the Midland Railway – one of the three or four major British systems – his influence was to spread throughout Britain and eventually the world. Allport had also visited North America and had travelled many thousands of miles in some of Pullman's more splendid cars. He even persuaded Pullman to visit Britain and describe his coaches. In 1874, the first Pullman sleeping car in Britain was introduced by the Midland Railway. The car was made in America, dismantled and re-erected in England. Its size, comparatively modest by American standards, positively dwarfed the home product. As a result of this importation Midland adopted bogie coaches as standard well before most other British companies.

Allport was quick to capitalize on his lead and, very significantly for the ordinary passenger, resolved that everyone should share in the higher standards established by Pullman and Wagons-Lits. In two short years, the Midland as well as introducing Pullman cars on the best services, in quick succession, admitted third class passengers

Above: The sumptuous interior of a Wagner Parlor car – one of the chief rivals to Pullman.

Right: A contemporary engraving of the famous Midland Railway 1st and 3rd class only coaches of the 1880s and a preserved example of the same genre at the British National Railway Museum, fresh from complete restoration.

Below: Combined European and American carriage building influences are illustrated on this South African train of clerestory coaches on a Hoedspruit-Pietersburg train seen leaving Goudplaas.

to all trains, abolished second class completely (but destroyed the third class coaches, thus providing the third class passenger with the former second class coaches at no increase in fare), and reduced first class fares to second class levels. Amongst the staid boardrooms of the other British companies, this reform was tantamount to revolution and the British rivals were not pleased.

If Pullman and Nagelmackers made a reality of the long-distance luxury train, Allport showed that a railway system could provide comfort for all passengers. The Midland was now a two-class railway and, by the first world war, most British companies had fallen into line. In America, two-class travel had virtually always existed. In Europe, the anachronism of multi-class travel finally succumbed in recent years to the basic and almost universal international standard – regardless of the specific labels on the coaches.

These events of the 1870s mark the start of real carriage evolution. Access to a lavatory was absolutely essential in the newly introduced sleeping cars and the day coaches were not long to follow suit. In America, where the centre gangway was universal, such access was readily available, but

in Europe the individual compartment with its limited seating capacity and its pair of facing sets of seats (entirely in the stage-coach tradition) was still the preferred mode. Thus the only suitable method was the side-corridor arrangement.

Side corridors inevitably caused an increase in coach weight per passenger and the European railways gradually realized the virtue of the American bogie coach concept for long-distance trains. Four- and six-wheelers were cheap to build and economical to operate. They were perfectly adequate for short-distance trains and remained commonplace. Thus the real inter-city express gradually became identifiable outside the American sphere of influence by its larger bogie coaches and gangway access to the essential lavatories. Evolution to a continuous connection between adjacent coaches was a slow process, but had become fairly widespread and continuous connection made its appearance by the latter part of the 19th century. Pioneer work was carried out by Waterbury and Atkins in the United States during the 1850s, while history suggests that the first real connection between adjacent coaches in Europe was seen in Queen Victoria's twin, six-

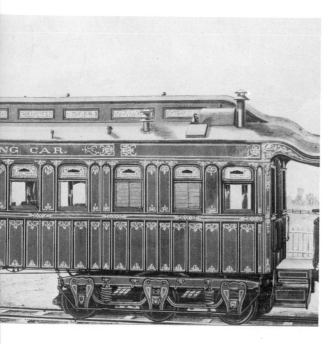

wheel saloons. These were built by the London & North Western Railway in 1869 and are happily preserved, now united on a single bogie under-frame, at Britain's National Railway Museum in York.

The real spur to widespread development was the introduction of dining-car services. Allied to the need for lavatories and sleeping accommodation on long-distance trains, was the need for refreshments. Commonly in early practice the train stopped at some suitable station for a short period to allow passengers to have a meal at the refreshment room. This solution was fraught with problems for the passenger. There was the inevitable rush for the refreshment room and unscrupulous proprietors were not above serving inferior food to this captive market – composed mainly of travellers unlikely to pass that way again for some time. Not infrequently the soup course would be so hot that passengers could not complete the meal before departure time – a splendid opportunity for profiteering by the restaurant proprietor who had (naturally) collected the cost of the full meal!

Passengers objected vehemently and some refreshment rooms gained real notoriety. The railways responded with the introduction of luncheon baskets – often of real splendour – which could be taken onto the train and by the first tentative attempts at dining cars. Refreshment room proprietors were unhappy and for many years (especially in Britain) insisted on trains, continuing to make meal stops. A combination of the elimination of meal stops to speed journey times, expiry of refreshment room contracts and gradual improvement of dining cars led to the permanent establishment of the train catering services as we know them today.

At the same time the provision of a dining car produced its own problems. A simple passageway within an individual coach provided adequate access to the lavatory but access to the dining car involved movement between coaches – hence the spur to develop corridor connections. At first, some railways took the view that not all passengers would wish to eat on the train – a perfectly valid assumption – and that those who wished to eat could join the dining car at the start of the journey, and remain with it throughout. Before long the more enterprising companies realized that though some passengers would not want to eat, there might be more hungry people than could be accommodated at one sitting in the dining car. It became more sensible to have the diner integrated with the rest of the train – the alternative being an undignified scramble between carriages at a station stop. Even so, the tradition of riding all the way in the dining car died hard and, in Britain at least, the Pullman car concept, renowned in America more for sleeping than for day coaches, became synonymous with a luxury 'meal at every seat' facility. Today the word 'Pullman' in British railway usage, now merely refers to this version of meal service.

With dining cars and continuous corridors added to the established sleeping cars and gangwayed day coaches, all the ingredients of the inter-city train had finally arrived. The 20th century has been more noteworthy for adaptation of these basic concepts than for any significantly new evolutionary moves. In essence, the inter-city train was evolved in the late 19th century and has matured in the 20th.

At the end of the Victorian period, the most effective and agreeable way of travel by land was by train. Whether one was rich or poor, the railway had a virtual monopoly, especially in long-distance travel. In this situation, one might have expected that service to the public would suffer – in most cases it did not. Even where no directly-competing rival company spurred development, most of the better railways of the world took their monopoly situation seriously and responsibly. Furthermore, they frequently provided trains of a quality over and above their minimum duty. The Wagons-Lits company provided superb services throughout Europe. Pullman cars in all their

Far left: Ornate scroll work elaborate lining, vestibule connections and six wheel bogies are typical of the wooden bodied Palace Car era of North American passenger travel.

Top: A Pullman drawing room and sleeping car.

Centre: Early Pullman style in Britain – a dining car of the Great Northern Railway.

Left: A contemporary engraving showing the vestibule connection between the American Pullman cars – note the extreme degree of elaborate external ornamentation.

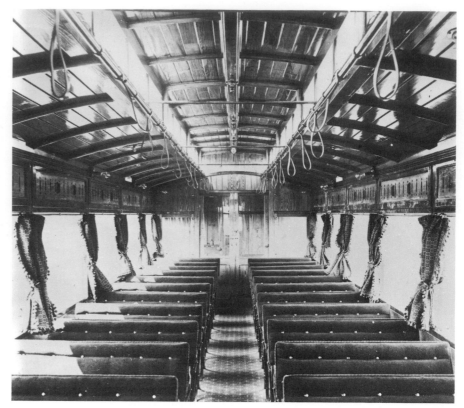

glory spanned the length and breadth of America, while in India and Asia fine trains were steadily increasing in number. Probably it was in Britain that the late 19th and early 20th century express train reached its high point of perfection – at least for the ordinary passenger.

Untroubled by political disturbances and unworried by the pressures of developing unexplored hinterlands (at least in the United Kingdom), Great Britain was basking in that Indian Summer of the Empire, the late Victorian and the Edwardian era – and the trains exuded the same confidence. Because of the limited British loading gauge, the trains were physically smaller than many of those found elsewhere in the world, and the distances covered were in no way comparable with the vast hauls of the major global transcontinental lines, particularly in America and Asia. Nevertheless, in terms of their general average speed they were immeasurably superior to all save the better trains in the USA. As far as comfort was concerned, only the various supplementary-fee luxury coaches elsewhere could compete with the best British coaches – generally available to any passenger without additional charge. At that time, nothing in the railway world matched the upholstered third class. This was a well-nigh universal feature of most reputable British railways at the turn of the century – even on less-prestigious trains. Furthermore, third-class passengers were commonly admitted to the vast majority of British inter-city trains. In many parts of the world no such provision was made.

This pre-eminent position was held by Great Britain for about 25 years prior to the first world war. In the late 1880s and early 1890s, the best British expresses, led by those of the Great Northern and Midland Railways, were generally averaging 64 km/h (40 mph) or more, where the rest of the world outside the USA and Australia

was hard-pressed to realize 48 km/h (30 mph). By the Edwardian period, the speed differentials had been eroded, but the standard of train still gave Britain the edge – possibly reaching an all time high when the London & North Western Railway in 1908 provided a superb set of 12-wheel coaches (at no extra charge) for its celebrated '2 p.m. all corridor' train from Euston to Glasgow and Edinburgh – first and third class only, note.

If the modern inter-city service underwent an adolescent phase before the first world war in which British influence was probably predominant, then its full adult maturity began during the 1920s, when the pacemaker was unquestionably the United States of America. As will be seen, the best American coaches had been without peer from a much earlier date but, until the 1920s, these superb coaches had carried a limited range of passengers. The inter-war years were to change all that. With the advent of the Pullman–Standard era, the emphasis changed to the complete train, a movement rapidly consolidated during the ensuing streamline era of the 1930s and 1940s.

The sudden improvement was in part a response to the growing threat of the motor car – especially amongst ordinary people. The USA was the cradle of the modern mass-produced automobile and, during the 1920s, these vehicles were produced at an astonishingly low unit cost. The ordinary (or 'coach' class) rail passenger of North America – equivalent to the British and European second or third class traveller – had not received much attention during the 'wood and varnish' era of the Pullman 'Palace' car and was still being offered a rudimentary ride. He proved a willing disciple at the shrine of Henry Ford and his fellow high priests. As a result, North American railways made strenuous efforts to win back favour and this time in a non-monopoly situation.

It had long been common US practice for rail-

Above left: An interior of a Sante Fe coach built in the USA in 1901.

Above: A third class suburban service coach used on Tyneside, England in the early 1900s.

Below: The London to Liverpool boat trains, catering for Transatlantic passengers were among the most luxurious in use in Britain in the early 1900s.

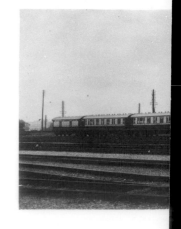

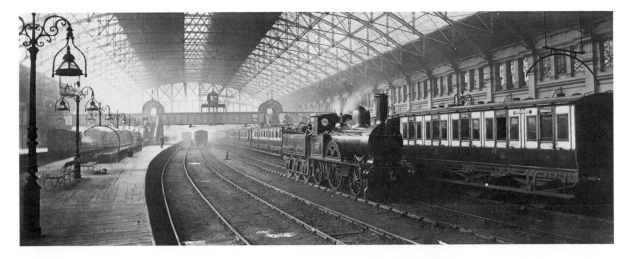

Left: New Street Station, Birmingham, photographed in 1884 showing third class coaches.

Below: A Midland Railways double-headed train of nine clerestory coaches needs the assitance of a banker to ascend a gradient.

DRAWING ROOM CAR – FOLKESTONE EXPRESS
SOUTH EASTERN & CHATHAM RAILWAY

INTERIOR OF THIRD CLASS DINING CAR GREAT NORTHERN

ways to buy equipment, whether locomotives or freight and passenger stock, from outside suppliers. During the first world war the United States Railroad Administration (USRA), formed to administer the railways during the national emergency, had standardized a limited number of vehicle designs. The advantages of standardization remained desirable when the companies had resumed full control of their affairs after the war, and provided Pullman (and others) with a splendid springboard from which to launch a re-equipment programme to provide North America with a vast fleet of new coaches.

From the outside, these massive 24 m (80 ft) cars looked much the same, whether Pullman owned and operated (in the traditional way) or Pullman built and company owned. Furthermore, Pullman was required to paint its own cars in the colours of the leasing railroad. But inside the vehicles every opportunity was taken to exhibit individuality according to the trends and fashions of the day and the particular idiosyncracies of the owners. Throughout the length and breadth of North America, the steel-built, Pullman-Standard car became the very epitome of rail passenger travel; the era of the 'Limited' had dawned.

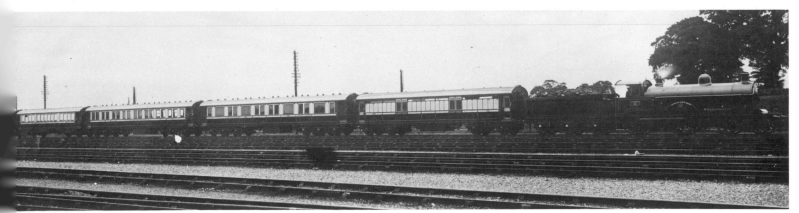

The name 'Limited' derived from the concept of a limited number of stops – thus a shortened journey time – but in some cases it was also legitimately applied to the limited number of people allowed to travel on the train. These trains were very popular and demand frequently outstripped supply. Though the motor car was not exactly routed, its competition over long and medium distances was certainly opposed determinedly. Speed was the essence of the 'Limited', and speedy trains were built. *Broadway Limited, Twentieth Century Limited, Blue Comet, Empire State Express, Yankee Clipper, Columbine* – the names read like a catalogue, made even more familiar by the tremendous influence of the Hollywood film industry.

When, in due course, the streamline fashion emerged in the 1930s and 1940s the railways were not slow to take advantage of it. More exotic names were added to the list and some supremely beautiful trains were built. Who but a man with no soul could fail to be moved by the 160 km/h (100 mph) flights of the Milwaukee Road's *Hiawatha*, the majestic sight of the Santa Fe's *Super Chief*, the *California Zephyr* as it traversed the unbelievable scenery of Colorado, or the progress through California of Southern Pacific's *Daylight* trains – acclaimed by many as the most beautiful in the world.

Sadly the great trains of North America were to enjoy something of a butterfly-like existence. Great trains emerged in all their magnificence,

but within barely more than a generation had succumbed to the aeroplane. If the motorized era after the first world war caused their birth, then the development of air traffic after the second great conflict just as surely killed them off.

This great era of North American railroading lasted long enough, however, to inspire not only imitators in the rest of the world, but also to affect profoundly the development of inter-city travel in general. The Canadians understandably were the strongest imitators and managed fortunately to retain the concept in rather better shape than did the USA itself. The Canadian transcontinental expresses have never fallen from grace. In continental Europe, superb trains like *Rheingold* and the Wagons-Lits' *Blue Train* were just as impressive as the North American 'Limited'. This same period produced in Britain not only magnificent trains like the streamlined LNER *Silver Jubilee* and the LMS *Coronation Scot*, but also stimulated considerable improvements in locomotive design. Sadly the war in Europe brought a stop to development along these lines earlier than in the USA.

Outside Europe and North America, the development of high-speed inter-city travel was a slower process. This was mainly because many areas were less highly industrialized or urbanized than the older (by railway standards) countries. Railways in Latin America and Africa were used more in the 19th century American 'colonial' fashion and, often of a narrow gauge, could not

Right: The original *Kingston Flyer* on the 3 ft 6 in gauge of New Zealand shows much North American influence.

Below: A classic North American standard steel express – Canadian style.

match the USA and Europe for speed. But by any standards, South African Railways' *Blue Train* was as magnificent a concept as any North American 'Limited', even though its average speed on the 1,067 mm (3 ft 6 in) gauge was slower.

In continental Asia, the Trans-Siberian Express, although not a 'flier' by global standards, indicated more than any other single service the ability of the railway to shrink distance and unify a large land mass during the pre-airline phase. The various trans-Indian trains of the pre-independence period were something of a unique institution. The railways of India were largely British in concept and operation and, in their later 19th century days, were not renowned for high speed. In view of the number of large towns, considerable areas of tolerably flat country and the ample supply of highly-qualified engineers both locally-trained and expatriate, it is surprising that the fast inter-city concept did not make greater headway. However, long-distance services were developed and made a considerable contribution to unifying this diverse subcontinent before independence.

Elsewhere in Asia, much development took place for economic reasons and utilizing substandard gauge systems. This inhibited growth of rapid inter-city services. At the same time, as in Africa, the choice of a narrower gauge did not prevent the long-distance train making its mark. For example, the Malayan State Railway, though modest in terms of network complexity, operated some fine trains from Singapore northwards to Kuala Lumpur and across the frontier into Thailand. At the other end of the scale, the Japanese achieved a remarkable degree of complexity on the 1,067 mm (3 ft 6 in) gauge.

The nearest approach to the classic European/American train occurred in Australasia, particularly in Australia itself. Australia was, and is still to some extent, bedevilled by its multiple-gauge problem, the origins of which recede into railway history. Within each state, distances between cities are considerable – more on the American scale than the European. Fortunately, the more densely populated states adopted standard or broader than standard gauges, which

Below: British streamlining – the 1937 LNER *Coronation* Express crosses the Royal Border Bridge at Berwick upon Tweed.

Bottom: A typical rake of vintage Chemin de Fer du Nord coaches of quasi 'Gothic' style on a Boulogne boat train. Note the very typical Wagons-Lits dining car also in the picture.

permitted higher speeds. Although the first steam trains did not run in Australia until 1854, by the 1880s the Australians were operating the fastest trains outside Britain and North America.

The trains displayed a curious mixture of British and American influence which, oddly yet accurately reflected the various periods of history. During the late 19th and early 20th centuries, British influence was predominant, especially in outward appearance; during the inter-war years and afterwards, trains exhibited increasingly American characteristics. If the pre-first world war *Sydney Express* looked as if it had escaped by magic from some London terminus, then the *Spirit of Progress* some two generations later would not have looked out of place at Grand Central station, New York!

New Zealand's ability to develop a true inter-city service was, like that of many of the developing countries, inhibited in speed terms by the use of the narrower 1,067 mm (3 ft 6 in) gauge. Construction did not begin in earnest until the 1870s and New Zealand was able to take advantage of the lessons and mistakes of earlier pioneers in other countries. Although much earlier equipment was British, American technology in the event proved more suited to New Zealand operations. By the 1920s, New Zealanders boasted some splendid 'Limiteds' built and operated on very similar lines to their larger American contemporaries. Furthermore, track had been upgraded to permit higher running speeds than were often possible on the narrow gauge.

By the 1940s, the long-distance train was the accepted norm for overland travel throughout the world. The motor car was well established and was already dominant over shorter-distance operations, but the inter-city express seemed secure. The express could out match the car in both speed and comfort over most distances above 160 km (100 miles) and, for those without cars, was a far superior alternative to the motor coach for anything but short hauls. This situation did not last long. Stimulated by vast orders for military equipment during the second world war, manufacturers had revolutionized aircraft construction. During the 20 years after 1945, a major revolution in long-distance passenger haulage took place. The airliner was no longer a somewhat temperamental plaything for the wealthy but afforded a means of mass high-speed communication for all and especially over distances above 480 km (300 miles) and more the inter-city train was under threat. Not only that – much improved motor cars and construction of motorways produced even more competition on the medium-distance journeys.

The longer-haul operators were the first to feel the effects. In spite of increasing efforts to modernize trains and devise more ingenious methods of entertaining travellers *en route*, the railways rediscovered that transit time between departure and arrival was the prime factor in many passengers' choice of transport mode. The railways should not have been surprised – after all, railways had used the very same argument in staving off early road competition. The great era of the 'Limiteds' and streamliners came to an end. Some sort of eleventh-hour reprieve was at hand however; stimulated this time by events far from the North American scene – back, in the original heartland of railways, in Western Europe, where road and air competition grew more or less simultaneously.

The motor car was invented in Europe but did not achieve mass ownership in this region until later than in North America – not until after the second world war. However, Western Europe faced the post-1945 world with a war-ravaged countryside and the urgent priority to rebuild shattered economies. The universal language was that of priorities. No place existed, at least initially, for the self-indulgence of private motor cars and intensive airline services. The railways had suffered huge war damage and were high on the list of priorities for rebuilding in order to restore commerce and industry. The dramatic effect of mass car-ownership and the newer threat of the airliner were delayed. The traditional express train had a chance to re-establish itself before facing the full competition of air and road. This delay gave European railways a chance to think out their attitude to the new order of things. The railways could not afford to be sanguine. To many millions of travellers mindful of the misery of wartime rail journeys, the chance to own a car or to sample the new glamour of air travel could not come too quickly.

As in many parts of the world, the most vulnerable area of rail travel was the longer-distance train and reductions took place in the face of air competition. In one respect Europe had a real advantage. Although many trains covered long enough distances to make the airliner a more attractive proposition in terms of total journey time, many passengers were not travelling the whole distance. The continent as a whole is compact enough for many services to remain competitive over these intermediate stages and this stems largely from delays to the air traveller going to and from the out-of-town airports. The railways were city-centre to city-centre routes and, provided that speed and frequency of service was maintained, could remain highly competitive on journeys up to 400 km (250 miles) and reasonably attractive over journeys of twice that distance.

Top right: British Inter-City – 1970s style – a 'Deltic' diesel on an air conditioned Anglo-Scottish express north of York.

Top: Passenger trains at Denver Union Station, USA. The two diesel locomotives are General Motors units equipped for passenger service. On the right is an observation dome lounge car of the stainless-steel design favoured by many US railroads in the 1950s.

Centre: A British Inter-City train of the final steam years. An ex-London Midland & Scottish Railway mixed traffic 4–6–0 on a train of flush clad but mostly timber framed coaches. Note the articulated vehicles at fourth and fifth position in the train.

Below right: A French inter-city train – 1970s style. The TEE *Stanislaus* leaves Strasbourg.

Below: A modern day New Zealand inter-city – the *Southerner*.

In response after the war, a fine network of high speed inter-city services was developed in Europe. This was usually scheduled with the businessman in mind and captured not only the public imagination but also heavy traffic. Aided by a complete change in attitude towards European unity, these services, spearheaded by the *Trans-Europ Express* (TEE) trains, cross Western European frontiers with a frequency which Georges Nagelmackers would have envied. The trains, moreover, are running over systems which, except for route alignment, have been totally re-built and re-equipped since 1945. They are thoroughly modern in concept. The modern *Rheingold, Mistral* and *Settebello* are totally in keeping with the last quarter of the 20th century.

Equally impressive are the giant strides made by the ordinary express trains of Britain and Western Europe. TEE trains still keep to the traditional 'limited' plan – in this case, first-class only (plus supplement) allied with limited stops – but, throughout Europe during the 1960s and 1970s, their success has stimulated similar improvements on non-supplementary fare trains. The 160 km/h (100 mph) train is now a commonplace, whereas, in the streamline era, it was the prerogative of a few specially equipped, prestige services.

The British railway system, brought under public ownership in 1948, faced the post-war world in a run-down state. Unlike the continental systems, the British system was still recognizably intact and usable and did not receive the same degree of priority in re-equipment and new investment. Intensive modernization did not begin until the late 1950s and early 1960s. Under these circumstances, rail travel was not always attractive and large parts of the network – generally marginal routes – were closed in the face of road competition. The inter-city network, however, survived. During the 1960s the inter-city service began to win back traffic in a spectacular way. Electrification of the London-

Manchester/Liverpool line with consequent faster services all but eliminated effective competition by the domestic airlines while a similar transformation took place on the East Coast route made possible by the high power Deltic diesels.

Spurred by these successes, European railways began in the late 1960s to rethink the whole question of the trains themselves. They were undoubtedly influenced by events in Japan. The Japanese economic recovery since 1945 is one of the most remarkable features of the modern world and the railways played a major part. Japan, like much of Europe, is a compact industrial area and the Japanese were quick to realize the value of a growing network of high speed inter-city trains, predominantly patronized by businessmen. However, Japanese railways run on 1,067 mm (3 ft

Left: This typical scene on the LMS Railway of Great Britain shows a streamlined 4–6–2 *Duchess of Gloucester* passing Rugby with a London bound train of non-streamlined coaches, c. 1939.

Centre: Present-day Indian trains still display characteristically deep body panels above the windows even though the train is thoroughly modern.

Below: Japanese National Railway's *Shinkansen* train of multiple unit electric vehicles as used on the New Tokkaido Line.

6 in) gauge and could not be developed to the high speed category. Great steps were made – up to 120 km/h (75 mph) – but the demand for speed continued to grow. In 1964, the Japanese opened the New Tokaido Line – a totally new 1,435 mm (4 ft 8½ in) gauge railway designed from the outset for really high speeds and along which enormous trains run at 210 km/h (130 mph) at frequent intervals. Its success was instantaneous.

The New Tokaido style lines in Europe (and elsewhere) have stimulated development of a new generation of trains built for speed. Construction has begun on two new lines on the Japanese fashion, Mannheim-Stuttgart in West Germany and Paris-Lyon in France, but many other routes are already capable of considerable upgrading without major rebuilding. Elimination of sharper than desirable curves, removal of 'bottlenecks' and the rationalization of track layouts have done much to improve matters and have permitted considerably increased speeds. Already in service, typifying the new order of things, are the 200 km/h (125 mph) high-speed diesel trains introduced in Britain in 1976, the futuristic West German inter-city multiple-unit ET 403, and the French turbo trains. Within a few years, if all goes well, the new British advanced passenger train (APT) will make London to Glasgow (640 km, 400 miles) in four hours.

The modern inter-city train on the Japanese/European pattern owes much of its success to patronage of business travellers. Railways have been far less successful at retaining the recreational traveller. The airlines – aided by the package-tour industry – have developed a virtual monopoly in longer-distance holiday travel; while the motor car, with its convenience and flexibility is still the first choice for the traditional family holidaymaker.

Modern airline travel is a time-saving, people-processing exercise rather than a worthwhile experience itself. This factor plus the general improvement of trains since the early 1960s and the boost to rail travel from the fuel crisis of the early 1970s, has caused many people to think again about the 'old fashioned' train. The environmentalist lobby has helped, by making clear that the railway is neither as prodigal of space nor as environmentally-polluting as the motor vehicle, motorway and airline. The railway is not as flexible as the car but makes more economic use of expensive fuel, and is infinitely more economical of fuel than the jet plane.

A most significant pointer to the rebirth of interest in the traditional long-distance train can be found in Australia – probably the first large country in which domestic airliners made impact. The completion of a standard gauge link across Western Australia in 1970 made possible through train communication, without change of coach, over the 3,960 km (2,461 miles) between Sydney and Perth for the first time ever. This had obvious economic advantages for freight haulage but a courageous decision indeed led to the establishment of a new passenger service over such a distance – particularly in the light of American experience during the 1950s and 1960s. A three-

day rail journey seemed unlikely to offer real competition to an eight-hour air schedule. Yet the *Indian Pacific* – as the new train was called – was an instant success. The *Indian Pacific* is a deluxe train of the old-fashioned type. Not only has accommodation on the train been increased since the service's inauguration, but service frequency has been doubled.

It is too soon to predict whether all these post-1945 developments will cause a major rebirth of rail travel in those countries most affected by alternative modes of transport. The signs are quite encouraging, even in North America where all seemed lost in the late 1960s. It is no exaggeration that, with the exception of commuter services and a few shorter distance hauls mainly on the Eastern seaboard, most US railroads had little time for the passenger train in the mid-1960s. A few noteworthy exceptions existed, like the Southern Railway and a few of the western lines, but in general the passenger was not welcomed. However, in 1971, prompted by pressure to maintain, for social reasons, a basic inter-city network of passenger trains, the Nixon administration introduced the most revolutionary change ever seen in American railroading – Amtrak.

This was a new corporation responsible for maintaining a basic inter-city passenger network throughout the USA and redeveloping some of the routes. Amtrak is effectively a quasi-nationalization of rail passenger travel and with few exceptions, the railroads were happy to hand to Amtrak the remains of their once fabulous fleets of 'Limiteds'. But painting old equipment in new standard colours and providing a new name did not, of itself, suddenly revitalize passenger travel.

The first years of Amtrak were touch-and-go. Motley collections of coaches, still at first decked in all the variety of their old company colours and not always in the best condition, bore no comparison with the superb trains of previous generations. Selective weeding out of the poorer coaches, gradual re-equipment with new stock and locomotives, and the unexpected bonus of the 1973 oil crisis together enabled Amtrak to survive its first five years. It seems that the worst may now be over. Interestingly enough, the USA is for the first time seriously examining the European concept of inter-city trains and has introduced European equipment on some services.

So much for the older traditional railway regions; but what of the rest of the world? Inter-city travel in the modern meaning of the phrase is essentially a feature of the developed industrial nations – hence the emphasis on Europe, North America and, to a lesser degree, Japan and Australia in this survey. Outside these areas, the long distance train, although it exists, has never been developed as extensively. This is explained in part by the stage reached in the economic evolution of the countries concerned. Curiously, this may be advantageous to the railways in the long term. As earlier mentioned, passenger railways in the developed world have reflected changes in social and economic conditions down

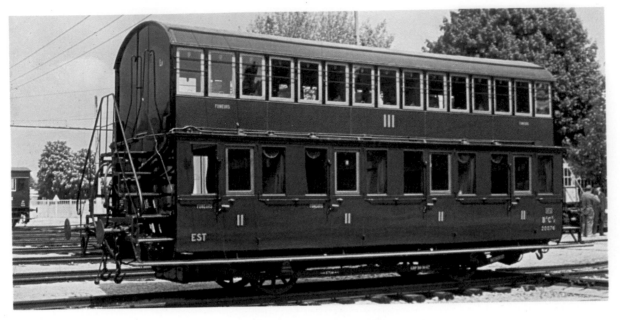

Top left: Beautifully restored second and third class four wheel French double deck suburban coach.

Top right: The modern stainless steel coaches of the Amtrak *Saint Clare*, about to leave Detroit for Chicago.

Centre: Double-deck commuting – American style. It should be noted that the train is carrying far more people than the sum total of all the road vehicles on the adjacent highway.

Below: The French TGV (Turbotrain à Très Grande Vitesse) designed for the high-speed Paris-Lyon route. Test runs have achieved speeds above 300 km/h (186 mph).

the years. The prerogative of the pioneer has always been to make the first mistakes as well as the first really progressive improvements – railways were no exception. The British pioneers of the mechanized railway built their bridges and fixed structures too small and consequently restricted development of the railway vehicle in a technological sense. The Americans were perhaps too ready to abandon the passenger train. Throughout much of the developed world, some lines may prove to have been abandoned overhastily.

The developing world will – hopefully – profit from these mistakes and the signs are tolerably encouraging. In areas, such as Latin America and the Indian sub-continent, where universal car ownership is still some time away, trains serve the same purpose that they did in Europe and America a generation or two ago. As only a small proportion of the population can afford long distance air travel, the long-haul express is still viable, though its overall speed is limited. New lines are still being built in many parts of the world. Unfortunately, we know comparatively little about activities in Russia and China where railways are still a prime means of moving both people and goods.

All told, therefore, the inter-city train does not appear quite such an obsolete institution as some of its detractors would have had us believe only a few years ago. The inter-city train can still, along with the ocean liner, be the most agreeable form of mass transport where time-saving is not crucial and can compete even in terms of the time factor over intermediate distances. No one would pretend that a crowded, slow moving, long distance train is an attractive alternative to the fast jet plane or the individual in his motor car but, given a balanced government approach to transport on a global scale, the inter-city concept can still make a contribution to the development of human activity.

The commuter train

If the inter-city train is the most prestigious and publicized passenger carrier on the world's railways, in one respect it takes second place – the number of passenger journeys made. Here the suburban commuter train holds first position.

The word 'commute', though now used for all forms of 'home-to-work' transport, has railway origins. A dictionary definition gives, *inter alia*, the following interpretation of commute: 'to pay in a single sum as an equivalent for a number of successive payments'. This gives the essential clue. The first commuters were those who pur-

chased a ticket permitting several repeat journeys on the railway. In other words, the commuters were regular daily travellers over the same line.

The growth of commuter transport can be traced to the point at which the 'limited stop' express train began to evolve. In order to carry passengers to the main centres from intermediate stations between the points served by the faster expresses, separate stopping trains were needed. At first, stopping trains were undoubtedly introduced for the benefit of those who lived at intermediate stations and wished to travel on the expresses, but before long someone realized that a regular stopping train to a nearby major centre need not be restricted to passengers travelling further afield. The stopping train afforded the opportunity to live in one place and work in another.

Today, when we are accustomed to the idea of domestic and work locations in different places it is hard to realize that this was rare before the railway age.

As with most major changes in lifestyle, the beginnings were tentative. At first, only the well-to-do would buy a house in the country and travel by train to work in the nearby town – and this development seems to have taken place spontaneously without pressure by the railways. Once under way, the railways realized that a potentially valuable source of revenue was available provided that more people could be encouraged to commute. In consequence, and vigorously promoted by the railways, the later Victorian period saw tremendous growth of the numbers living outside the main urban areas.

The idea then took root throughout most of the industrialized world. Whole new settlements grew in the vicinity of out-of-town stations. The new settlements became less and less like open country and more and more like the towns they served – 'sub-urban' in fact. A new word was added to the language. The more popular the notion became, the more passengers the railways carried. Soon specialized suburban trains evolved. Travel was cheap during this period of growth. For, given a partially-loaded suburban train, the additional cost of carrying extra passengers as they came along was minimal – and that

remained true until it was necessary to provide additional trains to cope with the loads.

To meet this situation, the railways developed high-capacity coaches. For passengers travelling only a short distance, refinements such as dining cars and lavatories were not essential. The main aim was to pack as many people as possible into a given train. In this context, the traditional compartment-type coach was particularly favoured. No space was wasted with gangways or corridors and the separate compartments were made to the smallest possible dimensions with the minimum of knee-room between seats. Everything was done to increase seating accommodation without increasing the number of trains. It was cheaper to widen coaches, lengthen platforms to accept longer trains, and even provide more powerful locomotives than to provide more trains. On the European mainland, with more generous structure clearance, double-deck trains were built from an early stage and some

particularly characteristic examples operated until well after the Second world war.

Those systems which had adopted the American centre-gangway layout found that the suburban operation posed problems. The gangway took up space at the expense of seats and the outside doors were confined to the ends of the coach which slowed down the loading and unloading of passengers. On the other hand, the gangway did offer opportunity for passengers to circulate within the coach. Some systems (for example the Southern Region of British Railways which has some of the world's busiest commuter routes) often combined the open gangway with a multiplicity of outside doors for quick passenger loading and unloading.

The success of the commuter train brought unique problems to management and many remain unsolved even today. In the early days, the coaches differed little from normal vehicles and many were used for other services outside the

morning and evening rush periods. In time the more specialized high-capacity stock became increasingly unsuitable for alternative use and stood idle for much of the day. Matters were complicated and made worse by the continued growth of the commuting habit.

To service these coaches, large depôts must be maintained and expensive land procured on which to store the coaches during the long periods out of use. Few major industrial operations in the world use their most expensive plant and equipment fully for only four hours in the day. This is the essential problem in the modern day and age. Although commuter trains are heavily loaded at peak times, they are now a basically uneconomic operation because of the lengthy period out of use. The railways no longer enjoy a total monopoly. To satisfy the commuter by providing more trains with more comfortable seats would merely exacerbate the problem for the railway; to reduce the number of trains and seats, although making life simpler for the railway, would infuriate the traveller who finds things bad enough already. One of the saddest side effects is that many a traveller knows no other form of rail travel than the commuter train.

To offset some of these problems, the railways have displayed considerable ingenuity in coach design on suburban trains. Viewed globally, some solutions are remarkably good and are receiving due praise but the fundamental problem is unlikely to be fully resolved unless basic changes are made in work patterns.

The railways invented the commuting habit. Had they foreseen the consequences, it is doubtful whether the railways would have encouraged the venture at all – at least as a commercial operation. To suggest that the railways should stop running commuter trains if they do not pay their way is no solution – nor to increase fares until they do; for the paradox is that modern city life would come to a standstill without the commuter train or something very similar. Some form of staggered working hours, spreading the peak demand, would partially fill the 'troughs' – but the basic problem would remain.

What is certain is that the commuter train remains a vital part of life in any urban area,

Top left: An Indonesian local train near Bandjar, Java. The coach design is typical of African and Asian practice.

Below: Rooftop commuting on a Calcutta local train.

Above: An all aluminium light alloy sliding door electric train of the '6000' series for the Teito Rapid Transit Authority of Japan.

Far left: A not untypically overcrowded Indian local train at Futwah on the Futwah-Islampur narrow gauge line.

Left: A modern British sliding door commuter train at Enfield Town. The considerable visual similarity to the Japanese '6000' train is apparent.

whether the service is economic to operate or not. Many cities throughout the world are building new commuter lines. Over the years, the commuter train has evolved into several highly-specialized categories. Foremost among these categories, are the various underground and rapid transit systems discussed elsewhere.

The rural train

At the opposite end of the operating spectrum comes the rural local train – probably derived from the same growth of specialization as its more frantic urban brother. The rural train is equally if not more significant in terms of social benefit – measured by qualitative rather than quantitative standards; wherever there are passenger railways in the world, then there is a universally perceived conception of the archetypal rural train. More books have probably been devoted to the rural train than to any other aspect of railways except the locomotive; it forms part of the folk-lore of many nations. Perhaps deep down we regard rural rail travel as a form on a more human scale than most sections of the railway.

The first train ever to traverse open country and stop at an intermediate location was a rural train, but the real rural train, as the term is generally understood, evolved as a special category.

The main-line services developed along the two lines of evolution already discussed. A third type of passenger and train began to emerge. Some of the intermediate stopping places were too distant from the main cities to afford any prospect of selection as residential areas for the new-style commuters. Such centres were too small to attract the patronage of the major expresses. Consequently, fewer trains stopped at these

stations and did so mainly to permit passengers to transact business at that station. These stations were not subservient to the demands of a nearby city but centres in their own right. The passengers were usually using the train in the course of their daily life as part of that particular community: the local shopkeeper, perhaps, travelling to town for the day to order supplies for the village store; or a farmer travelling to a nearby market town to inspect livestock. The variations are endless, but shared a relevance to the local community which other kinds of journeys lacked. Gradually there developed a direct involvement between community and railway – for these were the days when the railway represented the only form of speedy transport.

Top left: A Javanese mixed train from Kertosono to Bliter. Note the distinctive tropical sun blinds above the windows.

Above right: Many local trains ran either along or adjacent to the roads. This is an example at Surabaja, Java.

Below right: The ubiquitous diesel multiple unit. This British example is on the Leeds-Ilkley service near Calverley on the outskirts of Leeds.

Above: A multiple unit suburban train of the New Zealand Railways.

Below left: A mixed train near La Cumbre on the Bolivian Railway. Note the strong North American influence on the external styling of the coaches.

In time, the railways provided minor lines to feed their main routes and the era of the branch line began. Many of these grew to some importance and a number, even in the motor-oriented countries, survive today. These routes were more locally relevant than the principal main lines (whose function was essentially to connect larger centres) and they developed distinctive characteristics of their own. Their function, as far as the promoting railway company was concerned, was to provide additional traffic for the main lines. This was a two-way process, particularly in terms of freight traffic. Commodities from other areas were brought in by rail and, in this sense, the minor routes were branches. In originating traffic from the local centre, these lesser lines were the essential roots of the parent system.

From the passenger standpoint, the issues are less clear. Most rural lines were built more to carry freight than people. Rural lines afforded a means of distributing the products of the new manufacturing industries more widely and psychologically helped the rural dwellers feel part of the larger community. But rural communities were (and often are) largely self-sufficient. Why should rural dwellers want to travel on the trains? The railway ensured the all-important commercial contact with the wider world without need for travel on the train – surely that was sufficient. In many instances, it was, and passenger travel was minimal. To attach the odd passenger coach to the regular freight train often sufficed and produced that characteristic phenomenon of the rural railway, the mixed train.

Development was more rapid in some areas. The growing pace of industrial activity even in the smaller towns attracted the population away from the rural areas to man the growing number of factories and workshops. Industrial working conditions were mixed but at least offered a prospect of regular employment – not always guaranteed in the farming areas – and the wages were often more attractive than in agriculture. Then as now the lure of the town was strong. Rural depopulation became a real threat. The coming of the railways to rural areas enabled some people to remain in the villages and to work in the nearby town. It was a miniature repetition of the commuting pattern already established by the railways around the larger cities – but with one important difference. The growth of city commuting led to the development of suburbs – work people were encouraged to move out of the city and to live in the countryside. In the rural areas, the growth of the commuting habit enabled some of the isolated settlements to retain a community identity simply because the railway afforded a means of taking surplus manpower to a source of employment without depopulating the settlement.

Some evidence exists in the British population statistics, that in some parts where a rural railway was present (or a station on a main-line railway), the shift of population to the towns was less.

With the growth of flexible motor traffic, the rural train is, at least in the developed world, no longer seen as a vital factor. It is more sensible to load cattle onto a motor vehicle and take them direct to the destination without the two intermediate transhipment operations which rail haulage would imply. This applies to many other freight operations and, not surprisingly, this aspect of the rural railway has witnessed decline in many parts of the world. Unfortunately, without freight revenue, the passenger services are unable to cover operating costs on their own. The rural passenger services are threatened. Since not everyone possesses or wishes to possess their own mechanized transport, the threat to the passenger service is serious.

This chain of events has often been repeated in the older industrial regions, such as those of Western Europe and North America, and there is no guarantee that it will not spread to other areas of the world in time. As with the commuter train, so with the rural train, social problems are posed.

Possibly some sort of compromise solution will emerge. In addition to the rural branch-line train, which only in exceptional circumstances has a promising future, were services to the intermediate centres from the main lines passing through rural areas. Many of these intermediate centres have been closed to local traffic although the main line service still exists. Perhaps there is more hope in these cases. In north-west England, on the main line between Leeds and Carlisle, a limited restoration of local passenger services has been experimentally promoted by the Yorkshire Dales National Park in collaboration with British Railways. Essentially this affords a monthly opportunity for the citizens of the surrounding industrial areas to enjoy a day in a strikingly beautiful and remote rural region, while the balancing workings of the trains allow local

inhabitants of the National Park to make a day excursion for shopping and so on to the nearby cities. This has been strikingly successful and has managed to cover its direct operating costs.

One principal exception to this general picture ought to be mentioned – namely the intermediate train. Over the years, many countries have developed a type of passenger train not easily categorized. It was not an inter-city express, nor did it cover vast distances. Neither was it rural or commuter-like in its operation. Covering distances in the 50 to 200 km (30 to 125 mile) range, this train carried various names depending on the country of operation. In the English-speaking world, it was named 'semi-fast', 'cross-country', 'inter-district' or whatever. Since it offered connectional intermediate services on reasonably busy lines, its survival rate has been good – in even the most motor-conscious regions. Indistinguishable in its early days from more celebrated trains (save to the expert) it has latterly been monopolized world wide by the multiple-unit train, propelled by an internal combustion engine – usually diesel.

Despite the question mark over the future of the rural train, where it still survives, its past is unquestionably a significant part of railway history. Yet its long-term contribution to the evolution of passenger travel was probably minimal. Unlike the inter-city train which has constantly changed to suit the circumstances of the day, unlike the commuter train which inevitably has had to respond to increasing passenger traffic, the rural train changed little. For the most part, the rural train has made do with 'cast-off' rolling stock from the rest of the system.

Some noteworthy exceptions to this trend can be identified. During the early phase of road competition, many railways experimented with small self-propelled railcars. The idea was basically sound. In theory the operating cost from self-propelled railcars, whether steam-propelled or driven by some form of internal combustion engine, was cheaper than that of the conventional locomotive and separate coaches. Unfortunately the early railcars lacked flexibility. At times of peak loading the railcars were too small, yet lacked sufficient power to haul additional

Above left: A vintage Sentinel steam railcar at San Bernardo, Seville, Spain.

Above right: A stainless steel diesel railcar of the Canadian Pacific at Montreal.

Below left: a homemade railbus introduced to compensate for lack of passenger trains on the more lightly utilized eastward section of the Rio Mulato-Potosi-Sucre line in Bolivia.

Below right: A characteristically British early 20th century steam railcar of the Belfast & County Down Railway.

coaches, although some valiant attempts were made. Neither could railcars collect the odd freight wagon with the same facility as the locomotive-hauled train. Nevertheless, they provided a vital service for many years and their lineal descendants, in the form of the various diesel multiple-unit trains, can be seen throughout the world on intermediate services.

Another and predominantly British innovation, which was partly a response to the needs and problems of the rural railway, was the so-called 'push-pull' train. In this type of train, a conventional locomotive is semi-permanently coupled to a small number of carriages (generally one or two) and, with the minimum modification, altered for driving remotely from a small compartment at the opposite end of the train from the engine. This avoided the job of uncoupling the locomotive at the end of the journey. The 'push-pull' train was successful and lasted well into the 1960s. First, it solved the problem of augmenting the train at busy times, since the locomotive was capable of hauling several additional coaches. Second, the modification was tolerably inexpensive to install. And third, the locomotive could be detached from the train to perform additional revenue work of an unrelated kind.

In passing, note that the push-pull principle has been successfully employed on a grander scale in recent years as a partial solution to the commuter train problem. In Germany, France, Britain and the USA, to mention but four, many suburban trains are operated in the push-pull mode. This saves turnround time and, as with its rural ancestor, releases a valuable locomotive at off-peak periods for other duties.

Finally, we must not forget the multiplicity of rural railways which were built to narrow gauge. Again the aim was provision of an essential and economic rural service. These lines should not be confused with those widespread main line systems on the metre and 1,067 mm (3 ft 6 in) gauges

such as those found in Africa, Asia and New Zealand, or even the 914 mm (3 ft) gauge lines built in many parts and particularly the south west of the USA. In concept and operation, these systems rank with standard gauge railways.

The rural narrow gauge systems were self-contained small units and, like the similar specialist mountain railways, are dealt with elsewhere. In respect of passenger stock they differed from standard gauge branch lines. Gauge difference prevented operation with older main-line stock. Consequently they used purpose-built stock – often miniature versions of contemporary main line coaches.

Special trains
A large variety of trains and services do not fit the broad and simple classification of rail passenger service discussed so far. The mechanized railway has carried passengers throughout the world for a century and a half. Inevitably, over this period, a wide variety of specialized uses has emerged.

More than any other invention, before or since, railways revolutionized attitudes to travel. Before the coming of the railways, society (save for the wealthy) was predominantly static. A visit of even a few kilometres was planned with great care and not undertaken lightly. The railway made possible travel over distances formerly considered beyond the reach of the ordinary man. At first, the expense of such a venture was an inhibiting factor but before long countries realized, sometimes reluctantly, the railway could not be confined to the wealthy. As early as 1844, the British parliament under Gladstone obliged all railways in Britain to carry third class passengers at no more than a penny a mile on at least one train a day (the so-called 'Parliamentary Train'). From this seed grew the universally accepted principle that economically priced railway passenger travel should apply to everyone.

Inevitably, the first regular services were

directed to the daily needs and requirements of the local population. Stimulated by the growing acceptance of rail communication the railways (and the public) were soon to develop more specialized uses of the new mode. It is uncertain when specialized trains could first be identified, but the earliest recognizable class of specialization was the excursion train. We do not know whether the first excursions were designed to use equipment otherwise lying idle, or whether the railways were seeking methods of encouraging people to sample rail travel for the first time.

The earliest excursion journeys were those which could be completed within a day and were confined to areas where specific towns and cities lay within a few hours' travelling time one from the other. Fare levels were kept low because a full load for the whole distance was a virtual certainty – a basic principle utilized later by modern package air tour operators. The excursion idea was not wholeheartedly approved. One particularly contentious aspect was the Sunday excursion. A six-day working week was normal and annual holidays were vestigial. Sunday was the only day for an excursion for many folk despite the objections of the clergy and the more privileged.

Things were changing in a way which can only be understood from hindsight. In spite of constant objections and fulminations, the excursion train survived. Any excuse justified an excursion. Trains were run to the seaside for benefit of the children. Trains were operated in connection with race meetings, football matches or any other sporting occasion. As railways penetrated more rural regions, the attractions of the countryside received attention and scenic excursions were arranged – with specially designed observation coaches to attract more customers. Nor were the rural dwellers forgotten. Excursions took them to the nearby cities and towns.

More than anything else, the railway excursion helped to promote the holiday habit. The realization that seaside towns and rural beauty spots lay within a few hours' travelling time stimulated an appetite in the growing industrial regions for an annual break from the work routine and the 'day at the seaside' gradually turned into the 'holiday week'. For reasons connected with economic operation of the railway system, it made sense to carry as many holidaymakers as possible on one day. If all the employers in one town could be persuaded to cease operations during the same week, the railway could gain some very profitable business and yet keep fares to an absurdly low level. The trains which took holidaymakers from town X during one week, could be moved to town Y the following week if town Y could be persuaded to close its business premises at a different time from town X.

The resorts approved of this. Properly organized, this kind of holiday traffic could guarantee fully booked hotels and guest houses during the holiday season, promising highly-competitive accommodation charges. Small seaside villages were transformed almost overnight into thriving holiday centres, as the popularity grew. It needed only a stretch of beach, close to centres of high population density and a railway willing to build a connecting line and to provide a station with a multiplicity of tracks to cater for the procession of weekend holiday excursions. The entrepreneurs made sure that hotels, shops and the like were built apace with growing traffic; a whole new life style became possible for the ordinary family. That this life style persists and thrives under the greater flexibility of the road motor coach or the package-tour airliner should not blur the fact that the railway made possible that life style in the first place.

As society was at last liberated by the train from

Above: The former Canadian National Hotel, Ottawa.

Below left: Enthusiast Travel (i) – a tourist train at Main Street Station, Greenfield Village, Detroit, USA.

Below centre: Enthusiast Travel (ii) – Britain's last main line steam locomotive (2–10–0 No 92220 *Evening Star*) preserved at the National Railway Museum, still operates fan trips from time to time.

the more objectionable characteristics of 19th century life, the railways were developing sophisticated methods of attracting other categories of specialist travel. The realization that travel itself was pleasurable prompted the idea of the rail tour. Pullman and Wagons-Lits had shown the enjoyment possible in a railway journey in the right conditions, but this type of travel was a means of making a necessary journey more agreeable. Gradually the notion of spending a whole holiday on a train became viable. The 'holiday cruise train' had arrived. Sometimes it was a mobile hotel and was equipped with sleeping and dining cars. At other times, its journeys were co-ordinated with night stops at suitable locations where the railway had thoughtfully located one of its own hotels.

One cannot separate the growth of railway hotels from the ever-increasing elaboration of railway travel. Though the hotels were not part of the train, the reality of their existence was very much part of the transport 'package' which the more ambitious railways felt obliged to provide. Whether located in cities, principally for the benefit of business travellers, or at holiday centres, railway hotels blossomed wherever there seemed likely custom – and though many have been maligned, many more were very impressive. Though it is invidious to single out particular instances if one of the later examples can serve for the whole, then a prime contender is the Gleneagles hotel in Scotland, opened by the London, Midland & Scottish Railway in 1924. This edifice (no other word will do) was a latecomer, arriving almost at the close of the great railway age. The Gleneagles hotel had (and has) almost everything. Brand new and set amidst incomparable scenery, it was matched by incomparable service and a fine provision of trains. In addition, as it was situated in Scotland it was

naturally given a stupendous golf course by way of bonus. One wonders if any of today's golf addicts on the pilgrimage to Gleneagles to watch their modern demi-gods compete realize that they are walking over a part of transport history.

Varied and sophisticated modes of modern transport together with the tendency to stagger annual holidays has removed a considerable portion of the railway's dominance in this field of travel. But the railway remains important in the leisure field and the railways have been valiant in attempts to fight the competition of road and air.

Of all the threats to rail passenger travel, the private automobile has proved the most serious. Once across the rubicon of car ownership, the average traveller is not convinced of the economic advantages of rail travel. The financial disadvantages of car ownership, such as loss of interest on capital; depreciation; garaging and maintenance costs; taxes and insurance; these are all overwhelmed by the sheer convenience of personal door-to-door transport. 'Freedom of the road' seemed a tempting concept to which railways at first offered no alternative; and nowhere has the private car had greater impact than in leisure travel.

Obviously, the more developed nations were first to experience the problem and at first were unsure of the best solution. Excursion and holiday trains were reduced in number and scope as traffic dwindled. Once busy excursion platforms at holiday centres became less and less used until many were abandoned altogether (often becoming car or motor coach parks in the process). The whole *raison d'être* of the marginal 'holiday' railway was often destroyed and the lines closed completely. But the success of the private car carried the seeds of a major problem. The railways fought back, making their appeal to the pleasure and comfort of the rail excursion as an

Below right: Enthusiast Travel (iii) – Victorian and Edwardian veterans from Britain's National Railway Museum (LNWR 2-4-0 *Hardwicke* and Midland Railway compound No. 1000) hauling a model railway club excursion train near Weeton, Yorkshire, in April 1976.

alternative rather than substitute for the car.

A more spectacular development of the rail service has been designed with the motorist in mind. The prime innovation has been the growing network of car-carrier trains over the past 20 years. From the start of the motor age, railways have been willing to carry motor vehicles as freight and have designed a whole variety of special wagons. Attachment of genuine passenger coaches to the car-transporter wagons enabled the motorist to drive his car – a container for his bulky luggage – onto the train, and repair with his family to the comfort of the coach. The railway takes care of the tedious first few hundred kilometres of the holiday journey. The addition of sleeping cars provided an overnight option and there is now a well established network of this new form of inter-city travel in Britain and Europe.

Water is no particular obstacle. From an early stage, railways developed shipping services to connect with and extend their train services. These were originally passenger services. The passengers would leave the trains and embark in the conventional way. In time came the introduction of the rail ferry which carried trains across the water barriers. The only Wagons-Lits operation which penetrates into Great Britain (the Paris–London *Night Ferry*) crosses the English Channel by rail ferry. Ferry boats which carry railway coaches can also carry car-transporters – this has been developed. For the motorist without need of the train, the railway-owned 'roll-on/roll-off' car ferries – and hovercraft – are doing splendidly.

Competition with the airlines has been less easy; much of the long-haul trade has been abandoned to air. Occasionally, the railway has been able to co-operate with the airlines to provide integrated services. These services usually take the form of a high-speed rail link to newly-built stations at out-of-town airports. In favourable conditions an integrated rail/air/rail service can prove extremely attractive. A good example is the *Silver Arrow* operation between Paris and London.

Holiday and excursion traffic has, down the years, been a noteworthy example of socially-significant railway passenger specialization.

Top left: Services on which passengers are accompanied by their cars are becoming increasingly widespread. Here a British Rail 'Motorail' train takes holidaymakers through Devonshire.

Centre left: A special train with living quarters for the track gang converting the Climax to Leadville, Colorado, line from narrow to standard gauge.

Below far left: A British travelling post office sorting van from the era of steam with apparatus for picking up and putting down mail at speed.

Below left: The London – Paris *Night Ferry.*

Below right: The interior of a British travelling post office in about 1900.

Below far right: A modern British Rail sorting coach, showing letter racks inside.

Pride of place goes to the mail train. This seems an unlikely candidate for passenger patronage, but such an assumption ignores the facts. From the beginning postal authorities throughout the world realized that the railway offered the most speedy and efficient method of carrying mail over long distances. The small volume of passenger traffic in the early days meant that mail could be loaded easily into a small portion of the passenger train. Postal authorities, predominantly interested in swift and reliable transit, negotiated terms dependent on the railway's ability to keep schedules. In consequence, mail trains became the fastest on the system and passengers appreciated the fact. The nature of the services was largely indistinguishable from orthodox inter-city operations though travelling by 'The Mail' was always something special. Reliability and timekeeping was of a higher order since mail trains received absolute priority over other traffic. Penalty clauses were written into mail contracts obliging railways to make financial compensation in the event of delay to the post.

The early mail operations were so successful that many intermediate towns and cities wished to be included in the service. To do so would have increased the transit time and displeased the postal authority. The railway's solution was to develop the travelling post office. Mail was not only collected and delivered to the lineside without stopping the train, but also sorted *en route.* The first example emerged in Great Britain as early as 1837. Though trackside pick-up and dropping of mail ceased in Britain a few years ago, the system is still used in operations elsewhere and the *en-route* sorting of mail is universal wherever mail trains operate.

As the volume of mail increased it became necessary to provide additional mail coaches.

Only some were equipped for pick-up and dropping of mail and for postal sorting, since the volume of 'end-to-end' traffic was increasing. Over the years certain mail trains became almost exclusively utilized for mail with little of the train available to passengers. In accordance with what became a universal custom mail coaches travelled at the front, or 'head' of the train and, especially in North America, a whole train (save for one or two coaches at the rear) composed of so-called 'head-end' cars was a familiar sight. Mail trains without passenger facilities appeared in due course. These 'Solid Mails' were operated at speeds comparable to or even faster than orthodox passenger-carrying expresses.

The railway's unique and early ability to transport both people and goods with equal facility originally produced the 'special interest' train. It is impossible to describe all the variations of 'special interest' trains and it is sometimes difficult to decide whether or not the train is properly defined as a passenger service. If the broad definition that a *bona fide* passenger operation exists if people are legitimately and purposefully conveyed is an acceptable one then some very odd cases deserve a mention. The most unusual were those trains provided by the railways in pursuit of railway expansion. This sort of operation enjoys more scope where distances are greater. The special purpose train probably achieved its greatest variety in North America, though such trains were used over a much wider area of operation.

During the expansion into undeveloped territory, it was impossible to relate railway expansion to existing settlements – there were none. The workmen needed temporary housing and this took the form of a mobile settlement which moved forward to keep pace with the railhead advance. Not content merely to provide a normal

coach where men ate, slept and lived, the expanding railways took whole trainloads of portable buildings as well as an army of camp followers. At the end of the line, the whole infrastructure of a small town was offloaded from the flat cars. Within hours saloons, bars, shops, hotels and other less salubrious establishments sprang up. After a few weeks (or a few days), the whole township was dismantled, reloaded and moved to the next 'head' of the advancing line. Nicknamed 'Hell-on-Wheels' in the USA, they established a legend.

The special purpose train was a step away from the concept of 'promotional' train, in all its variety. The mobile exhibition train, aimed at commercial promotion, became an effective means of publicizing products over a wide territory. It carried a greater variety of goods, displayed in semi-permanent form, and were more effective than the lone salesman. Such trains are still with us generally converted from old passenger coaches. Their passengers, limited to company staff and potential customers, are a specialized charter category.

Such an enterprise is only marginally included in the category passenger train. Other special-interest activities are almost indistinguishable from orthodox operations. If a local charity group charters a train to take deprived children on holiday, the end-product is scarcely distinguishable from the conventional excursion. Train charter of this type has been widespread and is not insignificant. Nor is the interest in the actual railway by enthusiast groups who often charter trains to cover interesting sections of railway line, organize trips behind especially significant locomotives, arrange for the provision of particular carriages and so on. The most glamorous of all special-purpose trains is the provision made for Very Important Persons.

The essentials of VIP rail travel have always been luxury and privacy. Throughout railway history leaders have normally been provided with the most luxurious carriages available – insulated from the ordinary traveller. This provision ranges from exclusive use of one of the best coaches owned by the railway, to the other extreme –

provision and operation of a complete train of sumptuous coaches. The travelling entourage can then share some of the luxury.

Naturally the most impressive coaches have been reserved for heads of state. Since many railways developed under monarchical systems, the greatest variety is witnessed in the various royal trains down the ages. The longest continuous story is that of the British Royal Family, whose first saloons were provided in the 1840s and for whom two new coaches are being built at the time of writing. Interestingly these coaches, from a variety of railway companies, faithfully reflected contemporary railway fashions; fortunately, some have survived at the British National Railway Museum for posterity to examine. Some of these services in their own way were rather innovative. Queen Adelaide's saloon of 1842 was one of the first coaches to include sleeping

facilities in the form of a bed compartment; Queen Victoria's saloon of 1869 was, when built, two six-wheelers connected by a bellows gangway – the first European example of such a feature. Other royal coaches, such as those built for King Edward VII's superb train of 1903, tended to utilize the finest traditions of craftsmanship rather than introduce revolutionary new features; Queen Elizabeth II's saloon of 1941, now ending its service life, embodies the different fashions of the period of its construction, just as the air-conditioned 160 km/h (100 mph) successor reflects the ideas and fashions of the 1970s.

Outside Britain, royal saloons tended to lack continuity of evolution as many countries abandoned monarchy during the railway age. Nevertheless provision of coaches for heads of state continued to be important. Sometimes, the ideas and requirements of the new order differed remarkably from those of royalty. The coaches often reflected the differences. Nowhere can this be seen more strikingly than at the Transport Museum in Nuremberg where the astonishing baroque splendour of the Bavarian royal saloons (from the 1860s) stands in complete contrast to the severe austerity of the simple four-wheeler built over ten years later for Bismarck.

It is not generally known that most of the ultra-special saloons were actually owned by the railway itself and that the VIP travellers paid to ride in them like anyone else. Clearly the possession of a luxury coach was regarded as a status symbol by the railway. Most systems with pretentions to respectability felt obliged to have one or two in stock. Such coaches brought prestige to the owning company and an opportunity to display their best coach-building techniques.

In these instances it was not uncommon to provide what might be termed a general-purpose state saloon, equally appropriate to Kings or Presidents. In these cases, the precise title of the head of state mattered less and many of the vehicles survived in use after the original monarch had, perhaps, been replaced by a non-royal head of state. A venerable example of this type of carriage, dating from 1897 but much modernized later, is the state saloon of Coras Iompair Eireann (Irish Railways), originally built for royal patronage but afterwards utilized as a state coach; while the austerely grand Presidential saloon of French

Railways, now preserved at Mulhouse, represents a later version of a similar concept.

Acceptance from a very early date of railway travel by royalty and other influential people undoubtedly placed a seal of respectability on the railway which the companies were not slow to take up, and there developed a form of super first-class accommodation for the benefit of what might be termed 'other' VIPs. The coaches provided, whether they were called private saloons, special saloons, family saloons or whatever, generally had in common a degree of luxury and privacy which payment for their use entitled the traveller to enjoy. They were usually completely self-contained, incorporating day and night accommodation, cooking and toilet facilities, and were either available for private hire or reserved for the semi-exclusive use of senior railway officials on their tours of inspection.

Arising from these vehicles came the idea of the genuine privately owned saloon which, for a fee, the railway would agree to convey attached to one of its own service trains for the benefit of the owner. This was not a particularly common feature of the European scene, where travelling distances were generally quite modest and the railways could usually themselves provide a suitable vehicle from their own stock. But there were one or two noteworthy exceptions such as the Duke of Sutherland's private saloons in Scotland. At least three coaches were built for this wealthy Scottish

Top left: The sumptuous interior of the Grand Duchess of Luxembourg's saloon preserved at the French Railway Museum, Mulhouse.

Top centre: The businessman's exhibition train *Impact Europe.*

Above: The washroom in the *Impact Europe* exhibition train.

Below left: A modern dome car – as recently used on the TEE *Rheingold.*

Below: Interior of Queen Victoria's saloon, preserved at the British National Railway Museum.

landowner, of which two still survive, one in Canada and the other in the British National Railway Museum.

It was, however, in North America where the private saloon achieved its most magnificent expression. The distances covered by the railways of this continent, coupled with the prosperity which built them, made it a perfectly practical proposition for wealthy businessmen, railway officials, or private families to embark on a transcontinental journey surrounded by every convenience which the ingenuity of the carriage builder could devise. Just as in Europe, once the train became respectable as a result of patronage by the wealthy and influential, the idea took strong root. In this, as in many other aspects of passenger travel in North America, the influence of Pullman was considerable. He was not alone in this field of private saloon construction and other companies also built to order. However his company was of course, only too happy to build the coaches if so requested.

Externally, the American private coach kept pace with and differed but little from the normal coaches of the day, but inside the builders frequently ran riot. No specific interior layout was evolved, the customer being left to specify his requirements within a basically standardized bodyshell; but over the years most tended to incorporate open-plan day, dining and observation saloons, lavishly equipped private suites of sitting and sleeping compartments and, of course,

the inevitable open platform observation verandah. One could live in such a coach for weeks if desired and so popular did they become that they were not only built for private ownership but some were built as speculative ventures for hire. It was even possible to hire a complete train of them. Their interior appointments undoubtedly set many precedents for the great public trains of the Pullman Standard era. Their influence spread abroad and some were exported.

The special saloon, be it for an Indian Maharajah, an American railway president, a well-to-do family or the King of England was, without doubt, a highly-privileged form of rail travel enjoyed by but a minute fraction of the world's population. Yet, like so many other aspects of the passenger scene, it was an accurate reflection of society. Furthermore, although limited in numbers compared with common-user vehicles, their influence on the evolution of general service carriage design was out of all proportion to their numerical strength. Fortunately, because of their generally low annual mileage, many of them lasted well beyond the lifespan of their more mundane contemporaries and are available for us to examine in museums throughout the world.

Carriage design and evolution

So far, in this survey, attention has been concentrated on the passenger services provided by the railways with the coaches themselves being given but brief mention. However, the railway is an

Top left: King Ludwig II of Bavaria's baroque saloon.

Top centre: Ornate sleeping compartment in the German Kaiser's saloon.

Left: Exotic conveyance for Pope Pius IX.

Top right: Kaiser Wilhelm II leaving his train. The carriage styling is highly typical of early 20th century European practice.

Above right: The interior of King Edward VII's bedroom in the LNWR Royal Saloon of 1903, now preserved in the British National Railway Museum.

example of applied technology and development of the coach is an important aspect of the story. The human cargo is the only form of revenue traffic which can voice its feelings and needs to management and it is not too surprising, therefore, that the evolution of railway carriages has been more strongly influenced by social attitudes than almost any other aspect of the railway scene. Bearing in mind the dangers implicit in generalization, development of coaches can be divided into two main categories, the vehicle itself (its riding quality and safety), and the interior appointments provided to meet the differing requirements of the customers. To meet the requirements of one category would often influence the other.

The first railway vehicles were, literally, open boxes on wheels for conveyance of coal, minerals and the like. Simply made and totally unsprung, they sufficed for the cargo they carried. However, with the evolution of passenger travel, an unsprung and uncovered vehicle was no adequate substitute even for the road coach which, for all its slowness, was often quite elaborately sprung and appointed. Consequently, provision of cover and springing on carriages was an early point of departure from freight wagons. The early coaches

were, of course, four-wheeled and although some attempts were made to provide wheel springs on the road coach pattern, a much more acceptable method quickly achieved dominance. This took the form of a movable box, housing the bearings for the end of the axle, which was free to move vertically between two restraining guides fixed to the chassis. The axlebox itself was in turn attached (most commonly) to a simple leaf spring also fixed to the chassis, which absorbed vertical shocks.

However, vertical springing was not enough since the essence of railway operation was the use of a series of vehicles coupled together to form a train. The most common form of coupling was at first a chain link attached to a hook at the vehicle end, but since at first only the locomotive had brakes, whenever trains came to a halt the coaches inevitably came to rest by bumping into the vehicle ahead. It was thus necessary to provide some form of device to absorb end-shocks. At first these were simply projections padded with leather but in time they evolved into projecting, spring-loaded buffers, one at each of the four corners of the coach. This went some way to improve matters but the absence of carriage brakes, together with the loose chain connections, still caused jerking at the start of a journey and bumping and banging when the train halted.

Although some early carriages had brakes, most did not, but it was not long before the situation changed. Essentially, brakes took the form of blocks which rubbed against the wheel, thus slowing its rate of progress and they were operated by mechanical levers controlled by a guard or brakeman, who not infrequently rode on the carriage roof. It became quite an art to co-ordinate the braking on a series of loose-coupled vehicles and accidents were not unknown. Matters were improved somewhat, at least in Europe, by evolution of the screw coupling in place of the loose chain. In this device, invented by Henry Booth in the 1830s, the centre link of the chain was replaced by an adjustable screw link which enabled the couplings between vehicles to be tightened so that there was little or no slack between adjacent vehicles, thus reducing the end-shocks. Under these circumstances, some means of applying all the brakes in the train simultaneously became desirable and, after many and various experimental devices were tried and rejected, there evolved in time automatic brakes controlled by the engine driver.

It took some considerable time for all these processes to evolve in carriage coupling and braking, during which period other significant changes were taking place. The American coach quickly departed from its European counterpart in many respects, particularly size, and this too had its effect. The early European carriage builders were extremely conservative in their assessment of the potential size of a coach. Influenced strongly by the long tradition of road coach practice and often constructed by the same coachbuilding concerns, early coaches were distinctly modest in size and it was many years before there was much change from the original four-wheel concept. The broad-gauge trains of the British Great Western Railway had, however, shown that larger and wider coaches were possible and it was not long before other railways began to copy. In most cases the limit of width and height (determined by the size of fixed structures like bridges and tunnels) was fairly quickly reached and the only potentially expandable dimension was coach length. Mechanically, this necessitated more wheels to carry the extra weight and, because of this increased weight, not to mention the growing speed of trains, much-improved brakes and couplings were also essential. In consequence, there evolved in Europe the six-wheel coach, which is still common.

To enable rigid six-wheel vehicles to negotiate curves, some form of sideways wheel movement is essential on all but the most gentle of curves if the vehicle is not to derail. Furthermore, vertical changes in track alignment must also be kept strictly limited so as not to exceed the limit of tolerance of the vertical springing of each axle. In Europe, because of the substantial mileage of well-engineered line, this was not unduly difficult to achieve, but in North America, as has been previously stated, the pioneering nature of many early railways made an alternative solution necessary and stimulated development of the independently pivoting bogie or truck.

The carriage bogie is an extremely ingenious, yet basically simple device. It consists of four or, less commonly, six wheels, set quite close together and fixed to a rigid frame in which the wheels are sprung in the conventional manner. It is in the means of attachment of the vehicle itself to the bogie that the significance lies. Within the rigid frame of the bogie there is set a second structure or 'bolster' which is hung from the frame in such a way that it is free to move, vertically and laterally, quite independently of the main frame carrying the wheels. This, too, can be given its own springing for additional cushioning and restraint, and it is to this bolster that the carriage body is attached via a pivoting device. Thus the weight of the body actually hangs from the frame of the bogie on an independently movable frame. In turn this permits each bogie to adjust itself separately to track irregularities (both vertical and horizontal) and, because of the centre pivot, also allows the bogie to swivel at an angle to the coach body.

Development of this device in North America

Top right: Restored coaches show a method of carriage connection used in America in the 19th century.

Centre right: The articulated bogie and connection between coaches of a diesel railcar preserved at the Netherlands Railway Museum, Utrecht.

Below left and centre: Two views of a finely restored semi-open wooden seated third class coach at the Netherlands Railway Museum, Utrecht showing the coupling method.

Below right: Clerestory carriage styling on the Benguela railway.

quickly freed the coach from most of the size constraints hitherto experienced. Furthermore, the double springing effect occasioned by the use of an independently sprung bolster gave a very much more comfortable ride. Not surprisingly, the bogie coach became adopted world wide by most railways, especially for longer distance services.

Allied with development of the large American bogie coach was a very different approach to the question of coupling between vehicles. The simple chain link and side buffer was quite incapable of controlling the more massive structure of the American coach and there developed a central rigid coupling (or bar) between the vehicles. At first these were held in place by a simple pin dropped through a hole at the end of the bar into a 'pocket' at the end of the adjacent vehicle into which the bar coupling fitted. This acted both as a coupler and a longitudinal restraint, and the side buffer vanished from the American scene. It did not altogether eliminate the 'snatch' effect when starting from rest, but it did materially improve matters. In time, this method of coupling evolved into an automatic hook which engaged a similar hook on the adjacent vehicle which, on modern coaches, not only makes a physical connection but has been further developed to incorporate brake, lighting and other electrical connections.

In Europe, the centre screw coupling and side buffer, which became progressively improved throughout the four- and six-wheel phase remained the norm long after introduction of bogie coaches, largely to ensure compatibility between old and new vehicles, but the American-inspired 'buckeye' hook coupling was introduced on a progressively wider scale and is now widespread throughout Europe, and indeed the world, on modern coaches where it is often found combined with side buffers. It is often incorporated in such a fashion as to hinge out of the way to reveal the older pattern of screw coupler hook, in order that vehicles with the older coupling can still be incorporated in the train.

Much credit for the adoption outside America of this form of coupling, sometimes also referred

Left: Safety lights in a British Great Western Railway express buffet car in 1932.

Right: This disaster on a viaduct illustrates the weaknesses of non-box girder coach construction.

to as the 'Pullman' type, can be attributed to Nigel Gresley, much more famous during the 1920s and 1930s as a British steam locomotive designer. What is less well known is that prior to his involvement with locomotives, he was carriage and wagon superintendent of the British Great Northern Railway where, during the Edwardian period, he introduced a variety of modern innovations into carriage building. Apart from the adoption of American-inspired couplings, he was also responsible for perfecting a double-bolster bogie design, incorporating two sets of moving structures within the frame, and the idea of articulation whereby the adjacent ends of two vehicles were carried on one bogie mounted between them. This method saved valuable train weight and has been widely copied and adapted, notably on the British advanced passenger train and, at an earlier stage and in an applied form on the Spanish *Talgo* trains. In these ultra lightweight formations, each coach is carried essentially on a single axle only at one end, to which the non-axle end of the adjacent coach is attached by means of a flexible joint.

Allied to the question of ride quality, coupling and braking, is the general matter of safety. Much could be done by improved signalling methods which are covered elsewhere, but correct designs of coach bodies could play a considerable part in minimizing damage if, unfortunately, an accident took place. In this, as in other areas, American experience was to prove important.

The Americans, thanks to the use of the bogie, quickly developed a characteristic form of body construction which incorporated heavy longitudinal timber sections as integral strengtheners forming part of the body structure. In effect, the typical American coach of the 19th century was a semi-rigid box girder heavily constructed in timber with all the ancillary equipment fixed, as it were, on the outside. When such coaches were imported into other parts of the world, notably Europe, their rigidity was seen to give considerably better shock-absorbing qualities when involved in accidents. The traditional European coach, more lightly constructed and fixed to a separate chassis tended to break up completely when involved in a collision, whereas the body of an American-type coach, though not immune from danger, would often remain structurally intact after an accident even though all the wheels, brakes and other gear had become detached from the structure.

Unfortunately, marshalling heavy American-style coaches alongside their much more flimsy European contemporaries merely made the problem worse, since the American coaches could act rather like battering rams against the lighter vehicles. Consequently, although there was much agitation for safer coaches, European railways and those predominantly influenced by European thinking were rather slow to adopt heavier coaches. In time, however, it was discovered that whether on the American integral principle or the more traditional body-plus-chassis principle, a heavier and more massive coach was intrinsically safer than a small lightweight coach.

Another serious risk was fire, to which the timber coach, regardless of its type, was particularly vulnerable. Most of the fire risk, at least in Europe, was caused by interior coach lighting. Early carriages were lit by oil pot lamps and candles, both extremely dangerous unless adequately safeguarded and even when, towards the end of

Above: Link-pin coupling on a Canadian-built locomotive in use in Trinidad in 1968.

Above right: A detail of a British wood and alloy coach under construction.

Below right: Modern British Rail electrical multiple units under construction at York.

the evolution started with the increasing use of steel in the vehicle chassis, at first in combination with heavy timber sections, but later entirely on its own. This imparted considerable extra rigidity to the train and, in those areas where separate chassis were favoured, enabled the timber body to enjoy a new lease of life. In these instances, well exemplified by most of British practice, there was only a gradual change over to steel bodies as well as chassis. A favourite compromise was to use steel panelling on teak framing, but all-wood bodies were still being constructed as late as 1940.

Where, as in America, the concept of the integral body had already become well-established, transformation to the all-steel coach was more rapid, starting just after the turn of the century and reaching its famous high point during the Standard-Steel era, already discussed. The major disincentive to widespread adoption of steel vehicles was train weight. It was not just that steel coaches weighed more in themselves, 70 or 80 tons per vehicle being a quite common North American figure, but the demands of the passenger were simultaneously reducing the revenue load per coach as the number of ancillary fittings (lavatories, corridors, heating systems, air conditioning, and so forth) took up ever increasing amounts of space. Extra weight implied larger units of motive power to pull the trains, which in turn involved yet more capital expenditure. There was, therefore, every commercial incentive on the part of the railways to keep train weight down, made even more desirable by growing competition from road and air.

This problem is still relevant to carriage construction today, but the continuing improvement in metallurgy and development of alternative high-strength lightweight materials has enabled most railways to make substantial improvements, sometimes of a spectacular nature. Even in countries like Britain, where heavyweight vehicles were rather rare, a modern 72-seat open second-class coach with full air conditioning weighs little more than some turn-of-the-century corridor firsts with maybe only 24 seats, and is immeasurably safer and stronger.

As a result of these gradually improving techniques, the modern railway coach is probably the strongest and safest vehicle generally available for regular travel. Taking all factors into account, the railway passenger has always been at considerably less risk than in most alternative contemporary forms of public transport and the present day is no exception.

However, as speeds increased, even these improvements had their limitations. No matter how good the suspension and couplings may be, the intrinsic nature of a railway coach will cause the periodic vibration to reach an unacceptable degree of discomfort as speed increases. To some extent this is mitigated by a heavier coach whose periodic vibration is slower, and which, therefore, can attain a higher speed before reaching the threshold of discomfort. Consequently, as long as the faster trains were also increasing in weight, the onset of the problem was delayed and had

the 19th century, they were generally superseded by compressed oil gas, the incendiary risk was still high. It was only invention of a reliable form of electric carriage lighting that caused a real improvement to the safety factor. However, in North America, the greatest fire risk was the solid fuel heating stove.

Safety improvements did not take place simultaneously on all railways, some of which were distinctly sluggish in altering their ways; and some quite horrendous accidents took place long after development of safer types of coach. Much the same story was true of the change from all-timber to steel construction.

The use of steel in carriage building made a material contribution to both the rigidity of the vehicle and its fire-resistant properties. Basically, little influence on the development of coaches right down to the second world war period. All the same, onset of the streamline era began to make railways look again at the problem. The Americans, in general, managed to run their fliers of the 1930s at high speed largely because of their heavy weight, but those observers who were honest about the British streamliners of the late 1930s will confirm that the 160 km/h (100 mph) or more speeds achieved by the LMS and LNER trains often caused an extreme degree of discomfort and unease to the passenger.

Fortunately, the discomfort threshold is reached well before the normal limits of safety of the flanged wheel on steel rail. However, there is a world of difference in comfort terms between running a train at an average speed of 96 km/h (60 mph) with occasional short stretches at 145 to 160 km/h (90 to 100 mph) and trying to achieve the consistent high-speed performance which railways see as essential today. Coupled with their wish to reduce coach weight, railways therefore realized that the whole question of vehicle suspension had to be re-examined.

To a considerable extent they were assisted by the great improvements made in track technology. Deeper ballasting of permanent way and long stretches of continuously welded rail both served to reduce markedly the track-to-wheel shocks experienced by the train itself. However, improvements also took place in the vehicles. The whole question of wheel springing was critically examined. New forms of primary and secondary suspension, embodying increasing use of coil springs, torsion bars, and shock absorbers have all come into widespread use. Rather surprisingly, given these improvements, the old-fashioned bogie with its movable bolster has still proved to be the most effective means of connecting the coach body with the rail. Even the traditional wheel profile has been re-examined and it has been found that, by slight modification, the tendency of the wheel tread to oscillate slightly at high speed from side to side of the rail (until restrained by the flange) can be almost eliminated. On a modern wheelset, the flange hardly, if ever, comes into contact with the side of the rail except at points and crossings.

All these improvements have made it possible for modern trains to progress safely at steady speeds of up to 200 km/h (125 mph), even on

Above: British Rail's High Speed Train on trial. In service it runs at speeds of up to 200 km/h (125 mph).

Right: Conventional diesels lean with the cant of the track on a curve.

Far right: British Rail's 240 km/h (150 mph) Advanced Passenger Train employs a positive 'pendulum' suspension which enables the train to take a curve at high speed without discomfort to passengers.

Left: The Advanced Passenger Train at speed.

curves; but at this point their success tends to pose a new generation of problems. As is well known, negotiating a curve in a vehicle brings into play a familiar set of cornering forces. In its simplest form this is best illustrated by the need for a cyclist to lean inwards as he negotiates a bend. At its most uncomfortable it can be experienced by trying to negotiate a bend in the road too quickly in a motor car, when one experiences a sensation of being forced to the outside of the bend. Actually what is felt is the vehicle side pushing the occupant towards the centre of the curve.

In the railway context this problem is generally solved in two ways. First, as with modern roads, the track itself can be raised (or super-elevated) at the outside of the curve, thus causing the vehicle to lean inwards and, by its own weight, generate a force acting towards the centre of the curve which helps the vehicle negotiate the corner. The second is a by-product of the use of the bogie itself. Being free to move, via the bolster, within the bogie frame, the carriage body tends to move towards the outside of the curve it is negotiating. Because of the arrangement of swinging links by which the carriage hangs from the bogie, this has the effect of causing the outside link to adopt a near-vertical position while the link on the inside of the curve adopts a position at an angle to the

vertical. Since both links are the same length and fixed to the coach, the automatic effect is to lower the height of the coach on the inside of the curve, thus causing it to tilt inwards, which is precisely what the passenger wants.

The combined effect of these two factors can make it possible for a conventional coach to negotiate even quite severe curves with little reduction in speed. However, as speed increases, even though it would be perfectly safe to traverse sharp corners, the comfort threshold would be reached. To effect an improvement one must either increase the amount of super-elevation or alter the vehicle characteristics. To adopt the former approach might well produce a degree of super-elevation which is too great for comfort on slower-moving trains so most modern research has concentrated on the vehicle itself, culminating in the so-called 'pendulum' suspension which has now reached an advanced state of development.

In this system, electronic sensors detect when a coach is rounding a curve and actuate mechanisms that tilt the body into the curve even more than would naturally take place. This, in turn, enables higher speeds to be attempted without the need to rebuild whole stretches of line (or even build new railways), and thus has considerable appeal.

Increased speed and comfort of ride will in turn cause fresh developments in the brake, coupling and structural fields. The process is, as it has always been, essentially cyclic and is likely to remain so as long as there are railways responsive to the wishes of their passengers.

Change in interior amenities has continued. Upholstery fabrics, compartment and saloon finishing materials, and detail trimmings have faithfully reflected changing fashions down the years, from the heavy and dark button-down fabrics of the Victorian period with extensive use of wood veneer decoration, to the modern coach which makes increasing use of man-made materials in lighter and brighter colours. Lamps have changed from elaborately embellished pseudo-chandeliers glittering with polished brass to the modern flush-mounted electric arrangements; and heating has progressed from the non-existent via the footwarmer to the modern electrically heated coach with individually adjustable controls for the passenger to operate.

Allied to heating has been the change in carriage ventilation methods down the years. In early days, ventilation was achieved solely by opening a window, which often allowed more than fresh air to enter the coach. Even in the great days of American Pullman operations, one of the more common problems of travel was the unpleasant choice between open windows which let in the dust from the prairies or the soot from the engine, or closed windows which rendered the interior hot and unbearable. The problem was not confined to America, and most railways developed a variety of systems to cope with the difficulty. In general this took two forms. One was the roof-top ventilator which, while admitting air, could be so shaped as to deflect the air

into the carriage while trapping most of the unwanted matter. The second method was to provide ventilators over the tops of doors and windows which could perform similar functions. Both were under passenger control. Combined with opening windows they could at least provide some variation in fresh air supply.

The real saviour was air-conditioning. Introduced in North America to cope with the climatic extremes encountered over the vast distances involved, the air-conditioned coach is now a feature of better trains throughout the world. Above all it makes them cleaner inside.

It is not difficult to see why, in spite of detail improvements, the basic design of a coach has remained so consistent. Its fundamental object is to carry people and, setting all other considerations aside, the greater the number of people that can be carried per vehicle, the fewer vehicles the railway has to provide. This has obvious advantages in strictly economic terms and undoubtedly explains why coach sizes have increased down the years. Railways quickly discovered that to carry 100 people in one large coach cost them less, both in capital expenditure and running costs, than to convey the same number in two smaller coaches.

However, life is not as simple as all that. The passenger who will tolerate high-density seating for a short trip to the office will not accept similar accommodation for a longer journey. He will probably want more space within the vehicle and almost certainly wish to cater for his bodily needs on any trip lasting more than an hour or two. Hence, as has already been mentioned, the necessity for the railway to provide additional amenities on the longer-distance trains made itself felt at an early stage.

The trouble with providing auxiliary facilities is that, even at the level of the humble lavatory, they do not add to the revenue-earning capacity of the train. In fact, they actually reduce it in most cases. Consequently, provision of additional features inevitably raises the question of costs; it is not too surprising, therefore, that they have been most often provided in those countries where *per capita* income is high enough to meet this extra cost without the passenger feeling obliged to desert the railway. For the railway, this has always led to a very delicate balancing operation between improved amenities on the one hand and reduced accommodation on the other. Nowhere has this problem made itself more manifest than in sleeping and dining cars.

The necessity to provide sleeping and dining facilities on long-distance trains has taxed the ingenuity of carriage builders since the time they first appeared. The sleeping car, in particular, causes a fundamental problem, for it has to come to terms with the inescapable anatomical fact that, when we lie down to sleep, we occupy more floor space than when we sit on a seat. The ratio is approximately 3:1 and there is no way in which a train can suddenly treble its size without provision of a large number of additional vehicles. Furthermore, the problem is compounded by the distance over which the train is travelling. If the journey is of several days' duration, the train must provide both day and night accommodation, whereas if the trip can be completed in, say, 12 hours or so, then the vehicles can be provided to meet but one of the two prime considerations. This has led over the years to development of two basic types of coach, the sleeping car which is convertible for day use and the pure sleeping car which generally only operates at night.

The convertible sleeping car, inevitably, made its first appearance in North America with development of long distance and transcontinental routes. Not surprisingly, Pullman and his contemporaries were the prime movers. In this they were aided by the ever increasing size which the American style of open saloon was assuming. During the mid-Victorian period, the normal seating arrangement was in pairs on either side of

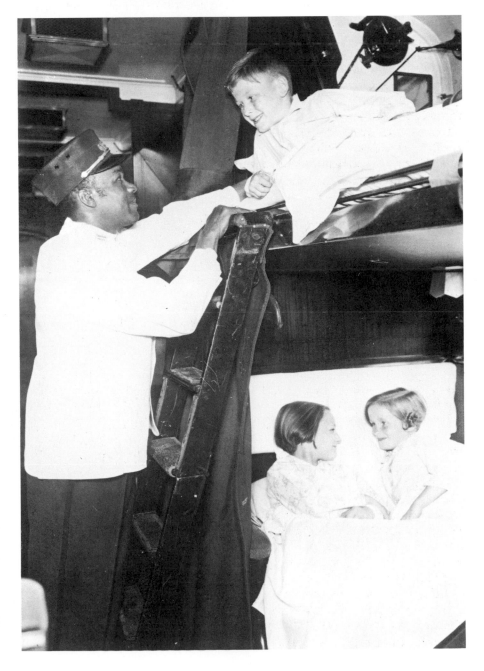

a central gangway. Often these all faced the direction of travel, with seat backs which were reversible at the end of the journey, but Woodruff devised the idea of adopting an arrangement of facing pairs of seats in which half the passengers rode with their backs to the direction of travel. He built coaches in which facing pairs of seats could be drawn together at night to form a bed – which would accommodate two of the four passengers. Utilizing the great height of American coaches, he then arranged for a second bed to be let down from the roof above the top of the window for the second pair of passengers, thus accommodating four sleeping passengers in no more floor space than four sitting passengers.

It had one particular advantage which none of the alternatives have totally managed to achieve. It was universally applicable to all degrees of luxury. At its most basic it could be applied to fairly rudimentary wooden or hard leather twin or triple seats, arranged in opposing pairs, while at its most opulent it could apply to facing pairs of luxurious single seats which would produce

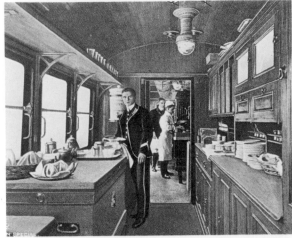

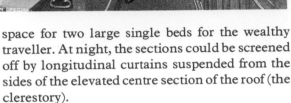

Far left: The butler's pantry of the London to Liverpool boat train, the American Special in the early 1900s.

Left: The setting for lunch on the London to Paris *Golden Arrow*.

Below: A Pullman Car of 1889 in use between Chicago and Cincinnatti.

space for two large single beds for the wealthy traveller. At night, the sections could be screened off by longitudinal curtains suspended from the sides of the elevated centre section of the roof (the clerestory).

When the American concept of sleeping cars was first brought to Europe, it was not altogether well received. The greater comfort of the massive American-style bogie coaches was much appreciated, but the open saloon arrangement and the lack of privacy were not always in accord with Victorian ideas of rectitude in the old world. There, the travellers much preferred their individual compartments. Furthermore, there was less need, particularly in Britain, for a dual-purpose sleeping-cum-day coach. In consequence, although some Pullman-type sleeping cars were operated, particularly by the Midland Railway in Britain, the general European trend was to try to adapt the familiar compartment to the sleeping mode. In Britain this led to the almost universal development of the pure sleeping car where no real provision was made for daytime riding.

Most commonly, therefore, the British sleeping car took the form of a conventional side-corridor compartment coach in which beds, arranged transversely, were located in the place normally occupied by the seats. This, with the corridor door closed, provided a private twin bed-room, much more to the liking of the British – moreover it could be fitted with a washbasin be-

tween the beds and did give space to disrobe. For the single traveller, a half compartment with but one bed was provided and in time became the standard form, still in use today. A double room could be contrived by unlocking a connecting door between two adjacent single berths.

In this type of sleeping car, the passenger had all the privacy he needed but the number which could be accommodated was, and still is, strictly limited, rarely exceeding 12 per vehicle. Not surprisingly, therefore, the cost of providing such a facility could only be met by the first-class passenger and it was not until 1928 that the lower orders were given sleeping accommodation in British trains in the form of compartments with upper and lower berths.

This problem was not, perhaps, very significant in Britain. Distances were short, overnight travel was not common and never involved more than one night on the train. Throughout the rest of Europe, however, things were different. The distances were not of American proportions but, since trains could take between 24 and 48 hours to make a journey, some form of convertible coach was essential; but still the Europeans did not like the open coach solution. Neither did Georges Nagelmackers. When he returned from North America, impressed by Pullman's ideas but not quite so enamoured of the standard Pullman sleeping section, he endeavoured with his Wagons-Lits vehicles to produce a compromise.

Many ideas, including Pullman-style coaches,

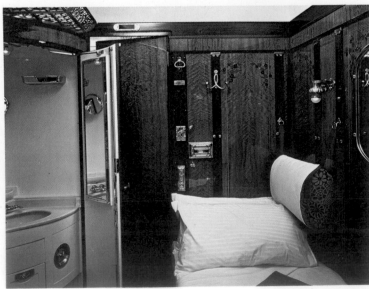

were tried but the most typical solution was to provide coaches with a series of half-compartments, connected by a side corridor. Within these compartments a conventional day seat was provided along one side, but at night a second bed could be hinged out from the partition above the seat to form a twin-bunk arrangement. Sometimes, if the height of the vehicle allowed it, a third berth could be thus provided and on other occasions, the high level berth folded out from above the window at right angles to the day seat. To make room for more compartments, it was common practice for the partitions between compartments which did not carry the seats/bunks to be set at an angle, thus giving a variable-width compartment whose average dimension was rather less than a purely rectangular arrangement. Washing facilities were provided in each compartment and, of course, space was available for undressing purposes. The Wagons-Lits, therefore, combined the privacy of the British sleeper with a greater passenger capacity and an ability to use the compartment during the day time.

Elsewhere in the world, high supplementary charges were a distinct disincentive to rail travel. They could only be sustained by the wealthy and yet in many developing areas widespread use of trains over long distances was absolutely essential if the general level of prosperity was to increase. The basic Pullman section did give relatively low-cost sleeping accommodation but it was only widely used where American influence was strong. In such vast countries as Russia, China and India, early development of railways was considerably influenced by European ideas and the fixation with the compartment took some time to change. Imperial Russia and China were strongly class-conscious societies; separation of the various classes of traveller was normal and the compartment concept proved ideally suitable. Nowhere was this more apparent than in pre-independence India where there were at least four classes of travel in places, and problems not made any easier to solve by the various religious differences.

There thus grew up a sort of basic overnight accommodation which took the form of triple tiers of bunks arranged within the confines of a normal compartment. Their furnishings were very simple and the bunks themselves were often no more than frames made from wood slats. They were no more austere in themselves than the basic Pullman section provided in the North American 'colonial' trains.

Sleeping accommodation provided in modern trains shows the influence of all these historical developments, overlaid with ideas borrowed from current hotel and airline practice, not to mention considerable cross-fertilization which has taken place between the various countries of the world. The European liking for privacy was taken back to North America where the traditional Pullman section was installed in private compartments to form small state rooms, bedrooms or roomettes, depending on precise size and accommodation offered. The reclining seat idea, dating back to

the 1840s, has been updated in open coaches to offer an alternative form of night travel. The high-density double- or triple-deck compartment berth arrangement has been introduced widely in Europe in the form of the *couchette* for low-cost sleeping accommodation, while the permutations within the super-luxury category seem to be determined only by the willingness of the traveller to pay for them or the inventiveness of the designer in thinking up new ideas.

Design and evolution of the sleeping car was basically governed by the need to balance the spatial requirements of a sleeping person and the need to keep within economic limits on the part of the railway and within the passengers' ability to pay; but at least it did provide revenue traffic. The dining car on the other hand is literally dead weight added to the train. Under these circumstances, the railway is in something of a dilemma and it has always been a moot point whether or not the dining car is a genuine revenue earner. On the one hand, the presence of catering facilities may well cause passengers to be attracted to the train; alternatively the absence of a dining car could cause the passenger to desert the railway. On balance, railways have tended to regard provision of meals as an essential part of their operations, if only as a 'loss-leader', ever since the unsatisfactory days of refreshment stops.

The classic dining car is a coach comprising a kitchen and pantry at one end with an open saloon equipped with tables at the other. It was, of course, derived from the pioneer open saloon coaches of North America. In order to tempt people to use it, the railways were obliged to enable passengers to gain access and then make the provision of meals a pleasurable experience. As a result, the vestibule connection between coaches was developed to meet the one consideration, and the appointments inside the coach were often made as elaborate as possible to meet the other.

There was and still is, a real sense of occasion in partaking of a meal in a well-equipped dining car. It probably appeals to some basic human need over and above the mere necessity of taking in regular supplies of food and, once the idea was introduced, railways were not slow to appreciate the possibilities. Here was a genuine shop window for their service which eventually came to be enjoyed by all, not just the wealthy. In fact it was not unknown for passengers to opt deliberately for a lower standard of accommodation in order that they could save enough on the fare to fully participate in the delights of the dining car *en route*. Properly planned, one could spend much of one's journey in these sumptuous vehicles and several railways positively encouraged the practice, particularly in Great Britain. Elsewhere in the world, the dining car was usually rather more of a travelling restaurant and the temptation to linger after the meal could well depend on the comfort of the vehicle itself.

As with most railway vehicles, the original dining car interior layout has stood the test of time and proved itself surprisingly adaptable to changing eating habits whether they be historic

Far left and left: A Wagons-Lits sleeping compartment in day use and made up for the night.

changes within one nation or contemporary regional differences between different nations. In fact on the international Wagons-Lits operations it is a feature of the service that, on crossing frontiers, the food and drink provided in the dining car can be changed to suit the country being traversed.

Not infrequently, the dining car evolved into what might be called the social focus of the train. Areas were provided for pre-meal drinks and, sometimes, a whole coach devoted to recreational activities (equipped with bar, piano and the necessary staff) would be connected to the dining car proper.

From the public dining car evolved in time such related features as the dining sections of private saloons or the exclusive club car. These latter were provided for, say, a group of regular users of the train who could guarantee to purchase enough meals and drinks to justify provision of semi-exclusive facilities. It was, in some areas, developed into a high-class commuter service – what a pleasant way to start and finish work. Even some normal service dining cars developed a sort of club atmosphere.

In more recent years, the dining car has undergone something of a transformation. The one-time universal 'full-meal' service has been augmented and in many cases replaced by a whole range of alternative facilities masquerading under a variety of pseudonyms, but generally embodying the buffet principle of self-service, tray meals or, at best, counter service. Some of these are very good, offering substantial fare at competitive prices while others are, frankly, squalid. Amongst the better offerings can be mentioned the recent re-introduction (1970 onwards) of rail catering on a modest scale but of a very high standard in New Zealand; British Railways' griddle cars operating in Scotland, which contain a pleasant saloon bar and a small dining saloon flanking a centre kitchen which can produce very tempting food; the modern cars operated by

Amtrak which are generally commendably clean; and a particularly civilized Wagons-Lits operation in France where a bar counter offering substantial food in addition to some excellent claret is placed in the same car as a supremely comfortable dining saloon. Vehicle design, too, has changed to take account of these altered eating habits.

Some of these changes have been occasioned by the need to reduce staffing levels in dining cars and others to take account, particularly in Europe, of the much reduced journey times which often no longer embrace a conventional meal time. Sadly, this has gone hand-in-glove with a distressing tendency towards 'instant packaging' of almost anything from French mustard to toothpicks.

However, it is still possible to have excellent ham and eggs cooked to order in the old solid-fuel heated wood-panelled blue Wagons-Lits cars after an overnight ferry passage to the Hook of Holland, or by contrast, dine in great splendour after a pre-meal aperitif in the beautiful modern refreshment cars of the *Rheingold*. Traditional afternoon tea with toasted teacake, real cups and proper teapots can still be obtained on British Railways while the cooked breakfasts are justly famous. In India traditional catering for the various religious persuasions continues at its customary excellence.

Outside the sleeping and dining car field, the change in emphasis from the original concepts of vehicle interior design, other than the obvious changes of upholstery material and interior trimmings, were more subtle. The traditional compartments changed hardly at all. They became more spacious between partitions on long-distance trains and, if possible, even more cramped for suburban and commuter service. For this purpose coaches were made as wide as possible with intermediate partitions close together to maximize seating. To help distribute passengers within the coach, interior passageways were sometimes provided along one or both sides, but they were not really proper corridors, while, to save expense, the intermediate partitions in some designs were not taken to full height. In this form, there was precious little difference between them and a conventional open coach, save for the full array of outside doors. Wooden or hardwearing leather seats were provided to reduce maintenance and many minor variations could be seen throughout the world.

The open saloon developed into such widely disparate vehicles as the special coaches already described, not forgetting observation and dome cars with glass areas at the ends or in the roof and, at the other extreme, high-density suburban coaches, both double and single deck. In more recent years these have often appeared with intermediate side doors, increasingly of the sliding variety, to speed up loading and unloading, while there has been, in some areas, a tendency to reduce the number of seats and increase the standing accommodation where it is impossible to provide a seat for every passenger at peak periods.

Top right: A 19th century Canadian Pacific dining car.

Top far right: A tourist dining car of the Indian Railways.

Centre right: A more conventional Indian Railways dining car.

Centre far right: A turn of the century third class dining car on the British Great Northern Railway.

Below left: A kitchen interior, Indian Railways.

Below centre: The west bound San Francisco *Zephyr* near Reno at breakfast time.

Below right: A preserved German dining car at the Deutsches Museum, Munich.

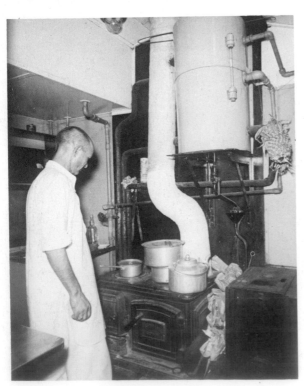

One final aspect of carriage design remains to be considered, and that perhaps the most obvious of all – its external appearance.

The external style of coaches has, for the most part, been a reasonably honest expression of functional form, but within the parameters imposed by the fundamental shape and size of the vehicles there has always been ample opportunity to display regional, national and even purely idiosyncratic differences. Coaches need doors and windows but the precise nature of either feature permits infinite variety in detail. A roof must be provided but the choice available is considerable. The vehicle needs side walls but the materials used and the favoured construction method can have considerable influence on the final style of vehicle. For this reason, perhaps, although carriage interiors may have displayed reasonably similar features on a global basis, exteriors tended to have more strongly marked regional or national characteristics.

In Europe, old-fashioned coach-building traditions were strong and the wooden-body coach evolved fairly harmoniously from earlier road vehicle practice. Bodies were made of timber frames covered with wooden sheets, whose joins were capped with raised strips (or beading) to prevent moisture entering. These raised strips gave considerable scope for decorative treatment, especially at the painting stage where they were often embellished with gilding and coloured lining to contrast with the main colour of the vehicle. Colour choices themselves were highly variable, often being copied from the old stage coaches; but fairly early in the development of railways it was realized that a standard colour scheme for all the coaches of one railway could have considerable publicity value. This led to some very attractive company liveries being developed, particularly in Britain and Ireland, many of which lasted right through until the 1940s, albeit with some reduction in variety after the various amalgamations of 1923 and later.

The British liking for colourful coaches did not apply to quite the same extent to the rest of Europe, where sombre and austere-looking coaches were the order of the day, usually

Above: A preserved Ringhoffer dining car at the Swiss Transport Museum, Lucerne.

Below: A modern Italian first class coach on the TEE *Mediolanum* about to leave Munich, 1976.

finished in plain varnished wood or very subdued colours with a minimum of lining or decoration. There were eventually a few noteworthy exceptions, such as the famous Wagons-Lits blue with gold trimmings (still to be seen today) and the rather brighter colours adopted for some special services, for example the purple and cream of the *Rheingold*.

Reverting to vehicle design, the traditional European style of coach building was only slowly modified, except for size. Eventually, however, steel outer panelling replaced the traditional wood finishes, and coaches gradually evolved into their modern form with an all-metal structure and smooth-sided exteriors.

The American-style coach was very different in appearance from its European counterpart. The favourite method of covering wooden trussed framework adopted in North America was with a series of close-boarded vertical planks between and below the windows with a wider horizontal board running above. Furthermore, American railways rarely adopted the common European technique of curving the sides in below the waist-line; their coaches were almost universally flat-sided. Another point of difference was that, being of integral construction, American coaches had no separate chassis as such and this characteristically visible feature of European-style coaches was absent from American vehicles.

Although there were eventually exceptions, especially from the 1920s onwards, such as the Milwaukee Road, which painted its coaches in orange and red, the characteristic colour schemes adopted by most American railroads during the bulk of both the wooden and Pullman-standard steel eras were rather sombre, partly because of the widespread standardization on Pullman-owned or Pullman-built equipment. Pullman green (a sort of darkish olive green with brown overtones) was commonly adopted by railways to produce a matching ensemble and even where this was not chosen, dark reds and greens were normal. However, the earlier wooden coaches were almost always lavishly decorated with a considerable degree of gilt ornamentation, they were frequently elaborately lettered and named, they

Above: A first class compartment interior, German Federal Railways.

Below: Vintage Wagons-Lits dining car still in service in 1976 between Austria and Italy, seen at Verona.

displayed considerable variety and artistry in window, door and verandah ornamentation, and they were, almost without exception, highly varnished. They looked, and indeed were, both dignified and opulent.

Perhaps the most characteristic feature of the American coach during its heyday was the roof shape. Most European coach builders of the mid-19th century adopted a fairly flat roof form, probably inspired more by stage coach practice than by any critical need to keep the height down to clear fixed structures on the railway. In America, however, the even larger structure gauge and the need for improved ventilation saw early widespread adoption of a high roof form with a conspicuously elevated centre section or clerestory. Fitted with ornately decorated side windows and, usually, terminated at the end of the coach by smoothly flowing downward curves, the American clerestory, sometimes also called a 'monitor' roof, was instantly recognizable. It was used throughout the wooden-body era and was retained during the all-steel Pullman-Standard period. Even during the move to air-conditioning, the structure remained a feature although often disguised from outside view. The lower side sections of the roof afforded a suitable location for air-conditioning equipment and many all-steel clerestory cars were thus modified with new sheeting over the whole roof structure giving the superficial appearance of a full-width high roof.

The other railways of the world were not slow to appreciate the virtues of the clerestory roof. It added light and air to the interior and could be made an outstanding decorative feature in its own

right. Although some railways did have structure clearance problems, many did not and they introduced the clerestory without serious difficulty. In Europe it even began to take on a character of its own. In Britain it was married to the traditional style of coach and was more commonly extended to the full length of the body, without the down-curved ends. Railways like the Great Western and the Midland found it so much to their liking that the feature became almost a company trademark, particularly on the Midland where the clerestory was so designed as to seem an integral part of the whole carriage, rather than an appendage on top. Other British systems favoured limited use of the clerestory for more important trains and for dining and sleeping cars.

However, it was on the mainland of Europe that the marriage of European and American coachbuilding styles probably achieved its finest expression and, as might be expected, Wagons-Lits played a major part. In the early part of the 20th century, there were built for this company some very elegant coaches which combined the American style of body with vertical boarding and varnish with a European-type chassis and a distinctive roof arrangement in which the clerestory was terminated slightly before the extreme end of the coach. Large windows were combined with recessed and angled end doors to produce a style which eventually became the hallmark of the great deluxe trains of Europe. Many countries adopted them and they were built throughout Europe.

Inevitably over the years, further cross-fertilization of carriage-building ideas took place world-wide. Australia, with its American-scale distances, tended to adopt American ideas for long-distance services, although remaining faithful to British concepts for its local trains. South Africa, too, followed quasi-American practice, but in other areas of British influence, quite different styles evolved. This was particularly the case in tropical regions where carriage design had to cater for quite different climatic conditions. In East Africa and India, elaborate screens, often extending from the roof nearly halfway down the body side, were fitted to the sides of basically

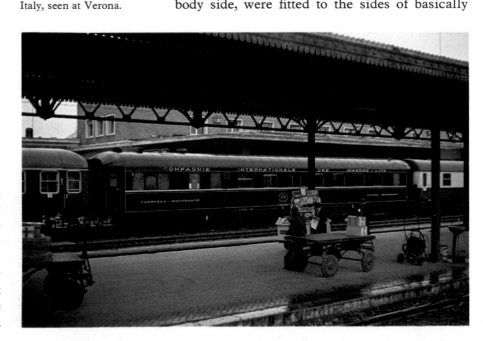

European-style coaches to shield passengers from the sun. Coaches were often given a double roof for the same purpose and pale colour schemes were commonly adopted for similar reasons.

The use of brighter colours on railway carriages is, apart from some early examples already mentioned, something of a latter-day phenomenon. In part, widespread adoption of dark colours in the early days was to offset the dirt created by the steam locomotive, but this is not the whole story. With the gradual erosion of the railway monopoly as a result of road and air competition, the railways had to rethink their publicity and it is not entirely without significance that introduction of bright, eye-catching, colour schemes together with stainless steel, dates in general from the streamline era. Led by the American examples but imitated world-wide with greater or lesser degrees of success, the train gradually took upon itself a less and less sombre hue until, today, almost any colour scheme can be witnessed.

Today, too, there are less obvious external differences between the trains of the world. Railways are not unique in this respect. With improved communications, all countries of the world are increasingly aware of developments elsewhere in all fields of human activity. The modern motor car, be it Italian, Japanese, German, British, or American is tending to become less regionally differentiated as the years go by. Interior design, furnishing ideas, town-planning methods and so on are tending to become increasingly similar and it would be surprising indeed if railways did not reflect this trend. Thus it is that as the world enters the closing decades of the 20th century, the train, as it has always done since it first came onto the scene, still represents a faithful barometer of the society it serves. Fortunately, however, it takes some time for ideas to spread globally, by which time there are new innovations to be seen, so there is still plenty of variety.

Above: A modern South African station scene with clerestory roofed coaches and refreshment trolley.

Right: High capacity non-corridor stock of the London Brighton & South Coast Railway in service around the turn of the century.

Below: A combination of the classic American style clerestory with a separate chassis on the railways of Ecuador.

Above left: A typically smooth sided modern dining car of the Swiss Sudostbahn.

Above right: The polished wood and leather interior of a Peruvian chair car/buffet.

Left: An elaborately appointed Canadian Pacific observation car in the grand style.

Below: A modern style open first class carriage of the French Railway system.

Conclusion

What of the future of the train? Honesty compels one to admit that, however pro-rail one might be, the passenger train can never again achieve the total dominance of inland transport which it once possessed. The railway itself was a product of change and, in its turn, it brought fresh changes. The railway all but exterminated its passenger-carrying competitors during the 19th century, so we should not be too surprised if, in its turn, the train itself is threatened by more modern modes of travel.

However, the train has shown far more resilience in meeting competition than did its 19th century forebears and this fact alone can permit a cautious degree of optimism. The infinite variety of uses to which the passenger train has been put during its long lifetime cannot be matched by any other transport alternative. Whether it be moving thousands of people to work in a crowded metropolitan area, conveying businessmen at high speed in great comfort, acting as an essential lifeline both in remote districts and developing countries, or providing a more relaxed alternative to the motor car, the train still has its place. The use of a fixed track has disadvantages in terms of total flexibility but it is now widely accepted that the railway causes less environmental disturbance and is more economical of energy than most of its competitors – possibly important points in its favour in the future.

On balance it seems likely that, as has already happened in the industrial world, so too eventually in the developing world, the passenger railway will tend to concentrate on those tasks which it can best fulfil. When there is no alternative, the train has to serve all purposes, some of which it is manifestly less able to perform than its competitors. However, the experience of the North Americans tends to suggest that the process of rationalization can go too far. One must hope therefore that those countries which still have passenger railways will assess the problem rather more carefully than has been the case with some of the older-established systems. The indications are that they probably will.

LOCOMOTIVE DEVELOPMENT

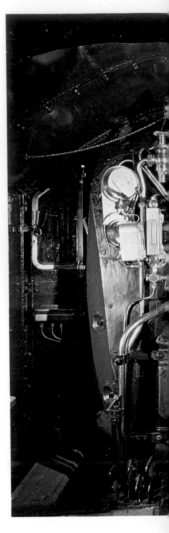

Above: Interior of the cab of *Caerphilly Castle*, a four cylinder simple 4–6–0 of the Great Western Railway, built in 1923 and now preserved in the Science Museum, London.

THE STEAM LOCOMOTIVE

Though steam locomotives have varied enormously in size, detail of design and construction, all orthodox ones have been variations on a basic pattern which took shape with the *Rocket* in 1829. The frames of the locomotive rest upon the axleboxes or bearing blocks, of the wheels, with springing provided by laminated plate or coiled springs of steel. The frames have slots in which the axleboxes can move vertically, called 'horns' or 'pedestals', and the springs of different axles may be connected by pivoted levers to 'equalize' the suspension. All locomotives have relatively large wheels, between about 1,219 mm (4 ft) and 2,133 mm (7 ft) in diameter on standard gauge, driven by the cylinders via connecting rods, wheel pairs being connected together by coupling rods. These wheels are fitted directly in the frames and provide the rigid wheelbase (small sideplay is sometimes allowed for). Most locomotives have additional carrying wheels of smaller diameter, which are not driven, and, if the locomotive has more than six wheels, carrying wheels are arranged in a subframe providing considerable sideways movement on curves. Two-wheel subframes are arranged to swing sideways with a radial movement, with a real or theoretical pivot nearer the centre of the locomotive. A four-wheel subframe, or bogie, can rotate about an approximately central pivot and is also provided with sideplay. These subframes are arranged with centring springs, or an equivalent device, to bring the locomotive to a central position over the track at the end of a curve, and to cushion the shock of entry into a curve so that this is not wholly borne by the leading wheels of the rigid wheelbase. All carrying wheels assist in bearing the weight of the locomotive through springs.

Most locomotives have two double-acting cylinders, which drive one pair of wheels directly, and others of the same diameter indirectly by coupling rods. The two cylinders may be outside, which means that their connecting rods work upon crank pins set in the wheel bosses, or they may be inside, in which case the driving wheels are mounted upon a cranked axle. The drive is horizontal or nearly so, so that the thrust is taken on the horns and does not disturb the springs. Locomotives with three or four cylinders have two outside, and one or two inside. In such cases the drive may be concentrated on one wheel pair or divided, with the inside cylinders driving a crank axle the wheels of which are coupled to those driven by the outside cylinders.

In the cylinders, steam is admitted to and exhausted from each side of the pistons in turn, by valves controlled by the valve gear. The valves may be flat 'slide' valves, working on a flat portface, or cylindrical 'piston' valves working within a cylindrical portface. Both these types of valve reciprocate at the same rate as the piston, though with a smaller travel. Poppet valves rising and falling upon seatings, usually four per cylinder, are sometimes found in modern locomotives. The valve gear makes it possible to change the valve timing for reversing, and also for early cut-off of the steam supply, to allow it to do work in the cylinder by expansion, which is essential for economical working. Each cylinder has a 'steam chest' within which the valves work.

The boiler has a horizontal barrel, and is supported upon the frame. At the rear end is the firebox, which is within the boiler, surrounded by water walls, with a grate at the bottom and an ashpan provided with air inlets and dampers below. The firing hole, in the boiler back, is covered by a firedoor. The front upper part of the firebox is a tubeplate, from which some 200 tubes lead the fire forward through the barrel to the smokebox. Between the fire itself, on the grate, and the tubeplate, the firebox is divided by a brick arch extending about two thirds of the way to the back of the box, and sloping gently upwards. The fire has to pass round this to reach the tubeplate, and this equalizes the draught in the tubes, improves combustion by turbulence, provides for mixing in of extra air from the firehole, and takes the flames close to the walls of the box. The waterwalls of the firebox are prevented from bursting under pressure by a large number of stays joining the inner and outer plates.

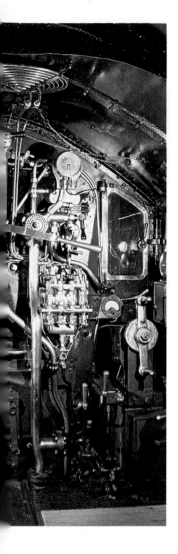

In the smokebox, the exhaust (or blast) pipe stands upright below the chimney, and each blast of exhaust produces a partial vacuum which draws the fire through the boiler. There is also a 'blower', usually a ring of fine steam jets surrounding the blastpipe, which can be used to draw the fire when the engine is standing, or running with steam off.

In a superheated locomotive, steam from the boiler is passed through a number of small tubes lying within extra large boiler firetubes known as superheater flues. The steam reaches the cylinders at a higher temperature than possible within the boiler at its correct working pressure, and this results in important economies in fuel and water. Locomotives without superheaters use 'saturated' steam.

The controls of a steam locomotive are the main steam valve, or regulator (throttle), the valve gear control, and the brake. In addition there are boiler fittings, such as live and exhaust steam injectors, or a feed pump, for maintaining the water level; water level gauges; the blower; safety valves and other valves used in connection with boiler cleaning. Pressure gauges are provided for boiler pressure and sometimes for steam chest pressure. They are also needed for the brakes and the steam heating apparatus for the train, if fitted. Lubricators are fitted at various parts of the locomotive, and those for the cylinders are sometimes in the cab, under the driver's eye. The brakes may be steam, air or vacuum operated, or a combination. Steam brakes are only applied to the wheels of the locomotive, but air or vaccum may be used in the train as well. The brakes are cast iron (in early days, wood) blocks pressed against the wheel treads.

Tank locomotives carry supplies of fuel and water on the main frame. Other locomotives have separate tenders coupled more or less permanently to them carrying larger supplies to give them a longer range or a longer period of continuous working.

The steam locomotive is unlike any other machine in one remarkable respect. Its various elements all interact, rather as they do in the body of an animal. The performance of the engine affects that of the boiler, via the action of the blast; with the result that the same boiler will perform differently when mounted on a chassis of different design. The engine part directly affects the behaviour of the locomotive as a vehicle on the track; and behaviour on the track has an influence on performance of the boiler, by the degree of disturbance produced to the fire. It is impossible, therefore, to determine the performance of the various elements by testing them separately. This interaction makes locomotives more powerful when running on the track than when running on rollers in a testing plant. In a diesel electric locomotive, the diesel engine, generator, and traction motors can all be tested independently. Their performance is not affected by their combination in a moving vehicle.

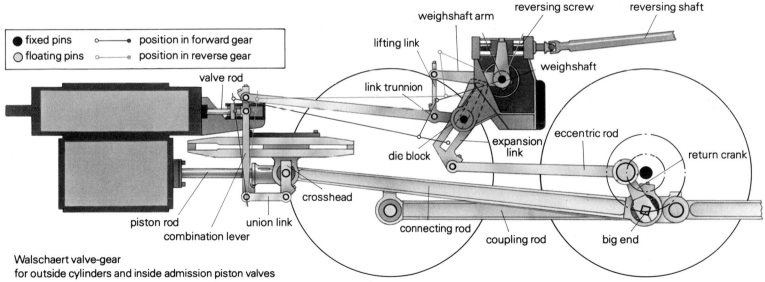

Walschaert valve-gear
for outside cylinders and inside admission piston valves

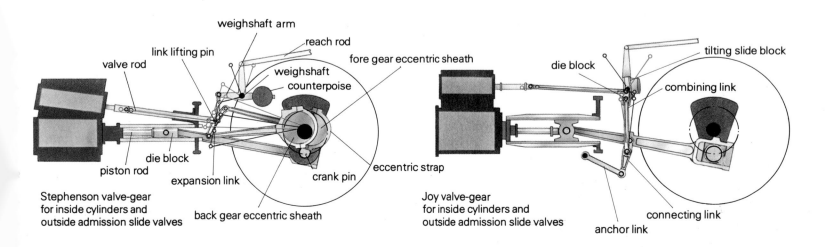

Stephenson valve-gear
for inside cylinders and
outside admission slide valves

Joy valve-gear
for inside cylinders and
outside admission slide valves

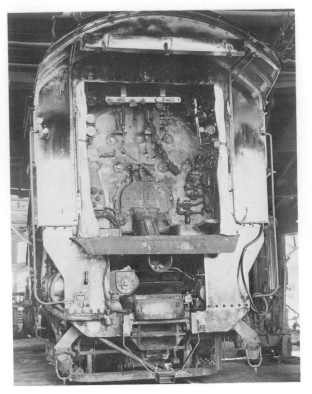

Far left and left: Mechanical stoker on an American locomotive. The screw conveyor on this tender (left) has a universally-jointed extension which works in the sloping tube rising to the firedoor (right).

Right: Trevithick's locomotive *Catch me who can* giving rides on its circular display track in north London 1808.

Far right: *Puffing Billy* of 1813, is the oldest steam locomotive in existence.

Some of the many important details of the steam locomotive should be briefly described. The two most important types of valve gear are Stephenson's link motion and Walschaert's valve gear. In the link motion, much the more common before 1900, each valve is controlled by two eccentrics whose movements are combined by a slotted link, from a point on which the drive to the valve is taken. By moving the link relative to the die block (which actually takes the movement to the valve), forward or reverse running is possible according to which eccentric is most influential. Intermediate positions give advanced timing and reduced valve travel to bring about earlier 'cut off' and more economical working at speed. Walschaerts valve gear, a Belgian invention, uses one eccentric (or, if outside, an equivalent 'return crank') which oscillates a centrally pivoted slotted link, from either end of which the drive to the valve can be taken. This drive is combined with a movement derived from the piston, to provide a constant advance of the timing independent of the shortening of the valve travel at the link, necessary for early 'cut off'.

Feeding of water into the boiler is usually continuous. Originally done by axle-driven pumps, it was later most commonly achieved by injectors, either using live steam from the boiler or exhaust steam extracted from the blast pipe. The injector is a system of cones through which steam and water pass in a continuous stream. It was invented by Henri Giffard in 1859 and has been greatly developed subsequently. Its operating principle is a matter of advanced physical science and cannot be briefly summarised. It involves conversion of the latent heat of steam into kinetic energy by condensation. Steam-operated feed pumps were used in recent years on most European and American locomotives, in conjunction with feed water-heaters deriving the heat from exhaust steam. Generally, these produced only marginally greater savings than exhaust steam

injectors, but they were rather more dependable.

For high-powered locomotives, hand-firing of coal is not practicable. Mechanical stokers were, therefore, adopted in America and for the largest locomotives in Europe and elsewhere. Most types were of American design. Coal was moved, usually by a screw conveyor, from the tender to a platform within the rear of the firebox, from which it was directed on to the grate by steam jets adjustable by the fireman. Oil firing, using jets of oil atomized by steam, was also common in the United States and Russia, and other countries where oil was cheap. Wood, for so long the staple diet of early American locomotives before 1880 was always hand-fired. It remains in use in a few places today as do a variety of waste materials which can be economically burnt in a locomotive firebox on industrial or agricultural railways.

The steam locomotive required vast quantities of water, delivered to its tender or tanks through large standpipes or water cranes. In Europe and especially in Britain (where, curiously, the world's longest non-stop run of nearly 400 miles was daily performed by Gresley's LNER Pacifics), water was picked up at speed by a scoop dipping into a trough between the rails. The quality of water available on various routes was a very important factor in boiler design. Water-softening plants were often necessary, and the French railways adopted a continuous water treatment system on the locomotive itself.

Early History
The first steam locomotive

produced by Richard Trevithick in 1804, and the first to pull a train successfully was his second, *Penydarran*, engine in 1804. His subsequent experiments ended with *Catch me who can*, which pulled a coach on a circular track in North London in 1808, and gave, for the first time, the opportunity of buying a railway ticket to ride behind a locomotive. As railways, using horses or steam

Above: A very early print of Blenkinsop's rack railway, 1812.

power with cable traction, were already fairly commonly found at the beginning of the 19th century, on private industrial sites, somebody was bound to produce a self-propelling steam engine for them before long. However, Trevithick had introduced the use of 'strong' steam (steam at a pressure well above that of the atmosphere – in fact, as much as four times as great). This made it possible to dispense with condensing, without which Newcomen or Watt type engines could not operate. This, in turn, made the engine lighter, as did the high pressure in itself, and opened the possibility of the self-propelling machine, which Trevithick quickly exploited.

The Penydarran locomotive proved able to haul 25 tonnes along a nine mile railway and back again without taking water on the way. It could climb the 1 in 36 gradient on the line and normally ran at 8 km/h (5 mph). It had a single, double acting, cylinder driving the wheels on one side through gearing giving a slight reduction of wheel speed. The boiler was cylindrical, with a single U shape flue having the firegrate in one end, and the chimney at the other. Trevithick found that when the exhaust (which passed through a silencer) was turned upwards in the chimney, it made the fire burn harder, and this observation was of the highest importance, because virtually every subsequent successful steam locomotive depended on this effect.

In 1812, the first commercially successful locomotives were constructed by Matthew Murray for John Blenkinsop, to work on the Middleton Railway near Leeds. Blenkinsop felt that a proper grip for traction was possible only if the rails had teeth and the locomotive had a gear-wheel engaging with them. The four locomotives originally built were the forerunners of the many rack locomotives used on mountain lines all over the world. They were also the first to have two double-acting cylinders driving cranks phased at 90 degrees to ensure positive self starting – always

the most common arrangement for steam locomotives. They could haul 100 tonnes at 5–6 km/h (3½ mph), replaced fifty horses and put 200 men out of work. The last went in 1834.

William Hedley, viewer (or manager) of the Wylam colliery on the Tyne, built *Puffing Billy* in 1813, after experiments carefully planned to establish whether a smooth wheel on a smooth rail would provide sufficient grip to enable a locomotive to haul a train on all but the severest gradients. *Puffing Billy*, with the similar *Wylam Dilly* and *Lady Mary*, were the first successful adhesion locomotives, and remained in service until 1861. They had Trevithick-type boilers, and their two cylinders drove the wheels through beams, rods, cranks, and gearing of considerable complication. Perhaps their low-operating speed (walking pace) and moderate loading (50 tonne trains) contributed to their remarkable longevity. Two are preserved in museums in Britain.

George Stephenson's first locomotive, the *Blucher*, appeared in the middle of 1814. It had vertical cylinders, set one behind the other in the boiler, their piston rods working upwards to connecting rods down each side of the engine. The final drive from the cranks to the wheels was by gearing. Though very like Blenkinsop's engines in general layout, it was an adhesion machine, and at one time had a chain drive to the front tender wheels to increase its grip. Stephenson experimented a great deal in the next ten years. In fact, almost all the work of developing the steam locomotive to a thoroughly practical machine was done by Stephenson in this period. He experimented with coupling the wheels by chains, conceived inside crank axles and inside coupling rods, and eventually adopted the outside coupling rods later standard on steam and many electric and diesel locomotives. He built perhaps a dozen locomotives and was established as the leading railway engineer by the time the Stockton & Darlington Railway was proposed.

SUPERHEATED STEAM LOCOMOTIVE
Sectioned diagram of Southern Railway (UK) 3 cylinder Schools class 4–4–0 locomotive

The source of power is the fire burning on the grate (43). Air for combustion enters the ashpan (44) through damper doors (42). Coal is fired (by hand shovel in this small locomotive) through the firedoor (23) which also admits a little warmed air. A deflector plate (21) prevents cold air entering the tubes when the door is open. The fire passes round the brick arch (16) and through the fire tubes (10) and superheater flues (9), drawn by the suction effect of exhaust steam passing from the blastpipe (3) to the chimney. If the engine is not working, steam jets from the blower ring (4) produce the suction. The firebox crown sheet (15) and other flat surfaces are tied to the boiler shell by

stays (18) and the whole boiler is lagged (11). The regulator handle (22) operates the main steam valve (12) in the dome. There is a 'steam stand' or 'fountain' (20) supplied by a collector pipe (14), from which steam is taken for auxiliaries, such as the injector (48) for feeding water to the boiler, and the vacuum brake ejectors working the locomotive brake cylinder (47) and the train brakes via the train pipe connections (1) at both ends of the locomotive. Steam is also taken for train heating via a reducing valve, to heating hose connectors (24) at both ends, and for the whistle (19). There are two safety valves (17).

When the locomotive is working, steam from the regulator valve (12) passes to the saturated or 'wet' steam header (7) of the superheater, then through numerous small pipes or 'elements' to the superheated steam header (5). In each element, the steam

water

saturated steam

superheated steam

exhaust (expanded) steam

makes four passes along the flue, the element having three 'return bends' (8, 13). A 'snifting valve' (6) on the wet steam header allows the elements to be cooled by air drawn in when the engine is coasting with the regulator valve shut.

Steam enters all three cylinders (only the middle one is shown) via two-headed piston valves (26) moved backwards and forwards by the Walschaert valve gear, which derives its motion from a single eccentric (38) and the crosshead (33), which is the junction of the piston rod (30) and the connecting rod (39) and is guided by slide bars (32). The connecting rod drives a crank (41) incorporated in the driving axle (40). The motion from the eccentric is taken forward by the eccentric rod (37) to the expansion link (36) which is pivoted in the middle. From this the radius rod (34) takes a movement variable in amount and also reversible, because its connection to the slotted link can be shifted up and down by the driver, via a lifting link and a 'weighshaft' (35). The radius rod movement is combined with that of the crosshead by a combination lever (28) connected through the union link (31). The resulting movements of the valves allow the running in either direction and for expansive working. Valve and piston rods enter steam chests and cylinders through steamtight glands (27).

The brake shoes (45) are connected to the brake cylinder (47) by beams and rods, known as brake rigging. The driving and coupled wheels are sprung with laminated plate springs (46), while the bogie has coil springs (25). In addition to pivoting at its centre, the bogie can move sideways controlled by transverse springs (29).

Deflector plates (2) at the front of the locomotive help to lift exhaust steam clear of the cab windows.

The Stockton & Darlington was a public railway, surveyed and built by Stephenson, which used steam locomotives for some of its traffic from the beginning. Its opening in 1825 is commonly regarded as the beginning of railways as a public transportation system. The locomotive *Locomotion* built by Stephenson for the opening was distinguished by the use of outside coupling rods, but was otherwise much like most of its predecessors, with rather elaborate driving gear, the cylinders being sunk in the boiler top as in the Middleton engines. It had a single flue, not doubled back. It was essentially a freight locomotive: such a boiler could not generate steam fast enough for rapid travel. Stephenson himself was, by this time, more concerned with the civil engineering of railways than with locomotives, and recommended Timothy Hackworth, who had helped to build *Puffing Billy*, for the job of looking after the Stockton & Darlington locomotives, while his own son, Robert Stephenson, took a major part in the development of locomotive building for other lines.

The *Rocket*

The *Rocket*, built by Stephenson, was the successful entry in the Rainhill trials held in 1829 prior to the opening of the Liverpool & Manchester Railway.

The *Rocket* incorporated a boiler proposed by Henry Booth, secretary of the Liverpool & Manchester company, having 25 small fire tubes instead of one large one. (At the same moment in history, Marc Séguin of the St Etienne to Lyon railway in France, was fitting a boiler with a large number of small firetubes to a locomotive of earlier Stephenson type, and, thereby, enormously increasing its steam raising capacity.) The *Rocket* had an external firebox at the rear of the boiler barrel, with water jacketed sides and top. The fire was drawn through the tubes by the action of the exhaust steam – following Trevithick – the two upturned blast nozzles in the base of the long chimney having slight constrictions to increase the intensity of the action. This feature may have been copied from Hackworth's *Sans Pareil*.

Another distinguishing feature of the *Rocket* was the direct drive from two outside cylinders onto crankpins in the wheels. All the essentials of the later steam locomotive were there, and the proportions of boiler, cylinders and wheels were notably good, so that this engine could reach

58 km/h (36 mph) in its original form, and over 80 km/h (50 mph) when the cylinders were lowered to a less steeply-inclined position.

The frames of *Rocket* consisted of a few iron bars, and the cylinders were 'outside' and inclined. These features were to become characteristic of the first successful and distinctively American type, the 4–2–0, especially as built by Norris of Philadelphia, and bar frames, in a highly developed form, were to remain standard practice in America throughout the history of the steam locomotive. Their derivation from *Rocket* may be traced through the designs of Edward Bury and his partner, Kennedy. Bury was engineer to the London & Birmingham Railway in the late 1830s and early 1840s. In 1830, he and Kennedy had built a four-wheeled coupled engine named *Liverpool*, which had a cranked axle and inside cylinders, and, therefore, a firebox overhanging at the rear. It also had bar framing. The firebox was more or less a vertical cylinder joined to the barrel at right angles. It was not wholly circular in plan, because it was flat at the front, to accommodate the firebox tubeplate. It was surmounted by a hemispherical top which acted as the steam dome – not at all an easy thing to make in those days. This was the style of almost all Bury engines, and his preference for four wheelers, coupled or not, eventually lost him his connection with the London & Birmingham, but these little machines were outstandingly good for their size. The bar framing and the boiler, with its overhanging circular firebox, were married in the Norris 4–2–0 locomotives to outside cylinders and a leading four-wheel truck.

Early American locomotives

The United States, like France, imported a few locomotives of pre-*Rocket* type from England. Like France again, they very soon started to make their own experimental types. The first was the *Best Friend of Charleston*, built by the West Point Foundry of New York for the South Carolina Railroad in 1830. Lack of manufacturing capacity caused the USA to import over 100 locomotives from Britain between 1829 and 1841.

Stephensons, having constructed a few locomotives like *Rocket*, but with more and smaller boiler tubes, enlarged the type slightly and incorporated the water-jacketed firebox within the boiler shell, producing the *Northumbrian* type. They then adopted inside cylinders, in

Far left: The remains of the *Rocket* in the Science Museum, London, showing the regulator handle and two steam pipes, the firebox tubeplate and backplate. The double-walled firebox shell has not survived.

Left: Close up of the left hand cylinder showing the drive to the slide valve and the arrangements for disengaging the valve drive and reversing the locomotive by hand, to allow the eccentrics to 'slip'.

Bar Framing and the North American Locomotive

Stephenson's *Rocket* of 1829, with bar frames and outside cylinders, set a style more closely followed in North America than in Great Britain.

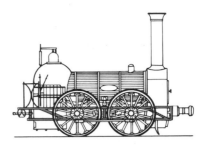

A Bury inside cylinder locomotive for the London and Birmingham Railway, 1838, with Edward Bury's typical bar framing and domed firebox copied by Norris.

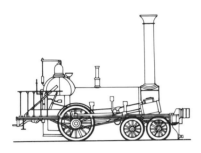

A 4-2-0 of 1839, by Norris of Philadelphia, clearly derived from the *Rocket* and Bury types, but well adapted for American conditions and successfully exported to Europe.

The addition of coupled wheels behind the firebox produced the first form of the classic American 4-4-0, which rapidly supplanted the 4-2-0 in new construction in the 1840s.

The Rogers Works were the first to lengthen the bogie wheelbase, bring the cylinders horizontal and fit the 'wagon top' boiler, so producing the later form of this wheel arrangement. This example was built by Daneforth Cooke in 1857.

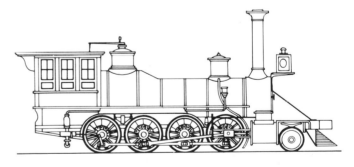

The 2-8-0 comes second only to the 4-4-0 in the history of North American motive power in the 19th century. This Leigh Valley Railroad example of 1886 was perhaps the first, and clearly derived from the 4-4-0, but profited by Levi Bissel's two wheeled truck invented in 1857.

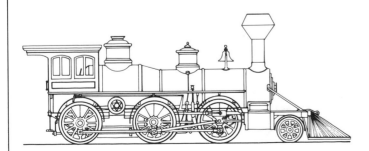

The usual type of 2-6-0 came slightly later, as a compromise type for general mixed traffic, and was never so numerous, though popular on secondary railroads. A Brooks example of 1877.

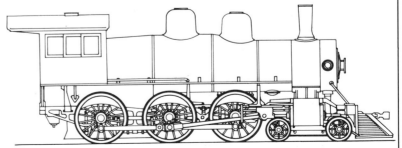

The American 4-6-0 was soon preferred for mixed traffic. This large 1900 locomotive on the Atchison Topeka and Santa Fe, shows how bar framing, compared with plate framing, permitted a wider but shallower firebox, between the wheels.

Typical superheated parallel boiler with Belpaire firebox

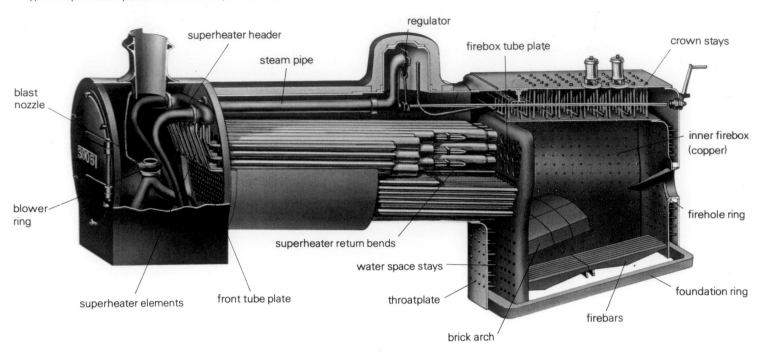

blast nozzle

blower ring

superheater header

steam pipe

regulator

firebox tube plate

crown stays

inner firebox (copper)

firehole ring

superheater elements

front tube plate

superheater return bends

water space stays

throatplate

brick arch

firebars

foundation ring

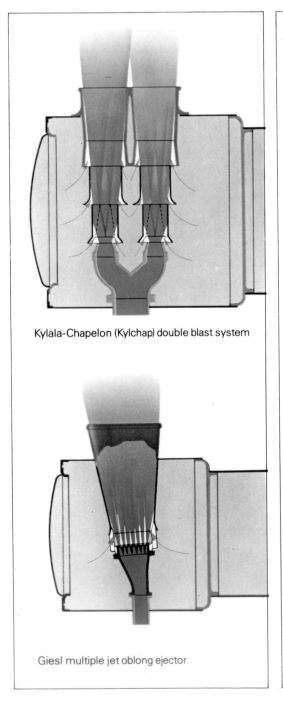

Kylala-Chapelon (Kylchap) double blast system

Giesl multiple jet oblong ejector

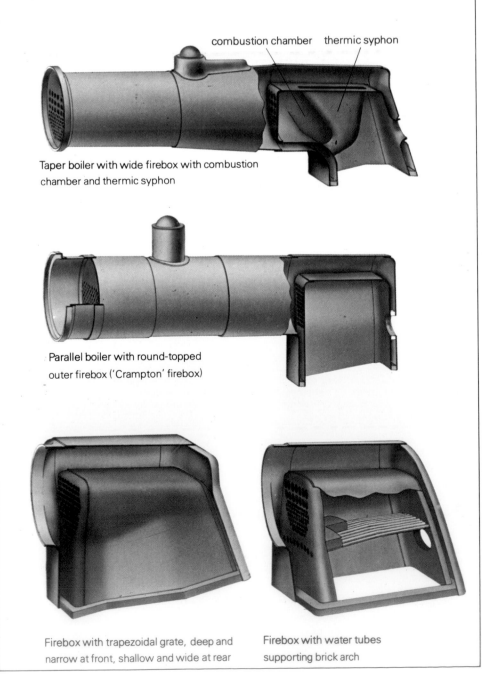

combustion chamber   thermic syphon

Taper boiler with wide firebox with combustion chamber and thermic syphon

Parallel boiler with round-topped outer firebox ('Crampton' firebox)

Firebox with trapezoidal grate, deep and narrow at front, shallow and wide at rear

Firebox with water tubes supporting brick arch

Below: Air brakes. Driver's control exhausts air from train pipe, while isolating locomotive reservoir. Triple valves on coaches respond to fall in train pipe pressure by admission of compressed air from reservoir to brake cylinder.

Bottom: Vacuum brakes. In running position, vacuum is maintained throughout the system by a small ejector or a pump. Admission of air to train pipe creates controlled pressure under the brake piston, while the ball valve preserves the vacuum above it. Brakes can be 'blown off' rapidly with the large ejector.

the bottom of the smokebox, driving onto a cranked rear axle just ahead of the firebox (the *Planet* type), and expanded this into a six wheeler by adding an extra axle behind the firebox. Four and six wheel engines of this type were exported to America, where most were eventually rebuilt. The short wheelbase engines were perfectly satisfactory on the finely engineered railways of Britain, where tracks were well aligned and supported, but they rode very badly on the light and usually irregular metals of the undercapitalized American pioneer railroads. These inside cylinder engines did not have the bar framing of *Rocket*, but a much more rigid system of plate and wood beam frames, generally six in number – outside the wheels, inside the wheels, and inside

each crank of the driving axle – to give the maximum support to the crank axle, which was liable to fracture. The rigidity of such machines proving unsuitable for American conditions, the American solution was the 4–2–0.

The first 4–2–0 was designed by John B Jervis and built at the West Point Foundry in 1832. Originally planned as an anthracite burner, and unsuccessful in that respect, it was soon altered to burn wood, and in that form it had a boiler of Stephenson type, inside cylinders in the bottom of the smokebox (which was widened to accommodate them because they were spread as wide apart as possible) driving a cranked axle at the rear of the firebox. The connecting rods passed on each side of the firebox. The front end of the

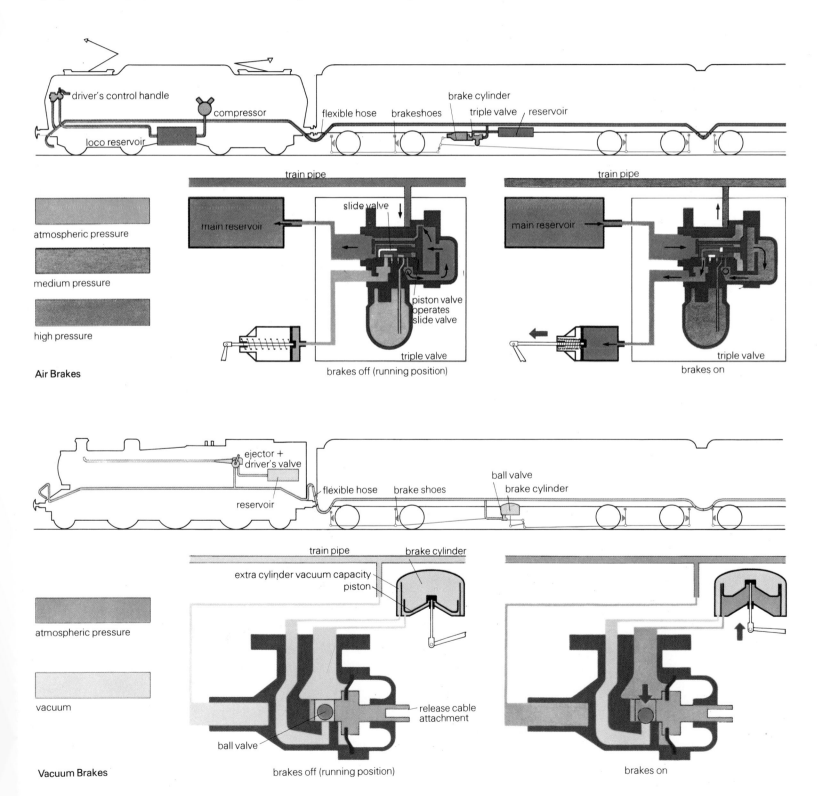

Air Brakes

atmospheric pressure

medium pressure

high pressure

train pipe · main reservoir · slide valve · piston valve operates slide valve · triple valve · brakes off (running position) · train pipe · main reservoir · triple valve · brakes on

Vacuum Brakes

atmospheric pressure

vacuum

train pipe · brake cylinder · extra cylinder vacuum capacity · piston · ball valve · release cable attachment · brakes off (running position) · brakes on

Baldwin Locomotive Works.

BURNHAM, PARRY, WILLIAMS & CO.,
PHILADELPHIA,
MANUFACTURERS OF
LOCOMOTIVE ENGINES

engine was carried on a pivoted bogie having four wheels. The long wheelbase and three-point support enabled the engine to ride steadily on twisting track, and the rotating bogie allowed it to take sharp curves easily. It was a success. Many of the imported engines were rebuilt to a similar plan. The one weakness was lack of weight on the driving wheels, and this was remedied in the classic design by bringing the driving axle ahead of the firebox, but, as the cylinders were outside, the driving axle did not need to be far forward to provide clearance for the cranks and big ends in front of the firebox.

The 4–2–0 type was an excellent machine of robust and simple construction, and was soon being exported to Europe. The reign of this wheel arrangement was short. These engines weighed between 7 and 10 tonnes, which soon proved insufficient. Around the year 1840, two thirds of all locomotives in America were 4–2–0s: a couple of years later they ceased to be built, having given way to the 4–4–0. The first American 4–4–0, by Henry Campbell of the Philadelphia, Germanstown & Norristown Railway, was completed in 1837. It was nothing more or less than a Stephen-son Patentee type 2–2–2, but with the rear axle coupled to the driving axle and a four-wheel swivelling truck in place of the leading axle. While it enjoyed the advantage of extra weight on the drivers, it was still almost as rigid as the English engines and was apt to derail. The true American 4–4–0 appeared in the next two years, and was essentially the 4–2–0 with a second coupled axle behind the firebox. The suspension of the four driving wheels was equalized – a vital feature for American tracks – due to the work of Eastwick and Harrison though its origins were in England. This preserved the three point support of the 4–2–0s. The leading coupled wheels were without flanges, because the bogies could only rotate and had no side play.

These early 4–4–0s mostly had Bury or Stephenson type boilers, inclined cylinders, and short wheelbase bogies. They were very lightly built, weighing between 15 and 25 tonnes, but the suspension and perhaps the none-too-smooth surfaces of the iron rails and tyres enabled them to pull very heavy loads at low speeds. The early ones were known to pull 400 tonne freight trains at 16 km/h (10 mph) or thereabouts, as well as light passenger trains at 30 to 50 km/h (20 to 30 mph). This versatility ensured a very long life of the 4–4–0 type in America, and it undoubtedly remained numerically predominant throughout the 19th century, though progressively superseded for freight work from about 1870. Around 1850, the type changed considerably in appearance. The cylinders came down to a horizontal position, and the bogie in consequence was greatly lengthened, while the boiler barrel became sharply tapered at the rear to fit a greatly enlarged or 'wagon top' firebox.

Stephensons' *Patentee* and long boiler designs
The Stephenson *Planet* type and its 2–2–2 derivative, the *Patentee*, were enormously influential in Britain. Locomotives with framing outside as well as inside the wheels continued to be built for

Top left: American locomotive manufacturer's advertisement of 1877.

Top right: The first railroad out of San Francisco opened in 1864 with a secondhand Baldwin 4-4-0 of the 1850s. The enormous spark-arresting chimney proclaims the engine to be a woodburner, like almost all American engines of the period.

Below: The *Best Friend of Charleston*, the first American-built steam locomotive, came from the West Point Foundry, New York, in 1830, for the South Carolina Railroad.

Left: Great Western 2,134 mm (7 ft) gauge 2-4-0 of 1865, essentially a standard gauge engine but with the wheels outside the outer framing.

Below far right: Stephenson's *Patentee* of 1837, the first of the long line of British multiple framed 2–2–2s which inaugurated so many new railways at home and abroad.

Right: *Le Maréchal de Saxe* was a Stephenson long boiler type 2-2-2 built in Paris in 1847 for the Paris-Strasbourg Railway (later Est). The raised crown and deep grate of the overhanging firebox are clearly visible. A very early photograph.

something like 70 years, and even longer on the Great Western. In the middle of the 19th century, 2–2–2s of *Patentee* type, built by British or Continental builders, were found all over Europe.

The double framed, six-wheel engine was not only built as a 2–2–2. Coupling the last pair of axles produced the 2–4–0, originally built for freight work, but later very popular as an express engine. The 0–4–2 was an alternative for slow service, and the 0–6–0 was soon preferred for the heaviest freight. All these types were really the same, with cylinders under the smokebox driving onto a central cranked axle, the motion work occupying the space between the frames in the front half, while the space between the second and third axles was occupied by the firebox.

Perhaps the greatest exponent of this type of machine was Matthew Kirtley of the Midland Railway, who steadily developed it from the mid-1840s to the 1870s. In this period the quality of iron improved, and, in the end, steel began to be available, both for the locomotive and for the track. Kirtley's designs were subtly improved to exploit the better materials, and in his last express 2–4–0s he finally dispensed with the outside frames: he felt that the crank axle was at last wholly dependable. To Kirtley also must go the credit for the simplest provision for burning coal instead of coke as previously preferred, in locomotive fireboxes. Under his direction, Charles Markham evolved the brick arch in the firebox, and the extra supply of air via the fireman's door (additional to that coming through the grate) which were copied universally.

The double-frame 2–4–0 was provided with a leading bogie in a few cases, though the general popularity of the 4–4–0 in Britain came after the heyday of double framing, at a time when engineering materials made it unnecessary. Large numbers of such 4–4–0s were exported to Holland, and were excellent machines which lasted till the end of steam, and Holland even saw the ultimate extension of the type into a 4–4–2. The Great Western Railway prolonged the type as a result of the broad gauge of 2,133 mm (7 ft) which Brunel had adopted and which lasted into the 1890s. For this gauge, Stephensons had built a large *Patentee* named *North Star*, the best of the early GWR engines. When Daniel Gooch took charge of the locomotive affairs he built a class of enlarged *North Stars*, and then, from 1847, produced a very remarkable 4–2–2 version.

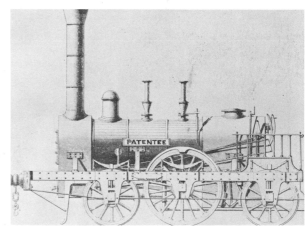

Wheel Notation Systems

Whyte system (steam locomotives)	Continental system (steam, diesel and electric locomotives)

English notation / Continental notation	front — rear	notation	front — rear
2-2-2 / 1-1-1		C	
4-2-2 / 2-1-1		1C1	
0-4-0 / 0-2-0		1Co1	
2-4-0 / 1-2-0		2C1	
4-4-0 / 2-2-0 American		2Co1	
4-4-2 / 2-2-1 Atlantic		D	
0-6-0 / 0-3-0		1Do1	
2-6-0 / 1-3-0 Mogul		1E1	
0-6-2 / 0-3-1		B-B	
2-6-2 / 1-3-1 Prairie		1B-B1	
4-6-0 / 2-3-0		1C-C1	
4-6-2 / 2-3-1 Pacific		2B-B2	
4-6-4 / 2-3-2 Baltic/Hudson		1B1-1B1	
2-8-0 / 1-4-0 Consolidation		Bo-Bo	
2-8-2 / 1-4-1 Mikado		Co-Co	
4-8-2 / 2-4-1 Mountain		A1A-A1A	
2-8-4 / 1-4-2 Berkshire		1Co-Co1	
2-10-0 / 1-5-0		Co-Bo	

The notation is derived from the numbers of wheels (axles in continental system) in each group: leading carrying wheels, driving wheels, trailing carrying wheels. A suffix 'T' is added to the notation to denote a tank engine e.g. 0-6-2T.

The notation is derived from the number of axles in each group of axles:- numbers for carrying axles, letters for driving axles: A=1, B=2, C=3 etc. Axles individually driven are suffixed 'o'.

Carrying (non-driving) wheels   Coupled driving wheel   Individually driven wheel

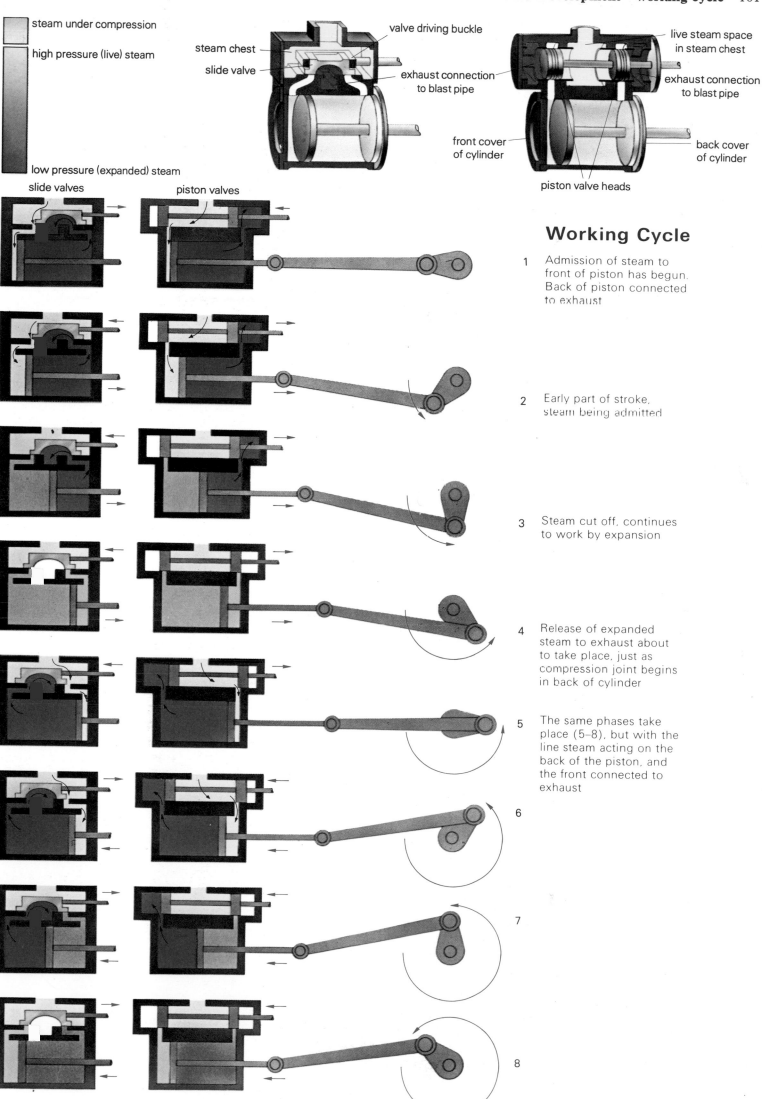

steam under compression

high pressure (live) steam

low pressure (expanded) steam

valve driving buckle

steam chest

slide valve

exhaust connection
to blast pipe

live steam space
in steam chest

exhaust connection
to blast pipe

front cover
of cylinder

back cover
of cylinder

piston valve heads

slide valves

piston valves

Working Cycle

1 Admission of steam to
front of piston has begun.
Back of piston connected
to exhaust

2 Early part of stroke,
steam being admitted

3 Steam cut off, continues
to work by expansion

4 Release of expanded
steam to exhaust about
to take place, just as
compression joint begins
in back of cylinder

5 The same phases take
place (5–8), but with the
line steam acting on the
back of the piston, and
the front connected to
exhaust

6

7

8

In 1841 the Stephenson Company patented its 'long boiler' locomotive. Although the name only refers to the boiler, this type was totally different from their previous productions in other important ways. The long boiler barrel lay above all three axles, with the firebox overhanging at the rear as in Bury's locomotives and the Norris 4–2–0. The smokebox was well forward at the front, in line with the cylinders which were outside and drove onto the central wheels. Although some were built with inside cylinders, the true long boiler type was not, and in the absence of a crank axle inside plate frames sufficed.

The reason for this design was to absorb more of the heat of the fire in the long fire tubes. The short-barreled *Patentee* type, when worked hard, was known to throw flames from the chimney, and often ran with the lower part of the smokebox front red hot. The short wheelbase and the large overhang of the weighty firebox at one end, and the cylinders at the other, made this design unstable at speed, and as a 2–2–2 it enjoyed a very short vogue. But as a six-coupled freight engine it became immensely popular on the continent of Europe. Usually known as the 'Bourbonnais' type, because of its particular early association with one route in France, it proved the ideal freight engine of the mid-19th century, and many lasted till the end of steam because they were able to negotiate sharp curves in factory or dockland goods yards. In Britain, the long wheelbase 0–6–0 was preferred.

There were two notable Continental derivatives of the six-wheel long boiler locomotive. One was the equivalent 0–8–0, of which the first example was the *Wien Raab* built at Vienna by John Haswell, one of the most distinguished of the British expatriate engineers who developed railway systems overseas, exhibited in 1855 and bought by the French Midi Railway. This was the prototype of the classic European heavy freight loco. Another was the long boiler 2–4–0, which was especially popular in France, and as speeds increased evolved into a 2–4–2. Many French 2–4–2s were large and powerful machines, and the type was the mainstay of the express services of the Paris, Lyon & Méditerranée, and of the Paris-Orléans railways for many years.

The finest were undoubtedly the PO engines designed by Victor Forquenot, some of which were still working light fast trains in the early

1950s, when around 80 years old. Their outside cylinders had slide valves on top, worked by external Gooch link motion, which gave unusually regular and precise valve timing. Some of these engines were rebuilt as two cylinder compound 4–4–2s, involving provision of a leading bogie, and the long boiler concept must be considered as underlying the development of the 4–4–2 or 'Atlantic' type, which appeared in Europe, with a narrow firebox, at about the time of its emergence in America in the middle 1890s.

Another British development of the locomotive which achieved greater success on the Continent than in Britain was T R Crampton's high-speed design, in which the large driving wheels were placed at the rear, their high axle being behind the boiler backplate. Unlike the original Jervis 4–2–0, it had cylinders outside, and valve gearing worked by eccentrics mounted on the crankpins. The front of the engine was carried on four, or in a few cases six, smaller wheels and the whole wheelbase was rigid. The idea was that in this arrangement the boiler could be placed very low down, to the benefit of stability. The weakness of the design was the small proportion of total engine weight that could be borne by the driving wheels.

Left: The typical European long boiler 0-6-0 goods engine; Eastern Railway of France. Some worked for nearly a century.

Below: A Crampton of the Eastern Railway of France, photographed circa 1900.

The Long Boiler Locomotive and its Development

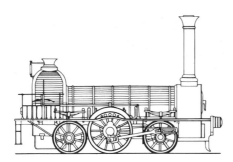

The original 2-2-2 layout, as built in the 1840s by the Stephensons and European builders, for passenger service. The overhang at both ends caused instability.

The slightly later 2-4-0 mixed traffic version, which was more successful because it operated at lower speeds. This one was built at Hanover in 1848.

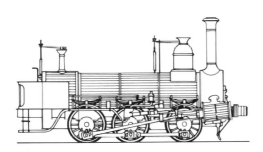

A long boiler 0-6-0 goods engine, built in 1849 to the design of E Flachat for the Paris-St Germain Railway. The type later received a pair of trailing carrying wheels.

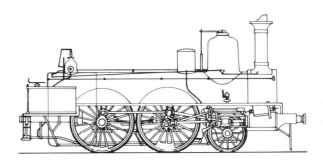

2-4-0 express locomotive designed by V Forquenot for the Paris-Orléans Railway in 1864. Later examples had a trailing carrying axle and were outstandingly successful and long lived.

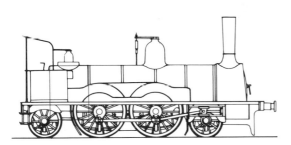

The 2-4-2 derivative of the long boiler locomotive was long favoured in France, but apparently first appeared in this locomotive built by the Stephensons for the Grand Luxembourg Railway in 1860, to the design of Robert Sinclair.

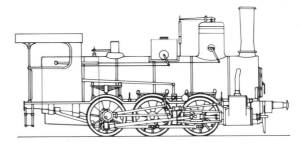

One of the most successful long boiler 0-6-0s was this, designed by Gölsdorf senior for mountainous routes in Austria, in 1874. Drive to the middle coupled axle was more common.

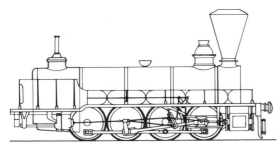

The first long boiler 0-8-0, the *Wien Raab*, designed by J Haswell and built in 1855 at the Vienna railway workshops. The prototype of a long line of European goods locomotives, it was bought by the French Midi Railway.

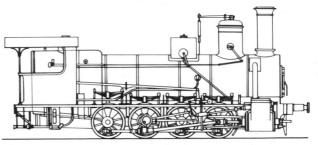

The large Austrian 0-8-0, built from 1870 onwards, was an example of the highly successful European heavy goods type which derived from the *Wien Raab* and was found in many countries until recently.

By the 1870s, the essential features of American locomotive design had long been stabilized along the lines described above. On the continent of Europe, there was some following of British patterns, but for the most part, outside cylinders and inside frames were preferred. The French favoured the long boiler pattern and its derivatives. The Germans made great use of the 2–4–0 for passenger service, in a layout combining outside cylinders overhanging the front wheels and a long coupled wheelbase embracing the firebox.

In Britain, inside cylinders were almost the rule. Two of the greatest designers, William Adams and Patrick Stirling, did persist with the use of outside cylinders for the largest locomotives until they both retired in the middle 1890s. Their locomotives, moreover, were probably the best in the country, and Adams especially can now be seen as a truly progressive designer. The earlier tradition of Crewe design was due to W Buddicom, who later worked in France, and involved the use of outside cylinders fixed between the plate frames in which the driving axles were located, and outer plate frames carrying the axleboxes of the small leading wheels. Later Crewe-built 2–2–2 express engines with outside cylinders, Ramsbottom's *Lady of the Lake* or *Problem* class, had single inside frames, but Crewe abandoned outside cylinders, except for the long series of Webb compound locomotives, after Webb succeeded Ramsbottom in 1871.

Between the complete multiple frame arrangement, as exemplified in Kirtley's Midland Railway engines, and the single inside frame arrangement, there were various mixtures of style. The most important style was one in which driving wheels were located in inside frames, and carrying wheels in outside frames. Though originated by one John Gray, this style was first notably used by David Joy in the *Jenny Lind* 2–2–2s, built by E B Wilson of Leeds and supplied first to the London, Brighton & South Coast Railway, and subsequently to many others. The four carrying wheels having the axleboxes outside made the engines very stable while the inside axleboxes of the driving wheels ensured good compliance with variations in track levels. A high centre of gravity could safely be allowed such engines. The type remained popular because there was scope for fitting quite large boilers.

Probably the finest development of the type was

Above: J Ramsbottom's Problem class 2–2–2s on the London and North Western dated from 1859.

Right: Sir Daniel Gooch's broad gauge 4–2–2s first appeared on the Great Western in 1847.

Below: Matthew Kirtley of the Midland, designed the beautiful 800 class 2–4–0s.

Bottom: One of the last of the beautiful and efficient '8-foot single' 4–2–2s.

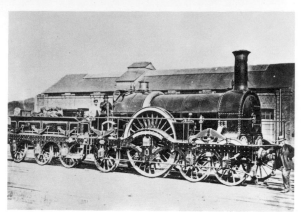

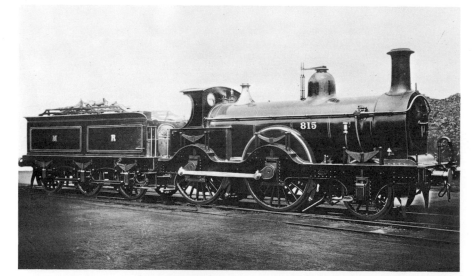

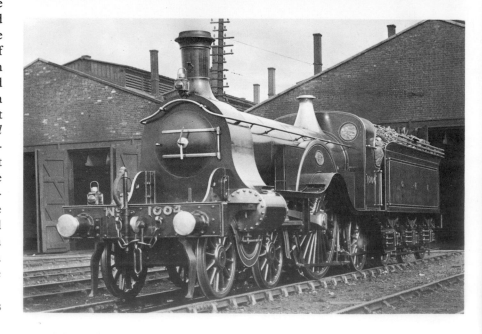

to be seen in Patrick Stirling's Great Northern 2–2–2s with 2,286 mm (7 ft 6 in) driving wheels, which were virtually as fast and powerful as his better known 2,438 mm (8 ft) wheel outside cylinder 4–2–2s. Also with 'mixed' frame arrangement were most of the larger 2–4–0 locomotives built well into the 1890s including Kirtley's last Midland engines, many Great Western standard gauge ones, the Fletcher and Tennant 2–4–0s of the North Eastern, the Great Eastern 2,133 mm (7 ft) and 1,727 mm (5 ft 8 in) driving wheel engines and many others.

Inside frames and the evolution of the British 4–4–0

In the first years of the 20th century, every major British railway was working express trains with inside cylinder, inside-framed 4–4–0s – except the Great Western, where the 4–4–0s had double frames, and the Great Northern, which used 4–4–0s for less important trains and preferred 4–4–2s for heavy trains and Stirling's 'single drivers' for the lighter ones. The universal goods and mixed traffic engine was the 0–6–0, again with inside frames and cylinders. Indeed this type was certainly the largest numerically, and probably earned more revenue than any in the whole history of steam traction in Britain – 0–6–0s were built new till 1940.

In addition to these two versions of the standard British layout, in which a cranked axle lies in the middle of the engine, with the cylinders and motion work ahead of it, and the firebox behind, there were essentially similar 4–4–2, 0–6–2, 0–6–0, 2–4–2, and 0–4–4 tank engines; and 2–2–2, 2–4–0, 0–4–2, and 4–2–2 tender engines; all these types with the characteristic short boiler barrel and, usually, deep firebox. In such a great range of types, built over so long a period, it is difficult to select examples for special mention, or to present a clear story of development, but there is one continuing line which may be judged to be the most important and which, perhaps, produced the finest examples of this basic type, and this line starts with William Stroudley.

Stroudley began his career with the Highland Railway, where his sole but significant innova-

tion was a very small 0–6–0 tank in which the pattern was established. Moving to the London, Brighton & South Coast Railway, he slightly enlarged this machine and produced the well known 'Terrier' in 1872. He also built 0–6–0 goods engines, 0–4–2 mixed traffic engines, and 0–4–2 and 2–2–2 express engines. His mantle fell in effect on the shoulders of Dugald Drummond, who followed him from the Highland to be works manager at Brighton, and who later became locomotive engineer of the North British, where he produced enlarged versions of some Stroudley designs, and also encountered the 4–4–0 engines of Thomas Wheatley – these engines were the first, rather primitive inside-framed inside-cylinder 4–4–0s in Britain.

Above: The outside cylinder 2–4–0 was very common in continental Europe from the 1850s. This German example was built in 1868.

Below: Holland favoured this large example of a typically British type. 175 of them were built in Manchester between 1880 and 1895, and were followed by 125 similar 4–4–0s.

Below right: Varieties of 4–4–0: British (GER) 1900; American c. 1860; French c. 1890 (derived from the Crampton type and with Brotan boiler); and a Prussian two cylinder compound of the mid-1890s.

Typical British Inside Cylinder, Inside Frame Locomotives

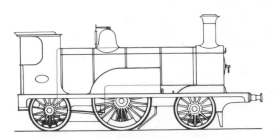

William Stroudley's Brighton Railway 2-2-2 of 1881 shows the deep narrow firebox and the neat outline resulting from the use of inside plate frames only, once suitable iron and steel were available.

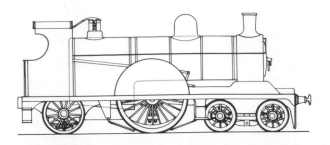

A much enlarged version with a leading bogie, typical of the late 'single wheelers' made possible by steam sanding: H Pollitt's Great Central 4-2-2 design of 1889. These were later superheated.

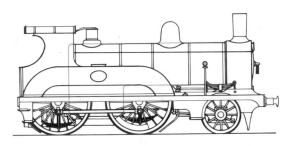

Great Eastern Railway 2-4-0 express engine of 1882. Coupled engines were only suitable for fast running after steel rails and steel tyres reduced tyre wear and track irregularity.

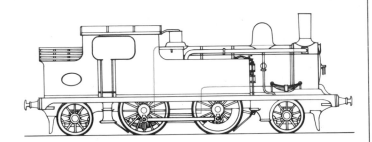

The Great Eastern suburban tank locomotive of 1884 was much like the 2-4-0 but with smaller wheels and lighter boiler. Both types were designed by T W Worsdell.

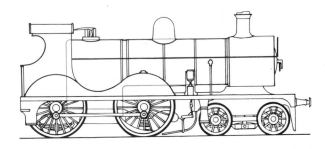

A leading bogie, for fast running and to take extra weight, resulted in the commonest and most elegant British passenger type, the 4-4-0. This is H Wainwright's class E, for the South Eastern & Chatham, of 1908.

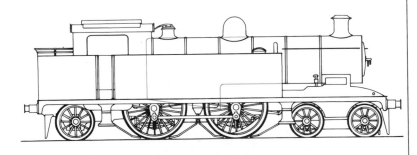

The large express tank locomotive of the London, Brighton & South Coast class I 3 was designed by D E Marsh. In 1910, this was the first British passenger locomotive to demonstrate convincingly the advantages of superheating.

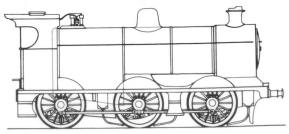

Henry Fowler's superheated Midland Railway goods locomotive of 1911 was built for 30 years in over 700 examples, mostly for the London Midland & Scottish Railway.

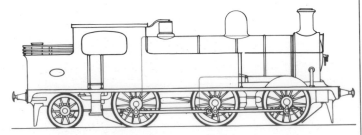

This Furness Railway 0-6-2 tank of 1905 is typical of thousands of saturated steam goods tank locomotives used in the last 100 years of steam. They were also used for passenger work, and later 0-6-2Ts were superheated.

Above: A shed scene of 50 years ago, with a Great Northern 4-4-0 under the smoke cowl, and an 0-6-0 goods to the right

Below: Probably the best British express engines of the 1880s and 1890s were the London & South Western 4-4-0s designed by William Adams.

After Drummond, Lambie and then J F McIntosh developed the Caledonian 4-4-0 into a truly formidable machine for its size, McIntosh, in particular, paying attention to the design of the boiler to enlarge the passage for the gases through the tube bank and eventually adding a superheater. The succession of McIntosh's Dunalastair classes, from the first to the fourth and finally superheated, provided as fine a 4-4-0 as any of the inside cylinder type.

Drummond joined the London & South Western Railway in 1895. He brought what by then might be regarded as the Scottish tradition with him, and built excellent locomotives until he attempted ten-wheelers. His design innovations were failures, and, in this, he was not alone: the challenge of the ten wheeler defeated many British designers at this time. Only two designers built large numbers of 4-4-0s to a wholly different pattern: David Jones of the Highland, who perpetuated the old Crewe type of framing in a long series of passenger locomotives of undoubted effectiveness and Adams, who started with 4-4-0 tanks on the North London, and, after a spell on the Great Eastern, produced a long and distinguished series of locomotives for the London & South Western.

Adams was one of the greatest of 19th century locomotive engineers, it was with the ideas of Adams, rather than those of Stroudley or Drummond, that the future of the steam locomotive lay. On the North London he found some 4-4-0 tanks with inside cylinders and equalized coupled-wheel suspension, and this experience led him to produce the first bogie with sideways movement. He soon added side control springs, at first of rubber and later of steel, and so created the locomotive bogie in its definitive form.

Next he adopted outside cylinders provided with unusually large capacity steam chests, well designed passages and large valves. The absence of a crank axle made possible some enlargement of the grate without lengthening the wheelbase. He standardized equalized suspension for all his subsequent 4-4-0s, giving them the three point support which had proved so important in North America, but with the refinement of the Adams bogie. Plate frames, as in all British 4-4-0s, permitted the usual deep firebox and he paid particular attention to draughting by providing an annular blastpipe arranged so that the hollow centre of the exhaust steam cone drew on the lower tubes of the boiler. This equalization of the draught over the tube bank was of particular importance, because most contemporary locomotives drew mainly on the upper tubes, with the result that the lower tubes were rapidly blocked with ash and steaming of the boiler was impaired. The annular blastpipe was the only effective improvement on the plain version before the introduction of double chimneys, but was more copied abroad than in Britain.

This development took place in the 1860s and 1870s, and Adams went on enlarging his 4-4-0 until his retirement in 1895, by which time his locomotives were certainly the best in England.

Early compound locomotives

In the whole history of the steam locomotive, only two major variations from the *Rocket* concept have been of lasting importance. One is the articulated locomotive and the other is compound expansion, in which the steam is used in a high-pressure cylinder first and then further expanded in a low-pressure cylinder of greater volume. There have been many types of articulated locomotive, but only two have been of worldwide importance, and of those two one was built in far greater numbers than the other. This was the type evolved by Anatole Mallet, originally as a compound design, in 1885. Anatole Mallet was also the first to build a practical compound locomotive of any sort, and his first was a small 0–4–2 tank engine for the Bayonne-Biarritz Railway in southern France. It first ran in 1877.

This first engine was a two-cylinder compound, and to ensure self starting, had to be worked as a simple expansion engine for the first few revolutions of the driving wheels. This was achieved by admitting boiler steam to the intermediate 'receiver' – in communication with the low pressure steam chest – at a reduced pressure, while the high-pressure cylinder exhaust was diverted directly to the blast pipe. More complicated starting devices were contrived by other engineers, but this was all that was needed.

The two cylinder compound possessed some advantages over the two-cylinder simple expansion locomotive, but one especially received attention – more economical use of fuel and water. It soon became popular on many European railways. The very large Prussian system, under the technical guidance of August von Borries, built over 6,000 saturated steam locomotives of this kind, in sizes varying from the small 2–4–0 to the 0–8–0 freight locomotive. Other countries followed suit and in England the North Eastern built many 0–6–0 goods, 0–6–2 tank, and 4–4–0 and 4–2–2 passenger engines, which did very well.

It should be recorded that one of the large compound 4–2–2 engines produced over 1,000 horsepower at 138.4 km/h (86 mph) when hauling a load of 270 tonnes inclusive of the tender. For a 40-tonne locomotive in the year 1890, this was outstanding. In later years, two-cylinder compounds were built with engine weights to about 90 tons. The large ones were mostly in North and South America: there were saturated 4–6–2s in the United States before 1900, superheated 2–8–2s and 4–8–4 tanks in Argentina, and, in fact, the two-cylinder compound was common in much of Latin America. In Europe its most permanent footing was in the east, notably in the many designs of the great Karl Gölsdorf for railways of the Austro-Hungarian empire, many of which remained at work until very recently.

The enlargement of the type was of course limited by the size to which a single low-pressure cylinder could be allowed to grow. It is also significant that, because of the emphasis on the economical advantage of the compound, it was considered worthwhile by the two European designers whose simple engines were already outstandingly efficient – William Adams in England and Victor Forquenot in France – both of whom converted individual locomotives to the compound system with inconclusive results.

Three-cylinder compounds were never very numerous. In England, F W Webb (one of the most eminent of engineers on the largest and most influential English railway) tried for 20 years to build good compound locomotives with very little success. His three-cylinder system involved two outside high-pressure cylinders of small diameter and one inside low-pressure cylinder of very large diameter. The logic of this lay in the restricted width of LNWR locomotives, affecting the outside cylinders, and the greater ease of accommodating adequate bearings for a single-crank rather than a double-crank axle.

Most three-cylinder compounds had the obvious arrangement: one high-pressure cylinder inside and two low-pressure ones outside. Optional working as a three-cylinder simple on heavy gradients was provided for in the designs of Adolf Klose for the Württemberg Railway in the 1890s, and copied elsewhere. The more usual arrangement, in which low-pressure cylinder volume is greater to provide for compound working under all conditions except the moment of starting, originated with a 2–6–0 locomotive built to the design of E Sauvage for the Nord Railway of France in 1887. Though very successful, this very advanced design was overshadowed almost

Above left: An Austrian two cylinder superheated compound 4–4–0 of 1908, designed by Karl Gölsdorf.

Above: North Eastern Railway No 1619 was built as a two cylinder compound, as shown here. In 1898 it was rebuilt on Smith's three cylinder system and was forerunner of the numerous Midland and LMS compounds.

Right: There were over 6,000 Prussian two cylinder compounds. Many ended their days like this one, in a foreign country, sent there as reparations after 1918.

Below right: No 701 of the Chemin de Fer du Nord was built in 1886 to the design of Alfred de Glehn. The experimental precursor of thousands of French and other four cylinder compounds, it is preserved, now with a leading bogie, at Mulhouse.

at once by the four-cylinder compounds of that railway, which were to prove so influential.

Only two really numerous classes of three-cylinder compound seem to have been built well into the 20th century. For the Jura-Simplon and, later, the Swiss Federal railways, Weyermann's 2–6–0 with divided drive was built in over 170 examples from 1896. Some of these were sold to Holland in 1945 and continued to give good service for several more years. In 1901, the first of the Midland compounds was built at Derby in England, to the joint design of Smith (of the North Eastern Railway) and Johnson (of the Midland). Of these there were eventually 245, building continuing through the 1920s.

Compound locomotives with four cylinders, two high-pressure and two low-pressure, were the most numerous and, as will be detailed later, eventually developed the greatest power to weight ratio, the greatest thermal efficiency, and some of the longest and most trouble free lives of any steam locomotives. In these best locomotives, the drive was usually divided, the high-pressure engine working one axle and the low-pressure another, the axles being, of course, coupled. This arrangement was evolved in France. In 1886, at the invitation of Gaston du Bousquet of the French Nord Railway, A de Glehn of the Alsatian locomotive works produced an experimental engine using a standard Nord boiler. Like Webb's first three-cylinder engine two years earlier, this had no coupling rods, but did have four cylinders, the LP ones outside. Du Bousquet exchanged the positions of the HP and LP cylinders, and provided coupling rods in his 4–4–0 version which appeared in 1891, and this engine established the form of many thousands of French and other locomotives built in the next half-century. Typical of these engines was the longitudinal separation of HP and LP cylinders, which went some way to equalizing the connecting rod lengths of the two sets. In the PLM (Paris, Lyon & Méditerranée Railway) system, which evolved at the same time, the four cylinders were all in a line across the engine, even though the drive might be divided. Although the PLM used the du Bousquet layout in some of its most successful earlier 4–4–0s and 4–6–0s, it returned to the all-in-line layout for its larger engines in the 20th century.

A number of two-crank four-cylinder compound arrangements enjoyed some popularity. Tandem cylinders, in which high-pressure and

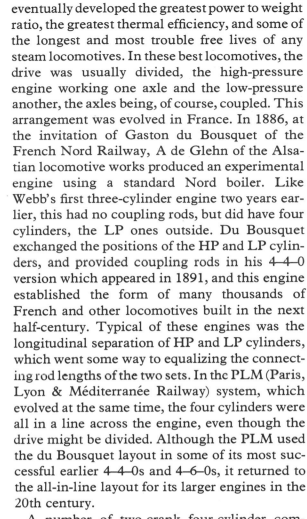

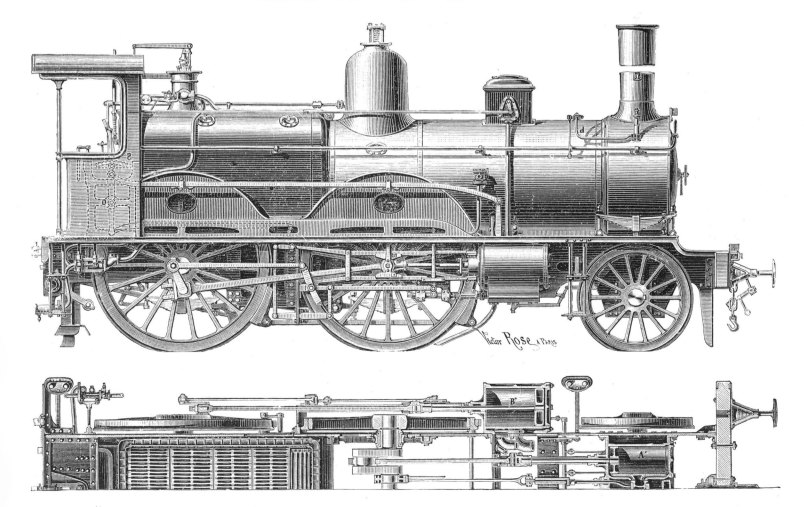

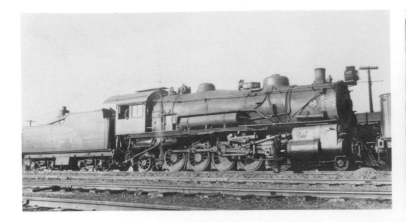

low-pressure cylinders were in line and worked the same piston rod, were much used in Russia and Eastern Europe around the turn of the century, and were favoured by the US builder Brooks. 'The Most Powerful Locomotive in the World' – a frequently transferred title – was for a time a 2–10–2 tandem compound of the Santa Fe railway. More numerous in America, and easier to maintain, were the Vauclain compounds, a speciality of the Baldwin locomotive works under Samuel Vauclain, in which HP and LP cylinders were placed one above the other on each side of the locomotive, with separate piston rods driving a common crosshead.

The well-known Mallet articulated locomotive was conceived as a compound. In this type the boiler is rigidly attached to a two-cylinder chassis at the rear end, while the front end is supported on another two-cylinder chassis coupled to the rear one, but able to swing sideways on curves, boiler weight being carried on a sliding saddle. Flexible steam connections are required for the front engine, and also flexible exhaust pipes. In the compound Mallet, the rear engine received boiler steam, and the front engine received the steam exhausted from the rear engine. The flexible connections were therefore not subject to full boiler pressure. The first engines of the type appeared in 1889, on an exhibition railway of 600 mm (1 ft 11⅝ in) gauge (a gauge which the Decauville company had chosen for light railway products of all kinds, and which is still the normal small contractor's railway standard. The first Mallet locomotives were commissioned by Decauville). The enormous development of the Mallet type for railways with sharp curves and steep gradients all over the world resulted mainly in large and powerful compound tank locomotives. In America, the type was adopted in the 20th century for main-line freight work. So

enormous did these machines become, that eventually it was impossible to accommodate low-pressure cylinders of sufficient diameter within the moving load gauge. The Virginian Railroad double ten-coupled Mallets of the early 1920s had the largest LP cylinders, of 1,219.2 mm (48 in) diameter. Beyond this power, four-cylinder simple expansion became necessary, and, in the advanced state of technology at this period, there was no problem with high-pressure flexible steam joints. It was also found that the simple engines ran more freely, because the valve design associated with very large LP cylinders was not really adequate. Henceforward, the simple expansion Mallet became popular in America, but in fact compound Mallets were built until 1952.

The compound locomotive can have certain advantages over a simple, assuming equally good design in both cases: the compound uses less fuel and water, produces a more even drawbar pull, is capable of better sustained acceleration, is more powerful for a given weight and rides better on the track. Against this, the compound is usually more expensive (though commonly longer lasting) and requires a more highly-trained driver. The compound has generally been most successful in countries where educational standards are high.

Above left: Santa Fe tandem compound 2–10–2. In 1903 this was the most powerful locomotive in the World.

Above: One of the greatest of all locomotive designs: du Bousquet's Nord Atlantic of 1899. These four cylinder compounds set new world standards of power for weight, and were in service for forty years.

Below: Southern Pacific (US) Vauclain compound Atlantic of c. 1900. The high pressure cylinders are on top of the low pressure ones, with a common crosshead.

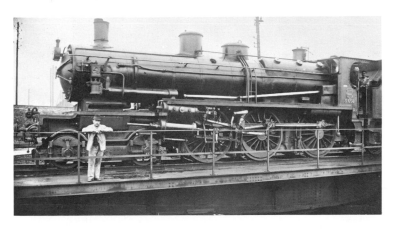

The big engine era

Around the turn of the 19th century, there was a worldwide increase in the weight of passenger and freight trains. Locomotive design standards evolved in the second half of the 19th century soon proved incapable of further enlargement. These classics, aptly symbolized by the British and the American 4–4–0 were still built but began to be relegated to secondary services by many of the larger companies.

In North America, there seems to have been little difficulty in designing and building larger locomotives. This was because the greater height of the loading gauge permitted higher pitched boilers, and because the use of bar framing had long resulted in the practice of having the grate above the frames in 4–6–0 and 2–8–0 locomotives. The fireboxes of such engines were wider than could be accommodated between the plate frames which were almost universal in Europe. In smaller wheeled locomotives the grate could be placed above the wheels, and in some 4–6–0s it could be fitted above the trailing wheels with some extension of the rear axle spacings.

In Britain, the progression from 4–4–0s and 0–6–0s to ten wheelers was not easy. The main trouble was the high rear axle of a 4–6–0, which resulted in a long, shallow firebox, to which the crews were not accustomed and which could be difficult to fire, because a shovelful of coal thrown to the front of the box sometimes hit the brick arch and fell in the middle. The rear axle usually interfered with the ashpan with the result that part of the grate became blocked quite early on a long run.

Ivatt produced Britain's first 'Atlantic' in 1898. It was mechanically much like the Stirling '8 footer' 4–2–2, with outside cylinders, and the low rear axle made it possible to fit a deep firebox which, though longer than that of the Stirling engines – over 2.41 sq m (26 sq ft) in area as against 1.86 (20) in the last few singles – was easy to fire, and could have a satisfactory ashpan. Four years later, Ivatt produced the first of his very numerous large 'Atlantics', identical except for their wide fireboxes and large boiler barrels. However, these engines only became outstanding performers after superheating. Aspinall pursued a similar policy, but as the existing locomotives were 4–4–0s with inside cylinders and 2,210 mm (7 ft 3 in) coupled wheels, he perpetuated these features in his 'Atlantics', which

Above left: The 4–6–0 version of the Nord Atlantic proved even more powerful. When superheated and fitted with improved blast system they could sustain 2,000 hp with an engine weight of only 70 tonnes.

Above right: The first generation of American Pacifics had the traditional inside link motion, and inside bearings for the trailing truck.

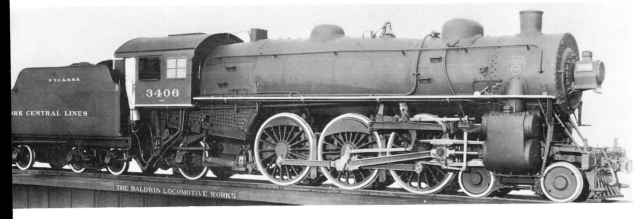

Left: This New York Central Pacific – precursor of the famous Hudsons – shows the outside valve gear and outside trailing truck bearings which had become standard by 1914.

Below: A curious revival of the 'single wheeler' was caused by the invention of steam sanding. The last built were of this Great Northern type, in 1901 – excellent but short-lived machines.

Left: Ivatt's famous large Atlantics of the Great Northern were mostly two-cylinder simples. The first appeared in 1902 and introduced the wide firebox to the European express locomotive.

Right: The first British ten-wheeled express locomotive, Ivatt's narrow firebox Atlantic of 1898, for the Great Northern.

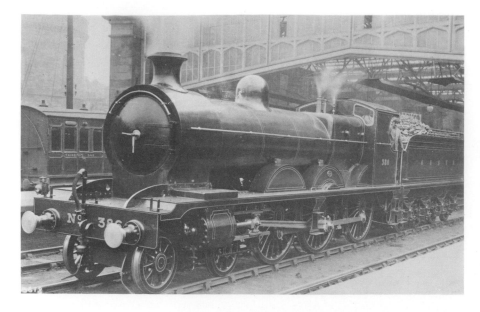

Above: Manson 4–6–0 of the Glasgow and South Western, at Carlisle in about 1905.

Above right: The first British four cylinder simple of modern type: Manson's G & SWR 4–4–0 of 1898. It lasted long but remained the only one of its class.

were extremely tall and most unusual machines, but also successful.

Most designers attempting the 4–6–0 type failed to produce engines which were noticeably more powerful than the 4–4–0s, and either adopted the 'Atlantic' or reverted to an enlarged 4–4–0 when stronger track and the advent of superheating made this possible. There were some inside cylinder 4–6–0s, among which S Holden's engines stand out as easily the most successful and long lasting.

There were, however, two successful early designs of saturated express 4–6–0 engines with outside cylinders, which appeared almost at the same moment, in 1902. These had more in common than is generally recognized. One of these designs was by Churchward of the Great Western, a great engineer whose work was extremely influential in Britain. His design was strongly influenced by American practice, though not to the extent of using bar framing. He adopted a raised Belpaire (square-topped) firebox and a

tapered boiler barrel. The valves were on top of the cylinders and driven by inside link motion, and he paid particular attention to the detailed design of the piston valves, cylinder passages and valve gear. The boiler was pitched very high and the ashpan was effectively in two parts, one ahead and one behind the rear axle. The competence of the Churchward 4–6–0 was never in doubt.

The other successful 4–6–0 was designed by James Manson. The Manson engines were restricted in weight, but incorporated many of the good features of the Churchward engines, plus the advantage of an increased rear-wheel spacing, allowing a fairly deep firebox. There was a marked resemblance between the Manson engines and the numerous standard 4–6–0s for the Indian broad gauge. These began to appear from the same works at the same time, and were built for some 45 years in large numbers. It was in Scotland that the first British 4–6–0 had appeared: David Jones' *Big Goods* on the Highland Railway in 1894, and the Manson engines,

Right: Jones *Big Goods* of the Highland Railway. The first British 4–6–0s, they appeared in 1894. Both Jones and Manson 4–6–0s influenced locomotive development for India.

Below: Churchward's Great Western 2–8–0 was built from 1903 till 1942. Boiler and cylinders were interchangeable with 4–6–0s. There was never a better British mineral traffic locomotive.

while not outstanding, were the first express locomotives in an important modern Scottish design development.

The eight-coupled heavy goods loco did not present the problems at the firebox caused by high rear axle, and from the beginning of the 20th century many British railways built 0–8–0s with inside or outside cylinders, and the 2–8–0 type followed quickly. Of the latter, the best were again Churchward's on the Great Western, which, like some other 2–8–0s, had the same boilers, cylindrs, valve gear and other components as 4–6–0 express engines.

When in 1923, the British railway companies were formed into four groups, the East Coast group (LNER) used very competent 'Atlantics' of the Great Northern, North Eastern and North British Railways on its long distance expresses between London and Scotland and other important routes. Eight-coupled heavy freight engines of Great Northern, North Eastern and Great Central types, and innumerable 0–6–0s handled the goods traffic. The West Coast group (LMS) used mainly 4–4–0s of which the best were the Midland compounds and the superheated simples of the London & North Western. There were also several hundred 4–6–0s which were less satisfactory, and double-heading of heavy trains was common. There were numerous eight-coupled goods engines, mainly ex LNWR – including Webb compounds with three and four cylinders.

The Great Western remained substantially unchanged, with Churchward's standard types fully capable of doing all the duties required of them. The Southern group only had ten-wheel express engines in small numbers: 'Atlantics' substantially of Great Northern design on the Brighton, and 4–6–0s on the London & South Western. These last included some of Drummond's unsuccessful four-cylinder machines, but also a number of modern type two-cylinder simples with external Walschaerts valve gear, designed by Urie.

Local services on all groups were mainly in the hands of inside-cylinder tank engines, but there were exceptions to this on the Great Western, which had numerous 2–6–2 tanks, and on what had once been the London, Tilbury & Southend, which had used outside cylinder 4–4–2 tank engines since 1880. Locomotives with more than two cylinders, for any service, were in a very small minority. The first three-cylinder engine of modern type was a 0–10–0 tank of the Great Eastern, built in 1903 to demonstrate acceleration superior to that obtainable with electric trains. Three-cylinder drive then became a speciality of the North Eastern, and later the Great Northern, and was to play an important part in locomotive designs of the London & North Eastern.

The first British four-cylinder simple expansion locomotive (again, apart from some very early experiments) was built by Manson for the Glasgow & South Western in 1898. It had a long life but remained unique on that system. More important were three French compound 'Atlantics' bought by the Great Western, which gave rise to the highly satisfactory four-cylinder simple 4–6–0s of the Star, Castle and King classes, and eventually, through those, to the Pacifics of the London, Midland & Scottish Railway.

Four-cylinder designs on the LNWR, and LYR, and the Great Central, were less successful. Three, and, even more markedly, four cylinders improve the balance of a locomotive. If all four drive on the same axle there is no 'hammer-blow' on the track, because the reciprocating parts are working as opposed pairs, and rotating weights in the wheels are not needed to balance them. Manson and others hoped, therefore, to be allowed to increase axle loading but were usually opposed by the civil engineers.

Below left: Outside cylinder 4–4–2 tank locomotives, originally designed by William Adams, were used from 1880 onwards by the London, Tilbury & Southend Railway. They were the first to carry water in the bunker as well as in side tanks. This is the 1900 version.

Below right: The Indian standard 1,670 m (5 ft 6 in) gauge 4–6–0 was built in many hundreds over some 45 years, with detailed improvements but little enlargement. Its resemblance to the Manson 4–6–0 shows its Scottish origins.

The early years of the 20th century saw the development of a practical system of superheating for locomotives by Dr Wilhelm Schmidt. The Schmidt system, like its derivatives known by the names of other engineers, involved the passage of the steam, after it had left the inside of the boiler, through a large number of small tubes inserted within enlarged boiler flues. The extra heat content reduced condensation losses within the cylinders and increased the power output, or, alternatively, reduced fuel and water consumption. In England, the virtues of the system were first strikingly demonstrated by a large 4–4–2 tank engine of the Brighton Railway, class I3, which proved able to handle a 250 tonne express over a distance of 90 miles without taking water en route and running mostly at over 80 km/h (50 mph) – doing round trips of 425 km (264 miles) on one heaped bunkerful of coal – some 3¼ tonnes. Comparative running with one of the excellent LNWR unsuperheated 4–4–0s so convincingly favoured the Brighton engine, that the LNWR proceeded to build a superheated 4–4–0, the *George the Fifth*; the first of a class which proved capable of power output greatly in excess of expectations based on its dimensions.

In Britain, superheating improved many existing classes, especially the larger and newer engines which had not yet produced power commensurate with bulk. There were disappointments: the rearrangement of boiler tubes sometimes resulted in poor steaming; the high steam temperatures led to lubrication difficulties; and, when piston valves were adopted in place of slide valves, less clear steam paths, often blocked by carbonized oil, as well as leaking valves caused locomotives to deteriorate rapidly after overhaul. These problems were resolved by the development of superior lubricants, by the use of narrow rings on the piston valve heads, and the increasing adoption of easier steam paths and long travel, long-lap valves. Eventually, high superheat played a vital role in outstanding performances from such different types as Ivatt's Great Northern Atlantics, Chapelon's compound locomotives in France, and the great North American locomotives – of which one engineer once remarked that he liked the steam so hot that the piston rod came blue out of the stuffing box on the rear cover!

Large American locomotives in the 20th century
The distinguishing feature of the large American locomotive was the wide firebox at the rear of the main framing – with a trailing truck beneath – with two or, from the middle 1920s, four wheels. The first form of wide firebox to receive much use was the Wootten type for burning anthracite. This appeared in 1877. Wide fireboxes for burning low-grade coal appeared early in Belgium. There were other European examples, but the normal modern type first became current in America in the early 1890s.

It was above all the 'Atlantic' (4–4–2) type which demonstrated the advantages of this type of boiler, some of the best express trains running in the United States were pulled by the Vauclain

compound 4–4–2s of the Atlantic City Railroad, first built in 1896. For competitive services, the Pennsylvania Railroad also used the Atlantic type, and the evolution of these locomotives on the Pennsylvania eventually resulted in the E6 class of 1910, which in its superheated condition was capable of developing 2,400 hp in its cylinders, and had an engine weight of some 110 tonnes. This was undoubtedly one of the finest American locomotives, and one of the finest 'Atlantic' designs in the world – with a power-to-weight ratio only surpassed slightly by the Atlantics of the French Nord Railway in their final form and nearly equalled by the Ivatt Atlantics with the large superheaters of the British Great Northern. Both these European types were, of course, much smaller machines.

The E6 class were two-cylinder simples, as were the vast majority of non-articulated American locomotives. The growth to enormous size in the 20th century did not change this state of affairs. American locomotive engineers were extremely practical and their situation was one in which thermal efficiency was altogether less important than the ability to run long distances with minimum attention and to haul enormous loads. Locomotive crews were expected to show courage and physical strength rather than intellectual quality. Physical strength of a high order was required to fire a Pennsylvania Atlantic, and even more, a Pacific, of the earlier series, before the mechanical stoker took over in the 1920s.

The Pacific type proper, with a wide firebox, was named after some small engines of the Missouri Pacific Railroad, which appeared in 1902. It was simply an enlargement of the Atlantic, with six-coupled wheels, and as often happened when extra wheels were added, the coupled wheels were smaller than those of Atlantics. The first American Pacifics retained the traditional inside link motion-driving outside valves through pendulum levers of rocking shafts – so long a feature of all American designs. The trailing wheels mostly had inside bearings. But by about 1910, external Walschaerts gear came into use, and the trailing truck had outside bearings, giving greater freedom for a capacious hopper-type ashpan.

Right: The Lima Locomotive Works developed the four wheeled trailing truck and enlarged firebox of later American locomotives, but Baldwins followed suit and turned out this 4–6–4 of the Santa Fe in 1937.

Below: The finale of North American steam power: Canadian National 4–8–2 and 4–8–4 locomotives at Toronto in 1957.

Below: The American export 2–8–2: a Baldwin-built 'Mikado' on the Nitrate Railways of Chile, with unusually small wheels for working on heavy grades.

Below: The classic American home and export locomotive of the 20th century was the mixed traffic 2–8–2. This entirely typical example has a 'Vanderbilt' tender.

There were innumerable American Pacifics. When hand-fired, they were probably the hardest locomotives in the world to work. Their true potential was realized only in the 1920s and 1930s with mechanical stoking. It is again to the Pennsylvania Railroad that we must turn for the finest examples of the type – the series which culminated in the K4s class of 1914. The earlier ones were, at one time, the most powerful locomotives in the world on a horsepower basis, and the last, with poppet valves, certainly the most powerful Pacifics, having developed 4,250 hp on test in 1942. This was slightly less than the maximum obtained from the French Chapelon 4–8–0 class four-cylinder compound at about the same time. The French locomotives were rebuilt from Pacifics with about three-quarters of the weight of the Pennsylvania engine.

This comparison is not one of merit: both American and French designs were of the very highest quality, and each perfectly adapted to the conditions of use. But it does illuminate the very different problems facing locomotive designers: the Americans were able to use high axleloadings and cheap fuel and catered for long distances and high speeds; the Frenchmen had to work within weight and loading gauge restrictions which required the use of four cylinders and eight-coupled wheels. The French had to reduce fuel consumption to the minimum.

The two equivalents of the Pacific type were the 2–10–0 and the 2–8–2 (or Mikado), both of which could use the same boiler as the Pacific, the small wheels of the 2–10–0 permitting the wide grate to pass above them. The 2–8–2 is perhaps the most typical American locomotive of this whole period. Not only was it built in large numbers for American home railroads, but was also the most extensively exported type. American Mikados of all gauges were to be found all over the world, their capacious fireboxes burning all sorts of fuel, their simple and robust mechanism defying the worst of maintenance and the most gruelling operating conditions. Moreover, the basics of American design, evolved when track was bad, made the Mikados well able to keep their feet on badly-maintained and severely-curving and graded routes – because of fully equalized suspension of driving wheels and trucks.

American and other articulated locomotives

Apart from articulated locomotives, dealt with in a separate section, the culmination of the American single-frame locomotive was the type with a four-wheeled truck under the firebox, first introduced by the Lima locomotive works in 1925 in the form of a 2–8–4, closely followed by a 2–10–4. The idea was to increase the steaming capacity sufficiently to enable a high tractive force to be developed at relatively high speeds. The once popular criterion of starting tractive effort (unrelated to boiler capacity) became insignificant. This philosophy, applied to the Pacific type, gave rise to the 4–6–4 (or Hudson), and the 4–8–4 was an enlargement of this. The 4–8–2 had never been regarded as a high-speed locomotive and was never built with very large coupled wheels, but this did not apply to the 4–8–4. Many of these types were given boosters in their early days. These were small steam engines driving two wheels of the trailing truck, to assist in starting, but able to be disconnected for running at speed. Their use was a result of the new locomotives replacing older ones with more coupled wheels, many of them Mallets.

The most famous of the 4–6–4 and 4–8–4 types were probably the Milwaukee *Hiawatha* 4–6–4s, the Santa Fe 3776 class 4–8–4s and those of the New York Central Railroad. These great locomotives habitually sustained very high speeds with very heavy loads – the *Niagara* 4–8–4s built in 1945 could manage 1,000 tonnes at 160 km/h (100 mph), and the whole class averaged a monthly mileage of 16,000, some regularly reaching 24,000 where the rosters permitted. In the final phase of American steam power, extraordinary attention was paid to ease and rapidity of servicing. In freight service, locomotives were often serviced without leaving their trains, during relatively short stops, and this was a vital factor in the achieving of large mileages. A Hudson had a maximum sustained cylinder hp of 4,700 on test, for an engine weight of about 160 tonnes. The *Niagara* 4–8–4 could sustain 6,600, with an engine weight of about 210 tonnes. For comparison, Chapelon's three-cylinder compound 4–8–4 could sustain 5,500 hp, with an engine weight of about 145 tonnes.

American and other articulated locomotives

If we exclude some primitive experiments, the history of the articulated locomotive can be taken as starting with the Semmering trials of 1851, the object of which was to find a type suitable for working the severe Semmering incline in Austria. Of the four competing machines the *Weiner Neustadt* foreshadowed the Meyer articulated locomotive in having two bogie engines beneath a long but fairly normal boiler. Another, the *Seraing* (named after the Cockerill works in Belgium) had two bogie engines beneath a double boiler arranged firebox to firebox, with chimneys at the extremities, and so was an example of what later was known as the Fairlie type after a later patentee. Both Meyer and Fairlie locomotives were successfully built in small numbers, and some still exist in running order, but these types are totally outweighed in importance by the Mallet and the Garratt arrangements.

It has already been pointed out that the Mallet was conceived as a compound, and was built extensively for some 30 years before being adopted in America. Until the Americans started building them, Mallets with separate tenders were rare, but some of the tank locomotives were very large for their time. The Gotthard 0–6–6–0 of 1890 weighed 85 tonnes, and the Belgian engine of similar wheel arrangement, used for banking up the Liège incline, weighed 110 tonnes. Perhaps more typical were the numerous Mallets constructed in Europe for service in the Dutch East Indies: the 2–6–6–0 tanks of 1902 weighed some 60 tonnes, which was quite large for the gauge of 1,067 mm (3 ft 6 in). Some of these are still in service. The Mallet was always regarded by Europeans as a 'colonial' or a mountain climbing type, and most of the very numerous European built examples were for service on narrow-gauge lines. In the 20th century, and perhaps with the American example, many large Mallet tender locomotives ran on 'colonial' railways, some built in America, and to cite the former Dutch colonies again, there were double eight-coupled locomotives of American and European build, followed by Swiss built 2–6–6–0s in the late 1920s, some of which were running in 1976.

Top left: Brazilian metre gauge 2–6–6–2 simple expansion Mallet articulated locomotive, built by Baldwin in 1950.

Above: One of the last South African steam types to be built, a class GMA 4–8–2 + 2–8–4 Beyer Garratt going off from the shed to work a train.

Right: In comparative trials held in 1921 by the South African Railways, the 2–6–0 + 0–6–2 Garratt locomotive (below) proved superior in power, speed, economy and smooth riding to the 2–6–6–2 Mallet (above). Most of its advantages were due to the shorter and fatter boiler, the greater flue area and simpler shape of which is seen in the diagram.

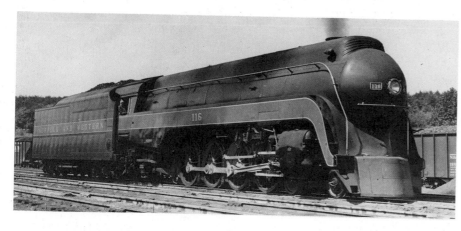

Above: The Norfolk and Western streamlined 4–8–4s had rather small driving wheels, which enabled them to develop over 5,000 hp at only 64 km/h (40 mph).

work, and even in a few cases to express passenger haulage.

The ultimate in size of the compound Mallet, was reached in 1920 with the 2–10–10–2 locomotives of the Virginian Railway, in which the low-pressure cylinders were of 1,219 mm (48 in) bore, adhesion weight was 280 tonnes and the horsepower developed at the slow speed of about 40 km/h (25 mph) (for which the locomotives were intended) amounted to nearly 7,000. There were also a few triple eight-coupled Mallets, with driving wheels under the tenders, on the Virginian and Erie railroads, but although the total adhesion weight reached some 350 tonnes, the power, and therefore the speed, was less than in the 'double Decapods'. Yet, one worked a train weighing 16,300 tonnes at 24 km/h (15 mph).

As already pointed out, the size of the low-pressure cylinders and the difficulty to provide adequate valves to deal with enormous volumes of low-pressure steam led to progressive replacement of compound by simple Mallets, by rebuilding and by new construction, but this was not without exceptions. Probably the last Mallets built were compounds of the Norfolk & Western class Y6b. Eighty Y6 locomotives were built between 1936 and 1952, the last being Y6b. They were 2–8–8–2s, capable of working 7,000 tonne trains on easily graded routes at speeds up to 80 km/h (50 mph). Their boiler pressure was 300 lb/sq in, driving wheels were 1,524 mm (5 ft) in diameter and weight was 270 tonnes.

The first American Mallet was a 0–6–6–0 built by the American Locomotive Company's Schenectady works in 1904 for the Baltimore & Ohio. It was a banking loco, and replaced two 2–8–0 locomotives, showing nearly 40 per cent reduction in repair costs and achieving something like 85 per cent availability in its first few years of service. As the builders had never constructed anything like this before, this must be taken as a remarkable tribute to the excellence of American design and construction, but the smoother operation of a compound locomotive, and the more rigid articulation of the two power units, as compared with two ordinary locomotives coupled together, must have helped a great deal. This was a 152 tonne engine, and its success led to an immediate popularity of the Mallet which was soon extended beyond banking to line freight

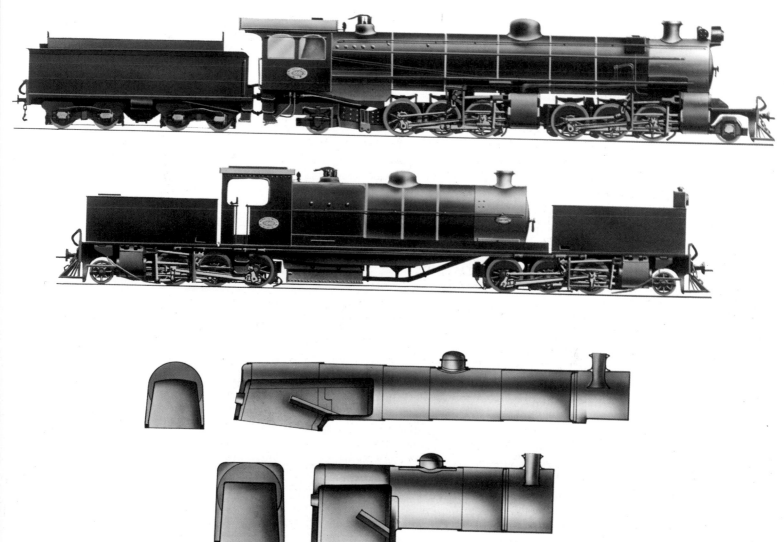

The use of simple expansion obviously made higher powers possible within the permissible width over the cylinders of the front engine. The later Mallets had improved control of the lateral movements of the front engine. It was in this way that the largest and most powerful of all steam locomotives were constructed, and here it must suffice to cite the Union Pacific 'Big Boy' 4–8–8–4s, and to give their particulars for comparison with the more modern but smaller compound Y6b class. The boiler pressure was the same at 300 lb/sq in, but the driving wheels were 228.6 mm (9 in) larger in diameter. Weight was 350 tonnes (without tender) as against 270. The firegates of these enormous locomotives were roughly 6,096 mm (20 ft) long and 2,743 mm (9 ft) wide, the firebox being extended forward in a combustion chamber and provided with water tubes supporting the brick arch. Used mainly on heavily-graded routes, they could develop 7,000 drawbar hp at low speeds – a remarkable figure because steam locomotives reach their maximum output when running relatively fast – and were able to run at 112 km/h (70 mph) with 3,000 tonnes on the level. Happily, many of these great engines are preserved in the country that was created by the railroad.

The Garratt locomotive was conceived by Herbert Garratt and became the speciality of Beyer Peacock & Company of Manchester, England. It was never built in the quantities of the Mallets, of which over 3,000 were built in the US alone, and more in Europe. There were certainly less than 2,000 Garratts in all, but most of these were large machines. In this design, the boiler is carried on a cradle slung between two engine units, and has no wheels beneath it. This is the great virtue of the layout: the barrel can be of large diameter and relatively short, and the firebox, almost always of the wide, square topped variety, can be deep, with a deep ashpan, and simple in shape (and therefore cheaper and more easily-designed to keep maintenance costs down, with simple direct staying of the water spaces around the fire).

The first Garratts were built in 1908 for Tasmania. They weighed only 33 tonnes and had four-wheeled engines pivoted to the central cradle, with, as in all Garratts, water and fuel supplies on the engine units. One engine was worked at high pressure, and the other at low, this first type being compound, though almost all later Garratts were simple expansion machines. The type progressed slowly until 1921, when a 134 tonne 2–6–0 + 0–6–2 was built for trials on the 1,067 mm (3 ft 6 in) gauge South African Railways. Compared with a British-built compound Mallet weighing, with tender, 180 tonnes, the Garratt proved faster with the same load and burned less fuel. It also rode very much better, thanks to the wide spacing of the pivots of the boiler cradle, which lie within the coupled wheelbase in Garratt locomotives to ensure that the weight of the boiler is well balanced on the engine units. On sharp curves, the front end of a Mallet boiler swings outwards, and the inertia of this can be detrimental to good riding.

The Garratt proving the better engine on all counts, South African Railways adopted Garratts for new construction, and because this railway system enjoyed a high prestige among engineers,

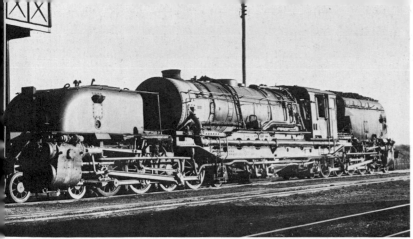

Above: On the more usual South African gauge of 1,064 mm (3 ft 6 in) a class GO 4–8–2+2–8–4 Beyer Garratt weighing 172 tonnes about to leave Lydenburg shed in 1970.

Left: The largest steam locomotive of all, the Union Pacific Big Boy 4–8–8–4 simple expansion Mallet, weighing 350 tonnes without tender. They could pull 3,000 tonnes at 112 km/h (70 mph) on level track, and handle far greater loads at moderate speeds.

Below: South African Railways 600 mm (2 ft) gauge 2–6–2+2–6–2 Beyer Garratt locomotives, the most powerful in the world on this gauge, weighing 60 tonnes.

other railways made increasing use of the type. In South Africa, the narrow gauge does not involve a small loading gauge, and does not preclude very heavy loads and speeds up to 88 km/h (55 mph) – indeed some steam 4–6–2 locomotives had 1,828.8 mm (6 ft) diameter driving wheels. To this day, the South African system is one of the most modern and efficient, and Garratt steam locomotives, though in diminishing numbers, work it.

While the Garratt (or Beyer Garratt as it later became known) was predominantly found in English-speaking countries, or those where British engineers and businessmen ran the railways, it was also used elsewhere, and built under licence by Continental builders. Some remarkable machines were made, of which the fastest were the 4–6–4+4–6–4 locomotives of the PLM Algerian system, which proved able to run with perfect steadiness at 136 km/h (85 mph). Among the last built were 42 4–8–4+4–8–4 for the standard-gauge New South Wales Railways in Australia. Like the last Y6b Mallets, they appeared in 1952, their total weight (being tank engines, like all Garratts) of 260 tonnes being closely similar to that of the Y6b without tender. The Garratt was found all over the world, except in North America, but it was above all the continent of Africa that depended most heavily upon them, and still does. From the express Garratts of Algeria, right down the continent, east and west, to Cape Province, this long, powerful and flexible machine worked many of the heaviest trains, passenger and freight.

The last development of European steam locomotives

No comprehensive survey can be attempted here but certain important lines of development can be traced. It was the appearance of the French Nord Atlantic at the turn of the century, and its remarkable feats of speed and load haulage, that really set the style for most subsequent French steam locomotives, and many British and German ones. In France, only the PLM kept to its own style of four-cylinder compound, while the British derivatives were four cylinder-simples.

The Nord Atlantic of G du Bousquet was a narrow-firebox engine, with some 2.69 sq m (29 sq ft) of grate, and the cylinder arrangement described under early compound locomotives above. On its first trials it developed 1,440 hp and in later saturated condition these engines produced some 1,600 in the cylinders, equally divided between high- and low-pressure groups. For a weight of only 69 tonnes, this was a standard not bettered anywhere and probably not equalled, and was the result of a careful study of steam flow in the pipes and valves of the whole double expansion system. Similar but larger engines, weighing some 77 tonnes, were built for the Paris-Orléans Railway, and these, again in fully developed saturated condition could be relied on to produce 1,800 hp, and reached nearly 2,000 hp on test.

Many French railways built 4–6–0s inspired by these engines. Superheating improved the Nord Atlantics, which were to remain on fast luxury trains of 350 to 400 tonnes weight until the late 1930s. A 4–6–0 version proved even more potent, thanks to a further review of what has since become known as the 'steam circuit', and, still weighing only 70 tonnes, these engines could be relied on to produce 2,000 hp without falling pressure or boiler water level. They first appeared in 1909, received superheaters before many had been built, and improved blast pipes and chimneys in middle life. They lasted till the end of steam, thereby proving that continual very hard work need not wear out a locomotive. The Nord 'Super Pacifics' of the 1920s and 1930s were derived from them and had narrow fireboxes of great length. Though lighter than other French Pacifics they were the most powerful, producing some 2,700 hp, until the Chapelon rebuilds appeared on the Paris–Orléans.

Above: SNCF class 141P, the Chapelon redesign of the PLM Mikado, was a brilliant machine, able to sustain 3,000 at the drawbar, but weighing only 110 tonnes without tender. Over 300 were built.

Far left: There were 44 of Eugen Kittel's 2–12–0 compound goods engines built from 1918 for the Württemburg State Railway. They ended their days in Austria after the last war.

Left: The first European Pacific type, on the way from the builders, the Société Alsacienne, to the Paris-Orléans Railway, in 1907.

The Paris–Orléans Pacifics were the first in Europe, and dated from 1907. They were scarcely more powerful than the Atlantics, and superheating did little to improve them. The maximum horsepower that could be obtained was about 2,200, and this was largely because their steam circuits were constricted. André Chapelon, perhaps the greatest locomotive engineer of the 20th century, examined their design critically and decided that it was not fundamentally bad, but required detailed improvement in several ways – no single remedy would transform them.

He rebuilt one with greatly enlarged steam passages, poppet valves worked by the original Walschaerts gear but giving much larger openings to steam and exhaust, enlarged steam chests to reduce the drop in pressure during admission to the cylinder (due to that fact that flow during admission greatly exceeds average flow in the superheater and steam pipes), increased the superheat to avoid condensation in the low-pressure cylinders, and devised a double blastpipe and chimney incorporating the Kylala exhaust splitter and petticoats at three levels to guide the steam, even when the blast was very soft, into the chimney and to even out the draught at different heights in the smokebox. The increased pump-

ing efficiency of the 'double Kylchap' exhaust greatly reduced the back pressure on the pistons. As a result, the power of the locomotive was raised to 3,400 hp, and a whole series was modified.

Later, further detailed improvements and an increase in diameter of the low pressure cylinders raised the power of a subsequent batch to 3,700, and finally in this particular development, the rebuilding of some of the small 1907 Pacifics into 4–8–0s, with the Nord type of long and narrow firebox, exactly doubled their output, from 2,000 to 4,000 hp, with a grate area of no more than 3.44 sq m (37 sq ft) and an engine weight of some 105 tonnes. Later rebuilds of this type produced 4,400 hp, for an engine weight of nearly 110 tonnes, and this power-to-weight ratio has never been improved upon in a steam locomotive. Moreover, these later, strengthened engines did not wear themselves out, because the blast arrangement produced a very even pull on the fire, further assisted by the relatively long cut offs at which compound locomotives work even when achieving a high overall expansion ratio. The long cut off also results in a more even turning moment and drawbar pull, both conducive to reduction in the wear of the mechanism. To

Above: One of the very numerous and elegant PLM Pacifics. Though famous for working the *Blue Train* they were poor machines until rebuilt on Chapelon's principles.

Top right: A German class 03 Pacific, as built c. 1938. This was a two cylinder simple expansion engine.

crown all this, these Chapelon locomotives produced the best figures for thermodynamic efficiency, i.e. fuel and water economy, of any steam locomotives, achieving a best figure of 12.8 per cent utilization of the calorific value of the fuel.

Chapelon principles were eventually adopted by other railways and other countries, and were found to improve simple expansion locomotives as well. In France, most of the larger locomotives were more or less altered, and some of the Etat and PLM Pacifics totally treated to achieve Chapelon-type results. There was also new construction of old designs modified according to these principles, notably of over 300 mixed traffic 2–8–2s (Class 141P) redesigned by Chapelon, which proved similar in power to the 4–8–0s, and of 35 4–8–2s (Class 241P) of PLM design, much transformed to be able to develop nearly 5,000 hp. There was also a unique 4–8–4, rebuilt by Chapelon as a three-cylinder compound, which achieved 5,500 hp, remarkably evenly divided between the three cylinders, for a weight of some 145 tonnes. This great machine was the experimental prototype for a series of three-cylinder compounds of 6,000 hp, planned to be built largely on American lines, with cast steel engine beds (the ultimate development of the bar frame in the USA). Unhappily, these were never built, but the performance of the 4–8–4 caused a rapid redesign of the electric locomotives then being planned for electrification of the PLM main line.

Preference for compound locomotives in Europe was severely upset by the invention of a practical system of locomotive superheating by Dr Wilhelm Schmidt in the first ten years of the century. In many tests superheated simples were found to be more economical than saturated compounds. In further tests, superheated compounds were found to be more economical still, but this did not prevent a complete change of policy on the Prussian State Railway (probably the largest single transport undertaking in the

world), where Robert Garbe, the locomotive engineer, worked closely with Schmidt in the production of a large series of superheated simples which dominated the working of all traffic except the fastest passenger trains within a few years. These engines were of superb mechanical design but low power-to-weight ratio, a combination which ensured long and trouble-free lives. Built in thousands, they were spread across Europe as reparations after both world wars, and their design principles were perpetuated in the standard locomotives of the Deutsche Reichsbahn, which were also superbly built, totally reliable in service, and rather undistinguished in performance.

The other German railways generally preferred compounds up to the time of their amalgamation into the Reichsbahn in 1920. The Bavarian system used numerous engines built by J A Maffei and designed by the firm's engineer and director A Hammel. These were remarkable machines, many of which were exported to other European countries. They were four-cylinder compounds with the drive concentrated on one axle, and they had bar frames. The Bavarian Pacifics in this style were perpetuated in new engines by the Reichsbahn in 1930, because its engineers were at the time unable to produce a simple expansion engine which was suitable for either the light, fast *Rheingold* express, or heavy work on steeply graded south German routes. The Württemberg and Saxon systems also used large compounds, of which the most noteworthy were the Württemberg 2–12–0 freight locomotives, designed by Eugen Kittel and built by Esslingen, which found their way to many steeply graded routes in central and eastern Europe after the second world war, including the famous Semmering route which had prompted the trials of 1851. It was perhaps because the Prussian system was relatively flat that the simple engine was preferred there.

Below right: The greatest French steam locomotive was Chapelon's 4–8–4 a unique three cylinder compound prototype, elegant despite its 145 tonnes and 5,500 hp.

Below: Many thousands of Robert Garbe's excellent Prussian class G8 superheated goods engines were built, and, as war reparations, they spread across Europe and into the near East.

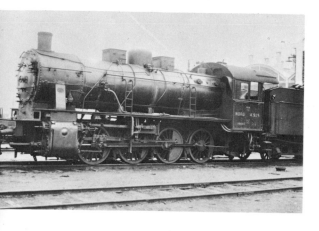

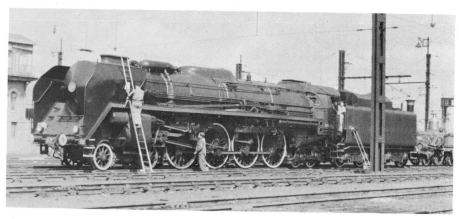

The railways of the Austro-Hungarian empire, and of the Eastern European countries which resulted from its disintegration, were for long dominated by the numerous locomotive designs of Karl Gölsdorf.

From the 1800s onwards he produced a great number of different designs for the greatly varying conditions of major and minor routes, but all were characterized by the need to keep axleloading down to very low figures for the sort of powers that were required. His designs were compounds, with two or four cylinders, and their appearance and construction were very different from any other designer's ideas. The framing was light and box-like, running plates and splashers over the wheels were largely suppressed, and boilers were tapered to reduce weight at the front, while working pressures were relatively low to enable thinner plates to be used.

Gölsdorf was undoubtedly a genius, and many of his locomotives survive even today to prove their durability and suitability. Perhaps his most celebrated express engine, and certainly his largest, was a 2–6–4 with enormous firebox, which was long associated with the *Orient Express*. A single equivalent 2–12–0 was highly successful; among smaller machines, numerous

Atlantics, 4–4–0s, and small compound tank engines gave long service, while the two-cylinder compound 0–10–0 was still to be found working recently in France and Italy as well as on more familiar ground.

In Britain, after grouping of the railways in 1923, the enlarged Great Western continued Churchward's designs with small additions, especially in the four-cylinder 4–6–0 type. The numerous Castles and the fewer Kings had the highest power-to-weight ratio of any British locomotives until the middle 1930s. A King weighing 89 tonnes could develop 2,000 hp (which was better than an unrebuilt Paris-Orléans Pacific but not as good as a Nord 4–6–0 in power-to-weight terms).

London & North Eastern locomotive affairs were in the hands of the imaginative Sir Nigel Gresley, whose three-cylinder simple expansion Pacifics, first built for the Great Northern, were progressively improved until one of them, the streamlined *Mallard* with a double Kylchap exhaust, achieved the world speed record for steam in 1938, at 202 km/h (126 mph). These engines could develop 2,700 hp in the cylinders, with a weight of just over 100 tonnes, which equates with the Nord Super Pacifics in France.

Above: An outstanding Austrian design of the early 20th century was the Gölsdorf 2–6–2, a four cylinder compound built to a low axle loading of 15 tonnes.

Below: A metre gauge 2–10–2, German built in 1937, comes round the mountain on the General Belgrano Railway in Argentina.

Left: *Sir Nigel Gresley*, the 100th Gresley Pacific on the London & North Eastern, represents the best in modern British express locomotives. In 1938, a similar engine, *Mallard*, set the World speed record for steam, at 202 km/h (126 mph). During the war, these three cylinder simple engines handled 20 coach trains with distinction.

Right: Boilers for Beyer Garratts on the Benguella Railway in central Africa.

Gresley used three-cylinder propulsion for almost all his designs, from 4–4–0s to 2–8–2s.

Three cylinders were also used in the Southern Schools class 4–4–0s of which 40 were built from 1930. These were the last and most powerful European 4–4–0s, weighing 67 tonnes. Later, when O V S Bulleid joined the Southern from the LNER, three-cylinder Pacifics based on Gresley's type but with many novel features were added to stock. The London, Midland & Scottish had inherited a very heterogeneous locomotive stock, without a single reliable large passenger engine. Although excellent mixed traffic 2–6–0 and 2–6–4T locos were produced, and large numbers of small reliable engines of pre-grouping design, it was eventually necessary to build a class of large three-cylinder 4–6–0s, the Royal Scot type, from 1927. But it was not until W A Stanier, from the Great Western, took charge that wholesale building of new standard designs began. Among these were a mixed traffic 4–6–0 and a heavy freight 2–8–0 with many parts in common, both excellent machines based on Churchward principles, with taper boilers. Stanier also produced four-cylinder simple Pacifics, based at first on the Great Western King class 4–6–0. The later examples, the Duchesses, were the most powerful class of British locomotive, one having developed 3,300 hp.

Locomotives for export
The countries which played the greatest part in the development of the steam locomotive were Britain, France, and the United States. Germany contributed superheating, and Belgium contributed the most widely used valve gearing and possibly the much favoured square-topped firebox. The emphasis in this account has been confined to the main development and most countries simply cannot be mentioned. These are those whose locomotives were built by, or inspired by the great locomotive exporting countries. Many were colonies of those countries, but others were not. In Europe there was no native locomotive style in Spain, or Holland, or many other countries. Countries not hitherto mentioned which had a native style and a substantial export trade were Switzerland and Czechoslovakia. The Swiss built very fine compound locomotives for their own system, until they

decided to exploit their own water power rather than import coal, and so adopted large scale electrification. They had a considerable export trade in steam locomotives, as they now have one in electric traction. The Czechs built what were probably the finest European simple expansion locomotives since the last war, and their exports were also to be found all over the world.

The main exporting countries were the United States, Britain, France and Germany. The railways of India, South America, Africa, and Asia were, and, in some cases, are, operated by imports from these countries, and in recent years indigenous new construction has developed the old imported designs well beyond their original capacity. This has happened most notably in India, South Africa and China.

Some special locomotives
There have been some notable heavy goods locomotives. In America, a most successful early type was Ross Winans' Camel 0–8–0 of the 1850s, with large overhanging firebox and the large driver's cab on top of the boiler. This position for the cab lasted long in American practice, there being 'Camelback' Atlantics and 4–6–0s as well as small wheeled goods locos. In the same period James Milholland, another great American innovator, produced a twelve-coupled engine on similar lines – a very early precursor of the Union Pacific 4–12–2 type of 1926 – which was not only remarkable for having twelve-coupled wheels but also most unusual among modern American classes in having three cylinders. In France, in 1867, Forquenot of the Paris-Orléans produced some 0–10–0 tank locomotives, the boiler dimensions of which were not exceeded in France until the end of the century. They were for banking purposes, but not long before Jules Petiet of the Nord had built some line freight locomotives for working coal trains from the north of France to Paris which were also tanks. They had twelve-coupled wheels in two groups of six, in a rigid frame, with four cylinders. They proved more powerful and economical than six-coupled locos in pairs.

Lastly, there have been some special locomotives built for high speeds. Francis Trevithick of the London & North Western built a locomotive with driving wheels nearly 2,743 mm (9 ft) in diameter, and put the boiler beneath the axle. It was later rebuilt in a more normal style, still with the big wheels, and is preserved after long service. This engine is the well known *Cornwall*. The largest coupled wheels in Britain were those of two 4–4–0s, North Eastern Nos 1869 and 1870, built after the races to Aberdeen in 1895, but never used for racing. They were 2,311 mm (7 ft 7 in) in diameter. J A Maffei built a compound 4–4–4 for the Bavarian State Railway, which reached nearly 160 km/h (100 mph) with a 150 tonne train in 1906. This was a special version of the Bavarian Pacific. Thirty years later, Deutsche Reichsbahn built a large wheeled 4–6–4 specially for record breaking. Its speed was at least equalled by the standard LNER streamlined Pacific *Mallard* in 1938.

ELECTRIC TRACTION

No generalized description, such as that given of the steam locomotive, is possible for electric traction, because it is only in the last few years that electric locomotives have begun to appear basically similar all over the world. This similarity is only appearing after some three quarters of a century of development which will be outlined here. Because of the long life of electric locomotives, and the relative ease of replacement of traction motors and control gear by more modern versions, a large proportion of the locomotives built over the development period are still in service, and it is possible in countries like Switzerland, with a long history of electric traction, to see locomotives working side by side which are fundamentally different in conception.

The steam locomotive came into existence, like the stationary steam engine, because there was a need for it. Its development was rapid, especially considering the state of engineering at the beginning of the 19th century. The electric locomotive, like the oil engined loco, came into existence because commercial firms were looking for new markets. The development of both types was very slow, in spite of the far more advanced state of engineering science and railway technology, because they had to establish their advantages over the steam locomotive. Moreover, these advantages were and are not financial, except in a few special cases. The main advantage was operating convenience, notably in the rapid acceleration of multiple-unit electric trains, and in a few instances the cleanliness of electric traction was important.

Early experiments

Oersted discovered electro-magnetic force in 1820, and Faraday demonstrated electro-magnetic rotation in the following year with a device which might be considered a sort of primitive electric motor. From then on, numerous experiments with electricity were carried out and among these were some attempts at propelling a vehicle on rails. Although the prototype of the alternator and dynamo was made by Pixii in Paris in 1831, generation of the sort of powers required for practical traction was not possible for another

Above: The first practical demonstration of an electric train, though on a miniature scale, by Werner von Siemens at the Berlin exhibition of 1879.

Below: The great American inventor, Thomas Alva Edison, built a few experimental electric locomotives, of which this one was tried in 1882.

Below right: A Tyneside electric train of the North Eastern Railway in 1904, an early British application of the multiple unit system invented by F J Sprague in 1897.

50 years, and these early experiments depended on chemical cells providing quite heavy currents at low voltages. The first experiment may have been that of Stratting and Becker, in Holland, in 1835, with a four wheel vehicle. In 1842, Robert Davidson made a primitive electric locomotive tried in Scotland, of which an illustration survives. The motor consisted of iron bars arranged on a wooden drum round the axle, which were attracted in turn by electro-magnets suitably mounted on the frame. It worked, after a fashion.

Many of this early work was on a very small scale, with what were in effect models. The history of engineering is full of examples of successes with models at times when the full-size device was still impossible, and it is with this in mind that we must consider the claim of Werner von Siemens to be the practical originator of electric traction with his miniature railway which operated successfully at an exhibition in Berlin in 1879. It was an effective demonstration, but the power required was only some 2,000 watts, the line was level and the all important question of control did not arise – very simple switchgear was all that was needed.

The first proper electric railway was that constructed by Magnus Volk along the sea front at Brighton in 1883, which still exists, though the original track gauge of 610 mm (2 ft) has been widened by 216 mm (8½ in), and the line is now longer than at first. Current at low voltage was collected from a third rail, and the rolling stock

Right: Electric tramway in Vienna, by Siemens and Halske, with two motor coaches and a trailer between.

Below: A recent scene on Volk's electric railway in Brighton, which opened in 1883.

was suggestive of a motorized horse tram. As this line was specially built along its own route for electric traction it is of great historical importance, and for this as for his many other electrical innovations, Volk, who was employed by Brighton Corporation, deserves recognition as a great inventor.

Among American pioneers of electric traction the most important were van de Poele (actually a Belgian expatriate) who seems to have been the first to use an overhead conductor wire in 1885 for a tramway, and above all F J Sprague who invented the multiple-unit train (1897), in which a single driver can control a number of motor coaches from either end of the train. It would be hard to overstate the importance of this idea, which has dominated electrification of suburban networks all over the world, and found application in a considerable number of long distance electric trains as well. The great inventor Thomas Alva Edison also took a hand, but his experimental electric locomotives were of small importance and it is his development work on electricity generation, not specifically for traction, which is of most relevance. Lastly, Leo Daft built two or more small electric locomotives in the 1880s, one of which was of 125 hp and pulled a train on trials on the New York Elevated Railway.

Curiously, it was in England, where the electric locomotive was very much a rarity until the 1960s, that a whole, more or less uniform, class of electric locomotives made its appearance as early as 1890. There were 16 of them at first, and they ran on the standard-gauge tube railway between the City of London and Stockwell, a suburb 5.6 km (3½ miles) distant to the south of the Thames. They were very small, with four wheels 686 mm (2 ft 3 in) in diameter, and each axle had a 50 hp motor, of which the armature was directly

Above: The Burgdorf-Thun Railway in Switzerland was one of the pioneers of three-phase traction, in 1899. Ten years later it received this 500 hp locomotive with rod drive on the bogies from central jackshafts. The double contact wire, and the sliding block drive to the coupling rods, to allow for axle springing, are noteworthy.

fixed on the axle and the stator mainly carried on axle bearings. There were thus no gears, but the unsprung weight was high. As the track was laid within a tube of rigid cast iron segments firmly bolted together it was doubtless well aligned, and was free of weather effects, so the unsprung weight may have been no disadvantage; in any case speeds were low, 40 km/h (25 mph) being the maximum. The locos were later converted with geared drive and higher speed motors, but one is preserved in restored original condition in the Science Museum in South Kensington. Current collection was by third rail, the supply being at 500 volts dc, control was by resistors, the motors being series wound. The Westinghouse air brake was fitted, but there was no compressor on the locomotive, the reservoirs being charged at each end of the journey.

The double bogie electric locomotive with four motors, now so familiar, first appeared on the Baltimore & Ohio Railway for working trains through Baltimore itself, to avoid smoke and steam which aroused protest in the city centre. The first of the type was built in 1894 and had the same sort of gearless lowspeed motors of great weight found in the London underground locomotives. Construction of this type continued for nearly 20 years, and all developed just over 1,000 hp and weighed around 90 tonnes. Supply was 650 volts dc with overhead contact rail. With these locomotives, mainline electrification had begun, and what might be termed the modern morphology had been arrived at, but although electric traction was established and successful, and quite widespread in tramway systems, evolution of the electric locomotive had hardly begun. To compress its complicated story into a few pages requires treatment under a few technical headings rather than a continuous chronology.

Mechanical arrangements

As the electric locomotive developed after all sorts of steam types, including various articulated ones, had been perfected, it was natural that for many years the new machines should be based on experience in building the old. Actual manufacture usually involved collaboration between an electrical firm and an established steam locomotive manufacturer. We can only guess to what extent the design of electric motors was influenced by this, but it is quite clear that the double-bogie electric locomotive with independent drive to each axle, was not favoured after its promising first appearance, perhaps because it was felt to be a glorified tramcar. So very large motors began to be used, mounted on steam locomotive type frames and driving the wheels through coupling rods.

The normal wheel classification of electric locomotives is by axles, the driving axles being represented by letters and the carrying ones by numbers. Thus a 2–D–1 electric locomotive equates with a 4–8–2 steam one. If this is written 2–Do–1, it signifies that the driving axles are uncoupled. The Baltimore & Ohio locomotives were Bo–Bo, as are great numbers of modern machines. One of the earliest Swiss electric locomotives was the B three-phase ac type of the Burgdorf-Thun Railway, in which the wheels were driven by coupling rods from a central jackshaft with external cranks. The jackshaft was driven by gearing from two motors of large diameter, one on each side of the locomotive, which were vertically above the jackshaft and overhung on each side. With this arrangement unsprung weight was at a minimum, and coupling rods are still used for this reason, though never in locomotives intended for high speed nowadays.

The B arrangement of the Burgdorf-Thun design appeared very soon in duplicate form – the B–B with central jackshaft on each bogie. Such were two of the experimental single-phase locomotives of the Swiss Seebach-Wettingen trial railway which started running in 1905, and very many others built in many countries. The concept was extended by addition of carrying wheels in many Swiss types, of which perhaps the most celebrated are the 1–B–B–1 locomotives built for working the Gotthard Railway, from 1919 into the 1920s. Some of these were still in service in 1976. Developing some 2,000 hp from a 15,000 volt single-phase ac supply, these machines weigh just over 100 tonnes. They have four traction motors, two geared to each jackshaft, and the buffers and drawgear are carried on the bogies.

For freight service, a double six-coupled type has proved effective in several countries, the Gotthard line, again, using 1–C–C–1 locomotives with jackshaft drive, the jackshaft being raised above the line of the coupled wheels to facilitate the layout of the rod drive. These machines were of several series, all with four traction motors, and in the later ones the driver's cab portion was reduced in length to a short central section over the articulation of the bogies.

There were some notable examples of this sort of layout in the United States, including heavy freight locomotives of the 1–B–B–1–1–B–B–1 type – i.e. two units permanently coupled – on the Norfolk & Western, from 1915. The later examples of the type, built in 1926, had two traction motors per unit and a total output of 4,000 hp, for a weight of 350 tonnes. A similar, but triple-unit machine of 7,000 hp was used by the Virginian Railroad for the same sort of very heavy, slow speed haulage on severe gradients.

The single frame locomotives with jackshaft drive were very much inspired by the steam locomotive. Typical of the primitive stage were the locomotives of the Prussian State Railway Dessau-Bitterfeld experiment. A single very large motor was carried high and connected by cranks and rods to a jackshaft, in turn connected to the driving wheels. The motor thus ran at wheel speed, without gearing. The passenger type was a 2–B–1 – one is tempted to call it an Atlantic. The freight version was a D without carrying wheels, and there were others. The large motors were of around 1,000 hp. Locomotives of this type were often arranged to work permanently in pairs, like the well known Pennsylvania 2–B–B–2 of 2,500 combined hp which appeared in 1910, also with a single ungeared motor in each unit.

The larger single frame locomotives sometimes required two jackshafts set above the line of the wheels, and some sort of driving yoke linking them to the main coupling rod system. Again, Switzerland provides several examples including the 2–C–1 2,000 hp machines of the mid-1920s, mostly still in service 50 years later. Two jackshafts usually meant two or even four motors, and there was at least one example of the yoke arrangement being unable to stand up to the

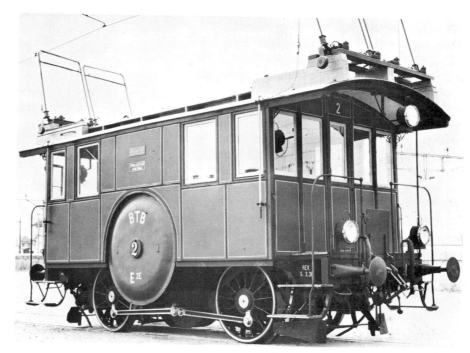

forces involved and disintegrating: this was on the 1–E–1 locomotives of the Berne-Lötschberg-Simplon Railway which started work in 1913. A much strengthened yoke was provided, but excessive weight in the rod mechanism was something to be avoided, because it gave rise to balancing problems like those associated with steam locomotives. So, although rod drive remains in use on many old locomotives still giving good service, in new construction it is confined to shunting types, and the independent drive is now the norm for everything else.

Top: In 1904, the North Eastern Railway electrified the goods branch to a Tyneside harbour, because of a horseshoe shaped tunnel on a steep gradient.

Above: The original three-phase two-speed locomotive of the Burgdorf-Thun Railway, 1899.

Below: Four-unit heavy freight electric locomotive of the Milwaukee Railroad.

The coupling of one motor to each axle has been done in two main ways. In one, a considerable part of the weight of the motor is carried directly on the axle, unsprung. The usual arrangement is called nose-suspension, in which bearings on the axle support one end of a frame, the other end of which is carried on the main or bogie frame and therefore spring-borne. The motor is fixed on the frame, its pinion in constant mesh with gear on the axle. Nose-suspended motors are still commonest on multiple-unit trains and diesel-electric locomotives. In Britain, they were used on the Metropolitan Railways' Bo–Bo machines of 1904 to 1906, also as later rebuilt in the LNER Manchester-Sheffield locomotives of 1940 to 1954; and even in some of the 50 Hz ac locomotives used on the West Coast electrified route. This arrangement is especially convenient when small wheels are used, and small wheels have always been preferred for electric locomotives in England. However, on the European continent, where, especially in Switzerland, the greatest use has been made of electric traction for all types of service for the longest period, fully spring-borne motors have long been preferred.

Two ways of connecting spring-borne motors to their axles are by means of a jointed shaft running to a pinion held in constant mesh with the axle gear, or by means of a quill, which is a hollow shaft mounted on bearings on the frame of the locomotive or bogie, within which the axle is free to move though coupled by some sort of spring network. A third way is the Büchli drive, much used on Swiss single-frame locomotives, and a speciality of Brown, Boveri. In the Büchli drive, the motors are over the axles and drive gears, outside the wheels on one side, which are mounted on stub axles in line with the driving axles. The drive is communicated by two short rods, cleverly attached to toothed quadrants pivoted on the gears in such a way that the drive is positive, but axle movement is permitted by the geometry. The rods have universally jointed ends, to permit lateral movement also. The main framing is inside the wheels, as in most steam locomotives, and auxiliary framing outside them, on the drive side, carries the stub axles and gear covers. With quill drives, the main frames are usually outside the wheels.

These individual axle drives with fully spring-borne motors were developed first in rigid frame locomotives having driving wheels of about 1,324 mm (5 ft) diameter, and carrying wheels at the ends. The Swiss 2–Co–1 machines of the 1920s were regarded as the standard express locomotive, and built in over 100 examples, whereas the rod drive equivalent, also of 2,000 hp, was considerd to be a mixed traffic locomotive, and only 60 were built. In fact, wheel diameter, gear ratio, and tractive effort were sensibly the same, but permitted maximum speed was 110 km/h (69 mph) for the individual drive machine as against 100 km/h (62 mph) for the other. The rod drive machine was slightly heavier, at about 98 tonnes. When a more powerful standard was required, 2–Do–1 individual

axle drive locomotives were built from 1927, and these were simply an enlargement of the similar twelve-wheeled ones, with power raised to 3,000 or more hp and weight up to 120 tonnes. All these individual drive machines had the Büchli drive.

Although undoubtedly it has been the Swiss who have led the development of electric locomotives for most of their history, important construction has taken place in many other countries, notably Hungary, Germany, France, Austria, and Sweden. Britain has not played a great role until recently, although a single very advanced electric locomotive was built for the North Eastern Railway in 1922. This was a 2–Co–2 with individual axle drive, built for an electrification between York and Newcastle which never took place. Although all countries are now wholly committed to individual drives, Sweden built large numbers of highly successful rod drive locomotives for all types of service. A characteristic of all these was the positioning of the jackshaft on the same horizontal line as the axles, making a perfectly normal steam locomotive-type coupling rod arrangement possible.

The application of fully spring-borne motors to bogie electric locomotives began very early in America, with such machines as the Boston & Maine 1–Bo–Bo–1 locomotives of 1911, but these had large wheels. Also, like so many double bogie machines, including a whole generation of those used for freight work, and many mixed-traffic locomotion such as the British LNER Bo–Bos built after the second world war, the bogies were directly coupled together, which does not con-

Above right: SNCF 3500 hp Bo-Bo electric locomotive for 25 Kv ac, 50 Hz, 1957 (weight 68 tonnes)
1. *Retracted Pantograph*
2. *High Tension Conductor*
3. *Air Circuit Breaker*
4. *Transformer*
5. *Ignition Rectifiers*
6. *Air Blower Motor*
7. *Transformer Oil Coolers*
8. *Air Brake Compressor*
9. *Traction Motor Air Cooler Blower*
10. *Traction Motor*
11. *Coupling Gearwheel Axle Bearing*
12. *Gearbox Housing*
13. *Master Controller*
14. *Tap Changing Transition Resistors (within cooling duct)*
15. *Smoothing Chokes*

Below right: Berne-Lötschberg-Simplon 1000 hp, 1-B-B-1, for 15Kv ac, 16 ⅔ Hz, 1920 (weight 70 tonnes)
1. *High Tension Conductors*
2. *Retracted Pantograph*
3. *Transformer*
4. *Traction Motor*
5. *Traction gearing*
6. *Jackshaft*
7. *Circuit Breaker*
8. *Radial Axle*
9. *Bogie Pivot*
10. *Sandbox*
11. *Air Brake Compressor*
12. *Driver's Controls*
13. *Traction Motor Cooling Air Blower*
14. *Transformer Cooling Air Blower*
15. *Resistance Housing*

Top right: 2,500 hp 1-E-1 locomotive of the Berne-Lötschberg-Simplon Railway, 1913. These were the first ten-coupled electric locomotives and after initial troubles with the driving yokes gave long and excellent service.

Top far right: The first of the Ae 4/4 class of the BLS railway, built in 1944. These locomotives set a new standard of power-to-weight ratio: 4,000 hp for 80 tonnes weight.

Left: Multiple unit electric trains of the Austrian Railways. The latest type is seen on the right.

duce to smooth riding. The essential of the modern bogie electric locomotive is that the bogies are not directly articulated, and the buffing and drawgear are mounted on the body ends. Another feature is wheels smaller than the driving wheels of single-frame locomotives, all these factors contributing to lightness.

With small wheels, and in the confined space of a bogie, an individual axle drive becomes more difficult to arrange. A most effective solution was devised for the Ae 4/4 class of the Berne-Lötschberg-Simplon Railway, built from 1944. Instead of a quill around the axle, the motor of each axle was provided with a hollow shaft. An inner shaft, flexibly coupled by a thin steel disc to the motor shaft at one end, was free to move within the motor shaft at the other, where it was flexibly coupled to what might be called a nose-suspended pinion in mesh with a large gear

rigidly fixed on the axle. The gear ratio was just under 6:1. The beauty of this was that the quill type arrangement was transferred from the axle, which has to be large to withstand track shocks, to the motor, and it could all be smaller because the power was being transmitted at a far greater rotational speed. The result was compact and light, and contributed to the remarkable power to weight ratio of these machines: 4,000 hp for 80 tonnes. These machines set the style for most subsequent double bogie electric locomotives, including Co–Co types, and not only in Switzerland, but their power to weight ratio has been improved upon since, and the quill drive surrounding the axle has been developed in lighter forms, including a variety in which the gear rotates upon a hollow stub axle, and carries elastic connections to a driving member fixed on the axle.

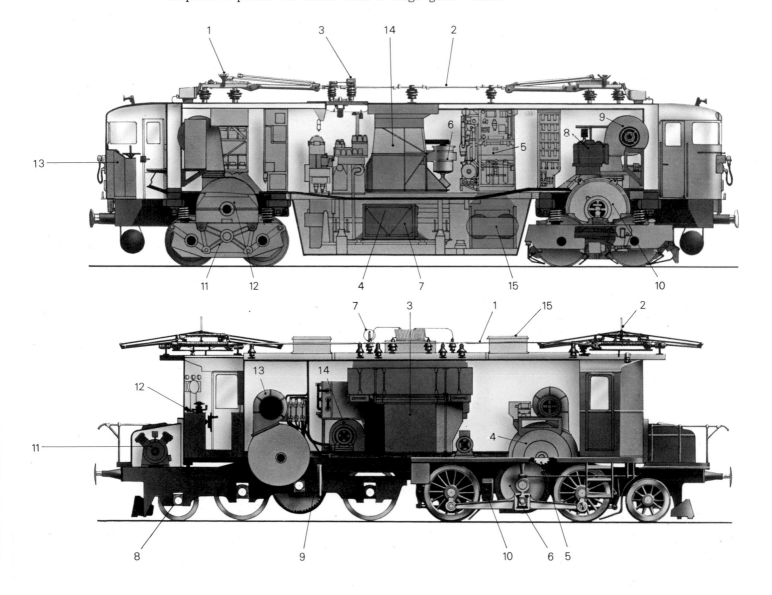

Left: Alignment of current collectors on one of the 800 hp 1–C–1 three-phase locomotives used for the opening of the Simplon tunnel in 1906. A four cylinder compound 2–8–0 steam locomotive of the Swiss Federal Railways does the pushing.

Below: In 1905, trains were worked into Grand Central Station, New York by this type of electric locomotive, steam being unacceptable in the central tunnels. A 1–Do–1 type, it weighed 93 tonnes.

Significantly different from the normal modern Bo–Bo locomotive is a French class designed in the late 1950s and built in some hundreds since. With a weight of 68 tonnes and a continuous power rating of 3,500 hp, this machine is a slight advance on the BLS Ae 4/4. Each bogie has a single traction motor, driving a large gear wheel in mesh with the gears coupled to each axle. To achieve this, the bogie wheelbase had to be short, some 1,524 mm (5 ft), and this in turn necessitated special arrangements for controlling bogie rotation. Two gear ratios are provided on these locomotives, one for freight working and one for passenger service, giving maximum speeds of 90 and 150 km/h (56 and 94 mph).

For the 25kV electrification at the industrial frequency of 50 Hz of the West Coast main line of British Railways, a long series of Bo–Bo locomotives have been built. The sixth series was equipped with axle hung motors in the belief that the unsprung weight associated with modern, relatively light, motors would not prove disadvantageous, but the latest machines have reverted to spring-borne motors design.

The design of running gear has by now changed completely from steam locomotive practice and traditional carriage design. Axleboxes do not slide in between vertical horns, but are usually guided by linkages incorporating rubber bushes, or bushed sleeves working on cylindrical guide posts. Bogies do not necessarily have central pivots but are similarly controlled by linkages and slides, and body weight is often carried at the sides of the bogie. A factor affecting design is the tendency of a bogie to tilt as a result of the tractive force, and thereby to transfer weight from one axle to another. To some extent this applies to the whole locomotive, but this can be countered by attaching traction links at suitable angles to carefully positioned anchorages. Multiple-unit trains increasingly use rubber springs and air springs in primary and secondary bogie suspension.

Electrical components
Direct current series-wound motors using low voltages were used in tramway practice and many early railway electrifications where the supply voltage was low. They are still used on the extensive Southern Region network of British Railways which uses a third rail contact system at some 660 volts, and at somewhat higher voltages, on locomotives taking 1,500 volts dc from overhead contact wires in Britain, and in other dc electrified systems. Recently, with the development of the rectifier locomotives taking ac at 25 kV and 50 Hz, the dc motor has become more common in traction applications. With dc supply, the series motor is controlled by connecting it in series or in parallel with its fellows, intermediate steps being provided by putting resistances in circuit for short periods. The characteristic of such motors is that the torque is greater at low speeds, so that a rising gradient which reduces speed will call forth a greater tractive effort. This is clearly a desirable condition, and matches the characteristics of steam locomotives. Some early ac electrification schemes used dc motors supplied by rotary converters. As all locomotives taking ac supplies are equipped with transformers, the converter itself could be controlled by varying the tapping of the transformer secondary. A modern rectifier locomotive can be controlled in this way, though other refinements are necessary.

The extensive use of 15,000 volt ac supplies in Switzerland and elsewhere at a frequency of 16 2/3Hz, single-phase, depended upon ac commutator motors of two types: series wound, and repulsion/induction. The series motor characteristics are the same with ac, and the repulsion/induction motor has the same behaviour, but with the advantage that it can be controlled by altering the angular setting of the brushes. With refinements of control based on tap-changing at the transformer the series type came to predominate.

The problem of all these traction motors was, and to some extent still is, the commutator and brush gear, which has to handle large currents, especially at low speeds, without excessive arcing. As motors have become individually smaller, these problems had reduced, but in early days they led to extensive trial of three-phase ac systems, which proved very satisfactory and

Above: The first British trunk route to be electrified was Manchester-Sheffield completed in 1954 though planned before the war. Here a 1500 volts dc Bo-Bo takes coal to Manchester.

Above right: Electric multiple unit train built in 1959, at present in service in the Manchester area.

Below: The most recent British suburban electric trains: 25 kV ac stock for Great Northern local services out of London, 1976. In the inner London tunnels, these trains operate on 600 volts dc collected from a third rail.

remained in use for a long time in, for instance, northern Italy. There were two disadvantages: the need for at least two separate contact wires, and the synchronous characteristic of three-phase brushless induction motors, which led to certain specific speeds being required during most of the running. The small B locomotives of the Burgdorf-Thun Railway, mentioned earlier, were three-phase machines with designed speeds of 19 and 36 km/h (11 and 22 mph).

Three contact wires were used on the remarkable Zossen-Marienfelde experimental line in Germany. They were arranged one above the other at the side of the track and three independent bow collectors were attached to the vehicles. On this line, in 1903, an electric railcar reached a speed of 216 km/h (135 mph).

The most successful three-phase system was that of the Hungarian firm of Ganz, whose chief engineer, Kalman Kando, is one of the few outstanding individuals, as distinct from companies, whose name is well known in the history of electric traction. From 1902 Ganz began electrifying mountain lines in Italy, using 3,000 volts and two contact wires. Locomotives developed for these lines were equipped with rod drive, a high proportion being 1–C–1 types, of which the earliest, of 1903, had a one hour rating of 1,200 hp for a weight of 62 tonnes. The success of these locomotives led to electrification of the Simplon tunnel line in a closely similar manner and to a considerable three-phase network in northern Italy. Control of the motors could be achieved by changing the effective number of poles in the stators, by switching connections. Commonly 8 and 16 poles were used. To this could be added cross connections between motors, called cascade connection, in which slip rings on one motor enabled its rotor to provide current for the second motor, to give slow running and good starting conditions. An element of rheostatic control was also needed for starting, and four economical running speeds were possible. The satisfactory results with three-phase traction motors led to the first extensive use of 50 Hz single-phase ac current for traction, which was again due to Kando. Between 1915 and 1920 he

Sectioned drawing of Swedish State Railways 2,580 hp, 1,500V, 16⅔ Hz ac electric locomotive, 1942

1 driving cab
2 transformer oil cooler
3 traction motor blowers
4 traction motors
5 transformer compartment and switchgear
6 transformer cooling oil pump
7 air compressor
8 pantograph
9 high tension busbars connecting pantographs

10 high tension busbar carrying current to transformer
11 main circuit breaker
12 pantograph operating cylinder and springs
13 relay cabinet
14 carrying wheels
15 driving wheels with elastic drive
16 main gear face
17 hollow axle
18 driving axle

19 sandboxes
20 sand delivery pipes
21 axle boxes
22 springs
23 compressed air reservoirs
24 brake shoes and hangers
25 buffers
26 drawgear
27 jumper cables
28 mainframes

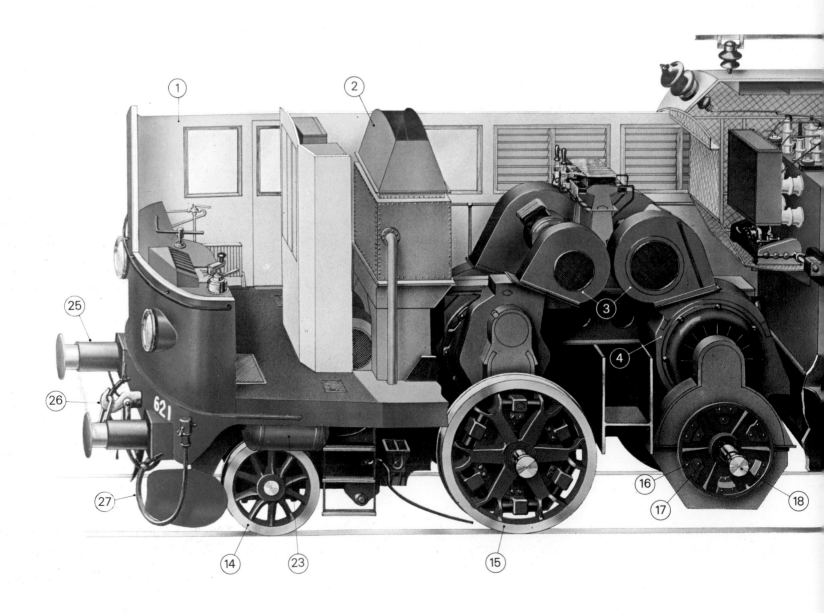

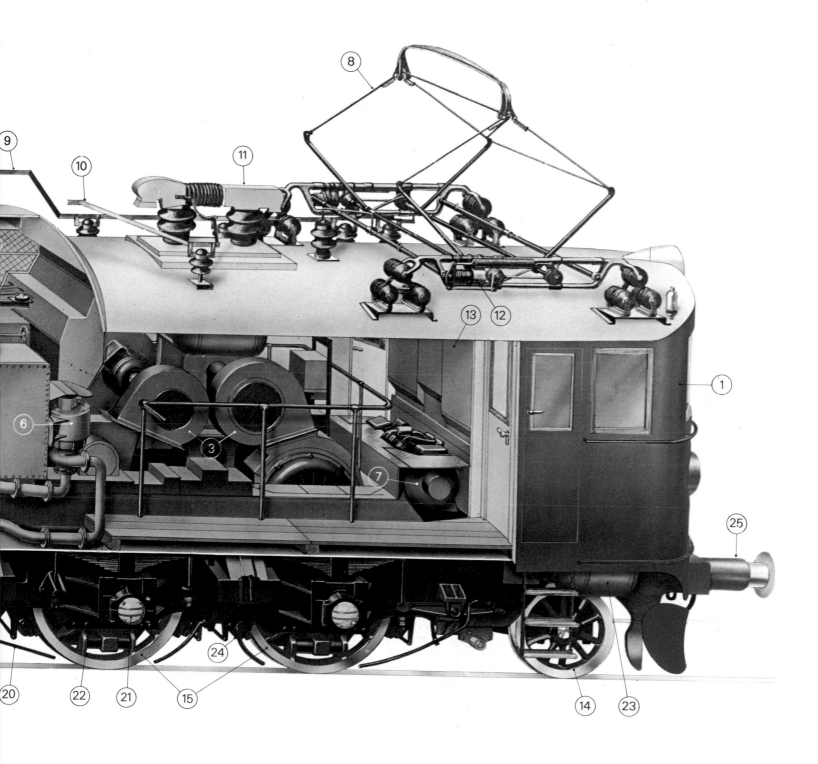

developed the phase converter locomotive, in which a rotary machine provided three-phase-supply for the traction motor. Thirty-two large locomotives of this type were later built, with single traction motors driving the wheels by rod drive, and with four possible groupings of the stator poles to give four economical speeds. These were very satisfactory and gave long service, while the advantage of drawing power at industrial frequency from the national electricity generating network has led to extensive adoption of 50 Hz supplies elsewhere.

Alternating current locomotives carry one or more transformers, which are the heaviest single pieces of equipment in the case of those handling the main traction current. Some early examples weighed as much as 20 tonnes. In double bogie locomotives this can be carried near the centre, but in many rod-drive and early individual-drive rigid-frame machines it had to be carried towards one end, where its inertia could cause rough riding on sharp curves. The transformer has to be cooled, as do the traction motors, and nowadays it is usually immersed in an oil bath, the oil being cooled in radiators under the locomotive. At one time the cooling pipes were conspicuous on the sides of some locomotives. The traction motors are cooled by blown air trunked to them.

Control by tap changing on the transformer used to be done on the secondary, low-voltage side, but is now commonly on the high-voltage windings, because the currents are much smaller. The moving contacts are largely protected against arcing by various devices, such as brief interruption of the current during tap changing,

using a separate, heavy, contactor with provision for arc quenching magnetically or by air blast. Air blast circuit breakers are also used to disconnect the supply from the pantograph when this is necessary for safety or protection of equipment. The main current collector today is the pantograph, which may be single or double sided, and is usually provided in duplicate. The actual surface which rubs on the contact wire may be of carbon blocks. Two-armed bow collectors were used in pairs on the Italian three-phase system.

The modern 25 kV 50 Hz single-phase locomotives are mostly fitted with rectifiers and dc traction motors. This has been largely because of the development of improved rectifiers. Some early use was made of mercury arc rectifiers, especially the simplified and more robust 'ignitron' produced by Westinghouse in the USA, but the real difference was made by solid state semiconductor devices, first the Germanium diode and then the Silicon diode. These have opened possibilities of electronic control in which rapid progress is currently being made. Solid state devices are smaller, lighter and intrinsically more robust that earlier mechanical control gear, and contribute to the increase of power-to-weight ratio of the electric locomotive, which has now reached the stage at which minimum weight is set by the adhesion, of what is now invariably an all-adhesion locomotive. Many locomotives and electric train sets are now used on international services in Europe which do not stop at frontiers. These are arranged to operate on different power systems, and to switch over while running at speed.

Electric traction offers possibilities of two

Above: The Pennsylvania 2–Co–Co–2 locomotives of the 1930s are the most numerous and still among the best in the United States. They weigh 212 tonnes and are of 4,680 hp.

Left: A modern Austrian luxury electric train.

Below: Swedish built electric locomotive in service in Denmark. Sweden is currently building some of the most advanced electric locomotives in the World.

kinds of electric braking: rheostatic, in which the motors acting as generators produce power which is dissipated in resistances on the locomotive, thereby converting the kinetic energy into heat to effect retardation; and regenerative, in which current produced by the motors is returned to the supply line. The latter is most used on very steeply graded routes, and allows a descending train to help pull an ascending one up.

Advantages of electric traction

It has never been convincingly proved that there is any cheaper way of pulling trains than by steam locomotives, but the operating advantages of electricity are great in all forms of traffic, so the

deciding factor is whether the traffic density is great enough to enable the high cost of the supply system, contact wires and so on, to be shared by enough traffic movements to make electrification economic. Those operating advantages are: cleanliness (absolutely necessary on such lines as the Simplon tunnel and the London tube, and highly desirable in all urban locations); availability of the power resource of a stationary power station instead of a moving one, especially on gradients, because much more power can, in fact, be drawn; high power available at low speed, which assists acceleration; and the mechanical possibility of the all-adhesion locomotive (possible with steam, but not for fast running), and the other possibility of fitting motors to the cars of a multiple-unit train, which can provide it with a high adhesion weight, a high tractive effort, and consequent rapid acceleration and hill climbing.

It should be noted that the powers of electric locomotives quoted here are those that can be sustained indefinitely, or in a few cases, for one hour. For shorter periods, higher powers are possible, at the cost of a rise in temperature of the traction motors, and for surmounting a short gradient at speed this is very useful. As the power demand in working a train fluctuates greatly over the route, the extra potential of the electric locomotive (and the power station) makes it a more effective traffic machine than it appears from its nominal rating. The same is true to a lesser extent of steam locomotives, which can put out short term powers above their continuous limit if the boiler water level is allowed to fall, and/or the boiler steam pressure. This does not apply to oil-engined machines, whose quoted power is the governed maximum of the Diesel engine, before electric (or in a few cases hydraulic or mechanical) transmission losses are deducted.

Above: The locomotive testing station at Vitry-sur-Seine in France, long used for scientific investigations into steam locomotives, now tests such machines as this latest SNCF Co-Co, able to use the traction supplies of several different countries.

Left: A three-unit electric locomotive returns light after taking a freight through the tunnel under Arthur's Pass, New Zealand.

Right: The lightly constructed overhead equipment made possible by the use of very high voltage supply current is clearly evident in this scene on the Norwegian Railways.

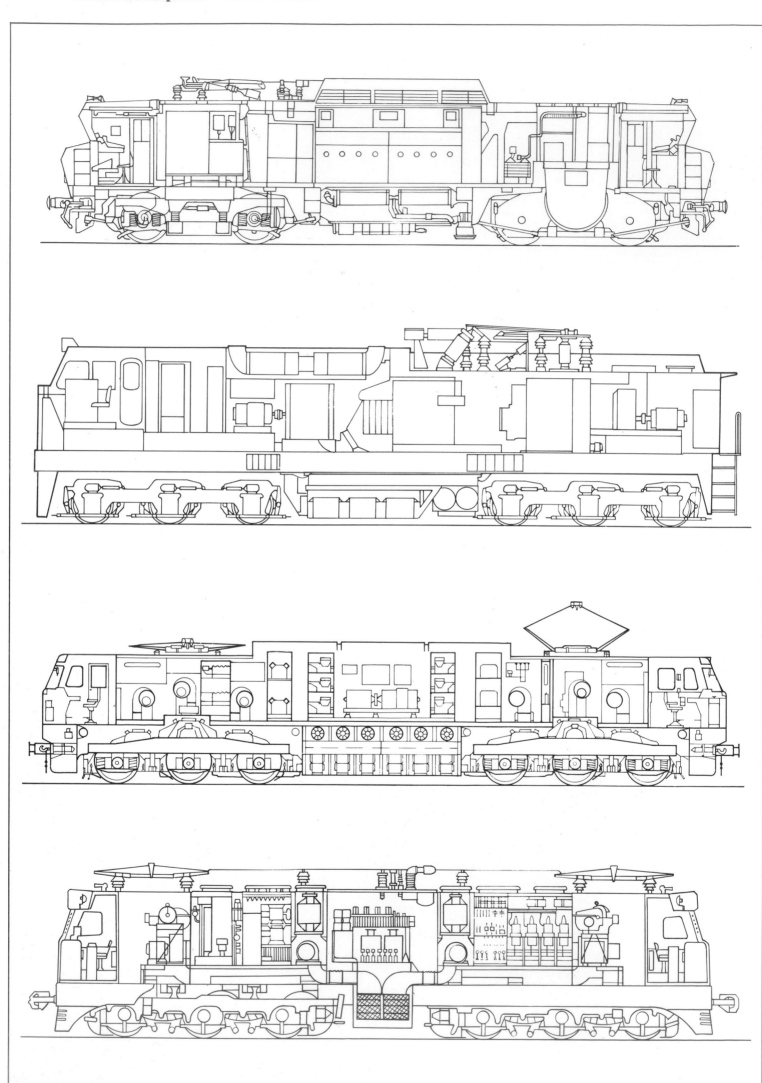

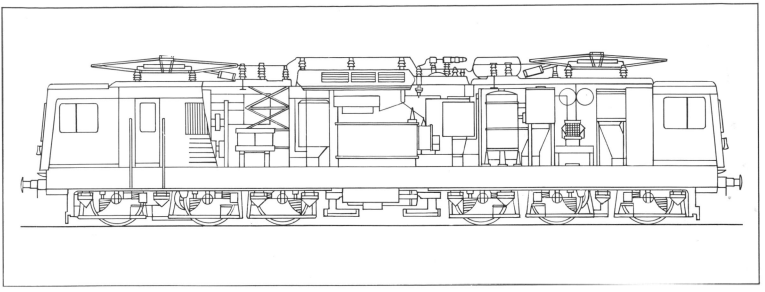

Above: Prototype ER200 high-speed electric multiple unit train of Soviet Railways. Currently on trial between Moscow and Leningrad, this 14-car train is designed for speeds up to 200 km/h (125 mph).

Opposite page from the top: Class 18 electric locomotive of the Belgian State Railways. This is a multicurrent design, able to work on Belgian 3,000-V dc, Dutch 1,500-V dc, French 25,000-V ac, and German 15,000-V ac systems. This class was built by the French Alsthom Company in 1973. Similar locomotives (Class 40100) have been built for the SNCF.

A 7,200 hp thyristor-controlled electric locomotive built in the German Democratic Republic. This locomotive (Class 250), is intended mainly for freight services; the prototype appeared in 1974.

Class E666 electric locomotive of Italian State Railways. A batch of these were ordered in 1975 for hauling 12-car passenger trains of 570 tonnes between Rome and Florence at speeds up to 200 km/h (125 mph).

A thyristor-controlled locomotive of British Rail. This unit, built in 1975, is basically of the 87 class, introduced for the West Coast main line; it was built in British Rail workshops with the assistance of GEC.

Right: German Federal Railways electric locomotive No.169 004-9 at Oberammergau in the Alps.

THE OIL ENGINED LOCOMOTIVE

The heavy oil engine appeared at the end of the 19th century and immediate attempts were made to apply it to rail traction in a number of primitive machines. The first successful use was on some railcars in Sweden in 1913, but as these were of small power and had the precedent of some petrol engined vehicles to follow, they hardly pointed the way to a locomotive of any considerable capacity. Early attempts at locomotives included the use of direct rod drive from oil engine cylinders, and pneumatic transmission, but in 1924 the diesel-electric locomotive, as it is today familiar, emerged in two places: Tunisia and the United States. The American machine was a Bo–Bo with four traction motors, and a 300 hp diesel engine. It was the joint product of Ingersoll-Rand (engine), General Electric (transmission) and the American Locomotive Company (vehicle). This locomotive was a shunter, and was the first of a long line of similar, very successful, shunters found all over the world today. Shunting is, in fact, the only duty for which oil-engine locomotives are used by virtually all administrations, for the obvious reason that electrified systems do not extend the overhead wires into all small yards, and usually not into privately-owned sidings.

Although the high-powered main-line diesel of the present day is simply an enlargement of the Ingersoll-Rand/GEC/Alco machine of 1924 (which might be likened to the *Rocket* in that respect) there was a period of experiment with rigid-frame engines having steam locomotive wheel arrangements, just as there was in the development of the electric locomotive. Some of these did quite well, like the Siamese 2–Do–2s of 1,000 hp which were appreciated because they did not require water. There were also the notable experiments of Lomonosoff in the USSR which established the advantage of electric over hydraulic or mechanical transmission for high powers; there were some Danish rigid-frame machines which gave good service; and above all, there were very many small shunters with four or six wheels in a rigid frame, some with mechanical, some with electrical, and some with hydraulic transmission. But the fact remains that, despite considerable progress with railcars, the diesel locomotive was essentially a shunter until after the Second world war.

In the USA oil at that time was cheap and its supply unaffected by international disputes and labour troubles, while coal was dear and effectively controlled by a particularly turbulent labour force. The diesel-electric locomotive, therefore, made rapid headway in the postwar reconstruction of motive power. The steam stock of the railways was run down, because steam locomotive builders, with their large-scale plant, had been engaged on war work and locomotive production had been greatly reduced. There was an opportunity for a mass-production oriented industry with spare capacity to produce relatively small diesel-electric locomotives which could still haul the heaviest trains because they could

Above: Two Co-Co diesel electrics forming a double unit haul the Santa Fe *Super Chief* and *El Capitan* combined expresses over the Raton Pass in New Mexico.

Below: Diesels in multiple arriving at West Palm Beach, USA.

be worked on the multiple-unit system. This opportunity was seized, by, for instance, the General Motors Corporation among others, which did the job with great thoroughness paying the greatest attention to proving the product on test beds and applying stringent quality control to the numerous components of what is a vastly more complicated machine than any steam locomotive ever was.

The relative prosperity of the USA enabled it to export these machines on favourable credit terms all over the world. Even in countries not techni-

cally dependent on American expertise, the example of the North American achievement established the modern diesel-engined locomotive as an effective and appropriate motive power tool, well able to supplant the steam locomotive if not the electric one.

The outstanding advantage of the diesel in the United States is multiple operation, which enables a very powerful traction machine to have a moderate axle loading, and cross section, and to take sharp curves easily. The excessive length is of no importance. In Europe multiple operation is

Above: The bogies, complete with traction motors, are interchangeable units. Here the body of a new locomotive is lowered onto them. The engine and generator unit, also interchangeable, can be lowered into the body subsequently.

Below: Already in the late 1930s the SNCF made great use of diesel-engined 'Autorails' for lightly loaded services.

Left: Just before the last war, the London, Midland & Scottish Railway started using diesel electric shunting locomotives on a small scale.

Above: The Deutsche Bundesbahn has a large fleet of these 2,000 hp diesels, the weight of which was kept down to 75 tonnes.

Below: Twin Co-Co diesel electrics of class TE7 at Leningrad in 1959.

not common and the single-unit diesel has been developed to higher powers. Elsewhere, diesels may be operated in pairs when necessary, but very seldom in threes, fours or even fives as is common in the United States. Everywhere the diesel shows a very high availability for service and is used intensively, but this is essential because its capital cost is very great, compared with an electric locomotive, let alone a steam one when all three types were in simultaneous production in many places, the cost per unit horsepower of a diesel-electric locomotive was about twice that of an electric, and five times that of a steam one. This has the effect of making some traffic unprofitable because its handling is incompatible with intensive use of the motive power. On the other hand, the light diesel railcar, often with mechanical transmission, can improve the economics of branch line operation for passengers.

Mechanical and electrical arrangement

All recent large diesel-engined locomotives are mounted on two bogies, and for high speed work these bogies follow electric locomotive practice closely in that each is independently attached to the body and exerts its tractive and braking forces through it. For shunting service the bogies sometimes carry the buffing and drawgear, but are not directly linked together, partly to improve the riding quality but also because the space between the bogies is usually needed for fuel tanks or other equipment. The first generation of mainline diesel electric locomotives on British Railways included a large number of 2,000 to 2,500 hp machines of the 1–Co–Co–1 wheel arrangement,

of which the bogies were built much like small steam locomotive frames, each with three individually-driven axles plus a carrying axle. The bogies were widely separated and carried buffers and drawgear. These locomotives are still in service. In overall length, number of wheels, and total weight (some 136 tonnes), as in power output, they equated very closely with a steam locomotive and tender used for similar duties. However, shortly afterwards, the all-adhesion Co–Co prototype *Deltic* locomotive showed a marked advance, having an engine shaft horsepower of 3,300 for a weight of just over 100 tonnes, and the production *Deltics* are slightly lighter. Although they date from 1960 these were the most powerful passenger diesel locomotives on British Railways until commissioning of the class 56 in 1976.

Where maximum power to weight ratio is not required, as in a very great number of North American diesels mostly worked in multiple, and also as in the British Brush Type 2 and other examples in other countries, the A–1–A + A–1–A arrangement is advantageous because the design of the bogie with only two traction motors simplifies the arrangement of the pivot, and the central carrying wheels reduce bogie stresses and axleloading, as compared with a two-axle layout.

Because the body has to accommodate a large diesel generator, the bogie units have to be kept low, and traction motors are not mounted above the axles as is common in straight electric machines. They are usually axlehung, but some recent high speed types have been equipped with wholly springborne motors using a layout with a partly axlehung pinion and a universal drive from

Left: The Victorian Railways use these 1,596 mm (5 ft 3 in) gauge class B diesels built in Australia.

Below right: Mixed traction in Italy: a diesel pilots a four cylinder 2–6–2 on a short, steeply graded section.

**Sectioned drawing of General Motors 3,600 hp
Co-Co diesel electric 'hood unit' locomotive,
1967**

1 horns
2 control desk
3 control cabinet
4 air intakes for engine room
5 traction motor blower
6 generator blower
7 exhaust stack
8 auxiliary generator
9 fans for dynamic brakes
10 engine water tank
11 radiator fans

12 radiator air intakes
13 sand pipes
14 air compressor
15 driving wheels
16 axle boxes
17 lubricating oil filter
18 brake cylinder
19 sand pipes
20 diesel engine
21 air reservoir
22 fuel tanks

23 air duct to rear traction motors
24 main generator and alternator
25 warning bell
26 traction motor
27 batteries
28 pilot (cow catcher)
29 buck-eye coupler
30 socket for multiple-unit control
   jumpers

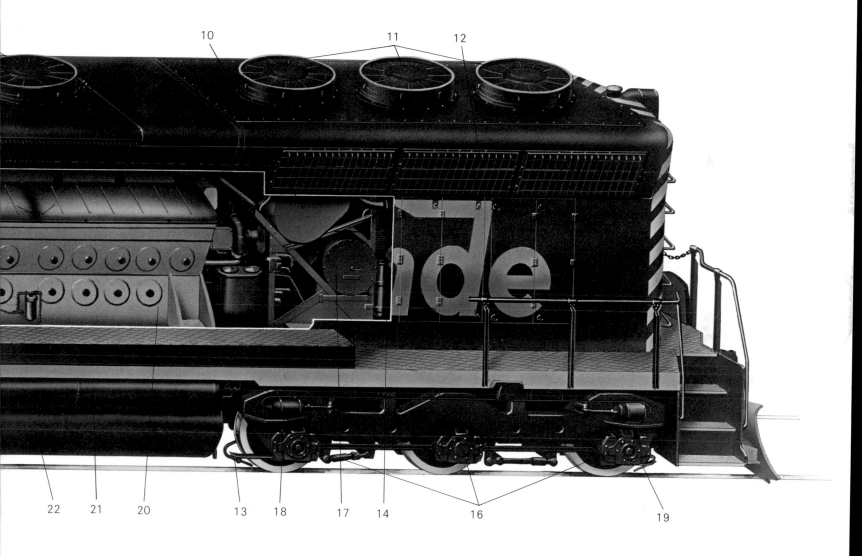

the motor, not unlike that described for the Berne–Lötschberg–Simplon Ae 4/4 locomotives.

The diesel engine may be a straightforward in-line machine, but is very commonly a Vee 12 or a Vee 16, and is mounted on a subframe with the generator. The *Deltic* locomotives have two engines and two generators, the engines being most unusual in having three crankshafts arranged in a triangular section, the cylinders between them with opposed pistons working on a two-stroke cycle. Sulzer has perfected a two-crankshaft design, with two rows of six cylinders side by side, which has been extensively used by British Railways in express locomotives.

The design of engines for railway traction has been complicated by unavoidable flexing of their mountings as the locomotive body responds to the movement of the bogies on the track. Taken with the need to keep the weight down, this has demanded a very careful study of structural design, not previously required for diesel engines.

Until recently, direct current was used for traction, and the generators were wound to provide characteristics matched to those of the traction motors and the diesel engines. This meant that the rotation speed was little varied, and the generator would deliver a lower voltage when a higher current was drawn from it. The diesel engine is protected against overload and possible stalling by suitable controls and the ultimate protection of a circuit breaker. Also there is usually provision for monitoring engine temperature at various sensitive points.

Above: British diesel for export: a Rolls-Royce engined diesel hydraulic railcar built for Jamaica by Metro-Cammell in 1962.

Below: The pageant of North American motive power: the Santa Fe proudly lines up a century of its history.

Above: Two power cars totalling 4,500 hp, 5 air conditioned luxury day coaches and two restaurant cars make up the trains of British Rail's Inter City 125 services, which run at 200 km/h (125 mph).

The undoubted complication of the control gear was a prime cause of failures in service in the early days of large-scale dieselization. This, and the weight penalty associated with electric transmission, led to a considerable use of hydraulic transmissions, most successfully in Germany. In one such, the Mekydro, a hydraulic torque converter is used at roughly constant speed and drives through a gearbox. In the Voith transmission there is no gearbox, a system of fluid couplings providing the necessary speed and torque variations. These systems have given improved power to weight ratios, but have declined in importance as development of straight electric locomotives has improved the characteristics of electric transmission. In particular, the use of alternators in place of direct current generators, made possible by the development of the solid state rectifier, has not only removed the rather troublesome commutator and brushgear, but has opened the way to designing the rest of the electrical gear more closely in line with modern straight electric practice.

The heating and braking of trains, having been developed with the steam locomotive, has presented some problems for the diesel designer. Steam heating has necessitated the provision of a boiler, usually oil-fired, which takes up space otherwise usable to increase the size of the main engine. Some diesels run with train heating vans attached in winter, so that the working of heavy summer traffic shall not be impaired by the need to carry around an unused boiler. Electric heating is powered by the main generator, or an auxiliary mounted on the same shaft, and takes proportionately more power from the engine than steam heating did from the boiler of a steam locomotive. Air brakes require a motor-driven compressor, which is at least as efficient as the steam locomotive's air pump, but much heavier, while vacuum brakes require a motor-driven exhauster which creates the vacuum more slowly than the large ejector of a steam locomotive. These are problems only where a high power to weight ratio and a limited length are desirable – in fact they are problems only in Europe.

In electric locomotives, power for auxiliaries can be drawn from the contact wire without affecting that available for the traction motors, so train heating boilers, if fitted, are usually electrically-fired; and compressors or exhausters can be built as large as may be needed. It is also possible to fit pantographs on vehicles of the train for some power requirements, such as cooking in the restaurant cars.

Gauges and Standards

In the space of 150 years mankind has covered the habitable portions of the globe with 1,500,000 km (900,000 miles) of railway, ranging from more than 200 m (650 ft) below sea level in Arabia to over 4,500 m (14,750 ft) in South America. For carrying goods and people en masse overland, the railway principle, by which two parallel steel rails provide guidance, support and almost frictionless running for pairs of flanged metal wheels is a form yet to be bettered.

Railways began their existence more as feeders to canals or ports rather than transport systems in their own right. Indeed, they were certainly in use with timber rails by the 16th century. Railways as we now understand them, with reliable mechanical haulage, became a practical proposition for general long-distance public transport by the 1830s. In order to take advantage of the new possibilities, gradients and curves usually had to vary considerably from those of the natural lie of the ground and accordingly cuttings had to be dug or embankments and viaducts provided to make up the difference. Fortunately, considerable experience in construction of big civil engineering works had been gained during the building of

Below: Flanged rails with a swelled upper edge laid on blocks. This waggonway, situated at the head of the Derby Canal in England, was built in the 1790s and ceased operation in 1908. It was used to carry coal to the canal for transhipment.

canals, the requirements for which had a certain amount in common with railways. For crossing rivers, experience in bridge-building had been accumulating since the days of the Roman Empire.

At first, it seemed absurd to worry that George Stephenson's railway between Liverpool and Manchester should be incompatible in gauge with Brunel's under construction between London and Bristol. Nevertheless, the two systems met at Gloucester in due course and there were serious problems of interchange. These problems were repeated in many countries and in some, notably India and Australia, are not resolved today. Palliatives, such as arrangements for wheel-changing and dual gauge track, can only be seen as partial solutions.

Before starting to build a railway, four separate standards must be considered. Second thoughts on any of them are apt to be expensive. First comes the track gauge, the distance between the rails. Oceans of ink have been expended on arguing the merits of different gauges when, in fact, the actual gauge – within wide limits – is not too significant. What is crucial is that a railway should have the same track gauge as any likely or unlikely neighbours.

One cannot but commend the countries of continental Europe (with the exception of Russia, Spain and Portugal) for adopting Stephenson's rather odd dimension of 1,435 mm (4 ft 8½ in). One and a half centuries later, we find the principal standardized main line gauges in the world to be as follows:

1,676 mm (5 ft 6 in)	India*, Pakistan, Argentine*
1,600 mm (5 ft 3 in)	Ireland, Australia*, Brazil
1,524 mm (5 ft 0 in)	Russia, Spain, Portugal, Finland
1,435 mm (4 ft 8½ in)	N. America, China, Egypt, Turkey, Iran, Japan*, Peru, Britain, Europe, Australia*, Brazil, Mexico
1,067 mm (3 ft 6 in)	Japan*, Australia*, Sudan, W. Africa, Southern Africa, New Zealand
1,000 mm (3 ft 3⅜ in)	E. Africa, India, Malaya, Chile, Argentina*

*countries with more than one 'standard gauge'

Much more important than the track gauge is the height and width of the largest rolling stock which can pass, known technically as the loading-gauge.

Brunel's GWR, locomotives and rolling stock were built to a width of 3.25 m (10 ft 8 in) and a height of 4.55 m (15 ft) compared with those of what he contemptuously called the 'coal-waggon gauge', with which the railways in Britain are even now saddled, of 2.75 m (9 ft) in width and 3.95 m (12 ft 11 in) in height. This is the most restrictive loading gauge of any 'standard-gauge'

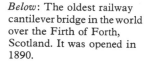

Above: Conversion of the Great Western Railway's broad gauge (2134 mm–7 ft) to the British standard gauge of 1435 mm, near Plymouth in 1892.

Above right: Dual gauge track is still necessary in many parts of the world.

Left: Checking the track gauge (in this case 1524 mm–5 ft) in the USSR.

Below: The oldest railway cantilever bridge in the world over the Firth of Forth, Scotland. It was opened in 1890.

country. The rest of Europe permit 3.1 m (10 ft 2 in) width and 4.5 m (14 ft 9 in) height, while in America even more room is available up to 3.3 m (10 ft 10 in) horizontally and 4.9 m (16 ft 2 in) vertically. Russia has the greatest loading gauge of all, 3.4 m (11 ft 2 in) wide by 5.3 m (17 ft 4 in) high.

The third point to consider is the weight of the trains. As regards the track, the load on each axle is important and in respect of bridges it is their combination that is significant. A balance between the permitted size and weight of rolling stock is important too; it is no use having a big structure gauge if, as was for many years the case in Russia, track and bridges are too weak to carry locomotives and loads to use it properly. However, rectification of this particular matter is the least onerous of the four. Bridges can usually be strengthened and light rails – which in any case wear out – can be replaced with stronger ones. In Britain, the railways have recently upgraded part of the network to take 25 tonne instead of 20 tonne axleloads at little cost beyond that of necessary renewals. On the other hand, to improve the structure gauge to the European standard would be prohibitive both in cost and in disruption. Most bridges, tunnels and station platforms would need complete reconstruction.

The fourth civil engineering standard to be defined is the minimum radius of curves. Although speeds may be seriously affected, (the effect of this is discussed under choice of route) compatibility is normally no problem until curves come down to about 150 m (7½ chains) radius, below which difficulties arise with long vehicles or, say, locomotives with a long rigid wheelbase.

Far left: British standard joint in flat bottomed rail. Note the gap between rails to allow for expansion.

Left: Typical bullhead rail track as used in Great Britain.

The conventional panacea for sharply-curved railways was to reduce the track gauge and, accordingly, many subsidiary lines were built to a narrower track gauge than standard. This was particularly so in mountainous areas, because of the saving of cost that arises in such places through the use of sharp curves and smaller tunnels. Here again there has sometimes been confusion between loading gauge and track gauge. Standard-gauge lines of light construction often exist with curvature sharper than many narrow-gauge lines possess, although it is true that very, sharp curves, down to 20 m (1 chain) radius can only be laid on the narrowest gauges. Engineers have, however, seldom taken advantage of this facility.

Again, could one imagine smaller tunnels than those of the standard-gauge tube lines of London Transport whose trains are a mere 2.9 m (9 ft 5½ in) high? The new Moelwyn Tunnel under construction for the Festiniog Railway – 600 mm (1 ft 11½ in) gauge – has a cross-sectional area much greater than a tube tunnel built for 1,435 mm (4 ft 8½ in) gauge. The advantage gained from compatibility of gauge is that, at least, the trains from the subsidiary line can run out on the main line – as tube trains now run out into the suburbs – even if the converse is not possible.

Though the concept may have been a false one, much subsidiary narrow gauge track exists in countries with 'broad gauge' as standard and certainly adds a good deal of variety and interest to the world railway scene. Variety is the word for, in countries with wider standard gauges, lines built to 600 mm (1 ft 11½ in), 610 mm (2 ft 0 in), 686 mm (2 ft 3 in), 750 mm (2 ft 5½ in), 760 mm (2 ft 6 in), 800 mm (2 ft 7½ in), 914 mm (3 ft 0 in) and 1,000 mm (3 ft 3⅛ in) gauges – to mention the commoner ones – can be found. Very few countries today are bereft of little railways.

It should be added, perhaps, that no railway achieves exactly its specified gauge throughout its length. Gauge is widened deliberately on very sharp curves to ease passage of long rigid vehicles; railways in Britain specify up to a 19 mm (¾ in) increase to 1,454 mm (4 ft 9¼ in) in such circumstances. Gauge can also widen involuntarily if tracks work loose, which happens occasionally on the best regulated railways.

Permanent Way

The term 'Permanent Way' arose in order to distinguish the temporary lines of contractors from those on which the permanent traffic of a railway would run. On the first railway to use mechanical haulage for all traffic wrought iron rails were used, held in chairs fixed by iron spikes and wood plugs to stone blocks. However, the flexibility of the formation over the swamp of Chat Moss led George Stephenson to try there the idea of timber cross-ties or sleepers, which have since become universal. Usually wood is used, but occasionally steel and now today frequently concrete. Steel rails began to replace iron in the late 1870s, with advantages in the increased quality of both strength and wear.

Chaired track with steel bullhead rail, was normal both in Britain and in a few other countries until the 1950s. A quarter of a century later huge lengths of this type of construction remain in use on secondary routes and on rapid-transit railways.

The world standard, however, from earliest days, was the flanged or flat-bottom rail spiked to timber sleepers.

Rails have steadily increased in size from 100 mm (4 in) depth weighing 16 kg/m (32 lb/yd), to a section nearly twice as deep and weighing 77.5 kg/m (155 lb/yd), occasionally used in the USA, but a typical main line rail currently in use world-wide has a height of around 160 mm (6½ in) and a weight of 50 kg/m (100 lb/yd). The wheelload a rail can safely carry depends not only on its weight but also upon the space between adjacent sleepers; more sleepers are necessary for lighter rail. For example, in Britain, sleepers are normally spaced at around 760 mm (30 in) centres, whilst in America, where axleloads are heavier, they are placed 500 mm (20 in). Furthermore, as wear takes place over a period of years, the weight of rail will decrease by 5 kg/m (10 lb/yd) or more, and this loss must necessarily be taken into account.

The standard fishplate joint, with the sleepers arranged one on each side at or near the normal spacing evolved fairly quickly. It superseded the superficially attractive but inferior idea of arranging a sleeper or block under the joint. This illustrates the way in which permanent way design appears simple but is actually subtle. Faults in

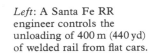

Above left: The highspeed *ligne des Landes* running from Bordeaux to Hendaye, France.

Above: Modern track with rubber chairs used in France.

Left: A Santa Fe RR engineer controls the unloading of 400 m (440 yd) of welded rail from flat cars.

Below: Flat bottomed track on wooden sleepers with Pandrol fastenings.

design will be discarded very quickly – it is less obvious that a design idea is a correct solution.

Joints are a serious weakness in the track and nowadays the solution is to eliminate them by welding rails into continuous lengths. (In fact, it is a case of re-welding, for they leave the makers' rolls in continuous lengths, but have to be cut up to be loaded at the steelworks). Once rewelded electrically, and loaded up under a special gantry they can be run to site on a specially fitted train capable of carrying 300 m (1,000 ft) lengths or more. These rails can then be pulled off the back of the last wagon direct on to the sleepers, existing short rails held by a minimum of fastenings, are unclipped and tipped out in the short intervening space. The long rails are themselves then welded together *in situ*.

Expansion and contraction is catered for as an internal compression or expansion stress in the welded rail. These stresses are limited by laying the rails (and, if necessary, re-laying them at a later date) when they are at a temperature which is a mean of the highest and lowest likely to be experienced. The man in charge has to take the temperature of the rails as a check. Concrete sleepers and additional ballast further reduce the liability of welded track to deform under stress.

A crucial component in satisfactory permanent way is the broken stone ballast which, when clean and sharp, performs its proper function of spreading the loading which occurs under the sleepers and is too concentrated for normal ground. Ash or sand is occasionally used in place of stone on

secondary lines and tracks. Beneath an adequate depth of ballast this loading is reduced to an amount which normal ground can bear. If ballasting is inadequate, serious problems will soon occur as the overloaded ground formation undergoes progressive failure.

The latest development in permanent way is concrete slab track, which is expensive and very disruptive to instal on existing lines but is largely maintenance free. The largest known installation is on the recent 396 km (630 mile) extension to the Japanese (Shinkansen) high-speed network which includes 272 km (435 mile) of slab track.

Junctions are made up from simple turnouts, diamonds, and single or double slips. These items are composed of pairs of points or switches and common and obtuse crossings. Short, sharp turnouts suitable for low speeds are used in sidings, whilst at the other end of the scale components for high-speed junctions are available on which speeds up to 120 km/h (75 mph) can be run comfortably on the diverging route. In some cases where very flat angles are involved, the crossings have to be moveable as well as the switches.

For many years crossings were fabricated from rail. A typical common crossing would have two 'wing' rails and a crossing vee made up from two other blocked and bolted between them. Nowadays, however, steel monobloc castings are used for main lines.

The impermanence of permanent way has already been mentioned; coping with this impermanence used to be a matter of endless and painstaking work with hand tools. Lining with bars, lifting with jacks, packing with shovels, and changing sleepers by hand, was the order. In recent years, much of the hardest work has been taken over by mechanization of various kinds, such as tracklaying cranes lifting, lining and tamping machines and mobile compressors and generators to run power tools.

Choice of route
Having settled the basic standards, the engineer must now consider how to lay out his railway in relation to the ground surface so that a proper balance between cost of construction and cost of working is achieved. It has been mentioned that the sharpness of the curvature with which a railway is laid out affects the speed of trains. In quantitative terms, typical maximum permitted speeds would be as follows:

Curve of radius
4,000 m (200 chains) 256 km/h (160 mph)
1,000 m (50 chains) 128 km/h (80 mph)
 500 m (25 chains) 80 km/h (50 mph)
 200 m (10 chains) 30 km/h (20 mph)
 100 m   (5 chains) 15 km/h (10 mph)
Note: before metrication the radius of railway curves were normally specified in chains – 1 chain = 20.12 m (66 ft), 80 chains = 1.609 km (1 mile).

These speeds allow for banking the track, that is, providing cant or super-elevation by raising the outer rail of a curve above the inner to compensate for the centrifugal force. There is practical limit of around 150 mm (6 in) because slow running or stationary trains – which have to be catered for as well – are liable to derail on curves with any greater super-elevation.

The sharper the curve the easier it is to go round hills rather than through them, and rivers can be crossed economically at right angles rather than obliquely.

Not only speed but also load is affected by another factor, the maximum gradient. Of course, the amount of curvature does affect the load that can be hauled, but this is a secondary effect. In approximate terms, the load a locomotive the whole of whose weight is available for adhesion, might be expected to haul on various grades is as follows:

On a grade of 1 in 20 2½ times its own weight
On a grade of 1 in 25 3 times its own weight
On a grade of 1 in 40 6 times its own weight
On a grade of 1 in 100 14 times its own weight
On a grade of 1 in 200 20 times its own weight

It follows that heavy gradients mean catastrophic increases in the cost of haulage. Yet easy grades also mean going through hills not over them and perhaps high bridges over rivers rather than low ones, so an easily graded railway in hilly country is extremely expensive.

Above left: New track laid on ballast which is in turn laid on sand to make a foundation.

Above centre: Earth moving plant being used in the relaying of track. New ballast is being spread to receive the replaced track.

Above right: A Santa Fe RR track gang laying 400m (440 yd) lengths of welded rail near Stanton, California.

Right: The 1067 mm (3 ft 6 in) gauge used on South African Railways enables trains to negotiate tighter curves than would be possible on a wider gauge. Shown here is the Mossel Bay-Johannesburg express climbing to the summit of the Lootsberg Pass.

Very often financial stringency means that a railway has to be built cheaply first in the first place. Then, when revenue begins to flow in and traffic increases, a new and more expensive alignment becomes worthwhile. For example, in 1904, the Southern Pacific Railroad in the USA by-passed its original heavily-graded and sharply-curved line which wound around the shore of Salt Lake in Utah and, incidentally, included the famous spot called Promontory where in 1869 the golden spike was driven. The by-pass, 212 km (132 miles long), saved 44 miles and was excellently aligned including a dead straight 37 km (23 miles) trestle bridge – the

longest continuous bridge ever constructed. A further improvement, completed in 1950 after many years' work, was conversion of the bridge into an embankment but the same argument of balancing a cheap railway which is expensive to run against an expensive railway which is cheap to run continued to apply.

The normal way to adapt the lie of the ground to a railway grade is to excavate cutting and tip embankments 'cut and fill'. The most economical conditions occur usually if the route has been adjusted to balance the amount of cutting to that of filling. The slopes of both cuttings and embankments vary according to the material encountered. Typically a slope of 1½ to 1 (34 degrees) will suffice to give stability, but the sides of cuttings in material such as chalk or rock can approach the vertical, with enormous reductions in the amount of digging. Cuttings in treacherous clays – rock hard in dry weather, like porridge in wet – need, for example, much gentler slopes. The amount of excavation and area of land required for the railway can be reduced by building retaining walls on either side of the line, but

Above left: herring bone drainage system on cutting on the London to Ramsgate line.

Above right: Back-to-back rack locomotives head a freight train over a ravine in Yugoslavia.

Right: Simple trestle bridge on the Vale of Rheidol Railway in Wales.

Below: The Alte Trisannabrücke in Austria.

unless there is some special reason – say, very expensive land – the cost is much greater. Sometimes, as at Sonning on the Great Western Railway in England, it is convenient to widen a deep cutting with small retaining walls.

Originally cuttings big and small were dug by hand and the material removed by horse and cart, but, by degrees, machines have taken over. First came temporary tramways using steam haulage to move the material from cutting to embankment, then early and crude steam shovels, finally developing into the armoury of earth-moving plant available to today's civil engineers.

Vitally important – but hidden and consequently perhaps a little uninteresting – in any cutting (or for that matter, tunnel) is a drainage system to keep dry and therefore stable the formation on which the track is laid. In clay material, drains are often needed on the face of the cutting slope, to do the same job. Each drain consists of a trench along the bottom of which runs a pipe – with manholes at intervals. After laying the pipe, the trench is back-filled with broken stone or large gravel.

Depending on circumstances, as the depth of a cutting increases, there comes a point where boring a tunnel becomes cheaper.

Embankments, tipped from loose material, need to be consolidated and it is usually a while before the track laid on top ceases to need extra attention. Before embankments are tipped, bridges, culverts and any retaining walls needed must be complete. As with a cutting, there comes a point when a viaduct is cheaper than a high embankment, with what could be, in effect, quite long tunnels for any roads and rivers running through it at the base.

BRIDGES AND VIADUCTS

Beams and girders

Bridge-building must be one of the most satisfying activities known to man. Millions of years have elapsed since early man first deliberately caused a tree to fall across a stream so that he could cross dry-footed. Pairs of tree-trunks, with a little squaring-off to make them into timber baulks about 350 mm (14 in) square, provide excellent railway bridges up to about 5 m (15 ft) span and many thousands are in use.

The term 'span' means the distance between bridge supports, or 'abutments' as they are usually termed. If a bridge has more than one span the additional central supports are referred to as 'piers'.

Our squared tree trunk is the model for the most common family of railway bridges, the beam or girder bridge resting on simple supports at either end. Unfortunately timber lacks durability as well as strength compared with iron and steel, but still has a place in bridge building.

In any solid beam the material in the middle contributes less to its strength than that in the top and bottom and early on this suggested a beam in the form of an iron box. This also has the all-important virtue of resistance to any tendency to buckle under load.

When in the 1850s Robert Stephenson was faced with the problem of taking the Chester & Holyhead Railway across the Menai Straits in Wales and conditions required two spans of 139 m (460 ft), which was several times that of any railway girder bridge previously built, he chose just such an iron box. The depth required to give adequate strength and stiffness was such that the trains could run inside, which they continued to do from 1856 when the structure (known as the Britannia Bridge) was opened, until 1971 when a disastrous fire damaged the original girders beyond repair. The modern steel-arched bridge which then replaced it is of a very different concept.

The cost of a beam increases in much more than direct proportion to its span. A big span is only justified if intermediate piers would for any reason be extremely expensive or in some way would not meet the requirements. In the case of the Menai, both reasons applied; the central piers or towers stood 69 m (230 ft) high and there were navigational objections to more than one in the centre of the channel.

Left: Brick arches on the Ouse Valley Viaduct in England.

Below: The Alexandria Bridge across the River Chenab on the Lahore to Peshawar line in Pakistan. Each of the 17 spans is 40.5 m (133 ft) long.

If one takes a box shape and moves the sides together to the middle, the result is an I. This is another economical shape for a beam or girder. These are very commonly used for all except the longest spans, either in the form of rolled steel sections or built up from steel plates. This was done at one time by riveting, but now usually by welding. Built-up girders are sometimes made bowed along the top or bottom flange (occasionally both) in order to make the beam deeper in the centre, where the maximum strength is required to resist the greatest bending forces which occur there. It must be remembered that the majority of bridges on the world's railways are small, carrying trains over roads or streams or roads over the railway. Nowadays such bridges almost invariably consist of solid concrete beams, reinforced with steel wires and bars, but many, thousands of small plate girder or I-beam bridges exist and offer few problems except a continuous battle against the effects of corrosion.

For large spans and very deep girders it is better to replace the vertical plate by individual members – usually diagonals with or without verticals – to form a truss girder. The Fades Viaduct in south-eastern France is such a bridge, built in 1905 with a span of 144 m (473 ft). Until recently, it was believed to be the highest in the world, being 132 m (435 ft) from rail to river.

Eclipsing Fades, the Mala Rijeka Bridge on the new line from Belgrade to Bar in Jugoslavia was opened in 1976. Here, the height is 201 m (660 ft) and the largest span 151 m (495 ft).

There is one important difference between these bridges. On the Fades bridge, trains run on the deck of the girders, while on the Mala Rijeka they run through between them. This latter arrangement makes a system of secondary girders necessary because the main girders must be sufficiently far apart to pass the trains.

The plain girder bridge with the greatest span is the Metropolis Bridge carrying the Burlington Northern Railroad across the Ohio River at Paducah mid-western USA. It is 222 m (720 ft) span and the height of truss necessary to achieve this is 33 m (110 ft).

Slightly greater girder spans have been economically achieved by connecting adjacent girders together, making a continuous structure across the piers. Each span both makes and receives a measure of strength and stiffness to and from its neighbours. Amongst those with the greatest spans is the Huey P Long rail and road bridge built in 1938 over the Mississippi River at New Orleans. The maximum span is 240 m (790 ft) and the Southern Pacific Railroad retains the world record with the 7 km (4.4 mile) length of this bridge now that the Salt Lake crossing is classed as an embankment. The mile-long double-deck rail and road bridge over the Yangtse River at Nanking, one of the great achievements of the People's Republic of China, is designed on this principle. There are ten spans of 160 m (525 ft).

Most long girder bridges have many spans and are usually a combination of the types mentioned, perhaps, like the 3.2 km (2 mile) Strorstron

Bridge in Denmark, opened in 1937, with riveted plate girder deck-type spans on the approaches and through-type truss spans on the main navigational openings. Of similar arrangement, but with lattice instead of plate girders on the subsidiary spans is that which still remains the longest bridge in Europe, the 4.2 km (2.6 mile) Tay Bridge in Scotland; the original structure succumbed to wind pressure during a gale while a train was crossing on December 29, 1879, only 18 months after opening. A new structure was opened in 1887.

We have been speaking, as is customary, of bridges which are 'the longest' or 'the highest'. Civil engineers are not particularly impressed with either of these criteria. They do take off their hats, however, to bridges with the longest spans, because design problems more than quadruple for each doubling of the length. In respect of height, it is not that measured from river level which impresses; instead, one should think of the height above the base of the foundations, which may be much greater.

As an illustration of this point, consider the bridge which carries the railway a modest 9 m (30 ft) or so above high water across the Mawddach river estuary at Barmouth in Wales. At 690 m (2,253 ft) it is the longest in Wales. But, being formed of 117 spans, mostly of timber, the superstructure is attractive but technically of little account. However, the central foundations of the main span, which was originally arranged to swing aside to allow vessels to pass, go down 27 m (90 ft) to bedrock; the men who did this could fairly call themselves engineers.

Such a depth is by no means a record; in the plains of India with their fathomless alluvial deposits, early British engineers took foundations down as far as 50 m (165 ft) below river level, as at the Hardringe Bridge now in Bangladesh over the River Ganges. An idea of the work involved is gained when one considers that the hidden parts of the double piers of the 1875 river Chenab Bridge north of Lahore add up in depth to over 5 km (3 miles).

The Hawkesbury river bridge, in New South

Above: A goods train on the Makohine Viaduct, New Zealand.

Above right: Sydney Harbour Bridge, which has the largest steel arch span in the world.

Below: The Bio-Bio Bridge at Concepción, Chile.

Below right: Steel arch and box girder bridges on the Feather River Canyon, California.

Wales, with seven truss girder spans of 126 m (416 ft), completed in 1889, had foundations as deep but settlement occurred and cracks appeared in the piers. The speed of trains was restricted to 8 km/h (5 mph) for a long period until a new bridge – with foundations up to 55 m (183 ft) below river level – was opened in 1946.

Nowadays, various types of timber, steel or concrete piles driven into the ground (or, in the latter case, cast into bored holes) enable these sort of conditions to be tackled less painfully.

In some cases, river bridges must be provided with opening spans for navigational purposes. The commonest way is to pivot the bridge about a vertical axis and swing it clear. Alternatively, a bridge can be lifted either vertically – in which case the obstruction is merely raised – or at one end with a horizontal pivot or rolling path at the other. Examples of the three types are illustrated. First, there is the swing bridge at Selby carrying the main London-Edinburgh line over the river Ouse in Yorkshire. Second is the surprisingly handsome Buzzard's Bay Bridge of 95 m (544 ft) span, opened in 1935, carrying Conrail trains across the Cape Cod Canal, Massachusetts, USA. Lastly, we return to 'ole man river' for the Atchison, Topeka & Santa Fé Bridge at Fort Madison, Iowa, completed in 1927 and including one lifting draw span of 160 m (525 ft) in its overall length of 1,020 m (3,347 ft).

A rare type is a true drawbridge; in this the opening span is drawn away from the bridge into a recess under the tracks. One existed at Newport in the Isle of Wight (UK) for many years, crossing the river Medina.

On the Furka Oberalp Railway in Switzerland a liftable bridge exists, which is opened all winter when the line is closed to provide free passage for avalanches.

Trestle bridges

So far it has been assumed that piers and abutments are made from brickwork, masonry, or concrete. However, in many cases, piers are made of steel or timber, and then the structure is usually described as a trestle.

The timber trestle railway bridge opened up the American West. It was quick and cheap to build but had the disadvantage of impermanence and most are now rebuilt in steel or replaced by embankments. A famous mountain example which survived until 1951 was at Ophir, Colorado on the Rio Grande Southern.

Typical of modern steel trestle bridges is the Mohaka Viaduct on the Hawke's Bay line in New Zealand, built in 1937 and at 96 m (318 ft) the highest in that country. The trestle bridge has one particular advantage, namely, its adaptability to a curved alignment, and this is well illustrated by the El Polvorilla Viaduct near San Antonio de los Cobres in the Argentine Andes, opened in 1948. A height of 89 m (290 ft) makes this eight span bridge a most impressive structure.

Cantilever bridges

The giants of the bridge world are the mighty cantilever structures. The very large spans achieved with this type of bridge have something of sleight-of-hand about them. The trick is done by bracketing out from piers and abutments and supporting girders of lesser span at the ends of the brackets or, as they are called, cantilevers.

The largest span railway bridge existing in the world today is at Quebec over the St Lawrence river carrying the Canadian National Railway line. The span is 549 m (1,800 ft). It was completed in 1917 after many vicissitudes including a failure of one of the main cantilevers in 1907 and the dropping of the suspended span while being lifted into position during 1916.

A little more famous, perhaps, is Scotland's Forth Bridge which has two main spans of 520 m (1,710 ft) and which dates from 1890. A feature is that all the main members are tubes, which, while structurally ideal, make for very expensive shaped platework at the points where they need to be joined at various angles.

Arched bridges

The arched type of bridge is one which has competed successfully with girders and beams throughout history for the whole range of spans from the smallest to the largest. Arched bridges are also very ancient and, built in stone, brick or concrete, they normally have no real limit to their lives. As time goes by, the filling placed on top of the arch consolidates to become part of it, thereby enhancing strength. However, if there should be any movement of abutments or piers which affects the points from which the arch is sprung, bad trouble results.

If individual openings are short enough, arched bridges and viaducts can be adapted to fairly sharp curves. An exceptional example is the Landwasser Viaduct on the Rhaetian Railway in Switzerland where the whole structure is on a curve of 100 m (328 ft) radius and, incidentally, a gradient of 1 in 29. The top arch is sprung on one side from a sheer precipice and on the other from a pier 65 m (213 ft) high. An end-on view shows that the flowing curve is in fact a series of straights, as an arch curved in plan is a structural nonsense.

Above left: A wooden trestle bridge in Mexico.

Above: The Cize-Bolozon Viaduct in France.

Below: The masonry arch viaduct above the Landwasser River in Switzerland. It carries the Rhaetian Railway.

Right: The steel arch bridge across the Zambezi River at Victoria Falls. The bridge carries a rail link between Rhodesia and Zambia.

Below right: A Canadian Pacific tanker train headed by four diesels on the Lethbridge Viaduct over the Oldman River in Alberta. The viaduct is the highest in Canada, being 95.7 m (314 ft) high.

The stone or brick arch bridge with the greatest span is Ballochmyle Viaduct in south-west Scotland, built in 1896, with 55.2 m (181 ft). For larger spans, masonry arches present problems in ensuring stability, but if reinforced concrete is used much greater spans become possible.

For still greater spans, arched bridges made of steel can be used. A steel arch could be regarded as a special case of a girder which, to ease its tendency to bend in the middle, is held and squeezed horizontally inwards low down at the ends. The steel arch itself can either be below or above the track; both types are visually most attractive. Of the former, easily the most famous is the Victoria Falls Bridge of 152 m (500 ft) span, built in 1905 and now joining Rhodesia and Zambia railways. Notable also is the unusual arch at Gambit in southern France, of 165 m (541 ft) span, bearing the unmistable hall-mark of its designer, Gustav Eiffel, better known for the Paris tower. It was built in 1884. The new Menai Bridge in Wales, referred to earlier, is also of this

Above: The Caronte swing bridge in France.

Top right: The steam pump of the tunnel under the River Severn in England.

Centre right: The entrance of the Lötschberg tunnel in Switzerland.

Bottom right: The lift bridge at Lachine in Montreal, Canada.

Below: Wilmington swing bridge at Hull, England.

type, with two spans of 138 m (460 ft).

For many years the greatest railway arch in the world has been the one of overhead type, the famous Sydney Harbour Bridge built in 1935 and having a span of 500 m (1,650 ft). It carries road traffic as well as a four-track railway.

Suspension and other bridges

Road bridges of more than three times the span of the conventional arch have been constructed, using the suspension principle. In the early days of railways suspension bridges were tried, a notable failure being the 1827 River Tees Bridge on a branch of the Stockton & Darlington railway in the U.K. The concentrated loads and vibration characteristic of a steam railway proved too much for the flexibility inherent in the suspension principle. A few railway suspension bridges have existed, a charming one being in the French Midi near Tulle, once carrying a single line of the narrow gauge tramways de la Corrëze. The longest span which has ever carried a railway is the San Francisco Bay Bridge; there are two 704 m (2,310 ft) suspension spans, but the inter-urban trains concerned no longer run.

A few engineers have had the courage to go their own way and there remain some notable structures that ingeniously combine more than one of the principles of those already described and, accordingly, defy categorization. To take

one example, the Denver & Rio Grande Western Railroad on its course along the bottom of the Royal Gorge of the Arkansas River at one point needed to cross over. There were problems in placing a pier in the rapids and also concern at its possible effect on the flow. The solution was the famous hanging bridge, suspended from a pair of girders pitched like rafters in a roof and fixed into the sides of the canyon, which is 300 m (1,000 ft) deep at this point.

Finally, there are the two 138 m (455 ft) spans of the Royal Albert Bridge at Saltash in England which carries the main line across the river Tamar near Plymouth. The bridge combines the principles of the arch, the beam and the suspension bridge. The main trusses are in effect self contained girders, but each derives its strength partly from an arched tube, whose thrust balances the pull of a set of suspension chains which also contribute to the structure's strength. Construction is of wrought iron, a material much weaker than steel, but much less subject to corrosion; hence we find this famous old bridge still carrying the much heavier loads of the present day. It was the last work of the famous engineer Brunel, who barely lived to see its completion in 1859.

Tunnels

Tunnels are, like bridges, a means of overcoming natural obstacles and at the same time keeping gradient and alignment of the railway within the standards set by the traffic which it is expected to carry. The earliest railway tunnel known, but which is unlikely to have been the first, was built in 1770 near Newcastle-upon-Tyne; its railway had wooden rails, was worked by horses, and it lasted until 1810.

Tunnels are bored through mountains and hills, whenever boring would be cheaper or more practicable than digging a cutting. Similarly, tunnels are built under water when the normal alternative of a bridge is less attractive. In the old days tunnels were occasionally built or even made artificially to hide trains from the superior gaze of a landlord looking out of the windows of his stately home.

Such environmental considerations are coming back into fashion in England; a good deal of the proposed high-speed line from London to Dover in connection with the Channel Tunnel was to have been situated underground for the same reasons. The consequent cost escalation was a primary reason for the project's abandonment in 1975.

Another common reason for tunnelling is to gain height with spirals or reverse loops. Examples of such arrangements are described later.

Tunnel construction, in general, is always hazardous and not to be undertaken lightly.

For posterity there is the rather sad fact that the work and the craftsmanship which goes into construction is – almost by definition – hidden from view.

The material through which a tunnel is driven is a crucial factor and this varies from the hardest of rock to the swampiest of ground, each presenting its own problems. Occasionally a material is

found – like the stratum of chalk that lies beneath the English channel – which is the perfect compromise, easy to dig yet with no problems of support. This would make the 50 km (31 mile) Channel tunnel – should it ever come about – rather less of an achievement than the underwater Seikan tunnel of similar length, through fissured granite, which is to connect the Japanese islands of Honshu and Hokkaido by 1980.

Very difficult conditions occur when strata of rotten rock are encountered deep inside a mountain. During construction of the 5.8 km (3.7 mile) Albula Tunnel in Switzerland from 1898 to 1902, a rate of drive around 25 m (27 yds) per week was achieved to begin with. Then came a period when, 1,100 m (3,600 ft) in from the southern portal, it was a case of two-and-a-half weeks per metre. Massive support timbering and an immensely thick stone lining had to be constructed in impossible conditions throughout the bad section. Experience gained during this traumatic period, however, enabled double the rate of drive (50 m per week) to be achieved in the sound rock beyond.

Inrushes of water from underground springs present major hazards. Long underwater tunnels, with their lowest point at the centre and so normally driven downhill, are particularly vulnerable. When the Great Spring was encountered during the building of the 7.2 km (4½ mile) Severn Tunnel connecting England with South Wales there was a delay of 14 months while steam pumping machinery capable of dealing with 7 million litres (½ million gallons) of water an hour was installed. Oddly, none of the spring water comes from the River Severn itself, but its pressure was such that flooding reached 45 m (150 ft) up the shafts.

Although it can normally drain away with the gradient, water encountered deep inside a mountain is liable to be scalding hot or under very high pressure. Construction hazards have included such things as an unsuspected cleft in the ground above, which in the case of the Swiss Lötschberg tunnel led to the loss of 25 lives and the abandonment of 2.5 km (1½ miles) of bore and a diversion with three curves to avoid the problem area.

Excavation in rock is conventionally carried out by first drilling holes using percussive means, usually compressed air jack-hammers, and filling them with explosive. The charges are detonated in a controlled manner so as to remove rock only where desired and also to shatter it into pieces small enough to allow easy removal. In the early days black powder was used; later on, the search for more powerful explosives led to such desperate measures as the use of that notoriously unstable liquid, nitro-glycerine. Modern explosives in skilled hands are, however, relatively safe and easy to use, as well has having sufficient power.

In soft ground it is normal to excavate and build the tunnel lining – of masonry, concrete, rings of brickwork or iron segments – within a shield. In the absence of boulders and such-like, some kind of mechanical rotary excavator can often be incorporated. There has to be a means of forcing the shield forward, usually by hydraulic jacks as well as – for all tunnels – a way of removing spoil. This latter task is usually one for a narrow gauge tramway and in that sense even a water or a road tunnel is temporarily a railway one. Sometimes the ground is so soft or waterlogged that excavation has to be done under pressure behind air-locks or, alternatively the earth has to be consolidated by freezing or chemical means before digging begins.

In urban areas particularly, tunnels are sometimes built by cut-and-cover methods, that is to say by excavating a cutting, then either building up side walls and roofing over or forming an arched roof. Whilst certainly within the definition of a tunnel, such an arrangement is constructionally much more a long bridge. London Transport's Circle line is a prime example.

Underwater tunnels made from prefabricated submersible sections have also appeared in recent years; a notable example is Bay Area Rapid Transit's 5.75 km (3.6 mile) long tunnel beneath San Francisco Bay.

The simple criteria of length is a good one on which to rate a tunnel. Setting aside the 27.7 km (17.3 mile) of continuous underground tube which exists on London Transport's Northern line the reigning King for over 70 years (but not for much longer) is the 19.7 km (12.3 mile) Simplon Tunnel between Switzerland and Italy opened in 1906.

Very close – and the longest underwater tunnel in the world – is the 18.9 km (11.8 mile) New Kanmon Tunnel in Japan for the Shinkansen, linking the islands of Honshu and Kyushu. It was opened in 1975.

With regard to the difficulties of great achievements at great altitudes, the world's highest tunnel is worthy of mention; this is the 1.2 km (3,960 ft) Galera Tunnel on the Central Railway of Peru, situated at 4,760 m (15,620 ft) altitude.

Finally, Brunel's Box Tunnel near Bath in England, opened in 1838, is remarkable in that

Above far left: Excavation of
a cutting on New Zealand's
Auckland to Wellington
trunk line in the 1900s.

Above near left: Entrance to
the excavations for the
Simplon Tunnel,
Switzerland.

Above right: Snow galleries
on the Rhaetian Railways,
Switzerland.

Right: Tunnels through hard
rock outcrops in
mountainous country.

Below left: Cut and cover
construction on London
Transport's Circle line.

Below right: Construction of
the Seikan Tunnel between
Honshu and Hokkaido,
Japan. The left hand tunnel
provides access to the main
bore on the right.

the rays of the rising sun shine through the bore
on one day of the year only, 18 May, the engineer's birthday, a circumstance that can hardly be a
coincidence.

Protecting the lines

Not only has a railway to be built and maintained
for safe running of trains, but the right-of-way has
also to be protected against adverse natural forces
and other hazards. Most frequently seen is the
fencing which a great many (but not all) railways
are obliged legally to provide to separate off their
property. Not very interesting but a considerable
source of expense and anxiety for those responsible. George Stephenson remarked that it would
'be the worse for the cow', yet large creatures do
inflict real damage on the trains that hit them –
especially now that the rugged steam locomotive
has given way to more vulnerable forms of power.

A good deal of unseen work goes into such
tasks as draining and supporting cutting slopes
with herring bone drains and counterforts in
order to prevent material slipping down on to the
line. Even natural slopes need attention – loose
rocks must be watched – and in some cases the
line needs to be protected by a device to detect any
that should fall. A famous installation existed for
many years in the Pass of Brander in Scotland on
the Callander & Oban line. If any of a set of
tensioned wires at the trackside were broken, a
series of semaphore signals automatically
returned to danger. On one occasion a rock
bounced over the wires and derailed a train with
some damage, but fortunately without injury to
those on board.

A surer but altogether more expensive way to
avoid rockfalls is to make a gallery to cover the
track; this is particularly suitable when the line
passes beneath cliffs.

Deep earth movements are very destructive to
railways. In Japan, where earthquakes are known
to be more than very occasional happenings, on
the new high-speed (Shinkansen) lines, a seis-
mograph is provided in the control room. When
this instrument detects an earth tremor above a
certain magnitude, the traction current in the
area where the trouble lies is automatically
switched off, bringing all trains there to a stand.

Snow is an implacable enemy of railway operation; in many snowy places tracks have been
roofed over as complete protection. The Central
Pacific Railroad (USA) constructed 60 km
(37 miles) of snow sheds in the Sierras above Sacramento, even before the line through to the east
opened in 1869, in order to keep construction
trains flowing right through the winter. A problem before oil-fired steam locos were used was to
keep the timber sheds from catching fire.

Lesser protection against drifting snow –
which is the real danger – is given by snow fences
arranged in patterns the choice of which, judging
from the variety which can be found, is more an
art than a science. If drifting is kept away, it is rare
for falling snow to bank in such a way that trains
cannot run, except in one place – behind the
blades of switches, where it prevents them from
closing properly. Gas or electric heating is now

frequently provided; especially where points are remotely controlled.

Accumulations of snow, even drifts, are usually more embarrassing than dangerous, but not so when the accumulations take place high above the railway and come down on it in the form of avalanches. Some protection can be given by planting forests or constructing strong fences in danger areas and, where avalanche tracks are known about, by bridging or gallery construction. However, the unpredictability of avalanches can be measured by the fact that buildings in the Alps, unscathed for 500 years, are from time to time destroyed.

Protective works, usually in the form of dumping blocks or setting gabions, are often needed to prevent rivers damaging bridges and embankments when they get out of hand or decide to change course. Examples occur where several spans of a bridge have, in time, come to stand in the middle of a wood whilst the river does its best to go through the embankment at the far end.

Most marine civil engineering work is affected by the times of the tides and the sea is a very demanding adversary. Any weak spot in a sea wall will be enlarged by the ocean in no time at all.

Many railways run along the seashore – it was always a deceptively easy choice for a route but protection is always difficult and expensive.

Ten Great Railways

The individual structures and the major considerations governing the construction of a railway have been reviewed. To demonstrate the interlocking of these, ten railway construction feats – from a hundred or more worthy of selection – have been chosen as examples.

Central Railway of Peru. 'Highest and Hardest' is the description given to the Central Railway of Peru in South America. The track began at the coast and in the Andes the main line reaches 4,818 m (15,806 ft). This is marginally the highest in the world – higher than the neighbouring Antofogasta (Chile) & Bolivia Railway whose oblique approach to the mountains is far longer and less severe.

The American engineer Henry Meiggs began the Central in 1869. It was completed in 1892 after his death in 1878. By setting the grade at a very demanding 1 in 23, he managed an alignment with the use of 21 zig-zag reversing stations. In some cases the stop blocks overlook sheer precipices and the remains of the odd locomotive or so far below. Operations on such gradients exact extreme penalties for the smallest mistake. Elsewhere, magnificent steel trestle bridges span gorges of breath-taking depths. Chaupichaca Viaduct is outstanding – the name is believed to be an onomatopoeic word for steam locomotive.

Above left: An electric locomotive on the metre gauge Rhaetian Railway in Switzerland.

Above: An open-air spiral on the Darjeeling-Himalaya Railway.

Below left: The sea wall and breakwaters protecting the line near Teignmouth, south-west England.

Below: The Chaupichaca Viaduct on the Central Railway of Peru. The wreckage of a train that fell from the viaduct can be seen in the ravine.

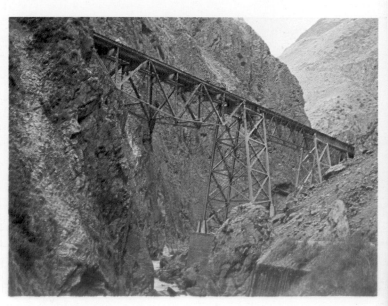

From Lima to Oroya, Meigg's course takes 221 km (130 miles). The price paid for such an alignment is a commercial speed of only 34 km/h (21 mph) for the daily passenger train. Air competition was limited for years, because none of the airlines operating on the Pacific coast were equipped with planes capable of reliable flight at that altitude.

Rhaetian Railway. Similar only in that it connects a high mountain valley with the outer world, is the metre-gauge Rhaetian Railway in Switzerland. In contrast, it serves not one of the roughest mining areas of the world, but some of its plushest tourist resorts. The method used to overcome the height is not the time consuming Z-reverse but a series of spiral tunnels of 120 m (6 chain) radius. A train climbing up St Moritz at 1,778 m (5,833 ft) threads four – no line in the world has more – including a unique case where two, the Toua and Zuondra tunnels, are vertically above one another in the same mountain. Beautiful arched masonry viaducts are founded in the stable rock formations of the Alps, in place of the steel trestles appropriate to those of the Andes, which are rather more loosely put together. With gradients similar to those on the Central of Peru, commercial speeds of 43 km/h (27 mph) are achieved by the Rhaetian Railway's electric express trains.

Kicking Horse Pass. Moving from the Alps to the Rocky Mountains of North America, the Canadian Pacific Railway originally crossed the range via the Kicking Horse Pass with grades of 1 in 23. In 1920, after 25 years of traumatic operation, a new alignment involving two spiral tunnels was constructed with a ruling grade of 1 in 45. Under the new conditions, two locomotives

could haul 40 per cent more than before at a cost of 4 km (2.5 miles) additional distance. In steam days, conditions inside the spiral tunnels were severe and hoboes 'riding the rods' on freight trains used to alight at the entrances, climb on foot to the exit some distance higher, and wait for the train there. The train crew no doubt wished to do the same. In really steep places such as these, legs have the advantage over trains.

Darjeeling–Himalayan Railway. One mountain range still remains uncrossed by rail – the Himalayas. However, the 600 mm (1 ft 11½ in) gauge Darjeeling–Himalayan Railway reaches the foothills at a trifling 2,255 m (7,400 ft). It does this with the minimum of engineering works – no tunnels and only very small bridges on the mountain section – by a masterpiece of surveying, using five zig-zags and four open-air spirals. From a traveller's point of view these open spirals are much preferable to spirals in tunnels. On a typical mountainside and for a typical railway, the tunnel arrangement is cheaper. However, the DHR is certainly not a typical railway and curves down to 20 m (1 chain) radius, combined with gradient up to 1 in 20 allowed open-air spirals to be laid out with the minimum of construction work. The penalty for these convolutions is reflected in the fact that the amazing 88 km (55 mile) journey takes over 7 hours.

Khyber Pass Railway. The point has been made that, to be successful, a railway must have traffic commensurate with the cost of its construction. An exception is the strategic 40 km (25 mile) Khyber Pass railway in Pakistan, built in connection with defence of the north-west frontier of British India. Success in this case has meant absence rather than presence of the traffic

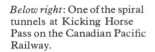
Below right: One of the spiral tunnels at Kicking Horse Pass on the Canadian Pacific Railway.

it was built to take and, in fact, there has never been more than one token out-and-back train a week since completion in 1926. Of very solid construction (to reduce the risk of malicious damage), in addition to a zig-zag on the descent to the Afghan border, there is a spiral zig-zag – the two main climbing modes combined – at Changa on the ascent. The summit is at Landi Kotal 1,065 m (3,493 ft), and the ruling gradient 1 in 33 coming up from Peshawar.

In discussing mountain gradients, no mention has been made of very steeply-graded railways where the adhesion between wheel and rail is supplemented by some more complex mechanical arrangement, usually a rack-and-pinion. Correctly such systems belong in the mountain railway section.

Rimutaka Incline. However, a few major routes have faced mountain obstacles and been forced by financial circumstances to adopt – usually as a temporary measure – such devices. One was the North Island main line of New Zealand Railways from Wellington to Napier, where the 1 in 15 Rimutaka incline was equipped with a Fell centre rail. After 77 years of difficult operation, in 1955, a diversion was built involving 16 km (10 miles) of new mountain line plus the 8.8 km (5½ miles) Rimutaka Tunnel, the longest in the Southern hemisphere. The new summit in the tunnel was 203 m (666 ft) lower than the old one and the distance 15 km (9½ miles) shorter. Running time over the diversion for locomotive-hauled trains (railcars had previously done a little better) was reduced by 2 hours to just over 30 minutes, an improvement of 440 per cent in average speed.

Festiniog Railway. An example of a rather different sort of gradient planning is the narrow-gauge Festiniog Railway in the mountains of Wales, which was designed to utilize as motive power for loaded trains (mineral traffic was all in the downhill direction) that well-known discovery of Sir Isaac Newton, the force of gravity. At the same time economy was pursued with the use of a very tight loading gauge and extremely sharp curves, down to 50 m (2½ chain) radius, so that only one valley had to be crossed and one ridge tunnelled through in the 20.8 km (13 miles) from Blaenau Ffestiniog to Porthmadog. The grade averages 1 in 90, but is slightly steeper on the longer curves to compensate for the extra friction which might allow a gravity train to stick.

This is the reverse of normal practice, which provides for easing the gradient on curves to compensate for the extra haulage effort required by ascending trains. Ascending trains on the FR were mainly composed of empty wagons so that haulage was not a problem. Nowadays, however, in its role as a major tourist carrier, this is not the case and, indeed, construction of a deviation (with the only railway spiral in Britain as well as a new tunnel) to avoid a reservoir, means that the gradients no longer lie all one way.

Key West Extension. An outsider amongst these mountain lines is a glorious folly that crossed the sea for 182 km (114 miles), not to reach a destination, but merely to shorten the sea passage bet-

Above left: The weekly passenger train near Shahgai on the Khyber Pass Railway in Pakistan (1963).

Above centre: The Key West Extension of the Florida East Coast Railway, USA. This section is 10.85 km (6.75 miles) long.

Above right: Portmadoc (Porthmadog in Welsh) station at the lower end of the Festiniog Railway. The locomotive is an 0–4–0 saddle tank with a tender for coal.

Right: A school excursion train approaching the summit tunnel on an ascent of the Rimutaka Incline, New Zealand (1955).

Left: A reinforced, pre-stressed concrete viaduct on Japan's Shinkansen line.

ween Florida and Cuba, then an important commercial and tourist link. The Key West Extension of the Florida East Coast Railway, USA, completed in 1912, included 27.5 km (17 miles) of bridging. There are 32 km (20 miles) of embankment in shallow water and the remainder is laid on the coral reefs known as Keys. In 1936 a hurricane put paid to railway operation, but the 'permanent' way was subsequently reconstructed as a road.

Sierra de la Culebra Line. Soon after the civil war ended in 1938, the Spanish government began building the long planned Sierra de la Culebra line which would, by directly linking Zamorra with Santiago de la Compostella, save more than two hours travelling time for traffic between Madrid and such places as Corunna in the north-west. Twenty years later it was ready for traffic; the time taken indicates the nature of the work, which included 182 tunnels totalling 78 km (49 miles) – 27 per cent of the length of line – and the remote Esla Viaduct near Andarias (referred to earlier), as well as numerous other structures. The ruling grade is 1 in 66 and minimum curve 400 m (20 chain) radius.

The Culebra is claimed as the most heavily-tunnelled line in Europe, but since 1975 this claim has been overtaken.

Shinkansen Extension. Leaving big mountains behind, we consider next the 1975 Shinkansen extension from Okayama on the main Japanese island of Honshu to Fukuoka on Kyushu. The standards set for the line were a running speed of 260 km/h (163 mph), which involves a minimum curve radius of 4,000 m (200 chains), and a maximum grade of 1 in 66. Tunnels, including the New Kanmon undersea tunnel already mentioned, amount to 222 km (139 miles) – more than half the line is underground. Bridges and viaducts, mostly constructed from reinforced prestressed concrete beams, aggregate to 117 km (73 miles), leaving a modest 56 km (35 miles) of plain railway building. From this may be guessed the nature of the cost of providing for such high speeds. Further extensions amounting to another 2,900 km (1,800 miles) are planned for the future. Until China begins to cover Tibet with high-speed railways, the Shinkansen will represent by every possible criterion an unparalleled railway engineering achievement.

GREAT TRAINS

THE BLUE TRAIN

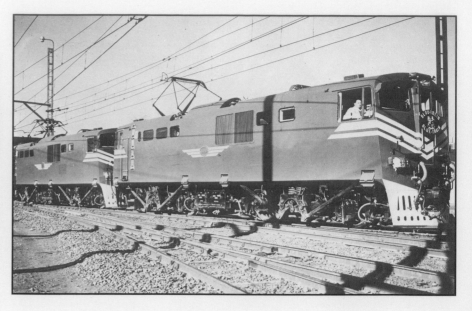

After the establishment of the Union of South Africa in 1910 and the amalgamation of the former Central South African, Natal Government, and Cape Government railways into the South African Railways, the luxury express train running between Cape Town and Pretoria, introduced in 1903, in connection with sailings of Union Castle mail steamers from England, was named *Union Limited*. It was one of the finest long-distance trains to be found anywhere in the world. Although the gauge was only 1,067 mm (3 ft 6 in) the carriages were very wide, and gave no impression when inside of being on a substandard gauge railway. At that time the train ran twice a week, in accordance with the steamer sailings. It left Cape Town at 10.45 and reached Johannesburg at 16.30 on the second day, after a run of 1,540 km (956 miles). The *Union Limited* remained the crack train of South African Railways until 1939 when the *Blue Train* was put on. Because of the war little was known of it outside South Africa; but afterwards it soon became established as one of the great luxury trains.

The original function of this great train from the cities of the Reef to Cape Town, as part of the direct and most favoured line of communication to and from England, has largely disappeared with the development of air travel. The *Blue Train*, however, has remained extremely popular with patrons who are not in a desperate hurry, and who like to enjoy gracious living on their travels. The rolling stock is air-conditioned throughout, and provides noise-free, vibration-free running, and all the amenities of a first class hotel. The private suites, compartments, and dining car are sumptuously appointed. Every compartment, to say nothing of the private suites, is furnished with loose cushions on the seats and writing tables with headed notepaper, while an excellent valet service is always available. There is an observation lounge at the rear end of the train. The northbound run now takes 26 hours, representing an average speed of 58½ km/h (37 mph). Departure from Cape Town is at 12.00.

When the *Union Limited* was first put on it was steam-hauled throughout, but right until the introduction of entirely new coaching stock in 1972, the train was hauled by steam over the

Above: A pair of standard electric locomotives at work with the *Blue Train* of South African Railways. Electric locomotives, formerly built entirely in Britain, are now assembled in South Africa itself.

Below left: An eight-coupled locomotive of the type which hauled the *Blue Train* in the days of steam. Passenger vehicles of the type shown are no longer used in the *Blue Train*, but still serve other long-distance trains.

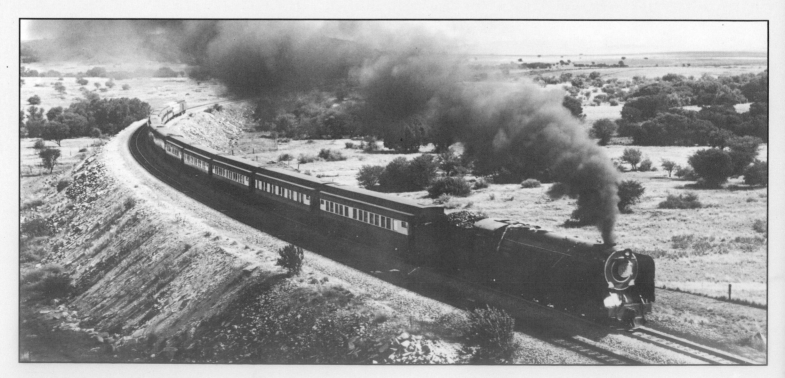

central part of the journey, between Beaufort West and Kimberley. The sections between Cape Town and Beaufort West, and between Kimberley and Johannesburg are electrically-hauled. Since the introduction of the new stock, diesel locomotives specially painted to match the coaches are used over the run. In the central part of this run, the line crosses the Great Karoo desert and the high veldt country north of De Aar Junction. Passengers on the *Blue Train* do not see much of this remarkable countryside because it is traversed during the hours of darkness. They miss the spectacle of freight trains speeding along hauled by two of the enormous Class 25 4–8–4 steam locomotives. On the other hand, the spectacular ascent of the Hex River Pass, in Cape Province, is made in the late afternoon and the sight of this from the observation saloon at the rear end is impressive.

On level stretches of line across the veldt speed is normally about 90 km/h (55 mph), though on the electrically-hauled section in the Transvaal higher speeds are permitted. But as the Reef area is neared the railway becomes extremely busy; there are many junctions and speed restrictions. The principal interest to a visitor as journey's end is neared are the distinctive golden-coloured pyramids of waste from the gold mines.

In April 1969, the Historic Transport Association of Johannesburg, with the co-operation of SAR, ran a special anniversary trip from Johannesburg to Cape Town and back to celebrate the 30th anniversary of the inception of the *Blue Train*. By special arrangement the train was steam hauled throughout. It was made a festive occasion by all concerned. South African Railways, with plenty of headroom available, does not suffer from the restrictions imposed on British Railways from the danger of an electrical flashover if steam locomotives pass beneath the overhead electric wires, and every one of the locomotives concerned was given a positively exhibition finish. The cabs, in the polish bestowed upon all their fittings, glittered like the

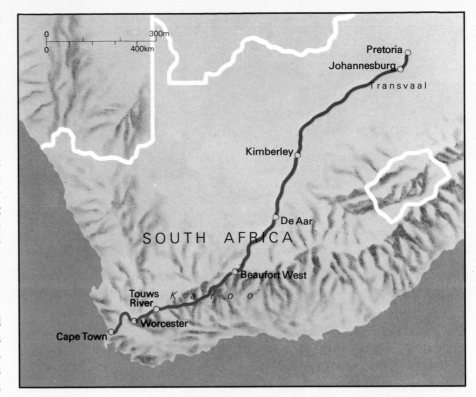

interior of so many jewellers' shops. On this run engines were changed at Klerksdorp, Kimberley, De Aar, Beaufort West, and Touws River, and opportunity was taken to use three of the types of steam locomotive most distinguished in the past history of *Blue Train* operation.

To ride the *Blue Train* today is the very height of opulence in travel. It has those touches of elegance that used to accompany the great trains of Europe and America before the coming of the jet age. The staff are specially selected to ensure the highest standards of public relations, just as, in former days, were the Pullman conductors on the *Golden Arrow* and the *Queen of Scots*. In the meantime less extravagant passengers can enjoy the same route and no more than a slightly reduced standard of service and speed, on the *Trans-Karoo Express,* which also makes good time between Cape Town and Johannesburg.

Below right: The present-day *Blue Train* against a backdrop of mountains, which are never far from the train's route.

GREAT TRAINS

THE CANADIAN

Speaking at the Guildhall in London, in May 1908, King George V – then Prince of Wales – said: 'We have seen how the Canadian Pacific Railway has helped to make a Nation.' It was in building the link to the province west of the Rocky Mountains that CPR forged what has been called the 'Steel of Empire', and it is not surprising that the transcontinental expresses of that railway became some of the great trains of the world, though naturally not among the fastest. The aim was to provide regular and reliable transport, and in days before the establishment of commercial airlines and majestic highways, speed was a minor consideration. Fifty years ago in 1926, principal transcontinental trains were *The Imperial* and *Trans-Canada Limited*. *The Dominion* was only introduced about 1930. The distance from the former city is 4,650 km (2,882 miles) and the journey time, entirely with steam haulage, was 87 hr 20 min. At that time one of the fast, highly-competitive inter-city trains between Montreal and Toronto was named *The Canadian*, but another 30-odd years were to pass before *The Canadian* became the name of the premier transcontinental express of the CPR.

It was in April 1955 that some splendid new stainless steel passenger stock was introduced to provide a second transcontinental service between Montreal and Toronto, and Vancouver. This new train was named *The Canadian*. For ten years *The Canadian* and *The Dominion* worked together, but in 1965 in face of dwindling passenger business *The Dominion* was reluctantly withdrawn.

The Canadian is a beautiful train. The coaches were built by the Budd Company of Philadelphia, and in 1954 the contract was for no fewer than 173. This might seem an extravagant provision, but even today, with one service daily in each direction, *The Canadian* needs seven sets of cars in continuous use. There are seven different varieties of car.

1. Baggage dormitory car, including living accommodation for the dining and buffet car crews and the stewards.
2. Deluxe coaches, each of which seats 60 passengers in comfort, with reversible reclining seats, adjustable foot rests, and comforts for a night journey.
3. Scenic dome coach, available to non-sleeping car passengers, including buffet, snack lounge, and coffee shop.
4. Dining cars.
5. Sleeping car: Type 1, with open sections, bedrooms, roomettes and a compartment.
6. Sleeping car: Type 2, with open sections, bedrooms, duplex roomettes and a drawing room.
7. Tail end dome observation lounge, with bedrooms and a drawing room.

All cars except the baggage dormitory, the coach domes, and the 60-seat coaches are named.

The Canadian is diesel-hauled throughout. In the eastern provinces and across the prairies two units of 1,500 to 1,750 hp are usually adequate, but in the tremendous mountain country west of Calgary a third is necessary.

On the westbound run the two sections, leaving Montreal and Toronto at 11.15 and 15.30 respectively join up at Sudbury, Ontario, in the evening, and daylight comes in time for passengers to enjoy the fascinating run along the north-

Below: A passenger train in the days of steam, passing through the Rocky Mountains on the Canadian Pacific's transcontinental line.

Right: *The Canadian* passes through the Rockies at a point long favoured by the photographers of the Canadian Pacific's publicity department.

Below right: The observation dome car of *The Canadian* standing at Ottawa, the first stop after leaving Montreal.

Below far right: Inside an observation dome car of *The Canadian*. Similar vehicles were used by several US railroads to exploit the train's advantage over the airliner for viewing the passing scenery.

ern shores of Lake Superior, where the line in places is carried on a ledge cut out of the vertical rock walls that rise sheer from the water's edge. For most of the way the line is single-track, with traffic regulation through continuous colour light signalling and electronic interlockings. Thunder Bay is reached in the early afternoon, and there watches are put back one hour. Another long stretch lies ahead, 675 km (419 miles) to Winnipeg and the beginning of the prairies. That great junction is reached around 20.00 on the second day out. The vast prairie lands through Regina, capital city of Saskatchewan, are traversed during the night, and at Moose Jaw watches are put back another hour. There the zone of Mountain time is entered, and the distant line of the Rockies can be seen across the western sky soon after noon, when Calgary is neared. The transcontinental expresses stop for half an hour at this major junction, and for one dollar passengers can take the lift up the Calgary Tower to gain a magnificent panoramic view from this high sky-scraper.

In the failing light of late afternoon *The Canadian* passes through some of the grandest scenery to be seen from a railway train; and on during the third night through the wild canyons of British Columbia to reach Vancouver, eventually, on the fourth day of the run, after entering yet another time zone, Pacific time. The actual time for the complete journey from Montreal to Vancouver is 69 hr 10 min.

When the diesels were first introduced they were painted in a livery of grey and Tuscan red, similar to that of the steam locomotives they had superseded; but when the great reorganization of the company took place, and its various activities were named CP Rail, CP Ships, CP Air, and so on, a new locomotive livery was adopted, of scarlet and white, as significant of the new image, and the coloured bands on the stainless steel coaches of *The Canadian* were also changed from Tuscan red to scarlet to match the locomotive style. The sight of this great train winding its way round the curves in the western canyons is one of the most spectacular railway events one could wish to see.

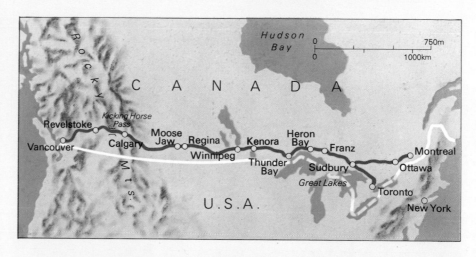

GREAT TRAINS

THE FLYING SCOTSMAN

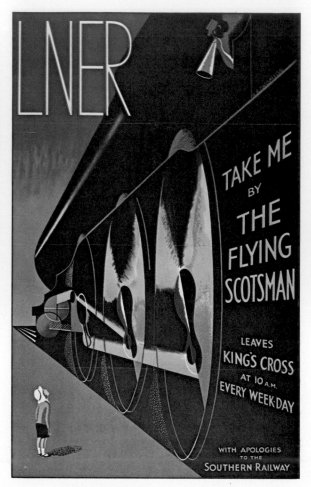

TAKE ME BY THE FLYING SCOTSMAN

LEAVES KING'S CROSS AT 10 A.M. EVERY WEEK-DAY

WITH APOLOGIES TO THE SOUTHERN RAILWAY

Above: One of the *Deltic* type diesel-electric locomotives, No 9001, passing Selby with the *Flying Scotsman*.

Top left: A pre-war poster advertising the *Flying Scotsman* service. The picture is based on a poster previously used by the Southern Railway; hence the wry acknowledgement.

The Great Northern main line between King's Cross and Doncaster was completed in 1852, and ten years later a *Special Scotch Express* was put on, leaving London at 10.00. Except at times of national emergency there was a train leaving for Scotland at that time, on weekdays, throughout the steam era. Within two years of its inception its speed had become something of a legend. It ran the 123 km (76.4 miles) to its first stop at Peterborough in 92 min at an average of 80.5 km/h (49.8 mph) and earned the *nickname* of the *Flying Scotchman*. Like all prestige trains of that era it carried only first and second class passengers. The overall time for the journey to Edinburgh was 10 hours, and included a stop of 30 minutes at York, for lunch. Then, anticipating the completion of their new independent route to Carlisle, the Midland Railway, in March 1872, announced that they would carry third class passengers by all trains. In due course the East Coast companies did the same, except for the *Flying Scotsman*. But they underlined the high prestige status of that train by quickening the time by a full hour, stopping only at Grantham, York, Newcastle and Berwick, and reaching Edinburgh at 19.00.

The rival train leaving Euston also at 10.00 carried all three classes of passengers and took 10 hours from London to Edinburgh. But when the East Coast companies decided, late in 1887, that their *Special Scotch Express* – as it was still known officially – would carry third class passengers as well, rivalry began in earnest, and resulted in the first 'Race to the North' at the height of the 1888 summer season. Little-by-little the booked times were reduced until the King's Cross train was scheduled to reach Edinburgh in 7¾ hours, and its rival from Euston in 8 hours. Both sides ran substantially ahead of time, and excitement was intense. As a result, an agreement was made fixing the minimum times as 7¾ hours from King's Cross and 8 hours from Euston, and this

Left: A locomotive man using the corridor tender, which enabled crews to be changed on the steam-hauled London to Edinburgh non-stop run.

Far left: A pre-war publicity photograph showing the old single-driver locomotive No 1 of the former Great Northern Railway and its modern equivalent *Sir Nigel Gresley*, an A4 Pacific of a type which in later years hauled the *Flying Scotsman*. The photograph was made at Stevenage, on the London to Edinburgh line. Both the locomotives are now preserved.

Left: The Gresley Pacific *Donovan* with the *Flying Scotsman* in 1933, before the advent of the streamlined A4 class.

Right: Inside a first-class restaurant car, as used in the pre-war *Flying Scotsman* service.

agreement was honoured even after the introduction of restaurant cars, which made the luncheon stops unnecessary. Actually these minimum times were exceeded in practice on the daytime trains between London and Edinburgh which, until 1932, took 8¼ hours by both routes.

It was after the grouping of the railways in 1923, and preparations were in hand for the British Empire Exhibition at Wembley in 1924, that the train was officially named and carried its name on the carriage roof boards. At the same time the Gresley Pacific engine No 4472 chosen for exhibition at Wembley was named *Flying Scotsman*. Then, for the summer service of 1928 came the remarkable development of running the train non-stop between King's Cross and Edinburgh, 633 km (392.7 miles) but still in the agreed time of 8¼ hours. The speed was not high, but to run such a distance non-stop was a severe test of locomotive reliability, and required two separate engine crews. To enable one crew to relieve the other at the half way point, just north of York, the locomotives were fitted with special tenders with a corridor, through which men could pass from the footplate to the leading coach of the train. By mutual agreement between the London & North Eastern and the London Midland & Scottish Railways, acceleration of the Anglo-Scottish services began in 1932, and by 1939 overall time by the summer non-stop *Flying Scotsman* had been reduced to 7 hours between King's Cross and Edinburgh, an average speed of 90.5 km/h (56 mph).

During the winter months the traditional stops were made at Grantham, York, Newcastle, and Berwick, while during the summer intermediate traffic was catered for by a second train, leaving King's Cross at 10.05 and nicknamed the *Junior Scotsman*. The *Flying Scotsman* itself, whether running non-stop or calling intermediately, had a high reputation for fast, smooth and punctual running, and the handsome varnished teak carriages with their characteristic bow ends matched the traditional green locomotives of the East Coast route. Towards the end of the 1930s, however, there came a change in locomotive styles. Introduction of the high-speed streamlined trains and their magnificent A4 Pacific locomotives brought some units painted in silver, for the *Silver Jubilee* train, and others in garter blue, for the *Coronation* of 1937. Eventually it was decided that all the streamlined engines should be blue; as more of these were built and became available for ordinary express trains as well as streamliners. Blue streamlined engines could be seen hauling the *Flying Scotsman*.

The general disruption of British train services during the second world war reduced speeds, increased loading, and resulted in chronic overcrowding. It could not be avoided. Locomotives that had previously taken 12, 13 or 14 coaches at high speed were then required to take 20 and sometimes more. In the recovery period that followed from 1946, the summer non-stops were reintroduced, but not on the *Flying Scotsman* itself which retained its 10.00 departure. The advance non-stop was first called *The Capitals Limited*, and from 1953, *The Elizabethan*. The latter train, a direct descendant of the non-stop *Flying Scotsman* of 1928 was eventually accelerated to a 6½ hour run from London to Edinburgh and sometimes attained a speed of 160 km/h (100 mph).

With the change to diesel traction the splendid Deltic locomotives became the standard motive power for the *Flying Scotsman* from 1961 onwards. Since then further acceleration has taken place, mainly through improvements to the route and the elimination of certain speed restrictions. The load is now one of 11 coaches, about 400 tonnes, and the cruising speed on level track 150 to 160 km/h (93 to 100 mph). The overall time between King's Cross and Edinburgh, with just one stop, at Newcastle, is now (1976) 5 hr 43 min.

GREAT TRAINS

THE INDIAN PACIFIC

Inauguration in 1970 of this remarkable transcontinental service from the shores of the Indian Ocean across Australia to the Pacific, could be regarded as the final liquidation of a great folly in railway pioneering, committed rather more than 100 years previously. By 1845 Great Britain was experiencing the acute difficulties of having railways with more than one gauge, and a Royal Commission was sitting to try to resolve them. Naturally enough the War Office, which then had responsibility for developing the infant colonies of Australia, urged them to make them all the same gauge. How Victoria and South Australia on the one hand, and New South Wales on the other, came to have different gauges is a monument to pigheadedness. Queensland decided that the Irish gauge of 1,600 mm (5 ft 3 in) adopted in Victoria and South Australia and the British 1,435 mm (4 ft 8½ in) were too expensive, and decided on 1,067 mm (3 ft 6 in), while in splendid

isolation out in the far west beyond the limitless, desert lands of the Nullarbor plain, Western Australia, after one or two false starts also decided upon 1,067 mm. A present day historian might condemn the whole development as muddled and shortsighted; but apart from the really inexcusable confrontation between New South Wales and the two southern states it was sound business. In Queensland and Western Australia the over-riding task was to open up the country, and both states could build a far greater network of railways on the 1,067 mm gauge than they could on 1,435 mm.

But what was good business in the latter part of the 19th century became a major problem when, on the formation of the Commonwealth of Australia in 1901, it was necessary to establish railway communication between east and west. Whatever gauge was decided upon for the connecting link across the Nullarbor plain there would be at least one break of gauge between the capital cities of Adelaide and Perth. Planning with a far-sightedness notably absent in earlier days the Commonwealth decided on the British standard gauge, at that time used only in New South Wales; but nearly 70 years elapsed before there was a standard-gauge link right across Australia. The new line in Western Australia, from Kalgoorlie to Perth and Fremantle, was primarily a conveyor belt project to carry iron ore in vast quantities; but its opening in November 1968 enabled it to be used by through sleeping-car trains from Port Pirie, South Australia, where connection was made with the 1,600 mm (5 ft 3 in) gauge system. Then the chain of railway communication across Australia included the 1,067 mm section from Port Pirie eastwards to its connection with the New South Wales system 348 km (216 miles) to Cockburn. The decision to convert this and to upgrade nearly 750 km (446 miles) of line across New South Wales from the border eastward to Parkes was a colossal undertaking not finished until the end of 1969; but on March 1, 1970, the *Indian Pacific* began through running over the 3,968 km (2,461 miles) between Sydney and Perth.

It is a journey of extraordinary contrasts. Leaving the teeming suburbs of Sydney, electrically-hauled, it heads straight for the barrier of the Blue mountains, climbing in magnificent scenery past the popular hill resort of Katoomba, with broad vistas along the range, with the distinctive blue haze rising to the upper crags from the forests of blue gum trees below. The summit level is 867 m (2,844 ft), and the line then descends for its long run through the night across the backlands of New South Wales. The next day brings the train down to tide water again, at Port Pirie, and after a second night there comes the unforgettable run across the Nullarbor plain, where the track is literally straight for 478 km (297 miles). 'Nullarbor' means 'no trees'; but there is little of anything else either – hills, rivers, water, animals! The beautiful train is completely air-conditioned, and one travels in comfort while outside the sun beats down from a cloudless sky on the desert land. Riding the *Indian Pacific* is

Above: Another view of the on-train services provided for passengers of the *Indian Pacific*, the lounge car with cocktail bar.

Below left: The economy class club bar of the *Indian Pacific*, designed to encourage Australian-style conviviality.

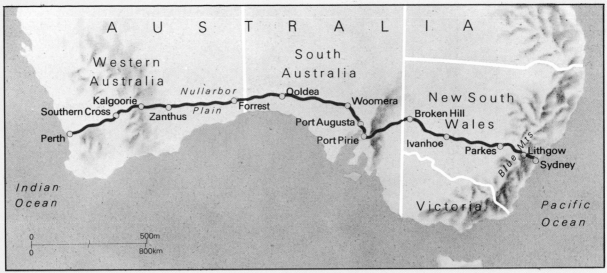

rather like being on board ship. There is an attractive lounge car, with piano; fellow passengers meet together at meal times and the handsomely-styled menu cards have spaces for autographs and other mementos of a journey together.

The *Indian Pacific* does not break any speed records. Across the plains, diesel-hauled, it makes a comfortable 105 to 110 km/h (65 to 70 mph), and out on the locomotive another characteristic of this extraordinary railway becomes evident. As in mid-ocean, one can sense the curve of the earth's surface. When nearing an intermediate station, where engine crews are changed and mail business is done, the buildings appear little by little as with approaching ships at sea, over the curve of the earth. Across the Nullarbor plain the train is hauled by locomotives of the Australian National Railways, the third administration since leaving Sydney. The working is as follows:

Section	Distance km	Railway	Motive Power
Sydney-Lithgow	156	New South Wales	electric
Lithgow-Cockburn	1,018	New South Wales	diesel
Cockburn-Port Pirie	350	South Australian	diesel
Port Pirie-Kalgoorlie	1,787	Australian National	diesel
Kalgoorlie-Perth	657	Western Australian	diesel

The westbound train leaves Sydney at 15.15 and arrives at Perth at 07.00 on the third day, a total journey time of 65¾ hours. Initially, two complete train sets each made a round trip from Sydney to Perth and back once a week. Since July, 1975, however, delivery of new rolling stock enabled the service to be increased to four per week in each direction. The average speed throughout the three-day journey is approximately 61½ km/h (38 mph).

Below: The *Indian Pacific* in Western Australia, hauled by a WAGR diesel unit. Because of the flat terrain, fewer diesel units are needed to haul a train of this size than would be the case in North America.

GREAT TRAINS

THE MISTRAL

The one-time Paris, Lyon & Mediterranean Railway was one of the best known continental routes to English tourists of Victorian and Edwardian days. It led to the French Riviera, and some of the finest, and most expensive trains in the world at that time traversed its tracks. Those who were interested in locomotives would be familiar with the queer-shaped fronts of the 4–4–0s that hauled the crack trains – an early form of streamlining – and although the speeds were higher than those of many French trains of the period the discerning wondered why this air-smoothing of the exterior should have been necessary. South of Avignon the line crosses the wide, limitless flats of the Rhone delta, and at times the tremendous *mistral* wind sweeps down from the Maritime alps. It was to combat the effects of this wind that the locomotives had those peculiarly-shaped fronts and became known as the *coupe vent machines*: the windcutters. To protect the line from the effects of that wind, thick hedges of cypress trees were grown on both sides of the track across the exposed stretch over the delta. And when in the post-war electric age French National Railways put on one of the fastest trains ever yet to run in France, what better name for it than *Le Mistral*.

It is one of the truly great trains of the world: a heavyweight, consisting of the sumptuous *grand confort* coaches, and running as near as practicable to 160 km/h (100 mph) all the way from Paris to Marseille. It is however only beginning to reach its ultimate destination when it arrives on the shores of the Mediterranean, though by that time it has run the gauntlet of wind buffeting on the delta, if the *mistral* is blowing. At Marseille it turns eastward, and running near to the sea for most of the way serves Toulon, St Raphael, Cannes, and Antibes, before terminating at Nice, at 22.25, having left Paris at 13.20. It does its major speeding between Paris and Lyon, with an opening dash over the 315 km (195½ miles) to Dijon in 2 hr 19 min. This average of 135 km/h (84 mph) is more remarkable than it might appear, because from Paris, and more particularly after Laroche is passed, the line is steadily climbing and eventually reaches an altitude of 405 m (1,324 ft) above sea level where it crosses the ridge of the Côte d'Or mountains, at Blaisy Bas.

Today electric locomotives of roughly 8,000 hp haul this train, and so well are curves and junctions laid out that no restrictions are called for; the train glides along at a steady, almost imperceptible 160 km/h (100 mph). Gradients make little difference. As the inclination steepens so the driver adjusts his controls to take more and more current from the overhead line, and at that summit point in the mountains the speed is still 150 km/h (93 mph). South of Dijon the train speeds at 160 km/h through a country where the station names seem more like a wine list than a railway timetable: Gevrey Chambertin, Nuits St Georges, Mâcon, and so on. In steam days there were many changes of engine, and special 4–8–2s were designed for the mountain section from Laroche to Dijon. Now one electric locomotive works through over the 863 km (536 miles) from Paris to Marseille, with changes of crew at Dijon and Lyon. The speeds are not usually quite so high south of Lyon, but nevertheless the complete run of 863 km (536 miles) from Paris, inclusive of the four stops at Dijon, Lyon, Valence and Avignon, takes only 6 hr 51 min – an average of 121.5 km/h (75½ mph).

Marseille is a terminus, and trains for the line

Top: A centre-aisle open vehicle as used on the *Mistral*.

Above: The small shop provided on board the *Mistral*.

Right: The present-day *Mistral*, photographed at Marseille in the charge of a type BB 9200 5,230 hp electric locomotive, built in the late 1950s.

Below: Pullman day coaches on the SNCF in steam days. This type of luxury vehicle has now been replaced.

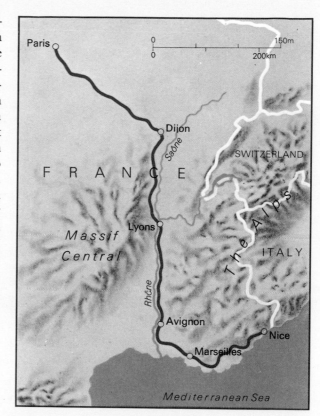

along the Côte d'Azur have to reverse their direction before proceeding towards Nice. The section along the coast was one of the most recent to be electrified, and for many years after its first introduction *Le Mistral* was steam-hauled east of Marseille. The locomotives used were of much interest because they were selected units from a bulk purchase of 1,100 general utility 2–8–2s that the French government ordered from American manufacturers to set the railways on the way to recovery from the vast destruction of the war. These locomotives, differing in many ways from traditional French practice, proved extremely successful and very popular with drivers and firemen. Although designed for general duties in rehabilitation of the railways, it was found they could be used in express passenger service so a batch of them was set aside for working all trains along the Côte d'Azur between Marseille and the Italian frontier, passenger and goods alike, including such a celebrated train as *Le Mistral*. The speeds, even since electrification of the route, are not so high as those between Paris and Marseille, but the scenery is at times breathtaking.

Northbound, *Le Mistral* leaves Nice at 14.32, so that the scenery along the coast can be enjoyed in daylight. Very fast running begins at Marseille, and Paris is reached in no more than 9 hr 3 min from Nice. The overall average speed inclusive of seven stops (one involving change of direction and locomotive) is 120 km/h (75 mph). The coaching stock and refreshment and other services are in keeping with the speed and smooth riding of the train. In addition to the full restaurant car there are lounge cars adjoining a buffet, and every facility to make the journey free from fatigue. Although not an international train itself, it is one of the famed *Trans-Europ-Express* (TEE) network, which by international agreement and collaboration ensures the highest standards of modern passenger train travel.

GREAT TRAINS

THE ORIENT EXPRESS

This famous named train is perhaps better known in fiction than in fact, to such extent indeed that some persons of today have asked whether there is really such a train as *The Orient Express*. The service was inaugurated in June 1883 to provide through connection between Paris and Constantinople. At that time one did not go all the way by train. The express from Paris ran via Vienna, Budapest, Bucharest and to the north bank of the Danube at Giurgevo. Then one crossed by ferry to Routschouck on the Bulgarian side, and continued by train to Varna, on the Black sea. The journey to Constantinople was completed by packet steamer of the Austrian Lloyd company. It was not until 1889 that the entire journey was made by train. Then instead of going via Bucharest the express went south from Budapest to Belgrade and then through Nisch and Sofia direct to Constantinople. The route was only 65 km (40½ miles) shorter, but the total journey time over the 3,000 km (1,857 miles) from Paris was 67 hr 35 min as compared with 81 hr 40 min via Varna. The train continued to provide through carriages between Paris and Bucharest.

The *Orient Express* of those days was not an easy train to run. No fewer than seven countries were involved in the complete run, and in Germany four different state administrations (Alsace-Lorraine, Baden, Württemburg and Bavaria) took their turns. The speeds were not heroic, and it was only in France that the speed between stops was as much as 65 km/h (40½ mph). The coaching stock was provided by the International Sleeping Car Company, with fine bogie vehicles designed on American lines, but although the company maintained continuity of service throughout the long journey, the organization was not welcomed in all countries. Prussia, for example, would not accept any stock belonging to the Sleeping Car Company. Another difficulty was that food consumed in the restaurant car had to be bought in the country concerned. No food of any kind could be carried across an international frontier.

After the opening of the Simplon tunnel, in 1906 a rival service known as the *Simplon-Orient*, or nowadays the *Direct Orient*, was inaugurated. In France it used the Paris, Lyons & Mediterranean line, instead of the Eastern, passing through Switzerland – Lausanne and the Rhone Valley – and through the Simplon tunnel to Milan. Afterwards it continued serving Venice and Trieste and came to Belgrade. Nowadays its through carriages are taken forward by two separate trains, the *Athens Express*, and the *Marmara Express*, the latter going to Istanbul. It is curious that while through first and second class accommodation is provided from Paris to Athens, nothing more than second class is available daily from Paris to Istanbul. Today the *Orient Express* proper runs daily between Paris and Vienna and Budapest following the traditional route via Strasburg, Munich, and Salzburg, and through

Above: An 05 class 4-6-2 of the Yugoslav State Railway heads the *Direct Orient Express* at Kreven Krst.

Below: Haydarpasa terminus, on the eastern shore of the Bosphorus. *Orient Express* passengers travelling onwards into Asian Turkey took their trains from this station.

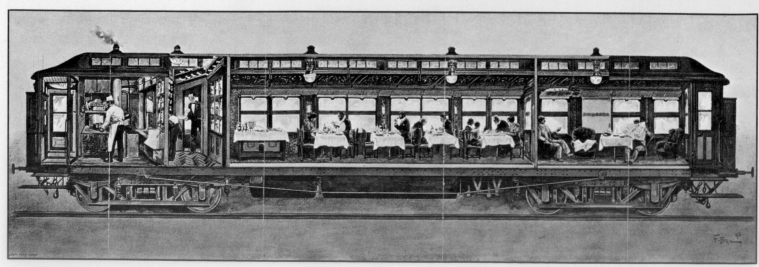

carriages between Paris and Bucharest are carried on four days a week. When the train was first put on in 1883, the time for the 1,350 km (837 miles) from Paris to Vienna was 26¾ hr, leaving Paris at 19.30 and reaching Vienna at 22.15 on the following evening. Today it takes no more than 16 hr 10 min. The respective overall average speeds are 50.5 km/h (31.3 mph) and 85.5 km/h (52.9 mph).

The westbound service is a particularly pleasant one to travel. Vienna is left at 15.00. The variety of scenery in the valley of the Danube can be enjoyed in the late afternoon, and then after dinner there is a comfortable night's rest, to arrive in Paris at 07.35. This is not quite such a fast run as eastbound, although there is some very speedy travel on the French part of the run. The haulage is electric all the way.

The Eastern Railway built a new class of locomotive in 1883 specially for the *Orient Express*, a powerful 2–4–0 with outside cylinders. Original make-up of the train consisted of two sleeping cars, one restaurant car and two four-wheeled baggage vans. Now, in France, the *Orient Express* is hauled by electric locomotives

of 5,000 hp which run at 160 km/h (100 mph).

At one time there was yet another offshoot of the original *Orient Express*, which used the Eastern Railway from Paris, passed into Switzerland at Basle, and continued via Zurich into Austria by the Arlberg route. This became known as the *Arlberg-Orient Express* and served Innsbruck and Salzburg on the way to Vienna. But the name *Orient* has now been dropped from the title of this train. In Austria the *Orient Express* itself, and the one time *Arlberg-Orient*, were the most important and popular trains between Salzburg and Vienna. Like so many long through services today there are few travellers who ride from end to end, but many who use them over intermediate stages, and between Salzburg and Vienna they are always crowded. It used to be a prestige run for Austrian steam locomotives before the first world war when the great engineer Karl Gölsdorf was director of mechanical engineering, and the railway itself was known as the Imperial Royal Austrian State. His steam locomotives were among the most elegant on the continent of Europe.

Left: A cut-away impression of the restaurant car of the *Orient Express*. The limited space for food preparation, typical of all restaurant cars, is effectively shown.

Right: The *Balkan Express*. World War 1 cut the route of the Orient Express but the so-called *Balkan Express*, which features in this picture, maintained northern Europe's rail route to Turkey during the war years.

Far right: Electric traction over part of the *Marmara Express* route in Turkey.

GREAT TRAINS

THE RHEINGOLD

The comprehensive and complicated extent of this famous German express service today is symbolic of the heterogeneous build-up of the route that it follows in West Germany, quite apart from the international feeder lines at its extremities. In broad terms it is a service from Holland and north-west Germany to Switzerland and Italy, though carrying a great number of through carriages. The parent stem is the dining car section. At one time this train ran from the Hook of Holland to Basle in Switzerland. At a later time the northern terminus became Amsterdam, while now the parent dining car portion runs from the Hook of Holland to Geneva. At that earlier time the train used to enter Holland at Venlo and run via Eindhoven and Dordrecht to Rotterdam, but now it travels via Arnhem, and much remarshalling takes place at Utrecht.

Entering West Germany at Emmerich, it comes on to the tracks of the one-time Right Rhine Administration in the days of imperial Germany, and the route lies through Duisberg and Düsseldorf, giving connections into the Ruhr, and northwards to Bremen, and Hamburg. It continues Right Rhine until Cologne, where it crosses to the left bank, to the great station almost in the shadow of the famous cathedral. The express proceeds from there on the former Left Rhine tracks, and calls at Bonn. In the days of the Third Reich a non-stop run was made from Cologne to Mainz, 186.5 km (115.7 miles), but now, in addition to Bonn there is a stop at Coblenz. At Bingen, the area of one of the old private railways is entered, the Hesse Louis Company, on whose tracks *Rheingold* continues to Mannheim, after which it is Baden State for the rest of the journey to the Swiss frontier.

Today, *Rheingold* is one of the most international of all continental express trains, and one becomes particularly aware of it on entering the restaurant car. The smart young waitresses wear flags on the lapels of their tunics representing the countries whose language they speak, and it is rare to see one who speaks fewer than three. English, French and German are virtually basic requirements, with Dutch and Italian in the way of optional extras. The coaching stock and dining cars are magnificent, while a particular attraction was the scenic dome car (no longer in use) which had a glass roof that gave additionally fine glimpses of the scenery in the lower part of the Rhine valley. On summer days, however, it was inclined to be rather hot under that glass roof, while the light construction of the framing sometimes gave rise to an occasional creaking.

The track is superb, and for most of the way along the winding course of the Rhine the speed

Right: A class 112 electric locomotive, one of 31 units built in the early 1960s by Krauss Maffei, at the head of the *Rheingold*.

Below right: The southbound *Rheingold* starts its journey in the dockside terminus at Hook of Holland. The locomotive is a former British Railways passenger unit, sold to the Netherlands Railways after the end of passenger services on the Manchester-Woodhead-Sheffield line.

Below far left: The *Rheingold*, hauled by a DB electric locomotive, passing along the bank of the Rhine.

Below left: Inside the dining car of the *Rheingold*.

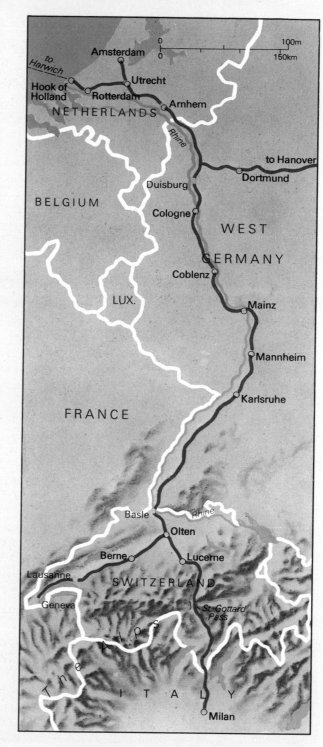

is 120 to 130 km/h (75 to 80 mph). On the north-bound run this is the time for dinner, and it would seem that part of the training of those young waitresses is to learn how to keep their feet, and balance well-loaded trays, when the train is rounding curves at high speed. The timing of the train is based on the arrivals and departures of the English cross-channel ferries at the Hook of Holland, leaving that port soon after 07.00 in the morning, and arriving from the south about 23.00.

Exciting though it can be on the curves beside the Rhine, the train makes its fastest running farther south, over the tracks of the once very slothful Baden State Railway. The fastest speeds are sustained between Karlsruhe and Freiburg with a maximum of 160 km/h (100 mph). The traction is, of course, electric throughout, with the change from the Dutch 1,500 volts dc to the German 15,000 volts ac 16⅔ Hz. Locomotives are changed at the frontier station. The German E10 class are 5,000 hp and provide for very rapid acceleration from rest. Although the gradients on the route of the *Rheingold* are almost level throughout, in following so closely to the course of the river, high power is needed to regain speed after the various speed restrictions for curves and junctions. It is because of curves, for example, that the 62 km (38.4 miles) between Basle and Freiburg are allowed as much as 34 minutes from start to stop, even though the train runs at 160 km/h for part of the distance. The really fast stretch is the 136.4 km (85 miles) between Freiburg and Karlsruhe, allowed 58 minutes and involving a start-to-stop average speed of 141 km/h (87.5 mph). The speed is 160 km/h for 50 km (31 miles) continuously between Gundelfingen and Niederschepfheim, and again after slowing down for the Offenburg curves until Baden-Oos is passed.

GREAT TRAINS
THE SHINKANSEN HIKARI

With all other trains in this series one individual service is concerned, leaving at a definite time of day, even though this may have varied slightly with the years in the case of long-established trains. But with the Japanese *Hikari* or lightning trains, there is one every quarter of an hour from Tokyo to Osaka, from 06.00 in the morning till 21.00 at night, in each direction, all alike, covering the 517 km (320 miles) in 3 hr 10 min inclusive of two intermediate stops. A similar procession is travelling from Osaka to Tokyo at the same time. The original main line of Japanese National Railways southward from Tokyo followed the ancient Tokaido trail. It was laid to Japan's standard 1,067 mm (3 ft 6 in) gauge and followed a rather meandering course along the east coast of the country, including many steep gradients and sharp curves. It could not be upgraded into a fast express route, and 100 km/h (62 mph) was the highest speed regularly run. By the 1930s the increasing industrialization of the east coast of Japan was leading to serious traffic congestion on this line – the Tokaido – and plans were made for a new direct line on the American and European standard-gauge of 1,435 mm (4 ft 8½ in) on which high-speed trains could be run.

The project was of course very much delayed by the war, and it was not until 1964 that regular passenger services began to run on the New Tokaido Line. Those who visited Japan for the Olympic Games held in Tokyo that year brought back first impressions of travel on the *Shinkansen,* or new line, but it was not until October of the following year that the full high-speed service of *Hikari* trains was introduced. In total contrast to the geography of the old Tokaido line the new one is carried on an alignment such that a speed of 210 km/h (130 mph) can be sustained for practically the entire distance. The track is carried on viaducts high above the towns, across valleys, over rivers, through mountains – directly through or over any natural obstacle. All *Hikari* are exactly alike, and have seating for 1,400 passengers. In Japan there are no classes as such, though one can pay a small supplement to travel in 'green cars', which provide greater comfort. This how-

ever is only relative, because Japanese passenger trains, whether on the *Shinkansen* or elsewhere, are very comfortable.

With a service frequency of only 15 minutes passenger handling at the terminal stations has to be very highly organized. Load factor all the year round is 67 per cent, so each train is carrying on an average 950 passengers. At the busiest times every seat is taken. Seats are reserved by computer at the time of booking. If, for example, the 15.15 departure from Tokyo was fully booked, a passenger would be reasonably certain of getting on to the 15.30, or at the very latest the 15.45. While the booking arrangements are so regulated the movements on the platforms are equally streamlined, both for trains and passengers. A single island platform is all that is necessary, and its two faces are used for alternate departures. Although the shortness of the journey times does not justify full restaurant car service the *Hikari* are liberally supplied with refreshment facilities, and the way in which the trains are serviced at the terminals is part of the overall streamlined procedure. The following is a typical example of normal working, at one of the platform faces:

15.00 *Hikari* departs for Osaka, 1,300 on board.
15.05 *Hikari* arrives from Osaka, 1,100 detrain.
15.10 Cleaners and servicing staff enter.
15.25 Cleaners and servicing staff leave.
15.26 Passengers enter.
15.30 *Hikari* departs for Osaka, 1,350 on board.

With only 4 or 5 minutes for passengers to enter, everyone is queued up on the platform, according to their seat reservations, exactly opposite the correct coach door, and the moment the cleaners are out, in go the passengers.

Travel in the air-conditioned coaches is quite deceptive. It is difficult to appreciate that one is going so fast. The fact that for most of the way the *Shinkansen* is carried on viaducts, high above surrounding buildings, reduces the impression of high speed. Trains going in the opposite direction pass silently, in a flash, and the long tunnels are quite unobtrusive. Travelling is very smooth, from the meticulous attention given to maintenance of track and rolling stock.

Far right: The bullet nose of the *Hikari*-type train. Unlike pre-war streamlined trains, the *Hikari* is fast enough to make streamlining worthwhile in terms of energy consumption as well as publicity.

Right: A fully-loaded vehicle of a *Hikari* train. The high-density seating enables each train to accommodate 1,400 passengers.

Right: On the New Tokaido Line, a *Hikari* train crosses the Fuji River against a background dominated by Fuji San.

Below: In the driving cab of a *Hikari* electric multiple unit train on the Tokyo to Osaka line.

The traction system is electric, at 25,000 volts ac 60 Hz, with overhead current collection. Every axle of every car is motored, thus resulting in a perfectly smooth distribution of power throughout each train. The total is no less than 16,000 hp for each train, and this provides for very rapid acceleration from rest, as well as for the maintenance of high speed. These trains can attain their full running speed of 210 km/h (130 mph) in 4 minutes from leaving the station.

The line between Tokyo and Osaka is no more than the beginning of the *Shinkansen* network in Japan, and on extension lines to north and south the tracks, fixed structures and trains have been designed for a maximum running speed of 260 km/h (161 mph). One of the differences has been to space the tracks a little farther apart so as to minimize the effect of air turbulence when two trains pass each other at maximum speed. Because no less than 55 per cent of the distance from Osaka southwards will be in tunnel this is a necessary provision on a train service on which much store is set upon the amenities of travel.

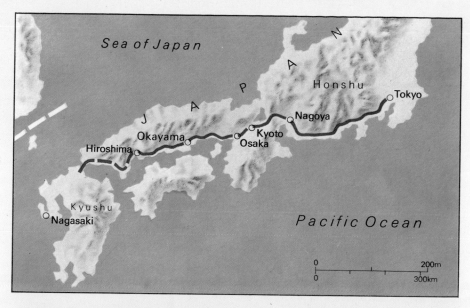

GREAT TRAINS

THE RUSSIA
[TRANS SIBERIAN EXPRESS]

To anyone who wishes to make the longest through journey on the railways of the world, longest both in distance and time, the *Russia* is of compelling interest. It runs between Moscow and Vladivostok daily in each direction. The distance is 9,297 km (5,778 miles), and the journey takes approximately eight days. The route taken today is, for much of its length, not that by which through communication between Moscow and Vladivostok was first established.

Construction of railways in Russia began to extend beyond the European boundaries in the 1880s, and by 1890 a line had been completed as far east as Chelyabinsk, about 1,700 km (1,054 miles) from Moscow. It was then that strategic needs prompted the amazing project of a line across the barren steppes to reach Vladivostok. The distance proved to be 7,416 km (4,608 miles), and construction began from both ends simultaneously in 1891. At its eastern end the line had to take a somewhat circuitous route. The more direct line was made possible by making use of the Chinese Eastern Railway through Manchuria to Vladivostok; but for political and strategic reasons an all-Russian route was always the ultimate target. Eventual link-up of the two sections, working east from Chelyabinsk and west from Vladivostok, took place in 1904.

Since then many additional lines have been built, and there are now three main routes from Moscow to the city of Omsk, which could be called the grand junction of the steppes. The original line from Moscow, via Ufa and Chelyabinsk, is now so heavily utilized by freight trains that the *Russia* takes the more northerly and longer route via Kirov and Sverdlovsk to join up with the old line at Kurgan, about 230 km (143 miles) east of Chelyabinsk. Omsk, 2,716 km (1,680 miles) by the present route, is reached in the small hours of the third day out from Moscow. Up to then progress has been thus:

Km	Moscow		Dep. 10.10	First day	Average speed km/h
957	Kirov	arr.	0.23	Second day	67
		dep.	0.38		
1,818	Sverdlovsk	arr.	13.15	Second day	66
		dep.	13.30	Second day	
2,716	Omsk	arr.	01.54	Third day	72

Stops at the principal stations are each of 15 minutes duration.

The train is advertised in having both 'hard' and 'soft' cars. On Soviet Railways a 'hard' car is one in which the accommodation provides only for sitting up, and are either of the compartment type entered from a side corridor, or of the open type as in the latest passenger coaches on British railways, and always favoured in North America. A 'soft' car is one that has 'places for lying', to quote the description in the timetables. On the Trans-Siberian run there are also some more luxurious cars described as 'soft first category', and these are equivalent to the sleeping cars run elsewhere. The *Russia* has a restaurant car throughout from Moscow to Vladivostok, though like those run on many other Soviet trains they do not seem to be extensively patronized as yet. Long distance passengers can always buy farm produce from peasants at rural stations en route.

The run from Omsk to Irkutsk, through the monotonous scenery of the steppes, is the most tedious on the entire lengthy journey, the 2,475 km (1,539 mile) run taking the daylight hours of two whole days. Progress is thus:

Right: On the Trans Siberian Railway during the Civil War in 1919. At this time services were few, irregular, and primitive. The photograph shows wood fuel being taken on board to heat a passenger vehicle provided in a freight train for priority travellers.

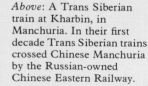

Above: A Trans Siberian train at Kharbin, in Manchuria. In their first decade Trans Siberian trains crossed Chinese Manchuria by the Russian-owned Chinese Eastern Railway.

Left: On the Trans Siberian Railway in about 1910. The train, hauled by an 0-8-0 freight locomotive, is probably a railway workmens' service.

Right: The interior of a standard post-war Soviet Railways restaurant car, as running in the *Russia* service. Such cars are provided by the Ministry of Railways, but are staffed and supplied by the Ministry of Internal Trade.

Distance from Moscow km	Station	Time	Day out from Moscow	Average speed km/h
2,716	Omsk	dep. 02.14	Third	
3,343	Novosibirsk	arr. 11.02	Third	70
		dep. 11.17	Third	
4,104	Krasnoyarsk	arr. 23.15	Third	63
		dep. 23.30	Third	
5,191	Irkutsk	arr. 19.34	Fourth	55

It is unfortunate that it is late evening by the time the train leaves Irkutsk, because passengers are then unable to enjoy the most beautiful part of the whole run, where the line skirts the shores of Lake Baikal, and where the route was blasted out of solid rock and taken through no less than 42 tunnels in a relatively short distance. The westbound *Russia* fares no better from the sightseeing point of view, for this picturesque stretch is crossed at night.

Trains from Moscow to Peking use the Trans-Siberian line as far as Chita, 6,204 km (3,845½ miles) from Moscow, following thence the former Chinese Eastern Railway via Shenyang; but the quicker route to Peking diverges at Ulan Ude, 5,647 km (3,509 miles) from Moscow. The *Russia* continues thus:

Distance from Moscow km	Station	Time	Day out from Moscow	Average speed km/h
5,191	Irkutsk	dep. 19.49	Fourth	—
5,647	Ulan Ude	arr. 03.55	Fifth	34
		dep. 04.13	Fifth	—
6,204	Chita	arr. 14.14	Fifth	55
		dep. 12.49	Fifth	—
7,313	Skovorodino	arr. 13.29	Sixth	—
		dep. 13.44	Sixth	48
8,531	Khabarovsk	arr. 22.00*	Seventh	—
		dep. 22.20*	Seventh	77
9,297	Vladivostok	arr. 12.35*	Eighth	55

* Local time: 7 hours earlier than Moscow

Allowing for the difference in time between the two terminal points the journey takes 7 days 19 hours 25 min. On the westbound run the train leaves Vladivostok at 23.15 local time and arrives in Moscow at 12.10 on the eighth day.

GREAT TRAINS

THE 20TH CENTURY LIMITED

Above: A postcard of pre-first world war days, showing the *Twentieth Century Limited* at speed.

Operation of fast trains between New York and Chicago, and the rivalry between the New York Central and the Pennsylvania routes, dates back to 1891, although the first regular service at high-speed coincided with the famous Chicago Exposition of 1893. It was however on June 15, 1902 that the New York Central introduced the *Twentieth Century Limited*, running the 1,542 km (958 miles) between New York and Chicago in the level 20 hours. Average speed including all stops was a shade under 77 km/h (48 mph). The load was five of the massive clerestory-roofed cars then customary in the USA, and speed was limited to a maximum of 113 km/h (70 mph). For one brief period before the first world war the timing was reduced to 18 hours; but the acceleration was not popular. Neither track nor rolling stock were ready for faster running, and a reversion to 20 hours followed. So it remained until the year 1932. By that time the *Century*, as it was always known, had become so popular that it was run regularly in at least three sections, each of which consisted of about 13 cars.

Its departure from Grand Central Terminal, New York, at 14.45 every day had the precision of a military parade. The three sections, with their tail ends exactly in line at the buffer stops of three adjacent platforms, moved out simultaneously, and only took their places, first, second and third, in line ahead when they had entered the long tunnel that comes immediately after leaving the station. The three sections were electrically-hauled as far as Harmon, 52 km (32 miles) out, and then the giant 4-6-4 Hudson type steam locomotives took over. A stretch of some 1,500 km (930 miles) remained to be covered with steam traction; and in 1930 engines would be changed twice in this distance, at Syracuse, and Toledo. Crews were changed at Albany, Buffalo, Cleveland, and Elkhart in addition to the places where the engines themselves were changed. The longest non-stop run, and then the longest in the USA, was the run through the night over the 295 km (184 miles) from Buffalo to Cleveland.

A typical make-up of the train in these last years

of the 20-hour run was, from the engine rearwards, club and baggage car containing bathroom, barber's shop, steward's pantry for serving soft drinks, smoking lounge; five sleepers; two dining cars; then five more sleepers, the last having an observation lounge at the rear. The rolling stock was all of very massive construction, and the 13 cars would weigh about 1000 tons, or more than double the weight of a British express train of that period. The sleeping accommodation was of varying kinds, ranging upwards in luxury from the berth type, with the passenger sleeping lengthwise to the train instead of in transverse berths as in Great Britain and in Europe, to private suites with bedrooms and private drawing rooms. Although the *Century* was basically a night train, there was a late afternoon and evening of travel before turning in for the night. The arrival in Chicago was at 09.45.

In the days before air travel and the proliferation of modern highway transport, the *Century* became very popular with top businessmen, some of whom used to travel on it once a week regularly. There was a stenographer service, where letters could be dictated, typed, and posted en route; stock market quotations were posted on a notice board in the club car, and at each station stop telephone connections were made by land line, so that calls could be made from the train itself. Nor were the comforts of a good hotel confined to the business clientele. On each section of the train there were skilled lady's maids, beauty specialists, and porters available to render personal service.

Despite the general business depression of the 1930s not only were new Pullman sleeping cars put on to the *Century*, but from 1932 there began a notable quickening of the run, first to 18 hours overall, and then in 1938 to 16 hours. By that time great strides had been made in track maintenance, and in the ride quality of passenger rolling stock, and the much higher running speeds necessitated by these accelerations could be sustained without any discomfort to passengers. Cruising speed of the train now became 130 to 136 km/h (80 to 85 mph). Unlike the rival Pennsylvania route from New York to Chicago, which cut through the heart of the Allegheny mountains, and involved some heavy gradients, the

Upper right: Grand Central Station in New York as it used to be.

Centre right: One of the 4-6-4 locomotives which hauled the fastest New York Central trains in the 1930s. The Railroad had 275 units of this wheel arrangement, but only a handful of them were streamlined.

Bottom right: Three General Motors diesel units haul the post-war *Twentieth Century Limited* along the so-called 'Water-Level Route' beside the Hudson. Modern signalling and reduced train frequency had by this time permitted the removal of one pair of tracks from this section.

New York Central line was little removed from level throughout, over which the end-to-end average speed became 96.5 km/h (59.9 mph).

At the time of these notable accelerations new streamlined rolling stock was put on, providing an increased degree of luxury in travel; but by the year 1939 the effect of competition was being felt. Although patronage remained good, the American love of novelty was tending to attract some passengers elsewhere. In keeping with the streamlining of the rolling stock the selected Hudson class locomotives working the *Century* were also streamlined, and painted in a striking silver-grey style with dark blue horizontal bands. These huge engines, which weighed 160 tons without their tenders, developed 4,700 indicated hp at 125 km/h. On the more favourable stretches of line the *Century* ran at 153 to 160 km/h (95 to 100 mph).

It had never been an exclusively New York and Chicago train. At Albany the third section attached a through sleeping car portion – usually three cars – from Boston. The train, or rather all sections of it, were very much in demand during the second world war, when it was used extensively by high-ranking service chiefs and government officials; but when the war was over, despite the change to diesel traction, the rapid decline in popularity of railway travel in the USA led to such diminution of patronage that eventually the *Century* was taken out of traffic. This was only one outward sign of the increasing financial difficulties of the New York Central Railroad itself. Today there is no through passenger service at all between New York and Chicago by the former NYC route.

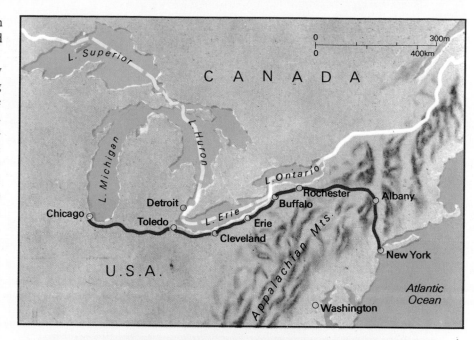

RAILWAY OPERATION

Introduction – the operating organization. The term operating, in its railway technical sense, covers all facets of working concerned with running the trains. In railway organization the commercial departments, in consultation with and as directed by top management, specify the type, frequency, and speed of trains needed to meet traffic requirements. Sometimes the need is already there; at others new services are projected with a view to attracting additional traffic. It cannot always be a case of precise specification of demands. There has to be consultation, because on most railways of the world, large and small, the operating departments have wide-ranging ramifications.

While organizations differ in detail on many railways, the most usual set-up today is for all staff connected with train movement to be included in the operating department – that is locomotive men, and other trainmen, signalmen, traffic regulators, telecommunications operators. The technical engineering departments provide the necessary tools, in the form of locomotives, rolling stock, signalling and telecommunications equipment, and maintain it in good order; while a further consideration affecting operating is the track and fixed structures, which determine the maximum speed that may be run over each part of the line, and the loads that can be carried on each axle.

From the operating viewpoint, railways can be divided into three broad categories:
(a) the 'Mixed', carrying a large volume of heavy traffic of various kinds and at varying speeds;
(b) the 'Special Purpose', carrying a single class of traffic, at a single level of speed, often at high density;
(c) the 'Sparsely Used', in remote or developing countries.

The mixed railway. This is the most difficult to operate. It is found in the developed countries of the world where commercial needs demand provision of high-speed inter-city express trains during daytime business hours; high-density commuter services; and freight services giving an acceptable level of fast city-to-city transit. At the same time this type of railway needs to have facilities to run extra trains, both passenger and freight, when demand requires it, often at very short notice, and superimposed upon the regular timetables. On many railways it is frequently arranged to operate the heaviest volume of freight at night, when inter-city passenger travel is confined to sleeping car services that are not required to run at such high speeds as the daytime trains. To provide for ready insertion of extras, timetables usually have space left to be taken up when needed.

The special purpose railway. This can be one of several kinds, examples of which are to be found in many countries:
(a) The rapid-transit railway, concerned solely with mass-handling of intense commuter traffic during relatively short periods, morning and evening.
(b) The ultra-high speed passenger line, specially constructed on an exceptionally favourable track alignment, to permit continuous running at 250 km/h (155 mph) or more, carrying no other traffic, and operated by completely standardized motive power and rolling stock.

Below left: Gantry of standard Indian semaphore signals at Agra Cantonment Junction.

Below right: Fig 1. Example of timetable graph, showing paths of trains of different speeds.

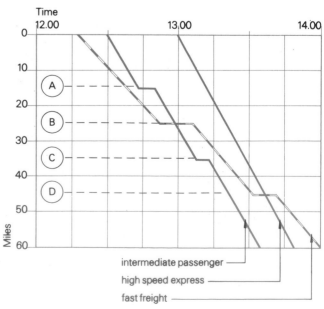

Above: On CP Rail: Bracket signal structure carrying searchlight signals providing speed signalling aspects.

Below right: The 'Spreader-Ditcher' is a composite machine used in railway construction and maintenance as a spreader, ditcher, ballast plough, ballast and roadbed shaper.

(c) The belt-conveyor type of mineral railway, built as an integral part of a unified commercial enterprise to convey a pre-determined tonnage of minerals or other freight from one centre of activity to another – year in, year out. Railways of this kind are usually privately-owned by the industrial enterprises concerned.

(d) A development of (c) is one that is completely automated, with driverless trains, though so far operating over a relatively short distance.

The special purpose railway is the easiest to operate, in that its trains run to the same speeds, and have identical running and braking characteristics. The timetable is pre-set, without any complications of extras, and variations only occur in the exceptional instance of some emergency.

The sparsely-used railway. This will be single-track, and because of the low utilization the loops, where trains running in opposite directions can pass each other, are often long distances apart. Equipment and methods of working on such lines are largely dictated by what the economics of the situation will justify. If the entire traffic over 24 hours does not amount to more than four freight trains and one passenger train in each direction, with occasional extras, a highly sophisticated system of remote-controlled colourlight signalling is not called for. The North American system of telegraphic train orders, in which written instructions are given to the enginemen at intermediate locations, is probably adequate. No signals of the orthodox type would be used at all.

On some newly-constructed railways in this category the telegraph is not used, and orders are conveyed into the locomotive cabs by means of a short wave radio network. With heavier traffic, still of a mixed nature, and not requiring more than a single track, the train order system is too slow and cumbersome for traffic to be efficiently regulated, and the Centralized Traffic Control (CTC) system of colourlight signalling with remotely-controlled electrical operation, has been installed to great advantage. The various techniques are described later.

Planning the timetable. The basis of all railway operating, however intense, however sparse the traffic, is the timetable graph, and its build-up and underlying parameters are now described. Fig 1 shows the sheet of graph paper applying to a section of double-track railway 70 km (43 miles) in length over the period from 12.00 to 14.00. A section of double track is chosen by way of explanation to avoid, at first, the complication of crossing opposing trains. Highest priority during this period must be given to an express passenger train entering the section at 13.00 and running continuously at 140 km/h (87 mph). Its timetable 'path', to use the recognized term, is shown by the thick diagonal line reaching the lowest line of the graph at 13.30.

There is also a freight train, running at 80 km/h (50 mph), entering the section at 12.10, with the path shown by the dotted line, and between the two is a fast intermediate passenger train, running at 120 km/h (75 mph), but making two station stops at A and B, shown by the thin continuous line

There are two intermediate stations C and D, at which neither of the passenger trains stop, but which have lengthy loop tracks. Into that at C the freight train is turned so as to give the first passenger train a clear run from A to B. Between the two passenger trains the freight is progressed from C to D, where it is side-tracked again to give the high-speed priority train a clear run. This is what is planned on paper. In implementing even this simple timetable a number of practical considerations have to be taken into account.

A few of these may be enumerated:

1. The freight might be running late.
2. One of its wagons might have an overheated axlebox required to be detached.
3. The first passenger train might be exceptionally loaded, requiring extra time at both stopping stations.
4. The priority high-speed train might be running well, and gaining on its booked time.

One can see readily how any of these factors, or a combination of them, could supervene to disrupt the planned pattern of train movement on the timetable graph in Fig 1. The question then arises as to how close succeeding trains may be

allowed to approach one another, in safety, without causing delay in running, and how the man in charge of operation on this section of line can alter the priorities so as to deal with local difficulties to the best advantage of the service as a whole.

The equipment of the line, and of the rolling stock running over it, must next be considered. This is where the operator must state his requirements. For example, the facility of running high-speed passenger trains at 140 km/h (87 mph) at intervals of 5 minutes at certain times of the day. This would immediately establish certain parameters for the signal engineer in providing the necessary safety equipment. He in turn would be dependent upon the locomotive and rolling stock designer, not so much in providing the power to pull but in the means of stopping.

Signalling and brake power. The relationship of signalling to brake power is fundamental in any timetable and operational planning. A driver will not be able to maintain his scheduled speed unless he is continuously receiving clear signals; but if it is not safe for him to proceed at full speed the warning signal must be placed so that he has full braking distance in which to bring his train to rest short of an obstruction. Positioning of signals along the line is vitally linked up with the brake power of the trains, and in this lies one of the great difficulties in planning the timetable for, and operating a mixed railway. Not all types of train have the same braking characteristics, but without taking into account this complication, the relationship between signalling and brake power can be seen in a simpler way.

The following statistics relate to the rolling stock of one modern railway:

Speed km/h	Service braking distance on level track	Time to run distance of 3 km
120	1,200	1 min 30 sec
160	2,020	1 min 7 sec

Thus while an increase in speed from 120 km/h (75 mph) to 160 km/h (100 mph) increases the braking distance necessary by nearly 70 per cent the higher speed trains would be clearing the signal sections quicker, and could therefore be run at closer headway one behind the other, if necessary. A driver working a train at 160 km/h would, from the above figures, need a warning distance of 2,020 m (2,209 yd) of an obstruction ahead; and if the signal was placed at that distance he could, theoretically, continue at absolutely full speed up to the moment of actually passing the signal. But in practice, psychological considerations intervene, and at such a speed a driver would almost certainly shut off power the moment he saw a warning signal in the distance. The margin of safety is thereby increased.

Traffic density. On a section of plain line, that is one without any intermediate junctions or stations with siding connections, the type of signal depends upon the density of traffic. If, for exam-

ple, trains are not required to run at more frequent intervals than 10 minutes, signals displaying only two indications – 'stop' and 'proceed' – would be adequate. Each of these would be preceded by a caution signal placed at full braking distance for maximum line speed in advance of the stop signal (Fig 2). If the line was one used by trains permit-

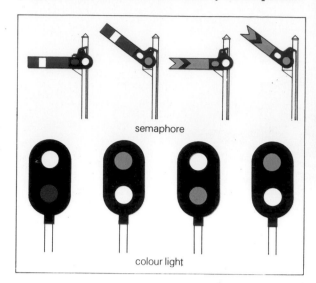

semaphore

colour light

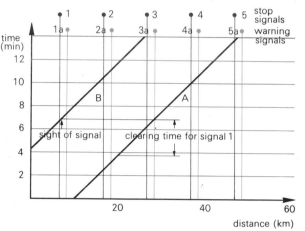

ted to run at 160 km/h (100 mph) the situation would be as shown in Fig 3. The stop signals are spaced 10 km (6½ miles) apart with the warning signals 2 km (1¼ miles) in advance. Train A passes No 2 signal 3¾ minutes after signal No 1, while train B, running at an interval of 8 minutes would reach the 'warner' for signal No 1 about 3½ minutes after the first train had passed signal No 2. But on straight plain line the driver might have a sight of this warning signal ½ km before reaching it, 23 seconds earlier. The time lag between this signal clearing, and the driver getting a first sight of it would thus be about 3½ minutes and

Top left: Fig 2. British semaphore signals – upper quadrant – and corresponding colour light aspects.

Above left: Fig 3. Spacing of signals in relation to train returning speeds.

Above: Maintenance man lighting up oil-lit semaphore signal.

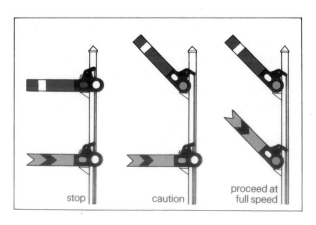

Below left: Fig 4. Three-indication semaphore signals using two arms.

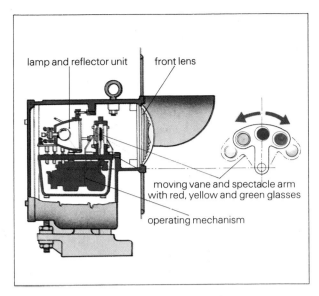

this allows a comfortable margin for any slight variation either way from strict timetable paths.

If it is required to run at closer headway the spacing of the signals along the line becomes closer, and the position is neared when the location of a stop signal almost coincides with the warning, or distant, signal for the next. Then the two functions are combined. In the case of semaphore signals in both British and German styles this is done physically, by putting two arms on to the same signal post, as shown in Fig 4. Then the three aspects signify, stop; pass this signal, but next one is at danger; all clear. The corresponding night indications involve the use of two lights.

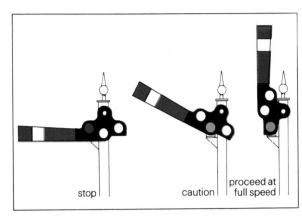

American use of semaphores in the upper quadrant made possible a three-position semaphore (Fig 5) using only a single light for each of the night indications. From this the day colourlight signal was developed, showing red for stop, yellow for caution, and green for all clear. Two varieties of three-aspect colourlight signal are in current use today in different parts of the world, the multi-lens (Fig 6), in which the col-

Top right: Fig 7. Mechanism of searchlight type colour light signal.

Above right: Fig 5. Three-position upper quadrant semaphore signals.

Right: Fig 6. Lens unit of colour light signal – multi-lens type.

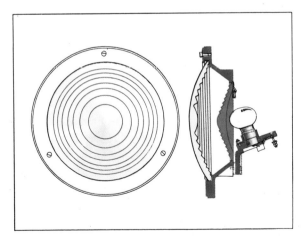

Below right: British Railways diesel hauled train passing standard mechanically worked upper quadrant signal at Edale (Sheffield-Manchester route).

ours are displayed from separate lenses, and the searchlight type (Fig 7), in which the controlling relay mechanism is in the signal case, and the red, yellow, or green indication as required is projected through the one front lens. The multi-lens is generally favoured in Great Britain and on the continent of Europe, and the searchlight in North America.

From the foregoing, the commercial departments having specified the traffic densities to be provided for during the day and night, the signal spacing can be determined and their locations plotted on the timetable diagram.

So far, consideration has been given only to level track. On railways in most parts of the world gradients make an appreciable difference to the speed of trains and the time they take to clear successive sections between signals. But in recent years on the busiest routes in developed countries, such has been the enhancement of tractive power, primarily through the provision of electric traction in its most modern forms, that there is very little difference between the speed on level track and when climbing the steepest gradients, with both passenger and freight trains. Of course, while the speeds may be similar the braking distances will vary considerably on a line with steep gradients, being considerably less when going uphill, due to the assistance of gravity, and more when descending the same incline.

Although the modern freight train, consisting entirely of bogie wagons and multiple-headed, sometimes with four or five diesel-electric locomotives, is run at relatively high speed, up to 120 km/h (75 mph), its speed, because of the running characteristics of the rolling stock does not approach that of the maximum speed passenger trains at 160 to 200 km/h (100 to 125 mph). If such freights are to run at headways of 5 to 7 minutes during the night hours, their performance can be the governing factor in the layout of signals along the line.

Basis of everyday working. On many railways the timetable graph is the basis of everyday working for the operator at control centres where operation of extensive areas of railway is being co-ordinated. A printed copy of the graph, with the paths of all regularly-scheduled trains is supplied daily. Certain key signalboxes are designated as reporting posts, and it is the duty of the staff there to report by telephone the time at which every train passes. This is duly noted on the printed copy of the timetable graph, and by connecting up successive entries with ruled lines the actual path of each train can be seen, in comparison with the scheduled path.

By this continuous reporting and plotting, the controller has constantly before him the gradually evolving pattern of the day's running and can judge whether any adjustments to priorities are necessary. For example, it may become apparent that for some reason a particular train is making poor time and causing cumulative delay in its rear. It might be necessary to stop it and provide additional locomotive power or other remedial action. Compilation of the daily graphic record not only provides a most valuable tool of operating for the controller, but a record is kept at headquarters from which day-to-day performance over many months may be studied. This is invaluable, indicating what adjustments to the timetable might be desirable at the next revision.

Regulation of train movement with the timetable diagram as a basis is only one part of the function of central traffic control. It is of inestimable value in dealing with problems of late running, passenger amenities, missed connections, and such like. Today, all over the world, the trend is to run main-line express trains in block-load formations, and to provide services on subsidiary lines by advertised connections rather than the older practice of attaching or detaching through carriages. A long-distance train making such a connection from an important branch might be seriously late, so that 20 or more passengers arriving by the branch train could have a wait of an hour or more at the junction instead of the timetabled 10 minutes. Then Control would step in and arrange for a train that normally passed that junction without stopping to be stopped specially to pick up those waiting passengers, after a wait of no more than 20 minutes.

Signalling at junctions. So far the only signalling considered has been that along plain line, but in turning to methods of operating at junctions distinction must be made between geographical signalling and speed signalling. The latter is the standard method of working in North America.

The geographical system tells the driver for what route the points are set, and more than 100 years had passed after the building of the first railways before a degree of finality had been attained in both principle and in the type of apparatus most favoured. Earlier practice was to provide a separate semaphore arm, or other mechanical device for each line; and while this could be clear enough at a simple bifurcation, it became very complicated at the approach to a

busy terminus, where there were many platforms in which a train could conclude its journey. It was even more elaborate if such a station was approached by several running lines parallel to each other. The result was huge gantries spanning the tracks and carrying 20 or more semaphore signals.

There is nevertheless a difference between the main-line bifurcation, beyond which two long and important routes diverged, and the approach to a large terminal station. In the first all the driver needed to be told was whether the route was set for left or right. The location would be approached and passed at relatively high speed, and the signal display needed to be something that could be seen and interpreted from some distance ahead. In the approach to a large terminal station the driver needed to know the platform into which he was being routed.

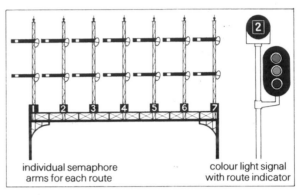

individual semaphore   colour light signal
arms for each route   with route indicator

Because of these differing conditions the main-line junction signal remained of the so-called splitting type (Fig 8) for many years after the introduction of route indicators, where no more than short range observation and low speeds were concerned. Fig 9 shows how the task of identifying the route was simplified by the use of route indicators. The type now most favoured is the theatre sign, in which there are no moving parts, and the figure or letter required to be displayed is obtained by selecting, electrically, the combination of lamps necessary (Fig 10).

At fast-running locations the splitting principle was used in many early installations of colour-light signals; but the close positioning of one signal unit abreast of another led sometimes to an optical embarrassment, where these signals could be sighted from a considerable distance. Red and green are complementary colours optically, and although the beams of light are very concentrated, there is a small amount of spread, and at long range red and green abreast of each other mingled to make an indistinct cluster of white light. It was to avoid this that the illuminated direction indicator was introduced – now standard for fast-running junctions in many countries of the world. With this type it is possible to specify three different divergencies on each side of the main line, as explained in Fig 11. In Great Britain no direction sign is shown for the main line, permitting unlimited speed; but in certain other countries an additional direction sign pointing vertically upwards specifies a movement along the principal route.

The principle of speed signalling informs the

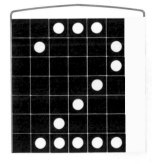

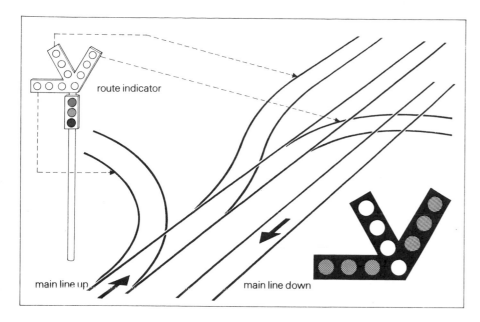

driver not necessarily of his route, but of the range of speed in which he must run his train. In the standard North American code a great number of different indications are included by the permutations made possible by having three signals of the searchlight type mounted in a vertical line, with each of the individual signal units able to display, as required, a red, yellow or green light. All three signals are continuously lit. Six specimen indications from the code, and their meaning, are shown in Fig 12. Indications to reduce speed are given on the approach to junctions where the train concerned has to make a diversion movement, which may mean that it is turning on to a branch line, or that it is being crossed over from one set of tracks to another parallel one.

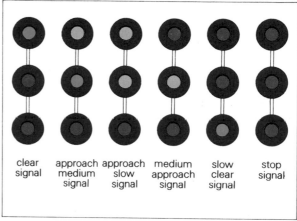

| clear
signal | approach
medium
signal | approach
slow
signal | medium
approach
signal | slow
clear
signal | stop
signal |

Line capacity. On American railways, and to a lesser extent elsewhere, many stretches of multiple-track route are signalled for running in both directions, instead of the conventional arrangement in which one track is reserved for eastbound trains and one for westbound. At different times of the day the preponderance of traffic may be in one direction, both passenger and freight, with little or nothing in the opposite

direction. If everything was confined to the normal eastbound track, for example, congestion might be such as to require an additional eastbound running line.

The point can be illustrated by an example in central France, on the main line from Paris to Marseilles and the Riviera. In the late evening southbound traffic is very heavy both in freight and sleeping car expresses to Swiss, Italian and Riviera resorts. The timetables have been so arranged that during the hours of greatest pressure no northbound trains are scheduled on the critical section north of Dijon, and both lines are made available to southbound traffic. In the early hours of the morning the position is reversed. The signalling is necessarily more elaborate, and facilities are provided to cross trains from one track to the other at all intermediate stations by the layout shown in Fig 13.

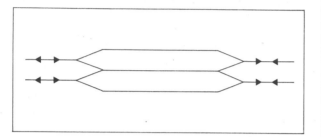

The problems of a mixed railway in having to provide for a variety of trains with different running speeds, and sometimes differing brake power, are nowadays capable of a neat solution by skilful use of multi-aspect colourlight signals. Earlier in this chapter reference was made to use of the three-aspect type; but the case for more than three aspects is illustrated by consideration of a line in the suburban area of a large city. In the morning and evening peaks the route has to carry an intense service of commuter trains, and at others high-speed long-distance passenger trains at speeds of 145 km/h (90 mph) on the same tracks. Between stops the commuter trains do not exceed 100 km/h (62 mph) and it is necessary to run them at the closest possible headway. The service braking distances of these two classes would be roughly 1,500 and 700 m (1,641 and 766 yd) – one twice the other. If one provided the distance required by fast trains solely between the yellow signal and the red, the commuter trains would be penalized and not able to run as frequently as desired; but by including a fourth aspect, the preliminary warning of the double yellow, both classes of service would be satisfied. Fig 14 illustrates how this can be done. The commuter train, because of its much shorter braking distance, can take the double yellow as its all-clear, full-speed indication, because there is full braking distance for it between the single yellow and the red.

The track circuit. Automatic working of a series of colourlight signals on plain line, such as has so far been considered, is dependent upon track circuits, which are the very cornerstone of safe, modern railway operation. The line is split up into a series of sections (Fig 15) insulated from

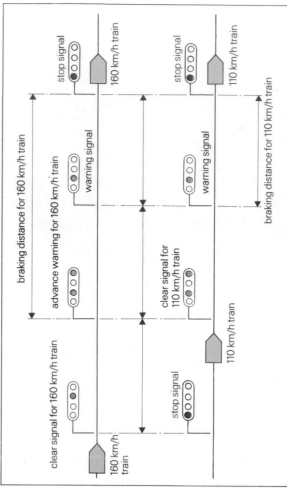

Far left: Fig. 13. Crossing station: typical passing place on double-track main line having reversible road working.

Left: Fig. 14. Four-aspect colour light signalling. The diagram shows aspects displayed with, at left, two high speed trains needing the braking distance between three signals, and, at right, medium speed trains for which the distances between two successive signals is adequate for braking.

Below: Old style French signal box with mixture of manual (large levers) and electric (small levers) operation.

each other by non-conducting joints in the rails. A source of electrical supply is connected across the rails at one end, and at the other is a precision instrument called a relay, which acts as a switching device. When there is no train or vehicle on the line current flows down one rail, through the relay and back down the other rail. With the relay thus energized certain contacts are closed, to complete control circuits; but if there is any interruption the relay becomes de-energized and the contacts are opened. This takes place when a train enters the track circuit, and opening of the contacts breaks the control circuit to the signal at the entrance to the track circuit, and changes its aspect from green to red. It is thus impossible to display a clear signal if the line is occupied by a train.

This is no more than the beginning of the chain of safety features in modern railway working that all stem from the correct functioning of the track circuit. With it is bound up the fundamental principle of fail safe. This is literally all-embracing. It applies to mechanical features of equipment, the intricacies of circuit design and wiring up, and extraneous factors, such as the electrical power supply. In general terms, if anything goes wrong the failure must be on the side of safety: a broken connection, a broken wire, the fracture of a mechanical member, must all cause the signal at the entrance to the section of line concerned to go to danger and remain so. Traffic must be held up until the cause has been found, and if it cannot be quickly rectified, the service can be restored only under very restrictive conditions, until complete repair has been effected.

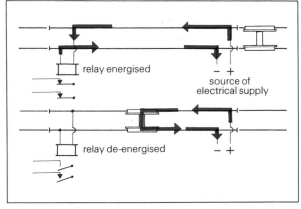

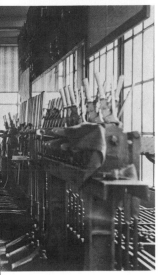

Top far right: Fig 15. Principle of track circuit, showing how relay becomes de-energized by train on line.

Top right: A typical British signal box of semaphore days: Gipsy Hill.

Below left: Paris, Gare de l'Est: view of control room.

Below right: Paris, Gare de l'Est: illuminated diagram and operating console.

Illuminated track diagram. Introduction of track circuits paved the way for one of the most important tools of railway operation – the illuminated track diagram. The track circuit relay is equipped with many contacts, closed or opened according to whether the relay itself is energized or de-energized. These contacts are used as 'make and break' switches in a number of different and independent control and indication circuits. One of these latter, on track circuit relays, is used for lighting lamps on the illuminated track diagram, which is designed to provide a clear geographical representation of the railway complex under the control of the signalbox concerned. The occupancy or otherwise of every track circuit in the area is shown on the diagram by illuminated strips or rectangles, and the diagram as a whole provides an instant picture of all train movements. Before the introduction of illuminated diagrams it was essential for signalmen to see every train. Nowadays in many modern signalboxes the men do not see a single train during their hours on duty. They work entirely from the illuminated diagram.

The earliest examples of these diagrams were used solely for indication of the track circuits. The first ever was installed in 1905 on what was then the Metropolitan District Railway, at Acton Town, West London, a station then known as Mill Hill Park. Operation of the points and signals in the area was by compressed-air regulated by electrically-controlled valves. The operating machine had a large number of miniature levers. At that time, although the advantages of power operation of points and signals was becoming appreciated, convention required that a miniature version of the ordinary signal lever should be used. While the physical position of the levers at any time was some indication of the actual lie of the points, or the position of the signal arms, it

was felt that this was not enough, and that some positive evidence that the apparatus had responded to the movement of the levers was essential. This was provided by indication lights on a facia board immediately behind the levers: red and green lights to indicate the position of the signals, and stencils N or R (for Normal and Reverse) to indicate the lie of the points. Thus began the fascinating history of the evolution of the modern power signalbox.

Evolution of the power box. The great principle of lever interlocking had been fully established during the 19th century. It ensured that no routes could be set up, nor signals cleared, that could result in a collision; and although there were many different types of mechanism invented to perform this function, as many companies patented their ideas and strove to secure contracts, they all involved mechanical interlocks. As more and more inventors entered the field so the designs became more complicated, because naturally the simplest ways of doing it had been adopted and patented by those first in the field.

When the miniature lever machine was introduced the interlocking between levers was a reduced version of the simplest mechanical type. But as sophistication in station control methods grew, particularly after the first world war in Great Britain, so mechanical interlocking mechanisms grew more complicated. The requirements presented a challenge to designers that was accepted and met; similar conditions, with the distinctive types of interlocking machines favoured in those countries, developed in France, Germany, Switzerland and the USA. It was in Great Britain, however, that the first move away from conventional lever interlocking between levers was accomplished electrically, instead of mechanically. This epoch-marking change was followed by rapid adoption of this type of machine in many overseas countries as well as in Great Britain.

Then, having dispensed with the need for physical mechanical connection between levers, the next step was to dispense with the lever itself and substitute small thumb-switches. Another great step forward in the interlocking principle was thereby involved. So long as the lever remained, if conditions outside precluded operation of the function it controlled, the signalman was prevented from pulling it. The lever was locked. No such positive interlock could be put on to a simple thumb switch or a push button, and interlocking to prevent setting up of a dangerous condition had to be effected through interaction of electrical circuits. You could turn the switch or press the button, but if unsafe conditions would have resulted the circuitry did not respond. One factor was immediately apparent from the replacement of positive lever interlocking by circuit interlocking – that was a great reduction in the size of the control instrument, and an equal reduction in the amount of physical movement a signalman had to make. The outcome was that a first-class man could look after a much wider area than previously, and because he had a broader picture on his

illuminated diagram of all that was going on the regulation of train movements was much improved.

In the days of mechanical signalling, and to a lesser extent in the days of the miniature lever electric apparatus, there was generally a separate lever for each function. But with circuit interlocking and thumb switch actuation, the practice developed of route setting, with one or two operating members setting up a complete route. Furthermore, when all the points in that route were correctly lined up, the signal giving authority to proceed was cleared automatically.

At one time two distinct methods of doing this were being developed and installed simultaneously. In one, a separate thumb switch was provided for every route, and they were mounted in groups on the facia board below the illuminated diagram. The signalman had to select the one he required, and turning just that one switch set up an entire route. This system, initiated in Great Britain, has been widely adopted elsewhere, on the continent of Europe, and in countries of the Commonwealth. The second method, generally considered to be simpler for the signalmen and now adopted as standard on the nationalized British Railways and elsewhere, places the operating members actually on the track diagram. Adjacent to the position of a signal on the diagram is a thumb switch, at the entrance to a route, while at the terminating point, or exit, is a push button. The entrance point may provide for several diverging, or alternative routes, and the signalman sets up the one he requires by turning the switch at the entrance, and pressing the button at the appropriate exit. This system, known as

Left: Paris, Gare du Nord: interior of new signal box, showing part of illuminated diagram, and of operating console, having 319 push buttons.

Above: Power signal box Frankfurt-Main.

Right: Fig 16. Frankfurt-Main: diagram to show 'chain of command', from overall supervisors to signal and point operating men.

Below: 'Chain of command' at Frankfurt: view in the control room, showing traffic regulators, and their track diagram.

Entrance-Exit, or NX, originated in the USA in the 1930s, and has been extensively adopted since.

The panel signalbox is at present passing through as marked a process of evolution as the details and technology of interlocking, as represented by the gradual transition from levers mechanically-locked one against the other to circuit interlocking on the Entrance-Exit route setting system. Even with the great advantages of compactness apparent there was a reluctance to incorporate exceptionally large geographical areas under the control of one signal-box.

In certain cases strategic considerations made it unwise to put all signalling 'eggs' into one basket. In others the cost of cabling from a central position to outlying functions 13 to 16 km (8 to 10 miles) away were prohibitive, while in others the lingerings of old-time orthodoxy resulted in installation of two large panel boxes at each end of an important junction complex, less than 1½ km (1 mile) apart.

Recalling that the operating officer had the responsibility for manning these novel appliances, and seeing that they were used to the best advantage, it is not surprising that some senior men were inclined to be cautious in their acceptance, and to stipulate parameters of utilization that did not at first make the most use of their potential. But the engineers had produced a tool of operation that was technically without limit in the scope of its application. How its application was developed showed different operating philosophies in different countries.

It is in these differences that the relation of signal and point operation to the overall control

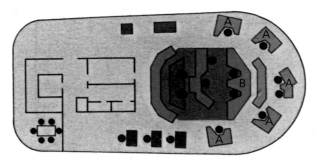

Signal Control Tower, Frankfurt, W Germany

command of the railway is shown. In the huge multi-storied control towers at major centres on the German Federal Railway, for example, there is a three-tier chain of command (see Fig 16). The highest level maintains a broad non-detailed surveillance over traffic on the outer approach lines, aided by an illuminated track diagram, but principally having regard to the effect in the terminal area of arriving trains, movement of freight in the outlying areas, and communication with major centres on the various radiating lines. The intermediate level maintains a detailed observation of all arriving and departing trains under the guidance and instruction of the highest level. The third group consists of a series of operating panels from which points and signals in the complicated approach and central areas of the terminal station are actuated. The men on these panels are signalmen working limited areas under direct instructions from No 2 level of command.

In the latest developments in Great Britain the panel boxes cover very wide areas, usually extending from a major junction. They include surveillance of long stretches of line where there are few junctions and on which the majority of the intermediate colourlight signals work automatically. These panel boxes are in effect traffic control centres in which the signalmen are themselves the controllers, handling the entire traffic for most of the time except when any pronounced divergence from punctual running occurs. Then matters are referred to the regulator for a decision on any special steps to be taken. The regulator's position in the control room is such that he has the invaluable information of the illuminated diagram before him, often covering more than 80 km (50 miles) of busy main line. With so comprehensive an overall picture he is in the best possible position to decide on the best course of action, in revising train priorities, arranging for assistance to a disabled train, or other incidents.

Train description. In the era of mechanical signalling the numerous signalboxes along the line were connected by telephone, and advice of approaching trains was passed from box to box in a code of bell signals. Signalmen saw every train as it passed, and from the type of rolling stock and motive power individual trains could readily be recognized. With the introduction of power signalling, and the extension of the areas controlled from individual signalboxes this old-fashioned chain of communication along the line was no longer acceptable. From the inception of electric traction on the Metropolitan District Railway in

London in 1906, automatically actuated 'next train' indicators were installed on the Inner Circle line using a technique known as train description. Mainly for the benefit of passengers, information of first, second and third trains approaching was displayed; but with the desirability of superseding the old telegraph and telephone links along important main lines, the train description principle was applied as a tool of operating, a valuable aid to the signalmen themselves.

Switching to the most modern conditions one could have a length of double-track railway on which there is no intermediate signalbox for 150 km (93 miles). All the intervening junctions, sidings, or crossings are remotely controlled from one or other panel signalbox at either end. There could be ten or more trains on each track at the same time, all travelling at high speed, and it is essential to have some means of identification. In the service timetable every train, passenger and freight, has its reporting number. In certain cases this number is carried on the front of the locomotive, though this is not essential nowadays when signalmen do not need to see the trains in order to carry out their duties.

What they do need to know is the reporting numbers of those many trains that are indicated by the constantly changing lights on their illuminated diagrams. At numerous locations on the diagrams there are dark rectangular spaces above the tracks. The basic principle of train description, with electronic computerized control, displays the train numbers in those rectangles, just as the pioneer installation of 70 years ago displayed the destination of trains on stations of the Metropolitan District Railway. Today, signalmen have instant information as to the whereabouts of any train on the line, and can act accordingly.

An example from the London Midland Region of British Railways illustrates how train description, together with a comprehensive illuminated diagram, can expedite train working. Because of traffic delays earlier in the journey, a maximum tonnage freightliner train conveying 60 containers was running late when it came within the area controlled by Preston panel box. It was being followed closely by the Anglo-Scottish postal special – a train of the highest priority, but which had a station stop to make at Preston. The freightliner was limited to a maximum speed of 120 km/h (75 mph), whereas the postal could run at 160 km/h (100 mph). The controller at Preston judged that the freightliner could reach a running loop at Carnforth, 42 km (26 miles) ahead, be berthed briefly there, and follow the postal to Carlisle. It worked with complete precision. The freightliner, passing through Preston under clear signals, quickly regained its normal running speed of 120 km/h. It made good time to Carnforth where, still under the surveillance of the Preston panel box, it was turned into the loop and stopped in time to give the postal train a clear run. This duly passed, running at a full 160 km/h. Less than a minute later the signalman at Preston, 42 km away, set the points and cleared the

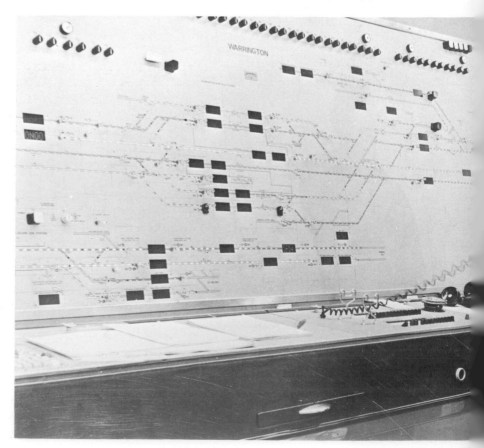

signals for the freightliner which then regained the main line and proceeded on its way to Carlisle.

Reference was made earlier to some proposals for remote control that had to be abandoned because of the high cost of cabling over the distance between outlying junctions and the controlling signalbox. Carnforth, with signals and points between 42 and 44 km (26 and 27½ miles) from Preston, could have been a case in point; but today the use of modern electronic devices enables the controls to be sent over the intervening distance on a minimum of line wires. Carnforth,

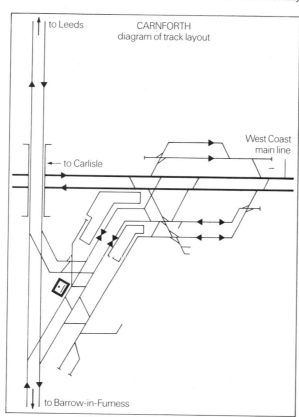

CARNFORTH
diagram of track layout

to Leeds

West Coast main line

to Carlisle

to Barrow-in-Furness

as Fig 17 shows, has quite an extensive junction layout of its own, and the various signals and points have all the essential safety features in their interlocked controls to prevent anything in the way of a dangerous situation being set up, even though the man in charge is at Preston. The link is electronic, giving instant response to control commands sent from the panel box, to indications sent back of the actual position of trains, and in the response of signals and points to commands sent from the signalman at Preston.

In West Germany the principle of train description has been carried a spectacular stage further. There the reporting numbers of trains, as carried on the locomotives, form a link in a remarkable system of automatic setting of the route a train is to follow at a junction. In Great Britain the panel signalmen set the routes according to the train numbers which are displayed on the illuminated diagram.

In some of the latest installations in West Germany a photo-electric scanner at the lineside reads the reporting number of the train as it passes; this is then transmitted to a computer, which processes the data and initiates the controls for setting the points. This, of course, applies when all trains are running to time, and in their correct

sequence. In the case of late running, as with the freightliner mentioned earlier, some intervention by the signalman or regulator would be necessary. In the British case in normal circumstances both the freightliner and the postal train would follow the main line through the Carnforth junctions.

Automatic train control. While numerous interlocking and safety features in the signalling system provide safeguards against the chance of a signalman setting up a dangerous condition, it is equally important to provide against a driver's misjudgment, or misinterpretation of signals, especially at the high speeds and traffic density now operated in so many countries. Under the general heading of automatic train control can be grouped a variety of systems designed to assist the driver, ranging from simple warning systems to full automatic control. In the application of these systems psychology plays almost as important a part as engineering, and a brief reference as to how the different approaches to the problem originated is necessary by way of introduction.

In Great Britain the catalyst was the difficulty of seeing signals in fog, and the first steps were taken in the closing years of the 19th century. Something to supplement the wayside signals was needed in the locomotive cab. A parallel development began in France with an important difference based upon a different philosophy of signal indications. British signalling with semaphore arms had been built up on the basis of providing dissimilar positive indications for 'stop' and 'proceed', whereas the French had a positive enough indication for stop, but no signal

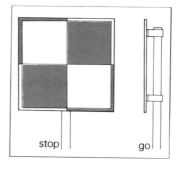

stop   go

at all for 'all clear', as shown in Fig 18. So, when it came to devising signals to be given to the driver in his own cab the British had the more complicated problem.

Then the question arose, is a simple warning enough? What will happen if a driver misinterprets that warning, or even ignores it? Steam traction was then almost universal, and a locomotive footplate at express speed could be a noisy place, with much going on all the time. In the USA the situation was far more urgent. In the first years of the 20th century the safety record was bad, and eventually the Interstate Commerce Commission made orders instructing certain railroads to install apparatus for automatically stopping the train if a signal indication was misjudged or misinterpreted. It ushered in a busy time for inventors and manufacturers of both brake and signal equipment.

In the meantime, in England, the Great Western Railway had brought to an advanced stage of development its own system of automatic train control, the principles of which were ultimately adopted as the nationwide standard by British Railways. It was felt that control of the train should not be taken out of the driver's hands except in emergency. So while providing in the locomotive cab two distinctly different audible indications – the ring of a bell for 'all clear' and the sounding of a siren for 'warning' – if the driver acknowledged the warning, and by so doing silenced the siren, he could remain in control, applying the brake ready to stop at the next signal, and releasing it if in the meantime that signal had cleared. If he failed to acknowledge, however, control of the train was automatically taken out of his hands, an emergency application of the brakes made, and the train brought to a stand.

In the USA, four different systems were developed:
1. Intermittent cab signalling, with visual indicators in the cab.
2. As above, with the addition of full brake control.
3. Continuously-controlled visual cab signals.
4. As above, with continuous control of the brakes, providing high, medium and low speed running according to the signal indications.

In system 3, which was ultimately standardized on the Pennsylvania Railroad, the cab indications were a repetition of those displayed by the wayside signals, whereas in system 4 the cab indications showed the speed that could be run, by the letters H, M, and L. The orders issued by the Interstate Commerce Commission varied according to the nature of the railroad concerned; but in due course system 3 became generally accepted as suitable for high-density, heavy-trafficked lines.

In both France and Germany the mixed railway provided problems when extra high-speed trains were introduced, with continuous running at 200 km/h (125 mph) on certain routes. In both countries multi-aspect colourlight signalling, generally similar to that in Great Britain, was considered adequate for speeds up to 160 km/h (100 mph) but that for higher speeds something more was needed. Though the methods differed the effect on the railways of both countries was the same, namely that a visual indication should be provided in the locomotive cab of two signals beyond the range of the ordinary four-aspect system. Normally the first warning of a signal at 'danger ahead' comes two signals previously, with a first warning, and at the next signal a final warning. With a 200 km/h train the first warning comes only in the locomotive cab, four signals previously. While the wayside signals continue to show green the driver will reduce speed, so that by the time he reaches the first wayside signal giving the warning indication he will have reduced speed to 160 km/h (100 mph) and have ample braking distance to stop at the red. The special trackside equipment has no effect upon ordinary trains, only on locomotives equipped for 200 km/h running.

Overall operating problems. Apart from the large modern panel signalboxes in which all matters concerned with the regulating of train movements are dealt with, there is the overall operating

Below left: Aerial view of Alyth mechanized hump marshalling yard near Calgary, CP Rail.

Below right: View ahead from cab of radio-equipped diesel locomotive, as it approaches a micro-wave installation.

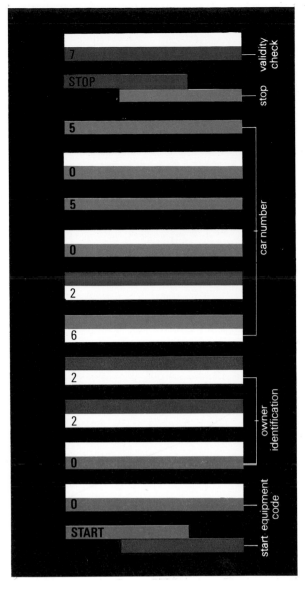

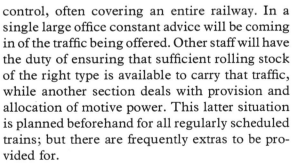

Right: Fig 19. Automatic car identification in North America: colour code panel on the side of cars.

control, often covering an entire railway. In a single large office constant advice will be coming in of the traffic being offered. Other staff will have the duty of ensuring that sufficient rolling stock of the right type is available to carry that traffic, while another section deals with provision and allocation of motive power. This latter situation is planned beforehand for all regularly scheduled trains; but there are frequently extras to be provided for.

Defects in locomotives develop when out on the run, and sometimes substitutions have to be made at short notice. The locomotive controller has to be aware of the routes over which various classes of locomotive can run, and in making a substitution care has to be taken to ensure that the complete duty can be worked. If not, another substitute may have to be provided at a further intermediate point. The manning of locomotives requires special vigilance to ensure that trains are worked within normal hours of duty; that reliefs are on hand when needed; and that balanced duties are available. It is manifestly uneconomic for locomotive crews to have to return to their home stations travelling passenger – deadheading as it is termed in North America. All these practical points in operating, and countless more, have to be dealt with in the central control office.

The telecommunications network is a vital fea-

ture in the entire set up, and on the larger railway systems private trunk dialling telephone systems are installed. One system makes use of a series of Zone Centres located at major centres of traffic. There are trunk dialling links between these, and from each there are extension links to lesser stations. In the day-to-day handling of traffic the number of trunk calls can be very large. Records taken from one relatively small geographical area showed an average of 220,000 trunk calls per week.

An equally important part of the telecommunications network is the teleprinter service, whereby routine reports can be sent to headquarters and other areas concerned. A recent development, however, is the automatic reporting of train movements. On railways that do not use the graphic method of train control, with the constant attention of a number of men that it needs, it has been the practice for routine reporting of train movements to be made by telephone from selected timing points on the line. They were then entered on records in the central control office. Later this work was done by teleprinter, but in some recent installations it is done instantly and automatically by an addition to the train description apparatus. As trains enter the track circuits that initiate the display of their reporting numbers on the illuminated diagram, a tape record is also produced giving the time, the train number, and the number of the signal it is passing. This tape is continuously fed through to the central control office.

Wagon control. On a mixed railway, the volume of freight traffic may vary from day to day, and is dependent in many ways on factors external to the railway, such as arrival of ships bringing traffic from overseas, seasonal variations in domestic requirements, and delay or disruption due to bad weather. Accordingly it is necessary to keep the closest possible control over wagon movements, to ensure that an adequate supply of the right type is available at originating points of traffic. In all countries today railway services are subject to severe competition, and it is necessary to ensure that delays do not occur because insufficient or unsuitable wagons are available where they are wanted. At the same time efforts are made to reduce to a minimum the empty wagon mileage, though in certain cases this cannot be entirely avoided.

Within the limited geographical confines of Great Britain recently much has been done to minimize the fluctuating factors in freight train working. Block-load coal trains, known as 'merry-go-round' trains, of fixed formation are run between certain collieries and electric generating stations, eliminating marshalling. Many special trains are chartered by large industrial organizations for their exclusive use and run to regular timetables, while the policy of closing a large number of country stations and their goods handling facilities has greatly simplified the overall freight operating problem.

What can be done in a small geographical area is not possible in large continents, and in North

Left: A railroad dispatcher in a centralized traffic control installation, providing control of signals and points up to 100 miles distant.

Right: At New Tilford yard, Atlanta, Georgia, a loaded freight car descending from the hump enters the master retarder.

America there are some two million wagons liable to be exchanged between the various railways. Any one of these is liable to be anywhere between the Mexican border and the Canadian lines that penetrate almost to the Arctic Circle, creating vast logistical problem, for the operators. In an attempt to solve these, the Association of American Railroads decided to install a system of automatic car identification (ACI). On the side of all rolling stock and motive power there is a composite label of coloured reflective strips. The entire label is a rectangle about 60 cm (24 in) high, and about 25 cm (10 in) wide. It includes 14 horizontal strips of colour, in combinations of red, blue, white and black. By varying the relation of the adjacent colours one with another a very large number of codes is obtained, and these are used to signify the type of vehicle and the owning railway (see Fig 19).

At key points along each line, such as the entry to major marshalling yards or other interchange points, the labels are read as the wagons pass by a photo-electric scanning device, which translates the code read from the side of the vehicle into an electrical signal. This signal is fed into a computer, and the information collected forms a complete record, up to the minute, of any vehicle and where it is. The various individual railways can have the whereabouts of any of their wagons rapidly traced. The great advantage of this comprehensive system of monitoring is that it improves the utilization of wagons, controls terminal operations and marshalling, and secures more rapid turnround.

Marshalling yards. Shunting wagons in and out of sidings can be a laborious process, and as early as the 1880s steps were taken to reduce engine power by introducing artificial mounds, or humps, from which wagons could gravitate to their correct sidings. The next stage was to operate the points by power, either compressed air or electrically. But the biggest breakthrough towards complete mechanization of marshalling yard working came shortly after the end of the first world war in the USA, with the wagon retarder,

which was in effect a remote-controlled air brake (see Fig 20). Instead of being fitted on the wagons themselves, these retarders consisted of brake beams mounted on each side of the running rails, which by the application of power could be made to close in and grip the wheels of a wagon as it passed through. To provide the necessary flexibility, the beams – often 22 m (70 ft) long – were articulated, with joints about every 3 m (10 ft).

One of the earliest yards to be so equipped was Mystic Junction, on the Boston & Maine Railroad, in 1927. It was a particularly awkward place for a pioneer installation because of the limitation in space; but it is important in that it was the first ever to have the group system of track layout, in which four to six classification tracks were grouped into a separate lead. Fig 21 shows this principle in diagrammatic form, while Fig 22 shows how ingeniously it was applied to the confined space available at Mystic Junction.

Developments came rapidly, both in the USA and on the continent of Europe. In 1929 the first British yard to be equipped with retarder was the yard at Whitemoor, Cambridgeshire. While a form of automatic setting of points leading from the hump was satisfactorily established, operation of the retarders themselves was controlled manually from a separate console, with reliance placed upon the operator's judgment as to what degree of braking he applied to each wagon. There are always great differences in the running qualities of individual wagons. Some run freely; others with bearings in poor condition are very stiff, and the operator had to judge from the way the wagon accelerated after passing over the crest of the hump whether it needed much or little braking. Account had also to be taken of the number of wagons already in the siding into which it was being routed.

It was no easy task, even for the most experienced of yard men, and it was complicated when two, three, or more wagons were propelled over the hump coupled together to go into the same siding. Though the use of retarders eliminated the need for shunters in the yards to ride on the wagons and to apply the brakes by hand, the

Above: In the control room of a marshalling yard control tower, French National Railways.

Right: In Alyth yard, Calgary, CP Rail, a freight car passing through one of the retarders.

difficulty of the task imposed upon the brake operators in control led sometimes to damage from rough shunts – when wagons running into a siding came into collision with those already there. Other wagons stopped short, and had to be pushed down by locomotive power when hump shunting was finished for the particular train. It was these difficulties that led to a further development in yard mechanization – automated control of brake force applied by the retarders. There are many variable factors that affect the running of wagons, all of which have to be recognized if the braking is to be made completely automatic. There is first of all rollability, a measure of whether it runs freely or not; then whether the wagon is loaded or empty, because this can affect the influence of the next factor, the direction and strength of the wind. The modern North American boxcar has a very large surface area, and an empty one would be much more susceptible to a strong wind than one that is heavily loaded. Then there is the factor of siding fullness, showing how much clear track there is for a wagon to run before it buffers with those already there, and finally there are the physical characteristics of the route to be taken. Curves impose a far greater retarding effect than a straight line, and one has only to study the track layout at Mystic Junction (Fig 22) to realize how different some of the routes leading from the hump in the outbound yard are.

In the case of new yards laid out in territory where there is plenty of space every effort is made to design the track layout to include approximately equal curvature from the hump into every siding. This can be appreciated from a study of the layout of a typical modern marshalling yard. In a fully-automated yard details of all these factors are fed into a computer, which duly processes the data and provides the answer in the form of the brake force to be applied to each wagon, or group of wagons, as they pass through the retarders.

The master control is in the yard tower. This American term, which applied also to what is known in Europe as a signalbox, has been adopted universally for the nerve-centre of a marshalling yard. The control floor, with such complete automation as has been described, has become much simpler than in the earlier retarder installations. To give operators the best possible lookout many of the earlier American yards were equipped with as many as three separate towers, and Fig 22 shows a typical case of how the spheres of control were allocated between them.

With complete automation a single control desk sufficed, and it became British practice to build these in semi-circular form so that the one operator had all the various controls readily to hand, while having a wide panoramic view over the yard as a whole. By positioning such a tower to one side of the tracks abreast of the first group of retarders the operator could see the progress of wagons as they were propelled over the hump, and in the opposite direction watch their running afterwards, with the classification sidings. Some of these control towers were of considerable architectural merit, and the automation processes proved very effective.

With the evolution of British freight train operating towards running block-load trains that need no marshalling, use of this type of concentration point is declining, though it is being actively developed on the continent of Europe, in North America, and also in India and Australia.

Automation has been carried to its furthest extent so far in the great yard at Alyth, near Calgary, on the Canadian Pacific. Even in the large modern yards installed in Great Britain and elsewhere, the destination of all wagons arriving in the reception sidings had to be ascertained prior to humping by men walking the length of the train, and then the information was sent, usually by pneumatic tube, from the Yardmaster's office to the Control Tower. At Alyth, however, no men are employed on this job. At each entrance to the yard there are photo-electric scanners which read off the destinations of all incoming wagons in their correct order, and the make-up of the train is transmitted automatically from the recording scanner to the main computer, which issues the various controls that regulate humping and classification of the train. At Alyth the only thing that is not automated is the actual uncoupling of wagons from each other into successive 'cuts' as they pass over the crest of the hump.

The sparsely-used single line railway. In many parts of the world railways were built through remote, mountainous, and undeveloped areas for colonizing purposes, or to provide connection between scattered communities whose only means of transport previously had been the trek cart or the horse-drawn covered waggon. Traffic on such lines could not be heavy, and on lengthy sections traffic movement was regulated by written train orders, transmitted by telegraph from a central office to the few stations along the line where facilities existed for crossing trains running in opposite directions.

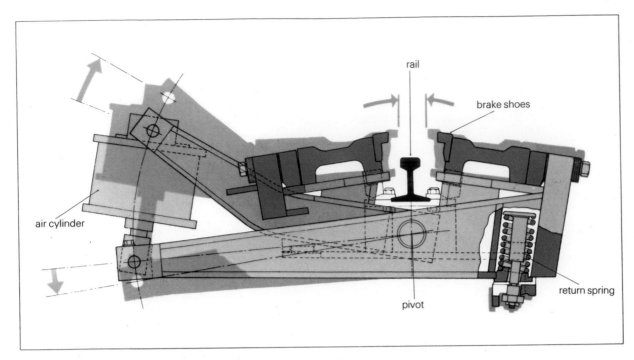

rail

brake shoes

air cylinder

return spring

pivot

The driver of a westbound freight train would receive an order telling him to proceed to station A, where he would meet eastbound train No XYZ. If it was not there when he arrived he would draw in to the loop and wait for it. On the way he might have passed several other stations, all of which would be equipped with a specialized form of semaphore signal designed for this type of line. This is a train order signal. If the arm is pointing in the upward direction it means that no additional or contradictory orders are awaiting the train, and it can pass through. If the arm is inclined diagonally upwards, it means 'I have an order for you, which you can collect without stopping'. If the arm is horizontal the train must stop for instructions.

Even with written instructions there could be mistakes. The following rules apply:
1. To prevent conflicting instructions and to ensure safety, no more than one man can dispatch trains on the same track at the same time.
2. That the dispatcher be kept fully advised of all delays, present or prospective, and the position of every train on the road.

3. That orders must be so clearly expressed as to render misunderstanding impossible.
4. That trains running against other trains under special orders must be able to recognize each other – complied with by giving the number of the engine of every train mentioned in the order.

It must be added that the dispatcher is the man in charge at the central control for the whole line, and operators are the men at outlying stations. It is a simple and very cheap method of operation. There is no more than one man at each of the few stations, a semaphore signal operated by hand, and the points at the entrance to the loop tracks are worked by hand usually by the train crews. Communication between stations and with the dispatcher is by telegraph. While being simple and cheap, it is also cumbersome and slow, and the dispatcher is made aware of the changing line position only by telegraphic reports from the various operators at the stations.

Centralized Traffic Control. In the 1920s the remote-control system of signalling known as Centralized Traffic Control (CTC) was introduced in

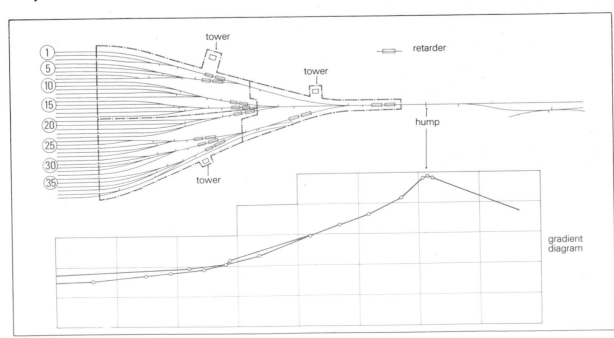

tower

retarder

tower

hump

tower

gradient diagram

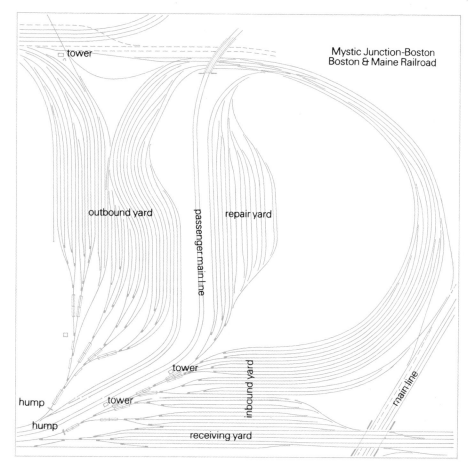

tower

outbound yard

passenger main line

repair yard

Mystic Junction-Boston
Boston & Maine Railroad

tower

tower

hump

hump

inbound yard

main line

receiving yard

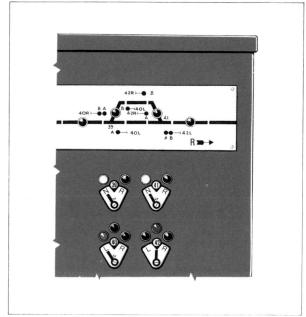

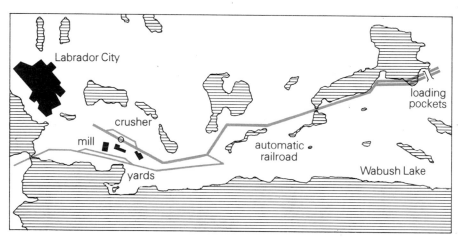

Labrador City

crusher

mill

yards

loading
pockets

automatic
railroad

Wabush Lake

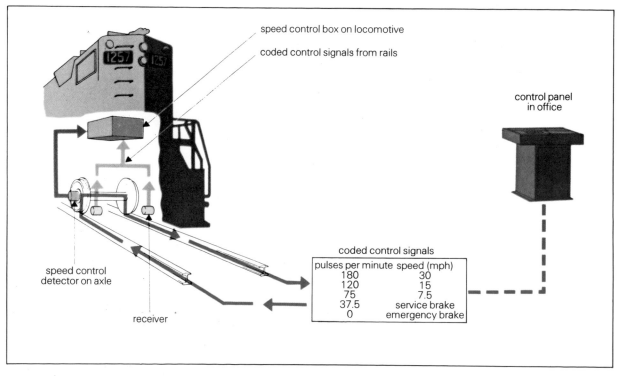

speed control box on locomotive

coded control signals from rails

control panel
in office

speed control
detector on axle

receiver

coded control signals

pulses per minute	speed (mph)
180	30
120	15
75	7.5
37.5	service brake
0	emergency brake

North America. It provided a means of speeding up train movements on single-track routes by giving the dispatcher a direct means of conveying his orders to each train without any intermediate steps in transmission, and without relying on cumbersome methods of communication. Orders are given to trains, not on pieces of paper, but directly by signal indication. Operators at intermediate stations no longer had the job of passing on the dispatcher's orders to train crew. The operator was provided with a control machine, on which representation of a simple passing station would be as shown in Fig 23. There are four thumb switches, two for the points, and two for the signals. On the complete control machine there might be ten or more such stations, and the most distant could be 160 km (100 miles) away. CTC permits such a single-track section to be controlled on no more than two line wires, with all signals and points electrically-operated.

The principle of operation can be likened to that of the ordinary automatic telephone with its dialling system. If the dispatcher required to move the points at station D for a westbound freight to enter the loop track to clear the main track for an eastbound passenger train, his turning of the point switch No 39 (Fig 23) from Normal to Reverse is like dialling a telephone number. The individual thumb switch No 39 sets up the necessary code, transmits it down the two line wires, and only at Station D would that code be picked up, decoded, and translated into the necessary action by the local apparatus to move the points. When those points are correctly set, an indication code would be transmitted back to the dispatcher and shown in a visual lamp indication beside his thumb switch No 39 on the control machine. Then he knows he can clear the signal leading into the loop track. The whole line is track-circuited from end to end, and indication lights on the track diagram show the dispatcher when the westbound freight train has arrived and is completely berthed in the loop. Then he can reverse points No 39 back to normal and set the signals for the eastbound passenger train to run through. It can be well appreciated how much simpler and more expeditious the CTC system is from an operating point of view, though the sophisticated electrical equipment needs constant and expert maintenance.

This original CTC system, with its control and indication codes transmitted by electro-mechanical stepper switches as used in automatic telephony, has its limitations when the need for remote control of busy areas is considered. The transmission time of the codes is approximately 4 seconds each way; and while this is minimal in the case of a sparsely-used single-track railway, it could be critical when applied to remote control of a junction like Carnforth (Fig 17) from Preston. In the 8 seconds taken from transmission of a code to the indication received back that the function has correctly responded a high-speed express train could have travelled 0.4 km (¼ mile). At busy times the transmission lines would be severely congested and trains delayed because the signal controls could not be made quickly

enough. But the whole situation so far as busy rather than sparsely-used lines are concerned has been transformed by the use of electronic remote-control methods, in which the transmission times are a small fraction of a second. This has enabled the CTC principle, in its most modern form, to be applied to busy, high-speed routes, with concentration of control at no more than a few major traffic centres.

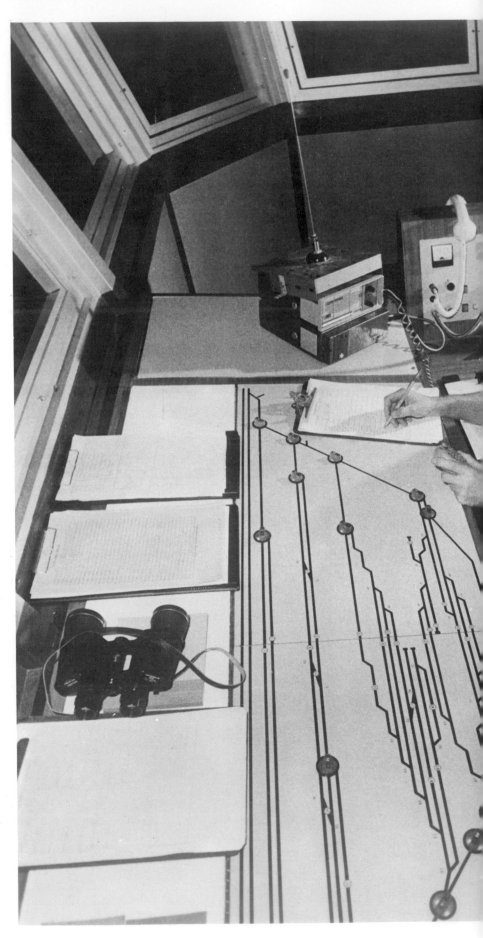

Below: Centralized traffic control console near Dampier, Western Australia, on the iron-ore carrying railway of the Hamersley Iron Company.

The single-purpose railway. One of the most intensively-used of all single-purpose railways is the London Underground, and on this has been installed the nearest yet to complete automation in operating. On most routes traffic working is regulated automatically by an instrument called a Programme Machine. It carries on a punched tape full details of the train service for an entire day. There is one of these machines for every pair of points on the line in question, and from the information on the tape it sets the routes for trains over the junction in timetable order. Each train, on passing, causes the tape to advance one step, thereby initiating any change in the setting of the points that is required for the correct routeing of the next train.

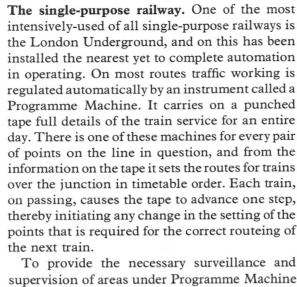

To provide the necessary surveillance and supervision of areas under Programme Machine control, there are small supervisory rooms with illuminated track diagrams showing the whereabouts of every train. The controller in one of these rooms is necessarily a very busy man, often with 20 or more trains on the illuminated diagram at once, and so the Programme Machines have a feature included in them which sounds an alarm if a train is more than a predetermined number of seconds late in approaching the junction. Similarly, but without calling anyone's attention, it delays the clearing of the starting signal at a station if a train should be ready to start before its time. This could cause complications at the next junction. One of the largest areas now on Programme Machine control extends from South Kensington on the District line westwards to Turnham Green, Putney Bridge and the complex of junctions at Acton Town, with such a station as Earl's Court included in this extensive area worked entirely without signalmen.

Having advanced so far in automating route setting and signalling controls, London Transport went one further on the new Victoria line tube, opened in 1969 by Her Majesty Queen Elizabeth II, by introducing automatic driving. In everyday terms it could be said that on this line the signals drive the trains, once the attendant on board has pressed simultaneously the two starting buttons. Once again track circuits provide the heart and soul of the system, though these are of a special kind. Once the starting buttons have been pressed the train runs without any human intervention until it stops with spot-on accuracy in the platform of the next station.

The automatic driving is a dual system, divided into what are termed vital and non-vital parts. The vital part is analogous to the ordinary signalling, which applies the brakes automatically if the train should be approaching a signal in the danger position, signifying that there is another train a short distance ahead. The controls are based on the fundamental safety principles universal in modern signalling. The non-vital part concerns actual driving of the train, applying power to the traction motors, maintaining speed until approaching the next station, and then receiving and implementing instructions received from electrical devices at what are termed command spots on the track, initiating the

reduction in speed necessary to bring the train to rest at the exact point on the station platform. There is a constant electrical inductive link between train and rails, ensuring the highest degree of safety.

It would be possible to run the trains on the Victoria line tube without any attendant on board, because the starting buttons could be so positioned as to be operable by a man on the station platform. But from the general operating point of view it was considered desirable to have a man on the train. Automation of such a kind cannot yet cope with the human side of any incident that might occur from delay, or any other cause. For this reason the train attendant who rides in the front cab is able to communicate with passengers by loudspeaker.

No such considerations apply, however, when the same system of automatic driving is applied to a belt-conveyor railway serving a great iron ore plant, as in the remarkable Carol Lake Railway of the Iron Ore Company of Canada. The first section of this project was no more than 9.7 km (6 miles) long, from a vast mountain deposit that is nearly 40 per cent solid iron ore to the crushing plant near Labrador City. The daily task was to convey 80,000 tonnes of ore over this route (see Fig 24). The method of working was to have four trains each of 19 wagons, each carrying 100 tonnes of crude ore, shuttling back and forth all day under complete automatic control without any men on the trains themselves. At only two points in the cycle of operation is the procedure subject to any human agency. There is an operator at the loading plant who presses a button to start a loaded train, and another at the dumper to move a train forward after it has arrived and stopped automatically on the approach tracks (see Fig 25). No one rides on the trains.

The Japanese Shinkansen. This is as much a single-purpose railway as the London Underground, or the Carol Lake Railway, except that the standard running speed between stations is 210 km/h (130 mph). There is one of the *Hikari* (lightning) trains every 15 minutes from 06.00 to 21.00 from Tokyo to Osaka, each carrying about 1000 passengers, taking no more than 3 hr 20 min to cover the 510 km (320 miles) inclusive of two intermediate stops. Interspersed between some of these very fast trains are others stopping at all intermediate stations, but also running at 210 km/h between stops. These are known as *Kodama* (echo) trains. The *Shinkansen*, or new line, is exclusively for high-speed passenger trains, and the entire line is controlled from a single centre in Tokyo. Operation is very closely monitored, with the running of every train automatically recorded on the timetable graph, and an actual graph drawn, superimposed over the planned timetable path. Information to enable this to be done is derived from the passage of trains over track circuits, recorded instantaneously in the Tokyo control centre even though the actual train may be 450 km (280 miles) away or more. In that control centre one can see train movements over the whole line.

FREIGHT TRANSPORT

From their earliest days railways have succeeded because they are uniquely good at performing one major task: that of moving bulk loads in consistent quantities; loads which require a minimum of handling and which travel more than a few miles. This remains the foundation of rail freight today. Railways compete for other categories of freight traffic but this is where they are most vulnerable and where profitable operation is less certain. In particular, much highly-rated, valuable traffic has been lost to road in most of the industrialized countries. Even so, freight operations on rail are largely profitable whereas only a very small percentage of the world's railways can boast of passenger services which consistently pay their way.

Railways are an expensive form of transport and the extra facilities needed for passenger services demand heavy expenditure. On the other hand, the existence of passenger services and the consequent need to maintain maximum levels of safety have forced railway administrations to provide high standards of track and signalling. This has meant that more efficient and commercially attractive freight services can be provided. The converse of this is all too apparent today: some US railroads have rid themselves of passenger trains and reduced track standards and freight service reliability has suffered. In developing countries a more consistent balance of freight and passenger train speeds has avoided this problem.

Whether predominantly passenger-carrying or not, railways must maintain a high level of investment to remain competitive. It is clear that a very high proportion of the estimated annual investment in the world's main-line railways is for freight services. The biggest growth in main line railway traffic has been in freight – particularly in the movement of raw materials. In fact, the greatest success of rail transport today is in carrying the very types of traffic which led to the construction of railways in the first place.

History

The pre-history of rail freight is extensive – even with horse motive power some waggonways in north east England were moving 1,000 tonnes of coal per day by the 1730s. These early railways carried coal and did not accept general goods traffic. From the late 18th century, the canals in Britain set the basis of the whole freight carriage system which not only survived the hey-day of inland waterways but which has set the pattern for rail-freight business to the present day. The canal companies set canal tolls as a charge for the use of the waterway. This practice was followed by the railways – certainly from as early as the toll-rates authorized in 1801 for the Surrey Iron Railway – in Britain. The earliest railways followed canal practice in that traffic was handled by carriage contractors. The contractors used their own wagons which were hauled by their own

Above: Typical modern marshalling yard, SNCF, France.

Below: Freight railways often started as feeders to canals, such as the Little Eaton tramway.

horses or locomotives. Indeed, the Stockton & Darlington Railway found this a better proposition than handling the traffic itself. The Act of Parliament authorizing the Liverpool and Manchester Railway in 1828 was historic in setting out conditions permitting the company not only to charge tolls on cartage contractors' goods but also to act as a common carrier of goods itself. The maximum tolls per tonne per kilometre (per tonne per mile) were established for different categories of goods, together with maximum rates for traffic carried by the company. Very quickly, railways dispensed with the practice of conveyance of traffic by outside operators in favour of the obvious advantage of a single authority for all traffic movement.

The system of rates structure (which followed the pattern set by the Liverpool & Manchester Railway) was based on the principle of charging a price related to the bulk and value of the goods carried, yet which would still undercut competition. Apart from railways constructed specifically to move types of traffic such as coal, freight rates were set to attract the highest classes of traffic at the highest rates.

Three principles established during the early history of commercial freight operation now provide severe obstacles to competitive performance. The principle of a railway as a common carrier compels the operator to accept all types of traffic offered whether or not profitable. In many cases, railways have been compelled to maintain their common carrier obligation and to provide a system-wide service for customers, even at a heavy loss.

Charging 'what the traffic will bear' was a relevant method of fixing freight rates in the absence of effective competition. Yet increasingly, the method has left the railways to carry bulk traffic at low rates; traffic in which other freight operators are not interested. Attention has, therefore, been diverted from competition for high-value and profitable freight. As labour costs and operating costs have risen adherence to an unrealistic charging system which is not based on the actual cost of moving freight, has prevented rail freight rates from achieving profitability. Government intervention in the fixing of freight rates during the 19th century, and subsequently, has saddled many railways with a service run at an uneconomic cost. In more recent times, public and customer resistance prevents increases to a realistic charge.

Consequently, railways throughout the world have been trying to escape the stranglehold of past legacies. The ideal solution has been the emergence of a freight policy which allows the railway to choose what traffic to carry, to fix special rates related to operating costs and to concentrate on those traffics which are most profitably carried by rail – long-distance, bulk freight.

By the late 1860s and early 1870s, a whole range of opportunities and influences set the picture for freight operation. Expansion of the railways throughout the world benefited existing systems: Britain exported 15,000 tonnes of rails to the United States in 1867 and 515,000 tonnes four

years later. More powerful and efficient locomotives were increasingly matched by more satisfactory wagons.

By 1890, the United States' railroad network was virtually complete. Through freight loadings made long-distance rail shipment competitive and successful. In 1893, US Federal law made the fitting of automatic couplers to wagons compulsory – halving, incidentally, the number of accidents to shunters. Towards the turn of the century, American practice was in the forefront of railway development. British and European railways sent staff to study the systematic control of train working, the collection of statistics and types of high-capacity wagon. Railways became more businesslike in controlling their freight traffic and identifying costs. Some were hampered by outside influences: British railways found it difficult to modernize their own wagon stock when the bulk of coal wagons were owned by collieries loath to adopt higher capacity wagons or to appreciate the advantages of vacuum brakes in place of the outdated 'pin down' variety.

The first world war saw the world's railway systems stretched to the limit with war freight. At the same time, war experience proved the value of the lorry. Railways were still expanding, however, particularly in countries like Canada. Total railborn freight was still increasing.

In Europe, railways reacted to road competition by working with or buying out road haulage companies. Schemes of road/rail co-ordination frequently worked to the disadvantage of rail. This happened in Northern Ireland where the combination of railway-owned and private road haulage was disastrous for rail freight. By the late 1930s, the old rigid freight-rate structure was a serious embarassment to effective competition with road transport.

In the post-war period, the pattern of freight operation began to change radically in the face of road competition – although, in nearly all countries, the overall volume of traffic carried by rail increased. Rail's share of the total freight movement in most industrialized countries started to fall by the mid-1950s. In 1962, rail was responsible for handling 43 per cent of freight in the USA, 46 per cent in Germany, 64 per cent in France, 37 per cent in Japan and 52 per cent in Sweden. During the next two years, rail's freight share had dropped still lower in each case.

Types of freight train

The well established rail freight service consists of the movement of individual wagons – in *wagonloads*. Almost everywhere, the traditional wagonload service relies on a large number of local railway-owned depots throughout the network – usually with collection and delivery by railway-controlled road services. The commercial basis is a quotation for individual consignments on the basis of published rates. The railways make up wagonloads or part-loads in their depots. The wagons are collected on local 'pick up' or 'trip' trains and moved between marshalling yards in 'rough' or unmarshalled trains.

Far left: A goods depot of the 1840s – Camden, London & Birmingham Railway.

Left: Goods collection/delivery is largely by railway-owned vehicles. Steam lorry, Lancashire & Yorkshire Railway *circa* 1922.

Left: Piggyback operation; loading a road trailer on to a low loader in the USA.

Right: The Trans Siberian Railway is one of the world's great freight routes. A train loaded with tip-up trucks passes the Trans Siberian Express.

Far right: Britain pioneered the specialised container train. A portal crane loads a maritime container at the Leeds Freightliner terminal.

All the wagons are 'common user' and none are designated for particular services. Until the application of computerized systems, there was little reliable control over the whereabouts of wagons in transit. Within yards, trains were made up on a 'first come-first served' principle. Consequently, railways were unable to guarantee the precise arrival of the wagon to the consignee – unless special monitoring procedures were observed. Universally, such services are regarded as obsolete and are loss-makers. The reasons are that the making up of wagonloads in many small depots leads to below-optimum pay loads and loss of control over the wagons. Because these are common user wagons, they can spend much time awaiting traffic and wagon turnround is, consequently, poor. Every time a wagon is 'handled' – placed in a yard or coupled or uncoupled to a train – costs increase because movement and shunting charges are high. Transhipment at depots to road vehicles is expensive and frequently leads to damage or pilfering. Such freight services cannot compete with road transport unless the road haulage system is subject to Government-imposed restrictions.

In the last ten years railways have rationalized the traditional wagonload service by closing small, inefficient freight depots and by cutting out part-loads. Railways have tried to opt out of the common carrier principle by refusing traffic that cannot cover costs.

Freight services have been concentrated by restricting depots to main centres, by making up complete wagonloads and by delivering or collecting traffic by road in a radius of between 30 and 50 km. Trains of economic payload can then be made to run between yards or the depots themselves.

Efficient traffic information facilities have been introduced using either the telex or computerized systems. Marshalling yards have been modernized and automated to reduce handling costs. However, marshalling yards, even the most efficient, represent a break in transit that lengthens journey times. The trainload working in combination with rationalized wagonload services is, therefore, becoming increasingly widespread.

Increasingly, railways have moved towards trainload or inter-block services. These are scheduled services operating, as far as possible, as complete blocks of wagons. Instead of remarshalling in yards, sections or blocks of wagons are coupled and uncoupled often without entering major yards at all. This service is becoming the pattern in Britain, Japan, Denmark and France. The wagons are loaded and unloaded in private sidings managed by companies and within their own works. The principle is to concentrate on door to door services between factories and to avoid expensive road/rail transhipment. The block trains are operated at fast speeds and are completely restricted to suitable wagons. Fully-computerized information ensures control over wagon location at all times. Often the wagons are permanently allocated to a particular service or customer to reduce turnround times.

Unit trains are often company trains designed to carry one commodity for one customer: high density, bulk movement quite often over distances of 50 to 70 km or typically, coal, iron ore, cement and phosphates. The trains act as a conveyor belt between mine and port, steelworks, major manufacturing plant or power station. The name, unit train, is significant in that this designation permits the railway to quote a special competitive rate based on the movement costs of a given tonnage or shipment. The wagons are often owned by the customer, restricted to the particular type of service, and designed specially for it.

To maximize use of the wagons special loading and unloading facilities are normally provided and the wagons are not remarshalled – but are frequently permanently coupled. Some unit trains load and unload on the move; this is known as 'merry-go-round' working in Britain and Canada. This railway operation is competitive with pipeline or shipping (rather than road) for such movements.

Inter-modal services combine road and rail, lorry or truck trailers being loaded onto low, flat wagons. The system is known as piggyback (in France, as *kangourou*). This type of traffic has developed considerably in North America, Germany and France, providing long, fast transits, often with a network of special services. In Europe, where strict control over permits for international lorry movements is in force, piggyback services are allocated a special quota to encourage road hauliers to use road/rail facilities. Rail rates are competitive for hauliers in the face of increased oil prices. Other combina-

Below left: A British Rail 'merry-go-round' coal train which loads/unloads on the move.

tions such as roadrailers in which the vehicles have road and rail wheels – enjoyed short-lived popularity in the 1950s to 1960s but were often inefficient in operation.

Container trains are a system of special trains of flat wagons for 7 m (20 ft) and above freight containers which run between specially built road/rail transhipment depots. The trains are operated at 120 km/h (75 mph) maximum. Pioneered in Britain this system has been followed in a number of countries such as Japan and on an increasingly expanded network throughout eastern Europe. A European network of trains between special terminals in major industrial centres is operated by Intercontainer, a company set up by 23 European countries. Such trains are known as TEC – Transports Européens Combinés. Containers are also moved in ordinary long distance fast freight trains particularly when only maritime containers are handled.

Freight services – worldwide

The 12,900 km (8,000 mile) Trans Siberia Railway (TSR) is one of the most remarkable feats of railway construction and a massive challenge to train operation because it covers such a wide range of geological and geographical conditions. Apart from the eastern section beyond Irkutsk, the TSR is electrified. The potential of the TSR within the Soviet Union for transcontinental operation has always been obvious but the container revolution in deep-sea trade has seen the TSR develop as the central section of a major rail/sea route between the Far East and Europe.

The Siberian landbridge operation was planned in the 1960s to secure a share of the growing general merchandise traffic between Japan, eastern Europe and inland points in western Europe. Russian and Japanese container ships provide the sea link from Japan to Nakhodka, northeast of Vladivostok, the eastern terminal of the TSR. More recently, a new container port has been constructed at Vostochny. Traffic is predominantly westbound from Japan, the imbalance being three or four to one. Despite this disadvantage and all the problems of empty working of container trains, traffic has grown from 1,000 7 m (20 ft) container equivalents in 1971 to some 60,000 in 1975. At present, only dry cargo is accepted for TSR shipment but specialized traffics will be handled in due course. The journey time via the 12,900 km (8,000 mile) TSR is some 30 days over a typical sea/rail haul such as Yokohama to western Europe. What is remarkable is that the Siberian landbridge, which offers a short transit time combined with low freight rates, is fully competitive with many throughout-sea transits. The TSR also carries heavy flows of conventional rail freight, mostly minerals, as well as passenger services. Growing transcontinental traffic together with planned exploitation of rich coal and mineral resources in Siberia has led to the construction of a new 3,200 km (2,000 mile) railway known as the Baikal–Amur line which will be completed in 1982. This will cut several hundred kilometres off the TSR route for container traffic passing through the Russian Pacific ports and will make the

Below right: A 50,000 gallon American tank car being loaded with liquid chemicals.

Siberian landbridge an even more formidable competitor for maritime shipping.

The potential of the TSR for other flows of container traffic is also being exploited, particularly for the growing Japanese to Middle East trade. This movement has risen steeply in the last year or so particularly in cars from Japan to Iran.

The North American continent has also looked towards the development of a landbridge. The Canadian Pacific 5,220 km (3,350 mile) route between Vancouver in the west and St John could provide a four-day transit for container traffic moving between Japan and North America or Europe. Although no sizeable volume of containers has yet moved by this route, much work has been done to develop a system in which the transfer between ship and rail through a container port is smoothly achieved. Current scheduled freight services across Canada already provide an impressive facility and usually consist of a mixture of boxcars, road trailers on flatcars and containers loaded on flats. The sight of one of these trains made up of over 100 wagons hauled by three large diesel locomotives moving at passenger train speeds across the prairies of Saskatchewan or Manitoba underlines the capability of rail for long distance freight. Train 902 of the Canadian Pacific is typical of these services. Leaving Vancouver at 10.50 pm on day 1, train 902 runs through to Toronto (4,320 km-2,700 miles) via Calgary, Medicine Hat, Winnipeg and Thunder Bay to give an arrival in Toronto at 3.35 pm (local time) on day 3 – a transit time of 83 hours, at an average speed of 52 km/h (32.5 mph) including 6½ hours for traffic stops. From the container port at St John, New Brunswick, complete container trains are run to Montreal conveying through maritime containers from Europe and the US mid-west. In the United States, the Missouri Pacific and Union Pacific railways handle a large traffic in maritime containers moving from Japan to the mid-west for on carriage to Europe via east coast US ports.

In Australia it has taken time for through freight transits across the continent to develop into an integrated service. This is because of variations in the track gauge between the seven railway systems. Only since the 1970s have Sydney, Perth, Brisbane and Melbourne been linked by standard gauge. Interstate freight traffic has only really built up in comparatively recent years. During 1973, interstate rail freight from the eastern states to Western Australia increased by about 15

per cent. Unfortunately wagon shortages have affected the growth of this traffic – an average shortage of about 3,000 modern bogie wagons.

Through freight transits by rail across Europe and the Middle East to Asia are difficult because of breaks between railway networks. The United Nations Organization has, however, encouraged the concept of a through Europe – Asia – SE Asia rail route for some time. From 1971, a standard gauge rail/ferry link between Iran, Turkey, the Mediterranean Coast and central and west Europe has been in existence. The route is through Tabriz, Razi, Van, Tatvan using the Lake Van and Bosphorus train ferries which avoids the previous transhipment problems caused by the break between the standard gauge Iranian and 1,524 mm (5 ft) gauge Russian systems. The link through Turkey was made possible by the construction of a new impressively-engineered railway between Sharifkhaneh (Iran) and Van (Turkey). As yet, the limited capacity of the Lake Van ferries restricts capacity for through freight but direct rail transits from Europe to Iran via Turkey take some 30 days. Growing traffic between Europe and the Middle East has led to such huge increases in lorry movements that it is vital for rail to develop attractive services. Plans for development exist but have been shelved – a line along the shore of Lake Van will probably be delayed for 10 years.

Within Europe, close co-operation in providing through freight transits has existed since the 1900s on the mainland and since the 1920s by train ferry between Britain and continental Europe. Because of differences in gauge, no train ferries have operated between Ireland and the rest of Britain, although there have been through container services since the late 1960s. Many of the technical problems between European railways have been simplified by the close co-operation of railway administrations through the work of the UIC (International Union of Railways) – standardized wagon dimensions – and RIV (see European wagons section) – wagon design standards. Within the last two decades, European railways have worked together to develop rail links between countries. To exploit rail's advantages for container movement, Intercontainer

Above left: Steam still plays its part in Poland. A narrow-gauge 0–8–0.

Above: Interfrigo manages refrigerated wagons in Europe. These modern examples are at Dover en route by train ferry to Europe.

Right: A French electrically-hauled express parcels train passes by Lac du Bourget.

was founded in 1968 as the agency for more than 20 European railways' container services. This has led to the development of a network of Trans Europ Container Expresses such as those between Paris and Cologne and Rotterdam and Paris. In addition, there is the longer-established system of Trans Europ Express Marchandises (TEEM) trains. These are made up of ordinary wagons but also convey container traffic. An earlier co-operative agency in Europe is the Interfrigo company, founded in 1949, which manages perishable refrigerated traffic for over 20 railways and which has its own fleet of more than 7,000 refrigerated wagons.

More generally, the European railways have worked together through UIC towards an efficient uniform railway network providing fast inter-city passenger services, greater carrying capacity and direct freight routes between the main centres of population and industry. The outcome of a series of studies was the UIC Master Plan for the development of the European network published in 1973. Apart from identifying traffic bottlenecks for elimination the Master Plan emphasized the need for a new standard gauge line between the Spanish/French border, Madrid and Barcelona – an important development for freight in view of the considerable traffic which now originates from Spain even with the present break of gauge between Spain and France. One further aspect of the development of an improved rail network in Europe is continued interest in the Channel tunnel – despite abandonment in early 1975, the European Economic Community has supported the development of better rail links between member countries and has recently published a proposal for EEC financing of infrastructure improvements. This proposal could hasten realization of the UIC Master Plan and, possibly, the Channel Tunnel.

Some international freight links across Europe have experienced vast increases in traffic over the last 20 years, interrrupted only by the recent industrial recession from 1974 to 1976. In particular, there are the international routes via Switzerland's north–south St Gotthard, Simplon and Lötschberg lines – most of the traffic being in transit to and from Italy. By 1969, 45 m tonnes of

freight was being moved across the Alps in a year – rail taking some 41 per cent or 19 million tonnes. Between 1968 and 1969 alone, traffic grew by 10 per cent. The Swiss Federal government accordingly drew up a major plan for improving the Trans-Alpine routes involving the construction of a new Gotthard base tunnel, new cut-off routes and double-tracking schemes. Between 1974 and 1975, because of the worldwide recession, freight traffic fell by 30 per cent removing the need for immediate improvements. Plans for the improvement of the Lötschberg route are expected to go ahead eventually.

Eastern European railways have also been planning major improvements for international freight traffic – rail has the major share of all land freight movements in the Comecon nations. Cooperation has progressed through Comecon to improve the capacity of major routes by electrification, increased dieselization, streamlined transhipment facilities at the breaks of gauge with the Russian system, and the introduction of international container trains. Better integration is being achieved by wagon pooling and computerized freight traffic management.

The major advantage of rail for transporting goods over long distances is underlined by the determined efforts of governments and railways to improve international rail links the world over. Apart from breaks between the railways of neighbouring countries, other difficulties exist such as changes in track gauge, transhipment differences in loading gauges and the need to provide satisfactory trans-shipment facilities. Many of these problems are emphasized by the success of road freight in taking advantage of major growth in trade, by its greater flexibility and by absence of many limitations.

National systems – Europe
Throughout the European Economic Community and western Europe generally, rail freight has grown steadily – although rail's share of all freight has been falling – and widespread investment, modernization and rationalization has taken place. In Belgium, there was a dramatic increase in solid fuels, ore, metal products and oil traffic – about 9 per cent per annum in the early

Below right: Railways prospered in Australia from cattle traffic. A Queensland Railway train being loaded at Julia Creek.

1970s – and further electrification is planned to improve freight. The Netherlands moves a comparatively small amount of freight by rail – with a recent decline because of the closure of the national coal mines. Rail has a 50 per cent share of freight traffic in France and a third of the traffic is international. Particular effort has been put into container, piggyback and import/export services. Private sidings have been opened at a rate of one per day over the 1973–75 period. Freight service handling is becoming fully computerized. West Germany introduced a transport policy – the Leber plan – in the late 1960s to divert freight traffic to rail. Much effort has been put into service modernization and the construction of private sidings. Deutsche Bundesbahn has enjoyed considerable recent success in carrying more container traffic in 1976 than ever before, in establishing a piggyback block train network for transporting heavy lorries in 1,500 tonne trains and now operating some of the heaviest freight trains in Europe – 5,000 tonnes. Britain carries a comparatively small amount of its freight by rail (20 per cent) but British Rail has recently launched a major freight drive by building on its successes with company trains, improving private sidings and expanding ferry wagon traffic to Europe. Rail freight has gained much of the North Sea oil traffic and will benefit from the development of the proposed Selby coalfield. Wagon control has been fully computerized. Italy is rationalizing its conventional freight services, developing its international freight traffic – likely

to benefit by new 'cut-off lines' – and since 1975 has built-up a wagonload liner-train network. Typical of recent modernization is the major marshalling yard at Alessandria with a capacity of 3,200 wagons daily. Eire is in the process of centralizing and rationalizing its conventional freight traffic and developing the growth of unit trains. Eire's target is to maintain the present volume of trade with a third of the existing wagon fleet.

Outside the European Economic Community, Austrian railways have seen continuous growth in rail freight but future expansion depends on route modernization across the Alps. In Switzerland, international freight traffic growth (despite the downturn in 1975) is the main target for improvement – helped by the recent construction of major marshalling yards such as Basle, Lausanne and Zürich. Thirty-seven new or improved marshalling yards will gradually take over the work of ninety existing ones. The 1977 railway modernization plan in Spain is based on phenomenal freight traffic growth since the early 1970s which outstripped the plan target. By 1980, the volume of traffic will be three times that of 1972. Although already moving more than 50 per cent of the country's freight, Spanish railways actually increased their share of the total market in 1972. By contrast Portuguese railways have had only a modest growth in traffic since the 1950s – Portuguese freight is still very largely moved in wagonloads. Some 3,000 wagons have recently been ordered for delivery over five years.

In the Scandinavian countries the most impressive developments in rail freight have been in Finland and Sweden. The Finnish railways have been considerably modernized since the 1950s and the upgrading of lines has particularly benefited freight. Traffic has grown at about 5 per cent per annum since the mid 1960s and this is expected to continue. Major effort has been put into improving long-distance freight traffic with the USSR. A new marshalling yard at Vainikkala (the border with USSR) is being built to handle two thirds of the eleven million tonne import/export traffic and will coincide with electrification of the through route. In Sweden freight

Below left: A typical unit train movement – iron ore.

Below: A typical North American freight train with five diesel locomotives in multiple. The train includes loaded piggyback wagons, car-carriers and box-cars.

Far left: The Swiss Railways' international container terminal at Basle-Zeughausmatte.

Left: A modern freight-handling depot with automated conveyors of the Santa Fe Railway.

traffic by rail has benefited from severe restrictions on long-distance heavy goods vehicles imposed since 1974. A quadrupling of rail traffic with East Germany through Trelleborg has led to greatly increased train-ferry capacity. In Denmark, a fifteen-year plan aims to concentrate all general freight into a network of block trains. In Norway, there are plans to move North Sea oil by rail over a new 240 km (150 mile) railway from Narvik to Tromsø, which would then be the most northerly terminal of the European standard gauge network.

The railways of eastern Europe all carry a substantial share of their countries' freight and although statistics are lacking, this share averages out at 45–75 per cent. Rail is especially suited to the heavy industrial bias of many of the Comecon countries and their own modernization contributes considerably to the volume of freight traffic.

The giant of all rail freight systems is the USSR. The expected achievement – to carry half of the world's freight by 1975 – seems to have been exceeded as the 1975 plan target was met one year early.

More than three million million tonne/kilometres of freight were carried in 1974. Some 4,800–6,400 km (3,000–4,000 miles) of new routes were constructed from 1971 to 1975. Electrification has been imperative for heavy freight working on many lines where freight trains of 9,000 tonnes operate. The maximum speed is 80 km/h (50 mph) for most freight services but some operate at up to 120 km/h (75 mph). Apart from the new Baikal–Amur line in Siberia already mentioned, a 720 km (450 mile) railway was opened in 1973 to serve the Siberian oilfields. An extensive container train service is operated.

The railway's share of freight movement in Czechoslovakia is probably the lowest of any country in eastern Europe – along with Yugoslavia. The Czech rail freight volume is increasing slightly, although much less than in the 1960s. A great deal of investment is going into a container service network. There is similar emphasis on containerization in East Germany where there has also been much investment.

National systems – North and South America

The importance of railways in moving long distance freight, particularly bulk traffics, is well demonstrated in Canada. The two main railway systems – Canadian National and Canadian Pacific – together with the various state and private administrations move a large proportion of Canada's freight. Major new lines for freight have been built in recent years such as the Great Slave Lake Railway to tap Canada's vast resources of minerals and coal. The volume of traffic has increased by some 10 per cent annually in recent years. Most of the major expansion has occurred in coal movements – export coal moved by Canadian Pacific increased by nearly 200 per cent in 5 years in the west. Forecasts suggest that there will be a five-fold expansion of export coal moved by Canadian National over the next five years and the railway plans to invest heavily in new equipment and facilities. Some of the traffic is moved by 'merry-go-round' trains. Recent studies by Canadian National demonstrate that a new railway from Alberta to the Mackenzie river delta would compete economically with a pipeline in transporting oil and natural gas. The railway could move two million barrels of oil per day and three billion cubic feet of gas transported in trains of 225 tank wagons hauled by seven 3,000 hp locomotives.

Transcontinental freight has grown so much in recent years that major schemes of doubling and upgrading main lines across the Prairies and in the Rockies are in progress by both national railways. Future increases in traffic have led to major studies advocating electrification of 13,000 km (8,000 miles) of railway across the Prairies and in the Rockies over the next 25 years. Merchandise freight movement has contributed a large increase in revenue and a number of marshalling yards have been re-equipped. One of the most notable developments has been the growth of piggyback loadings over long distances. US to Canada fast freight services have been introduced – such as that between Montreal and Washington – some 1,200 km (750 miles). Both railways operate a large mileage of uneconomic branch lines in the Prairies serving wheat-growing areas and, as part of a rationalization programme, both railways want to close about 6,500 km (4,000 miles) of track out of the present 30,000 km (19,000 mile) rail network.

Rail freight operations in the United States are fittingly on a massive scale. The US railroads are predominantly freight carriers – over 97 per cent of the 309,600 km (193,500 miles) of line are freight only. US government statistics show that two-thirds of rail freight movement is carried over a fifth of the network. In general, the US railroads do not have an impressive productivity record – wagon turnround in days is nearly four times worse than West Germany, for example, and the traffic moved per motive power unit is under half that of the French railways. The problem is the large number of independent railways, duplication of services and a multiplicity of marshalling yards. Even so, the railways carry 40 per cent of all freight moved in the US. Coupled with strict control over freight rates imposed by Federal regulation these factors have spelt bankruptcy for a number of major companies.

US railways have generally found it difficult to attract new investment and much of the rolling stock, track, signalling and yards have become obsolete particularly in the north east. Between 1961 and 1970, seven major railways went bankrupt in all, operating 43,200 km (17,000 miles) of track. The US government accordingly has set up a new independent corporation with the stock held by the Federal government. The corporation, known as Conrail, will control 24,000 km (15,000 miles) of railway in the north east, and is expected to cut the present $300 million loss by half in five years by more efficient working and by reducing the mileage by one quarter.

This is the gloomier side of the picture. Many railways are profitable – such as the huge Union Pacific Railroad, the Southern Pacific and the Southern. Major investment is going into new equipment, particularly into rolling stock and facilities for the current and projected growth in coal traffic. Rail moves some 65 per cent of all US coal produced and from carrying 388 million tonnes in 1974 will hope to increase tonnage to 650 million by 1985. Most of this will be moved in unit trains made up of 60–110 wagons of around 100 tonnes capacity at speeds of 64–96 km/h (40–60 mph). It is expected that the railways will need to buy about 8,000 more locomotives and 150,000 wagons in the next ten years.

Other solutions to achieve greater efficiency are being found in the construction of new marshalling yards and national box car pools. The proposed St Louis yard would handle 10,000 wagons daily and replace 63 existing marshalling yards operated by 19 companies. The boxcar pool entered into by 40 railways will acquire 10,000 units and achieve more efficient working by the operation of a national fleet.

Until the early 1970s the railways of Central and South America seemed set for stagnation if not decline, bankruptcy and abandonment. One problem was the isolation of national systems, isolated lines within countries, different track gauges and outworn equipment. Many of the countries, particularly in Central America, operate railways of comparatively localized importance, often owned by overseas companies and restricted to particular traffic such as fruit. In South America, there had been a period of rapid expansion in the 19th century leading to fairly intensive networks, particularly in Argentina and Uruguay, but with a record of traffic moving to road in recent years.

Recently this picture has changed dramatically. After expanding the road network in the 1960s, the government in Brazil decided to recast its transport policies in favour of railway modernization to exploit the huge mineral resources and open the inland areas for industrial development. A major plan was drawn up in 1973 to cover railway improvements and traffic developments over the next 25 years. The more ambitious proposals have since been modified or deferred but the Brazilian railway strategy, largely calculated to

boost rail freight, is one of the most impressive testimonies to the potential of railways in the world.

Basically the plan involves the following:

Brazilian Federal Railways (RFFSA)

Upgrading of lines for higher axleloads, increased speeds and longer trains.

Large scale standardization of track gauge.

The construction of a new 400 km (250 mile) electrified railway in the State of Minas Gerais 'Ferrovia do Aço' for iron ore traffic.

Investment to increase rail freight carryings by over 200 per cent in six years.

Improvements to about 14,400 route km (9,000 route miles) of existing railways – with some new construction – to create rail freight export corridors and to move bulk freight to ports.

A major expansion of the wagon fleet. Ten thousand wagons are currently being delivered and 3,000 per year will be constructed in Brazil from 1979.

The São Paulo State Railways (FEPASA)

Major upgrading of 2,400 route km (1,500 route miles) of existing lines together with some new construction to give higher axleloading for heavier trains up to 2,000 tonnes – financed by the Federal government.

Finance for the purchase of 5,000 more wagons and more locomotives.

In addition, work is going ahead on the construction of a 960 km (600 mile) electrified railway in north east Brazil to carry iron ore for export.

By comparison, other countries' projects appear modest, although Venezuela has major plans for a new network of railways to boost industrial growth inland and to carry export iron ore which would treble rail freight within fifteen years. Chile has plans for a trans-Andean link with Argentina. In Argentina, the railways face a major task in rehabilitating equipment and slimming an under-used network in order to regain traffic lost to road.

Other major developments are the proposed electrification of the steam-worked system in Paraguay to link with Argentina and new links between Bolivia, Brazil and northern Chile. In Peru the rail system is fragmented, which inhibits through freight movement, but rehabilitation of lines is taking place. The Southern Peru Copper Corporation is constructing a 64 km (40 mile) extension to its railway serving copper mines which will be notable for having no less than 27.2 km (17 miles) of tunnel on its route.

National systems – Asia

The value of a railway system in contributing to the growth of a developing economy can be seen in the dramatic growth of India's rail freight. The volume of traffic grew by 80 per cent between 1953 and 1961; in the next fifteen years it rose by 65 per cent and, between 1975 and 1989, the increase will be 100 per cent. Eight basic bulk commodities dominate Indian rail freight: coal, iron and steel products, ores, limestone, cement, fertilizers, grains and petroleum products. Most

Above: Southern Pacific Railroad westbound freight in the Sierra Nevada Mountains, California.

Below: US freight operation old-style. A 4–8–4 locomotive No 3038 hauls 14 wagons from Nopala southbound.

of these traffics move in heavy flows on a dozen or so major routes. This is ideal for rail to exploit its advantages. Such movements involve relatively low speeds – about 80 km/h (50 mph) maximum – and are suitable for transport in large capacity bulk wagons which can then be worked as unit trains. Indian Railways aim to improve the railway infrastructure – signalling, track, running loops and motive power so as to work most of it in 4,500 tonne air-braked trains. More efficient working and the replacement of steam by diesel and electric traction has enabled the Indian Railways to keep pace with the huge growth in traffic. Compared with 1950, traffic volume has doubled but only 30 per cent more locomotives have been added to the fleet.

India's railways are administered as nine zonal systems and consist of a mixture of broad and metre gauge lines. Work is in progress to convert the most heavily used lines to broad (1,676 mm; 5 ft 6 in) gauge to cut out transhipment problems and increase capacity. Other problems revolve around freight rates since, as with so many railways, there are statutory controls on rates which mean that traffic is carried at uneconomic charges. Examples are food grains for famine areas and industrial coal. For this reason, despite moving the bulk of the nation's freight, Indian railways have to fight to retain high rated merchandise traffic.

New railways are being built such as the Banspani-Jhakpura line for mineral ore traffic in Orissa. At the end of 1974, for example, over 320 km (200 miles) of new railway had been approved for construction and nearly 960 km (600 miles) of new construction or major reconstruction of existing lines was in progress. Indus-

Above right: Despite the doubling of traffic since 1950, the Indian Railways' locomotive fleet has increased by only 30 per cent. Steam is responsible for a declining share of freight movement.

trial systems in India such as those serving steelworks are major railways in themselves. A good example is the Bokaro steelworks system in Bihar which has 256 km (160 miles) of track and handles 40 million tonnes of traffic annually with its fleet of 70 locomotives.

Pakistan too, has seen much the same pattern of expansion in industrial traffic as India although on a smaller scale. The new massive marshalling yard under construction at Pipri will be able to handle 2,500 wagons daily.

In Bangladesh 'consultants' studies in 1973 indicated that the railway would be the most important form of transport in the Chittagong to Dacca corridor moving about 45 per cent of all land freight. A major programme of upgrading and investment is in progress.

The railway system in the People's Republic of China is the major carrier of surface freight with the heaviest traffic consisting of coal, grain, cotton and pig-iron. Evidence suggests that, during harvests, the railways work at full capacity to move the millions of tonnes of grain. The railways are still thinly spread over the huge landmass. Since the Revolution, major railway construction has taken place: some lines like the Chuchow to Kweiyang line are to open up the interior and others such as the Chengtu to Kunming line are to tap natural resources – in this case shale-oil.

Many of the problems of freight operation faced by railways in industrialized countries afflict Japanese National Railways. The JNR freight services lost Y405,200 million in 1975 and efforts are being intensified to stem losses by closing marshalling yards and freight depots and by reducing services. A major plan launched in 1973 is aimed at reorganizing the freight business and concentrating on services that the railways can do best. There is a successful network of block container trains modelled on the British Freightliner system. Wagonload services have been remodelled making extensive use of computer control of wagon movements. Marshalling yards have been extensively modernized. Over 30 per cent of freight tonnage moves in single commodity unit trains carrying coal, limestone, petroleum products and cement. Overall rail freight volume has remained stable, rail steadily losing its share of the total freight business.

One of the most remarkable and least known railway systems is in Mongolia, nearly 14,400 km (9,000 miles) in length and constructed between 1938 and 1955 to the Russian 1,524 mm (5 ft) track gauge. The 1,152 km (720 mile) main line from north to south forms part of the main USSR–China link. Freight traffic over the whole system has quadrupled between 1955 and 1967 and includes much timber and coal.

In the Middle East, after a long period of neglect, improvements are in hand on a number of rail systems to develop through freight.

Existing lines are being upgraded or new lines built for bulk freight in Iraq, largely for sulphur and oil traffic and in Jordan, for phosphates. Major development plans are in being or are planned to provide new links between principal towns and cities and ports in Iran, to Bandar Shahpour, in Israel and Saudi Arabia. High capacity lines are being created from existing routes by upgrading in Iran, Iraq, Syria and Turkey. The result should be that by the late 1980s a collection of previously under-invested and declining systems will provide a modern infrastructure for through freight – having benefited from investment from Middle Eastern oil revenue. A major international loan is being used to develop the Egyptian Republic Railways as a major carrier of agricultural products. There is also a plan for a 560 km (350 mile) phosphate export railway to a new port on the Red Sea. One most interesting prospect is the proposal for linking the Sudanese and Egyptian systems.

National systems – Africa

African railways are developing rapidly from the fragmented pattern of lines running in from major ports to the interior, principally for trading products. The exceptions to this pattern were in the north and south where more complete networks were built. Since the 1950s major new railways, principally for freight, have been built right across the continent. There has been a virtual explosion in railway construction since the mid 1960s with extensive railways constructed or planned in Cameroun, Gabon, Guinea, Malawi and Morocco. The most spectacular and significant development is the Tan-Zam Railway

opened in 1975. This railway, built with Chinese assistance, would appear to inaugurate a new era in African railways by directly connecting the east and central African markets and by providing a major new outlet to the sea.

This development has also proved correct the vision of railway administrations, for the World Bank doubted that the 1,866 km (1,160 mile) railway linking land-locked Zambia with Dar-es-Salaam would be an economic proposition. Less than 300,000 tonnes of traffic per year was anticipated after construction. Within a year of opening, the line carried one million tonnes of freight. African countries have recognized that the lack of an integrated railway network inhibits economic development and have established the Union of African Railways to explore ways of unifying the African railway networks – amongst other major tasks.

As in the case of other developing countries, major African railway projects are tapping the vast resources of raw materials. A 320 km (200 mile) section of the Trans-Cameroun railway was opened in 1974. A 320 km (200 mile) railway with standard 1,435 mm (4 ft 8½ in) track gauge is under construction in Gabon and is expected to carry 1 million tonnes of traffic annually, mainly timber. A 1,200 km (750 mile) system is being built in Guinea for bauxite and iron exports.

Of the railways in the north, the systems of Algeria, Morocco and Tunisia are experiencing record traffic levels, particularly of iron ore and phosphates. Other notable bulk traffic railways include the Lamco Railroad in Liberia which moves 13.5 million tonnes of iron ore annually over 274 km (170 miles) in its 12,000 tonne trains. The Mauritanian national system has a 640 km (400 mile) line which transports 12 million tonnes of iron ore each year in some of the heaviest freight trains in the world.

Many railways have had a phenomenal growth rate in freight business in recent years. Nigeria doubled its traffic between 1974 and 1976; Algeria doubled its volume in four years and the Ivory Coast is expecting freight tonne kilometrage to have tripled between 1970 and 1990.

South African railways have an established

Above left: South African Railways still rely on steam for much of their freight traffic. A GEA class 4–8–2/2–8–4 Beyer Garratt locomotive on empty fruit vans.

Above right: A typical modern marshalling yard. A wagon passes over the retarder to slow its descent into the yard at the Te Rapa yard in New Zealand.

Below left: Australian railways are increasing their long distance business. An impressive load of containers, piggyback traffic and double-decked car-carriers nears the end of the 3940 km (2460 mile) run from Sydney to Perth.

Below: The Tan Zam Railway has been a resounding success since opening in 1975. Timber is being loaded in China for use in construction of the line.

32,000 km (20,000 mile) system. It is planned to increase the electrified network by 80 per cent between now and the early 1990s by which time 80 per cent of freight traffic would be electrically hauled. As in the case of the United States, Japan and India, considerable effort is being put into moving bulk traffic in unit trains principally to carry iron ore and coal. With the imminent containerization of maritime traffic to South Africa, a major container train network is being built up. Wagonload business is being modernized by the use of computerized information systems, terminals rationalization and the modernization of marshalling yards. Current investment in freight is about three times that of passenger service re-equipment. Two major new freight routes have recently been or will shortly be completed: a 480 km (300 mile) line, partly new, partly reconstructed, from Vryheid (Transvaal) to Richards Bay (near Durban) for coal exports and an entirely new 896 km (560 mile) export iron ore line in Cape Province running from the ore field at Sishen to a new port at Saldanha Bay. The Richards Bay line has the annual capacity for some 30 million tonnes of coal exports to be moved in 5,500 tonne trains.

National systems – Australia and New Zealand

Australian railways' general freight problems have been discussed earlier. One of the most interesting developments has been the construction of new high capacity mineral railways. The most spectacular of these is the Hamersley Railway largely built in 1965–66 and now extending over 384 km (240 miles) from the iron ore fields at Paraburdoo and Mount Tom Price to Dampier in Western Australia.

The heaviest trains are 23,000 tonnes gross and 1,750 m (1,800 yards) long. Annually the line at present carries some 22 million tonnes of traffic, expected to increase to 40 million tonnes in the future. The three major iron ore railways owned by mining companies in Western Australia – including the Hamersley Railway – carry about 62 million tonnes of freight a year over nearly 1,280 km (800 miles) of railway – a striking example of railway productivity. Other major bulk freight operations are in Queensland – coal and phosphates – and New South Wales, mainly coal. Freight traffic is booming in New Zealand where in 1975–76 the system carried more freight than ever before and a successful container train operation for export/import traffic has been built up.

Throughout the world, distinct trends are evident in rail freight. In Europe and Japan a determined effort has been necessary to rationalize conventional freight services to make them competitive with road and to pay their way. This has been done by withdrawing from the very general, small load merchandise business and concentrating on building up block wagonload services, container train networks or piggyback facilities. In North America, many of the rationalization processes are only just beginning. In developing countries the expansion and modernization of freight railways is seen as integral to economic development. In Africa, South America and Asia efforts are being made to build up a continental network of lines so that railways are more fully effective in their role as long-haul carriers. Universally, the opportunities for rail to provide conveyor-belt movements of coal and mineral traffic are being optimized so as to ensure that railways will continue to be an indispensable part of national transport systems throughout the rest of the 20th century and into the 21st.

Freight train motive power

Steam freight locomotive designs were characterized by small driving wheels. The object was to maximize the tractive force available at the wheel rim. Therefore the rule was, the smaller the wheels the greater the power. With high tractive force the locomotive is able to use more of its own weight for adhesion. Even better use of adhesive weight could be achieved by more driving wheels which when coupled in series made the locomotive more sure-footed.

Above: Road/rail transhipment the modern way. A portal crane transfers a container at an SNCF container terminal.

The larger the number of driving wheels the less is the load on each axle. So, the powerful steam freight locomotives had small wheels and were limited to freight train working by virtue of their speed. Whatever the railway, the formula was the same from the 19th century to the last of the breed which were probably a batch of freight locomotives built in China as late as 1976.

To make optimum use of the power available, diesel locomotives have small wheels but are not limited by the technical problems of high piston speeds which kept the speeds of small-wheeled steamers low. In the case of diesel locomotives suitable characteristics for freight working are achieved by adopting lower ratio gearing. From the 1930s onwards, with the advent of large scale diesel locomotive production, most types have been produced in low-geared freight and higher-geared passenger versions. For many of the world's freight railways a compromise can be reached because general operating speeds of both freight and passenger trains are low – particularly where the track is obsolete or worn.

The limiting factor of diesel power is the output or rating of the diesel engine designs available. There are virtually no diesel engine units available above the 3,000–4,000 hp level. So, without twin engines in one power unit, the most powerful single units are around 4,000 hp. Such types are now in production in the USA and have been supplied by French and German builders to China. In the USSR, the most powerful diesel freight locomotives are 6,000–8,000 hp and these are twin units.

For greater power, locomotives are operated in multiple, that is, coupled together and controlled by one unit. Perhaps the record for the number of units in one regularly scheduled freight train is held by Canadian Pacific's 11,000 tonne coal trains in the Rockies which have four 3,000 hp locomotives at the front and two 3,000 hp slave (remote controlled locomotives) in the centre. These then need the further assistance of four

3,000 hp banking locomotives on the steepest grades.

Not surprisingly, there is a better solution – electrification. Greater power output is available from electric units than from diesel locomotives of corresponding size and they weigh less. Installed power equipment can be almost unlimited and the restrictions are set by the axleloads that can be permitted. High voltage electrification (at 25,000 volts or 50,000 volts ac) can provide all the power required for the heaviest and most frequent freight currently considered. Typical electric freight locomotive 'heavies' are as follows:

7,350 hp 25 kV ac Co-Co built in France for China, 1972

8,150 hp 15 kV ac Co-Co, West Germany, 1973

8,450 hp 11 or 25 kV ac Bo-Bo-Bo, USA Prototype, 1976

13,000/16,000 hp 25 kV ac Bo-Bo-Bo-Bo, USSR Prototype, 1971–75 (twin unit).

A number of major freight railways are considering electrification at high voltage ac to match the predicted increases in traffic for the future, particularly in Canada and the USA.

Other interesting motive power developments involve automated train operation. The remote control of 'slave' diesel locomotives situated in the middle of trains has been mentioned but to reduce manning costs in areas where labour is scarce completely automatic train operation has been introduced. This is easily achieved where all the trains are of similar type, speed and operation. The locomotives are usually electronically controlled through track circuiting, or, by transponders/responders mounted respectively between the rails and on the locomotives.

Control signals activate acceleration and braking. Radio control of locomotives from the trackside has also recently been used on an electrified lignite railway in Texas. The principal automated electrified lines are as follows, all built in the 1960–1970s:

9.6 route km (6 route miles) – Carol Mine Railway, Labrador, Canada

24 route km (15 route miles) – Muskingum Electric Railroad, Ohio, USA

Right: Long distance freight transits in Australia have benefited from the transcontinental standard gauge line completed in the late 1960s. This train is hauled by a typical diesel-electric 'hood' unit.

Far right: Typical US diesel-electric units of the 1940s/1950s. A cab unit is coupled to a 'B' (non-driving) unit.

125 route km (78 route miles) – Black Mesa and Lake Powell Railroad, Arizona, USA

There are also a number of automated railways within mines and, perhaps the grandfather of them all, the mail-carrying Post Office Railway in London dating from the late 1920s.

For shunting locomotives, power ouput has steadily increased so that 1,000–1,200 hp diesel shunting locomotives are now common around the world for the heaviest tasks.

Apart from locomotives a range of shunting and wagon moving systems are used in sidings. These include rail tractors, adapted fork lift trucks, road-rail lorries and rail mounted 'pushers'. Some between-the-tracks systems are available particularly for use in marshalling yards, usually cable, electrically or hydraulically worked. Linear motor propulsion is used in the modernized Shiohama marshalling yard of the Japanese National Railways.

Wagons

Wagons have steadily become more efficient in terms of payload carried against tare weight and with better braking and more effective couplers. The limiting factor is generally axleloading. Few railways are able to permit wagons with more than 20–25 tonnes loaded on each axle resulting in a maximum gross weight for wagons of 100 tonnes. Substantial modifications to track would increase axleloads to 30 tonnes – as planned for some routes in the USSR.

Over the last 100 years all-wood and steel underframe/wooden bodied wagons have given way to all-steel types. More recently materials such as aluminium and glass-reinforced plastics have been used for wagon bodies.

Four-wheel wagons make up a large proportion of many railways' wagon fleets such as in Europe, India, Australia, and the USSR. In many respects four-wheel wagons can still offer the best solution giving good payload/tare weight ratios and an ability to run at speeds of up to 120 km/h (75 mph) at least. For railways with lightly, poorly laid track bogie wagons were popular from early days – this being particularly true in North America.

Above: Modern French high-sided sliding roof wagons.

Heavily-loaded bogie wagons can often cause severe damage to track unless the bogies have satisfactory suspension design. Braking systems are now mainly air with tread brakes acting on the wheels although these are increasingly giving way to disc brakes.

Current trends in wagon requirements reflect the pattern of freight service developments with its emphasis on more efficient wagonload working, unit trains and specialized traffics. The most common types being delivered to the world's railways include standardized open and box-bogie wagons; bogie hopper wagons – many with self-discharge – for unit trains; low loaders for container and piggyback services; refrigerated box cars; car-carrying wagons and pressure assisted and ordinary discharge tank cars for petroleum products, gas and chemicals. Recently, there has been a growth in orders for wagons to carry powders or pellets in bulk – chemicals and plastics products. There is a continuing trend towards standardized wagon designs in Europe, the USA and on major railways such as those of India and South Africa.

Careful design has enabled high payload tare/weight ratios to be achieved. Good examples include the South African-built hopper wagons for the Iscor Sishen to Saldanha Bay line iron ore

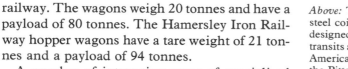

railway. The wagons weigh 20 tonnes and have a payload of 80 tonnes. The Hamersley Iron Railway hopper wagons have a tare weight of 21 tonnes and a payload of 94 tonnes.

A number of interesting types of specialized wagons are being built. Covered wagons (box cars) are being built in Europe with fully sliding sidewalls to facilitate the loading of standard commercial pallets. In one Czech design the roof can be slid back to allow crane loading into the wagon. Several railways operate special heavily insulated torpedo ladle cars to carry molten iron between steelworks. An American builder, GATX, has developed a tank train: an integral train of tank wagons which has a through loading/discharge pipe system between the 40 cars and is able to carry one million gallons. Another US builder has designed the sandwich car, a tank car with temperature control provided by urethane foam insulation and which has no metal-to-metal contact making it particularly suitable for acids and food products.

Above: Truck traffic such as steel coil requires specially designed wagons for safe transits and easy loading. An American 'breadbox' car of the Pittsburgh & Lake Erie RR.

Probably one of the heaviest specialized wagons is a 32 axle wagon built in the USA for Sweden and designed for transporting heavy electrical plant. The wagon is 68 m (220 ft) long with a tare load of 230 tonnes and weighs 700 tonnes fully laden. The centre of the wagon can be displaced sideways while on the move so as to clear trackside obstacles.

The International Union of Railways (UIC) has been responsible for promoting the standardization of wagon designs used by the major European administrations. The major European railways also work together within co-operative administrations such as the Europ wagon pool – for the control of wagons moving between sys-

Left: An interesting steel-coil wagon operated by SNCF with sliding body sections.

Right: Railways the world over have increasingly put into service air/gravity discharge wagons for powdered/pelletized traffics, such as this Italian example.

Below left: Shunting can be carried out by cheap 'wagon pushers' in private sidings.

Left: A typical heavy load transporter – the load being carried by multi-wheeled units at each end – 32 axles in all able to carry a 500-ton load.

tems – and within the conditions of RIV (Regolamento Internazionale Veicoli), the International Wagon Union, which prescribes standardized dimensions, fittings and equipment.

The UIC is working towards a standard range of 12 wagons in Europe covering bogie vans, flat wagons, hopper wagons, opening roof vans and container wagons. As well as standardizing designs of two-axle wagons there is also an agreed standard bogie for speeds of up to 96 km/h (60 mph). The UIC aim of specifying automatic couplings on all European wagons by 1980 has been deferred due to the recession in traffic during the mid 1970s. Throughout Europe there is a sizeable fleet of privately owned wagons – 15 per cent of a total of 1 million – for special traffics – and these are either owned by industries or by leasing organizations.

The Irish Railways (Coras Iompair Eireain) exemplify the change in European wagon fleets from predominantly general user open and covered wagons to specialized types, increasingly for trainload working and mechanized handling. Such wagons are often privately owned. New types on the CIE comprise gypsum hopper wagons, a design for bagged cement traffic, a bogie palletized bagged fertilizer wagon and tar-bitumen tankers.

Some railways' requirements for new wagons in recent years have been really extensive, generally as part of major re-equipment programmes. Bangladesh Railways intended to purchase over 8,400 wagons during 1976 to rehabilitate its fleet. The Soviet Railways alone put over 70,000 wagons into service in one recent year against which the French Railways' orders of 5,000 a year, although quite sizeable, pale into insignificance.

Wagon building is a growth industry. Major wagon producing countries are Brazil, France, West Germany, India, Japan, Spain, Yugoslavia and most of the eastern European states. Wagon exports are quite considerable. Probably one of the most notable orders in recent years was that for 10,000 wagons placed with France by East Germany in 1970. In India, the nine manufacturers have a capacity of over 20,000 wagons a year. Just one of the Soviet Wagon works – that at Abakan in Siberia which opened in 1973 – has double the capacity of all the Indian works.

Even so, wagon building is not a mass production industry for despite orders in tens of thousands, ordering is uneven and designs are still very varied so that even the most efficient works are doing well if they turn out 20–25 new wagons daily.

Controlling wagons

Individual wagons, unlike lorries, have no driver and unless their movements are strictly supervized they are subject to delay or misrouting. Railways are ideally suited to control systems using computers since all facilities are under one control and all vehicles are guided. Consequently, an obvious application for computers has been to control wagons moving over rail networks. A data bank of wagon numbers, types and loading capacity is developed together with full details of train services, marshalling yards and terminals. Information is then fed into the computer at yards and terminals so that the computer system can provide details of the movement and location of wagons and ensure their full utilization. The computer information systems can also furnish information on whether wagons are loaded or empty, the total wagon stocks and their availability.

This faculty gives railway operators' an up-to-the-minute and comprehensive picture of freight movement to aid train and yard working. Material is available for accounting and location enquiries and to give the customer advance information on wagon transits. Computerized freight information systems are a vital stage towards making wagonload and general freight operation efficient and competitive. Over twenty US and two Canadian railroads have comprehensive systems with teleprocessing equipment using teleprinters or visual display units for information presentation. Computerized systems are also in use on the national railways of Britain, France and Japan.

Another modern aid to efficient wagon control includes automatic wagon identification by optical or microwave scanners – usually with input to the computer information system. The scanner system is particularly worthwhile in North America where wagons can travel anywhere on the Continent from Northern Canada to Mexico. One other vital monitoring aid is the 'hot box' detector. This detects overheated axlebox bearings and enables the defective wagon to be quickly located for removal from the train before further damage to itself or derailment of the whole train.

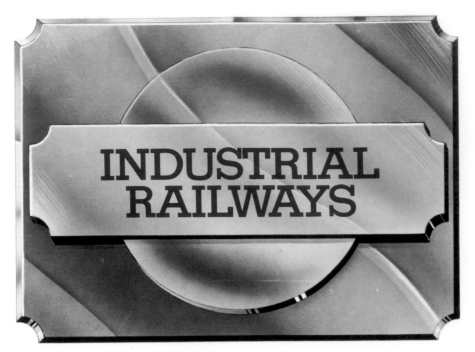

Definition

An industrial railway is defined as a railway provided as a link in an industrial activity where the operator is not in business as a provider of freight transport for reward. Industrial railways perform a supporting role secondary to the main function of the owning company. There are borderline cases, of course, such as the railway provided for the transport of minerals and owned by the mining company, but which also operates a public passenger service. Legal distinctions cannot be made, because they vary from country to country. Broadly, a railway ceases to be an industrial line as soon as it offers a public freight service – in other words it becomes a 'common carrier' of goods traffic – even if such public freight is an insignificant element in the railway's activity.

There are, however, no such problems of definition with most industrial railways. They are self-evidently so, even if the description covers an almost infinite variety, from a single works siding to a major mineral railway, hundreds of kilometres in length; from a short brickworks line with one wagon pushed by hand to an elaborate network serving a vast steelworks complex.

Industrial railways may be divided into four main categories, although these divisions overlap considerably. Many railways fall in, or between, two categories, while the more extensive systems can encompass all four functions. The classification has been adopted here purely to illustrate the scope of the subject.

First, there is the feeder to a main line railway. If the industrial premises are alongside a public railway there will be sidings within the works leading from the reception sidings to enable wagons to reach loading or unloading points. If the industrial plant is some distance from a public railway, then the works line will in effect be a branch connecting the works with the main system.

Secondly, there is the internal works system, providing a transport service within the works complex. This could be completely isolated from a main line system and therefore of any gauge to suit its particular function. It could provide a general service throughout the works, as in many steelworks, or perform a specific function such as ash disposal from a boiler plant.

Thirdly comes the railway carrying raw materials to a manufacturing or processing plant. This includes railways connecting mine or quarry with works and also agricultural railways taking produce from field to factory.

Finally, there are the railways conveying raw materials from mine or quarry to a transhipment point for transfer to another mode of transport for onward conveyance to destination. The best-known examples are the long mineral railways connecting mine with deep sea port, but there are also canal and river feeders and examples where a short rail haul precedes a trunk movement by road. Narrow-gauge feeders to main lines of a different gauge fall into this, rather than the first, category.

History

The early history of railways is concerned solely with industrial railways, which had been developing for more than 250 years before the appearance of the first public railways early in the 1800s. One of the first recorded railways served a German mine about 1550. This had wooden rails and the

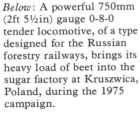

Below: A powerful 750mm (2ft 5½in) gauge 0-8-0 tender locomotive, of a type designed for the Russian forestry railways, brings its heavy load of beet into the sugar factory at Kruszwica, Poland, during the 1975 campaign.

timber wagons were pushed by hand. Railways reached England in the 1600s and developed with the Industrial Revolution, for the transport of ore, coal and limestone to the furnaces. By the mid-1700s the coal mines were served by horse-worked wooden tramroads, while elsewhere quarries were connected with the rapidly developing canal network by primitive tramways.

Iron replaced wood for wagon wheels; wagons were coupled together into trains; cast iron rails appeared, and later wrought iron. The first steam locomotive in the world made its debut on the Penydarren tramroad in South Wales in 1804.

The first railways were industrial railways, and they form an essential part of systems throughout the world. About 90 per cent of the freight carried in the industrially-developed countries is generated by rail outlets from industrial premises or industrial railways. In many of the developing countries the only railways are industrial ones – either mineral or agricultural.

With the spread of public railways throughout the world in the last century, some industrial railways developed alongside them with compatible equipment. Many lines, however, grew up independently of the main lines. These were the self-contained railways with a specific purpose and no main-line outlet, or else they had been built long before the main line reached the district. Many were of narrow gauge, either because of the nature of the country traversed, for reasons of economy in construction and equipment, or simply the whim of the engineer building them.

Many of these self-contained railways retained outdated concepts long after they were discarded elsewhere. As innovators they had no precedents to follow. They developed their own techniques and had no reason for costly change.

There were even some industrial railways laid to a broader gauge than the country's standard. A 7 ft 0¼ in gauge railway taking stone to a break-water may still be in use in the Azores. The widest gauge ever used for a conventional railway was 3,327 mm (10 ft 11 in), on which three strange-looking steam engines served the coke ovens at a Glasgow steelworks for 40 years from 1885.

Scope and variety

Industrial railways vary from short cable-worked brickworks lines and hand-worked lines serving watercress beds or sewage works to the great systems. There are long and intricate networks serving groups of collieries in Britain, France and Germany; the ironstone railways of Western Europe show a wide variety of lengths and gauges. The narrowest practical gauge ever employed was 457 mm (1 ft 6 in). An extensive network of this gauge served the needs of the Royal Arsenal in London for many years. The sugar industry, both cane and beet, relies heavily on railways to bring produce to the mill. The sugar beet railways of Western Europe have largely disappeared, but an enormous mileage survives in Poland. Wherever sugar cane is grown, there are railways covering considerable distances between field and mill. Finally there are the long mineral railways of Spain, Africa and Australia, some of very recent construction and using very sophisticated technology, carrying ironstone, phosphates, coal, and so on from mine to sea.

Just as public railways are best suited for bulk transport, so too are industrial railways usually to be found serving heavy industry. In the days of the horse and cart many quite small factories had their own railway, but these have progressively

Above: A colourful fireless locomotive, with a touch of humorous advertising about its livery, hauls a wagon of beer to the main line from Salmen Brewery, Rheinfelden, Switzerland, on a spring day in 1973.

Below: The lightly-laid portable feeder tracks which run right into the sugar-cane fields cannot bear the weight of locomotives and animal power is more common, as in this scene from Fiji.

changed to road vehicles for both internal and external transport since the turn of the century. Most of today's industrial railways are associated with extractive or heavy manufacturing industries although the less-developed countries still have their agricultural railways, using this term somewhat loosely to include forestry and plantation work. This survey of typical industries served is by no means exhaustive, but illustrates the variety that can, or could, be found.

Collieries

Just as coal gave birth to railways in the first place, so today it features prominently in the freight hauls of railways throughout the world; most coal moves by rail, even over short distances. Main-line wagons must have access to the coal screens and most collieries have a main-line connection. Many public railways serve collieries direct (they were often built for that very reason), in which case the colliery railway is a modest one – just a fan of sidings for wagon reception and storage and the lines under the screens.

Other collieries are some distance from the nearest railway and operate their own link to the main line. Colliery railways five and more kilometres long are common in Europe while much longer lines serve South African mines. These operate on a grand scale with large steam locomotives. The collieries of northern Spain tended to be located in places inaccessible to the main lines of 1,676 mm (5 ft 6 in) or metre gauge, and it was the practice to locate the screens alongside the main line, with narrow-gauge lines bringing coal from the pithead to the screens. Gauges varied from 550 to 750 mm (1 ft 9¾ in to 2 ft 5½ in) and the lines were anything up to 30 km (19 miles) in length, sometimes serving several collieries. One or two of these lines still survive, but most have now gone.

Then there are the great colliery networks. These gather coal from a number of collieries (usually under the same ownership) to hand over at one or more main-line exchange points. Quite often they move coal from several shafts to a central washery for screening. They are (or were) complete railway systems with large fleets of locomotives and wagons. Their workshops would build their wagons and sometimes complete locomotives, such as at Anzin in France.

The Valenciennes area collieries in northern

Above: Easy-discharge hopper wagons move coal efficiently from mine to port or power station. This metre gauge (3ft 3⅜in) system is in Spain.

Below: The Dona Teresa Cristina railway is a metre gauge (3ft 3⅜in) coal carrier in Brazil. The 100 per cent steam roster includes massive American-built 2-10-4 and 2-6-6-2 types. 1941 ALCO 2-8-2 No 154 loads coal wagons from the conveyor belt at Capivari in October 1974.

France have a main line 39 km (24 miles) long, with several branches, which even crosses the frontier to connect with Belgian railways. A public passenger service was worked at one time and in steam days there were more than 60 locomotives. In the Pas de Calais there were six such systems, operating over 250 locomotives between them. The Dutch State Mines had a system in Limburg which required more than 40 locomotives even in diesel days. Similar networks exist in the Ruhr area of West Germany. The South Maitland and J & A Brown railways in New South Wales convey coal from a large number of collieries to the state railway and the coal port of Hexham. Their main lines are about 25 and 50 km (15 and 30 miles) long respectively, but at various times the colliery branches have reached more than double this. Their motive power for many years was large 2–8–0 tender locomotives which had at one time worked on British main lines.

In more recent years railways have been built to convey coal direct to power stations. In the Spanish province of Teruel, massive 4–8–4 tank locomotives haul 1,000 tonne trains over 50 hilly kilometres (31 miles) from the lignite mines at Andorra to the power station at Escatron on the river Ebro. Similar large-scale operations exist in the brown coal area south of Cologne in West Germany. These lines are electrified and trains up to 2,000 tonnes are handled. Another very

recent example is the Black Mesa & Lake Powell Railroad in Arizona, an electrified line 125 km (78 miles) long equipped with the latest in bulk mineral railway technology. Two 6,000 hp locomotives haul trains of over 8,000 tonnes to the generating station on Lake Powell. Ultimately planned to carry 17,000 tonnes daily, it was designed for fully-automatic unmanned operation, but teething troubles dictate a two-man crew on each train for the time being.

Even more impressive, because they are achieved by steam engines on the narrow gauge of 750 mm (2 ft 5½ in), are the feats of the Rio Turbio Railway in the far south of Argentina. The twenty 2–10–2 locomotives built in Japan in 1956 and 1963 haul coal trains of 1,700 tonnes unassisted for 260 km (162 miles) to the Atlantic port of Rio Gallegos.

Other mineral railways

Another reason for early railways was iron ore, a mineral which later became a prolific source of industrial railways. Long railways in West Africa, some of recent construction, connect the mines of the remote interior with the sea. Likewise the mines of Australia supply iron ore to Japanese steelworks via modern railways using the latest equipment.

Spain was once rich in narrow-gauge iron ore railways. The lines around Bilbao were anything up to 23 km (14 miles) long and were worked with British equipment until all were closed in the late-1960s. On the Mediterranean coast the metre-gauge Sierra Menera was the longest industrial railway in Europe, 205 km (128 miles) from the mines at Ojos Negros to Sagunto steelworks, a journey of 9¾ hours. Big engines were the rule, sixteen 4–8–0s at first, later joined by Mallets and Beyer-Garratts. Diesels appeared in 1964 but the line closed not long afterwards when traffic was diverted to the parallel Spanish National Railways line. Two copper companies in the south of Spain still operate 80 km (50 mile) railways with diesel locomotives. The 1,067 mm (3 ft 6 in) gauge Rio Tinto line had a roster of over 100 steam engines at one time and still boasts the biggest locomotive shed on a European industrial

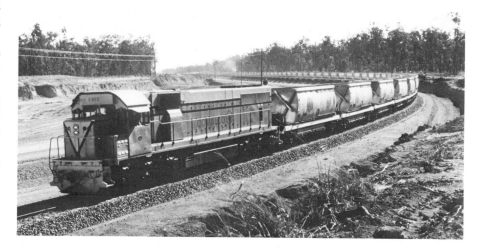

railway. The Tharsis line, also, running to the port of Huelva, has the unusual gauge of 1,219 mm (4 ft). Over the border in Portugal the copper and manganese mines at São Domingos were connected to the River Guadiana by a 17 km (10½ mile) 1,067 mm gauge line using exclusively British equipment, some of it quite primitive. Locomotives built in 1865 were still shunting at the port of Pomarao when the mine closed 100 years later.

The gold mines of the Transvaal vie with the collieries as operators of big steam power. Beyer-Garratts jostle with 4–8–2 tanks on the standard South African gauge of 1,067 mm. Minerals the world over have their railways – phosphates in North Africa and the Pacific Islands, platinum in South Africa, copper in Zaire, chrome in Rhodesia and bauxite in West Africa.

Quarries

Quarries of all types, particularly chalk and granite, had railways unless they were very small. Usually narrow gauge within the quarry itself from the working face to the crushing, grading or processing plant, they were then connected to the main line by either narrow or, more usually, standard-gauge tracks. The larger quarries used standard gauge to the working face because of the size of stone or the quantities to be handled. Although a handful survive, most quarry internal railways have been replaced by dumper trucks or

Above: Modern industrial railway. Diesel-hauled bauxite train of high-capacity rapid-discharge wagons on the 18 km (11¼ mile) Comalco Railway at Weipa in the Cape York Peninsula, Northern Queensland.

Below: A Hunslet 0-6-0T heads a train of slate away from Dinorwic Quarries on the Padarn Railway in North Wales. To avoid transhipment the 580mm (1ft 10¾in) gauge quarry wagons were carried over the 1,219mm (4ft 0in) gauge to the port on transporter wagons. The 12·9 km (8 mile) long railway lasted from 1824 to 1961.

conveyor belts. Many quarries despatch their product by rail, however, so have retained their external rail connections. Indeed, railways themselves are among the principal customers of granite quarries, for track ballast. Quarry railways have experienced something of a revival in recent years in heavily-populated Western European countries where growing environmental consciousness has forced this sort of traffic away from road and back onto rail for its trunk haul.

Like coal and other minerals, some quarry railways transport their product direct to consuming plant – limestone to steelworks, chalk to cement works, and so on, with quite long hauls in some cases. An interesting variation is the railway taking stone to a breakwater to maintain the sea defences.

Cement works

Transport economics dictate the location of cement works adjacent to a chalk quarry, while coal is brought in from elsewhere. Cement works railways perform two main functions, therefore, and are operated as separate systems. Sometimes, as at Dunstable in England, they are not physically connected, although of the same gauge. The internal railway, often quite primitive in equipment, brings chalk from quarry to works, and is often narrow gauge. The main-line connection brings in coal and takes out the finished product. In many cases the quarry section has been replaced by a non-rail movement, but some quite long railways still survive. An Indian works uses 1,676 mm (5 ft 6 in) gauge custom-built tender locomotives on its quarry haul. The cement works at Perus, near Sao Paulo in Brazil, has a 600 mm (2 ft 11⅜ in) gauge railway with no less than 16 steam locomotives.

Sandpits

Before development of dumpers and long-distance conveyor belts, an essential part of the equipment at nearly all sand and gravel pits was a 600 mm gauge railway over which small diesel locomotives pulled trains of tiny tipper wagons (known as skips) from the workings to the washing and screening plants. The tracks were basically portable, although the layout usually included a more or less permanent 'main' line. Where such railways have survived there is usually a special reason – one near Canterbury runs across a narrow causeway through a swampy nature reserve. This causeway could probably not withstand the punishing effect of a continuous procession of loaded dumper trucks.

The numerous sandpits near Leighton Buzzard in England could muster a fleet of small diesel locomotives running into three figures, and were connected with each other and with the main-line railway by an 8 km long, 600 mm gauge light railway. Another unique railway ran until 1967 in Upper Silesia, that part of Germany which became Poland after 1945. It carried sand to collieries at Gleiwitz, where it was used for filling-in old mine workings to prevent subsidence. This called for as much as 5 million tonnes of sand a year, moving in 1000 tonne

Above: Gasworks railways are now a thing of the past. British-built Hudswell Clarke 0-4-0ST propels coal wagons to the top of the retort house at Østre Gasworks, Copenhagen, in April 1961.

trains over the 23 km (14 mile) line. Massive power was necessary, and the 136 tonne 2–10–2 tank locomotives were the biggest non-articulated locomotives in Europe, if not the world.

Brickworks

At one time it would have been difficult to find a brickworks without a railway to carry clay from the pit. This often included a cable-worked incline from the pit bottom up to the kilns. Many were entirely cable-worked even on the level pit floor. Some were short – just a wagon or two propelled by hand. The commonest, and there must have been thousands of them throughout the world, had a haul of about one kilometre from the foot of the incline to the working face, and up to half-a-dozen small diesel locomotives on 600 mm gauge track.

Some were quite fascinating, such as that at Volos in Greece, where, until closure a few years ago, two old steam engines brought the clay a kilometre or so over this 600 mm gauge line, which included a level crossing over one of the main roads on the outskirts of the town.

Many smaller brickworks became uneconomic and have closed, while others now use conveyor belts in place of their railways, but there are many brickworks railways still working, particularly in Holland, Germany and Switzerland.

Below: Hohenzollern-built 0-4-0T raises the echoes at Esch-Belval steelworks, Luxembourg, in September 1972 as it sets out for the slag-bank with a train of slag ladles.

Steelworks

Virtually all steelworks, including the most modern, employ railways, both for raw materials and finished products and for internal transport within the works complex. Concentration into fewer and bigger works has resulted in some quite massive railway systems with large locomotive fleets. Some of the operations are quite specialized, such as slag disposal. A steam locomotive pushing enormous slag ladles up a tip and then the tipping of the molten slag, is an unforgettable sight and sound, especially at night. Very few steelworks still use steam locomotives and onerous conditions and continuous duty have given rise to a particular breed of robust diesels, which even so have a relatively short life. A steelworks in the Saar still uses narrow-gauge steam locomotives on slag disposal, while Bilbao (Spain), and Judenburg and Donawitz (Austria) still have extensive narrow-gauge internal systems worked by steam at the time of writing, although their days are most certainly numbered. Two or three steelworks in India still operate fleets of steam locomotives.

Gas works

Manufacture of town gas from coal has been largely replaced by natural gas, but at one time every town of any size had its municipal gasworks, with sidings on which one or two small tank engines shunted coal wagons. The largest gasworks in the world, at Beckton, London, had a railway to match. As recently as the late 1950s this works, with its associated by-products plant, had over 50 steam locomotives operating an elaborate internal system. Several of Glasgow's works had narrow-gauge railways running right under the retort houses to remove coke, employing what must have been the smallest serious steam locomotives ever built. There were other examples in Rotterdam and at Piraeus near Athens. One of the Paris works had a steeply-graded line and used massive Mallet articulated locomotives.

Power stations

A large proportion of the coal mined today is used in power stations and much of it passes by rail. Many power stations therefore have extensive sidings for the reception of coal (and oil); many of them are electrified. They have also been frequent users of fireless steam locomotives, with many still at work, notably in Germany. Power stations have also retained traditional coalfired steam locomotives long after other industries. In Britain the second biggest operator of steam locomotives in 1976 (after the National Coal Board) is the Central Electricity Generating Board. Other steam users are power stations in Washington (USA), Warsaw, Moscow and Rosherville (Johannesburg), but there are many others.

Agriculture and Forestry

The sugar beet factories of the northern hemisphere use rail transport extensively and most have railways for exchange of traffic with the main lines. Virtually every country in Europe and North America has examples. Some countries have gone in for networks of narrow-gauge rail-

Above: A 70-year-old Krauss 0-4-0T hauls the molten slag away from the blast furnaces on the 785mm (2ft 7in) gauge internal system at Völklingen steelworks, Saar, Germany, in 1972.

ways radiating out from the factory direct into the growing areas. Such lines were once common in northern France, often using surplus railway equipment left behind after the first world war, but they have all gone now. Denmark still has some, now diesel-operated, particularly on the island of Lolland, but Poland retains an extensive network. The flat countryside between Warsaw and the German frontier is covered with hundreds of kilometres of 600 or 750 mm gauge track which lies dormant for nine months of the year and suddenly springs to life about the end of September. Scores of little green steam locos venture forth anything up to 45 km (28 miles) from the factories to gather in beet from the fields. After three months of feverish activity they hibernate again until the following September.

In the USA, the biggest operator of non-preserved steam locomotives is probably Great Western Sugar. There are at least five factories in Colorado which still use steam locomotives during the season.

Cane sugar and narrow-gauge railways are almost synonymous. Although beginning to succumb to road transport (the Natal lines of South Africa were the first to go), they are still a rich source of enjoyment for the steam enthusiast. The two main islands of Fiji once had 750 km (470 miles) of 610 mm (2 ft) gauge sugar railways mustering 90 locomotives, including the 465 km (290 miles) Rarawai-Kavanangasau line with its free passenger train. The surviving lines are mostly diesel-operated now, as are the lines in Queensland, but steam reigns supreme in the canefields of Brazil and the Philippines, while the finest system of all must be that at Sena in Mozambique, now alas inaccessible to Western visitors.

In the Indonesian island of Java there are over 50 sugar factories, with an estimated 5,000 km (3,100 miles) of 600 and 700 mm gauge railway operating nearly 500 steam and over 100 diesel locomotives. There were at one time many kilometres of cane railways in Cuba. They are probably still working – we shall see when the country is again opened to tourists.

The forestry railways of the world are diverse in character, equipment and operating practice. The USA had hundreds of miles, notably in Pennsylvania. In their early days some used wooden rails made by sawing tree trunks down the middle, and laying them end-to-end with curved side uppermost to guide double-flanged wheels on locomotives and wagons. A whole range of steam locomotives was evolved specially for lumber work. The Shay-geared locomotives combined tremendous power with slow speed and a low axleload for poor-quality light track. They were built in the USA for logging lines throughout the globe, and some are still at work in Formosa and the Philippines.

The principle was the same everywhere, a network of lines radiating from a central sawmill deep into the surrounding forest. Several such railways are still in use in eastern Poland close to the Russian frontier, totalling hundreds of kilometres, and there are almost certainly vast

systems in Russia. New Zealand had a number but they have all gone now. Pakistan has the Changa Manga forest railway which, on Sundays, runs passenger excursions into the forest for picnic parties.

Before the development of road transport, the eastern counties of England had their potato railways. In the Gezira area of Sudan there are many miles of 762 mm (2 ft 6 in) gauge railways serving the cotton fields. The famous Edaville Railroad in the USA state of Maine is operated as a tourist attraction, but was first conceived to serve the owner's cranberry bogs.

South-East Asia is the best place to look for plantation railways. Vast numbers of diesel locomotives were built in England for the rubber plantations of Malaya, while in northern Sumatra there are several lines serving palm oil plantations, for one of which there emerged from Hunslet's Leeds works in 1971 the last serious steam locomotive to be built in the British Isles.

One area in which railways are definitely not on the way out is the peat industry. In various parts of Britain and Germany peat is gathered for agricultural purposes and lightly-laid narrow-gauge railways are the only sensible way to transport peat to the milling and packing sheds. The waterlogged moors cannot, especially in winter, support the weight of tractors. In Ireland it is a major natural resource and the industry extends to all parts of the country. It is highly-mechanised and a major transport operation; peat is the fuel for four power stations. There are about 20 separate systems, some feeding peat direct to the power stations. Mostly 914 mm (3 ft) gauge, they total several hundred miles of track and employ almost 300 diesel locomotives.

Miscellaneous railways

We have covered the major industries using railways, but the list goes on and on. Factory estates often have railways linking the various tenant factories with main lines – Trafford Park (Manchester), Graz (Austria), Venice, Neuss (Germany) and Copenhagen are examples, while the

Left: Rotary coal tipplers turn wagons completely upside-down to discharge their load. This example is at Rio Gallegos on the Rio Turbio Railway in Argentina.

Far right: The Austrian forestry railways were as attractive as any in Europe. Two locomotives built by Krauss for the Austrian military railways haul a light load on the 600mm (1ft 11½in) gauge Lanckoransky'sche Waldbahnen at Steinhaus.

Below: A Hudswell Clarke 0-6-0ST poses with its crew on the grass-grown tracks of the Wissington Light Railway, which collected sugar beet from the fields of the English Fen district until closure in 1957.

many terminal railroads of the USA undertake the same function.

Major ports and harbours of the world all have (or had) their railways taking wagons to warehouses or alongside ships. The Port of London railways have gone now, but at one time operated 46 steam locomotives on three separate systems. The Manchester Ship Canal railway follows the canal for most of its length between Birkenhead and Manchester, serving factories and docks on the way, and works the Trafford Park Estate line. The great ports of India have enormous railway networks – Bombay and Calcutta are the biggest. The latter still operates more than 30 steam and 20 diesel locomotives, facilities include a port-owned hump marshalling yard for exchange of traffic with Indian Railways. The Italian ports, notably Genoa and Savona, do not work their railways themselves, but employ shunting contractors to do so.

When dealing with collieries and other mines

Methods of traction

we only looked at the surface installations. Virtually all mines use railways underground and they are a complete subject for study in themselves. Pit ponies were the traditional motive power, but diesel locomotives for mine use began to appear in the early 1930s. Where there is no fire hazard, a simple exhaust filter is the main requirement, but a whole range of 'flame proof' locomotives was later produced for use in coal mines. Alternatively, battery-electric locomotives are used, while some mines (mostly drift mines where the railway runs straight into the hillside with no pitshaft) have straight electric locomotives with a relatively low-voltage overhead current supply.

In the past many public works contractors kept a stock of locomotives and railway equipment of a portable nature for use on major contracts, such as transport of materials to site, or removal of spoil. Railway construction itself saw this type of temporary industrial railway, also harbour contracts and even building the big London housing estates between the wars. After the second world war narrow-gauge railways were used to clear the rubble from bomb-damaged German cities prior to reconstruction. Major dam and reservoir construction gave rise to a number of quite long railways in Britain and India, and some remained in use after completion of the works for maintenance purposes. Contractors today use quite different equipment, and this type of railway has largely disappeared. However, narrow-gauge railways with battery locomotives are an essential ingredient in all tunnelling contracts.

The earliest industrial railways were worked by horses or mules, sometimes over quite long distances, and horse-worked railways survived in Britain until recent times. A peat railway near Doncaster was still using horses in the early 1960s. The sugar cane railways of the Philippines use horses to work wagons over temporary tracks into the fields themselves, and there may be other examples.

To all intents and purposes, however, horses ceased to be a serious means of power with the advent of the steam locomotive in the early 1800's (pit ponies excepted). All the early steam locomotives were built for industrial railways, from the first at Penydarren in 1804, built by Trevithick. Blenkinsop built one in 1811 for Middleton colliery, Leeds, and Hedley followed with several for collieries in north-east England. The oldest locomotives still in existence – *Puffing Billy* and *Wylam Dilly* – were built by Hedley for Wylam colliery in 1813. It was not till 1814 that the famous Stephensons built their first locomotive for Killingworth colliery, and there were many steam locomotives in industrial service before the opening of the Stockton & Darlington Railway in 1825.

Just 100 years later, industrial railways were the first to experiment with internal combustion. The very first locomotives powered in this way appeared in the late 1890s and a number had been tried out by 1914, but it was the first world war which gave a much-needed boost to locomotive

Left: Andrew Barclay supplied many fireless locomotives for use in British paper mills. One is seen here on the Thames pier of Gravesend Paper Mills, Kent, in July 1975.

Below: An Australian-built diesel locomotive at work on a narrow gauge sugar cane railway in Queensland.

Bottom: Built for army use in the 1939–1945 War, many of the Austerity 0-6-0ST later worked for British collieries. One approaches the central washery from St. John's Colliery on the Maesteg system in South Wales in March 1973.

development. Both sides produced and perfected petrol-engined locomotives of 600 mm gauge for the trench tramways of France and Belgium. Development of petrol, and later diesel locomotives proceeded during the 1920s by a number of builders in Britain, America, Germany and France. They were mostly small machines for narrow-gauge use, or limited standard-gauge shunting, and it was only during the 1930s that the diesel locomotive became a serious competitor to steam in industrial service. Since 1950 steam has steadily declined in most countries of the world, with its almost total elimination in industrial use in North America and some countries of Western Europe.

Another source of power appeared a little earlier than oil – electricity. This has never been very popular for industrial railways due to the high cost of the fixed equipment, but in appropriate circumstances they were quick to adopt it. A colliery system at South Shields near Newcastle was electrically-worked by 1908, and other obvious candidates, such as power stations, followed. Where traffic density justifies the cost of installation, or where the company produces its own electricity, it is generally used. Examples are steelworks in Luxembourg and France, colliery systems in the Ruhr, copper mines in Zaire, gold mines in South Africa, and anywhere where the railway runs underground for any appreciable distance.

Another application of electric power is the battery locomotive, particularly useful for work inside buildings where smoke or fumes are undesirable. Its use is limited, however, to low-powered locomotives for relatively light work.

The steam locomotive is a versatile machine and can burn many things in its firebox. Other than coal and oil, any locally-available fuel has been used. Wood burners are common, especially on logging lines. Peat, sugar-cane waste, and palm husks have all fueled steam locos.

A variant of steam traction only found on industrial railways is the fireless locomotive, charged with high-pressure steam from a works steam main. It is particularly suitable for factories with a fire hazard, or where plenty of steam is available as part of the industrial process. From early beginnings in Switzerland about 1900, the idea was perfected for use in munitions factories during the first world war. Paper mills and chemical works are large users, also power stations and oil refineries and storage depots. Fireless locos are cheap to run and easy on maintenance, with a long life. Many are still in service in the USA and Britain, while the Germans, Swiss and Austrians are particularly fond of them, one being built for a refinery near Vienna as recently as 1973. Many have been observed at power stations east of the Iron Curtain.

The locomotive industry

The early locomotive requirements of main lines and industrial railways were similar, and manufacturers supplied both markets, but from the middle of the 19th century a locomotive industry began to emerge specifically to meet the needs of industrial railways. Distinctive industrial types began to appear. The four- or six-coupled saddle tank was almost universal in Britain, while continental builders produced larger six- and eight-coupled side tanks of simple and sturdy design. The well tank (water tank between the frames) was popular in Germany. Locomotives with vertical boilers were common in Belgium. The USA also favoured saddle tanks, although bigger than the British version, but the Americans tended to think bigger and many of their industrial locomotives were large tender machines.

The older industrial countries dominated the world market – Britain, Germany and the USA in particular, although other European countries built for their home market and their colonies. Some small firms produced their own distinctive types for a particular local market, such as the

DeWinton vertical boiler locomotives for the North Wales slate quarries. Bundaberg Foundry built steam locomotives exclusively for the Queensland sugar railways. But these were exceptions. Names like Hawthorn Leslie, Henschel, Barclay, Bagnall, Krauss, Baldwin, Porter, Hunslet and Orenstein & Koppel became famous throughout the world as builders of industrial locomotives, leaving others to concentrate on larger machines for the main-line railways.

In later years attempts were made to compete with diesel development. Such ideas as the Sentinel-geared steam locomotive were relatively successful and found temporary favour where the work was not too arduous.

Meanwhile the diesel-locomotive industry was developing between the wars and many of the successful diesel builders had never produced a steam engine. New names like Ruston, Deutz, General Motors, and Moyse were leading the field, although some steam builders, like Henschel and Hunslet, made a successful transition and are still in business today. The other steam builders slowly but surely ceased production as demand tailed away.

Another major source of steam locomotives for industrial service was the second-hand main-line market. Standardization or changed traffic requirements have frequently led to the premature withdrawal of locomotives with years of life left in them. This applies to diesel as well as steam locomotives. Many an industrial railway engineer with an eye for a bargain has obtained his locomotives this way. Some English collieries relied entirely on second-hand main-line shunting locomotives, while when the time came to replace steam on the Corby iron ore system, a whole fleet of prematurely withdrawn diesels was purchased from British Railways. The long rambling line owned by Zambesi Sawmills in Zambia was powered entirely by elderly steam locomotives that had been pensioned off by Rhodesia Railways.

Second-hand military equipment was also a rich source of industrial railway equipment after the two world wars. Steam locomotives built in large numbers by the Germans and Americans for the trench tramways gravitated after the war to sugar beet and forestry lines and some turned up in the most unlikely places. The German *Feldbahn* type was particularly successful, and at 60 years of age they still work in the forests of eastern Poland and, of all places, the sugar-cane estates of Mozambique. Their American counterparts, built by Baldwin, turned up in Greece, South America, and France. One even went to a Queensland sugar railway via a slate quarry in North Wales, and two are still working at an Indian colliery.

After the second world war, British War Department saddle tanks were nearly all sold into industrial service and some are working at British collieries to this day. The Dutch collieries also used them. The American version, with side tanks, also found its way into European industrial service, such as in Holland and Jugoslavia.

Rolling stock

Many industrial railways own no wagons. If their function is exchange of traffic with main-line railways, common-user railway-owned wagons are handled. On the other hand many firms own their own wagons which carry their traffic over main lines to their customers. Many standard-gauge railways rely on second-hand equipment which is quite fit for use at the slow speeds encountered, long after it has been discarded by the public railways which have to maintain much higher standards. Wagons built for industrial service generally follow main-line practice, but there are specialized types. Quarry lines require wagons with easy discharge – either tipping bodies, or bottom door. Steelworks have a whole range of specialized wagons – slag ladles, low-floored flat wagons for carriage of hot ingots and massive torpedo wagons carrying 100 tonnes of molten steel gross 250 tonnes on six bogies. Timber railways use skeletal wagons or even simply put a bogie under each end of the log and tow it that way. There are transporter wagons for carrying narrow-gauge wagons over standard-gauge tracks and vice versa. Whatever specialized job an industrial railway does, a wagon has been designed for it.

Recent developments

In recent years industrial railways have experimented with novel methods of propulsion. In Britain, the NCB unsuccessfully tried out an electro-gyro locomotive and another which ran on methane gas. But the real goal of industrial railway engineers is the fully-automatic railway. Remote control (which is not the same thing) has been successfully applied for years. Indeed, self-acting inclines, where the descending loaded wagons pull up the ascending empties, date from the earliest days in North Wales and north-east England, and all cable-worked railways are remote controlled by definition. The Post Office tube railway runs for 10 km (6½ miles) under the streets of London, and its driverless trains have carried the mails over its 600 mm gauge tracks at more than 50 km/h (35 mph) without serious incident since 1927. It is controlled entirely from switch cabins along the route.

Radio control is a more recent step. It is still in

Above: A flameproof diesel locomotive waits at a junction underground at Lea Hall Colliery, Warwickshire, England.

Above right: Turon Colliery in Asturias had a narrow gauge railway typical of Northern Spain. The 600 mm (1 ft 11½ in) gauge *Turon 3* was built by Jung in 1914.

Below right: A locomotive of the electrified railway at Kearsley Power Station, near Manchester, England.

Below left: The Guinness Brewery railway in Dublin, Ireland.

its infancy, but has been applied to diesel locomotives at a Dutch steelworks, a Belgian colliery and a nuclear power station in Scotland, and there must be other examples. The automatic mineral railway has made its appearance in the USA with the Carol Lake and Muskingham, and the Climax Molybdenum's Henderson project in Colorado, which uses techniques previously applied successfully at a Polish coal mine.

Since the invention of the petrol engine, road transport has become more suitable for many of the tasks industrial railways used to perform. Other competitors, such as the conveyor belt, have been developed. Heavy industries have regrouped into fewer larger plants. Mines and quarries have become worked out.

The survival of traditional industrial railways reflects the degree of development of individual countries and also the survival of steam locomotives. The disappearance of the colliery and iron ore networks in northern Spain has been the direct result of the improvement in the country's economy in the last 20 years. Sugar-cane railways illustrate this to a marked degree. They have all but disappeared in South Africa; they remain, but are diesel worked, in Fiji; they are still steam worked in Indonesia and Brazil, representing the three stages in the transition.

Throughout the world industrial railways are still performing yeoman service for industries of all types, and will continue to do so for many years. New specialized mineral railways are taking the place of the old systems, and are proving that rail is still the best means of land transport for bulk commodities over long distances.

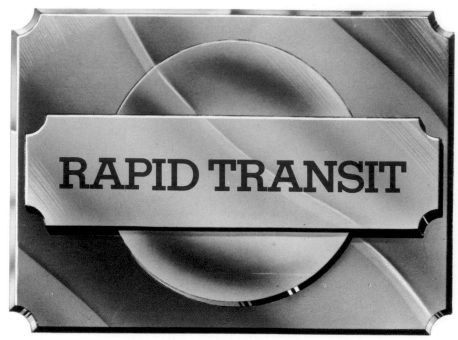

The term 'rapid transit' is self-explanatory, but, over the years and especially in the USA, it has come to have the specialized meaning of swift movement in towns and cities. Traffic conditions in modern cities make automobile movement anything but swift, so it is recognized that a means of rapid transit needs its own reserved track. This in turn has meant that until very recently rapid transit was always rail transit and the underground railways and metros of the world were its rapid transit systems. In the older cities and many of the younger ones this is still true, but it is now realized that buses or trains of tramcars on reserved tracks can also give a rapid transit type of service, as could several of the monorails and other less orthodox means of transit if they had tracks to themselves.

Full-scale rapid transit railways are expensive, especially when they are under the ground or (to a lesser extent) on elevated structures, so the tendency is to put the tracks underground in the centre of cities and bring them to the surface or on to elevated structures in the suburbs as soon as traffic conditions allow this to be done without feeling the effects of congestion. There is a tendency, especially in Germany, to put tramways underground in city centres, designing the tunnels to be suitable, if traffic increases sufficiently, for 'heavy' or full-scale rapid transit with trains at a later date. The period with tram operation is the 'pre-metro' phase, with the 'metro' itself following when required. Experience shows that a well-designed tramway can carry about half the traffic which can be handled by a full-scale rapid transit system. The tramway is enjoying a renaissance in the USA at present under the name of 'Light Rail Transit' (LRT), and in some cases it is becoming increasingly difficult to differentiate between rapid transit and light rail transit, especially when the latter has its own tunnels or reserved track. Once, only cities of more than a million people could afford to build a full rapid transit system, but there are now exceptions.

One aspect of rapid transit, the importance of which is only now being fully understood, is the need to provide swift and easy interchange at stations between rapid transit lines themselves and with complementary means of transport such as buses and cars. Most rapid transit tunnels are just below the surface (often under main streets) and built by digging a deep trench for the railway and then roofing it over and restoring the street above. Such lines can be reached easily by short flights of steps, but some cities, especially London, also have deep lines in tunnels bored with a cylindrical tunnelling shield. Deep 'tube' lines of this type need elevators (lifts) or escalators to get people to or from the platforms as quickly as possible. There is no point in providing a two-minute journey between stations if the passenger has to spend three minutes at each end getting down from, and back to, street level. Unless underground lines always follow the streets above, the deep foundations of modern high-rise buildings can make deep tunnels essential.

Right: Rush hour, it seems, never changes! In this Doré print of 1875, workers are crowding to board the train. The engine was typical of the tank engine types used on the underground system for some years. They had no cab; the driver was protected only by a weather board.

Top left: Metropolitan and Bakerloo Line trains stand at Wembley Park, The train in the foreground is one of the Metropolitan 'A' stock 'silver' trains.

Two new developments are 'people movers' and 'personal rapid transit' (PRT). Both share similar characteristics in that they would use reserved tracks in the busiest areas of cities. In practice this would normally be a track supported by concrete pillars above normal traffic heights. The pillars would usually be along the pavement or sidewalk edge with the track either over the pavement or cantilevered out over the road. People movers correspond to buses and PRT to a taxi system. Both would be driverless and highly automated.

Great Britain

London was the first city in the world to have an underground or rapid transit railway. It was built for the same reason that such lines are being built today – to avoid street congestion. This first line, 6 km (3.75 miles) long and opened on January 10, 1863, was worked by steam trains and linked the Great Western Railway at Paddington with Farringdon Street on the edge of the City, then London's principal business area. There were five intermediate stations, two of which served the main line stations of Euston and King's Cross. Trials with a fireless locomotive were unsuccessful and in the event ordinary steam locomotives,

Above: The overhead monorail at Wuppertal-Sonnborn Station on the Schwebebahn in West Germany.

Below left: An artist's impression of the interior of the station hall and concourse of King's Cross, London.

Above: A Bakerloo line train pulls away from Neasden on the London Transport underground system.

fitted with equipment to condense the exhaust steam, were used without any untoward trouble from fumes. The trains were very comfortable for their day and the service was an immediate success. In the first six months it was used by an average of 26,500 passengers a day. This early line was built by the Metropolitan Railway, and from that name the term 'metro' has spread as a name for underground railways all over the world.

The Metropolitan Railway was built largely on the trenching system already mentioned, usually known now as 'cut-and-cover'. More cut-and-cover lines were added over the years by the Metropolitan, the Metropolitan District, and other companies and these were also linked to surface sections. One important result was incorporation of parts of these lines into a 'circle' line which encloses most of central London and links nearly all the main line stations. At one stage, through a quirk of railway history, the Metropolitan reached out into the Buckinghamshire countryside as far as Verney Junction and Brill, both 80.5 km (50 miles) from London, but the service now ends at Amersham and Chesham, 38.6 km (24 miles) and 46.7 km (29 miles) respectively from London. Nevertheless, this is still much further than one would expect from a normal rapid transit railway. Electrification of the 'sub-surface' lines began at the turn of the century, the first electric service starting in 1903.

London is also the only city in the world to have an extensive network of deep-level 'tube' lines. The early tube lines were also built by private companies and owe their existence to the invention of the tunnelling shield by Sir Marc Brunel in 1818 and its adaptation and improvement by Peter William Barlow and his pupil James Henry Greathead from 1862 onwards to make it eminently suitable for building deep tube railways. A second factor was the existence under much of London of a bed of blue clay, an ideal tunnelling medium because the surface cut by the tunnelling shield will support itself long enough to allow rings made up of cast iron (or concrete) segments to be placed in position as a permanent support. The first tube line was the City & South London Railway, opened on

December 18, 1890. All tube railways were electrified from the beginning. There are 119 km (74 miles) of railway in deep-level tubes in London, many of the lines rising to the surface in the suburbs.

Although there had been a good deal of co-operation between London's underground railways before that, they were formally brought together in 1933 by an act of parliament setting up the London Passenger Transport Board. This took over responsibility for all public transport in the capital except main line railways and taxicabs, and the position has been consolidated by later acts. The present London Transport Executive has 381 km (237 miles) of railway, collectively known as the 'underground' even though only 156 km (97 miles) are actually in tunnel. This figure includes both sub-surface and tube lines which between them give a dense network of communications in central London with radial routes stretching out to the north, east and west. Mainly because of the number of suburban railways in the south, the underground does not penetrate so deeply into south London although one tube line runs to Morden, 16 km (10 miles) from London.

Underground trains also run over some British Railways lines, bringing the number of miles worked by London Transport's trains to 408.8 km (254 miles). One example is the service to Wimbledon worked by District line trains over British Rail Southern Region tracks.

There are two main types of underground trains in London. Those which run on the sub-surface lines have dimensions similar to those of main-line railways, but the tube trains have to run in tunnels of roughly 3,666 mm (12 ft) diameter and are much smaller in profile, though not in capacity. All trains are electric. Most of the modern rolling stock has bodywork of unpainted aluminium alloy. They serve 278 stations, closely spaced in the city centre but farther apart in the suburbs. Including stops, the average speed is 32.8 km/h (20.4 mph). On an average weekday some two million passengers are carried in London Transport's 4,400 cars.

Below: A prototype rapid transit car, destined for the Tyneside 'Metro' system, is shown here on the test track.

Right: Display console, track diagram and signal switches in the control room of a London Transport signal box.

London has eight underground lines. The Metropolitan 88.5 km (55 miles), District 64.4 km (40 miles), and Circle 21 km (13 miles) are sub-surface, while the Bakerloo 29 km (18 miles), Central 83.7 km (52 miles), Northern 57.9 km (36 miles), Piccadilly 64.4 km (40 miles) and Victoria 22.5 km (14 miles) are all tube lines. Some of these lines use parallel or common tracks for parts of their lengths.

The Victoria line, begun in 1962 and opened throughout from Walthamstow to Victoria in 1969 (with an extension to Brixton opened in 1971) was at that time the most highly-automated and technically-advanced underground railway in the world and the first on such a scale to have all trains automatically driven. A new line, the Fleet, is under construction to run from north to east London. The first stage will take over the Stanmore to Baker Street branch of the existing Bakerloo line and run to a new combined station at Charing Cross. The second stage, to Fenchurch Street, has parliamentary approval but the final eastern destination had not been decided at the time of writing. Another new line, the River, is under consideration to break off from the Fleet line and serve the dockland areas of London. A new south-west to north-east route which would incorporate some existing lines in its outer sections is also under consideration. The Piccadilly line is being extended westwards to Heathrow airport and is expected to begin serving the airport terminals in 1977.

London has another short tube line. This is the Waterloo & City line which is operated by British Railways and runs from Waterloo to the Bank, a distance of 2.4 km (1.5 miles), without intermediate stations. It was opened in 1898.

The only other city in the British Isles with a true underground railway is Glasgow, where the 10.46 km (6.5 miles) circular route is entirely underground and the only way to take a train out for maintenance is to lift it through the roof of the tunnel. The line was built partly by shield, using compressed air to keep water out, partly without a shield but in compressed air, and partly by cut-and-cover. The greatest depth to the top of the tunnel is 35 m (115 ft) and the least only 2,134 mm (7 ft). It passes under the river Clyde at

two points. There are twin 3,353 mm (11 ft) diameter tunnels without connections between them and when the line opened in 1896 trains were hauled by cable. Glasgow Corporation purchased the railway, known as the Glasgow Subway, in 1923 and in 1935 it was electrified while still at work under cable haulage. The two-car 1,219 mm (4 ft) gauge trains were adapted for electric traction. There is a three-minute service and the circuit is covered in 28 minutes.

One of the difficulties with this line, apart from the very old rolling stock, is that few of the 15 stations are conveniently placed for interchange traffic. Under a £12 million modernization plan, which will include new rolling stock and new track, the Greater Glasgow Passenger Transport Executive, now responsible for the Subway, intends that 11 of these stations shall become useful interchange points with cars, buses, or trains, and escalators are to be provided at the busier stations. Before modernization began, traffic on the line amounted to 30 to 35 million passengers a year.

There is another underground railway system in Merseyside, but this is really part of British Railways' electrified network in the area. It began with construction of a line by the Mersey Railway to link Liverpool and Birkenhead by tunnel under the river Mersey. The line opened in 1886 with steam traction and was electrified in 1903. Connection with other lines in 1938 greatly improved the scope of this underground link, and in the early 1970s work began on a two-mile underground loop and a short-link line which will serve three main line stations and give much better interchange facilities in the city centre. These new tunnels are expected to be operational in 1977.

In Manchester, there are proposals for a 3 km (1.9 mile) underground link line with three intermediate stations to link Piccadilly and Victoria main-line stations. Government grants for this work were withheld in 1976, however, and apart from planning work the scheme is at a standstill.

On Tyneside, busy but obsolete British rail tracks will be brought to life again, with some additional underground track and a bridge over

the Tyne, to form a new rapid transit system to serve both banks of the Tyne from Newcastle and Gateshead to the coast, operating on tramway principles. There will also be new stations in the centres of the two towns. The line, about 55.4 km (34.4 miles) in length, will be worked by two-car electric light rail sets locally known as 'super-trams'. There will be 42 stations. The cost, estimated at £65 million in 1973, had soared to perhaps £175 million by late 1976 and there were warnings then that the government share might not, after all, be available on the scale expected.

Recent studies suggest that Dublin could have underground links between existing main-line railways. This would enable stations to be provided to serve the city centre and permit commuter services to two new towns to be built to the west of Dublin.

Europe

The first underground urban railway in Europe opened in Budapest in 1896. It was 4 km (2.5 miles) long and was built instead of a surface tramway with correspondingly closely-spaced stations, only 400 m (0.25 miles) or so apart. This small line was modernized in 1973 and the original rolling stock has at last been retired. Budapest today has one of the most modern rapid transit systems in Europe. The first 7.2 km (4.5 miles) section of the 10.1 km (6.3 mile) east to west line opened on April 4, 1970 and there are plans to extend the system to a total of 65 km (40.4 miles) by the year 2000. The trains are Russian-built and resemble those used on Russian rapid transit lines. Each car has seats for 42 with room for 128

Above: Schlesisches Thor Station on the Berlin U-bahn at the turn of the century.

Right: Modern rolling stock on the Berlin U-bahn, 1973–75.

Below: Tempelhof-bound train on the Berlin underground system.

normal flanged railway wheels mounted inside the rubber wheels; in the event of a puncture the tyre deflates to allow the steel wheel to drop down on to the rail underneath so that the train can proceed in safety. At turnouts, also, the concrete tracks descend so that the steel wheels come into play and the change of route is accomplished using normal points or switches.

Paris also has a fast east-west line which is the first stage of a 'Regional Metro', and the existing Sceaux line is being extended and developed as the north-south element of this new network, expected to have 92 km (57 miles) of track by 1978.

Two other metro systems are being built in France. A two-line 10.3 km (6.4 miles) rubber-tyred system for Lyons should start operation in 1978 and an 8.8 km (5.5 mile) nine-station line for Marseilles, also using rubber-tyred stock, should be ready by 1977.

Berlin's first underground rapid transit railway, 5 km (3 miles) long, opened between the Potsdamer Platz and Stralauer Tor on February 18, 1902. The system grew into a close-knit and effective network which had the distinction, from 1929, of being one of the first to serve an airport – Tempelhof. The division of Berlin after the war also divided the rapid transit system and the two sections (with minor exceptions) are now operated independently. There have been considerable extensions and improvements in West Berlin, which now has 116 km (72 miles) of track and 100 stations, and there are also improvements in East Berlin, with 25.5 km (15.8 miles) of subway.

After Berlin comes the extensive system in Hamburg, (where the first line was opened in 1912) with its 89.9 km (55.9 miles) of route and 79 stations. Like Berlin, Hamburg uses conventional electric trains, as does Munich, where the first 18.7 km (11.6 miles) of a system planned to reach an eventual 100 km (62.1 miles), with 40 km (25 miles) underground, is already in operation.

Germany, in particular, is a country where distinctions between various types of rapid transit

to stand (260 in crush conditions), and is 19.2 m (63 ft) long. There are four pairs of double power-worked doors. All axles are motored with four 88.5 hp motors in each car.

The Paris metro is basically different from most others in that there is a dense concentration of lines in the area once enclosed by the old city walls. This formed the metro boundary for many years after the first line opened on July 19, 1900. In the 1920s the metro began to spread beyond the walls and to take on a somewhat different character, but originally the lines lay just below the street surface and were reached quickly by flights of steps. The metro in those days – and to some extent still – served as an underground tramway and had closely-spaced stations and a single flat fare. Much of the original engineering work was paid for by the city authorities. The greater part of the Paris metro, now 175.3 km (108.9 miles) in length with 165.1 km (102.6 miles) underground, is worked by normal electric stock on standard-gauge track. However, in the postwar period experiments were made with rubber-tyred rolling stock and the whole of Line 11 (Châtelet-Marie des Lilas) was converted to this system by the end of 1957. Several other lines have been converted since, and new metros in Montreal, Mexico City and Santiago all use this type of stock. The cars have bogies fitted with pneumatic tyres. These run on concrete surfaces laid outside normal track and are guided on the special surfaces by horizontally-mounted pneumatic-tyred wheels at each corner of the bogie; these press against guide rails mounted outside the running tracks. The cars still have

Above: An automatic ticket dispenser in service at a surburban (Paris region) station of the SNCF.

Below: SNCF local trains provide urban transport in Monte Carlo.

Left: A shot of the interior of a shuttle service train on the Swiss Federal Railway (Schweizerische Bundersbahn or Chemins de Fer Fédéraux Suisses).

tend to fade. Some underground lines are really sections of tramway being upgraded; there are full-scale underground railways (as already noted); and some cities may have a 'Stadtbahn' (generally worked by trams) or a 'Schnellbahn' (S-Bahn) network operated by the main-line railways. All are capable to a greater or lesser degree of performing rapid transit functions. Cities actively engaged with S-Bahn projects include Stuttgart, Cologne, Hamburg and Frankfurt, though Hamburg and Frankfurt already have underground (U-Bahn) lines and Stuttgart and Cologne intend that sections now open as tramways shall be developed to full U-Bahn standards. Munich also has an S-Bahn, and a comprehensive S-Bahn system is being developed for the Ruhr area. Sub-surface tramways are also in operation and being extended in Bielefeld, Hanover and Nuremberg, which also has about 8.5 km (5.3 miles) of its first 14.2 km (8.8 miles) U-Bahn line in operation.

The USSR was quite late in the field with underground or rapid transit railways, but the first line, opened in Moscow in 1935, rapidly became famous for the grand scale of its architecture and, thanks to lavish use of manpower, its cleanliness and efficiency. Since then the Moscow underground has been under almost continuous expansion and, though not on such an ambitious scale as in 1935, still has excellent stations. The total length is now 161 km (100 miles) with 97 stations, but expansion continues. It is the busiest metro system in the world, carrying nearly 1,850 million passengers a year, more than a third of all passenger movement in the city. Expansion to a network of 320 km (199 miles) is envisaged under the current 25-year plan. There is a very low flat fare of five kopecks. Trains are mainly made up of the standard stock mentioned in connection with Budapest.

Outside Moscow, the largest system is that of Leningrad with 56 km (34.8 miles) of route. There is an immediate construction target of 116 km (72 miles) with 90 stations, to be increased eventually to 240 km (149 miles) and 140 stations. Leningrad has the same type of rolling stock and the same flat fare as Moscow. Other Russian cities with existing metros are

Baku, Kharkov, Kiev, and Tbilisi: lines are also under construction or planned for Dnepropetrovsk, Gorky, Kubichev, Minsk, Novosibirsk, Sverdlovsk, and Tashkent, amongst others.

Vienna opened its first rapid transit line on May 8, 1976, much of it replacing parts of the former Stadtbahn which was worked by trains of trams. By 1978, 13.7 km (8.5 miles) should be in service. The eventual target is a four-line 32.4 km (20 mile) system with 44 stations.

Spain has two main rapid transit systems, in Madrid and Barcelona, but has plans for more in the near future. Madrid opened its first 3.6 km (2.2 mile) line on October 17, 1919. There are now seven lines with a total length of 66 km (41 miles) and the system is being rapidly extended. In Barcelona the network is under more than one control and of two different gauges, but works quite satisfactorily. There are 81.7 km (50.8 miles) of route and here, too, considerable expansion is planned. At the end of 1976 work was about to begin on an 8 km (5 mile) line in Seville. Also in Iberia is a 12 km (7.5 mile) line in Lisbon, the nucleus of an eventual 40 km (25 mile) three-line system.

Italy, too, has two metro systems, the more important being the 26.5 km (16.5 mile) system in Milan, which will eventually reach a length of 51.7 km (32 miles) with 67 stations. The Milan metro authority is helping to design a two-line rapid transit system for Naples which will have 26.2 km (16.3 miles) of route with 39 stations. Italy's first rapid transit line, in Rome, is also being extended. It opened on February 9, 1955 and is 11.3 km (7 miles) long. A second 14.5 km (9 mile) line is being added.

In the north, Stockholm has an important rapid transit system of which the first section opened in 1950. It is now 78 km (48 miles) long with 78 stations. Extensions will bring the number of stations to 97 by 1980.

In Finland, Helsinki is building the first 11 km (6.8 miles) of what will eventually be a 45 km (28 mile) system. The six-car trains will be computer-controlled and the first line should be open by 1981.

Below: One of the new trains, which are gradually replacing the old trams waits at a station on the Stadtbahn, Vienna (Stadtwerke Verkehrsbetriebe).

Holland has a 17 km (10.6 mile) rapid transit line in Rotterdam which gives a useful route under the river Maas, which bisects the port. The first section of a metro for Amsterdam is under construction and may open in mid-1977.

The major cities of Belgium decided some years ago to build subways for use by trams on the pre-metro basis, the tunnels being built to dimensions which would ensure that they could be used by full-scale rapid transit trains at a later date. The first city to convert a line to full metro is Brussels, where on September 20, 1976 train services began between Place Ste-Catherine, Tomberg and Beaulieu on the east-west line. Two services covering 14.3 km (8.9 miles) and seven stations are involved.

There are plans for numbers of other metro systems in Europe. One likely to take shape soon is that designed for Warsaw. After long delays it now seems that the first 7.4 km (4.6 mile) line may be ready for service by 1980 with another 4.4 km (2.7 miles) to follow by 1988 with 23 stations in all. The first 6.7 km (4.2 miles) of the Prague metro opened on May 9, 1974 and plans call for a three-line system to be completed by 1986. Total length will be 32.6 km (20.3 miles) with 40 stations. Long-term plans would add another 92.7 km (57.6 miles) and another 104 stations. Russian-type rolling stock is used.

America

The United States was fairly late in the field with underground railways or 'subways' as they are usually known in the USA, but New York was

Above: A six-car, computer-controlled train of the Helsinki metro system.

Left: The escalator (travelator bande neve) at a new deep-level station in Milan.

Below: Excavations in progress for the new metro system in the centre of Helsinki, Finland. A short trial section is already opened.

early with a rapid transit system of sorts – the elevated railway or 'El', the first short trial line of which was built by its designer, Charles Thompson Harvey, in 1867. The El, with steam traction at first and electric trains later, carried a million passengers a day at one time. Work on the first subway, a cut-and-cover line, did not begin until 1900, but when it opened in 1904 other lines were authorized and already being built. Today the New York City Transit Authority has 371.2 km (230.6 miles) of route, 220.6 km (137.0 miles) of which are in tunnel. It has 461 stations and nearly 6,700 cars, and carries 1,100 million passengers a year. A feature of the New York operation is the provision of multiple tracks, enabling express services to be run without interfering with stopping trains, to and from which passengers can change at selected stations. The system is still expanding and some remaining elevated lines are being replaced by tunnel sections. A new spur is being built to connect Kennedy airport with central Manhattan and a new 17.7 km (11 mile) line is being built to serve most of the east side of Manhattan and the Bronx.

A separate New York subway system is operated by the Port Authority of New York & New Jersey through its Port Authority Trans-Hudson Corporation (PATH), which began with two privately-built tunnels under the Hudson carrying passengers between Manhattan and Hoboken. By 1911 Newark was also being served. The PATH system is 22.4 km (13.9 miles) long and has 13 stations. It carries 40 million passengers a year in its 298 air-conditioned cars.

Chicago also began with an elevated railway, opened in 1892, and its first subway line, the 7.9 km (4.9 mile) State Street line, was not opened until 1943. Although Chicago has 143.1 km (88.9 miles) of rapid transit route only 17.1 km (10.6 miles) are in subway, partly in tube and partly in cut-and-cover construction. This extensive system, with 154 stations, is interesting in that it operates successful 'skip-stop' services. Trains stop at every other station, that is one train stops at stations A, C, E, and G, and the following train at stations B, D, F, and G. The common stop at G is to allow interchange. Chicago was also very early with the idea of running rapid transit lines in the median strip (the strip between lanes running in opposite directions) of motorways. The system has about 1,100 cars, many of them very modern, and carries over 100 million passengers a year. Another unusual feature is a 1,036 m (3,400 ft) long underground platform which runs all the way from Congress Street station to Lake Street station on the State Street line. Access is from many entrances but there are only three stopping points on this long platform.

Philadelphia's rapid transit system is now about 62.8 km (39 miles) in length and has 30.9 km (19.2 miles) in subway. There are two operators, the Port Authority Transit Corporation (PATCO) and the Southeastern Pennsylvania Transportation Authority (SEPTA). The first line, part of the Market Street Elevated and Subway route, was begun in 1903 and opened in 1907. Now there are 65 stations, 53 on the

Top left: A train waits at Center Station on the new Washington subway.

Left: An interior shot of a BART (Bay Area Rapid Transit authority) 72 passenger car with carpeted floors, wide tinted windows, well-upholstered seats, temperature control and a new style of lighting.

Bottom left: A stainless steel car working on the Market-Frankford subway elevated line in Philadelphia. These are 40 per cent lighter than the cars they replace, about one third roomier (56 passengers) and considerably faster (maximum speed 88 km/h; 55 mph).

Above: Chicago Rapid Transit Authority's train, *Ben Franklin*, leaves a downtown station on the Chicago loop.

Below: One of the cars designed for BART (Bay Area Rapid Transit Authority) enters a station at Oakland, California, in 1976.

SEPTA routes and 12 on the 23.3 km (14.5 mile) PATCO line to Lindenwold, which was not opened until 1969. This is a highly-automated line with automatic train operation. It is also a high-speed line – its trains are scheduled to cover the 5.1 km (3.2 miles) between Haddonfield and Ashland stations in 3 minutes, for example. The cars are all air-conditioned. Parking space and easy interchange with private cars appeal to the motorist and 80 per cent of passengers arrive at stations by private car. Tickets are sold and checked by machine in much the same way that automatic fare collection is being adopted by rapid transit lines all over the world. PATCO's stations are unmanned; they do, however, use closed-circuit television surveillance – again a feature of many other modern systems. The SEPTA system works in harmony with commuter lines of the main-line railways and between them they operate a well-organized network covering the whole Philadelphia region, with plans for extensions and improvements, including a link to the International airport.

Boston has a rather smaller rapid transit system with 48 km (29.8 miles) of route, 15 km (9.3 miles) of which are in subway. A tramway subway completed in 1898 was used by Elevated Railway trains between 1901 and 1908, marking the first subway line. About 350 cars are now in use and there are plans to replace all cars used on two lines (about 190 vehicles) with modern stock. Many other improvements are in hand or contemplated, including replacement of remaining overhead sections.

A small but important rapid transit line is that of Cleveland, 30 km (18.6 miles) long with only 0.6 km (0.4 miles) underground. It carries nearly 13 million passengers a year and the first section was opened in 1955. A notable feature is the massive provision for car parking but its claim to fame is that it was the first rapid transit line in the USA to serve a major airport.

One of the most exciting rapid transit railways in the world has been built in the San Francisco Bay area. Exciting because when the Bay Area Rapid Transit District (BART) decided rapid transit was needed it determined to ignore everything already done in the field and to think everything through from first principles, taking advantage of the latest aerospace, computer, and other technology.

After considering monorails, trains, buses, ground effect vehicles, and many other types of transport, rapid transit trains running on two rails came out on top.

The trains were to be capable of high speeds, be attractive and comfortable enough to compete with the private motor car, and every passenger was to have a seat. A 6.4 km (4 mile) underwater immersed tube would carry trains under San Francisco Bay and make it possible to travel between the business centres of Oakland and San Francisco in eight minutes. The system as built is nearly 120.7 km (75 miles) long, with 37 km (23 miles) underground or in tunnel, 43.5 km (27 miles) on the surface, and 40.2 km (25 miles) on elevated structures.

Work began on June 19, 1964 in Concord and by April 12, 1965 a test track to try out the modern methods and techniques proposed was completed and at work. On September 11, 1972 the first 38.6 km (24 mile) section opened. Since then, section after section has opened and the whole line, with all but one of its 34 stations, was open to traffic on September 15, 1974.

The air-conditioned, carpeted trains are operated automatically by a central computer which is designed to run all the trains simultaneously, keeping proper distances between them, bringing them to a stop at stations, opening the doors, closing the doors again and driving away. An on-train attendant monitors the automatic equipment, announces the stations, and can drive the train manually if required. The trains run on track with a gauge of 1,676 mm (5 ft 6 in), and each car is 21.3 m (70 ft) long. Top designed speed is 128 km/h (80 mph) and average speed, including stops, is 67.6 km/h (42 mph). Trains consist of between two and ten cars.

The stations are attractively and individually designed with decorative features worked out by well-known artists. There are special facilities for the handicapped, including ramps for wheelchairs. Passengers buy their tickets from vending machines, obtaining change, if needed, from other machines. The ticket is inserted into a mechanism which opens a gate allowing the passenger onto the platform – often reached by escalators. Passengers can also buy 'stored-fare' tickets from which the fare for a journey is deducted automatically by the gate mechanism at the end of each trip until the whole value of the ticket has been used up.

Largely because it attempted to put so much new technology into a single package, BART has had extensive teething troubles and may not achieve its full operating capacity for some years, but it has taught the whole world a great deal about rapid transit techniques as well as bringing about a revolution in travel habits in San Francisco.

The latest metro to open in the USA is that in Washington DC, where the first 7.4 km (4.6 mile) section, from Rhode Island Avenue to Farragut North, came into service on March 29, 1976. When completed, Washington and the surrounding areas of the District of Columbia and the states of Maryland and Virginia will have 157.2 km (97.7 miles) of rapid transit route, 76 km (47.2 miles) of them underground, 12.8 km (8 miles) on elevated structures and the remaining 68.4 km (42.5 miles) on the surface. There will be 86 stations, 53 of them underground. Construction began on December 9, 1969. As with most modern rapid transit lines, the system is highly automated. The trains are operated by a computer-based control system known as AUTOPOS (Automatic Train Protection, Operation and Supervision) which accelerates the trains away from stations, runs them at the appropriate speeds, brings them to a stop at the next station and opens the doors. It also adjusts train speeds to compensate for delays to trains ahead or make up a gap in service by speeding

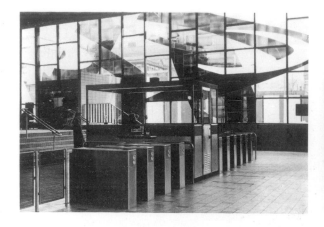

Far left: Passenger entrance hall and ticket barriers at a suburban station on the Montreal Urban Community Transit System.

Near left: Pneumatic-tyred electric train for the Sapparo Subway's east west line, Hokkaido, Japan.

trains up or shortening station stops. The trains themselves are capable of 120 km/h (75 mph) and will maintain an average of 56 km/h (35 mph), including stops, over the whole system. In all, 556 carpeted, air-conditioned cars will be needed by 1990, when the system is expected to be carrying a million passengers a day. Tickets, including stored-fare tickets, are sold by automatic fare collection methods.

There are many other cities in the USA with rapid transit plans well on the way – Atlanta, Baltimore (both under construction), Detroit, Pittsburgh, St Louis, San Francisco, Seattle, Dallas, Cincinnati, Houston, Los Angeles, Minneapolis-St Paul, and Miami among them, as well as Honolulu.

Recent need for economy has led to light rail transit being considered as an alternative to a full-scale system, and Pittsburgh, Buffalo, Dayton, and Denver are among the cities considering the change – equivalent to the European premetro. Canada already has two major rapid transit systems, one in Toronto, based largely on British practice, and the other, in Montreal, based on French principles. The Toronto line could be said to have been built by popular acclaim, for the plans were approved by the citizens by a majority of ten to one. This first line, opened on March 30, 1954 and then known as the Yonge Street Subway, ran north and south under Yonge Street, which practically bisects the city. The line's curious gauge of 1,495 mm (4 ft 10⅞ in) came about because it matched the existing tramway gauge. Like most of the subsequent extensions, the original section was built by cut-and-cover methods. The original 104 cars came from Britain, but subsequent orders were placed in Canada. The system has 42.6 km (26.5 miles) of track, of which 39.3 km (24.4 miles) are in tunnel, and 49 stations. It carries about 170 million passengers a year.

The Montreal metro is much more recent. It opened on October 14, 1966, uses rubber-tyred trains like those on some lines of the Paris metro, and has 25.6 km (15.9 miles) of track, all in tunnel. There are 28 stations, many of considerable artistic interest, and almost 130 million passengers a year are already being carried. There are plans for considerable extensions which will raise the length of the network to 76 km (47.2 miles). Other cities in Canada contemplating rapid transit include Ottawa, Calgary, and Vancouver (LRT), while Edmonton is building a

7 km (4.5 mile) LRT route for opening in 1978.

In Central America, Mexico City has a 40.8 km (25.4 mile) three-line subway system based on rubber-tyred trains of the Paris metro pattern. The system opened the first section, between Chapultepec and Zaragosa, on September 5, 1969. It is the highest metro system in the world as Mexico City is over 2,135 m (7,000 ft) above sea level and in some ways presented engineering difficulties in that the whole city rests on the dry bed of a lake which has waterlogged clay just below the surface. Cut-and-cover construction was used, with 'bentonite' walling, and special precautions are built-in against seismic tremors. Operation of trains is computerized and electronic coding of tickets is employed. Many of the stations are architecturally notable. Extensions are in hand. Proposals for a 50 km (31 mile) four-line network in Guadalajara have met with setbacks and the first section, 5 km (3.1 miles) with two surface and five underground stations, is expected to be worked initially by trolleybuses.

For many years South America had only the Buenos Aires rapid transit system, opened in 1913 and extended steadily to its present 31.5 km (19.6 miles) and five lines. There are 57 stations and traffic amounts to over 400 million passengers a year. Extensions, amounting to more than 10 km (6.2 miles) are in hand and there are plans for three new routes with 52 stations.

Buenos Aires has now been joined by São Paulo (Brazil), which opened the first 7 km (4.3 mile) section of its 17 km (10.6 mile) 20 station metro on September 14, 1974. Eventually, it is planned to have four lines and 47 km (29 miles) of route and 68 stations. The six-car trains have a capacity of 1,998 passengers. Rio de Janeiro has the first 20 km (12.4 miles) of a 67.6 km (42 mile) 55 station network under construction and may open it in 1977. The cars to be used have only 24 fixed and 30 folding seats but will take 333 people under peak-hour conditions.

Caracas, in Venezuela, has begun work on the first section of a 49.7 km (30.9 mile) line. The first 6.7 km (4.1 miles) of the 19.7 km (12.2 mile) Line 1 will have 22 stations, 19 of them underground. Services began on September 15, 1975, on Santiago's Line 1, which is 15 km (9.3 miles) with 22 stations. Rubber-tyred cars of the latest Paris type are used and trains are automatically driven. Bogota, which had ready plans for a full metro, has now had to go ahead with a light rail scheme because of shortage of funds.

Below: Trains head out of town to the suburbs on Toronto's Rapid Transit system.

Right: A series '700' car now operating on the Yurabucho line – the newest rapid transit line in Tokyo.

Asia

The rise of rapid transit systems in heavily-populated Japan has been surprising in recent years, but the first line in Tokyo opened as long ago as 1927. It was then 2 km (1.25 miles) long. Today, the Teito Rapid Transit Authority and the Tokyo Metropolitan Transportation Bureau between them operate 163.2 km (101.4 miles) of underground railway, and some 138 km (85.8 miles) of their lines are in tunnel. Extensions are in hand, some of them giving connections with urban electric railways which, publicly or privately owned, carry a great deal of Japan's commuter traffic. They are so closely allied with rapid transit systems – often including through running over each other's tracks – that they could be counted as part of the rapid transit systems. All Japanese rapid transit lines tend to be busy, efficient, and to use the latest engineering techniques while remaining essentially workmanlike and functional in appearance.

Osaka's first 3.2 km (2 mile) line opened in 1933. The system has now grown to 70.2 km (43.6 miles) with 60 km (37.3 miles) in tunnel. Nagoya began with only 2.4 km (1.5 miles) of line but has grown to 38.1 km (23.7 miles). Kyoto has a 3.5 km (2.2 mile) stretch of line of a rapid transit nature, but this is effectively part of a much longer interurban line. A new 11 km (6.8 mile) line is under construction which will connect with a private railway at the southern end. Kobe has a 13.6 km (8.5 mile) line under construction, almost entirely underground. The first 5.6 km (3.5 mile) section is due to open in March 1977. The remaining 8 km (5 miles) is expected to open in 1981. Yokohama has 11.6 km (7.2 miles) of rapid transit railway, the last 6 km (3.7 miles) of which were opened in 1976.

The most unusual rapid transit line in Japan is that in Sapporo, which uses pneumatic-tyred trains. The track is much less complicated than the French system, however. The main wheels run on concrete strips but the guidance is carried out by horizontal rubber-tyred wheels running on the sides of a central 'I' beam placed between the running tracks. There are no standby steel wheels and rails as in Paris, but the main wheels have substantial steel rims on which the car could run for a limited distance should the tyre puncture. The 12.1 km (7.5 mile) Sapporo system is being extended.

China has a rapid transit line which runs across Peking east-west and which apparently can be used only by those who hold cards to show they live or work near the line. It is 22.4 km (13.9 miles) long and has 16 stations. Another 20 km (12.4 mile) line is being built. The first line is entirely underground and was built by cut-and-cover. No recent figures are available and it may be that the railway is now open fully to the public. The four-car trains have 240 seats and can take 1,200 passengers in crush conditions.

In Hong Kong, the initial route of a projected 52.6 km (32.7 mile) system is in hand. This initial route is 15.6 km (9.7 miles) long and will include twin 1.3 km (0.8 mile) immersed tube tunnels linking Hong Kong and Kowloon under the harbour. Hong Kong is the most densely-populated city in the world and this will be reflected in the size of the cars to be used, which will carry 400 people each under crush conditions. Average speed will be 32 km/h (20 mph). Tunnels will be bored, but stations will be built by cut-and-cover using steel decks to maintain the road surface above during construction. Trains will be automatically driven. Test running is expected to begin in 1979, with public service starting later the same year. The full initial system should be working by 1980.

In Korea, the city of Seoul, which has grown enormously since the end of the Korean war and now has some six million inhabitants, opened its first 9.5 km (5.9 mile) rapid transit line on August 15, 1974. A very much larger system, totalling 156 km (97 miles) with 150 stations, is envisaged for the future. Other Far Eastern cities considering rapid transit include Singapore, Bangkok, and Taipei (Taiwan). Pakistan is considering a 9.7 km (6 mile) metro in Karachi and a feasibility study has been made into the prospects of a rapid transit line in Lahore. In India, work on a 16.5 km (10.3 mile) rapid transit line for Calcutta began in 1972 and completion is expected in 1979. Subway systems are also under consideration for Delhi, Bombay, and Madras.

Africa
There are no rapid transit railways in Africa at present, but at least two cities, Cairo and Johannesburg, are thinking seriously about them. A study of Johannesburg's passenger traffic pub-lished in 1969 suggested than an underground railway would be needed by 1985, previous proposals for monorail systems having been rejected. A further study was made by London Transport and Mott, Hay & Anderson, consulting engineers, in 1971 and more studies, during which City Council officials visited overseas rapid transit systems, were carried out in 1973. So far, a basic 23 km (14.5 mile) system with 23 stations has been proposed.

Cairo has been studying the possibilities of rapid transit, with outside help from France, Britain and Japan over the years. Current proposals are based on the Sofretu (French) report of 1973 and would include a five-station 4 km (2.5 mile) underground line linking two suburban railways across the city to form a 41 km (25.8 mile) regional metro. The 1973 plan also suggested two other routes totalling 21 km (13.2 miles) and serving the city centre. No action seems to be proposed for these at present, but an extra 44 km (27.7 miles) of double-track tramway are proposed.

Australia and New Zealand
There are no rapid transit railways in Australia or New Zealand, though there are, or have been, plenty of proposals for such lines and there are suburban railway developments of a quasi rapid transit nature. For example, a scheme which would have provided Auckland with a 5 km (3.1 mile) three-station underground loop and a 26 km (16.2 mile) urban line stretching out south of the city to Papakura has been ruled out by a recent report because it could not justify its cost by any benefits it could bring. It is thought that improvements to existing lines will be sufficient. Similarly, a 5 km (3.1 mile) underground railway with six stations was proposed early in the 1960s

Left: Tunnelling in progress at Parliament Station on the Northern line loop of Melbourne's Underground Rail Loop Authority.

Right: Construction by the 'cut and cover' method of excavation at Melbourne's Museum Station.

Below: A double-deck train on the Sydney-Gosford scenic route – New South Wales' Public Transport Commission.

for Wellington, though this was modified later to a 3.2 km (2 mile) line with only four stations.

In Australia, a transport plan for the city of Perth, announced in 1972, envisaged some 8.9 km (5.5 miles) of electrified railway, of which 6.4 km (4 miles) would have been in tunnel under the central area of the city. An underground outer loop line was also suggested. No action seems to have been taken on these proposals. Melbourne, however, is building an ingenious underground loop to connect with suburban railways and serve the business district of the city. The loop consists of four parallel tunnels in pairs at two levels, each 3.2 km (2 miles) long with three city stations served by all four tunnel lines. It is likely that two of the tunnels could be open for traffic by 1978 and all four lines by 1980.

In Sydney, the 11.2 km (7 mile) underground line being built to serve the eastern suburbs is an approach to the rapid transit concept. It runs under busy streets and will, when complete, have 11 intermediate stations. All but 1.6 km (1 mile) of this route will be underground and bus/rail interchange will be a feature at a number of stations. There is already an underground loop which connects the shopping and business areas and serves Circular Quay. The new line will be operated by standard electric suburban railway stock. There are proposals for a north-south underground railway line in Adelaide, but this is a long-term project.

The Middle East may soon need underground railways, and a line for Cairo has already been mentioned. Other Middle East cities with rapid transit systems in mind include Baghdad, where a two-line system has been proposed. Beirut, where Russian consultants carried out a feasibility study in 1968, has ideas for a 37 km (23 mile) system with four lines, and in Kuwait a north-

south line is a possibility. In Haifa there is already a rapid transit railway – a funicular line with trains capable of 30 km/h (18.6 mph) in tunnel up the slopes of Mount Carmel, a high-class residential area of Haifa. It is 1,752 m (5,748 ft) long and has six intermediate stations.

Rapid transit is not confined to the methods and systems already listed. At Wuppertal in West Germany a monorail, with its cars suspended from a massive overhead track, has been running safely and reliably since 1901. It is 13.3 km (8.3 miles) in length and has modern rolling stock with all-electronic control, giving particularly smooth acceleration and braking. There is another monorail, 12.9 km (8 miles) in length, which has linked Tokyo with Haneda airport since 1964. The cars on this line run on top of a concrete beam with steering and balancing wheels in skirts which extend down on each side of the beam.

Personal rapid transit (PRT) is having its first full-scale service trials in a US government-sponsored demonstration project at Morgantown, where 8.5 km (5.3 miles) of track link the central business area with the campus of West Virginia university. The present three stations and 45 cars may possibly be increased to five stations and 78 cars.

A number of other types of PRT have been invented and many have reached the stage of running over short demonstration lines owned by their manufacturers.

'People movers', which have cars carrying perhaps 30 to 50 people against the four or five carried by PRT cars, are already in use at some airports, such as the Dallas/Fort Worth, for travel between the terminals, but there is no full-scale people mover system at work in urban conditions anywhere at present.

Major rapid transit systems

City	Length of route		Length in tunnel		No of lines	No of stations	Passengers carried (mill. per year)	Date first line opened	Remarks
	km	miles	km	miles					
Baku	18.5	10.3	16.0	9.9	1	10	41	1967	Being extended
Barcelona (all lines)	81.7	50.8	45.9	28.5	6	86	400	1863 (Section which then formed part of surface steam railway)	Being extended
Berlin (W)	116.0	72.0	72.0	44.7	8	100	271	18.2.1902	Being extended
Berlin (E)	25.5	15.8	22.5	14.0	2	34*	61		*Plus 11 not in use
Boston	48.0	29.8	15.0	9.3	3	48	95	1901	
Brussels	5.5	3.4	5.5	3.4	2	7	–	20.9.1976	First pre-Metro lines converted to full rapid transit
Budapest	4.0	2.5	3.5	2.2	1	11	150	1896	Original line
	10.1	6.3	8.9	5.5	1	11		4.4.1970	Modern system
Buenos Aires	31.5	19.6	31.5	19.6	5	57	400	1913	Extensions in hand
Chicago	143.1	88.9	17.1	10.6	9	154	104	1892	(Elevated)
								1943	(Subway)
Cleveland	30.0	18.6	0.6	0.4	1	18	13	15.3.1955	
Glasgow	10.5	6.5	10.5	6.5	1	15	15	14.12.1896	Being reconstructed
Haifa	1.8	1.1	1.8	1.1	1	6	6	6.10.1959	
Hamburg	89.9	55.9	31.6	19.6	3	79	188	15.2.1912	Being extended
Kiev	18.2	11.3	12.7	7.9	1	14	178	22.10.1960	
Kharkov	17.9	11.1	12.1	7.5	1	13	–	1975	
Kobe	13.6	8.5	13.0	8.1	1	11	–	About to open (1977)	
Kyoto	3.5	2.2	3.5	2.2	1	4	–	–	Being extended
Leningrad	56.0	34.8	55.2	34.3	3	27	400	11.1955	Being extended
Lisbon	12.0	7.5	12.0	7.5	1	20	70	30.12.1959	Extensions planned
London London Transport									
(owned)	381.0	237.0	156.0	97.0	8	248	601	10.1.1863	Being extended
(run over)	409.0	254.0				278			
British Rail	2.4	1.5	2.4	1.5	1	2	–	11.7.1898	
Madrid	66.0	41.0	60.2	37.4	7	99	530	17.10.1919	Being extended
Mexico City	40.8	25.4	30.8	19.2	3	48	437	5.9.1969	Being extended
Milan	26.5	16.5	24.5	15.2	2	38	120	1.11.1964	Being extended
Montreal	25.6	15.9	25.6	15.9	3	28	129	14.10.1966	Being extended
Moscow	161	100	141.4	87.9	8	97	1850	15.5.1935	Being extended
Munich	18.7	11.6	13.9	8.6	2	19	60	19.10.1971	Being extended
Nagoya	38.1	23.7	35.6	22.1	3	41	179	11.1957	Being extended
New York NYCTA	371.2	230.6	220.6	137.1	32	461	1100	27.10.1904	Being extended
New York PATH	22.4	13.9	12.6	7.8	2	13	40	1908 (As PATH, 1.9.1962)	Extension proposed
Osaka	70.2	43.6	60.0	37.3	6	56	683	5.1933	Being extended
Paris Metro	175.3	108.9	165.1	102.6	16	274	1250	19.7.1900	Being extended
Regional	75.0	46.6	15.0	9.3	3	51		12.12.1969	Being extended
Peking	22.4	13.9	22.4	13.9	1	16	20	1970	Being extended
Philadelphia	62.8	39.0	30.9	19.2	4	65	112	4.3.1907	Extensions planned

City	Length of route		Length in tunnel		No of lines	No of stations	Passengers carried (mill. per year)	Date first line opened	Remarks
	km	miles	km	miles					
Prague	6.7	4.2	6.7	4.2	1	13	–	9.5.1974	Long term plans for 125 km (78 miles) system with 144 stations
Rome	11.3	7.0	6.0	3.7	1	11	22	9.2.1955	Second line under construction
Rotterdam	17.0	10.6	3.2	2.0	1	8	28	1968	Being extended
San Francisco (BART)	120.7	75.0	37.0	23.0	4	34	26	11.9.1972	
Santiago	12.9	8.0	11.3	7.0	1	11	–	– About to open (1977)	
Sao Paulo	17.2	10.7	15.0	9.3	1	23	260	14.9.1974	Being extended
Sapporo	12.1	7.5	7.3	4.5	1	14	–	1972	Rubber-tyred system
Seoul	9.5	5.9	8.8	5.5	1	9	175	15.8.1974	Being extended
Stockholm	70.6	43.9	26.7	16.6	2	78	187	1950	Being extended
Tashkent	16.2	10.1	–	–	1	14	–	About to open (1977)	Being extended
Tbilisi	12.6	7.8	10.2	6.3	1	11	75	1965	
Tokyo	163.2	101.4	138.0	85.8	8	146	1613	1927	Being extended
Toronto	42.6	26.5	39.3	24.4	2	49	170	30.3.1954	Being extended
Vienna	3.9	2.4	–	–	1	–	–	8.5.1976	Being extended
Washington	7.4	4.6	7.4	4.6	1	5	7	29.3.1976	Eventual system 157.2 km (97.7 miles) with 86 stations
Yokohama	11.6	7.2	11.6	7.2	1	6	–	12.1972	Being extended

Below: Digging a tunnel for the new rapid transit system in Helsinki.

Above right: A rope-worked incline up Mount Vesuvius in Italy from the foot to the rim of the crater.

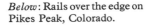

Below: Rails over the edge on Pikes Peak, Colorado.

Rope-worked inclines

Mountain railways imply steep gradients and the history of such lines is the history of the means by which steep gradients were conquered. On the colliery tramroads of north-east England inclined planes, as they were called, often had to be built to carry coal down from the upland mines into the river valleys where it was put into ships. By the 1820s some of these inclines were being worked by stationary engines operating the ropes that pulled waggons up or lowered them down under control. Early steam locomotives were not very powerful and they too were rope-assisted by stationary engines up steep gradients. For a few years the gradients on either side of the Rainhill level on the Liverpool & Manchester Railway were thus equipped and similarly, for a few years after opening in 1837, trains were aided up the bank out of Euston station in London. A longer lasting rope-assisted operation on a main line railway was up 1.8 km (over one mile) of 1 in 42 gradient out of Queen Street terminus station in Glasgow. This lasted from 1842 to 1913. The Ans incline in Belgium carries a main line down into the valley of the river Meuse at Liège. It is 6.5 km (4 miles) long and the greater part of it is at a 1 in 31 gradient. Rope working started in 1842 and lasted until 1866 for passenger trains and 1871 for freight. It is of interest that today the

Class 15 electric locomotives of Belgian State Railways are prohibited from hauling Brussels-Liège express trains because of the Ans bank. The locomotives are designed for a top speed of 160 km/h (100 mph) but not for climbing steep gradients at low speed. The later Class 16 can tackle both jobs.

In Brazil, the Santos-São Paulo-Jundiai railway has to climb a *serra* a few miles out of the port of Santos on the sea coast. The British surveyor, D. M. Fox, had to spend months in the tropical rain forest that covered the mountainside before he found a way to the top. In addition he was constrained in his work by the promoters of the railway, who limited the amount of capital that they were prepared to spend. This made spiral tunnels and other expensive means of gaining height impossible. Eventually, Fox laid out four successive inclined planes, each at a gradient of 1 in 9.75 and proposed working by stationary engine and rope. The Santos-Jundiai Railway, together with the inclines, was opened to traffic in 1868. During construction many trees were cut down and the undergrowth cleared, which was unfortunate because the roots held the soil in place. Throughout its history right up to the present day this mountain section has been plagued by landslides.

The four inclines are 1.95, 1.77, 2.09 and 2.14 km long (6,388, 5,842, 6,876 and 7,017 ft) and they surmount a height of 776 m (2,500 ft) in a distance of 8 km (5 miles). The arrangements for working the inclines were modelled on those at Ans, that is to say the inclines were separated one from another by a train's length of 1 in 75 gradient. A stationary engine was sited alongside each head-of-incline. The inclines had funicular-railway characteristics, that is to say that an ascending train is aided by the weight of a descending train at the other end of the rope as well as by the stationary engine. Again just as in a funicular the upper part of each incline was laid with three rails for trains in either direction, the centre rail being common to both directions. Such a layout of the track aids running of the haulage rope over its pulleys. In the middle of each incline there is a stretch of double track so that the two trains can pass each other. Below that is ordinary single track.

Trains on this original incline consisted of four coaches or wagons, together with a special brake wagon and a tank locomotive for incline use. Each train took an hour to go up or down the whole series of inclines. Traffic on the line increased and a second series of four inclines was opened in 1900, using steel wire in a continuous length on to which trains hitched themselves. Because the rope was in a continuous length, three-rail construction had to be used both above and below the double-track passing place in the middle of each incline. The complete series of inclines rose 793 m (2,601 ft) in 11 km (just over 6¾ miles).

São Paulo is now one of the great cities of the world with more than 7 million inhabitants and most of the traffic to the seaport at Santos goes by road. Indeed, until a few years ago powerful road

Right: Serra Inclines, Santos-Jundiaí Railway in Brazil. The *Comet* diesel express for Santos descends from the summit at Poranapiacaba behind a Stephenson steam brake locomotive.

interests successfully blocked most Brazilian railway improvement schemes. Nevertheless the original series of inclined planes was reconstructed and opened in 1974 as an Abt rack railway. It is electrified and uses Japanese-built 3,000 volts dc rack-and-adhesion locomotives. Traffic is still increasing and the 1900-built inclines remain in use and are still rope-worked.

Fell Railways
Captain Ericsson of the Swedish Army (co-designer of the locomotive *Novelty* for the Liverpool & Manchester's 1829 Rainhill trials) and Charles Vignoles, remembered for the flat-bottomed rail, suggested as long ago as 1830 that a locomotive could be helped to climb a steep gradient by an additional pair of horizontal wheels gripping a central rail. This design was also suggested for the locomotives to work a proposed railway across the Panama isthmus in 1848. Fifteen years later a locomotive of this type, designed by A. Alexander to the requirements of James Barraclough Fell was tested. Fell was an engineer in association with Thomas Brassey the contractor and he was building railways in Italy for the latter when he proposed a 'Fell railway' over the Mont Cenis pass across the Alps, pending the completion of the Mont Cenis (Fréjus) tunnel.

Two trial locomotives were built, the first by Canada Works, Birkenhead, in 1863 and the second by J. Cross of St Helens in 1864. The first of these locomotives had four cylinders, the two outside driving the rail wheels in the usual manner and the two inside powering the horizontal wheels. The horizontal wheels were arranged to be pressed by powerful springs against a centre rail laid down the centre of the track. At first a screw handwheel was used to apply the pressure

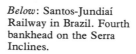

Below: Santos-Jundiaí Railway in Brazil. Fourth bankhead on the Serra Inclines.

Right: The Fell centre rail section of the line between Bocco do Mato and Teodoro de Oliveira in Brazil.

Below: Mount Washington Cog Railway's locomotive No. 10, *Colonel Teague*, ascending from the base station. The Mount Washington line is North America's only steam cog railway.

through a system of bevel gears and levers. The second locomotive only had two inside cylinders, the piston rods of which drove the horizontal wheels at the rear and also projected at the front of the cylinders to drive a rocking shaft that was coupled in turn to the rail wheels.

The mechanical design of the two-cylinder machine was not good, but as the boiler of the other locomotive showed itself incapable of supplying four cylinders with steam for any length of time the two-cylinder design was chosen for later locomotives for the Mont Cenis. The French builder's workmanship was unfairly blamed for the design defects when the Mont Cenis Railway was in full operation.

Fell had his locomotives built for the gauge of 1,100 mm (3 ft 7⅜ in) and a temporary track of this gauge some 730 m (800 yards) long was laid out adjacent to the 1 in 7 rope-worked Bunsal incline near the Whaley Bridge terminus of the Cromford & High Peak Railway in Derbyshire. It included gradients of 1 in 12 and 1 in 13½, and one curve as sharp as 60 m radius. The four-cylinder locomotive (later No 1 of the Mont Cenis Railway) was tried out at Bunsall during 1863 and showed itself capable of hauling 24 tons up the gradient without trouble.

In 1865 it still seemed that the Mont Cenis tunnel would not be completed for over ten years, so Brassey and Fell formed a company to build a railway over the pass. After demonstrating the mechanical practicability of their proposal on a short section of the line above Lanselbourg, on the French side of the pass, they obtained concessions from the French and Italian governments, though it was required that the railway must close after the tunnel was opened for traffic. In the mid-1860s it seemed that this would occur not for more than ten years. The Mont Cenis Railway, for the most part, followed the road across the pass (the way Hannibal had taken his elephants that so dismayed the Roman armies). Consequently there were sharp curves and gradients as steep as 1 in 10. The line was 80 km (50 miles) long. After opening in 1868, it had to close again in 1872 because of the opening of the tunnel earlier than expected in 1871. At the time, the railway was the last link in a route for the *Bombay Mail* from Calais to Brindisi. In addition to the two trial locomotives, Alexander had 16 more built for the line in France.

The next Fell railway was in Brazil and used 1,100 mm gauge track partly lifted from the Mont Cenis. Indeed a 1,600 mm gauge (5 ft 3 in) line that ran inland from Porto Caixas near Rio de Janeiro was converted to 1,100 mm gauge when an incline up the mountain was built to reach the coffee-growing areas about Nova Friburgo. The incline opened at the end of 1873 and was 12.5 km long (7¾ miles) with gradients of up to 1 in 12. The owning company, the Cantagallo Railway, had four-cylinder locomotives built for the incline section, with enlarged boilers to provide the necessary steam. Three of these were built by Manning, Wardle & Co in England and two by Gouin in France.

When new locomotives were next needed by the Cantagallo they went to The Baldwin Locomotive Works at Philadelphia. Baldwin built six-coupled tank locomotives for ordinary adhesion working on the incline, although the locomotives were fitted with centre-rail brakes. The incline was worked by steam locomotives with the Fell rail in use for braking only until its closure in 1956.

The best-known and longest-lived of all the Fell railways was that up the Rimutaka incline in New Zealand. This was on the North Island not far from Wellington on New Zealand Railways' 1,067 mm (3 ft 6 in) gauge line to Masterton and Woodville. The gradient facing southbound trains from Masterton averaged 1 in 15 for 4 km (2½ miles) of the 5 km climb from Cross creek to summit. Four four-cylinder locomotives were built in England in 1875 and another two in Scotland in 1886. These half-dozen 40-tonne locomotives struggled up the incline for many years with all kinds of trains, and ample traffic kept them busy throughout their lives. Indeed, to watch some of the heavier trains with three or four locomotives, occasionally even five, cut in at intervals along the train was something of a tourist attraction. One locomotive was rated to take 65 tonnes up the incline (60 tonnes if a passenger train) and four could take a freight train of 260 tonnes, each locomotive cutting into the train at the head of its rated load. Eventually, in 1955, the incline was closed when it was bypassed by a cut-off railway through the 8,800 m (5½ mile) Rimutaka tunnel. Two other short inclines in New Zealand were equipped with a Fell central rail for braking purposes only. One of these was closed in 1960. The centre rail was removed from the other in 1966.

The electrified Snaefell Mountain Tramway on the Isle of Man is the only line still operating with a Fell centre rail for braking purposes.

Above: Fell railway up the Rimutaka incline in North Island near Wellington on New Zealand Railway's 1067 mm (3 ft 6 in) gauge line to Masterton and Woodville.

Below: Locomotive, with extra horizontal wheels, on the Mont Cenis Railway across the Alps in Europe which was opened in 1868.

Marsh cog wheel railway

The most usual method of running a train up a steep gradient is the rack railway, known as a cog railway in the United States. Rack railways have been tried from time to time since the earliest days of railways. John Blenkinsop's celebrated locomotives with rack-rail propulsion built from 1812 for the Middleton Railway at Leeds are the best known. Other examples briefly ran up steep inclines in the United States but were defeated by the inability of wrought iron to stand up to the duty.

Nevertheless it was in the United States that Sylvester Marsh first successfully applied the idea for a tourist mountain railway. He proposed the Mount Washington Cog Railway in New Hampshire and built the line halfway up the mountain in 1868, reaching the top the following year. The railway is still operating and it is still run by steam locomotives to add to the tourist's satisfaction as he is borne upwards over gradients that are as steep as 1 in 5 in places.

It was Marsh's idea to run a rack rail the whole length of the railway. The rack comprises two steel flange plates on edge and close together, connected by a series of tubular bars. The flange plates are laid on the sleepers and the bars are pitched at a 51 mm (2 in) spacing. In effect the assembly looks like the rungs of a ladder. The teeth of a driven pinion or cog wheel on the locomotive engage with the rungs and thus the locomotive is able to pull itself up the gradient.

Above: No less than five locomotives struggle up the Rimutaka incline in North Island, New Zealand.

Above right: A hand-operated 'traverse' on the Amsigenalp, 1350 m (4,429 ft) high and about half-way up the Pilatus Rack Railway.

Riggenbach rack railways

Niklaus Riggenbach was the mechanical engineer of the Swiss Central Railway and he devised his rack railway at the same time as Marsh. In 1866, when Marsh was first demonstrating his cog-wheel locomotive, Riggenbach was doing the same on the Kahlenberg Railway in Vienna. This line was delayed until after other Riggenbach rack lines had been built, but it opened to traffic finally in 1874 to serve Grinzing and the famous Vienna woods. Riggenbach's rack was very similar in construction to that of Marsh, although it is held that his cross-bars were more closely adapted in shape to the job in hand and thus more successful than Marsh's simple round bars. In any case the loosening or breakage of these bars in traffic is one of the drawbacks of this sort of rack railway.

The Rigi mountain outside Lucerne in Switzerland was a popular tourist viewpoint and Riggenbach determined to build a railway to it from the lakeside below. The line was ready in 1870 apart from the rails, because the outbreak of the Franco-Prussian war in the same year had made them impossible to obtain. Eventually a supply was found, although the rails were iron rather than the steel which Riggenbach wanted. The Rigi Railway opened from Vitznau on the lake to Staffelhöhe up gradients of 1 in 5, in 1871. The top of the mountain was reached in 1873 at Rigi-Kulm.

The popularity of the Rigi was such that another railway, the Arth-Rigi, was opened from the other side of the mountain in 1875. This started from Arth-Goldau, a station on the main line from Lucerne towards the St Gotthard pass. It ran to Staffelhöhe and Rigi-Kulm, the latter section alongside the earlier Rigi Railway. The Arth-Rigi had similar gradients to those of the

Rigi and both had a rack rail throughout their lengths. The Arth-Rigi line was electrified in 1907 but the Rigi did not follow this example until 1937. Both are still open to traffic.

Riggenbach's success with his pioneer rack lines led to a number of others. Vienna had its first in 1874 and so did Budapest, the latter going up to the hills on the west bank of the Danube which are a popular walk away from the city. The Kahlenberg Railway in Vienna was electrified but it is now closed; the Budapest line was electrified in 1929 and then re-equipped from 1973 with an Abt rack. There were other railways in Switzerland and industrial lines in Austria and Hungary.

Overseas in Brazil the Prince of Grand Pará Railway opened a rack extension up to Petropolis in 1883. This was metre-gauge and the whole railway was converted to metre from 1,600 mm gauge through from Rio de Janeiro at the same time. Also at Rio, a rack railway was opened up the Corcovado mountain in 1884.

The Pilatus Railway

The Pilatus Railway in Switzerland has a good claim to be the most remarkable railway ever built, crawling as it does round and up an almost-sheer mountain face. In its whole 3.5 km (2¼ miles) length it is more steeply inclined than any other rack line and it is only rivalled by some funiculars. The steepest gradient is very nearly 1 in 2 and just like steep funicular railways the carriage compartments are stepped. That is the floors of each compartment form in effect the treads of a staircase built on the carriage frame, so that, when on the severe gradients, the floors are level and rise one above the next.

Colonel Locher-Freuler devised a special rack for the very severe incline, a rail laid horizontally with rack teeth machined into it on each side. The motive power has a pair of pinions that grip the rack on both sides and is provided with a second pair of pinions that are used solely for braking during the descent. The Pilatus line opened to traffic in 1889, was electrified in 1937, and is still working to provide one of the world's most dramatic railway rides.

Abt rack railways

Roman Abt was chief engineer of a mountain

railway firm founded by Niklaus Riggenbach in 1875. Abt devised an improved form of rack involving an upright steel plate (known as a blade) into which the rack slots were machined. Machining of the locomotive's pinion teeth and those of the rack blades could be matched more closely to ensure precise meshing, which in turn meant more effective propulsion as well as decreased wear and tear and greater safety.

Most Abt rack railways have two rows of blades along the sleepers, the blades being bolted on each side of a steel spacer which holds them the right distance apart and which in turn is bolted to the sleepers. The rack teeth on one row of blades are staggered in relation to the teeth on the other row. The teeth are pitched at 120 mm (4¾ in) and this staggering means that the locomotive is able to push itself along on a tooth every 60 mm (2⅜ in). A pair of coaxial pinions on the locomotive have their teeth staggered similarly to match. With an eye to tourist railways to the tops of mountains, Abt claimed that staggered teeth were more effective in ice and snow conditions.

The first Abt rack railway ran 28 km (17 miles) from Blankenburg to Tanne up in the Harz mountains in Brunswick. Rack sections of this line opened to traffic in 1886 and the rack-equipped sections in it occurred in open track, amounting in all to a length of 5.5 km (3½ miles). The railway was highly successful – not least with the people of the surrounding countryside who proposed more Abt rack railways in all directions in the Harz mountains – a number of which were built. Still greater was the fame of the line among engineers in other countries, so much so that the 1890s became the decade of the rack railway and examples were built all over the world. The Blankenburg Railway was one of the first to have rack sections starting in open track and most of the new railways were similar. Instead of all the line being laid with a rack only the steepest gradients on it were so equipped.

Below: Europe's first rack and pinion railway, the Vitznau-Rigi; locomotives with an upright boiler were built only during the first ten years of the Vitznau-Rigi Railway. These locomotives are working at Vitznau Station in the 1880s.

Above: An early shot of the Pilatus Rack Railway's No. 5 steam coach, built in 1888 and characteristic of the Pilatus passenger car.

Left: A reconstruction of the Locher rack system used on the Pilatus Railway.

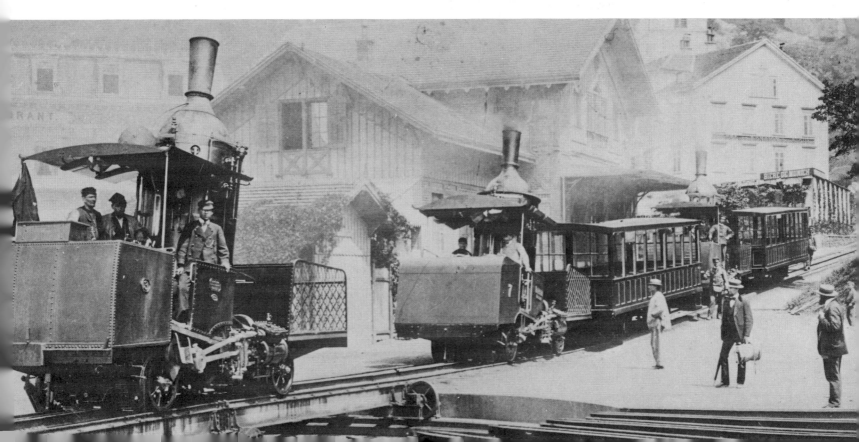

Rack sections in open track are approached dead slow, but they bring the problem that the locomotive's rack pinions often strike the toe of the rack very heavily where it commences. Not only the rack on the ground but also the locomotive's rack pinions can suffer damage and wear. It is usual to support the toe of the rack on a spring rather than on a sleeper so that it will give a little if hit, while sometimes the locomotive's pinions are so assembled that the teeth are sprung in relation to the axle that carries the pinion. Final drive axle-mounted gear wheels with sprung teeth of this nature are frequently fitted to electric and diesel-electric locomotives of high power to avoid shocks from the rails being transmitted to the traction motor pinion.

Providing and assembling a two-row Abt rack rail, with blades bolted to a spacer bar and the latter bolted to the sleepers, is expensive and maintenance of the assembly is also costly. Hence the modern Abt railways is equipped with a single blade of greater breadth. Moreover it has a flat foot for direct fastening to the sleepers. The Abt rack has become similar to that of the Strub system noted below, the only difference being that the teeth are machined in a slightly different shape.

An Abt rack-equipped tourist line was opened in the United States in 1891 – the Manitou & Pike's Peak Railway in Colorado. The line has gradients of up to 1 in 4 to reach an altitude of 4,302 m (14,110 ft) above sea level at the summit, the highest point reached by rails outside the Andes in South America. Venezuela followed with a 61 km (38 mile), 1,067 m (3 ft 6 in) gauge line from Puerto Caballo to Valencia. This had rack sections to scale the coastal *sierra* and was opened in 1894. In the same year a main line was completed north-westwards from Tokyo over the central mountain range to Takata on the opposite side of the main Japanese island Honshu. This included a rack section with a 1 in 15 gradient between Usui and Toge (the latter name means summit in Japanese). The rack section was electrified at 600 dc volts in 1912.

The Snowdon Mountain Railway, another tourist line, opened in Great Britain in 1896. Sumatra gained a rack railway in 1897 (followed by Java in 1905) and in south India a metre-gauge line was built from the sweltering plains up into the cool of the Nilgiri hills in 1898, rising on the rack up to Coonoor and then having an adhesion section as far as Ootacamund. In Africa the line from the Transvaal to Lourenço Marques (Maputo) had a rack section in the same year (long since by-passed by a cut-off). The Benguela Railway in Angola also had a main line Riggenbach rack section when it opened in 1909, by-passed 30 years later. There were many other lines, particularly in Europe.

Strub rack railways

The Strub rack was devised in the middle 1890s as a simplified version of the Abt rack. The Abt, with blades to be bolted to a spacer and the latter to be bolted to the sleepers, was expensive to produce and maintain. Strub flat-bottomed rails were rolled at steelworks in the usual way, but they were rather higher than usual with wider and deeper heads. The rack slots were machined into the head, after which the rail could be laid on the sleepers in the same way as the running rails.

A notable Strub rack line is the Jungfrau Railway in Switzerland. Most of it runs in tunnel inside the mountain and the greater part of the tunnel section is at a continuous 1 in 4 gradient. The line is electrified using the three-phase method, electric services being started in 1889. The Gornergrat Railway, another Swiss rack line in the vicinity of the Matterhorn, was three-phase electrified in the same year. These two, as well as being very nearly the earliest three-phase lines, are now the last in the world using this electrification method.

Italian State Railways Strub rack-equipped a number of the steeper gradients in open track on their 950 mm (3 ft 1⅜ in) gauge railways in Sicily from 1912. On one of these lines, with rack sections and other steep gradients, a passenger and mail train over 61 km (38 miles) only averaged 11 km/h (7 mph). The train ran from Magazzolo to Contuberna – in effect from nowhere to nowhere – and undoubtedly passengers and letters were few. There were also two standard-gauge lines similarly equipped on the Italian mainland.

All these rack railways are out of traffic now, except the Paola to Cosenza line in Calabria. This has a claim to be a main line rack railway for the Cosenza through coach to and from Rome is still hauled up and down the rack in the small hours of the morning. A 15 km (9¼ mile) tunnel is being driven to replace the rack sections. At Paola a great spoil heap of pale green rock exists, so extensive that it does not seem possible that all the rock came out of the little hole to be seen in the mountainside. Tunnelling is slow because of lack of money, so the Paola to Cosenza rack trains will operate for some years yet. Most passenger services are worked by diesel-mechanical railcars equipped for rack-rail braking.

Motive power

In the days of steam traction a point that worried the pioneer builders of locomotives for rack-equipped steep gradients was the level of the

Above: Empties returning from Rothorn Kulm to Brienz on the Brienz rack line in July 1958. The first train of the day had run in three parts instead of the usual one with the result that the return service was also in triplicate, one for passengers and two empties.

Top left: Jungfraujoch Station at 3454 m (11,333 ft); Jungfrau Railway, Switzerland.

Centre left: The toe at the start of a Strub rack rail section on Italian State Railways. The train approaches the rack section in open track at walking pace with the rack pinion spinning at an appropriate speed.

Below left: Rack mechanism of a Sicilian R370 locomotive.

Below: Axle with Abt double pinion from the Snowdon Mountain Railway.

Below right: Terminal of the Snowdon Mountain Railway.

water in the boiler. On a steep gradient either the firetubes at the front of the boiler would be tilted up so far that the water would fail to cover them or, even worse, if the locomotive was travelling in the other direction the top of the firebox would be uncovered. In either case there was a likelihood of boiler failure, even explosive failure. Both Marsh on the Mount Washington Cog Railway and then Riggenbach on the Rigi guarded against trouble by building their first locomotives with vertical boilers. This reduced the dangers of tilt to the boiler diameter measurement. Furthermore, both men installed the boiler so that it was tilted forward in relation to the locomotive frames, that is to say so that when the locomotive was on a gradient the boiler was as near vertical as possible. Because of its fancied resemblance to a travelling sauce bottle, Marsh's locomotive was nicknamed Old Peppersass.

Almost at once it was realised that conventional boilers could be fitted to tilt towards the front so that they were level on gradients and the Rigi had three locomotives so built in 1873. From then on this became the normal method of locomotive construction for very steep gradients – similar locomotives appeared on Mount Washington in 1874. The dividing point between normal and tilted boilers came at a gradient of 1 in

8.3. Less steep than that ordinary boilers sufficed, steeper and the boiler had to be tilted. Thus the Budapest rack railway with a 1 in 9.75 gradient was provided with three locomotives in 1874 with non-tilted boilers, whereas five almost indentical locomotives but with the boilers tilted forwards were supplied in 1875 for the Arth-Rigi with its 1 in 5 gradient.

Rack railways built in the 1870s had little or no level track and were equipped with rack from end to end. The locomotive's cylinders drove the rack pinion and that was the only means of propulsion, the four wheels running on the rails being for carrying purposes only. Because the locomotives were the main source of braking power they were always placed at the downhill end of the train to prevent breakaways. Again as the firebox was the most vulnerable part of the boiler it had to be kept covered with water, so the chimney end always faced uphill and was next to the coaches.

There are exceptions to every rule and one of the Budapest locomotives had a Brown boiler. In this the firebox rises high above the boiler barrel, the latter being full of water always as the level is carried high up inside the firebox. Perhaps just to show that it could be done, this locomotive was put on the rails the wrong way round at Budapest and worked out its life of over 50 years with the chimney at the downhill end.

Locomotives provided with rack pinion propulsion only are not always what they seem to be at first glance. Later on, particularly when the Abt rack came into use, it became popular to mount a pinion on each carrying axle and to couple the axles together. The locomotives of the Snowdon Mountain Railway in Wales are of this type and there were others in Switzerland. Discounting the position of the cylinders and the indirect drive provided, the Snowdon locomotives look as if they were built for adhesion working with four-coupled wheels. This is not so for the wheels run loose on the axles and it is the rack pinions only that are driven.

It will be recalled that when Roman Abt equipped his first line from Blankenburg in Germany in 1886 the rack sections made up only a small portion of the route and that they occurred in open track. The idea was in the air at the time and the Brünig Railway that opened in 1888 (now part of the Swiss Federal system) equipped open-track sections with a gradient of up to 1 in 8.3, using the Riggenbach rack in this case. Such railways called for locomotives that could work both by rail adhesion and by rack propulsion.

The first locomotives provided for the Brünig in effect were six-coupled units – the first and last axles were used for adhesion while the centre axle carried a rack pinion but had no rail wheels. Because of the gradients they encountered these locomotives had tilted boilers and were used to push trains up to the summit of the line using the rack. At the top they were turned round and put at the head of the train to descend the rack-equipped gradients on the other side. Later rack-and-adhesion locomotives for the Brünig had ordinary non-tilted boilers and hauled trains from end to end of the line in the usual way.

Left: A model of one of the Jungfrau Railway's locomotives in 1906.

Rack-and-adhesion locomotives in which the rack pinion is coupled to the driving wheels (and locomotives in which driving wheels and rack pinion are on the same axle) have the disadvantage that the driving wheels do all the work and leave nothing for the rack pinion to do. Only when the limit of adhesion of the driving wheels is reached and the wheels slip does the rack pinion take over. Fortunately the reverse occurs going downhill, for the pinion is a better means of braking than the wheels.

To maximize the locomotive's hill-climbing ability while retaining the rack pinion's superior braking power it is necessary to have a separate drive to the rack pinion and another for the adhesion wheels. Four-cylinder locomotives were the answer and they were built with two completely separate engines, one for the adhesion wheels and one for the rack pinion (or in many cases two rack pinions coupled together). Not only did each drive have its own pair of cylinders but also its own valve gear and regulator for the driver in the cab. Locomotives of this type approaching 50 years old are still working on the Erzberg line in Austria, handling iron-ore trains, and on the Caransebeş to Subcetate country branch line in Roumania, both lines with rack sections in open track.

Below: An early steam locomotive with an upright boiler, built by the Swiss locomotive and machine factory in Winterthur, photographed in Vitznau at the Vitznau-Rigi Railway's centenary exhibition.

One detail on these four-cylinder rack locomotives may be overlooked by the casual observer. On approaching a rack section in open track the driver starts up the rack pinion engine so that the rack pinion is already spinning to mesh with the rack-rail teeth. The rack section is approached at around walking pace to avoid undue meshing shocks. The pinions should be revolving at the same speed as the driving wheels, but there is no way in which the driver can see that this is so. To give him a visual indication a vertical shaft is provided (driven from the pinion's valve gear at a suitable speed) on the top of which, in the driver's line of sight, is a small disc, typically painted white one side and red the other. As the engine for the driving wheels is operating, puffs of steam are going up the chimney. All the driver has to do is synchronize the revolutions of the disc with the puffs from the chimney and he knows that both pinions and driving wheels are revolving at the same speed.

With four cylinders, compound rack-and-adhesion locomotives are a possibility and the SLM Winterthur firm worked out an arrangement after the turn of the century that is known now as the Winterthur system. Compounding had been applied to rack locomotives before that – the original 1891 rack-pinion locomotives of the Manitou & Pike's Peak Railway in the United States were Vauclain compounds. In a Vauclain compound the high- and low-pressure cylinders on either side of the locomotive are mounted one above the other and the piston rods of both are connected to a common crosshead and crank pin. The crank pins on either side belong to a jack-shaft which was geared to the rack pinion shaft on the Pike's Peak locomotives. In the Winterthur system the high-pressure cylinders are connected to the adhesion driving wheels, while the low-pressure drive the rack pinion, each pair of cylinders with its own valve gear. In the ordinary way, while the locomotive is hauling a train away from

Above: Clouds of steam are emitted from two tank locomotives hauling a trainload of iron ore over the Austrian Alps on the Eigenertz line.

Left: Austrian rack engine with Giesl ejector.

the rack, the high-pressure cylinders are used alone and the exhaust from them is directed up the chimney. The low-pressure cylinders are then idle.

When a rack section comes into sight the high-pressure cylinder exhaust is turned into the low-pressure cylinders, the rack pinion starts to turn, and the locomotive begins to work as a compound. To ensure compound working, normally the volume of the low-pressure cylinders must be greater than those of the high-pressure cylinders, typically 2.1 times as great as the high pressure. A peculiarity of the Winterthur system is that all the cylinders are of the same volume and usually they all have the same cylinder and stroke dimensions. This is possible because the low-pressure cylinders drive a jackshaft which is geared down to the rack-pinion shaft in a ratio of 1 to 2.1. Thus the pistons of the low-pressure cylinders sweep the volume of their cylinders 2.1 times as often as the pistons of the high-pressure cylinders and compounding is made possible.

A combination of lightweight track, sharp curves and a desire to haul as great a load as possible, has led to building of articulated rack locomotives on occasion. The 760 mm (2 ft 6 in) gauge Bosnia & Herzegovina Provincial Railway running from the Adriatic sea to Sarajevo included a mountain section with Abt rack rail-equipped 1 in 16 gradients approaching a summit from both sides – the total length of rack rail working was 18.5 km (11½ miles). Two Mallet compound locomotives were built for this line in 1908. Normally the high-pressure cylinders drive the rear group of driving wheels in a Mallet while the front articulated bogie wheels are driven by the low-pressure cylinders. In these 760 mm gauge locomotives the high-pressure cylinders were connected to six-coupled driving wheels but the front bogie had four carrying wheels only and the low-pressure cylinders drove two rack pinions. On non-rack rail equipped sections, only the high-pressure cylinders were used.

On the metre-gauge Abt rack-equipped Trans-andine Railway between Chile and Argentina opened throughout in 1910, with rack gradients of up to 1 in 12½, Meyer-Kitson articulated locomotives were tried from 1907. These were carried on two bogies, the front with eight-coupled wheels and the rear with carrying wheels only but with two rack pinions. At first the front bogie was provided with a rack pinion as well and an auxiliary engine to drive it. This led to various troubles, not least that the boiler was not large enough to provide steam to six cylinders, and the extra rack pinion was removed. What may be supposed to be the last of these Meyer-Kitsons was to be seen doing some desultory shunting of wagons at the Argentine end of the line in 1975. Altogether the Transandine Railway had nine Meyer-Kitsons between 1907 and 1912 and it added an Esslingen articulated locomotive on the same general lines in 1911. Esslingen articulated locomotives had a resemblance to Mallets, with a different arrangement of articulation for the front truck. The Chilean part of the railway with the

Above: Eduard Locher-Freuler, 1840–1910, engineer and designer of the Pilatus Railway, Switzerland.

Right: Steam coaches on the Pilatus Rack Railway, Switzerland.

Below: Locomotive No. R370-044 of Italian State Railways.

Below right: One of the ten Bhe 1/2 biaxial motor-coaches on the Pilatus rack railway.

steepest gradients was electrified in 1928 at 3,000 volts dc.

The advent of electric traction greatly simplified the task of the design engineer in providing rack locomotives and motor coaches, particularly for rack-and-adhesion applications. The rack pinion and driving wheels can be powered by quite separate electric motors and if both are required to revolve at the same speed that can be ensured by electrical circuitry. Similarly, construction of diesel-electric locomotives and motor coaches is simplified. The modern tendency is to build diesel-hydraulic railcars, possibly because the inevitable shocks and stresses of rack-rail propulsion are taken up more readily by the hydraulic converter. On some rack-and-adhesion railways it has been found that a normal diesel-mechanical railcar can sail up gradients as steep as 1 in 10 without using the rack. In such cases, railcars are provided with a rack wheel on one of their driven axles for use in braking during the descents.

Braking

When working trains up and down steep gradients braking assumes considerable importance. On rack railways five different brakes are usually fitted. First of all, as on every locomotive or its tender since locomotives began, there is a screwdown handbrake applying blocks to the wheel treads. Then there is the normal vacuum or air brake throughout the train, also applying blocks to the wheel treads. Rack railways often are narrow-gauge and the vacuum brake has tended to linger longer in use on such lines. Then there is the counter-pressure brake, which involves injecting a small quantity of steam into each cylinder as the piston is moving towards it. The steam is compressed and acts as a cushion to slow down the piston and through it the wheels or the rack pinion. The steam is exhausted during the reverse stroke of the piston, during which the piston is compressing a further quantity of steam injected on the other side of it. Air-braked locomotives substitute compressed air for steam with water for cooling.

All these brakes have been used on ordinary railways, even the counter-pressure brake was fitted during the 19th century until it was noted what a destructive effect it had on crosshead and crankpin bearings if used at any great speed. Two other brakes are used that are peculiar to rack locomotives, the first being a band brake on a drum carried by the jackshaft that drives the rack pinion. A steel band embraces the drum and this band is tightened on the drum by a handwheel on the footplate. Second, grooved drums are mounted on the rack pinion shaft to which grooved brake blocks are applied, normally by the train's automatic vacuum or air brake.

Occasionally other brakes have been used, thus on the Mount Washington Cog Railway two vertical flanged plates hold the rack rail bars. A brake was used that grips the underside of the parallel upper flanges of the plates, in effect locking the locomotive more closely to the rails.

On railways equipped with a rack from end to

end (that is those with the steepest gradients) the locomotive with its brake system is placed at the downhill end to prevent the coaches of the train running away. On rack-and-adhesion railways this cannot be done as the locomotive's normal position is at the head of the train. On these lines a brake van is provided at the rear, equipped with conventional handbrake and a valve to apply the automatic train brakes. In addition the van carries a rack wheel and braking gear to apply the brake on grooved drums.

On electric and diesel-electric rack locomotives rheostatic brakes can be applied. That is the traction motors are turned into electric generators going downhill and the turning wheels of the locomotive are slowed down by the necessity of supplying power to generate electric current. The power generated is used to heat up resistances, which in turn are cooled by air fans. Sometimes it is possible to mount some of the resistances in passenger compartments to provide heating.

Rack locomotive builders

Niklaus Riggenbach was mechanical engineer of the Swiss Central Railway and as such he was in charge of the Olten workshops of the line. During the 1860s the shops built some locomotives for the Swiss Central and a few for industrial concerns. The Rigi Railway not unnaturally placed orders on Olten for its motive power and the first three upright-boilered locomotives for the line were built there in 1870, followed by another three in 1872. For a few years Olten built no more rack locomotives, but in 1883 they built four for the Prince of Grand Pará Railway in Brazil and followed this up with two more for the Corcovado metre-gauge line in 1884, also in Brazil. These locomotives for Brazil were four-wheelers with rack pinion propulsion and a boiler tilted forward on the frames. Riggenbach founded the International Company for Mountain Railways in 1875 with workshops at Aarau, and this works built 12 locomotives between 1875 and 1877. In the first year five locomotives were built for the Arth-Rigi Railway, three for the Rorschach-Heiden Mountain Railway, and a later product was a locomotive for the Budapest Rack Railway.

The Swiss Locomotive & Machinery Co of Winterthur (universally known as SLM Winterthur) started up in 1873. In initial production the same year were the first rack locomotives with tilted normal boilers, three of which went to the Rigi Railway. The firm has built plenty of orthodox locomotives, but it has become known as the world's leading manufacturer of rack locomotives and maintains that reputation today. In 1976 they were building two diesel-hydraulic railcars for the Manitou & Pike's Peak, following up a previous order supplied in 1969. As an example of continuity, SLM Winterthur built the first three steam locomotives for the Budapest Rack Railway in 1874, followed up with eight electric locomotives in 1929 when the line was electrified, and supplied seven motor coaches when the rack was changed from Riggenbach to Abt in 1973.

Charles Brown (1827–1905) was a British engineer born in Uxbridge who came to SLM from Sulzer Brothers (the latter a firm noted today for diesel engines). As recorded previously he designed a special type of boiler that was applied to a rack locomotive in 1874. Brown boilers went on a few other rack locomotives, but they were applied principally to steam tramway locos, another type that was an SLM speciality between 1877 and the turn of the century. Subsequently Brown was employed by the Oerlikon Engineering Works and then went to England in 1885 to work for R. & W. Hawthorn & Co, where more Brown-boilered tram locomotives were built. Then came a brief period after 1889 with a shipyard at Pozzuoli near Naples before he retired in Switzerland.

Brown had a son, another Charles (1863–1924), who passed through the technical college at Winterthur and then went to work for Oerlikon, becoming manager of the electrical-engineering department there when his father left for England. At Oerlikon too the younger Charles Brown met a German engineer Walter Boveri (1865–1924), who turned out to be as capable in business matters as Brown was skilled as an electrical engineer. Together the two of them set up the firm of Brown, Boveri & Co in 1891 – today one of the great international electrical engineering concerns and leaders in electric-locomotive design, including in their time the later rack locomotives for the Usui-Toge section in Japan and those for the Transandine Railway in 1927 and 1957.

Among other locomotive builders concerned with rack locomotives, Floridsdorf of Vienna built chiefly the four-cylinder simple type, while Beyer, Peacock & Co of England gained a modest reputation for rack locomotives of all types as called for by their customers. The Mount Washington Cog Railway's 1874 locomotives with normal boilers were built by the Manchester Works, New Hampshire, a firm that was swept up into the American Locomotive Co (Alco) later. Also in the US, the Baldwin Locomotive Works built rack locomotives for railways overseas.

The Esslingen works in Germany had a great reputation for both steam and electric rack locomotives (it built the 1911 electric locomotives for the Usui-Toge rack line in conjunction with the electrical firm AEG) and it was the last manufacturer to build steam rack locomotives in Europe. Among these were a pair of twelve-coupled tank locomotives with two rack pinions and a pair of carrying wheels under the bunker, produced in 1954. These were for the metre-gauge General Belgrano Railway and worked 400 tonnes up an Abt-equipped 1 in 16 gradient in the Jujuy province in the far north-east of Argentina.

Rack railways are obsolete now because of the improvement in road transport. Both uphill and downhill speeds greater than 10 to 15 km/h (6 to 10 mph) cannot be achieved on rack-equipped sections. Any greater speed would cause so much wear and tear on both rack pinions and rails that the expense would become impossible.

Above: A train climbs to the summit of the Snowdon Mountain Railway, 1064 m (3,493 ft), Britain's highest railway.

Right: A rack 0-8-2 tank locomotive of the Austrian State Railways (OBB) Mo 97–210 pounds out of Vordernberg up the mountain railway on the 0820 hours Vordernberg – Hierslau train.

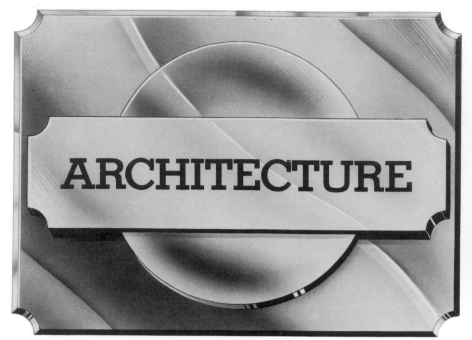

From the earliest days of passenger railways, the station has had an attraction and romance that even the passing of the steam engine has not dispelled, whether it be a great 19th century edifice in stone, iron and glass or a modern reinforced concrete structure. There is about the railway station an atmosphere which its rival, the airport, can never possess.

This distinctive aura has been recognized by artists. Monet found inspiration in the high roof of his 'Gare St Lazare', dim in a haze of steam; Frith's 'The Railway Station' depicts all the animated bustle of a departure from Paddington in 1862; the importance of the railroad depot in the daily life of a small New England town in 1867 is faithfully recorded in the gathered baggage, coaches and farm carts as passengers and well-wishers congregate around the quaint, steep-gabled wooden station portrayed in E L Henry's 'The 9.45 a.m. Accommodation, Stratford, Connecticut'. Stations have also been widely drawn on as a setting for films and novels for the same reason.

Yet for all this, externally the station has no easily recognizable form. In plan, its layout is influenced by the terrain, the track formation and the land available. Internal appearances are stylized by function: platforms, awnings, roofs, variations according to size and local or national custom, yet easily recognizable as the components of a station. Outside it can resemble anything from a country cottage to a royal palace, a wooden hut to a modern office block. Architecture acknowledges nothing as specific as a station form for the station has simply mirrored changing architectural expressions and tastes from the 1830s to the present day. Indeed, so many stations have been built on the world's railways that they probably form the most faithful and comprehensive record of 19th and 20th century architectural development of any single class of building.

Because the railway evolved and grew faster in Britain than anywhere else, British practice has had a considerable world-wide influence, particularly in former dependencies or in the British sphere of influence.

For similar historical reasons, in the broad field of architecture, most of the world's cities strongly reflect British and European styles, particularly in North America; most of the important railway architecture is, therefore, concentrated in Europe and the United States. Again, because the railway is a 19th century creation, its structures are still predominantly of the last century – despite the rapid developments of recent times.

The first passenger lines took their cue from the stage coaches and used nearby inns for selling tickets and providing accommodation for passengers. The term 'booking office' derives from the coaching practice of tearing handwritten tickets from a book – a practice adopted at first by the railways until the invention of the Edmondson card ticket in 1837. From some of the inns the stations took their names, later to bestow them on the settlements that grew around the railway. However, the companies quickly realized that purpose-built stations were needed, although there were odd instances of existing buildings being taken over by the railway.

The station's basic function is to afford the passenger facilities to buy his ticket, await his train, board and alight. The railway, on the other hand, needs accommodation for its trains – whether passing through, starting or terminating – varying degrees of servicing facilities and staff accommodation. Some stations need room for railway operating and administration. Large stations catering for heavy traffic flows need a concourse or circulating area for controlling the movement of passengers, together with refreshment rooms, shops, bookstalls and so on.

The basic small station layout consists of one or two platforms, varying from the traditionally high platform of the British station to the low ones of Europe and America or, in many Eastern countries, merely a space beside the line. Some of the earlier British types had staggered platforms, often on either side of a level crossing, a unique feature not found elsewhere. Small junctions might have one or more bay platforms for the branch trains, or an island platform. At awkwardly-sited junctions it might be necessary

to place the platforms in the angle of diverging lines, and in England there were even two stations that had sets of connected platforms on all three sides of a triangular junction.

Geography, too, governed junction-station layouts, particularly where platforms were added to an existing station to serve a later connecting line. Sometimes it meant that the station platforms had to be placed on a different level. Here and there stations were built where two railways crossed, with high and low level platforms, either for the convenience of serving the locality from a common point or for easy exchange of traffic, or for both.

The most noticeable difference between a British through-station and one elsewhere in the world is in space. British stations tend to be more compact, partly because the more restricted loading gauge only needs 1.8 m (6 ft) between tracks compared with the wider loading gauge in most other countries, and partly from the tradition of strictly confining passengers to the platforms and footbridges or subways which connect them. The lower platforms in other countries, and greater freedom to walk about the tracks, give an impression of spaciousness.

A number of the more important through stations in Britain at one time had a single long platform serving trains in both directions, with scissors crossover tracks in the centre. Brunel in particular favoured this type on the Great Western Railway though it was used at some other stations.

A single platform was similarly considered adequate for both arrivals and departures at the

Above left: The simple unmanned New Hadley Halt in Shropshire, England.

Above: The red-bricked station in Sucre, Bolivia's legal capital, shows the influence of earlier civilizations.

Left: An interior view of Grand Central Station, New York City.

Below: Crisp modern functionalism from Den Haag Central Station in the Netherlands.

first terminals, adjoining the station building. Liverpool Crown Street and Mount Clare, Baltimore, both opened in 1830, were of this type and many more followed. The first to provide separate arrival and departure platforms was London Euston (1838), although the buildings were still on the departure side only. King's Cross and Paddington had similar layouts. The latter for a time had the added disadvantage of a retractable drawbridge to connect the two platforms. Separate entrances and exits were provided, sometimes, like waiting and refreshment rooms, sub-divided for first-, second- and third-class passengers.

The 'head' type of terminus was certainly the most convenient. In it the entrance and exit were contained in a block of buildings built across the inner ends of the platforms behind a cross-platform. David Mocatta used it at Brighton in 1841 and George Townsend Andrews at York in the same year. That example extended part way down the sides as well, in the form of a squared U. Thereafter it proliferated in various forms, the first Gare du Nord in Paris (1847) adding the

Above: The railway office and station at Crown Street, Liverpool, in the 1830s.

Below: One of designer Edward Bury's 0-4-0 locomotives, nicknamed 'Copperknob' because of the boiler shape, stands in front of Camden Freight Shed, London, in the 1840s.

refinement of a concourse which, thenceforth, became an increasingly important feature. There were also a few T-shaped head stations – Versailles in 1838 and Stuttgart's Neuer Bahnhof in 1868, where the buildings forming the stem extended down the middle of a broad central platform.

Split-level stations with platforms on an embankment or in a cutting and buildings at ground level below or above, or on an overbridge, were built on some early lines although they did not become common until the second half of the 19th century. On the London & Birmingham Railway, opened throughout in 1838, Coventry and Tring had a building fronted by a terrace and steps leading down to the platforms in the cutting below, while the Gare de la Place de l'Europe in Paris, also of 1838, was one of the first to be built on a bridge over the line. Some city termini were built on the end of a viaduct, like Greenwich Station (1840) on the London & Greenwich Railway, a line built entirely on arches. The Anhalter Bahnhof, Berlin (1880), was one of the largest terminals to be built in this fashion. Brunel built his Bristol Temple Meads Station (1841) as an elevated terminus with all the offices along one side at ground level and the company's administrative headquarters in a three-storey block across the head.

Intermediate stations on elevated railways frequently had the entrance building and booking hall underneath, the Liverpool Overhead, New York's Elevated and parts of the Vienna Stadtbahn being examples, although a good many had no entrance building at all but simply a flight of stairs from the street and a booking office on a landing or separate ones on each platform.

The first covered stations were little more than barns derived from local farming practice. On the Stockton & Darlington Railway of 1825 the Dar-

Left: A view of Brunel's roof, recently renovated and restored, over the modern platforms and passenger concourse at Paddington Station, London.

Below: An artist's impression of the old Friedrichstrasse Station in Berlin, Germany.

lington terminus was a converted warehouse, while Stockton passengers had to put up with a wooden coach shed. Often such a building would serve for passengers and freight traffic, while in the United States such stations were actually called train barns. Some served a triple purpose, being used for stabling engines overnight. As they were nearly all wooden it is not surprising that a number burned down.

The concept of the passenger train-shed was first introduced at Liverpool Crown Street, which had one platform and two lines of rails beneath a wooden-trussed overall roof. From a contemporary engraving the roof has every appearance of an afterthought, as one side is supported on a screen wall while the other, instead of springing from the station building, rests on the edge of a flat canopy over the platform, supported by wooden columns. It was only 9 m (30 ft) wide and the second pair of rails was used for the movement of locomotives and storage of carriages. Such storage was the secondary purpose which train-sheds were to serve for many years until the need for more platforms encouraged the construction of separate carriage sheds.

At Bristol and Bath Brunel began his series of distinctive wooden train-sheds. Bristol and Bath had mock hammer-beam roofs which disguised cantilever construction to take the thrust of the trusses; Bristol's was in an ornate Tudor style with a span of 22 m (72 ft). Brunel's trusses varied, some being entirely of timber, others having light iron rods, and some were composite types. They were all functional, decoration being mainly confined to the gable screens which had semi-elliptical cutaway sections and glazed openings in a variety of attractive shapes.

The wooden train-shed was extensively used on colonial railways. Ballarat (1862) on the Australian Victoria Railways had a Brunel

Left: Locomotive No 688 with a local passenger train pauses at Abhanpur Junction in India. As in many developing countries the station does not have a raised platform.

imprint, strongly reminiscent of his first Windsor station with coupled pilasters and a cutaway gable screen, Storlein in Sweden had a steeply pitched two-bay roof not unlike G T Andrews' at Richmond, Yorkshire, one of a few he built with vertical gables. Andrews designed many stations in north-east England with distinctive iron-trussed slated roofs having hipped gables on decorative light iron cross girders.

In 1839 James Green built a small triple-arched shed at North Shields, Northumberland, comprising curved laminated wood ribs resting on iron columns, with a central arch 8 m (25 ft) wide. The station was covered by a straight-pitched roof. At King's Cross, London, Lewis Cubitt erected a magnificent curved roof on laminated wooden arches in 1852, each of the two 32 m (105 ft) wide spans springing from arcaded walls. They were elegant and spacious, compared with which the wooden ribbed 24 m (80 ft) single arched roof at the first Munich Hauptbahnhof of 1849, by Friedrich Bürklein, was heavily over-powering with its elaborate cross-bracing. Nonetheless, these roofs displayed an impressiveness which was not lost on railway proprietors and engineers when the potential of the wrought iron arch was fully appreciated a few years later.

The need for wider spans without intermediate supports revealed the limitations of the wooden roof and after the early 1850s, wood was used only at small stations, iron taking its place. Side-by-side with timber, highly-elegant pitched iron roofs were an early development. Robert Stephenson designed the iron sheds at Euston (1837) in conjunction with Charles Fox, on plain iron columns and decorated spandrel brackets, and those at Derby (1840) with Francis Thompson. They were covered with closeboarding overlaid with slates. Euston had a series of glass lights over the platforms; Derby had continuous glazing along the ridge of each bay (making it much lighter) and columns which were fluted without brackets. The Euston roofs were later fitted with vertically-glazed gable screens, curved across the bottom.

Pitched iron roofs were used in France long after they had been superseded elsewhere. To a lesser degree, they suffered from the same width limitations as the timber roofs, requiring construction in bays, although the problem was eased at the second Gare du Nord in Paris (1865) where the engineer, Léonce Reynaud, inserted columns beneath the wide single span towards the sides, resulting in a high ridge and deep multi-glazed gable screens of distinctive two-tier design. The same style of screen was used at La Rochelle to terminate a much steeper roof.

Once more the variety was enormous. The light iron shed at Oporto's Sao Bento Station had delightfully slender columns; Oslo West had a shallow pitched roof on side walls, no gable screens and simple arched trusses with a large circle at the apices producing a considerable degree of elegance. Externally, the station roof profile could be made or marred by the ventilators needed to let out steam and smoke. Usually they

Right: Reading Old Station in England exhibits the characteristic solidity of major stations built during Great Western Railway's heyday.

Below: Ballarat Station in Victoria, Australia. A Victorian Railway R Class 4-6-4 waits at the platform.

formed a clerestory running along the length of the ridge with vents along the side. At Cardiff Queen Street they were large and ungainly, spoiling the appearance, while others like Budapest West (1877) were so delicate as to be barely noticeable. The Town Station at Calais had ventilators in series running down the pitches of the roof in customary French fashion. Great pains were taken to incorporate decoration in the cast ironwork, columns and brackets being favourites. In Britain, bracket spandrels often were used to display the initials or emblem of the railway company, floral work or designs carried the favourite wheel motif, all in cast iron.

The pitched iron roof sometimes might be extended outwards as an awning on one or both sides, as at the Chicago & North Western's station at Milwaukee in 1889 and as late as 1903 at Monte Carlo, where the awning was canted upwards at a corresponding angle to the main roof. The old Nord-West Bahnhof in Vienna (1872) had an imposing shallow-pitched single span roof, very slightly curved, with tall, handsome Romanesque end-glazing.

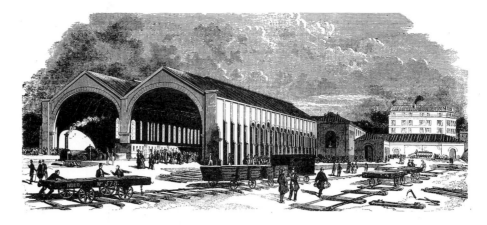

Top right: Considerable activity in the sidings and passenger hall at the first Gare du Nord, Paris – illustrated in an engraving by a German artist.

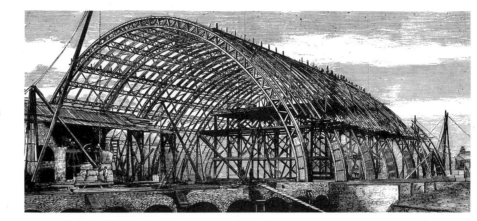

Right: The railway station in St Enoch's Square, Glasgow, during construction.

Below: An early view of Bristol's Temple Meads Station on the Great Western Railway.

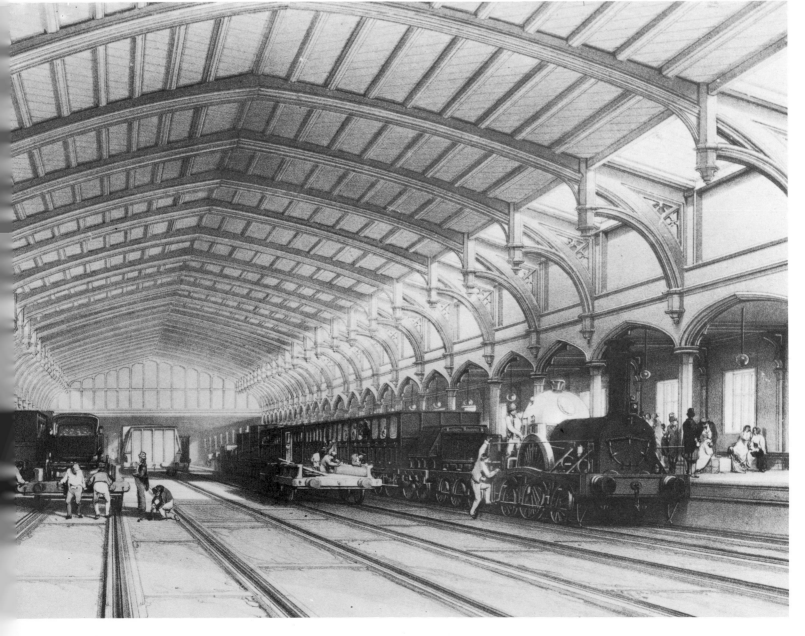

The desire to cover even wider spaces in one span gave impetus to development of the arched iron roof, the dramatic impact of which, more than any other, epitomizes 19th century structural engineering. It was an impact that was fully exploited by the railways as one company after another sought to build bigger and better train-sheds from the 1860s onwards, particularly in America. As older stations became obsolete or outgrown they were replaced by larger, more grandiose structures which, without a great arched shed, would have been considered incomplete.

The breakthrough was first made in Britain by Joseph Paxton's giant greenhouse for the Duke of Devonshire at Chatsworth House in 1840, followed by Decimus Burton's Palm House at Kew Gardens in 1848. Like the pitched sheds, the first arched iron roofs were built in bays.

The opening of Paxton's Crystal Palace in 1851 introduced two new principles from Chatsworth: transverse ridge-and-furrow glazing, and construction of cross-halls or transepts to break up the main arcade, using iron vaulting. Added to them was prefabrication. Characteristically it was Brunel, always the innovator, who adopted Paxton's system at Paddington, London (1854), aided by the architect Matthew Digby Wyatt, with columns supporting only every third arched rib. Ridge-and-furrow roof glazing was used extensively for the rest of the century in arched roofs and in the much less interesting horizontal profiles.

Then in 1854, still in England, the great crescent-trussed roof at Birmingham New Street was completed, at 64 m (211 ft) then the widest span. A narrower but loftier roof was built over the Schlesischer Bahnhof in Berlin in 1869, and 1873 saw completion of the crescent roof at Zurich Hauptbahnhof, having nine wide, curved, transverse ridge-and-furrow bays terminating at each side with a gabled window, a unique combination created by J F Waner. In 1852, François Dusquesne completed his 29 m (97 ft) tied arch roof, with latticed ribs to reduce weight, springing from side walls at the Gare de l'Est, Paris.

Above: Hamburg's Central Station, extensively damaged during the second world war, is now rebuilt and again deals with all main line traffic in a busy sector of Germany's rail system.

Above right: An old railroad station with charm and character at Midland City, Ohio, in the USA.

Below: Dresden Station, showing the wide central shed flanked by two narrower ones.

Five years after New Street the London Chatham & Dover Railway completed its new London Victoria station with segmental arched roofs on latticed ribs, handsomely tied with radial fan-wise struts giving yet another new dramatic effect. At Glasgow Queen Street (1875) the crescent shape was combined with struts to produce a bow-string roof. Charing Cross and Cannon Street in London (1864 and 1866), and Belfast Queen's Quay, were loftier, wider examples of single span crescent-trussed roofs. The spectacular vista at Cannon Street was punctuated by a pair of Baroque towers overlooking the Thames.

The next step was to use the latticed arch to achieve a completely clean, uncluttered roof by dispensing with struts and ties. London St Pancras led the way in 1868, 74 m (243 ft) wide in one great leap, slightly-pointed Gothic arches springing directly from the platforms which were at first floor level and therefore had the effect of ties. Designed by W H Barlow and R M Ordish, it was followed by W J Cudworth's immensely lofty but narrow Gothic roof at Middlesbrough in 1877 and Barlow's Manchester Central in 1880, both built on similar principles. Europe and America

were quick to follow, Germany and the USA rapidly outpacing the rest in size and span: New York's first Grand Central by Buckhout and Snook in 1871; Berlin Alexanderplatz in 1885; and Dresden Hauptbahnhof in 1898 with a 59 m (161 ft) central span flanked by two narrower ones. Whole series of great arched sheds were built side-by-side: five at Frankfurt-am-Main by Eggert and Faust (1888), the widest 56 m (184 ft); five at Milan Central ascending in size from each side to a 72 m (236 ft) wide central arch, designed in 1913 but not completed until 1930; Leipzig Hauptbahnhof (1915) with six, four of them 45 m (148 ft) wide, by the engineer Louis Eilers. Hamburg Hauptbahnhof, completed by Reinhardt and Sossengüth in 1906 possessed an unusual 73 m (240 ft) wide roof in one span, 'Early English' in outline, with transepts – it was magnificent. The widest single span roof was the second Philadelphia Broad Street of 1893, by Wilson Bros & Co, at 91 m (300 ft).

Elsewhere in the world such size was not needed. Nevertheless, smaller station roofs were no less impressive, such as Brisbane's 30 m (100 ft) semi-elliptical span, Algiers, the old Capetown station and the attractive Madrid Atocha.

From beginning as a practical way of providing shelter, overall roofs became status symbols for powerful companies eager to demonstrate their success by sheer size and ostentation. Although, as we have seen, new roofs continued to be built well into the next century, it was already becoming clear in the 1890s that construction and maintenance costs were becoming prohibitive. Individual platform awnings, although much poorer at keeping out the weather, were seen as a cheaper alternative. Long used at smaller stations, they began to replace the great overall roof for a big city terminal.

Their origin lay in the small, neat awnings attached to the country stations of Britain. There from the earliest beginnings on which an awning or canopy was designed as an integral part of the structure. Many of Brunel's small stations on the Great Western had a flat awning around all

four sides of the building. Later developments included a wide variety of shapes – flat, canted forward or backward, curve-topped, ridge-and-furrow – some in wood, others iron and glass. Island platforms had umbrella-type awnings supported by a row of columns and brackets, often elaborately decorated. A particularly British feature was the vertical wooden valance along the outer edge designed to deflect smoke, steam and driving rain from the platform, quickly to become a prominent decorative feature. It was probably used first by Brunel, and was clearly derived from Regency porches and balconies.

Above: Decorated edges to the wooden valances of the station roofs and ornate brackets were features of British 19th century station architecture which spread to many parts of the world.

Below: The fine vaulted roof of Brighton's station in southern England.

Use of platform awnings throughout the British Isles spread beyond to British-inspired railways all over the world and to some extent to Europe. One can still see French, Swiss and Spanish stations with frilly-edged valances on the rather angular, utilitarian iron awnings favoured on the continent. The form of decoration and degree of intricacy was endless, from plain sawteeth to the most delicate fretwork. Standardization grew as the century progressed. By 1900 most British railways could be identified by their platform awnings which were copied further afield. Arequipa Station, in Peru, had an awning with a frilly valance that could have been made by Britain's Great Eastern Railway but for the light iron railing around the top, and Bulawayo in Rhodesia had a serrated wooden valance that could have come straight from the Great Western.

So far only the working parts of the station have been considered – layout, platforms and coverings – which took on a form of their own – a form which belonged to the railway and nothing else. Conversely, the buildings that fronted them, viewed from the outside, had no obvious association with the railway and generally were deliberately designed to look like something else. The 19th century was an age of architectural copyists that later it became fashionable to decry but which are now appreciated. European ideas of building were to incorporate in the design the very latest improvements, but to clothe the building in a style of the past. During the century all large cities acquired halls, hotels, theatres and other public buildings that looked remarkably like a Greek temple or Bavarian castle. The spread of European influence carried its architecture with it, to become mixed with vernacular styles. The age was an architectural free-for-all that exploded in the rapid expansion of North America. Against the background of this feverish activity station buildings must be appraised.

Railways spread over the world and in country districts, the triumph of the railway was expressed by the great viaducts, tunnels and bridges built to overcome natural barriers. But they were

not enough. The pride of the pioneers needed equal expression in the towns where the public could see and be impressed – so arose the concept of the grand entrance. For their initial inspiration, engineers and architects turned to the fashionable style of their day, the classical idiom.

In Britain, Philip Hardwick built his Doric Arch, or propylaeum, at Euston for the London & Birmingham Railway in 1838 and a smaller but complementary classical entrance at the other end of the line at Birmingham Curzon Street. Sir William Tite did the same for the London & Southampton Railway at Nine Elms and Southampton Terminus stations, and others followed. The finest was at Huddersfield (1847), its magnificent giant Corinthian portico flanked by long colonnades and pavilions – one of the most eloquent symbols of the triumph of the railway.

Above left: The head of Knucklass Viaduct in England in the style of a medieval castle.

Above: Luxembourg station exhibits a mixture of styles

Below: The imposing Doric Arch (demolished 1962) which formed the entrance to the London & Birmingham Railway Station in Euston Square, London. The Doric Arch and Great Hall at Euston were designed by Philip Charles Hardwick, opened in 1849 and were ranked among London's major architectural features.

Other companies favoured different styles. Italianate was so popular, accompanied by campaniles and turrets, that it was dubbed 'the English railway style' and later spread across Europe. Smolensk Station, in Russia, was built in an Italianate style, complete with campanile, that could well have been on the Great Northern Railway in England. Other styles were used with equal freedom – Gothic, Venetian, Byzantine, even a monolithic Egyptian at Dublin's Broadstone station of 1850 – all dignified and handsomely executed, with none of the raw brashness that came later. One of the finest stations in Europe was Sancton Wood's Dublin Heuston (formerly Kingsbridge) of 1850, based on Inigo Jones' classical Renaissance Whitehall Banqueting Hall. Three distinct types were built for the first stations in Boston, Massachusetts. The Bos-

ton & Lowell Railway Station (1835) had three Romanesque arches supporting a broken pediment. Haymarket Station (1845) was composed of a giant pediment on a series of Ionic columns set in front of a flight of steps leading up to the entrance doors. Kneeland Street (1847), on the other hand, was a straightforward study in Italianate without frills.

The idea of a station as a gateway caught popular imagination, and architects rose to the occasion. Euston was called 'the gateway to the north'; the classical screen fronting Liverpool's first Lime Street Station was pierced by tall Roman arches with Doric columns; the Delftsche Poort Station in Rotterdam was entered through an elaborate Gothic screen with crenellated towers. It was a pity that the early trains themselves were so unspectacular. After passing

Above right: Quebec Station has been described as 'Canadian Pacific Gothic'.

Below left: Part of the roof and platform awning at Marylebone Station, London.

Below: A station built in neo-Slavic style at Moscow in the USSR.

Above: Flinders Street Station in Melbourne, Australia.

Left: The main passenger hall of Grand Central Station, New York. The station was built on a grandiose scale in 1869 and was rebuilt even more grandly in 1912.

It was otherwise in Europe. A popular centrepiece for a large frontage, there were numerous examples of the use of roof profiles. Rome's first Stazione Termini of 1874; the Porta Nuova station, Turin (1868); the Anhalter Bahnhof, Berlin (1880); Budapest Ost (1881); the Gare de l'Est (1852) and the second Gare du Nord (1865) in Paris; and above all, Tours (1898), where the gable screens of Victor Laloux's twin sheds virtually were the frontage.

From the 1850s dignity and form rapidly gave way to commercial ostentation as one company sought to outclass a competitor or was persuaded it ought to enhance a city from which it drew its traffic. As train-sheds became wider, huge office or hotel blocks were built to mask them, in every conceivable design. The personal aggrandisement of a railway tycoon was often the driving force. Commodore Vanderbilt had visions of a station to out-rival those of Europe. New York's first Grand Central was the result in 1869, to be rebuilt on an even greater scale in 1912. The hotel frontages at London's Cannon Street and Charing Cross stations reflected Sir Edward Watkin's ambition to control railways from Manchester to France, in which he would have succeeded had the Channel tunnel been built. Whatever the motive, the great stations of the second half of the century no longer represented the railways' achievements in overcoming time and space, but their establishment as the commercial lifeblood of the country.

Fast-growing traffic created the need to enlarge or rebuild many of the old stations. Some architects still respected dignity and form, but many produced highly-ornate designs from a whole riot of styles. One of the first and most incredible was Henry Austin's New Haven Union Station, Connecticut (1849), that contained elements derived from Italy, India, China and the Moorish tradition, including a dwarf pagoda. Towers were considered essential as a mark of importance, again in all conceivable styles, Chicago Grand Central's (1890) rising 76 m (249 ft). More modestly in keeping with Swedish conventions, Uppsala had four circular copper-clad conical turrets; in North Africa Oran

through such splendid station portals the cramped box-like carriages, or worse, the open third-class coaches, must have presented a considerable anti-climax.

In some countries the frontage of a head-type terminal was actually pierced by the tracks, like the first Thüringer Bahnhof at Leipzig (1844) where rails emerged from the shed through an arcade of Roman arches, complete with iron gates, on to a railed-off turntable in the square fronting the station. This practice was fairly common in the early days in the USA where trains ran down the main street mingling with horse traffic and pedestrians. The triumphal arch in the large Gothic gable-screen at Salem Station, Massachusetts (1847), again with lofty crenellated towers, had the rails running through; another of this type was the astonishingly ornate Italianate Harrisburg Union Station, Pennsylvania, of the 1850s.

The dominant feature of this type of frontage was the train-shed profile projected, as it were, from behind. In London, Lewis Cubitt used it at King's Cross in 1852 and George Berkeley at Fenchurch Street in 1854, but apart from Manchester Central (1880) – where the great roof gable formed the frontage more by accident, the intended head block was never built – and Buxton's remarkable twin termini (1863), this feature was rare in Britain.

Below: The clock and ornamentation above the entrance to Grand Central Station, New York.

Right: London's St Pancras Station is one of the great examples of the Victorian Gothic style. The station and the adjoining station hotel were designed by Sir George Gilbert Scott in 1865 and were opened in 1866 and 1873 respectively.

Below: A view of the Gothic vaulting of St Pancras Station

Below right: Aerial view of the harbour, docks, rail terminal and city centre at Wellington, New Zealand.

and Casablanca (Voyageurs) had towers; Accra in West Africa had a wooden broached spirelet like the bellcote of an English country church, and the Darjeeling terminus of the narrow-gauge Darjeeling Himalaya Railway was sufficiently important to sport an Indo-Italianate turret.

The prize in the western hemisphere must go to Sir Gilbert Scott's great Gothic fantasy at London St Pancras. Less fittingly in the East, Bombay Victoria and Delhi Junction in India were poor and misplaced imitations of Victorian Gothic in red brick, while Delhi's Churchgate Station, on the other hand, was an enlarged copy of an English black-and-white half-timbered *cottage orné*; a less appropriate style for India would be hard to imagine. None were to be compared with the quietly dignified symmetrical elegance of the 'Mogul' Gothic of Gwalior.

In South Africa, Pretoria (1855) had a quietly attractive Romanesque frontage and in Australia Brisbane Central was built with a Doric portico and a 31 m (100 ft) clock tower. Possibly the most fantastically oriental station in the world was Kuala Lumpur in Malaysia. Its profusion of spirelets, minarets and turrets outdid even New Haven Union, down to the smallest detail – including Moorish arches into the train-shed.

Eventually, with the 20th century, ideas began to change. Not only did awnings replace train-sheds; architecture began to lose its flamboyance and there was a return to a somewhat chunky form of classicism. Emphasis switched from large train-sheds to huge concourses. Concrete provided a new medium; the flat ceilings, moulded cornices and columns or open-trussed pointed roofs of the smaller Victorian concourse were replaced by grand halls of cathedral-like dimensions. Leipzig, completed in 1915 after eight years' building, had a great arched cross-platform; Washington Union Station of 1907 had lofty barrel vaults dwarfing pew-like seats. Both interiors were heavily panelled. New York Penn's 'General Waiting Room', whose giant fluted columns, immense height and arched windows almost rivalled the Vatican, had no seats at all.

The gradual change in style can readily be appreciated by looking at a representative sample of stations built up to around 1940. The debased classicism had none of the careful attention to detail and proportion of the late 18th and early 19th century classical revival. Such stations as Scranton, Pennsylvania (1907), the Pennsylvania and second Grand Central stations at New York (1910 and 1913), and Toronto Union (1934) were coldly monumental edifices which could easily have been mistaken for bank headquarters or seats of government. In New Zealand Auckland (1930) and Wellington (1937) followed the fashion, as did Adelaide in Australia (1930). The huge bulk of Milan Central, completed in 1931 after more than ten years' building, was the most excessively pompous of them all. The vulgarity of its immense halls and staircases, not to mention the sheer distance between entrance and platforms, reflected the late 19th rather than the 20th century, almost as though its designer, Ulisse Stachinni, was trying to dwarf the cathedral.

Accompanying and gradually overtaking this traditionally-based treatment was a movement to remarkably fresh designs. Karlsruhe (1913) and Stuttgart (1928) in Germany, Helsinki (1914) in Finland, dated now in present-day eyes, marked a new architectural awareness, employing traditional materials in new ways with clean, unobstructed outlines. Reinforced concrete came into its own, even in train-sheds, for several were built in the new material. The conoid roof at Rheims (1934) and the Gare Maritime at Le Havre (1936) were in concrete. Tall, slender, square-cut towers reflected the new 20th century idiom, like those at Havre's other station, Gare de la Ville (1936), Tampere, Finland (1938) and Surbiton, England (1937). The newly-formed Italian State Railways, once the excesses of Milan were out of its system, built some most creditable modern-style stations such as Florence in 1935, low and flat-roofed, and Spoleto, quietly traditional, in 1939. After the war Verona (1950) carried on the tradition. The great tent-like concrete and glass concourse at Rome Termini (1951), with its daringly cantilevered canopy, was a triumph of ingenuity. In Britain between the wars, Charles Holden designed a highly meritorious series of new surface buildings on London's Underground, yet the big four main line companies were still investing in clumsy neo-Georgian or classicism and America was still more behind.

It was in Africa and the Far East where the new European movement gained quicker momentum in station building, perhaps because in expanding economies there was more to be done. Johannesburg's fourth station, completed in 1958, with 14 through platforms, had a large concourse sensibly left open to the sky with fountains, shrubs and shady corners. Cape Town's new station had strong emphasis on contrasting vertical and horizontal lines, again in concrete and glass. Taipai, in Taiwan, added a Chinese overlay to Western styling, while Peking's new station of 1959 had four large vertical blocks punctuating its long frontage, each one surmounted by a small traditional pagoda. In Western Australia Northam fol-

Above: Cloistered walkways, arches, rotunda and a spire topped by a hammer and sickle weathervane adorn the entrance hall to Revolution Square station in Moscow.

Below: Columns and arches on the ground floor of the station at Chertsey and the 'town house' aspect of the upper storey blend well with the half-timbered frontage of the Tudor tavern next door.

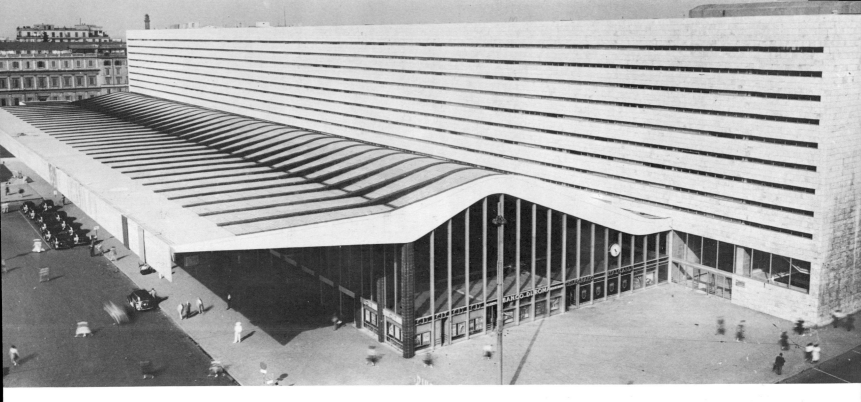

Above: Rome's new Stazione Termini, with its large tent-like concrete and glass concourse with cantilevered canopy, was opened in 1951.

lowed functionalism to the extent of an overhanging upper storey forming an awning, and in India Delhi's Shahdara station incorporated traditional open fretwork into its square, flat-topped tower. Japan, as would be expected, invested heavily in new stations in the 1950s and 1960s, Kure for instance having an attractive hipped roof.

Russia, like the USA, has been slower to adopt light modern styles. Only in recent years has there been a move away from the dull pomposity of the 1920s. Even the Moscow underground railway was encumbered with overbearing entrance buildings, heavily-decorated marble interiors and symbolic carved figures.

In China before the Revolution in 1949, both major and rural stations reflected, in the external decoration, trim, and choice of building materials, elements of the traditional 'pagoda' style and other features characteristic of the old China. Since the 1950s, and influenced largely by Soviet construction methods and architectural styles, major city stations, newly built or refurbished, have tended to be functional box-like structures in concrete, such as the huge, and uncannily deserted, concrete 'palace' at Peking.

Rural stations are often little more than halls with small concrete or timber sheds for station officials and the ever-present militia – at larger stations in the countryside, platform shelters of the pagoda-style are still common – sometimes elaborately developed to include a 'cathedral-cloister' frontage. Here, despite the predominance of concrete in construction, local building materials and ancient tastes overlap the familiar and universal rectangular concrete shapes with a superficial decorative touch that is characteristically Chinese.

Britain's contribution to large station frontages in the last decade has, with the main exception of the soulless glass front to the new Euston, largely been confined to building office blocks like those at Holborn Viaduct and Cannon Street in London, and at Leeds and Hull. They are like office blocks anywhere else; one almost has to search for the station.

The record in new medium-sized stations is much better. Coventry makes extensive use of glass and timber; Banbury and Stafford have their main offices over the tracks on a bridge and striking external lines; Portishead, near Bristol, although strictly functional, was saved from severity by the use of local stone facings. Folkestone Central has a particularly striking new frontage, built in 1961, incorporating the 19th century idea of a clock tower, but in the slenderest brick and concrete. Post-war reconstruction in Europe gave impetus to new station designs, too, fine examples being Venlo's sloping roof extended to form a frontage canopy – another modern station with a detached clock tower – and Amsterdam's Amstel Station, in Holland, and Seefeld in Austria, to name but three from a large and growing selection.

Although the great stations caught the public eye, a good deal of quiet charm rested in a number of the thousands of small country and urban stations which were built in the last century and a half, with a visual significance quite disproportionate to their numbers. The early railway builders felt that their rural and small town passengers needed reassurance to encourage them to travel by the new mode of conveyance. They built their stations in a domestic style using local materials which provided strong emphasis on the homely and the familiar. From the cottage-type stations with their steep roofs, overhanging gables and latticed windows to the more ambitious half-timbered work with fretted bargeboard and angled porch and the classical town house with elaborate finials and roof patterns, there was an insistence on scale and architectural good manners which ensured that the station fitted into its environment. It was a unique epoch which lasted for about 20 years.

The variety at times was bewildering. Stations were built to look like Italian and French villas, Gothic churches or Scottish baronial castles as confidence grew, interspersed with Tudor and Georgian mansions. 'Line styles' soon developed – an individual style or series of styles on one line.

Left: A view of a functional and modern railway station at Christchurch, New Zealand.

Top right: Elements of the pagoda-style decorate the simple single-storey railway station at Tai-Po in the New Territories, Hong Kong.

Centre right: An RDC3 (rail diesel car) of the Canadian Pacific Railway dominates this view of Mont Roland Station on the Mont Laurier line up-country to North Quebec, Canada.

Below right: The entrance hall at the Gare Montparnasse, Paris.

Below: Desert features can be detected in the design of Albuquerque Station in New Mexico, USA.

The small Lincolnshire town of Stamford, which a 17th century writer described as 'as fine a built town all of stone as may be seen', had two picturesque stations owned by different companies, each of which, though differently styled, was built in local grey stone and fitted perfectly into its surroundings. Anything else would have been disastrous, and the old railways fortunately recognized this.

Though the traditionally-styled railway building was less deep-rooted in European countries, owing to later and slower development, there were numbers of highly-localized stations, for instance in southern France, the Black Forest, Scandinavia and Switzerland. Some of the elaborate Swiss chalet stations were among the most charming, and in remoter areas the custom persisted well into the final decades of the 19th century. Small stations on the Trans-Siberian Railway were completely traditional like the pretty wooden buildings at Achinsk and Mariinsk, or the incredibly ornate Russo-Mongol-Chinese station and water tower at Oyash.

In the Americas, Africa and Australasia, the railway was the means of advancing western-style civilization. Construction was fast and wood offered the cheapest and quickest building material. There was no time for the finer points of design and what few flourishes there were appeared only at larger places. The development of suburban lines outside Europe brought more wooden stations, not to mention a good many in England. On the continent, generally, better taste

was displayed. The growth in the United States of the interurban line, a cross between a railway and a street tramway, involved little startling station work, although the amazing Indianapolis Traction Terminal of 1904 must be mentioned, comprising a multi-storey Italian warehouse-style office block and a train-shed covering eight tracks.

In Britain, the growth of railway companies brought increasing standardization without regard for local traditions. The London & North Western's standard wooden station, for example, was much the same at Wolverton in Buckinghamshire as at Marsden in the Yorkshire Pennines. Small stations elsewhere in Europe, after their bright beginnings, tended to follow a fairly dull pattern with no great pretensions to being other than a railway station. Generally, they were fairly large house-type buildings with staff accommodation included, although local styles predominated. There was some standardization here, too. The Upper Italy Railways, for instance, formed in 1865, followed a vigorous policy of producing standard buildings of all kinds.

The pre-eminence of rail transport in the last century is illustrated by the considerable number of private or special stations built for the royal family, nobility, local landowners, racecourses, ports, hospitals and factories, and such. Cemeteries even had special stations. Brookwood in Surrey, England, had its own private branch line and station, while Rockwood cemetery station in New South Wales, built like a Gothic church with a pair of angels guarding the rail entrance, was carefully dismantled after closure and rebuilt as a church near Canberra. The Hedjaz Railway in Arabia had specially-fortified stations to withstand the attacks of local tribesmen.

The rebuilding of war-damaged railways in Europe has given an opportunity for adventurous designs in smaller stations as well as the large ones. In the developing countries new railway construction has provided an incentive. Brassa in Cameroun is an example: the main building is a concrete cell-like structure, its flat roof extended as a platform canopy. Alongside is a small concrete shelter of remarkably advanced yet simple design, in section resembling a hairpin opened out, with the lower part foreshortened and the upper canted to form an awning. Nakuru station in Uganda is flat roofed in brick with a concrete footbridge and an interesting island platform awning profile, low pitched with equal-angled canopies on both sides.

Modern railway policy of providing only 'basic railway' facilities on secondary lines in recent years has meant the replacement of many elaborate Victorian buildings with small metal and glass 'bus stop' structures which provide only minimum shelter. The traditional canopies, waiting rooms, and lavatories even, are rapidly disappearing other than at important stations. No doubt this policy makes for economies, though such minimum shelters are hardly attractive to passengers in wintry weather, although even a very basic station is preferable than no station at all.

In the USA, the approximate number of steam locomotives on Class I railroads fell from 37,500 in 1946 to 1,700 in 1958. After the end of the 1950s, use of steam locomotives in the USA was very limited. In Europe, main line steam lasted a few years longer. The years which saw the end of steam in general use on some national railway systems were: Holland – 1958; Irish Republic – 1964; Belgium – 1966; Great Britain – 1968; Norway – 1970; Denmark – 1971; France – 1975. The same period has seen remarkable growth of live railway preservation – in various forms and under various names. Great Britain has preserved railways, the USA tourist railroads, France *chemins de fer touristiques*, Germany *Museums-Eisenbahnen*. In Switzerland, the Blonay-Chamby line calls itself simultaneously *chemin de fer touristique* and *Museumsbahn*. Norway has two *hobbybaner*. Railway preservation varies greatly in different parts of the world. At risk of over-simplifying a complex subject, preservation activities can be placed in three categories.

In the first category are railways run the whole time by preservation organizations. In some instances the organization owns the freehold, in others the organization operates under govern-

Below left: A working replica of George Stephenson's *Locomotion*, the engine built in 1825 for the Stockton and Darlington Railway. The replica is shown in action at the 1975 celebrations of the Railway's 150th anniversary.

Below right: No 92220, *Evening Star*. Built at Swindon Works in 1960, this was the last steam locomotive constructed for British Railways. It had a relatively short life before becoming a museum locomotive.

ment concession or has a lease. Often locomotives and rolling stock are provided by other preservation groups or individuals.

In the second category are some commercially operating railways, big and small, which have retained or even repurchased steam locomotives to haul tourist trains. In some instances, lengths of run are short and steam services regular enough to appear in public timetables. In others, distances are long and steam specials intermittent.

In the third category, locomotives and rolling stock owned by preservation organizations run on railways which otherwise provide a normal transport service. Again, there are in some instances regularly-scheduled trains over fairly short distances, and in others there are occasional specials over much longer routes.

The growth of live railway preservation has taken place largely in the countries of north-west Europe and in English-speaking countries elsewhere; USA, Canada, Australia, New Zealand. In those countries, the decline of the steam locomotive has been most rapid, and the railways have had to meet most competition from road and air. There appears to be no live railway preservation in communist countries, with one or two exceptions in eastern Europe, and there is little in Latin America, Africa and non-communist Asia. Many countries in those parts of the world retain in use railway equipment which would be preserved elsewhere. Japan is an exception: the end of steam on Japanese National Railways in 1975 has been matched by an upsurge of steam enthusiasm of truly Japanese thoroughness.

Throughout the world many locomotives are in static preservation – some individually, slowly rusting on pedestals, some as parts of small museums or general technical museums, and some as parts of great collections such as those at York (England) and Steamtown (USA) and Mulhouse (France), and those which are being built up in India and South Africa. Locomotives preserved throughout the world are listed in detail in the four comprehensive volumes of *Preserved Locomotives* compiled by Gerald Wildish and updated at intervals. His world-wide grand

total up to September 16, 1976 was 6,907 loco-motives. This includes both static and live pre-servation, and electric and internal combustion power as well as steam. The geographical spread was: Europe, 4,028 locomotives (including 1,547 in Britain); North, Central and South America, 1,897 locomotives (including 1,544 in the USA); Asia, Africa and Australasia, 981 locomotives. Many locomotives which worked in one country are now preserved in another.

By 1966 the *Steam Passenger Service Directory* (published by Empire State Railway Museum Inc., USA) was already listing 53 steam railway operations in North America. By 1976 the total had risen to 88. Several of those listed earlier had disappeared, to be more than offset by those newly opened. In Britain, the Association of Railway Preservation Societies was formed in 1965 with nine members. By 1976 the total of full and associate member societies was well over 100. These included both societies preserving locomotives and rolling stock, and those con-nected with operating railways. The association furthers mutual co-operation among members, promotes publicity for them and encourages them to achieve high standards. In Holland, where as recently as 1970 railway preservation was virtually limited to the excellent but static railway museum at Utrecht, there were by 1976 seven operating museum lines.

It is clearly impracticable in the following description to detail every organization or railway operating preserved steam. Nor are the great rail-way museums described here. Rather an attempt has been made to describe steam operations which are important, typical, or perhaps excep-tional, with brief details of some of the others. They must stand for the rest. There is one thing almost all steam operations carrying passengers do have in common, wherever they are located: they have come, by accident or by design, to be part of the tourist trade. Tourists and holiday-makers form the majority of their passengers, rail-fans the minority. To all, however, they offer an experience compounded of sentiment, education and entertainment.

Above: A 'Big Boy' 4–8–8–4 Mallet locomotive formerly belonging to the Union Pacific Railroad. This American design of locomotive is generally recognised as the world's biggest.

Left: A once well-known Canadian Pacific design for secondary passenger service.

Below left: A Shay-type articulated logging locomotive, now preserved for working on the Cass Scenic Railroad in West Virginia.

Below right: On the Torbay Steam Railway, later renamed the Torbay and Dartmouth Railway. The train is shown approaching the terminus at Kingswear behind No 4588, a 2–6–2 tank locomotive.

Britain

Back in 1951, the pioneers of the Talyllyn Railway Preservation Society were totally unaware that their activities would have such widespread consequences. One of the attractions of the 10.5 km (6½ mile) long Talyllyn Railway which is in North Wales, was that, in 1951, the railway still retained the two locomotives, four four-wheel coaches and brakevan with which it had been equipped as long ago as the 1860s. Except for a few hundred yards, the rails were original too. When the railway was built, heavy traffic of slates was anticipated, but this never developed. There had been neither cause to modernize the railway, nor money with which to do so. During the second world war, the railway was not considered important for transport, and so was not brought under government control. In consequence the TRC was omitted from the almost all-embracing list of British railway companies that were nationalized in 1948. In 1950, came the death of Sir Haydn Jones, to whom the company had belonged since 1911. The railway, already in bad condition, seemed likely to be closed and its equipment scrapped.

The TRPS was formed on October 11, 1950, and led by the late L T C Rolt. Sir Haydn's widow generously agreed to give the railway company shares to a new holding company controlled by the society. The society was to raise funds to operate the railway and made a tremendous start, carrying during the summer of 1951, 15,618 passengers, three times as many as in the previous year.

It was very nearly too successful. Rapidly-increasing traffic meant excessive wear and tear on ancient and dilapidated equipment. Talyllyn members rapidly came up against a problem which has plagued railway preservationists ever since: that to use historic railway equipment is the quickest way to wear it out. Everything from boilers to bearings has in due course to be replaced, and as each old part is discarded, so a little bit of history is destroyed. On the other hand, if a locomotive or piece of rolling stock is to be maintained indefinitely in precisely the same form as that in which it came out of service, then it must be kept unused as a museum exhibit.

The answer is that there is room for both. It is important that people should be able to visit a museum to see a locomotive in the knowledge that those very pieces of steel and brass created a particular speed record. But equally the essence of a steam railway is the sight and sound of a moving train, coupled with the skills of those who make it work, and it is these that are not so much preserved as kept alive by preserved and tourist railways.

Some 50 km (31 miles) to the north of the Talyllyn Railway is the Festiniog Railway, of 597 mm (1 ft 11½ in) gauge. In the last century it was more extensive and ambitious than the TR; by the early 1950s it was in an even worse state. It was opened in 1836 to carry slates from quarries near Blaenau Ffestiniog for 21 km (13 miles) to

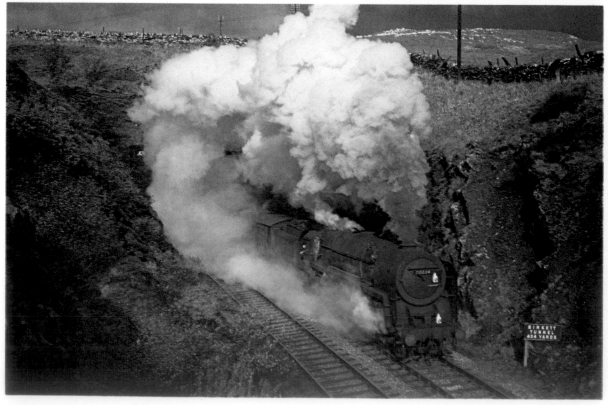

Above: Linda of the Festiniog Railway at the Railway's workshops near Portmadoc. This locomotive was originally used by the Penrhyn Quarry Railway, and has recently been converted for oil-burning.

Below right: On the present-day Talyllyn Railway. The locomotive *Douglas*, originally built in 1918 for an industrial railway, takes water at Dolgoch.

Left: The last days of steam on British Railways. The 4-6-2 passenger locomotive *Vulcan* hauls a freight on the picturesque Settle and Carlisle line.

the port of Portmadoc (now called Porthmadog). Until 1863, trains were powered by horses or gravity, but in that year steam locomotives were introduced, the first on so narrow a gauge, and two years later passenger trains, the first in Britain on a gauge less than standard.

By the 1940s, things on the Festiniog were very different, and declining traffic culminated in complete closure in 1946.

The Festiniog Railway Society originated from a public meeting held in September 1951 and with money and voluntary labour from the society, restoration of the FR commenced.

Above left: On the Talyllyn Railway, decades before the preservation movement was thought of.

Above right: A double-Fairlie locomotive, the Festiniog Railway's most interesting equipment. These patented locomotives were pioneered on this railway in the nineteenth century, when they seemed to promise high power outputs on winding narrow-gauge track.

Reopening throughout is scheduled for 1977. The Festiniog's revival has been even more of a success story than that of the Talyllyn. During 1975 it carried 441,000 passengers.

The air of main line competence, reminiscent of the FR of a century ago, has not been recovered overnight. It has been accomplished gradually since 1954. In the process, original locomotives and rolling stock, though overhauled and still in use, have to some extent been overshadowed by new or improved equipment. Rather than simply preserve the old, the FR has developed new techniques for small steam railways. Its new coaches have rubber suspension, and its locomotives burn a mixture of waste and diesel oil. It is in such developments, as much as in surviving physical equipment, that the spirit of the old FR lives on.

Two additions to the locomotive stock are of international interest. The first is No K1, the original Beyer-Garratt articulated locomotive built in 1909 for Tasmania's North East Dundas Tramway, and eventually repurchased by her builder, Beyer Peacock, and brought back to Beyer's works in England. When the works closed, she was bought by the FR. Pending eventual rebuilding and use, she is on loan to the National Railway Museum, York.

The other is *Mountaineer*, built in the USA by Alco (Cooke works) in 1917 for the British War Department to use on military light railways in France. She finished up in civilian use on the *Tramway de Pithiviers à Toury* and, when that line closed in 1965, was bought by the author, aided by the *Fédération des Amis des Chemins de Fer Secondaires* (Federation of Friends of Secondary Railways), brought to England and, eventually, to the FR. Following extensive overhaul she is regularly used on passenger trains.

The examples set by the Talyllyn and Festiniog railways have been widely followed elsewhere – in Wales, England and other countries from Sweden to Australia. In Wales, part of the

762 mm (2 ft 6 in) gauge Welshpool & Llanfair Light Railway (closed in 1956) was acquired from British Railways by enthusiasts in 1962 and reopened.

For the standard-gauge preserved railway, enthusiasts in Britain had to wait until 1960. Indeed, pessimists – or realists – among those connected with the Welsh narrow-gauge lines held that standard-gauge equipment was so bulky that it would be quite beyond the scope of volunteers. They have been shown to be wrong – but this indicates not that full-size equipment was any less massive, or its maintenance less laborious, than was supposed, but that some practical railway enthusiasts proved capable of greater determination than was expected.

In 1960, two very different standard gauge preserved railways appeared on the scene almost simultaneously: the Middleton Railway and the Bluebell Railway. The Middleton is urban and industrial with a history going back to 1758, when a waggonway was built to link Middleton colliery with Leeds. It has another remarkable claim to fame: although it does now offer a passenger service at weekends, the Middleton Railway has been, and continues to be, a preserved railway operated principally for freight.

The Bluebell Railway, by contrast, was the archetypal rural branch line. The Lewes to Horsted Keynes branch of British Railways had gained the nickname 'Bluebell line' from the spring flowers along its wooded course. When it was closed in 1955, local opposition discovered an Act of Parliament which obliged BR to reopen it. After it was closed a second time, a preservation society was formed in 1959.

The 8 km (5 mile) section from Sheffield Park to Horsted Keynes was considered to be short enough to be a practical proposition for preservation. There was no precedent for preservation of a British Railways branch (the W&L scheme was still in its formative stage) and negotiations were long and complicated. The solution which eventually emerged made use of late-19th century legislation intended to encourage development of rural transport by construction of light railways. First, trustees appointed by the Bluebell Railway Preservation Society formed themselves into a company called The Bluebell Railway Limited; then the Minister of Transport made a light railway order for the line, followed by a further order (a light railway transfer order) transferring it from BR to The Bluebell Railway. This company at first leased the line from BR; later the company purchased the line.

The Dart Valley Railway (Buckfastleigh to

Above left: A former Great Western 0–4–2 tank locomotive takes water at Buckfastleigh on the Dart Valley Railway.

Above: Another former Great Western locomotive on the Dart Valley Railway. An 0–6–0 pannier tank locomotive refuels.

Above right: On the *Puffing Billy* line in Australia, located in pastoral countryside near Melbourne.

Centre right: A diminutive 0–6–0 tank locomotive, once part of Class P of the South Eastern and Chatham Railway, at Sheffield Park on the Bluebell Railway.

Below left: A carefully restored Bulleid 4–6–2 of the former Southern Railway, *Blackmore Vale*, hauls a heavy special train on the Bluebell Railway in Sussex.

Below right: On the Romney, Hythe & Dymchurch Railway in 1929. The locomotive, though built in Britain, is styled to represent North American practice.

Australia

The train Australians call *Puffing Billy* runs on a 13.25 km (8¼ mile) 762 mm (2 ft 6 in) gauge branch line of Victorian Railways, from Belgrave, east of Melbourne, to Lakeside. For many years its operation has been a unique blend of government railway and voluntary preservation society. The line, opened in 1900, originally ran from Upper Fern Tree Gully through Belgrave and Lakeside to Gembrook. It passed through the picturesque Dandenong ranges and became so popular with excursionists that, when it was closed in 1953 following a landslide beyond Belgrave, a limited service of tourist trips continued between Upper Fern Tree Gully and Belgrave. But only until 1958: then this section was widened and electrified as part of Melbourne's suburban network.

Meanwhile the Puffing Billy Preservation Society had been formed in 1954 and aimed to reopen the line from Belgrave to Lakeside. Major tasks were to build a new station at Belgrave and to reinstate the line past the landslide; but a first section was reopened in 1962 and *Puffing Billy* eventually reached Lakeside again on October 18, 1975.

Puffing Billy locomotives are a distinctive class of 2–6–2 tank, Australian-built but based on a design by Baldwin Locomotive Works, USA, which built the first two of the class. Enclosed observation cars from the Mount Lyell railway in Tasmania were obtained to supplement Puffing Billy's own open-sided excursion coaches.

The railway has remained part of the VR system and the driver, fireman and guard on each train are always VR employees. Other tasks – such as selling tickets, maintaining track, repairing carriages, and publicity – are done by preservation society volunteers. As with early British

Totnes) and the Torbay Steam Railway (Paignton to Kingswear) are owned and operated by the Dart Valley company, and Great Western practices prevail. Two preserved lines which have recently opened, but which have been a long time in the formative stages, are the Kent & East Sussex Railway, in 1975, and the North Norfolk Railway in 1976.

There are other types of line to be considered. Some former industrial lines now carry passengers with steam trains – such as the Sittingbourne & Kemsley, Leighton Buzzard narrow gauge and Foxfield railways. Two famous long-distance miniature railways, the Romney Hythe & Dymchurch and the Ravenglass & Eskdale, have survived probable closure through rescue operations mounted by enthusiasts. And new narrow-gauge lines have been added to existing tourist attractions – such as the Whipsnade & Umfolozi in Whipsnade Zoo.

railway preservation schemes, the example of *Puffing Billy* in Australia has been followed by establishment of many other railway preservation groups.

Europe

The first steam-worked tourist railway in France was the brainchild of certain railway enthusiasts – notably Jean Arrivetz – who regretted the decline and disappearance of the light railways once common in that country. In 1959 the enthusiasts decided to build a new one: the *Chemin de Fer Touristique de Meyzieu*. It took shape as 1.6 km (1 mile) of 600 mm (1 ft 11⅝ in) gauge track on a roadside location – typical of French light railways – east of Lyon. The line was opened in 1962 and was a success. Locomotives came from industrial railways, and coaches included former tram trailers reduced in gauge.

When built, the line was in the country. But with the rapid growth of Lyon, the district started to become built up, and another location was sought. Eventually CFTM was given a concession to operate a 6 km (3¾ mile) line within an extensive 'leisure park' being created nearby. But the new line is not expected to be complete before 1985, and in the meantime the Meyzieu line has closed and its equipment is stored.

Meanwhile, the operators have undertaken a far greater task. In the mountains to the south of Lyon the *Réseau du Vivarais*, a metre-gauge system of immense character and great scenic attraction was closed in 1968. This closure challenged Arrivetz and his associates. They were aware of the success of the Talyllyn and Festiniog railways, and they had learned some lessons from Meyzieu. CFTM offered to work a 53 km (33 mile) section of the Vivarais, from Tournon to Le Cheylard, for goods and tourist passengers, in return for a local authority subsidy (this being the normal arrangement in France, except for the substitution of tourists for travellers). The authority refused. CFTM then offered to work the 33 km (20½ miles) from Tournon, where there was an interchange station with French Railways, to Lamastre at its own risk. This was met with amazement, but the concession was granted.

The line was retitled *Chemin de Fer du Vivarais* and a supporting association formed. Later, in 1972, CFTM changed its name (but retained its initials) to become *Chemins de Fer Touristiques et de Montagne* (Tourist and Mountain Railways).

The new régime ran its first public trains in June 1969. It got off to a shaky start, with avalanches of rocks on to the line, thefts of material, a collision between two railcars and, for a time, refusal by French Railways to let Vivarais trains into Tournon station over a length of mixed-gauge track. But passengers came, problems were overcome and additional rolling stock obtained. To the two handsome 0–6–6–0 tank Mallet locomotives which had been inherited from the RduV was added another, of similar type, resurrected from scrap; further locomotives and coaches have been added from many parts of

Above left: A Mallet
compound locomotive on the
metre-gauge Réseau du
Vivarais in France.

Above right: A
standard-gauge 2–6–0,
formerly of the Est Railway,
which AJECTA operates on
its line from Chinon to
Richelieu.

Bottom left: Another Mallet
locomotive at work hauling
tourists on the Vivarais line.
Mallet tank locomotives
were used by many French
and German narrow-gauge
lines because their pivoted
sets of driving wheels suited
them for winding track.

Below: A former Réseau
Breton locomotive at work
on the Vivarais line in
France.

France and from Switzerland. Only ten years ago, a single lightweight railcar with trailer, was generally adequate for passenger traffic between Tournon and Lamastre; now, the line sees steam-hauled trains of a dozen coaches.

Even before closure of the RduV, closure of another French light railway had already prompted preservation. This was the old-established 600 mm (1 ft 11⅝ in) gauge *Tramway de Pithiviers à Toury*. It closed in 1965, and used steam to the end. The *Fédération des Amis des Chemins de Fer Secondaires* first took steps to ensure survival of various items of equipment and then joined forces with AMTUIR (*Association pour le Musée des Transports Urbains, Interurbains et Ruraux:* Urban, Interurban & Rural Transport Museum Association), which already had a transport museum in Paris, to promote the *Association du Musée des Transports de Pithiviers*. With the support of local authorities, and the voluntary work of members, this live museum was opened on April 23, 1966.

The museum proper is housed in the former locomotive sheds and works of the TPT at Pithiviers, some 96 km (60 miles) south of Paris. Part of the TPT was retained as an operating line: it was later extended into a new terminus called Bellebat to give a route length of 3.8 km (2⅜ miles); the new terminus has more space for crowds than the old, and is complete with a turning wye.

Many other steam tourist railways have been established in France. Notable among them are the 700 mm (2 ft 3⁹⁄₁₆ in) gauge Abreschviller Forest Railway, a former logging line in a picturesque part of the Vosges, and the *Chemin de Fer Touristique des Landes de Gascogne,* a standard-gauge line in the south-west.

Belgium has long been good country for light railways, and an extensive system remains, though now electrified. In 1966 the *Société National des Chemins de Fer Vicinaux* (National Light Railway Company) conceded operation of 10 km (6 miles) of disused metre-gauge (3 ft 3⅜ in) line in a scenic part of the Ardennes to the *Tramway Touristique de l'Aisne* (Aisne Tourist Tramway). This had been set up by an association of light railway enthusiasts. SNCV provided railcars with which operations started; subsequently TTA has added steam locomotives, including some of enclosed tramway type.

In Holland also the term *tramweg* (literally, tramway) is used to describe light railways. *Tramweg Stichting,* the Tramway Society, is an offshoot of *Nederlandse Vereniging van Belangstellenden in het Spoor- en tramwegwezen* (NVBS), the Dutch association of people interested in railways and tramways. It has close links with three preserved lines. TS has 1,600 supporters, of whom about 10 per cent work voluntarily at tasks which include guard and engine driver – for these two they must pass an examination and be sworn in by a district judge.

The most interesting activity of TS is the *Stoomtram Hoorn-Medemblik* (Hoorn-Medem-

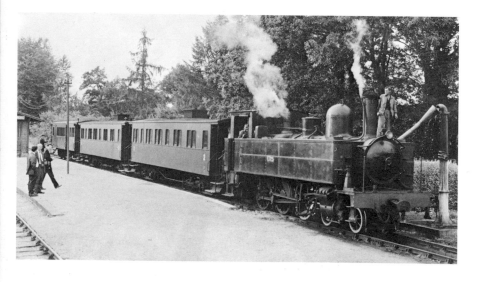

blik Steam Tram), a standard-gauge line 20 km (12½ miles) long. The number of passengers grew from 18,000 in 1971 to 70,000 in 1975 and is still increasing. In 1975 SHM took over operation of freight traffic on the line from Netherlands Railways. Goods wagons are added to passenger trains and traffic includes potatoes, rags and yachts which are sent from Medemblik via Hoorn to Rotterdam for export. Curiously enough, the Peterborough Railway Society in England has similar traffic (cabin cruisers for export) although its line is not yet open for public passenger service.

The other TS operations are at Hellevoetsluis, where locomotives and stock of the former 1,067 mm (3 ft 6 in) gauge Rotterdam Steam Tramway are operated over 1.8 km (1⅛ miles) of track relaid on the original roadbed, and near Amsterdam there is a museum line devoted to electric trams. Other standard-gauge steam lines are the *Stoomtram Goes-Borsele* in the south which, like the SHM, carries freight as well as passengers, and the line from Haaksbergen to Boekelo in the east. This line formerly ran to Enschede but has been truncated by construction

of a main road across its route. This type of problem is all too familiar on English lines (Lakeside & Haverthwaite, Kent & East Sussex, for example) – but on the Dutch line the crossing may still be used five times a year for service purposes.

When the *Östra Södermanlands Järnväg* (East Södermanland Railway), a voluntary organization, was set up in 1959 to collect, restore and operate material from Sweden's seven former 600 mm gauge passenger railways, it based itself on an industrial line belonging to a brickworks. After the 3 km (1⅞ mile) standard-gauge branch of Swedish State Railways from Läggesta to Mariefred was closed, the ÖSLJ was authorized to re-lay it to 600 mm gauge and reopen it. This it did, and moved its equipment, to reopen for regular traffic in 1966. In 1973 the Läggesta end of the line was extended for about 1 km to a new terminus called Läggesta Södra, near both the standard-gauge station and a main road.

The stock includes 8 locomotives and 12 carriages; locomotives include No 7 *Helganäs*, a 0–4–2 tank built in England by Hudswell Clarke in 1889, and No 2 *Virå*, an elegant 2–4–2 tank built in Sweden in 1901.

In Switzerland the Blonay-Chamby line, metre gauge (3 ft 3⅜ in) and 2.95 km (1¾ miles) long, is operated with both steam and electric traction, and in Austria the *Verein der Kärntner Eisenbahn Freunde* (Carinthian Railway Enthusiasts' Club) runs a 3 km (1⅞ mile) section of the 760 mm (2 ft 5¹⁵⁄₁₆ in) gauge line formerly called the *Gurktalbahn*. But in both these countries, the main stream of steam preservation has taken a different course. Museum railways are reported from Hungary, Czechoslovakia and East Germany.

North America

In North America, steam railways have become more closely involved with the tourist industry than elsewhere, and preservation for

Above left: A preserved Swiss locomotive of 1882.

Above: A steam tram in the Low Countries.

Above right: The Rhaetian Railway's pair of preserved 2–8–0 locomotives.

Right: Active relics of the Maine narrow gauge lines at Edaville, Massachusetts.

Left: On the Blonay to Chamby tourist railway in Switzerland. A Mallet 0–4–4–0 tank locomotive.

Below: The Tilburg-Turnhout tourist train in Holland.

purely historic reasons has tended more towards static museums. Notable among these are the Baltimore & Ohio Railroad Museum, the Smithsonian Institution, the National Museum of Transport at St Louis and the Canadian Railway Museum near Montreal. Some museums have amateur support, and some include short operating lines.

Ellis D Atwood had no thought of tourism in 1945 when, aided by Lindwood W Moody, he started to build the Edaville Railroad (named after Atwood's initials). Quite the contrary: the railroad, an 8.9 km (5½ mile) loop, was to serve Atwood's cranberry farm at South Carver, Massachussetts, and its passenger cars would carry him and his friends. Atwood was able to recreate a line resembling the 610 mm (2 ft) gauge railroads in Maine which he had known, and from which he had been able to purchase, after closure, locomotives, rolling stock and rails. The Edaville RR was completed with a traditional golden spike ceremony on April 7, 1947. Only when visitors started to arrive in ever-increasing numbers was the decision taken to start a revenue-earning passenger service.

After Atwood's death, his widow ran the railroad until 1955, and then sold it to F Nelson Blount, a distant relative. Blount expanded his activities to standard gauge, setting up the immense locomotive collection of Steamtown USA at Bellows Falls, Vermont, with live steam operations over the Green Mountain RR. In 1967 he was killed in an air crash. Until 1970 Edaville was run by Blount's right hand man and executor, Fred Richardson; then it was sold to the present owner, George E Bartholomew.

Edaville's workshops are extensive enough to have fitted new boilers to the four locomotives (two 2–4–4 tanks and two 0–4–4 tanks) obtained from the Maine railroads, and to have rebuilt a fifth, including fitting a new boiler and narrowing the gauge from 762 mm (2 ft 6 in). Passenger cars include 11 originals from Maine and 22 built out of Maine freight wagons. Today, 5 per cent of Edaville's business is railfan and 95 per cent is tourist: it is a mixture between a working museum and a tourist attraction.

Tourism was not uppermost in the minds of the group headed by the late Henry K Long which purchased the Strasburg Rail Road in 1958. The standard-gauge Strasburg RR is the USA's oldest short line, incorporated in 1832. It lost its passenger service in 1920, and in 1958 it faced total abandonment. Long's group wished to purchase the historic line and preserve and restore it by operating it as a hobby.

The purchasers acquired a 7.2 km (4½ mile) stretch of lush grass with railway track hidden somewhere beneath it, and a 32-year old petrol locomotive in need of heavy repairs. But the locomotive was restored, and track patched up enough, for freight traffic – a single incoming freight car – to start up again on November 8, 1958. This was followed by passenger traffic, using a coach purchased from the Reading Railroad, on January 4, 1959.

The railroad was desperately short of money for renovation. Freight revenue fell short of expectations, but passenger revenue more than made up for it so it was decided to concentrate on passenger business, and to restore the entire route to a typical short line steam railroad of the turn of the century.

It was the right decision. Passengers have increased from 8,712 in 1959 to over 360,000 a year at present. This has meant not only the acquisition of steam locomotives and passenger cars, but also construction of workshops and a passenger station, called East Strasburg. The station building is handsome and genuine, originally built in 1882 and re-erected at Strasburg in 1960. It was removed in sections from its original location 32 km (20 miles) away.

The railroad's first steam locomotive for 34 years, No 31, also arrived in 1960. It is an 0-6-0, previously owned by Canadian National. The next, No 4, is an 0-4-0 of the 'Camelback' type – regrettably too small for today's heavy trains, it is now kept as a static exhibit. Most striking among the other locomotives is No 1223, an elegant Pennsylvania RR 4-4-0 of 1905, which was preserved by that railroad in 1951. The Strasburg RR has been for some years both busy and profitable. But profit is ploughed back, and in addition to all its passengers, the railroad still hauls about 50 wagonloads of freight a year.

One of the most tourist-oriented of all American steam railroads is the 4.8 km (3 mile) long Tweetsie Railroad, near Blowing Rock, North Carolina. Each train is first held up by bandits, then attacked by Indians. Eventually it returns passengers to Tweetsie Town, a reproduction turn-of-the-century railroad town complete with a vaudeville show at the Tweetsie Palace.

A steam railroad of a kind much more familiar to a European railway preservationist is the Valley Railroad which operates approximately 8 km (5 miles) of standard-gauge track between Essex and Chester, Connecticut. Much work such as manning trains and maintaining track and rolling stock is done voluntarily by members of the Connecticut Valley Railroad Museum. The railroad operates over a former New Haven branch line

Above right: The narrow-gauge Silverton train in Colorado; hauled by one of the 4-6-2 locomotives once used by the Rio Grande Railroad on its 914 mm (3 ft)-gauge lines.

Below left: On the Tweetsie Railroad in North Carolina, an enterprise with a show-business approach.

Below: At Greenfield Village, near Detroit, a 4-4-0 locomotive with train forms part of a replica of a mid-nineteenth century American settlement.

which was reopened on July 29, 1971, 100 years to the day after the original opening.

Logging railroads, built to haul logs from forests to sawmills, were an important part of the American scene. In 1911 West Virginia had 4,800 km (3,000 miles) of logging railroads: today all are gone except the line now called the Cass Scenic Railroad. This standard-gauge line was last used for logging in 1960. In 1963 it began operations as a tourist railroad, owned by the West Virginia Department of Natural Resources. Shay and other geared locomotives haul trains over an 18 km (11 mile) route which climbs 700 m (2,300 ft) from Cass to Bald Knob and includes two switchbacks at gradients steeper than 1 in 10.

There are a great many other tourist railroads of various sorts in North America. Notable among them are the East Broad Top RR, 8 km (5 miles) of original 915 mm (3 ft) gauge in Pennsylvania, the Cape Breton Steam Railway in Nova Scotia, Canada, where the locomotives include former Southern Railway (England) 4–4–0 No 926 *Repton*, and the Cumbres & Toltec Scenic RR, 103 km (64 miles) of 915 mm (3 ft) gauge track sponsored by the states of New Mexico and Colorado. But most famous of all – indeed, world famous – is the Silverton Train.

Both the Cumbres & Toltec line and the 72.5 km (45 mile) Silverton branch are surviving remnants of a once extensive network of 915 mm (3 ft) gauge lines operated by the Denver & Rio Grande Western RR in the Rockies. The branch from Durango to Silverton was built in 1882 and has had a passenger service ever since. By the 1940s this was down to a thrice-weekly mixed train, but during the following decade, with the second world war well over, tourism began to build up and tourists in increasing numbers came to ride the Silverton Train. Its route is highly scenic: it passes through forests, clings to precipitous canyon sides, and has a background of high and snow-covered mountains.

The branch is still operated by D&RGW, though it is now isolated from the rest of its system, and long trains run daily throughout the summer. One-way passengers increased from 35,588 for the 1959 season to 97,176 in 1976.

Left: A former Canadian Pacific standard 4–6–2, No 1278, at work with a Steamtown to Bellows Falls tourist train.

Below right: Inside a restored passenger car running on the Cass Scenic Railroad in West Virginia.

There are 21 passenger cars, of which 7 are vintage and the other 14 have been built since 1963. Locomotives are three 2–8–2s so large that British visitors, accustomed to thinking of the 915 mm (3 ft) gauge in terms of the elegant but dainty 2–4–0tanks of the Isle of Man Railway, are surprised to find them as large as the biggest standard-gauge locomotives to have operated at home.

A few small American railroads have entered into the steam tourist-train business with enthusiasm. One such is the standard-gauge Arcade & Attica Railroad in New York State. It dates from 1882 but discontinued regular passenger service in 1951. Eleven years later, in 1962, it introduced steam tourist-trains. Now, a Baldwin 4–6–0 and an Alco-Cooke 2–8–0 power them at weekends throughout the summer between Arcade and Curriers, about 12 km (7½ miles). The railroad has a year-round freight service between Arcade and North Java, 24 km (15 miles) away.

Preservation by operating companies

State-owned railways have generally avoided operating regular steam train services for tourists, but New Zealand Railways is a notable exception. In 1971 NZR introduced the *Kingston Flyer*, which now runs daily throughout the New Zealand summer – from just before Christmas until just after Easter – and is now NZR's only steam train. The idea arose out of a review of branch lines with light traffic. The Lumsden to Kingston section, 60 km (37 miles), of the Invercargill to Kingston line carried but one freight train each way daily, but lay at the centre of a popular tourist area in the South Island. The location suggested a good route for a vintage steam train – so it has turned out.

The train has a 1920s flavour. Two handsome Class Ab Pacifics, dating from 1925 and 1927 and withdrawn in 1969, were restored to work it, together with seven wooden-bodied passenger carriages built between 1900 and 1925. The train is fed by many NZR road coach services, and makes two return journeys daily. Trains sometimes run mixed, and the first outward and last inward trains on weekdays are scheduled to run more slowly than others, so that four-wheel wagons may be added.

Above left: Another view of the Silverton train, photographed near Richmond on the Durango-Silverton line in Colorado.

Above right: Another view of the Canadian National's No 6060 at work with an excursion train.

Centre left: The *Kingston Flyer*, the vintage train of New Zealand Railways. The locomotive is one of the two Ab class 4–6–2 units retained for this service.

Far left: The preserved 4–8–2 of Canadian National Railways, the distinctive bullet-nosed No 6060, photographed at Hamilton with a Niagara Falls excursion.

Left: The former Canadian Pacific *Royal Hudson* No 2860, used for steam excursions by the British Columbia Railway.

Steam-worked narrow-gauge railways have lasted longer in Austria than in most West European countries. In fact steam has now been replaced by diesel for normal train services on most lines, but several have found it worthwhile to put tourist trains (the German word is *Bummelzug*, a little train that goes bumbling along) into their timetables, retaining steam locomotives to work them. First in the field were the *Steiermärkische Landesbahnen* (Styrian Provincial Railways) in 1968 on its 760 mm (2 ft 6 in) gauge *Murtalbahn*. In 1969 SL went one better and offered a steam locomotive for self-drive hire! Tourists may, at a price, themselves drive an 0–4–0 tank under supervision of a regular driver. The same concern operates timetabled steam tourist-trains in summer over its Weiz to Birkfeld line of the same gauge, though this no longer carries ordinary passenger trains.

The well-known 760 mm (2 ft 6 in) gauge *Zillertalbahn* also runs regular steam tourist-trains, and offers a self-drive locomotive; while the *Montafonerbahn*, a 13 km (8 mile) standard-gauge electrified line in the west of Austria, purchased a steam 0–8–0 tank with which to run its own tourist trains.

In Canada, the British Columbia Railway (owned by the provincial government) has since 1974 operated steam tourist-trains over 64 km (40 miles) of standard-gauge line between North Vancouver and Squamish. The locomotive is magnificent – former Canadian Pacific Royal Hudson class 4–6–4 No 2860, complete with stainless-steel jacketed boiler. The train makes

one return trip five days a week during the summer; the scenery, mountains and fiords, is spectacular.

Main line railway systems which maintain their own steam locomotives to operate steam excursions are rare, so one is all the more grateful for the actions of Canadian National Railways. CN has done more than simply run its own steam excursions – it recovered a locomotive which had been on static display for ten years and overhauled it to power them.

Before this, and following the end of steam on CN in 1960, the railway maintained 4–8–4 No 6218 and ran many successful steam excursions with her until the boiler reached the end of its useful life in 1971. Rather than reboiler her, CN decided to overhaul another steam locomotive, and preserve No 6218 as a static exhibit. The choice of replacement fell on No 6060, a U–2–f class 4–8–2. She was the right size, of a type not previously operated in 'nostalgia' service, and when restored to original condition would have a distinctive appearance with conical smokebox-front.

No 6060 was built in 1944 to haul fast passenger trains and incorporated advanced features of the last generation of North American steam locomotives. For example, her entire frame, cylinders and valve blocks and pilot are a single enormous steel casting. In 1962 she was placed on display on a short length of fenced-in track at Jasper, Alberta, where CN employees maintained her.

In 1972 she was taken to Point St Charles

shops for major repairs. These took time, because CN decided that an intensive diesel rebuilding programme should not be interrupted. But by September 15, 1973, she hauled her first public excursion.

In 1975 No 6060 hauled 27 excursions which carried around 13,700 passengers. Operation was profitable, and was expected to be so again in 1976. A typical run is from Toronto via Hamilton to Niagara Falls and back, approximately 130 km (80 miles) each way, with a 90 km (56 mile) side trip from Niagara Falls to Yager and return. This includes a photographic run-past on the wye at Yager where the train is turned, and another on the return journey. Air-conditioned stock is used, and the baggage car next to the locomotive has 110 volt power outlets for tape recording.

Southern Railway System in the USA operates many steam specials. Two of the locomotives used – Nos 630 and 722 – are 2–8–0s built by Baldwin for the Southern, later sold to short lines, and then re-acquired. The third locomotive, Baldwin 2–8–2 No 450, belongs to the Tennessee Valley Railroad Museum. Some of the trains are sponsored by groups such as the local chapters of the National Railway Historical Society; others have an educational bias.

Elsewhere, railway systems which keep a minimal number of steam locomotives include French Railways, which has 4–6–0 No 230G353 for films and hauling specials, Danish State Railways which retains a 2–6–4tank and other locomotives for specials, Victorian Railways in Australia, and the railways of Japan, Rumania and Malawi.

In Switzerland many of the independent railways have one or two steam locomotives with which they operate steam excursions, either for the public or on charter to groups. On the *Rhaetische Bahn* (Rhaetian Railway), Switzerland's most important metre-gauge railway, two 2–8–0s power steam excursions through mountain scenery second to none over a route which includes spirals on a grade of 1 in 29. The *Appen-*

zeller Bahn obtained a 2–6–0tank from the RhB in 1973 for steam excursions, and among standard-gauge lines the *Sihltalbahn* and the *Mittel-Thurgau Bahn* also run steam specials.

Netherlands Railways 4–6–0 No 3737 celebrated the end of steam in Holland on January 7, 1958 by hauling the last train, which was then preserved in Utrecht Railway Museum. In 1972 she was removed from the museum and restored to working order. She worked some specials in 1974; later that year and during 1975 she was hired to *Stichting Stoomtreinmaatschappij Tilburg-Turnhout* (Tilburg-Turnhout Steam Train Company) to work a regular tourist train service, but Netherlands Railways then reclaimed her to work specials on their own network. The SSTT operation continues with two Hunslet 0–6–0tanks built in the 1940s.

In Britain, British Rail's only steam operation is also its only narrow-gauge section – the 19 km (11¾ mile) 597 mm (1 ft 11½ in) gauge Vale of Rheidol line from Aberystwyth to Devil's Bridge in Wales. It was opened in 1902 for general traffic but has always attracted tourists because of its scenic route high up on the side of the Rheidol gorge. After 1930 the line ran exclusively for tourists in summer only, and when the rest of BR

Top left: A 4–6–0 of the former Paris-Orléans Railway, No 230G 353, now preserved. This locomotive was used in the film *Orient Express*.

Top right: Swiss Rhaetian Railway's pair of preserved 2–8–0s.

Centre left: *Flying Scotsman* in America, here pictured at San Francisco.

Centre right: No 8, one of the three 2–6–2 narrow-gauge tank locomotives operated by British Rail on the Vale of Rheidol line in Wales, takes water at Devil's Bridge.

Far right: Stephenson's *Locomotion* is confronted by the Duke of Edinburgh at the official opening of the National Railway Museum at York.

Right: Early coaching stock in the National Railway Museum at York.

went over to diesel and electric traction, the narrow-gauge tourist line continued to be operated with its three steam locomotives. These are 2–6–2 tanks; one dates from the opening of the line and the other two were built specially for it by the Great Western Railway in 1923.

The attitude of British Rail towards steam specials has varied widely over the years. Back in the late 1950s, *City of Truro*, the record-breaking GWR 4–4–0 with a claim to 164.6 km/h (102.3 mph) in 1904, was removed from the railway museum at York where she had been since 1931 and restored to work special trains. Then BR's Scottish Region repainted several pre-grouping locomotives in their original colours and used them on specials.

In 1962 A F Pegler started a trend when he purchased the famous 4–6–2 *Flying Scotsman* on her withdrawal by BR and had her overhauled. With great foresight he also obtained a legal agreement entitling *Flying Scotsman* to run over BR tracks, and she powered many specials.

As steam declined rapidly on BR many other locomotives were purchased by individuals or by preservation groups. They included A4 class Pacifics *Union of South Africa* and *Sir Nigel Gresley*, GWR 4–6–0 *Clun Castle*, LMS 4–6–2 *Princess Elizabeth* and many more. Many steam excursions were hauled by such locomotives.

But when its own last standard-gauge steam locomotives were withdrawn in 1968, British Rail imposed a ban on use of privately-owned locomotives on its lines, excepting *Flying Scotsman* with the benefit of her agreement. Reasons for the ban have never been made public.

In the meantime, several preservation groups had, like the SRPS, obtained locomotives and rolling stock and set up depots in which they might be stored and maintained. At Didcot, Oxfordshire, for instance, the Great Western Society (formed in 1961) has since 1969 used the former motive power depot to house most of its collection of locomotives and rolling stock. By 1976 this extended to 16 GWR locomotives and 3 others, and over 50 carriages and wagons. Not only are the locomotive shed and its ancilliaries – coaling stage, ash pits, water tower – maintained for their proper purpose, but locomotives and rolling stock are overhauled and maintained to a very high standard.

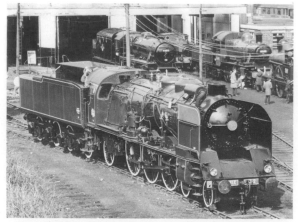

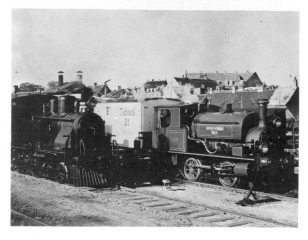

Centre far left: Preservation in Denmark; Sunday activity at Helsingfors.

Centre left: Another preserved Great Western machine, *Clun Castle*, a four-cylinder 4–6–0 somewhat smaller than *King George V*, but to the same general design.

Below: *Shannon*, an 1857 locomotive with a varied history, now preserved in working order at the Great Western Society's depot at Didcot, near Oxford.

Comparable depots have been established at Carnforth, Tyseley, Dinting, Hereford and elsewhere. Generally they include a length of track long enough to give a reasonable run for demonstrating trains.

It was at Hereford that the return-to-steam breakthrough came. While steam was being phased out on British Rail, BR itself had set up a national collection of historic locomotives and rolling stock. This exceeded available museum accommodation or storage space on BR, and some items were loaned to responsible preservation groups or other bodies. The famous GWR 4–6–0 No 6000 *King George V* was one of these: in 1968 she was transferred to H P Bulmer, cider makers of Hereford. Bulmer already had purchased from BR a rake of five Pullman cars to use as a travelling exhibition train. *King George V* was overhauled and joined the Pullmans at Hereford, where she was often steamed on Bulmer's private sidings.

In 1971 British Rail, after long negotiations by Peter Prior, Bulmer's group managing director, agreed that *King George V* might take the cider train on a tour, as an experiment to establish what difficulties were inherent in running occasional steam specials. After trials, the tour was made over four days in October 1971. It was an outstanding success; a return to steam was achieved.

Subsequently BR announced a limited programme of steam specials for 1972, over a number of routes which carried light traffic but which were far longer than those any preserved railways had to offer. There were 5 routes, and 23 locomotives were passed to run on them. Similar agreements were made in the years following, though both routes and locomotives have varied.

Late in 1975 BR announced a policy for four years ahead as an incentive to locomotive owners to invest in repairs and maintenance to a high standard. Fourteen routes were designated in 8 areas, and 23 locomotives were authorized to run.

The Railway Preservation Society of Ireland has been fortunate in the co-operation given by the Irish railway systems, *Coras Iompair Eireann* (Irish Transport Company) and Northern Ireland Railways, and was able to operate main line steam specials throughout the period of the steam ban in Great Britain. RSPI specials now range widely over almost the whole of the two railways and feature photographic run-pasts, lineside buses which take passengers to photographic vantage points and then meet the trains, and two-day trips using two locomotives either alternately or double-heading. A great achievement is the *Portrush Flyer*. This RPSI steam train runs regularly on summer Saturdays out of Belfast to take passengers for the day to the seaside resort of Portrush.

The RPSI was formed in 1964. It now has six locomotives and sufficient coaches to form its own trains; locomotives include J 15 class 0–6–0 No 186 of a classic Irish type. All stock is to the Irish standard gauge of 1,600 mm (5 ft 3 in) and is based on the society's depot at Whitehead, between Belfast and Larne. Plans include increasing its already extensive maintenance facilities by installing a foundry so that the society can cast its own firebars and brake blocks.

One of the Australian Railway Historical Society's activities is to organize steam specials powered by preserved locomotives. The society originated in 1933 and ran its first railtour in 1946, and it now has divisions in all Australian states. Many

Right: Three preserved locomotives lined up at Carnforth. On the left is a former Midland Railway compound 4–4–0, restored to its original condition. In the centre is a Great Western *Hall* 4–6–0, and at the right another two-cylinder 4–6–0 of the former London, Midland and Scottish Railway.

Right: *Clun Castle*, hauling a train over a short stretch of line at Tyseley, near Birmingham.

of these have their own museums of steam locomotives – at Melbourne, Adelaide, Brisbane and Perth – and some of the exhibits are maintained in working order for specials.

In New South Wales, the NSW Rail Transport Museum at Thirlmere, approximately 80 km (50 miles) south of Sydney, has a collection of about 40 steam locomotives. About eight of these are kept in condition for traffic – they include No 3801, a streamlined Pacific which in 1970 powered the first and only steam train to travel from Sydney to Perth, following completion throughout of the standard-gauge route. New South Wales has now relaxed a BR-style steam ban to the extent that the ARHS and NSWRTM are jointly permitted to have six steam train tours each year.

In Switzerland, locomotives of the short Blonay-Chamby line work special trains over neighbouring railways of the same metre gauge. In Britain, locomotives of the North Yorkshire Moors Railway sometimes haul specials over BR. There are further instances of intermittent long-distance excursion trains hauled by private or society-owned steam locomotives in Canada, USA, West Germany, Denmark, Sweden and France.

In several countries preservation organizations are able to arrange to operate their locomotives and rolling stock on regular timetabled tourist services over lines otherwise used by normal freight or passenger trains. One of the oldest-established ventures of this sort is in Denmark. The Danish Railway Club was formed in 1961 and acquired two locomotives and two carriages, and the standard-gauge Lolland Railway offered it the use on Sundays of its 7.2 km (4½ mile) branch from Maribo to Bandholm on which to run them. Passenger traffic had ceased on the branch in 1952, but it was still used on weekdays for freight. 'Museum Train' services commenced in 1962 on summer Sundays. Now they run on summer Saturdays, and steam locomotive stock has increased to nine, with railcars as well. In 1970 the club started a similar service on the 16 km (10 mile) line from Mariager to Handest.

The *Erste Museums-Eisenbahn Deutschlands,* or First German Museum Railway, was established in 1966 on a metre-gauge branch line of the *Verkehrsbetriebe Grafschaft Hoya GmbH* (Hoya County Transport Company), south-east of Bremen. Adjoining narrow-gauge lines had been converted to standard-gauge but the 8 km (5 mile) branch from Bruchhausen-Vilsen to Asendorf remained narrow and was still used for freight. On it at weekends the *Deutsche Eisenbahn-Verein* (German Railway Club) was able to arrange to run its museum trains. Stock now includes representatives from many German metre-gauge lines. DEV's example has been followed by other groups in Germany: for instance the *Deutsche Gesellschaft für Eisenbahngeschichte* (German Railway History Society) has regular steam trains on the 750 mm (2 ft 5½ in) gauge line from Möckmuhl to Dorzbach (east of Heidelberg) and on the standard-gauge line from Achern to Ottenhöfen in the Black Forest, which belongs to SWEG (*Sudwestdeutsche Eisenbahnen AG,* South-West German Railways).

Some of the Dutch preserved railways started off with the same system before gaining full control of their lines. Between Apeldoorn and Dieren, 21.7 km (13½ miles), the *Veluwse Stoomtrein Maatschappij* (Veluwe Steam Train Company) runs in summer a daily service of steam-trains over a branch line also used by Netherlands Railways freight trains.

In France, AJECTA (*Association de Jeunes pour l'Exploitation de Chemins de Fer Touristiques et d'Attraction,* which can be translated roughly as Youth Association for working Tourist and Miniature Railways) operates a regular weekend steam train service between Ligré-Rivière and Richelieu, Touraine, over a standard-gauge line otherwise used only for freight. A handsome small 2–6–0 hauls vintage carriages, including a Pullman car, all part of AJECTA's large collection which is otherwise housed at Longueville near Paris.

In Switzerland, the *Sensetalbahn,* an 11.3 km (7 mile) long standard-gauge railway near Berne carries a busy service of electric trains. But into this is inserted, on the first and third Sundays of

May, June, September and October, a steam train service. Locomotives and rolling stock belong to an enthusiasts' group called *Dampfbahn Bern* (Berne Steam Railway).

Of all these voluntary organizations, the one with the most extensive operations is Eurovapor. Its full name is *Europäische Vereinigung von Eisenbahnfreunden zur Erhaltung von Dampflokomotiven* (European Association of Friends of Railways for the maintenance of Steam Locomotives). Eurovapor was founded in 1962 and is based in Zurich, Switzerland. It has about 1,000 members and its steam trains operate over 5 routes in 3 different countries.

The busiest service is in Austria, where Eurovapor steam trains run on the 35 km (22 mile), 760 mm (2 ft 5¹⁵⁄₁₆ in) gauge Austrian Federal Railways branch from Bregenz to Bezau. Trains run on summer Sundays and also on Tuesdays, Wednesdays and Thursdays in July and August. The locomotive is a 0–10–0 tank on loan from the *Zillertalbahn.* Elsewhere, stock of Eurovapor steam trains is owned by the association, and operation is generally one Sunday a month during the summer. On the 750 mm (2 ft 5½ in) gauge *Waldenburgerbahn* (Switzerland's narrowest-gauge railway) an Austrian 0–6–2 tank hauls three Austrian coaches, and, also in Switzerland, on the metre-gauge lines between Worblaufen and Solothurn, and Worblaufen and Worb, a stumpy 1949-built 0–4–0 tank is used. In Germany, a typical small German light railway 0–6–0 tank hauls matching coaches on SWEG's

Top left: A varied assembly of equipment used on the preserved light railway from Haltingen to Kandern in southern Germany.

Top right: A Netherlands Railways 4–6–0, temporarily released from the railway museum at Utrecht, hauls a special train near Tilburg.

Above: A 700 mm-gauge train hauls tourists among the sand dunes at Katwijk in the Netherlands.

Left: A preserved 2–6–0 and a former Prussian State Railways 4–6–4 tank locomotive head a steam excursion in Western Germany.

Right: Preserved locomotives line up for the parade celebrating the 150th anniversary of the Stockton and Darlington Railway in 1975. A three-cylinder 4–6–0 of the 1930s, *Leander* of the former LMS Railway, is in the foreground.

13 km (8 mile) standard-gauge line from Haltingen to Kandern. Trains run through from Basle, over 5.6 km (3½ miles) of German Federal Railway main line, and replace regular diesel passenger services. Eurovapor has many other locomotives, ranging from an elegant Swiss 4–4–0 tank to a massive 01 class Pacific from the German Federal Railway.

There is a pleasant and increasing tendency for preserved steam locomotives to form part of the celebrations of important events. In 1972 Swiss Federal Railways celebrated the 125th anniversary of railways in Switzerland with a series of steam specials hauled by 4–6–0 No 705, and with an international steam festival at which eight preserved locomotives were in steam. The American Freedom Train carried a Bicentennial exhibition to every mainland state of the USA during 1975 and 1976. Its motive power included three steam locomotives. One of these, superb Southern Pacific 4–8–4 No 4449, was restored to working order, largely by voluntary labour, after 16 years of open-air static display.

In Britain, in 1975, 150 years of railways – that is, the 150th anniversary of opening of the Stockton & Darlington Railway – was celebrated at Shildon, County Durham. More than 50 preserved steam locomotives converged on British Rail Engineering's Shildon works from many parts of Britain, for an exhibition which culminated in a cavalcade on August 31 in which 30 of them took part, all but one under their own steam. It was a magnificent sight.

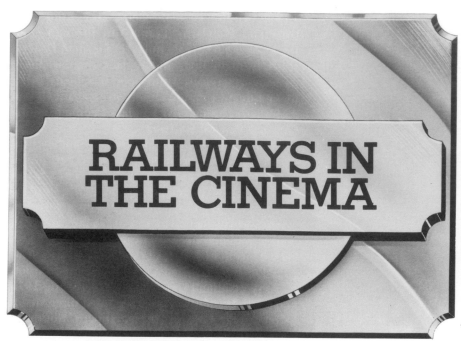

RAILWAYS IN THE CINEMA

The world's first public film show contained a railway scene. This was the Lumière Programme, first shown in the Grand Café of the Boulevard des Capucines in Paris on December 28, 1895 and now universally recognized as the original cinema presentation in the modern sense. One of the hits of the show was a study of a little 2–4–2 locomotive of the PLM railway arriving at La Ciotat station on a branch line from Marseille. It was shot in July 1896 when the two inventors, Auguste and Louis Lumière, were on summer holiday. The shot formed part of a basic 15-minute show which was, eventually, seen throughout Europe and America during 1896; the Lumière Programme came to London, for example, on February 20, 1896, first to the Marlborough Hall of the Regent Street Polytechnic and then, three weeks later, transferred to the Empire Music Hall, Leicester Square, now a regular cinema.

The Lumière Programme tremendously influenced the early film makers. Most of their catalogues contained reproductions of 'A Train Entering a Station'. In England, the pioneer, Robert Paul, filmed 'Express Trains', a single shot showing Great Northern locomotives and stock of both local and express trains passing at

Below left: From 'The Hazards of Helen' series (1914–1917). A silent movie heroine, tied to the tracks, makes a tricky escape from disaster.

Below right: An American railroad movie heroine prepares for a perilous leap.

Wood Green in 1896. In the same year, George Albert Smith made 'A Train Arriving at Hove Station' on the London, Brighton & South Coast Railway. In America, Thomas Edison filmed 'The Black Diamond Express' on the Leigh Valley Railroad *en route* from New York to Buffalo; in Germany, Max Skladanovsky made 'A Train entering East Station, Berlin'; and in France itself, the Lumières had their imitator when Georges Méliès made 'Arrival of a Train at Vincennes Station'. By the end of 1896, there already existed a substantial repertoire of railway scenes and film makers had discovered the fascination of the train as a cinema subject. The fascination endures to this day.

Next stage came the discovery that exciting shots could be obtained by filming from a camera placed on the front of a locomotive – the result was the view seen by the engine driver. These shots became known as 'Phantom Rides' and one of the earliest examples is 'A Railway Ride Over the Tay Bridge', taken from the front of a train as it crossed the famous bridge in 1897. It includes shots of a locomotive of the same class as the one which was lost when the bridge collapsed; twice we see a Wheatley North British Railway Class P 2–4–0 approaching from the opposite direction. A number of 'Phantom Rides' were made in 1898, including rides on the London & South Western Railway to Barnstaple and Ilfracombe, a run down the Queen Street incline at Exeter and a journey through Shilla Mill tunnel. In France, Méliès made 'Panorama Pris D'Une Train En Marche' (sic) in 1899. In America that same year, George C Hale launched his 'Hale's Tours' at the St Louis Exposition. The audience sat in a mock railway carriage and saw pictures of passing scenery taken by the 'phantom ride' process. Excellent films still survive of spectacular rides on American railways at the turn of the century, including a trip on the 'Georgetown Loop' in 1903, 'The Mount Tamalpais and Muir Woods Railroad', filmed in 1898 and 1903, and the 'Catskill Mountain Railway' taken in 1906.

In 1902, Edwin S Porter, working for the Edison company, made a publicity film for the Delaware, Lackawanna & Western Railroad called 'Romance of the Rails'. From this con-

Above: 'The Signal Tower' (USA). The film company at work in the Sierras before the first world war.

Below: 'Phantom Ride' (1900). A cameraman perches precariously on the locomotive during the shooting to obtain views from the engine.

nection, he went on to produce the first railway fiction story 'The Great Train Robbery' (1903). This famous little film, shot mainly in the vicinity of Paterson, New Jersey, and featuring typical American 4-4-0 locomotives of the day, launched the whole concept of the story film, and ensured that railway melodramas were to play an essential part in cinema development for the next ten years. Individual films included 'The Lonedale Operator' (D W Griffith, 1911), 'Hold-up of the Rocky Mountain Express' (Ulster & Delaware Railroad, 1906), 'The Attempt on the Special' (1911), 'The Lost Freight Car' (1911), 'The Switch Tower' (D W Griffith, 1913) and hundreds of others. In time, these melodramas developed into complete modern television series prototypes such as 'The Hazards of Helen', with Helen Holmes, which ran to 120 episodes, all with a railway background.

In Britain, similar films were made at this time. The first attempt seems to have been 'A Kiss in the Tunnel', made by G A Smith and using a shot of Shakespeare Cliff tunnel on the London & South Eastern Railway as background to a mild flirtation. The Bamforth company promptly made an imitation film with the same title, using a Johnson locomotive on the Midland Railway at Monsal Dale as background; both were filmed in 1900. There are shots of the American-built Dreadnought 2-2-2-2 locomotives bought by the London & North Western Railway in a film called 'When the Devil Drives', made in 1907. A British serial called 'Lieutenant Daring' often used backgrounds on the old South Eastern & Chatham Railway out of Charing Cross.

In France, Pathé made great use of the PLM Railway for backgrounds to their melodramas, including the famous 'Fantomas' series. The Italian company, Cines, frequently used the great Rome station for their melodramas. Turin station was used by the Itala Film company for some of the 'Cretinetti' comedies; this little comedian was known as 'Foolshead' in England and 'Boireau' in France.

The public's appetite for railway melodramas might have been blunted by an overdose, had it not been for a new trick. In 1914, the Vitagraph company staged the first genuine crash for their film 'The Wreck'. After the usual story of the runaway locomotive with villains at work to steal gold from the baggage car, this film reaches a climax with a real crash in which a light engine dashes headlong into an express train complete with stock. From then onwards, film companies bought all the old locos that could be cheaply obtained and smashed them in the cause of a good climax to a railway film. Some of these still survive and have not lost their impact (in every sense!). The railway idea was kept alive for the arrival of the silent feature film.

The first major use of a railway scene in a feature film was D W Griffith's race between an old car and a train at the climax of his film 'Intolerance' (1916). A man is about to be hanged in a prison yard for a murder he did not commit. His wife has obtained fresh evidence which will secure his acquittal but the evidence must be presented to the Governor who is the only person in the state who can grant a stay of execution. The Governor is on board an express train. The owner

Top left: 'The Iron Horse' (1924). Union Pacific No 116, doubling for No 119, in use in a reconstruction of the Golden Spike ceremony at Promontory Point, Utah, on May 10, 1869.

Top right: 'The General' (1927). Buster Keaton and admirers inspect the historic W & ARR 4-4-0 No 3 *General* in all her glory.

Below: 'The General' (1927). One of the two locomotives wrecked in the making of the film. The letters W & ARR cover the original owner's livery. An old wooden bridge, due for demolition, was blown up and collapsed into the river beneath for the film.

of an old racing car is willing to help. The chase is on! There are excellent shots of a rather old fashioned (even for 1916) Santa Fe locomotive racing along, intercut with scenes of the car in pursuit. Finally, the car comes alongside (in a dramatic shot taken from a camera car out in front) and eventually the train is stopped. The Governor orders the hanging to be postponed.

In France, Abel Gance made his spectacular film 'La Roue' over an extended period from 1919 to 1923. Much of the material was shot on the ever-helpful PLM, in the yards at Nice and also in the French Alps at St Gervais. For the main scenes, Gance got PLM to let him have 29 km (18 miles) of track as well as the exclusive use of two 4-4-0 locomotives.

In Germany, Fritz Lang made 'Spione' in 1927 with an international cast, which features an enormous model layout filmed at the Neubabelsburg Studios in Berlin as well as some superbly-lit night exteriors taken in the Hamburg area. The climax is a giant crash in a tunnel.

In Russia, the Turkestan–Siberian Railway was the subject of a major documentary in 1929, directed by Victor Turin; the best scene is an encounter between one of those solemn, black Russian 4-4-0s and a group of nomadic tribesmen who have never seen a steam engine in their lives. They decide to see if they can outpace the train on their horses.

In Britain, the two most important silent feature films were the original version of 'The Ghost Train' (1927) which has now been lost; and a modest little thriller called 'The Wrecker' (1928). Both were based on plays by Arnold Ridley, but much of the action was confined to stage settings. 'The Wrecker', however, contains one of those genuine railway crashes that enlivened any film in those days. The crash involved a collision between South Eastern & Chatham 4-4-0 No 148 pulling a set of eight-wheel coaches and a Foden steam lorry at Spain's Crossing near Herriard on the Basingstoke–Alton line. The same crash shots were used in 1937 for a film called 'Seven Sinners'.

Back in America, a large number of railway features were produced in the 1920s. John Ford made 'The Iron Horse' in 1924, which told the story of building the American transcontinental railway which opened in 1869. In those days there were still plenty of early locomotives about and the film has a breathtaking authenticity, right down to use of the original Union Pacific coalburner No 119 in the final scenes.

Excellent melodramas of the day include 'The Overland Limited', 'The Block Signal' and 'Transcontinental Limited'; but pride of place now goes to a comedy 'The General', featuring Buster Keaton and made in 1927. Based on the true story of an incident in the American Civil war (which was also the basis of 'The Great Locomotive Chase' made by Walt Disney in 1956), Keaton's film is notable for a magnificent lumber camp railway which he bought, together with six locomotives, 50 km (32 miles) of track and 20 pieces of rolling stock, just for the film. The main locomotive bears a striking resemblance to the actual *General* which is now preserved at Union Station, Chattanooga. In making

Bottom left: 'Seven Sinners' (1936). Harwood and Caryl, trapped in a single carriage which has been uncoupled – moments later follows one of the most dramatic of all railway crash shots.

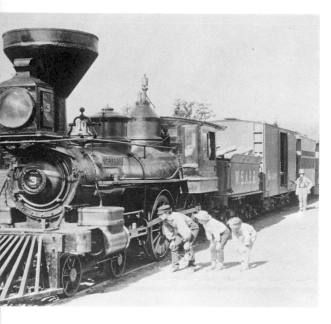

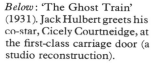

Left: 'The Ghost Train' (1931). Jack Hulbert in the cab of one of William Dean's standard 0-6-0 goods engines, No 2381, a class introduced in 1883 and not withdrawn officially until 1934. No 2381 was painted white for the film to show up in the dark.

Below: 'The Ghost Train' (1931). Jack Hulbert greets his co-star, Cicely Courtneidge, at the first-class carriage door (a studio reconstruction).

Below: 'The Wrecker' (1929). A Foden steam lorry loaded with cement was driven onto Spains Crossing near Herriard and a train, consisting of a Stirling SE & CR 4-4-0 No 148 and a set of eight-wheeled coaches, was run into the lorry at speed – the crash was recorded by 22 cameras and was subsequently edited into two crashes.

the film, two of the locomotives were destroyed, one by design and one by accident! Following the tradition of the day, Keaton did all the driving himself and made sure that every scene was shot with real engines and wagons; sometimes at enormous risk to life and limb.

Introduction of the sound film in the late 1920s produced a whole flood of railway films just when the attractions of the silent railway film were beginning to wane. In one case, the arrival of sound literally overlapped a production at Elstree Studios in England, where Castleton Knight, a newsreel director, was making a feature film called 'The Flying Scotsman'. The film featured a young and unknown Welsh actor who was then billed as Raymond Milland; later he went to Hollywood as Ray Milland. The film was a melodrama based on the morning run of the world-famous *Flying Scotsman* express which, in 1928, began to make the run from King's Cross to Edinburgh non-stop. Castleton Knight began work on a silent film and shot the first 30 minutes with titles and no sounds from either locomotives or actors. Then, as a result of the enormous success in London of Al Jolson in 'The Jazz Singer', the studio decided to install sound equipment – literally over the weekend. So the cast finished work in a silent picture on Friday and started again on a sound film on the following Monday morning! The result – on the screen today – is rather startling. Nevertheless, because he was a newsreel-trained man, Knight shows an extraordinary respect for reality by using the LNER Pacific locomotive No 4472, *Flying Scotsman* throughout the film. Many of the scenes were shot on the run from London to Edinburgh. The detailed work, including a terrific scene when the stunt girl, Pauline Johnson, climbs out on the side of the train and makes her way forward to the locomotive, were filmed when the company was given occupation of the Hertford loop on six successive Sundays, plus the exclusive use of No 4472.

The first 'all-talking' railway film was a remake of Arnold Ridley's play 'The Ghost Train', produced in 1931, with Jack Hulbert and Cicely Courtneidge. It used the Limpley Stoke–Camer-

ton branch of the GWR and featured one of William Dean's standard 0–6–0 goods engines, No 2381, painted white to show up in the dark! A year later came 'Rome Express', with Conrad Veidt, directed by Walter Forde. The film is interesting now because it has some shots of the *Orient Express* in its hey-day. Most of the main railway scenes, however, were shot with gigantic full-scale studio reconstructions of Pacific locomotives of the 231 class, built in the Shepherd's Bush Studios of the old Gaumont British company. Also in 1932, Alfred Hitchcock made his first excursion into thrillers with a railway background in a picture called 'Number Seventeen'. The film ends with a chase between a runaway goods train and a Green Line road coach, climaxing with an enormous crash into a

Right: 'Shadow of a Doubt' (1943). A dramatic scene from a Hitchcock thriller famous for the scene where the villain, attempting to push his niece beneath an approaching train, falls instead to his own death.

Below: 'Rome Express' (1933). A scene from a story of theft and murder on a train journey from Paris to Rome conveys an atmosphere of authenticity in the studios of Shepherd's Bush.

Channel ferry. The material was shot with the help of LNER, using the run from Liverpool Street to Harwich as the basis for the story. Some very good night shots of a Gresley Pacific are included, but the whole of the crash scene is composed of a vast model, laid out on the stages of Elstree Studios.

This picture was the start of a grand affair between Hitchcock and railways He used a run from King's Cross over the Forth bridge to Scotland as a main section of his film 'The Thirty Nine Steps' (1935), including location scenes at the main line station and also on the bridge itself. In 1936, he made a railway crash the climax of his film 'Secret Agent'. The film, 'The Lady Vanishes' (1938) takes place entirely on a train journey across Europe. For this, Hitchcock shot all the railway scenes on the Longmoor Military Railway in Hampshire. His film 'Shadow of a Doubt' (1943) has a nice scene when the villain tries to push his neice under an approaching train but falls to his own death. 'Strangers on a Train'

includes a famous symbolic finale as a train dashes into a tunnel (1951). These last two films were made in America.

A burst of film-making activity was released by the arrival of the centenary celebrations of various countries as they celebrated 100 years of railways. Britain came first with the official LNER film of the Darlington centenary celebrations of 1925 which features a spectacular parade of steam locomotives in action, including Gresley's K3, A3 and P1 class engines; Raven's C7 Atlantic and Pacific classes; Churchward's GWR 4700 and Castle classes; the Urie/Maunsell King Arthur locomotive *Sir Torre*; the Gresley Garratt U1, the largest steam locomotive ever built in Britain; plus a parade of the best preserved steam locomotives in the world at that time, including Stockton & Darlington No 1 *Locomotion*; *Derwent*, built by Timothy Hackworth in 1847 for the same company; the Stirling 8 ft single-driver of the Great Northern Railway (1870); Ivatt C2 class No 990 *Henry Oakley* (1898); the Fletcher/Wordsell tank oddity No 66 *Aerolite*, originally built for the North Eastern Railway in 1869; Robinson's *Lord Farringdon*, a B3 class locomotive of the Great Central Railway; a Holden Y6 class steam tram of 1897 as used in the docks at Felixstowe and Yarmouth by the Great Eastern Railway; a nice LNER Sentinel steam railcar that saw service in the Newcastle area; an experimental petrol-driven railbus for unremunerative branch lines (already a problem by 1925); a reconstruction of the 1837 GWR Robert Stephenson locomotive *North Star* (the Great Western smashed up the original in 1908!); and finally a glimpse into the far future in 1925 was the Raven experimental electric locomotive No 13 (a most appropriate number as it turned out), built for the LNER electrification of the line from York to Newcastle. The job has still not been carried out!

Next came America with the Iron Horse Centennial of 1927, organized by the Baltimore & Ohio Railroad. Here the parade included a replica of the original horse-drawn cars of the B&O which began in 1830 (the centennial was a slight cheat because 1827 was the year that the railroad company was incorporated and not the year when it ran its first trains!); the beautiful vertical boiler locomotives *Best Friend of Charleston* and *Atlan-*

Right: 'Der Stahltier' (The Iron Horse) 1936. A full-scale replica of *Der Adler* (The Eagle), the first German steam locomotive built in 1835 for the line from Nuremberg to Fürth, the first German railway, stands beside the Third Reich's No 10 150 in Nazi livery and insignia.

tic, built by Phineas Davis for the Baltimore & Ohio in 1835; the famous DeWitt Clinton engine and decorative stagecoach-style coaches; the fascinating Hayes Camelback of the Baltimore & Ohio, dating from Civil war days; followed by a vast assembly of characteristic American locomotives right up to 1927. Britain was represented by a replica of *Rocket*, a chorus girl clad as Britannia and the first public appearance of the Churchward GWR locomotive No 6000 *King George V*. The success of this show led eventually to the well-known American touring historical transport show 'Wheels A' Rolling', which used a number of the same exhibits.

In 1935, the scene moved to Germany, where Dr Goebbels, Minister of Propaganda to Hitler's new Nazi regime, commissioned Willy Otto

Zielke to make a film to celebrate 100 years of German railways. Called 'Der Stahltier' (The Iron Horse), Goebbels was the first to see it. He immediately banned it. Its maker, Zielke, was committed to an asylum, emerged briefly to film the opening of the 1936 Olympic Games for Leni Riefenstahl, and then promptly disappeared again. He was re-discovered long after the second world war by the American film maker, Kenneth Anger. In the meantime, a negative of the film had been secretly kept, was hidden away in France during the Occupation and finally re-emerged in 1969. What had obviously annoyed Dr Goebbels so much is the fact that Zielke paid so much attention to the early work of experimenters in France and England instead of extolling the triumphs of German pioneers. For example, the film begins with a superb reconstruction of the Nicholas Cugnot steam carriage of 1769 which he ran through the streets of Paris until the steam carriage got out of control and crashed into a wall. This is followed by William Hedley's *Puffing Billy* (known in the film as 'Puffen Willem') which operated at Wylam colliery from 1813, and by an enormously-detailed representation of the opening of the Liverpool & Manchester Railway in 1830, complete with full-size *Rocket* locomotive and the dramatic moment when William Huskisson, Member of Parliament for Liverpool, was struck down and fatally injured while crossing the lines to speak to the Duke of Wellington.

Only after all this does the film come to the opening of the first German railway in 1835 between Nuremberg and Fürth, using a full-scale replica in steam of *Der Adler* (Eagle), the first German steam locomotive; and even here the film points out that it was built in England by Stephenson and driven by an English engineer 'Mister Vilson', 'Der Stahltier' ends with a dazzling, impressionistic study of a 1935 German steam locomotive set to music. This anticipates the style of Jean Mitry's 'Pacific 231' with music by Arthur Honegger – shot in France in 1949.

By a strange coincidence, another film that seems hardly to have seen the light of day at the time was the Great Western Railway centenary film 'Romance of a Railway', made in 1935. Directed by Walter Creighton, with Carl Harbard as Isambard Kingdom Brunel and Donald Wolfit as Sir Daniel Gooch, it told how the GWR began as a company in 1835 at Bristol, decided on Brunel's recommendation to build to a gauge of 7 ft (2,132 mm), suffered bad times at the hands of Disraeli in the 1860s, finally converted to standard gauge in 1892, and was a thriving concern in 1935. Scenes include building the Severn tunnel and construction of locomotives at Swindon works, as well as some general publicity for the GWR on the industry and countryside it served. The full-scale replica of *North Star*, built for the Darlington centenary celebrations of 1925, was brought out again and used for the early scenes of the opening of the London to Maidenhead line; the modern scenes feature Hall, King and Castle class locomotives, including one shot of the peculiar streamlined, bullet-nosed King No 6014 *King Henry VII*. A boardroom dispute seems to have erupted at Paddington after the first private showings of the film and it was never released. The negative disappeared for a long time. It was eventually unearthed from the wine vaults of the old Marylebone Hotel by enthusiasts of British Transport Films.

Many fine factual films were made on the work of the railways in the Golden Age before the second world war. The London Midland & Scottish Railway was the first company to have its own film unit and in 1933 it filmed the tour by the LMS locomotive *Royal Scot* and a complete train through Canada and the United States, ending with scenes of *Royal Scot* hauling the *Broadway Limited* to the Chicago World Fair. In America, Gene Miller was making his films like 'Days of Steam on the L&N', Russia produced its famous films of the Moscow underground, Norway made 'Two Norwegian Towns' on the railway from Oslo to Bergen, and Britain produced the documentary 'Night Mail'.

'Night Mail' was made by John Grierson's General Post Office Film Unit in 1936 and featured the steam-hauled nightly run of the Postal Special from London to Glasgow. The motive power consists mainly of Royal Scot class locomotives but there are brief appearances by a Jubilee class engine as well as a 2–6–0 Crab and an old Midland Railway Compound. The first part of the film is a factual account of the journey of the travelling post office train up from London through Bletchley, a long stop at Crewe, then on through Preston, Carnforth, over Beattock summit and finally down into Glasgow Central. Rumour holds that the budget was overspent and money ran out for the last part of the film. There was only about £25 left for the sound track of the final reel. It was suggested that a poem might cover the absence of proper sounds. A search was made for an impoverished poet to compose some verses for a few pounds. He was found teaching in a school in Wiltshire; his name was W H Auden. And for a modest fee he wrote these famous lines for the film.

This is the Night Mail crossing the border,
Bringing the cheque and the postal order,
Letters for the rich, letters for the poor,
The shop at the corner and the girl next
    door.

There was now nothing left in the way of cash for the music. It was necessary to find a struggling and unknown composer willing to do the job for practically nothing. The man they found was Benjamin Britten.

At the end of the film, these two talents came together with the directors Basil Wright and Harry Watt to make one of the most fascinating experiments in sound and vision of the 1930s; all in the service of the railways.

During the 1930s, a number of attractive feature films were made including the classic 'La Bête Humaine', directed by Jean Renoir, with Jean Gabin as the engine driver. Produced in 1938, the film was based on the novel of the same name by Emile Zola and told of an engine driver who was subjected to a series of murderous brain-

Above left: 'Union Pacific' (1939). A raid on the pay train by a gang of frontier desperadoes – the basic train used on location consisted of six locomotives and fifty pieces of rolling stock – all classified as 'of the period of the 1860s'.

Above: 'Union Pacific' (1939). Joel McCrea and Barbara Stanwyck on the framework of locomotive No 60 – an old 1875 steam locomotive from the Virginia & Truckee Railroad, named *J. W. Bowker*, was used for the film.

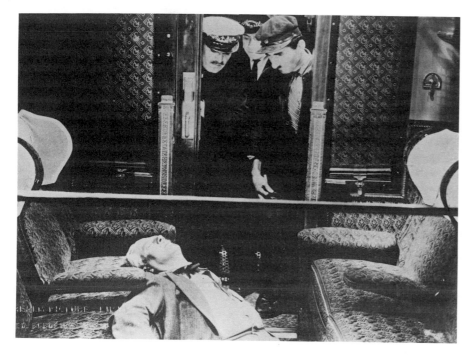

Above left: 'La Bête Humaine' (1938). The discovery of the body – a dramatic scene in this story of a French engine driver who murders for love and himself dies when he jumps from the locomotive at speed.

Above right: 'La Bête Humaine' (1938). The engine driver confesses his murder on the footplate of the Paris express, overpowers his fireman, and plunges to death from the tender – leaving the train to race to its doom.

Left: 'Streamline Express' (1936). A scene from a thriller set aboard a trans-continental streamline express on its inaugural run.

Below left: 'Night Mail' (1936). A GPO documentary which provided an excellent chance to observe the working of the LMS in the 1930s. The 4-6-0 Fowler Royal Scot locomotives are very much in evidence – notably No 6115 *Scots Guardsman*.

Below right: 'Night Mail' (1936). The famous signal box sequence where the signalman telegraphs 'Can you take the Postal Special?'

storms which eventually result in the death of a girl. In a fit of total depression, he drives his train (in one version) to unknown destruction; in another copy of the film, the train is stopped in the nick of time by the fireman. The basic railway scenes were shot on Pacifics running from Paris to Le Havre with the active co-operation of SNCF and Jean Gabin driving his own engine.

In America, there was an amusing little film made in 1936 called 'Streamline Express' for which a team of experts worked out the designs for trains that could operate at 240 km/h (150 mph). Special copper models were used. The trains were double-deck like a Jumbo jet and included a barber's shop, beauty parlour, gaming room and a small dance floor!

The great railway film of the 1930s was Cecil B DeMille's 'Union Pacific, made in 1939, with Joel McCrea and Barbara Stanwyck. For this, an old 1875 steam locomotive from the Comstock Lode line of the Virginia & Truckee Railroad by the name of *J W Bowker* was used. It followed the basic story of John Ford's earlier film 'The Iron Horse' and DeMille is said to have thought of the idea on a train from Omaha to Chicago – in the days when everyone crossed America by rail.

In Britain, many railway films were made at this time. 'The Last Journey' (1936) was the tale of an engine driver who goes mad on the footplate and drives his train to destruction. It was shot on

the main line from London to Plymouth, with special details shot on the Reading-Basingstoke branch. 'The Silent Passenger' (1935) was made with the help of the LNER and featured Liverpool Street, Stratford works and N7 class 0–6–2 tank engine No 2616. 'Bulldog Jack' (1935) was made on the Central line of the London underground, featured Jack Hulbert and was about an attempt to steal the treasure of Tutenkhamon from the British Museum using the disused British Museum underground station as an escape route. The British classic of the era was 'Oh! Mr Porter', made in 1937 at the Gainsborough Studios, Shepherd's Bush, London, by the comedy trio, Hay, Moffat and Marriott.

Marriott was no stranger to railway films; he had played the part of the engine driver in the early 'talkie' 'The Flying Scotsman'. The director was Marcel Varnel from France. The first part of the film features the LNER streamlined locomotive *Silver Link* being named at a specially-loaned station on the Hertford loop. The action then moves to the wayside halt of Buggleskelly on the fictitious Southern Railway of Northern Ireland; which in fact was Cliddesden station on the Basingstoke & Alton Light Railway. This line was the first to be opened under the Light Railway Act of 1896. It had opened in 1901, was shipped, rails, sleepers and all, to France in the first world war, set up again in

Above left: 'The Great Locomotive Chase' (1956). An obstruction on the line provides a critical few moments in the chase.

Above right: 'Titchfield Thunderbolt' (1952). Sabotage by steam roller! The train is towed away and swept to destruction over an embankment by a steam roller hired by the rival bus company.

Top far right and top right: 'Oh! Mr Porter' (1937). Two scenes from the Will Hay comedy in which a new stationmaster at Buggleskelly, on the Southern Railway of Northern Ireland, routs a gang of gunrunners after a hectic chase. 'Oh! Mr Porter' was filmed with SR rolling stock and locomotives on the abandoned Basingstoke – Alton line with Cliddesden Station as Buggleskelly.

Below left: Bandits reach the locomotive tender in a spectacular leap, which, though almost a Hollywood cliché, is nonetheless compulsive watching.

1924 and finally closed in 1936. The track was being lifted as the Will Hay film was being made in 1937. Motive power included Kent & East Sussex locomotive No 2 *Tenterden,* renamed *Gladstone* with suitable modifications; William Adams' London & South Western 0395 class 0–6–0 No 3509; and another Adams LSWR engine of the X2 class, No 657. As may be gathered, the Basingstoke & Alton was owned originally by the LSWR. The film includes a glorious chase, ending up with a crash staged in Basingstoke yard. The story became strangely topical again in the mid-1970s – it deals with the attempts of men of an illegal organization to smuggle guns and ammunition across the border between Northern and Southern Ireland. However, these trimmings are always incidental to the music hall type of comedy of the trio who appeared in a whole series of British comedies at that time.

The post-war years saw nationalization of the railways in Britain and the decline of steam in favour of diesel and electric traction. One film, 'Train of Events', was being made by Ealing Studios during 1948 and shots of the old LMS 4–6–0 Royal Scot class No 6126 *Royal Army Service Corps* had to be redone as British Railways' engine No 46126. Incidentally, this was one of those stories about a group of people thrown together on a train heading for disaster; this theme was used in 'Night Train to Munich', 'The Last Journey' and, in modified form, 'Murder on the Orient Express'.

In France, the story of Abel Gance's film 'La Roue' was remade with the then world's fastest electric locomotive BB 9004 in 1956, SNCF providing the motive power for a series of runs from Paris to Lyons with the new locomotive.

The next theme to occupy film makers was that of preservation. From Australia, came a film called 'Shades of Puffing Billy' about a delightful narrow-gauge preservation project in Victoria, as well as an account of the problems of the gauge differences between the states – this had for years plagued unification of the Australian rail system. In America, Carson Davidson made 'Third Avenue El' in 1956, followed by 'Toccata For Toy Trains' and 'Railway With a Heart of Gold', all on the concept of the preservation of the past.

Yugoslavia joined in with a film about the disappearance of the steam-hauled narrow-gauge line at Ochrid.

The British contribution was an Ealing Studios feature film called 'Titfield Thunderbolt', made in 1952. Inspired by the story of the Talyllyn preservation scheme in Wales, it was written by T E B Clarke, directed by Charles Crichton and acted by Stanley Holloway, George Relph, John Gregson, Godfrey Tearle and Sid James. The producer was Michael Balcon, responsible for 'The Wrecker', 'Rome Express', 'The Lady Vanishes' and 'Oh! Mr Porter'. The railway was provided by the Limpley Stoke & Camerton branch in Somerset and the surrounding countryside was well captured by the Technicolor camera.

The part of the locomotive *Titfield Thunderbolt* was played by a very real veteran *Lion,* a basic 0–4–0, built by Todd, Kitson & Laird of Leeds in 1838 for the Liverpool & Manchester Railway. This fine engine, loaned by the Liverpool Engineering Society Museum, was put into full working order and steamed throughout the filming. In the style of the earliest period of railway history, *Lion* is seen with the boiler and tank contained in a fine, wooden casing, offset by a brass hood over the firebox and a tall, elegant chimney, collared and crowned with sunbursts. Other locomotives used included two GWR 0–4–2 1400 class tank engines, Nos 1401 and 1462, as well as sundry Kings, Castles and Halls in the final scene shot at Temple Meads station, Bristol.

In 1963, a new story hit the headlines – armed robbery on trains. The British real-life version took place on the main line from Glasgow to London near Cheddington in Buckinghamshire. About £3 million was stolen from a Royal Mail coach in the 22 minutes from the time when the train was brought to a standstill by a false red signal to the moment when the thieves made their getaway. In 1967, Studio Hamburg and Nord Deutsche Rundfunk made a film of this great robbery but it did not get very far. Legal actions by the robbers prevented the picture from being shown in Britain or America and it eventually disappeared. In the same year, Paramount invested in a British version but only after a team

October 17, 1963; the boilers stayed in one piece, 100 journalists had a grandstand view, and the film unit finally left Acquigny. The remains of three locomotives and six demolished wagons littered the station. The tremendous accuracy of Frankenheimer's film is now acknowledged in the railway world – every locomotive is correct in its setting and even the sounds are all in order!

The story was based on fact and SNCF experts helped to recreate the tricks they had employed during the occupation to disrupt German lines of supply, including blocked points, jammed stop lights, fake arguments between staff members and so on. As is mandatory in these films, Burt Lancaster and Michel Simon had to learn to drive a locomotive properly.

Real crashes had returned to the cinema with a vengeance. For 'The Bridge on the River Kwaï', filmed in Ceylon, David Lean took over a couple of neat little Beyer Peacock tank engines supplied to the railways of Ceylon at the turn of the century, as well as long sections of track, 21 items of rolling stock and lots of accessories. For the film, Dorman Long of Middlesbrough built a complete wooden bridge across the river on a location about 40 km (25 miles) from Colombo and then arranged for the bridge to be blown up as a train crossed it. Sixteen cameras covered the scene. The timing had to be exactly right to catch the train on the bridge. The Beyer Peacock locomotive was approaching the main span when the charges blew. It crashed into the river below, taking with it the three carriages with specially strengthened couplings. Just to make sure that all the stock really went over the top, the hawk-eyed

of 20 lawyers had agreed on the script. It was shot on location at Husbands Bosworth, near Market Harborough, using a train almost identical to the one which ran on the night of the robbery. The stars were Stanley Baker, Frank Finlay and Barry Foster; this reconstruction of the event cost £2,600,000 to make!

Robbery was the theme of John Frankheimer's 'The Train' made in 1964. Filmed in France, this American production starred Burt Lancaster, Paul Schofield, Jeanne Moreau and Michel Simon; it dealt with the attempts of a German general to steal a large trainload of paintings from France and take them to Germany in the closing months of the war. The main railway scene was an actual crash, staged at Acquigny, a village in Normandy. First, an engine was derailed. This nearly led to a real-life disaster, for the locomotive ran out of control before the film unit was ready. The final crash was only captured by a small camera which tripped off automatically, filming from below the level of the rails. For the big crash, a second locomotive, running at about 90 km/h (55 mph) runs into the derailed engine. Families were evacuated from their homes in the area in case the boilers exploded. All gas and electricity was shut off for several hours before the shot was staged and a representative from Lloyds of London stood by in case compensation was needed for a café alongside the line and right in the path of the collision. The great stunt was staged on

Top left: 'Butch Cassidy and the Sundance Kid' (1969). Butch Cassidy and his partner survey the damaged mail coach after successfully stopping the train.

Left: 'Lawrence of Arabia' (1962). The film includes a sensational railway crash, tense fighting on the stricken train and various other railway scenes all shot on location in the Middle East with authentic locomotives and stock.

Above: 'The Bridge over the River Kwai' (1957). With the destruction of the large wooden bridge, built specially for the film, an ex-Ceylon Railway 4-4-0T locomotive and four coaches (pushed into camera range by a small diesel banker) plunge to the riverbed below.

Top right: 'The Train' (1964). Shooting on the film began in France in Autumn 1963. From the start, Frankenheimer kept his cameras in motion to capture in black and white the full cinematic flavour of his re-created wartime operations.

can spot the little baby petrol car that is pushing up the rear of the train and guaranteeing that all the wagons went into the river!

Trains played a big part in later Lean films – all made for Columbia Pictures. For 'Lawrence of Arabia', he blew up an old British-built Palestinian locomotive and carriage in the desert, while a specially-modified Spanish steam locomotive was used for the train scenes, supposedly in Russia, for 'Dr Zhivago' in 1966.

In Australia, a direct link between film makers and the early preservationists provided the railway background for two feature films. 'The Sundowners' needed an authentic steam-hauled train and Queensland Railways brought out and cleaned up two locomotives from cold storage, using local amateur groups to ensure that the detail was correct for the period of the film and the location. A complete train, steam hauled of course, was needed for 'Ned Kelly'. This provided a far more complex problem for the film company in view of the fact that the story went right back to Australia's formative years. Again, a preservation society, with help from the Australian railways, managed to take a locomotive of later vintage as well as three carriages and mock them up to provide a very reasonable representation of the days of the famous iron-masked outlaw.

In 1968, Poland made a film with spectacular steam-hauled scenes. Directed by Andrej Wajda, it was one of the more controversial political films

in the complex battle of wits between Polish film makers and their Russian overlords. Featuring a highly-individual and much-respected actor Zbigriew Cybulski, the action of the film centred on an accident at a railway station as the train pulls away. Tremendous atmosphere is built around the locomotive, the escaping steam and the first tentative movements of the wheels.

Japan made a fine film called 'The Engine Driver' in 1964 and their most internationally well known director Akira Kurosawa, produced a feature film of 'cops and robbers' variety, based on the New Tokaido high-speed train which remains the pride of the Japanese system. Although electric traction can, as David Shepherd once said, never equal the 'romance of the steam locomotive', Kurosawa captured terrific atmosphere as the train raced at 200 km/h (125 mph) through the countryside.

Railway stations have sometimes been the inspiration for film makers. The first picture made for the big screen by John Schlesinger was a study of Waterloo station, London, as it was in 1960, with steam still in evidence. As a result, he won the contract for 'A Kind of Loving', which also contains some nice steam scenes shot in Bradford. This was followed by 'Billy Liar' and 'Midnight Cowboy'.

One of the earlier works of the Italian director Vittorio De Sica, famous for 'Bicycle Thieves' and 'Miracle in Milan', was a study of a series of meetings and farewells in Rome's main station.

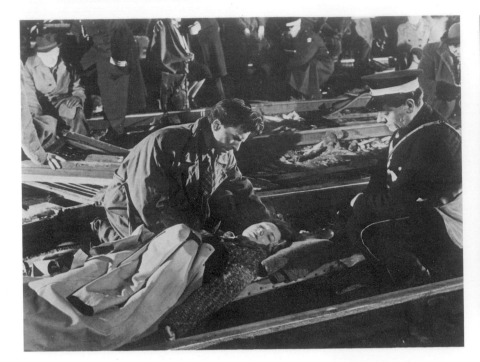

Called 'Stazione Termini' (made in 1952) with the English title 'Indiscretion', it was confined entirely to the station, with many lively steam scenes.

It is now forgotten that most people's first introduction to the Beatles was in 1964 in Marylebone station. Richard Lester used the station as a background to the titles and setting for the first number in the original Beatles film 'A Hard Day's Night'. Although by then diesel-orientated, the old Great Central Railway London terminus gave a good account of itself in providing a strange, almost baroque, atmosphere as the Beatles dashed through the booking hall, across the Victorian concourse and onto the platforms.

One of the most spectacular of the American preservation projects is the famous Durango–Silverton narrow-gauge line. It has enjoyed great success in recent years as a tourist attraction, complete with such transatlantic novelties as an arrival at Silverton to the accompaniment of a sheriff's posse and bandits firing on the approaching train. It has also featured in countless American film and television productions but never better than in 'Butch Cassidy and the Sundance Kid', which included two train holdups, ending in the blowing up of a wagon carrying the gold. The line has an excellent stock of old steam locomotives and fine restored coaches in the style of the Wild West.

One of the best of recent films with a railway background was 'Murder on the Orient Express'. Based on a book by Agatha Christie, it was directed by the American Sidney Lumet – the director responsible for 'Twelve Angry Men' and 'Long Day's Journey into Night', who assembled a large international cast including Albert Finney, Vanessa Redgrave, Sean Connery, Ingrid Bergman, Lauren Bacall and John Gielgud. Instead of the usual technique of preparing a studio mock-up of the coaches in the studio at Elstree, the authentic interiors of three actual Wagons-Lits and Pullman cars of the period were bought by EMI Films and assembled for filming

purposes. Thus the cut glass panels in the dining car, the art nouveau panelling and the superb cutlery are not props but the real thing. For motive power, SNCF provided locomotive No 230 G 353, a very proper 4–6–0 which was maintained in working order at Noisy-le-Sec depot near Paris. Built in 1922 by Batignolles, the engine was filmed, along with four genuine coaches of *Orient Express* style, at Landy goods station, Paris, for the Istanbul scenes and on an SCNF freight-only branch from Pontarlier to Gilley in the Jura mountains near the Swiss border for the snow scenes.

At first, there was not enough snow to fill the cutting so trucks were hired to bring vast quantities to the site. Then it snowed so heavily that the film unit were bogged-down and could not reach the location! For the rescue scenes, a 141 class 2–8–2 No R 607 from Nevers depot was used to push the snow plough. With its gleaming blue and silver carriages and the superb sight of a 1922 steam locomotive in the Jura mountains, 'Murder on the Orient Express' achieved a very high degree of authenticity.

Top far left: 'Train of Events' (1949). This story of lives linked by a railway accident was shot on the Midland Region of British Rail mainly at Euston and Wolverton.

Top left: 'Stazione Termini' (1952). Meetings and farewells in Rome's main station form the basis of this film which is confined entirely to the station and enhanced by lively steam scenes.

Right: 'Robbery' (1967). At an isolated railway crossing, the robbers cut their way through the rear and side doors of the high-value security van to overpower the mail sorters.

Left: 'Murder on the Orient Express' (1974). The passengers, isolated in the stationary train by deep snowdrifts, gather tensely in the dining coach during the murder investigation.

Below: North West Frontier (1959). Tribesmen chase a train, hauled by the locomotive, *Victoria, Empress of India*, across plains in the Himalayan foothills.

Below right: 'Doctor Zhivago' (1965). One of several splendid Russian railways scenes in a film which was actually made on location in Spain.

Yet, desite the claims of the exciting use of railways in feature films, the material most often remembered are the occasions when the newsreel and even the amateur camera has captured moments in railway history. In 1920 an unknown cameraman recorded the joys of the Lartigue monorail system used on the Listowel to Ballybunion line in Ireland, where the carriages were so finely balanced astride the single rail that two people were required to sit on one side to offset a large pig being carried in the opposite compartment. This strange little railway lasted from 1887 to 1924. In 1930 a cinema projectionist in Leek, Staffordshire, made a film of the Leek & Manifold Valley narrow-gauge railway which ran from Waterhouses to Hulme End. It shows the sturdy American style 2–6–4 tank engines *E R Calthrop* and *J B Earle* on a journey through the lovely countryside at the western end of the Derbyshire Peak District where the line ran.

In 1931, Pathé News staged a race between the *Flying Scotsman*, a de Havilland Puss Moth aeroplane, piloted by Geoffrey de Havilland, and Miss Elto Mycroft's outboard speedboat. An area near Huntingdon where the river runs close to the railway was selected and the crazy race took place, with the locomotive on the *Flying Scotsman* train starting off as Gresley Pacific No 4475 *Flying Fox*, changing to a Great Northern Atlantic and finally converting magically to another A3 Pacific No 2549 *Persimmon*, all supposed to be the same engine! In 1927, Pathé in America made a newsreel of airship No TC–6–241 picking up the mails from the roof of a Baltimore & Ohio train running at speed, which it then delivers to a ship already out in the Atlantic on its way to Europe! Canada made a lively film of the route over the Rockies in 1928, with speeded-up action giving a breathtaking impression of the run. France has provided a short film of its double-deck suburban service, recorded in 1927, whilst Denmark produced one of the best films about the end of steam railways – it includes an extraordinary survey of just about every class that ever ran, plus a simple but effective study of the working of a steam engine. The French film of the first tests in March 1955 of two electric locomotives that achieved 340 km/h (205.6 mph) still has the sort of magic that such an occasion engenders. Geoffrey Jones' two classics 'Snow' and 'Locomotion' are still admired as impressionistic studies of railways in action. South African Railways had films made as early as 1925; the record of the principal locomotives at that time is still unique in its detail.

Turning to more recent times, Locomotion Pictures produced a beautiful record of the passage of a Manchester-built steam tram through the streets of Java as recently as 1975; they also discovered a lovely little Manchester Sharp Stewart 4–4–0 still running after 100 years on a branch line to Ponorogo in Indonesia. From the

same source has come material on the sad sight of locomotives in steam in Vietnam, stationary because there were no main lines left, as well as impressions of the hundreds of British steam locomotives still running in India and Pakistan.

The Adams/Whitehouse film collection covers material from Italy, Yugoslavia, France and Ireland, including a superb account of the Tralee & Dingle Railway which ran only once a month on market day in its later years. British Transport Films have in their archives such gems as the original test runs of *Coronation Scot* in 1937 and one of the nicest films ever made about a run on a diesel 'John Betjeman Goes by Train'. The railways of the world have been well served by the film makers. But then, by the same token, the film makers have not done too badly by the railways!

Although the glories of the steam engine in action are at their best on the big screen, television was quick to recognize some possibilities. In 1937, BBC Television, based on Alexandra Palace, transmitted its first railway scenes from the lineside near Wood Green on the old Great Northern line, just as Robert Paul had filmed from almost the same spot in 1896. 1938 was the centenary of the opening of the London to Birmingham railway and was marked by a television transmission showing *Duchess of Gloucester*, a locomotive of the Coronation class 4–6–2s designed by Sir William Stanier. In America, an early outside broadcast using the RCA Zworkyn camera showed scenes on the old Third Avenue ell, the elevated system that was once the subject of an Edison film when still steam-hauled.

In many ways, TV has set the scene for successful feature films. For example, the original version of 'The Railway Children' was made by the BBC in 1967 with backgrounds shot on the Keighley and Worth Valley Railway, a background repeated in the later EMI production. The *Orient Express* was the subject of 'Nairn's Journey', made in 1971 on the rail journey from Paris to Bucharest. A mixture of electric and diesel then operated on this basic run, but there was a glimpse of steam in a postscript on the link from Bucharest to Istanbul. The feature film followed in 1974.

In America, the process has been reversed, with TV series based on old movies popular in their day. 'The Iron Horse' series used a basic stable of Santa Fe locomotives and stock that had originally seen service in Mack Sennett days and was kept in store on the outskirts of Los Angeles for forty years. 'Union Pacific' was a television series inspired by the Cecil B DeMille film, made twenty years before the television studios at Paramount-MCA caught on to the fact that they owned the rights both to the title and the script research. They even found an old replica engine on the Paramount lot. It needed only a bit of refurbishing before facing the cameras again. 'Casey Jones', with Alan Hale and Bobby Clark, was launched on the success of a commercial reissue of the song which dates back to the pioneer days of railroad operations in the States in the 1880s. Because the locomotives were so important, the company in this case commissioned the building of a brand new locomotive, based on a design of the period but with concealed diesel power behind its steam exterior. It ended its days in Disneyland.

For an episode in 'The Avengers', Patrick Macnee and Diana Rigg went to Stapleford Park, Melton Mowbray and used Lord Gretton's 10¼ inch gauge miniature railway as a background. In one scene, Diana Rigg is tied to the track as a train, hauled by locomotive No. 750 'Freelance' class 4–4–2 *Blanche of Lancaster*, approaches, only to be rescued in the nick of time by the redoubtable Stead. The original series of 'The Avengers' was shot between 1967 and 1969 at Elstree studios and used the station at St Albans for the episode 'Something Happened on the Way to the Station' as well as the abandoned LMS Stanbridgeford station on the Leighton Buzzard to Dunstable line for 'Death at Noon', a mild parody on the way a railway background had been so effectively used in the feature film 'High Noon'.

Most of the preserved lines in various parts of the world have been used by television companies. The Dart Valley Railway in Devon was used for GWR scenes in 'The Hound of the Baskervilles' in 1968. Another Arthur Conan Doyle

Right: 'The Railway Children' (1973). The villagers, grown-ups and 'railway children' celebrate the saving of the line.

Below: 'Murder on the Orient Express' (1974). Albert Finney, as Inspector Poirot, paces in thought beside the locomotive.

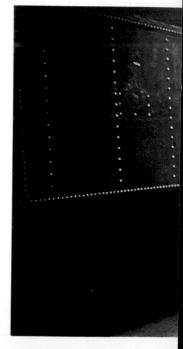

work 'The Seven Per Cent Solution' made extensive use of the Severn Valley line; this scheme, which began as a television film, was eventually converted to a full screen project. The Durango to Silverton line in America was used as a background for 'The Wild Wild West' show on a number of occasions, the French Seine Valley line was used in no less than five ORTF films in the 1960s and Italian television used the Settabello line for a documentary by the director, Visconti. Tasmanian television in Australia produced some good films on their narrow gauge lines, including 'Limestone Special', the story of an industrial railway (1963) and 'The Last Train', an account of a preservation society's final steam run.

One of the most famous of the television film series in railway activity was the 'Railway Roundabout' programmes put out from BBC Birmingham in the late 1950s and early 1960s. The men responsible for the material were Pat Whitehouse and John Adams, who had already made documentary films of railway subjects. 'The Bristolian in the Days of Steam', shot in 1958 with GWR locomotive *Drysllwyn Castle* is still regarded as one of the classics from the 'Railway Roundabout' series.

The accent has been very much on steam railways. Yet today, there is a growing interest in the departure of the early diesel classes. The famous 'Westerns' have already been the subject of two television programmes. The electric locomotive was honoured in such works as 'The Pennsy Electrics' originally made by Blackhawk in 1960 for television use. The humble DMU was the subject of a television documentary 'Gone Tomorrow', which featured the line from King's Lynn to Dereham, via Swaffham in Norfolk, in 1962.

Big screen or little screen, the fascination of the railway engine, whether steam, diesel or electric, will persist for a long time.

Far left: 'Murder on the Orient Express' (1974). Cross-examination of the suspect gets underway in the day saloon coach.

Left: Locomotive No 230 G 353, an ex Paris-Orléans Railway 4-6-0, at work on the Northern Region SCNF hauling a FACS tour, was the locomotive used in the film 'Murder on the Orient Express'. The locomotive is one of two surviving examples which are now employed exclusively for film making and enthusiast trips.

Right: 'The Railway Children' (1973). The children save the train from disaster after the collapse of the old tunnel.

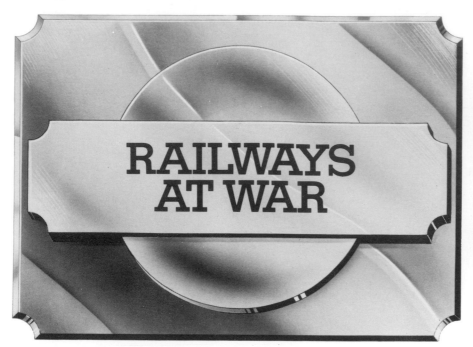

Introduction

For many centuries, armies marched when no water transport was available. Roads, even in Europe, had deteriorated so much since Roman times, that even as late as Napoleon's day, transport was more rapid by sea than by land.

The advent of railways was as much a revolutionary change for military thinking as for the civilians. Land transport, by rail, was more rapid than sea transport for the first time in history. It took time for the military planners to discover how best railways could be adapted for military transport. Manoeuvres were a very poor imitation of the surprises and mishaps of actual war, and planners were never sure if their plans were practical. Railways, while more rapid than other modes of transport, were inconvenient because vehicles were restricted to the rails. A damaged road could be by-passed, but not a damaged railway: repair was required.

By the end of the 19th century Defence Departments of many countries, especially Germany, were laying great emphasis on departments dealing with rail transport. It was a bitter

Above: A construction gang excavates a 'Y' during the American civil war. Brigadier General H. Haupt, Chief of Construction and Transportation, US Military Railroads, is supervising the work.

Below: The locomotive *Firefly* on a trestle bridge on the Orange and Alexandria Railroad during the American civil war.

German jest that 'geniuses juggled with timetables for three years, and then entered a lunatic asylum'. The problems of planning intensive traffic on a single-line railway with passing places unevenly spaced are such that there is an element of truth in this. The importance of railways to the conduct of war reached its peak in the first world war, where the mistakes and experiences of previous years were thoroughly learnt and applied to warfare.

The American civil war

By the time the American civil war occurred in 1862, the use of railways in war was beginning to be understood. Prior to this war, railways had not had decisive effects on any military actions. Railways had played a rôle in the Crimean war (1854–56) between Turkey, France and Britain, and Russia, and in the Italian war of liberation (1859). In both cases, railways were used to bring up supplies and evacuate wounded rather than for the mass movement of armies. Whereas the various European countries had well-developed road systems in pre-railway days, the United States had nothing but rough tracks or 'trails' as they were called. Such railways as existed in 1862 were, therefore, fully utilized. The first battle actually won by the use of railways was the first battle of Bull Run. The Federal army advanced from Washington against a wooded position behind the river held by Confederate troops under Beauregard which were known to be inferior in numbers. But, as the battle was about to begin, the Confederate General Johnston brought up his Corps by railway to Manassas Junction in the rear of their position and then marched his men to Beauregard's left flank and enveloped the Federal's right flank, causing their defeat. Had the Federals won this first big battle, it is just conceivable that the Confederates might have lost heart. As it was, the Confederates gained confidence – resulting in a long and costly war.

During the next two years, railways were increasingly used and proved the sole reliable link between the semi-independent campaigns being waged along the Atlantic coast and in the

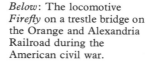

Mississippi valley. The Confederate defeats at Vicksburg and Gettysburg in the same week of 1863 proved the ultimate downfall of the Confederacy. Both battles were fought astride lines of communication but no special use was made of the railways, although they were used in the then normal way in bringing troops and supplies, and in taking away wounded after the battles.

Sherman's Atlanta campaign was fought along the railway from Chattanooga to Atlanta, and the railway was used for all supplies – indeed when a part of his forces diverged from the railway owing to strong Confederate defences in hilly country, they were on short rations until they returned to it. Sherman, having reached Atlanta, was bypassed by Confederate troops who destroyed eight miles of the railway track at Allatoona, in Sherman's rear. Fortunately for Sherman, he had already brought ample stores and ammunition to Atlanta. He was able to return northwards and to free the railway from the Confederates, establishing strong points at every bridge, with ample troops to guard the whole railway from raids. Shortly after his return to Atlanta, Sherman conceived the idea of his famous march to the sea. To do this, he intended to cut himself off from his lines of communication, and live on the country. Before leaving Atlanta, Sherman sent many trainloads of stores and ammunition northwards from Atlanta to Chattanooga and further north to Nashville. During the march to the sea, the railway from Atlanta to Augusta was destroyed.

During the final campaign, the Confederate surrender at Appomattox Court House was rendered inevitable by the Federal army, cutting the two railway lines that the Confederates had hoped to use in their retirement to Danesville. This broke the Confederate lines of communications and starvation rendered surrender necessary. There were some picturesque incidents during the war, such as the exploits of the locomotive *General*, which have been the subject of films.

Prussia's rise in Europe

Prussia waged three wars within five years from 1865. The Prussians, characteristically, were the first of the European nations to discover the role that railways could play in war, and sent many of their ablest officers to serve in army railway transport. The General Staff was always consulted on the siting and equipment of new railway lines to make sure that they could be useful both in peace and war. Military railways were built in increasing numbers.

In the first two of Prussia's wars against first Denmark and then Austria, railways played only a minor role. The third war was the Franco-Prussian war in 1870 when, allied with other German states, Prussia fought the French Empire. The Germans were then able to move their armies to their points of concentration by no less than six railway routes. The French had built railways very rapidly during the previous 40 years but these had been built for peaceful purposes, between the main centres of population.

The defence of France against attacks from across the Rhine has always been handicapped by

Above: A Federal armoured railroad car containing an artillery battery during the American civil war.

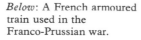

Below: A French armoured train used in the Franco-Prussian war.

the Vosges mountains which divide Alsace from the rest of France for over 200 km (125 miles) running north and south parallel to the Rhine. There were, at this time, only two railways crossing this mountain chain – one from Strasbourg to Paris and the other, 200 kilometres to the south from Mulhouse and Belfort to Paris. Consequently, when the French army under Marshal Macmahon was defeated at Wörth, north of Strasbourg, it was driven back from the northern railway from Strasbourg and had to retreat as best it could either on foot across the mountain chain, or back to Belfort and take train from there to Châlons-sur-Marne, the selected point of assembly. Macmahon's army was thus put completely out of action for two weeks, and during that time the German armies concentrated on the other main French army commanded by Marshal Bazaine which was retreating on Verdun by way of Metz. The Germans swept round the French southern flank and cut Bazaine's direct road of retreat to Verdun. Bazaine attacked these forces at Rezonville and Mars-la-Tour but did not succeed in clearing them off the road.

With the direct road closed, Bazaine's original intention appears to have been to retreat north-west by means of two railways and several secondary roads. He may well have been shocked to learn that the railway from Metz to Verdun some 15 km (10 miles) to the north was not yet completed, and this may have weighed with him when he decided against marching north-west at that time. Instead he withdrew to a strong position at Gravelotte, a few kilometres west of Metz. The Prussians attacked him and, after heavy losses, succeeded in enveloping his right flank and causing him to retreat to Metz itself. Two weeks later Bazaine failed to break through the Prussian cordon to the north and to use the railway to Montmédy where he hoped to join Macmahon, who had brought his army to this neighbourhood. Macmahon was pushed westwards to Sedan by very strong Prussian forces where he was surrounded and forced to capitulate. Bazaine also surrendered not long afterwards. It is interesting to speculate whether the French mis-fortunes in the Franco-Prussian war might have been avoided if the railway from Metz to Verdun had been completed.

French historians of the war comment on the lack of an efficient centralized organization to operate the French railways in the war zone. They describe the chaotic conditions which resulted from comparatively junior officers ordering trains from the local railway staff. Trains, they say, followed one another at close intervals, sometimes using both tracks uni-directionally. The result was, naturally, that trains became banked up, locomotive fires had to be dropped through shortage of water, and it took many hours to clear the tracks. The Prussians certainly, on this occasion, handled matters better. It should be added that ambulance trains were used by both sides, and gave good service.

The Boxer Rising

The Boxer Rising occurred in China in 1900. The spread of the railways was one of the causes of this conflict. The Chinese government, financially embarrassed after the great Tai-Ping rebellion, opposed the introduction of railways but yielded slowly to demands by progressive officials for railways for defence purposes and more rapid communications. In order to build these railways, it was necessary to obtain foreign loans, mainly from the British. Meanwhile the Russians succeeded in obtaining Chinese consent to the extension of the Trans-Siberian Railway to the Pacific coast across the comparatively flat lands of Manchuria instead of through the mountains in Russia north of the Amur river. This meant, in effect, that there was a strip of Russia, policed by Russians, across Manchuria. This hurt Chinese pride. There followed a curious scramble for railway concessions by the great powers and this added to the flow into China of foreign engineers, businessmen and missionaries. A rising tide of Chinese exasperation with the foreign influx

The AMERICAN view of the CHANNEL TUNNEL Scare.
Extracted from the American "PUCK."

The Lion can not face the crowing of the Cock.

Above left: A Russian troop train being shelled by Japanese artillery during the Russian retreat from Mukden in the Russo-Japanese war (1904–5).

Above right: British armoured train armed with a naval gun was used against the Boers in the South African war (1898–1902).

Centre right: The British volunteer town guard of besieged Kimberley pose by their armoured gun wagon in the South African war.

Below left: An American cartoon lampooning the alarmist British public opinion over the proposed Channel Tunnel in the 1890s.

Below right: Serbian machine-gunners man a camouflaged armoured train during the first world war.

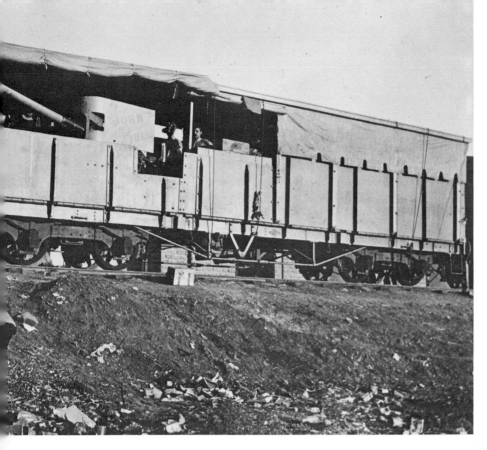

ended in the 'Boxer Rising' – so-called because it was headed by a society known as the 'Harmonious Fists'. The Boxers swept across north China burning, breaking, and murdering foreigners and Chinese Christians. The foreign legations in Peking were soon besieged, with the reluctant consent of a divided government, and the railway to Tientsin and the coast was cut. A small international force under Admiral Seymour was collected at Tientsin and proceeded towards Peking in four protected trains but was stopped halfway by the destruction of the railway tracks. After efforts to repair the track under fire had failed, the trains withdrew before the track behind them was cut.

Seymour's little force was then besieged in Tientsin until a second and larger international force could be collected at Tangku on the coast and advance on Tientsin along the railway. There was then a second advance on Peking using mainly river transport. The railway was repaired as the troops advanced, mainly by Russian engineers. In due course, Peking was reached and the legations relieved though not before friction occurred between the British and Russians over the railway – the main link of communication. The Russians claimed it 'by right of conquest' while the British claimed it because it had been built by an Anglo-Chinese staff. The German commander-in-chief settled this by appointing German military engineers to run the western section of the railway, leaving the Russians in control of the Manchurian section. When the German forces left China, the British Royal Engineers took over the former section of the railway until, two years later, the Russians released their section. The whole railway was then restored to the original Anglo-Chinese staff.

The first world war

The first world war (1914 to 1918) was the climax of the use of railways in war for, by this time, all nations had accustomed themselves to the military use of railways, and mechanical road transport had not yet reached a stage of development when it could replace, rather than supplement, railways for supplying armies in the field.

The Germans had made the closest study of how best to utilize railways for both strategic and tactical purposes. No new railway was built in Germany without the prior sanction of the General Staff, and large numbers of strategic lines were built for use in case of war.

The German Empire had been created in 1871 and by the end of the century the Germans were proud of the efficiency and power of their country and felt that it should have a seat at any International Conference of world importance. At these conferences they were not averse to speaking of the power of the German army, incomparably the most effective army in the world, and did so, to the alarm of their neighbours. This was the cause of the alliance between France and Russia, made in 1892 which perturbed the Germans and caused them to tighten their alliance with Austria and, on certain terms, Italy. This alliance was more powerful than the Franco-Russian alliance and it

began to appear that the only way to preserve the balance of power in Europe would be for Britain to become friendly with France and Russia. Britain, therefore, after several unsuccessful attempts to defuse the situation, formed an 'Entente Cordiale' with France.

The Franco-Russian alliance made it clear to the Germans that if war should come, they would have to fight on two fronts, even with the help of the Austro-Hungarian Empire – for the Russian army, when fully mobilized, was very large. Field Marshal von Schlieffen, the chief of the German General staff brought out a new plan for dealing with this situation. In this plan, only one German army would defend Germany against the Russians. The remaining seven armies would invade France in order to force a quick decision before the slow-moving Russians could complete their mobilization. Because the French border with Germany was protected by forts and defensive lines, Schlieffen decided that there would be insufficient time to force a way through these defences and that the German army must march through neutral Belgium and fall on the French flank. Schlieffen hoped that the Belgians could be browbeaten into allowing the German army to march through their country, but, if not, the Belgian army must be crushed even though the breach of the Belgian neutrality treaty should bring Britain into the war. Schlieffen was fully aware of the importance of railways to his plan.

By 1914 there were 13 double-track railways in Germany running towards the western frontiers and available for troop movement and supply, while on the Eastern front, in East Prussia, a network of strategic railways had been built which were intended to go far to offset the low numbers of the German defending forces.

The French railways were, in 1914, also in a high state of efficiency, and the faults found in

1870 had long ago been eradicated. The French General staff had reviewed the possible course of a war with Germany very closely and strategic railways had been built wherever they were regarded as necessary, while large numbers of locomotives and wagons were kept in reserve.

The Austro-Hungarian railways had a more open network than those of France and Germany, but were also in good condition and well directed. The Russian railways, though reasonably well administered, were widely separated and comparatively few in number. Even in Poland (then a province of Russia), the railways were inadequate in capacity for supplying large armies, and this had an effect on the Russian conduct of the war.

The first two weeks in August were taken up with mobilization by all the contestants.

The Germans put the Schlieffen Plan, as modified by the younger Moltke, into effect and 35 divisions broke through the Belgian defences and began an enormous wheeling movement through Belgium. But their hope of making use of the Belgian railways was a vain one, for the Belgians destroyed their railways as they retreated, especially the bridges and tunnels. This upset the German plans more than anything else. Moltke rushed all available motor transport to Belgium in an attempt to replace the railways, but they were fully employed in moving supplies, and the troops had to march the whole distance with increasing fatigue. This was not their only misfortune because they were taken utterly by surprise by the arrival of a British army on the left flank of the French which, with its rapid and accurate fire, took a heavy toll. The transfer of this British Expeditionary Force to France was a triumph of organization by the British and French railways. The Chemin de Fer du Nord used 339 trains to move them up to the Belgian frontier.

Above left: Soldiers of a German railway regiment standing beside a light railway behind the front lines in the first world war.

Above right: A German artillery regiment moving through Berlin in autumn 1914.

Right: Optimistic German sailors depart for their ships.

Below: The huge numbers of men and weapons transported during the 1914 mobilization required highly efficient timetable planning.

While the German armies plodded wearily through Belgium, the Schlieffen Plan was working in the east. The Germans' expertise with railways won them the momentous battle of Tannenburg. After an indeterminate fight against the Russian First Army at the eastern tip of East Prussia, the Russian Second Army came up from Poland on the German right flank and it began to appear that the German Eighth Army might be cut off. The Chief of Operations of the Eighth Army, on his own responsibility, moved the German First Corps round by railway through Marienburg to the neighbourhood of Tannenburg to reinforce the solitary German Corps already there. He also moved the two remaining corps by rail and road southwestwards to the right flank of the Russian Second Army. As a result the whole Eighth Army made a surprise attack on the Russian Second Army, surrounded it and destroyed it. Hoffman, the German chief of Operations was responsible for this brilliant manoeuvre. To organize and place the trains for moving the First Corps would normally take at least 48 hours. Hoffman did it in one night.

Moltke, in some trepidation, moved two army corps to the Eastern front at the time that Tannenburg was being fought, and this reduction, with other causes, opened a gap between the German First and Second armies advancing towards Paris. To close the gap the commander of the First Army moved south-eastwards, exposing his flank to Paris. Gallieni, the commander of the Paris garrison, saw his chance and begged Joffre to send him troops to attack this open flank. Joffre was intending to make a counter-attack within a day or two, but doubted the ability of the French railways to move at least two army corps at almost a moment's notice from east to west while already supplying the French armies of the centre with south to north traffic. One can picture Joffre, the transportation sapper, mentally reviewing the situation before giving the orders to French railways which paved the way to the victory of the Marne.

The Belgian retreat that followed the fall of Antwerp was aided by the British Seventh Division, newly landed at Zeebrugge and Ostend, and by improvized armoured trains manned by sailors who did useful work with their quick firing guns in discouraging the German advance. The Belgians and the Seventh Division retreated to Ypres and the Yser and there made a stand against heavy odds until the BEF was pulled out of the line after the German retreat from the Marne, and moved northwards to aid the Seventh Division and stop the German advance along the coast to outflank the allied line.

From that time onwards the Western Front became static in what was known as 'siege' or 'trench' warfare. This was a blessing for the British, for they were by the end of 1914 so short of ammunition that the limit imposed was one round per gun per day. The French shortage was not as bad as this, but they had none of the high-explosive shells needed for trench warfare.

Turkey had joined Germany and Austria late in 1914 and early in the new year set about invading Egypt. They were, however, stopped at the Suez canal by British, Australian and Indian forces, and after Kitchener had commented that they were not defending the canal – the canal was defending them, they pushed the Turks back into Sinai and then continued their advance towards Palestine. They built a standard-gauge railway as they went to act as their line of communications. A swing bridge was built across the canal at El Kantara to connect this railway with the Egyptian railways.

To take some of the weight off the Egyptian front, the Turks were attacked in Iraq by an expedition from India which, after using the Tigris and the Euphrates as lines of communication, built a railway up the Euphrates valley. This was built to metre gauge because materials for this gauge were plentiful in India. This expedition suffered several changes of fortune, but finally succeeded.

Meanwhile the Russians were suffering from a shortage of munitions of all kinds, and asked for some sort of military assistance from their allies. The British proposed to land in Gallipoli in order to attract Turkish forces away from the Russians, and the latter agreed. The landing was successfully made, and certainly tied down large numbers of Turkish troops, and aided the Russians to take Erzerum, but it failed to open the Dardanelles, take Istanbul, and bring in urgent supplies to Russia at the Crimean ports. Had the Gallipoli peninsula been taken and the British army advanced on Istanbul, light railway materials would have been assembled in Egypt for use as a line of communication.

Russia was still demanding supplies, and large quantities of war material were sent to Archangel in summer when the port was ice-free, and the Trans-Siberian Railway was bringing in American-made munitions and railway equipment (paid for by the British). The Government of India built a broad-gauge railway from Quetta to Zahidan in southeastern Iran and lines of motor-lorries then carried war material from railhead to Meshed on the Russian border. The Iranians were annoyed at this initiative but diplomacy and financial aid soothed their feelings.

The deadlock on the Western Front continued. The Germans, the French, and the British all tried unsuccessfully to break through the trench lines to open country beyond, and then roll up the enemy line in both directions. Deceptively, the British were nearly successful at Neuve Chapelle, but they failed to bring their reserves across the churned-up battle line as quickly as the Germans in undamaged country, and this remained a problem throughout most of the war.

The battle of the Somme, 'the big push' as it was called at the time, had failed to break the German line, although it remains a mystery how German machine-gunners survived days of intensive bombardment from thousands of guns. What the battle had revealed was that as soon as the immediate German trench lines had been taken the Germans dug themselves in afresh. It had been impossible to bring up adequate supplies to the attacking troops not only because of the churned-up trench lines, but because the railway and road lines of communication simply could not cope with the tonnage required. For the whole British army, it was something like 200,000 tonnes weekly. Forward-area transport preparations had to be much more thoroughly planned than hitherto. At the height of the Somme battles more than 20,000 tonnes daily had had to be distributed in advance of the main railheads. The War Office asked Mr Eric Geddes, deputy general manager of the North Eastern Railway, to visit France and to report on the transport situation in the British area. Among his recommendations he stressed that a proper system of tactical light railways should be built between the various standard-gauge railheads and the battle-front. This he considered essential because of the obvious inadequacy of road transport (mechanical or horsed) in a battle zone. Additional standard-gauge railheads were also recommended.

Both the French and German general staff came to the same conclusion about the same time, and hundreds of miles of light railways were built. By 1918, more than 1,300 km (800 miles) of 600 mm (2 ft) light railway were constructed and carried up to 200,000 tonnes of supplies each week to the British army alone. To explain these high figures, it should be mentioned that a single 18-pounder battery fired, during an offensive, no less than 240 shells per hour. Each battery, with ammunition wagons, had 150 horses and each horse needed a bale of hay and a sack of oats per day. On the British light railways there were no fewer than 687 steam and petrol driven locomotives of British and American manufacture. The total number of British locomotives sent to France and Italy for war service was 1,224.

Above: A Turkish prisoner-of-war construction gang work on the Stavros light railway line for the British Salonika expedition.

Right A working party of British troops going up to the front near Ypres by light railway, 1917.

Below left: Tanks of the British 2nd Brigade on flat trucks returning from the battle of Cambrai in 1917.

Below right: British troops unloading shells from a light railway during the 1917 battle of Ypres.

Despite Britain's great efforts to produce enough munitions, Russia was still critically short, especially after her largest arsenal at Ochta was blown up. The Russian army became increasingly discontented and ineffective. In March 1917 a revolution occurred, and Kerensky became head of a provisional government. The Germans, who had worked for a Russian revolution since 1914, watched hopefully but when Kerensky announced that the war would continue, realized that their main objective had not been achieved. The German general staff then arranged the passage of Lenin, Trotsky and their adherents from Switzerland through Germany in sealed trains to Russia in order to foment further unrest and force Russia out of the war. It was the finest piece of grand strategy the German general staff ever achieved.

Lenin created another revolution in October 1917, and succeeded by a narrow margin, but most of the Russian field commanders refused to accept the new government and fought a three-year civil war mostly along the lines of railway. The Germans, however, had succeeded in their main object of making a separate peace with Russia, and began moving their armies across to the west in order to achieve final victory.

In 1917, the Italians suffered a serious reverse at Caporetto from a combined offensive by German and Austrian troops along the Isonzo river, and had to fall back fighting until they reached the Piave river line. The Italian high command had selected this line because railway connections south and west were particularly good. Reinforcements were brought up by hundreds of trains from other parts of the front, and from training areas. They succeeded in stopping the enemy offensive before Franco-British help arrived. Four British divisions were moved south in 550 trains and six French divisions in 881

trains. The French railways provided these trains with their usual efficiency and the Italian railways proved equally good in receiving them, unloading them, and returning them. The whole operation was completed in three weeks.

In addition to their logistic function railways were also used for offensive purposes. Rail-mounted super-heavy guns were used by both sides. The British used 13.5 in, 9.2 in and 6 in guns and also 12 in howitzers, a considerable proportion of them being rail-mounted. The 13.5 in guns were mounted on 15 axles and the entire weapon and mounting weighed 230 tonnes. The weapon could not traverse and had to operate on curved track to give it lateral traverse. The 9.2 in guns and 12 in howitzers were mounted on special well-wagons, the centre section of which could be lowered to rest on the sleepers of a line of track, the bogie trucks being raised clear of the rails. When firing laterally to the track these weapons had to be secured from lateral movement by brackets with jacks, and by buried hold-fasts. It required 12 hours or more to bring them into action. *Big Bertha*, the German gun which

Above: A demolition charge laid by Colonel T. E. Lawrence's Arab irregulars explodes on the Turkish railway near Devraa.

Below: A girder bridge on the same railway. Lawrence tried unsuccessfully to destroy this structure.

shelled Paris from a range of about 60 miles, was also rail-mounted.

In March 1918 the Germans launched their anticipated offensives in the west, using troops brought from the Russian front. The British received the two first blows but, after an anxious period, they succeeded in preventing their lines from being broken. In these offensives the Germans experienced difficulty in maintaining momentum and keeping their fighting troops supplied because of the problems of crossing the churned-up areas of the old trench lines. They extended their light railway system across these areas with commendable speed, but not quickly enough to obtain a powerful breakthrough. The light railway systems built by the British and abandoned in the retreat were seldom usable.

The same thing happened when the Germans switched their offensives to the French. They succeeded in breaking through the trench-lines but their advance progressively slowed down while French and British reinforcements rapidly poured into the battlezones until stalemate ensued.

Ludendorff called August 8, 1918 'the black day for the German army'. The French, British and American armies had been making small offensives up and down the line in order to tire and unsettle the German troops. On August 8th, however, the British initiated a new form of offensive. This was a surprise attack by large numbers of tanks, which cleared the way for the infantry, in conjunction with low-flying planes machine-gunning the enemy troops. The British had tried this method of attack at Cambrai in October 1917. It had been very successful – indeed had penetrated the German lines so rapidly that the British reserves were taken by surprise and failed to make the battle decisive. This, however, was a positive advantage in the long run, because the Germans gained false confidence from repelling such an attack. No mistakes were made on 8 August and the victory was complete. The German troops began a long fighting retreat. The British, French and Americans had some hard fighting, but from that time onwards the retreat never ceased. The British and French railway troops were faced by enormous problems in extending the rail network to keep up with the fighting lines. Fortunately, the weather was better than in the previous year when the Passchendaele battle was fought to take pressure off the French in the wettest summer for forty years. During the advance in 1918 railways, both standard-gauge and narrow-gauge railways, proved the only satisfactory method of crossing the succeeding battle lines with their mud, shell-holes, wire and unexploded shells.

Meanwhile progress had been made on the other fronts. In December 1917 the British had captured Jerusalem and, after a pause during which the Sinai Railway was extended, they advanced further and fought the decisive battle of Megiddo which broke the Turkish army. The

right flank of the British army during its advance had been protected by Arab levies under the Hashemite King, with his liaison officer, who also acted as paymaster of the levies, T E Lawrence. This force not only guarded the flank of the army, but sabotaged the Hedjaz Railway running up from Medina to Damascus and Haifa, which had been useful in transferring Turkish troops. A total of 1,006 km (625 miles) of standard-gauge and 205 km (128 miles) of narrow-gauge railway were built in this war-zone worked by 75 British standard-gauge and 25 narrow-gauge locomotives hauling 1,675 standard-gauge and 767 narrow-gauge wagons.

At almost the same time as the Palestine offensive, the Iraq campaign which had bogged down awaiting the railway from Basra, began to move in favour of the British and ended in the retreat of the Turkish army from Baghdad, and, later, from Mosul. With the capture of Baghdad the standard-gauge Iraq section of the German-built Baghdad Railway came into British possession and was restored to working order as soon as possible. Twenty-two standard-gauge British locomotives and 113 wagons were sent to Iraq to improve the traffic capacity. The metre-gauge railway crossed the Tigris river above Baghdad and was extended towards Kirkuk. By the end of

Above: A camouflaged armoured train mounting 190 mm guns near Caix during the battle of the Somme 1916.

Below: A British 9.2 inch gun on a railway mounting.

Top: Locomotives used behind the Allied front lines belonging to the 19th Transportation and Base Section. The photograph was taken in November 1918.

Left: A second world war method of unloading tanks from transporters by merely driving them off onto the straw bales.

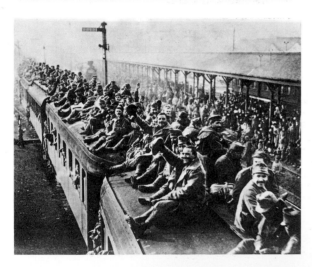

Left: Austrian soldiers returning home from the horrors of the front line.

Bottom: British troops servicing a locomotive in Russia during the civil war in 1920.

the campaign 156 locomotives and 3,140 wagons had been received from India for this railway. In all, 280 km (175 miles) of standard-gauge, and 1,126 km (700 miles) of metre-gauge railway were built.

A battle-zone not so far mentioned was that at Salonika where a Franco-British army, sent originally to help the Serbians, had been almost stationary for years. The good news from France acted as a tonic to this army and it began its own offensive against the Bulgarian and Austrian troops opposed to it. During its stationary period, many light railways had been built in imitation of those in France and these were extended as the troops advanced northwards towards Skopje. The standard-gauge railways were restored to working order as the advance continued up the Vardar valley. By the end of the campaign in this theatre 177 km (110 miles) of standard-gauge and 425 km (281 miles) of narrow-gauge had been built on which 54 standard-gauge and 69 narrow-gauge locomotives hauled trains drawn from 1,784 standard-gauge and 2,922 narrow-gauge wagons supplied by Britain.

By the autumn of 1918 the war was obviously drawing to a close and Turkey, Bulgaria and Austria–Hungary sued for peace, followed by Germany. Fighting ended on the 11 November. The efforts of the British, Indian and American railways and the railway industry during the war were truly phenomenal. 6,346 km (4,000 miles) of standard-gauge, 1,413 km (878 miles) of metre gauge and 6,994 km (4,346 miles) of narrow-gauge track had been supplied and laid. A total of 1,375 locomotives and 56,827 carriages and wagons had been supplied for standard-gauge; 206 locomotives and 4,340 carriages and wagons for metre gauge; and 806 locomotives and 19,909 carriages and wagons for narrow-gauge, together with 1,268 tractors, had been delivered.

The second world war

In September 1939 war began in Europe. The first two weeks were taken up by mobilization which worked very much as it had done in 1914. The British army was transported to France much as in 1914 and occupied part of its previous region. This spoke well of railway efficiency in all countries, even in Russia which, by reason of the signature of the Russo-German Pact, was partly on a war footing, and Italy where Mussolini had won his first, enduring and possibly only favourable comment by 'making the trains run to time'. The German railways were, according to Dr Dorpmüller, the Director-General, over-manned.

The role of railways in this war was less important than it had been in 1914 to 1918, at least in Europe. This war, unlike the previous one, was highly mobile. Nevertheless railways still had a vital role to play.

The first move by the Germans was to invade Poland, destroy the Polish army and divide the country with the Russians. Railways played a very minor part in these events.

The second phase of the war was the German assault in the West on May 10, 1940. In this attack the Germans imitated the British attack of August 8, 1918 but using armoured divisions and dive-bombers. The result was equally successful. The German armoured divisions emerged from the forests of the Ardennes, which the French had believed to be impassable, broke through the weak French line, and reached the Channel coast within a week. This cut the allied line in two and led to the evacuation of the British, and a part of the French, armies from the beaches at Dunkirk. They were landed at ports in the south-east coast of England and the Southern Railway did excellent work in running hundreds of special troop trains at very short notice. The French troops were taken to south-west ports and shipped back to France together with the First (British) Armoured Division and other British troops to give France what help was possible while the rest of the army remained in Britain for re-arming and re-equipping.

On 5 June the Germans launched their attack on the remainder of the French army which had already lost 30 divisions and much of its armour. The result was inevitable, although the French resisted strongly. The Germans had complete command of the air, and the French railways were heavily damaged by bombing, trains were gunned from the air, and bridges destroyed. France was compelled to cease the combat, and the British made a second evacuation, with heavy casualties. On 10 June, Italy declared war on Britain and France and the Italian railways performed creditably in moving the army up to the French frontier.

A pause for re-grouping followed and then the Germans began Operation Sealion – the campaign to invade Britain. The British felt much as they did during the Spanish Armada or Napoleon's threats of invasion; alone but defiant – illogically but completely confident of ultimate victory. The beaches were protected by tubular scaffolding brought by the trainload; all beaches were mined, defensive positions were prepared; rail-mounted super-heavy guns were brought to the vicinity of Dover to command the Channel and the beaches, while rail-mounted 9.2 in guns and 12 in Howitzers were distributed in key sites. Each was equipped with its train and locomotives in order to move to threatened areas at short notice (after experiments, it was possible to bring these weapons into action in only 21 minutes). Tanks were few in number. Tests were made to entrain and detrain them in the shortest possible time in order to improve their mobility. Sleeper stacks and even straw bales proved possible aids to rapid unloading. Railways in the invasion area were requisitioned and operated by the Royal Engineers, while 23 armoured trains were produced by the railways in a matter of days in order to supplement the remaining tanks. Even the 381 mm (15 in) gauge Romney Hythe & Dymchurch railway had two armoured trains: the only weapons that could pass through the tubular scaffolding, line upon line of which protected Dungeness. But, in the end, none of these precautions were necessary, for Operation Sealion depended on Germany's command of the air.

Top: Possibly the most unlikely armoured train ever. The Romney, Hythe and Dymchurch Railway on the English south coast prepares to repel the German invader in the second world war.

Above: Machine gunners inside an armoured rail trolley in Northern Ireland during the second world war.

Below: A heavy howitzer on a rail mounting near the south coast of England.

Bottom: Soldiers on exercise in Northern Ireland leap from an armoured rail trolley to attack the 'enemy'.

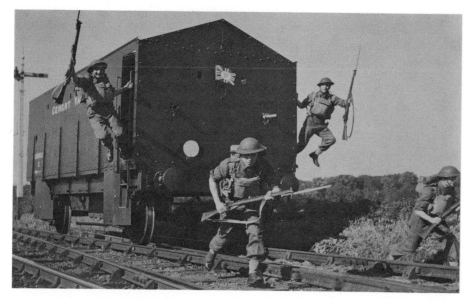

This failed and the invasion petered out. It was Hitler's first failure.

Three months later came the decisive victory of Wavell and O'Connor over the Italian army near Mersa Matruh in western Egypt. The remaining Italian forces retreated from Egypt and Cyrenaica back to the borders of Tripoli. Orders were at once given to extend the railway from Mersa Matruh westwards and this was done as rapidly as possible. It acted throughout as the main line of communication for the army, supplemented by road and sea transport. The German attack on Greece followed closely on these events and Greek railways were heavily used during the retreat of the Greek and British forces under constant air attack. This caused much damage to track and rolling stock. Before the evacuation of Greece, the remaining locomotives and rolling stock were sabotaged as much as possible in the limited time.

The Sudan Government Railway and East African Railways were used in the campaign against the Italians in Abyssinia which ended in the surrender of the Italian army. The British then liberated the Vichy-held territories of Syria and Lebanon, greatly helped by restoration of the Sinai railway, built during the first war, and its extension northwards using materials largely from India, British locomotives, and rolling stock from various countries.

In June 1941 the Germans broke the Russo-German pact and attacked their erstwhile 'friends' with three army groups. Secret preparations had been made some months in advance and among these were important plans for taking over and operating the Russian railways. Railways were of great importance because there were very few tarred roads in Russia; the ordinary secondary road was merely earth and sand which became a quagmire whenever it rained.

As Russia's railways are of 1,524 mm (5 ft) gauge it was necessary to convert them to 1,435 mm (4 ft 8½ in) gauge as the armies advanced. Fortunately for the Germans, this was a much easier task than the converse as all that

was needed was to move one rail inwards by 89 mm (3½ in), though points and crossings required alterations to the switch rails, and some bridges needed altering. Standard-gauge locomotives and rolling stock were needed in large numbers. German locomotive builders were already turning out the standard 2–10–0 'war locomotive' and increased production until over 7,000 were built, over 1,000 being equipped with condensing tenders for use in the arid regions in south-west Russia. Wagons were built on the same large scale.

As soon as the Russian frontier was crossed, the German railway troops began their work in day and night shifts to keep up with the armoured divisions which moved quickly, successively surrounding and taking prisoner bodies of Russian troops totalling over one million within the first three months. Railways were, therefore, absolutely necessary to bring up the minimum supplies necessary in the shortest possible time, and to bring the prisoners westwards before starvation set in. Traffic on the captured railways increased rapidly.

Top far left: Canadian-built tanks are moved by rail to the east coast for shipment to Europe.

Top near left: A squad of British civil defence workers specially trained to quickly repair damage to the railway network. They are wearing gas masks and protective clothing.

Centre left: Railways all over the world suffered heavily from bombing. This photograph shows an RAF attack on a Japanese-held railway yard at Mandalay, Burma, 1942.

Below left: The construction of a railway across the Western Desert in North Africa.

Below right: A British soldier takes his train back to the war, 1942.

The Russians demanded from their allies supplies of all kinds, including locomotives and wagons, and the British were soon sending thousands of tanks and other war materials to Murmansk, the northern ice-free port. They restored the supply route through Zahedan and Meshed, while the Trans-Siberian railway later began to bring in materials until Japan joined the war and stopped the port of entry. British (and later American) railway troops aided Iranian railways by supplying locomotives and rolling stock to transport war material to Tabriz, where it was handed over to the Russians.

At the same time the British had begun an offensive in North Africa which was only partially successful in clearing Cyrenaica and had to be followed by another five months later which had better success. The railway along the North African coast was stretched to the uttermost in meeting the requirements of these offensives, and had to be supplemented by road traffic on a big scale.

By 1941 the Japanese armies had occupied north China and the coastal areas of south China. Japan had also forced Vichy France to permit her to occupy Indo-China, including Vietnam, Laos and Cambodia. In July the American government froze Japanese assets and put an embargo on oil supplies until Japan agreed to evacuate not only Indo-China, but China itself. The Japanese could not face the enormous loss of prestige that this would have entailed, and so prepared for war. On 8 December Japan began the war by landing in Malaya one hour before attacking the American Pacific fleet in Pearl Harbor, after already violating the neutrality of Thailand by running in trainloads of Japanese troops from Cambodia and Vietnam.

The Japanese army in Malaya drove the British forces back southwards and used their command of the sea to outflank British defence lines by sea-borne landings. Japanese railway troops repaired the Malayan Railway as quickly as possible, using locomotives and rolling stock from Thailand whenever captured equipment proved insufficient.

The fall of Singapore completed the Malayan operation and the Japanese then attacked Burma at Moulmein from Thailand. The small British force was driven back and most of it was trapped because the Japanese reached the railway bridge over the Salween river before the British. The bridge therefore had to be blown up, and the troops on the other side were taken prisoner. With complete command of the air, the Japanese bombed Rangoon heavily, and the British, to save loss of life, evacuated Rangoon and retreated by railway to a line 150 miles south of Mandalay. This line was enveloped by the Japanese and the British were forced to retreat again, partly by railway and partly by river steamer.

The railway worked well throughout; much machinery from the workshops at Insein being transferred to Mandalay. But the collapse of the defence line caused the British to evacuate Mandalay and move westwards by train to Monywa, and then, partly by steamer on the Chindwin and mainly on foot, to the trail beside the telegraph line to India. Some of the troops had proceeded by train from Mandalay to the northern terminus at Myitkyina and then on foot across the mountains. Shortly after this, the Japanese began to build a line connecting the Thai and Burma railways, partly with prisoner-of-war labour.

The Germans, in attacking Russia, had intended to separate, penetrate and round-up the Russian armies by the speed and efficiency of their Panzer divisions. Many smaller units were thus destroyed and, as already noted, a million prisoners were taken; but nevertheless the Germans had failed in their prime object of forcing Russia to sue for peace. The Germans had not envisaged a winter campaign, and were forced to make great efforts to fit their armies for the

Ils sont encore nombreux là-bas, et la France les attend avec une naturelle et légitime impatience. Leur présence est indispensable chez nous, car ils représentent les forces vives de notre pays.

Ouvriers, qui partez librement pour l'Allemagne, regardez ces hommes que vous croiserez sur la route. Ils vous doivent leur liberté, ils ne l'oublieront jamais. La reconnaissance de la Nation toute entière monte vers vous.

Ces ouvriers qui partent me permettront de mieux défendre les intérêts de notre pays.

La fraternité — qui ne fut souvent qu'un grand mot — se traduit ici par une émouvante réalité.

P. LAVAL

Left: A German propaganda poster encourages Frenchmen to go to work in Germany. For every worker who went, a French prisoner of war was repatriated to France.

rigours of a Russian winter. Fortunately, German locomotives and rolling stock stood up well to very low temperatures and the railways continued to function without more than minor difficulties. During the winter, the Russians, who were more accustomed to winter conditions than their opponents, tried to counter-attack to stem the German advance but their success was limited because the Germans had converted towns and large villages near the lines into a chain of forts which they successfully defended throughout the winter. Most of these towns had railway connections and these were used to keep the forts supplied.

In the spring of 1942 came a big German offensive towards the south-east in an attempt to obtain possession of the oilfields in the Caucasus. They made the usual rapid advance and captured the Maikop field but failed to capture the Grosny and Baku fields. The Maikop field had been damaged by the Russians but the Germans put it in working order again and, after the railway had been repaired, trainloads of oil were sent to German refineries.

The German advance into the Caucasus alerted the British to the possibility of an invasion of Iran. Paiforce Command was therefore created and centred in Baghdad to protect both Iran and Iraq, and it made full use of available railways in both countries. Metre-gauge locomotives were brought to Baghdad from India, while standard-gauge motive power included locomotives brought from China, and Japanese-built units. A mixture of rolling stock of both gauges was also brought to Iraq, while large quantities of locomotives and rolling stock were supplied to Iranian railways by British and American builders. Very large tonnages were moved to Tabriz, where

trainloads were handed over to the Russians. The Russian victory at Stalingrad caused evacuation of the Caucasus by the Germans, and this reduced the significance of Paiforce, but the arrangements for supplying Russia continued and even increased.

During all this period the North African desert battle between British, German and Italian forces continued to fluctuate across Cyrenaica – victory sometimes with the British and sometimes with the Axis forces – by this time under Rommel. In June 1942, the British defeat at Gazala let the Axis forces advance not only to the Egyptian frontier but to El Alamein, only 60 miles west of Alexandria. There three critical battles were fought, the last of which decisively defeated the Axis forces. They were forced to abandon Cyrenaica and fall back, first to Tripoli and then to Tunisia. The desert railway from Mersa Matruh had reached Habata, on the western frontier of Egypt, earlier in the year and from that point had continued to supply the British until the retreat. Then El Alamein became the railhead until after the third battle, when the railhead advanced again.

Synchronized with the advance of the British 8th Army along the North African coast, a large Anglo-American force was landed in Algeria and Morocco in November 1942 with the ultimate object of taking Tunis and trapping the Axis forces in North Africa. In order to make themselves more acceptable to the Vichy French administration, the presence of the American forces was prominently stressed, though there were actually more British than Americans in the landings in Operation Torch. There was some delay while the French decided whether they would co-operate or not, and this gave the Germans in Tunisia time to take defence precautions. Vital to the whole operation was the standard-gauge railway running from Casablanca to Tunis, with narrow-gauge branches. Once the French had decided to co-operate, the railways and their French staff came under allied control and were soon in full use. The allies had been hoping to enter Tunis before Christmas, but torrential rain and well-planned German defence operations prevented this, especially when Rommel and his Afrika Corps arrived in Tunisia. This, however, caused Hitler and Mussolini to denude Sicily and Italy of troops in order to try and hold Tunis. Thus when the 8th Army arrived in the south and the defence was overwhelmed, about 250,000 prisoners were taken instead of the 40,000 present in December. The railways gave good service throughout. They were of great value in removing prisoners to detention camps in various places in North Africa and in feeding and supplying them afterwards.

The German evacuation of the Caucasus was made largely by railway and was aided by the fact that the Russians were impeded because two of their main railways through Stalingrad could not be used. This city was held by the Germans until their surrender on the last day of January 1943. The Germans had fallen back west of Rostov and the Russian railway troops then had the task of

Left: A German propaganda poster encourages Frenchmen to go to work in Germany. For every worker who went, a French prisoner of war was repatriated to France.

Right: An armed sentry stands guard over the British railways against the feared threat of sabotage.

Below: German war *materiel* being transported east to Russia. The vast distances and appalling roads made railways vital during this campaign.

reconverting the captured railway lines from 1,435 mm gauge to Russian gauge, which took several months because the German demolitions had been thorough.

Meanwhile the Chindits had penetrated deep into Burma and had begun to destroy the railways, and especially the bridges, which resulted in large Japanese forces being diverted to eliminate them. Though the Chindits did not have a vital effect on Japanese operations, they made the Japanese more cautious, and were one cause of the Japanese offensive on Imphal. This proved eventually to be fatal to the Japanese and led to a more rapid reconquest of Burma.

The allied invasions of Sicily began on July 10, 1943 and ended on 17 August. There was a rail network in the island but distances were too short for it to be of much use to the British and American armies, though the electrified line along the north coast was used by Patton's troops in their race to reach Messina before Montgomery.

The invasion of Italy began on September 3, 1943 when the 8th Army crossed the Straits of Messina. Mussolini's regime had been overthrown in July and many Italians surrendered to the allies. However the Germans quickly occupied most of the country and the war continued. The Germans put up a remarkable fighting retreat all along the peninsula and, as

they retreated, tore up the railways bodily using 'claw' wagons which acted as ploughs, breaking the sleepers in two and ploughing up the track-bed. This made the railways unusable until ship-loads of new sleepers could be received, for there was a limited amount of wood available in Italy. Italian railwaymen co-operated with the Royal Engineers and Transportation Corps in carrying out repairs not only to the track and bridges but also to the locomotives which had been sabotaged thoroughly.

Above: A Russian armoured train protecting passing trains loaded with troops and arms.

Below: 'Schwere Gustav' an enormous self-propelled gun used by the Germans in the siege of Sebastopol. It was protected by a whole regiment and a railway cutting. The curve of the reinforced track allowed the gun to be traversed.

Above: After the D-Day landings the British and French railways systems were linked across the Channel. Here wagons loaded with war supplies roll off a US landing ship watched by American army engineers.

All these difficulties naturally impaired the allied advance which was slowed down anyway after the first few months by withdrawal of an increasing number of good troops for the invasion of France. The Russians had been demanding such an invasion since 1942, but neither the troops nor the landing craft were available and tests, like the attack on Dieppe, were not encouraging.

In Burma there had been unsuccessful British attacks at Akyab. Then came a Japanese offensive in April 1944, the object of which was to disrupt the forthcoming British offensive of which the Japanese were aware. The Japanese advance caused some anxious moments, but Slim remained confident and, after a long struggle, the Japanese retired, having lost far more men than the British. The railways in this operation were used to keep the armies supplied and at the same time to move troops from one area to another more rapidly than the Japanese could march. In this the railways succeeded admirably. The railways then took an active part in the build-up for the reconquest of Burma, which was the next stage.

D-day was preceded and accompanied by intensive bombing and rocket attacks on the French railways to destroy not only trains, but bridges, yards and junctions. It was sad that the damage and loss of life was to Britain's ex-allies, but the destruction was absolutely necessary in order to prevent a successful German counter-attack that would push the allies into the sea. It achieved its objective. When Montgomery succeeded in concentrating the German armour at the east end of the landing zone he gave the Americans at the west end opportunity to break the cordon and flood into north-west France. The German armoured counter-attack, when it came, was weakened by shortage of supplies caused by bombing of the railways and failed. This led to encirclement, a rapid German retreat, and the liberations of Paris and Brussels.

As French railways came into allied possession, railway troops co-operated with the surviving French railwaymen to restore them to working order. This was by no means easy. As soon as some of the ports were freed, however, a mass of railway material was received, from locomotives to machine tools and spare parts. Less damage was done to the French and Belgian railways further east, and the big railway workshops at Lille were not in bad condition when they were occupied by British troops so repairs were expedited.

On the Russian front there had been a slow German retreat all through 1943 and 1944, although there were some brilliant German strokes which temporarily turned the tide, but the ebb westwards continued. The Germans carried out thorough demolition of the railways as they retreated, withdrawing all locomotives and rolling stock and using claw wagons to tear up the track, as well as blowing up all bridges. These tactics slowed the Russian advance, for millions of new sleepers had to be brought from Siberia and temporary bridges built, often of wood. One of the main delays was in machining new switch-blades, for planers were in short supply and consequently heavily used. Rail was mostly re-usable and water supplies were not seriously sabotaged. Most of the machine tools in locomotive depots were heavily damaged by the Germans before their retreat and, once trains began to run again this was a real difficulty, for most of the Russian locomotives were badly worn, and needed considerable running repairs at fairly short intervals.

By the end of 1944 the Russians were besieging Budapest and were just outside Warsaw while, in the south, they had captured Belgrade. There was a short pause for consolidation and to allow time for railways to be repaired.

On December 16, 1944, the Germans mounted their Ardennes offensive in the west. For a time it seemed that the Germans might repeat their success of May 1940 in almost the same location and cut the allied army in two. This time, however, they were faced by experienced generals and

Below: The opening of the strategic railway bridge over the Rhine at Mainz allowed war *materiel* to be poured into Germany in support of the Allied armies.

troops who, after the initial surprise, made a fierce resistance and were aided by an increasing shortage of petrol and oil for the German Armoured divisions. This shortage was finally decisive. The offensive caused complete interruption of railway communications in the battle-zone, but railway staff were by this time as battle-trained as the troops and modified their services immediately to suit the changing conditions of the battle.

In mid-January of 1945 came the next Russian offensive. The Russian generals were by this time as experienced and skilful as the German generals opposing them. The Germans in turn had learned how to cope with winter offensives, but the latter were now seriously short of men. The Russians had received so much British and American equipment that their armies were less dependant on horse transport to supplement the railways. Nevertheless railways were still vital. It was this offensive that forced the Germans to decide that defence of the Oder line in the east was more urgent than defence of the Rhine. This gave some help to the British and American forces in their drive towards the Rhine, though hard fighting continued. The allies in the west had now gained air superiority over the Germans and increased the bombing of German railway centres not only in the west, but also behind the German lines in the east.

In March 1945, the British and American armies crossed the Rhine in several places after sweeping the west bank clear of Germans, cutting off large bodies of German troops and driving eastwards with less opposition than before, except from fanatics. The Germans, both army and people, now despaired of a successful outcome of the war, and hoped that the British and Americans would drive as far east as possible before encountering the Russians. The allies now learnt how much damage railways could

sustain and yet remain operational. Some British railways had been heavily damaged by German bombing in 1940 and 1941, but traffic had been resumed in a matter of hours. They had, however, never been damaged so badly as were the German railways during the last year of the war – yet trains continued to run. Destroyed bridges were replaced by temporary structures; marshalling yards were partly, but never wholly, put out of action, locomotive depots, even turntables, were repaired, or replaced by triangles. The most difficult obstacles were blocked tunnels, but, even in these cases, mechanical diggers, bulldozers and belt conveyors greatly reduced the time required to clear them, and tubular scaffolding was used to support the forms for concrete lining when this was essential.

In Burma all had gone well for the British. The Japanese had hoped to hold the line of the Irrawaddy and to block Messervy's advance down the Sittang valley by rail and road, but the Japanese troops were not in a fit state to fight. Messervy reached Toungoo on April 22 where he headed off the Japanese 15th Army at almost the same time as Stopford's Corps bottled the 28th Army. At Kadok, 113 km (70 miles) from Rangoon, Messervy's troops met strong opposition for the Japanese were trying to keep open a corridor of retreat to Thailand. This was frustrated by Operation Dracula, a seaborne landing, following a parachute landing at the mouth of the Rangoon river. Rangoon was taken and a junction made with Messervy's troops and, as a result, less than 6,000 Japanese succeeded in reaching Thailand. The liberation of Burma was complete. During the British advance, the Japanese had continued to use railways as their main supply lines, despite increasing interference from guerillas. As they fell back they sabotaged the railways.

Left: Attacks by Allied air and land forces caused heavy damage to Germany's railways in the latter part of the second world war. This photograph shows Aachen station after the German surrender.

The over-running of Germany by the allied armies, the collapse of all organized resistance and division of the country into four zones for administration by allied Control Commissions was a post-war phase. But it should not be forgotten what a magnificent feat of rehabilitation and reconstruction was achieved by the Control Commissions during the autumn of 1945 in their efforts to save the German people from starvation, disease and cold during the winter that followed. The Control Commissions worked seven-day weeks in their unselfish and unrecognized efforts.

Although the war with Germany and Italy was over, that with Japan continued. The Japanese high command now realized that, with the collapse of the other Axis powers, the war would inevitably be lost, and were manoeuvring to achieve peace without loss of face. By this time the Japanese were retreating on all fronts, even in China, where the Chinese, after 14 years of war, were almost as tired as the Japanese. The increasing scale of bombing of Japan was reducing the high efficiency of Japanese railways, but not so seriously as in other countries. Shortage of oil was a very serious factor for the armed forces and the country at large, but this had only a minor effect on the railways, where motive power was nearly all electric or steam, using coal in both cases. Manchurian coal was still plentiful, though lubricating oil was becoming increasingly difficult to obtain, and railways turned to vegetable oil, with considerable success.

Japanese uncertainty was reduced by the dropping of the atomic bombs on Hiroshima and Nagasaki. The Japanese had nothing equivalent to these devastating weapons and could, therefore, surrender without loss of face.

The last noteworthy involvement of railways during the war of 1939 to 1945 was use by the Russians of the Manchurian railways during the brief campaign against Japan which began on 8 August and was over in a few days. The Russian attack, which had been carefully planned in advance, was so sudden and unexpected by the local Japanese commanders that they were either taken prisoner or escaped so rapidly that they had no time to damage the western section seriously during their retreat. They even lost locomotives

and rolling stock in Manchouli yard, the frontier station. The Russians had transported standard-gauge locomotives and rolling stock from Europe for use in Manchuria, and these were fully utilized. East of the Khinghan mountains, the Japanese had time to destroy most of the bridges, and this delayed the Russians somewhat, especially the big bridge over the Sungari River at Harbin. From Tsitsihar eastwards and southwards the Japanese had time to do rather more thorough demolition, especially to locomotives, rolling stock, and depots. The Russians were, therefore, extremely short of locomotives and rolling stock during their advance, which was both east from Manchouli, west from Vladivostok and south from Blagoveshchensk, joining at Harbin to go south to Mukden and Dairen, where they captured plenty of undamaged locomotives and rolling stock.

Above left: During the second world war the German requisitioned locomotives and rolling stock from all over occupied Europe. After the war some were returned to their original owners badly damaged, as can be seen by this British-built Dutch locomotive photographed in 1946.

Above: German civilians loot a supply train immediately after the German surrender.

Below: The completion of a temporary bridge over the River Orne in northern France allowed the Allies to move supplies from Cherbourg inland to Caen more easily.

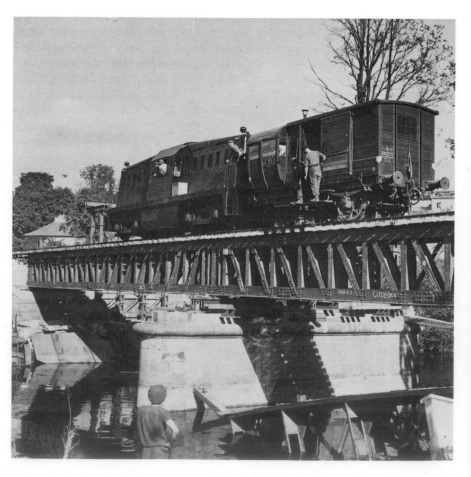

Above right: The ubiquitous American Willys 'jeep' fitted with flanged wheels for rail travel.

Below: The wholesale destruction of Europe's railway network in the second world war made the reconstruction of railways a major priority during the immediate post war period.

Conclusion

This account finishes in 1945 – over 30 years ago. Although railways have been used in the many wars that have since taken place, they were almost without exception rather scrambling and disjointed affairs which do not deserve close attention from a railway viewpoint.

Railways became increasingly utilized in war until by the end of the 19th century they had become essential to rapid mobilization, movement and supply of the large European conscript armies. It was the close study of railway utilization that gave the Germans one of their most important initial advantages at the beginning of the war of 1914. Yet the fact is that the Schlieffen Plan, on which the Germans worked, would have been possible 100 years earlier or 50 years later, when troop and supply movements were made by road, but was not possible in 1914, when railways were essential. Schlieffen had not counted on the wrecking of the Belgian railways and had not provided enough mechanical road transport to take its place. Despite this handicap the Schlieffen Plan nearly succeeded through the errors of Germany's opponents, but not quite. The ultimate consequence was Germany's defeat.

The period when railways were the dominant factor in war was already passing in 1914 – with the appearance of London omnibuses and Carter Paterson motor vans behind the British front. The type of static or 'trench' warfare, which machine guns and barbed wire had forced on the various armies, was the very type of campaign to which railways were best suited and led to a great increase in their use. Military planners had never been very happy with railways other than in 'trench' warfare, for they were not flexible enough for war of the manoeuvring type, when an army

had to be ready to move in any direction at short notice. In cases such as these, armies could make little use of railways and had to trust to road, tracked or horse, transport. The desert war of 1940 to 1942 was an example.

War has changed since 1945. Air observation is now so detailed that it is impossible to assemble large forces for attack without detection.

For rapid movements of troops, guns and armoured vehicles railways are still supreme and will be used as much as the enemy will permit. A picturesque phase of railways in war was the use of armoured trains. Their scope was limited, but in some operations they played an important role. They may yet achieve a new lease of life to fight off guerilla attacks and to rebuild damaged track under enemy fire, but in future conflicts their form will certainly change.

BIOGRAPHY

A

Abt, Roman Born Bünzen, Canton Aargau, Switzerland, July, 1850; died Lucerne, May 1, 1933 aged 82. Swiss locomotive engineer and inventor of the Abt system of rack railways. From 1869 he studied engineering at the Federal Polytechnic, Zurich, and from 1872 he continued his training under N Riggenbach (q.v.) at the Swiss Central Railway works at Olten. In 1875 he became engineer of the International Company for Mountain Railways at Aarau until 1879 when he was appointed chief engineer in the Swiss Railway Department at Bern. From 1881 he was chief engineer of the waterworks contractors C Zschokke & Terrier in Paris.

In 1882, he patented his famous rack rail system. This uses two, or three, toothed plates mounted side by side. In the double rack each tooth on one plate is opposite a gap in the other plate and in the triple rack opposite half a gap in the next plate. Thus, at least one tooth is in engagement.

The system was first used in 1884 on the rack and adhesion Harz Railway in Brunswick, using 11 rack sections.

From 1885 he worked on his own and in 1887 moved to Lucerne. In 1890, his rack system was used on the metre gauge Visp – Zermatt Railway, and, in 1891, on the standard gauge Erzberg Railway in Austria.

By 1914, 66 railways including 12 in Switzerland and 14 in overseas countries were using the Abt rack. In 1920 to 1929 a further six sections were built making a world total of 72 totalling 1,695 km (1,053 miles) to gauges of 600 to 1,676 mm (1 ft 11½ in to 5 ft 6 in) and gradients up to 25.5 per cent (1 in 3.9). Abt supervised construction of many lines himself in addition to designing locomotives and rolling stock.

Adams, William Bridges Born Madeley, Staffordshire, 1797; died Broadstairs, Kent, July 23, 1872, aged 75. Locomotive engineer and manufacturer, and inventor of the steam railcar. He was apprenticed to an engine builder named John Farey, but failing health forced him to seek recovery in Chile. He returned in 1837. In Chile he decided to become a railway engineer. In 1838 he invented a rail brake which gripped the sides of the rail but could not be used on track of that time.

In 1843 he founded the Fairfield works at Bow, London. He designed his first steam railcar, the *Express*, built and tested on the Eastern Counties Railway. His next, the *Fairfield* for the Bristol & Exeter Railway, had a saloon coach seat-

William Bridges Adams

ing 58. His third railcar, the *Enfield*, built in 1849 for the Enfield branch of the ECR, had a separate 2–2–0 locomotive. Adams patented a successful type of rail fishplate in 1847.

He is best remembered for his radial axlebox, first used on a 2–4–2 tank engine built in 1863 by Cross & Co of St Helens for the St Helens Railway.

Allen, Horatio Born Schenectady, New York, May 10, 1802; died Montrose, New Jersey, January 1, 1890, aged 87. Pioneer American locomotive and civil engineer. In 1821, he entered Columbia College

Horatio Allen

and in 1823 graduated with high honours in mathematics. He started in law, then changed to engineering and began his career with the Delaware & Hudson Canal Company under the engineer, Judge Wright. In 1824, he was appointed resident engineer of the Delaware & Susquehanna Canal and in 1825 to the same post at the summit level of the Delaware & Hudson Canal under John B Jervis.

Early in 1826 he visited England to examine Stephenson locomotives. He was asked by the D & H Co to purchase rails in England for 26 km (16 miles) of railway and also four locomotives. One of these, the *Stourbridge Lion* from Foster, Rastrick & Co of Stourbridge, was the first locomotive to run in America, in 1829.

In the same year he became chief engineer of the South Carolina Railroad, until 1837. In addition to acting as consulting engineer to the New York & Erie RR he was engaged in water works and the manufacture of steamship engines. He retired in 1870 and devoted his last 20 years to study and invention.

Allport, Sir James Born 1811, in Birmingham; died in 1892, aged 81. In 1839 he became chief clerk to the Birmingham and Derby Junction, and shortly afterwards general manager. But, in 1844, when the Midland Railway was formed by a major amalgamation, Allport was

Sir James Allport

Sir William Arrol

succeeded Joseph Armstrong at Swindon in 1877, George refused to take orders from him, and continued to rule at Wolverhampton until he retired in 1897 at the age of 75.

In his 33 years at Wolverhampton, he built 626 engines and rebuilt 513 – the number of men employed in the works increased from 750 to 1,500.

Armstrong, Joseph (senior) Born Bewcastle, Cumberland, September 21, 1816; died Matlock, Derbyshire, June 5, 1877, aged 60. Locomotive carriage and wagon superintendent, Great Western Railway. Trained at Walbottle colliery where he became friendly with George Stephenson and Timothy Hackworth (qq.v.). In 1836 he worked as engine driver on the Liverpool & Manchester Railway and in 1840 on the Hull & Selby Railway, later becoming foreman of the sheds and shops at Hull. In 1845 with his brother George he followed John Gray to the London & Brighton Railway. In 1847 he was appointed assistant and then locomotive superintendent on the Shrewsbury & Chester Railway. When the Shrewsbury & Birmingham Railway opened in 1849 it was worked as one railway with the S & C and in 1853 Armstrong was transferred to the newly opened shops at Wolverhampton. In 1854 the whole network as far north as Chester became part of the GWR forming a standard gauge division. Armstrong became responsible only to Daniel Gooch (q.v.) at Swindon for all the Northern Division locomotives. In his ten years at Wolverhampton he designed many locomotives. In 1864 Gooch resigned as also did J Gibson the carriage and wagon superintendent. Armstrong was appointed to both positions at Swindon, becoming the first locomotive, carriage and wagon superintendent on the GWR. He built few broad gauge engines, and established the Swindon carriage and wagon works. From 1874 new coaches were built as 'convertibles', looking towards the end of the broad gauge. Armstrong's most famous engines were his 2–2–2s, 0–6–0s, 2–4–0s and 2–4–0 tanks. In his 13 years at Swindon, 600 engines were built.

Arrol, Sir William Born Houston, Renfrewshire, Scotland, February 13, 1839; died Ayr, February 20, 1913, aged 74. Civil engineering contractor; builder of the Tay and Forth bridges. Began as a blacksmith. By the age of 29 he had saved £85, half of which he spent on a boiler and engine and in 1868 he started a small works of his own near Glasgow. The

works flourished and in 1871 he began the Dalmarnock works, adding bridge building to his work. His first contracts were for bridges on the Caledonian and North British railways, at Bothwell, Glasgow and Montrose. In 1882 he was awarded the contract for the second Tay bridge, completed in 1887, the longest railway bridge in Europe. Also in 1882 he began his greatest work, the Forth bridge. Following its completion in 1890 he was knighted by Queen Victoria.

Arrol was also responsible for the steelwork of the Tower Bridge, London; the new Redheugh bridge, Newcastle, three bridges over the Nile at Cairo, the huge Queen Alexandra bridge at Sunderland, the Scherzer lifting bridge at Barrow and the second section of the Clyde bridge at Glasgow Central station.

Ashfield, Lord, of Southwell Born at Derby in 1874; died 1948. He was the major developer of the London Transport organization but all his early experience of urban transport was gained in the USA. He was taken to America, and his career began with the street cars of Detroit. Before he was 28, he was general superintendent of the tramway system of that city, and in 1903 he moved to the Street Railway Department of the Public Service Corporation of New Jersey, first as assistant, and then as general manager. In 1907 Albert Stanley, as he then was, was appointed general manager of the Underground Electric Railways of London – which in time incorporated all the underground and tube lines except the Metropolitan. He later became managing director but resigned in 1916 when invited by Lloyd George to become President of the Board of Trade. He returned to the Underground in 1919 as Chairman, and, on the merging of all London transport activities in 1933, he was appointed Chairman of the London Pas-

---

dismissed as redundant. The great and notorious tycoon George Hudson engaged him for another of his lines, and he served on the York, Newcastle and Berwick until 1850, when he was appointed general manager of the Manchester Sheffield and Lincolnshire. He joined the Midland as general manager in October 1853, for 27 years of momentous and distinguished service in that office. He will ever be remembered in railway history for providing third class accommodation, at the Parliamentary fare of a penny a mile on all trains, regardless of their importance and speed. His policy dates from 1872. By New Year's Day 1875, second class was abolished, and all existing second class carriages designated *third*. Another great project, in which he was the prime mover, was the construction of the Settle & Carlisle line which gave the Midland direct access to Scotland. It was opened for passenger traffic in May 1876. He retired in 1880 and took a seat on the Board. He was knighted in 1884 for his service to cheap fare travellers.

Armstrong, George Born Bewcastle, Cumberland, April 5, 1822; died Wolverhampton July 11, 1901, aged 79. Northern division locomotive superintendent, Great Western Railway. From 1836 he was trained at Walbottle colliery, Northumberland, and in 1840 under John Gray on the Hull & Selby and London & Brighton railways. In 1848, after a period in France, he began work on the Shrewsbury & Chester Railway, from 1854 part of the GWR. When his brother Joseph was appointed locomotive superintendent at Swindon, George succeeded him at Wolverhampton, with William Dean as his assistant. When Dean

senger Transport Board. Under his management, the system was developed; the formerly distinct and individual tube lines were linked by ingeniously constructed junction systems, and the main routes were extended into country areas. He was re-elected chairman in 1940 for a further period of seven years. He was knighted in 1914, became a Privy Councillor in 1916, and received a barony in 1920.

Aspinall, Sir John A F Born in Liverpool in 1851; died in January 1937 at the age of 85. One of the greatest English railway engineers and managers. He was a pupil successively to John Ramsbottom and F W Webb at Crewe Works, LNWR. After his training and when only 24, he was appointed Works Manager at Inchicore (Dublin) on the Great Southern and Western Railway and in 1883 became Locomotive, Carriage and Wagon Superintendent of that railway. In 1886 he was appointed Chief Mechanical Engineer of the Lancashire and Yorkshire Railway, so beginning an illustrious career of 33 years in active service with LYR. He planned and brought into service the splendid new locomotive works at Horwich, and built there excellent locomotives of the 4–4–0, 4–4–2 and 2–4–2 tank types. In 1899 he had the rare distinction, for a locomotive engineer, of promotion to General Manager, a post that he held for 20 years. He retained his interest, and was an ever-increasing influence, in engineering matters. He was a leading pioneer in railway electric traction and was responsible for electrifying, as early as 1904, the network of lines between Liverpool, Southport and Ormskirk.

B

Baird, Matthew Born near Londonderry, Ireland, 1817; died Philadelphia, Pennsylvania, May 19, 1877, aged 60. American locomotive engineer. At 17, he was apprenticed in a copper and sheet iron works. From 1836 to 1838 he was superintendent of the Newcastle & Frenchtown RR shops and from 1838 to 1850 was foreman of the sheet iron and boiler department of the Baldwin Locomotive Works. In 1854 he bought an interest in the Baldwin Works. On the death of Baldwin (q.v.), in 1866, Baird became the sole proprietor. In 1867 he took in two partners. He was associated with the first spark arrester, invented by Richard French in 1842, and was credited with the first firebrick arch in a firebox, in 1854. He retired in 1873.

Baker, Sir Benjamin Born Keyford, Frome, Somerset, March 31, 1840; died Pangbourne, Berkshire, May 19, 1907 aged 67. Civil engineer; designer of the Forth Bridge. He was educated at Cheltenham Grammar School, and from 1856 to 1860 was apprenticed to H H Price at Neath Abbey Ironworks, Wales. After working with Sir John Fowler (q.v.) on the Metropolitan and District Railways in London, he joined J H Greathead in the building of the Central London tube, opened in 1900. He incorporated in this a scheme he had devised 20 years earlier – to make the line rise on entering a station and fall on leaving to reduce braking and starting power. With Fowler, he undertook several overseas works including railways in Australia and South Africa.

His greatest work was the design of the great cantilever bridge over the Forth in Scotland, begun in 1882 and opened on March 4, 1890. In the same year he was knighted.

Matthias William Baldwin

Baldwin, Matthias William Born Elizabethtown, New Jersey, November 10, 1795; died Philadelphia, Pennsylvania, September 7, 1866, aged 70. American locomotive engineer and manufacturer. He began as a jeweller but, after six years, entered into a partnership in an engineering firm. In 1832 he

A 2-4-2T locomotive designed by Sir John Aspinall and built at Horwich in 1889.

built his first locomotive, named *Old Ironsides*, for the Philadelphia & Germantown RR. It was in his second, the 4–2–0 *E L Miller* completed in 1834 for the South Carolina RR, that he introduced features which became standard American practice. In 1866 he introduced the 2–8–0, *Consolidation*, which gave its name to what became the most numerous locomotive type in America. The Baldwin Locomotive Works became one of the world's largest. The last of Baldwin's 75,000 steam locomotives was built for India in 1955.

Barlow, Peter William, FRS Born Woolwich, London, February 1, 1809; died Notting Hill, London, May 19, 1885, aged 76. Eldest son of Professor Peter Barlow and brother of William Henry (q.v.). In 1826, after private education, he became a pupil of Henry Robinson Palmer on the Liverpool & Birmingham canal and London docks. In 1836 he began work under Sir William Cubitt on the London to Dover Railway, later the South Eastern Railway, becoming resident engineer and, from 1844, chief engineer. He built many miles of SER lines. In 1851 he resigned and devoted the following years to bridge construction and railways in Ireland and Shropshire. He devised the idea of boring tube railways in the London clay and proved his theory by boring the Tower Subway under the Thames, opened in 1870. It was the world's first tube railway. It now carries a water main.

Barlow, William Henry Born Woolwich, London, May 10, 1812; died Greenwich, London, November 12, 1902, aged 90. Younger brother of Peter William (see above). He trained as a civil engineer at Woolwich dockyard and London docks. From 1832 he spent six years at Constantinople (Istanbul) assembling machinery and constructing buildings for the manufacture of ordnance for the Turkish government. In 1838 he became resident engineer on the Manchester to Crewe line and in 1842 began his association with lines which, in 1844, became the Midland Railway. Barlow was appointed chief engineer at Derby. Between 1862 and 1869 he carried out the MR extension to London. He was responsible for St Pancras station with the largest roof span in Great Britain (73.15 m [240 ft] and 30.48 m [100 ft] above rail level).

Between 1844 and 1866, he patented several items related to the permanent way. These included the saddleback Barlow rail, much used on the Great Western Railway, and patented in 1849.

He was a member of the court of inquiry into the Tay Bridge disaster of 1879 and was consultant for the design of the replacement bridge built by Arrol (q.v.) between 1882 and 1887.

Beatty, Sir Edward W Born in Canada in 1877; died in March 1943, aged 70. First Canadian-born President of the Canadian Pacific Railway. He was trained in law. He joined the CPR as an assistant in the law department in 1901, and rose very rapidly, to assistant solicitor in 1905, general solicitor in 1910. In 1913, he was appointed general counsel. By that time he was acquiring a complete mastery of every facet of the operation of this great company, and on the retirement of Lord Shaughnessy as president, in 1918, Beatty was elected to succeed him. On the death of the former in 1924, Beatty succeeded him in the dual role of chairman and president, which he held for 18 momentous years. He developed the steamship services of the company to a position of world eminence, and, with great skill, steered the CPR through the very difficult slump years of the 1930s. Major re-organization and development in the Angus Locomotive Works at Montreal and the Strathcona shops at Calgary, authorized by his administration, proved of inestimable value in maintaining the stock during the second world war and in undertaking much direct production of munitions. He was knighted in 1935. He retired from the presidency of the CPR in 1942, but retained the chairmanship until his death.

Behn-Eschenburg, Hans Born January 10, 1864; died near Zurich May 18, 1938, aged 74. Swiss electrical engineer and the pioneer of high voltage ac railway electrification. He studied under H F Weber and in 1892 entered Maschinenfabrik Oerlikon (MFO) where he was engaged in the development of transformers and traction machinery. He became chief electrical engineer in 1897. In 1902 he introduced a three-phase induction motor and in 1904 the first practical single-phase traction motor, tested on the Seebach to Wettingen line. This motor was used in 1913 on the Lötschberg and Rhaetian railways and subsequently on other Swiss main lines. In 1913, he became managing director of MFO, responsible for the manufacture of a great amount of railway electrical equipment.

Belpaire, Alfred Jules Born Ostend, Belgium, September 26, 1820; died Schaarbeek, January 27, 1893, aged 72.

Alfred Jules Belpaire

Locomotive engineer and designer of the Belpaire firebox. Studied at the Central School of Arts and Manufactures, Paris, and in 1840 gained an engineering diploma. He was then put in charge of the locomotive repair shops at Malines where his contemporary Walschaert (q.v.) began his career. In 1850 he was appointed director of the rolling stock department, Brussels. To obtain better combustion of poor fuel he produced his famous firebox, first in a round form, in 1860. In 1864, he designed the well-known square form which facilitated the use of vertical and horizontal stays. Subsequently, he introduced various improvements. He also invented a combined reversing lever and screw, and designed many locomotives for the Belgian Railways.

Berkley, James J Born October 1819, London; died, August 1862, at Sydenham, aged 42. Civil engineer, and builder of the first sections of the Great Indian Peninsula Railway. Began his engineering training in 1836, became a pupil of Robert Stephenson (q.v.) in 1839, and assisted him on surveys of railways in France, Germany and Belgium. In England, he was resident engineer on construction of the North Staffordshire Railway. In 1849, he was appointed chief resident engineer of the Great Indian Peninsula Railway, where he had the tremendous task of carrying not one, but two main lines up the Western Ghat range. The surveys alone took nearly six years, during which he adopted the zig-zag technique of mounting the jungle-clad escarpments to lessen the gradients. The present main lines from

Bombay to Madras, and Bombay to Calcutta, in their crossing of the Ghats are a monument to his work.

Betts, Edward Ladd Born Sandown, Kent, June 5, 1815; died Aswan, Egypt, January 21, 1872, aged 56. One of the most famous railway contractors. At the age of 18, he was given sole responsibility under Joseph Locke (q.v.) for the construction of the Dutton viaduct on the Grand Junction Railway. He was later responsible for much of the Chester to Holyhead Railway and other lines in North Wales. He then entered into partnership with S M Peto (q.v.) with whom he constructed many miles of railway in Britain and abroad, including the Grand Trunk Railway in Canada – with Robert Stephenson's great tubular bridge over the St Lawrence at Montreal. With Thomas Brassey (q.v.) he built the Balaclava Railway during the Crimean war. With T R Crampton (q.v.) he built the whole of the London, Chatham & Dover Railway.

Beyer, Charles Frederick Born Planen, Saxony, May 14, 1813; died Llantysilio, Wales, June 2, 1876, aged 63. Locomotive engineer and manufacturer. While at the Dresden Polytechnic he visited Manchester to report on cotton spinning machinery, he was greatly influenced by Richard Roberts of Sharp, Roberts & Co. He soon returned to Manchester and, in 1834, began as a draughtsman in this firm. In 1837, they began the manufacture of locomotives. Beyer designed the 'Sharp Standard' 2–2–2s and 0–4–2s. After the retirement of Roberts in 1843, Beyer designed all the locomotives. In 1853 he left the firm to form a partnership with Richard Peacock (q.v.) and found the firm of Beyer Peacock at Manchester. They bought 12 acres close to the Manchester, Sheffield & Lincolnshire Railway works at Gorton, where Peacock had been locomotive superintendent. The works were begun in 1854. The first locomotive appeared on July 31, 1855 – the first Great Western standard-gauge engine.

Many famous engines were built by Beyer Peacock, including the 4–4–0 tanks for the Metropolitan Railway and the Garratts (q.v. H W Garratt). The works finally closed down in 1966.

Borsig, Johann Carl Friedrich August Born Breslau, June 25, 1804; died Berlin, July 7, 1854, aged 49. Founder of one of Germany's most important locomotive works. He studied at Breslau Technical

Borsig's locomotive *Beuth*, built in Berlin in 1841.

School and at the Royal Industrial Institute, Berlin, and then trained in mechanical engineering at F G Eyells, Berlin. In 1837, he established a small works in Berlin. After the first ten years, the works had built 67 locomotives and the number of employees had grown to 1,200. Also in 1847 he established an ironworks at Moabit near Berlin where, from 1850, he produced iron rails.

Bouch, Sir Thomas Born Thursby, Cumberland, February 22, 1822; died Moffat, October 30, 1880 aged 58. Civil engineer. In January 1849, he became manager and engineer of the Edinburgh & Northern Railway, later part of the North British. In 1851, he left that post to engage in private practice.

He made numerous surveys and plans for railways and bridges. His over-riding weakness lay in his desire to carry out work as cheaply as possible, with the resultant expensive repair and reconstruction later. His lack of attention to work in progress led to faults in materials and construction.

His largest work, the first Tay Bridge at Dundee, a single line structure 3.552 km (2 miles 364 yd) long, was opened on September 22, 1877. The Tay Bridge suffered from weaknesses in construction and, in a violent storm on the night of December 28, 1879, the centre spans blew down while a train was crossing. Over 70 people were drowned and there were no survivors. The shock of this undermined Bouch's health and he died shortly afterwards.

Boveri, Walter Born Bamberg, Bavaria, February 21, 1865; died Baden, Switzerland, October 28, 1924, aged 59. Electrical and mechanical engineer and manufacturer of electric railway equipment. In 1884, after training in Nuremberg, he joined Maschinenfabrik Oerlikon (MFO) near Zürich where he worked under C E L Brown (q.v.) on the manufacture of electrical machinery. Later,

Sir Thomas Bouch's Tay Bridge after the disaster (1879).

when in charge of the erecting department, he supervised the development of the dc motor.

In 1891 he joined C E L Brown to found the famous Swiss firm of Brown, Boveri & Co, Baden (BBC). Its growth was rapid. From about 1896, the firm manufactured ever increasing amounts of equipment for railway electrification throughout the world.

From 1911 Boveri was president of BBC and its related interests and a member of the commission on the electrification of the Swiss Federal Railways.

---

du Bousquet, Gaston Born Paris, August 20, 1839; died Paris, March 24, 1910, aged 70. French locomotive engineer associated with compounding. He was trained at the State School of Engineering, Paris, and in 1862 began his career on the Nord railway of France where he spent the whole of his working life. In 1883 he became divisional locomotive superintendent at Lille, in 1889 chief locomotive superintendent and in 1890 chief engineer.

From 1886 he worked with de Glehn (q.v.) on compound locomotive designs. In 1894 he was elected president of the French Society of Civil Engineers. His best known engines were the very famous Nord 4-cylinder compound Atlantics, also the 0–6–2 and 2–6–0 articulated compound tank (1905). His great 4–6–4 was still unfinished at his death.

Brandt, John Born Lancaster, Pennsylvania, c 1785; died Lancaster c 1860 aged about 75. American locomotive engineer who pioneered the famous American 4–4–0. In 1832, after a period as assistant engineer on the Philadelphia & Columbia RR, he was appointed chief engineer of the Philadelphia, Germantown & Norristown RR. In 1839, he moved to the Erie RR and, in 1851, became superintendent of the newly formed New Jersey Locomotive & Machine Co, Paterson, N J During the period 1854–1855 he left to establish a locomotive works in Lancaster.

Brassey, Thomas Born Baerton, near Chester, November 7, 1805; died St Leonards-on-Sea, December 8, 1870, aged 65. Civil engineer and contractor. After his marriage, in 1831, he decided to become a railway contractor and he secured his first contracts on the Grand Junction Railway (Birmingham to Warrington) under Joseph Locke (q.v.) in 1835. He next undertook large contracts, again for Locke, on the London &

Thomas Brassey

Charles Brown (senior)

Southampton Railway, employing about 3,000 men, and on other Locke lines – the Chester to Crewe, (1838 to 1840), Sheffield to Manchester (1838 to 1845) and Glasgow to Greenock (1838 to 1841). In 1840, in partnership with William Mackenzie (q.v.) he secured the contract for the Paris & Rouen Railway. From 1843, Brassey & Mackenzie undertook the Havre & Rouen as well as lines in England, Scotland and Wales, Belgium, Holland and Spain.

At this time Brassey employed 75,000 men. In partnership with M Peto and E Betts (qq.v.), he built the Grand Trunk Railway in Canada (1852 to 1855) and other railways in France, Italy, Spain, Norway, Sweden, Denmark, Switzerland, Austria, Turkey, India and Australia. He built the first railways in South America. His total railway contracts amounted to 3,820 km (2,374 miles) at a cost of £28 million.

Brown, Charles Born Uxbridge, Middlesex, June 30, 1827, died Basle, Switzerland, October 6, 1905, aged 78. Founder of the Swiss Locomotive & Machine Works (SLM), Winterthur. He cut short a seven-year apprenticeship with Maudslay & Field, London, to establish his own workshop. In 1851 he was invited by a relative of Sulzer at Winterthur to build steam engines at the Sulzer works. He left Sulzer in 1871 to re-establish his own works which became SLM. His first locomotives were four rack machines for the Rigi Railway, numbers 7 to 10. His interest in the development of the Swiss electrical engineering industry led him

to join the Maschinenfabrik Oerlikon (MFO) in the late 1880s. He retired in 1890 and practised as a consulting engineer in Basle.

His son Charles Eugene (q.v.) was one of the founders of Brown Boveri & Co.

Brown, Charles Eugene Lancelot Born Winterthur, Switzerland, June 17, 1863; died Lugano, May 5, 1924, aged 60. Electrical engineer; son of Charles Brown (q.v.). He began his career at the Maschinenfabrik Oerlikon (MFO) near Zurich where, at the age of 23, he took charge of the electrical department. He began to build generators – at the time among the world's largest. In 1889, he turned his attention to alternating current equipment. He developed the first single-phase generators and motors. In collaboration with Dolivo-Dobrowolski, he developed multi-phase traction. In 1891 he resigned from MFO to join W Boveri in the founding of Brown Boveri & Co (BBC) – (q.v. W Boveri).

Brunel, Isambard Kingdom Born Portsmouth, April 9, 1806; died London, September 15, 1859, aged 53. Civil engineer; son of Sir Marc I Brunel. He began his engineering training under his father in 1823 and assisted him in the building of the Thames tunnel. His health was permanently damaged during this project.

In 1829, he prepared a design for the Clifton suspension bridge at Bristol and was appointed engineer but, because of lack of funds, work was suspended until

Isambard Kingdom Brunel

1860 when it was completed by W H Barlow and John Hawkshaw (q.v.).

In March 1833, Brunel was appointed engineer to the Great Western Railway and he laid out a magnificent line from London to Bristol to a gauge of 2,134 mm (7 ft). The line was opened in 1841 when he was still only 35. On extensions into South Wales, Devon and Cornwall he built the great bridges at Chepstow (1852) and Saltash (1859). His abilities as a mechanical engineer were poor, however, and the few locomotives built to his specification were failures, as was the atmospheric system of propulsion he adopted for the South Devon Railway. His 7 ft gauge was doomed from an early date, although it lasted until 1892.

Brunel achieved distinction with his great steamships, the *Great Western* (1838), *Great Britain* (1845) and the *Great Eastern,* begun in 1853. It was the anxieties and accidents during the construction and trials of that last ship which broke his health and led to his early death.

Brunlees, Sir James Born Kelso, Scotland, January 5, 1816; died Wimbledon, Surrey, June 6, 1892, aged 76. One of the most outstanding civil engineers of his time. He was trained under Alexander Adie, another Scottish civil engineer, and, in 1838, was engaged by Adie on the Bolton & Preston Railway. The first railways for which he was completely responsible were the Londonderry & Coleraine in Ireland and the Ulverston & Lancaster – with its viaducts across the Kent and Leven estuaries.

Brunlees carried out some very difficult projects such as the inclined planes between Santos and São Paulo, Brazil (1851), the Fell railway over Mont Cenis pass (opened 1868 and closed when the Mont Cenis tunnel was opened in 1871), the Solway Junction Railway and viaduct, and the Cleveland extension, Yorkshire, with a viaduct 54.86 m (180 ft) high. In collaboration with Sir Douglas Fox (q.v.), he built the Mersey Railway tunnel for which he was knighted.

Buddicom, William Barber Born Liverpool, July 1, 1816; died Mold, Flintshire, August 4, 1887, aged 71. Locomotive and civil engineer and contractor. From 1831 he was apprenticed to Matherm, Dixon & Co Liverpool, and in 1836 was appointed resident engineer of the Liverpool to Newton bridge section of the Liverpool & Manchester Railway. In 1838 he moved to the same situation on the Glasgow, Paisley & Greenock Railway. In 1840, he was appointed locomotive superintendent of the Grand Junction Railway and prepared the plans for the original Crewe works. Buddicom introduced the outside cylinder locomotive design which became known as the 'Crewe' type.

In 1841 he and William Allcard established works near Rouen on the Paris & Rouen Railway for the supply of rolling stock, eventually operating 628 km (390 miles) of railway. His company survived the revolution of 1848. He resigned his contract in 1860 to join Brassey (q.v.) and Charles Jones in building and stocking the Maremma Railway (completed in 1865) and in doubling the Rouen to Dieppe line. From 1863 until his retirement from engineering in 1870, he worked with Brassey in Italy and elsewhere.

Bulleid, Oliver Vaughan Snell Born Invercargill, New Zealand, September 19, 1882; died Malta, April 25, 1970, aged 87. Chief mechanical engineer, Southern Railway, England. In December 1912, he re-joined the Great Northern Railway at Doncaster as personal assistant to H N Gresley (q.v.) who had succeeded Ivatt as chief mechanical engineer.

In 1937, at the age of 54, he succeeded R E L Maunsell as CME of the Southern Railway. Here his inventive capacities were given freedom and he produced the Q1 0–6–0 in 1941 incorporating many novel features. His most revolutionary design was the Merchant Navy class 4–6–2, built from 1941 to 1949, followed in 1945 by a lighter version the West Country class. They incorporated thermic syphons, enclosed chain-driven valve gear, 'Boxpok' wheels and numerous other features some of which gave a lot of trouble. He also designed an electric locomotive, a diesel electric, and an electric train with double level seating. His last SR design, the C-C Leader steam locomotive, was barely completed before nationalization. His resignation from British Railways in 1949 came before the five Leader class locomotives had done any revenue earning service, so beset were they with numerous defects.

Edward Bury

Bury, Edward Born Salford, near Manchester, October 22, 1794; died Scarborough, November 25, 1858, aged 64. Designer and manufacturer of locomotives and machinery. His works in Liverpool were well established when he began his first locomotive in 1829 and, following the opening of the Liverpool & Manchester Railway in 1830, he decided to devote himself to locomotives. In 1838, he became responsible for the locomotives of the London & Birmingham Railway, establishing a light four-wheeled type with bar frames and dome-topped firebox. From 1847, he managed the locomotive department of the Great Northern Railway. On his resignation from the GNR in 1853, he closed down his works in Liverpool and moved first to Windermere and then to Scarborough.

C

Caprotti, Arturo Born Cremona, March 22, 1881; died Milan, February 9, 1938, aged 56. Inventor of the Caprotti valve gear. After training at the Royal Technical Institute and Pavia University, he graduated in mechanical engineering at Turin Royal Polytechnic College (1899 to 1904). After two years in automobile engineering and two years in experimental work, he carried out research in the application of poppet valves to locomotives. He took out his first Italian patent in 1916. His valve gear became used in many countries throughout the world.

Chan Tien-Yu (Tien Yow Jeme) Born Kwangtung, China, 1861; died December 1919 aged 58. The first Chinese railway engineer, and a founder member of the Chinese Institute of Engineers. He was educated in the USA and began his railway career in 1888 after

seven years in the Chinese Navy. In 1902, he was appointed chief engineer for the Peking to Hsiling line and, from 1905 to 1909, was chief engineer of the Peking to Kalgan Railway, to the Mongolian frontier, with many difficult engineering works. On this line, he established the standard gauge in China. From 1909 until his death, he worked on the Hankow to Szechuan Railway.

Chapelon, André Born St Paul-en-Cornillon, Loire, France, October 26, 1892. One of the most progressive engineers in the history of the steam locomotive. His enthusiasm for steam locomotives developed at an early age. He graduated as Ingénieur des Arts et Manufactures at the École Centrale, Paris, in 1921. His first railway appointment was at the Lyon Mouche depôt on the Paris, Lyon & Méditerrané Railway but, seeing little hope of promotion there, he left locomotive work in 1924 to join the Société Industrielle des Téléphones. However, he soon re-joined the railway. In 1925 he was in the research and development section on the Paris–Orléans railway. In collaboration in 1926 with the Finnish engineer Kylälä (who had devised a steam and gas exhaust device in 1919) Chapelon designed a new exhaust system, which he named 'Kylchap'. This produced an adequate draught with minimum back pressure. While still an assistant under M Bloch, he completely redesigned the steam circuit to reduce throttling losses, and these principles were applied to various locomotives achieving a high degree of efficiency. His greatest locomotive, which could claim to be the finest steam locomotive ever built, was his three-cylinder compound 4-8-4 No 242A1 of 1942 to 1946. Because of the transition to electric traction it was tragically scrapped in 1960. His giant treatise, *La Locomotive à Vapeur*, was published in 1938 – a revised edition was published in 1952.

Churchward, George Jackson Born Stoke Gabriel, Devon, January 31, 1857; died Swindon, December 19, 1933, aged 76. Locomotive carriage and wagon superintendent and afterwards chief mechanical engineer Great Western Railway. At the age of 16, he was articled to John Wright, locomotive superintendent of the South Devon Railway, at Newton Abbot. When the SDR became part of the GWR in 1876, Churchward was transferred to Swindon where he worked in the drawing office. He progressed to Locomotive works manager in 1896 and then chief assistant to Dean. Churchward eventually took office as chief in 1902. Churchward led British locomotive design in his use of coned boilers with Belpaire firebox, large diameter long-travel piston valves and standardization of components. In 1908, he produced his largest locomotive, No 111 *The Great Bear*, the first British Pacific. He retired at the end of 1921. On December 19, 1933, he was out on the line at Swindon on a misty morning trying to locate a 'hanging' rail joint when he was struck and instantly killed by a locomotive.

G. J. Churward's 4-4-0 *City of Truro*

Conrad, Frederik Willem Born 1800, near Haarlem, Holland; died 1869 at Munich, aged 69. Engineer Director of the Railway Company of Holland: civil engineer, consultant to H H Said Pasha, Viceroy of Egypt, on construction of the Suez canal. Conrad's earlier work was

André Chapelon's unique three cylinder compound locomotive No 242 A1 (1946).

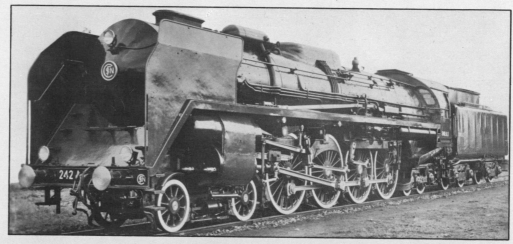

concerned with waterways, canals, building of dykes, and river works. Building of the first railway in Holland, from Amsterdam to Rotterdam was so involved with crossing waterways and in producing a firm foundation on unstable, spongy ground that the government appointed him engineer director in 1839. He afterwards described the works, and the numerous types of bridges he had designed in a paper presented in London to the Institution of Civil Engineers – of which he was a member. In 1855 he began his association with the Suez canal. He was elected President of the Commission, and, later, Commissioner for the Viceroy in the consortium that undertook that great work. In Holland, his railway has become, over the years, one of the busiest of all main lines in Europe. He died in Munich on his way to witness the opening of the Suez canal.

Thomas Cook

Cook, Thomas Born Melbourne, Derbyshire, November 22, 1809; died Leicester, July 18, 1892, aged 83. Founder of the famous firm of travel agents. He began as an assistant gardener, was next apprenticed to a wood turner and afterwards worked at Loughborough for a printer who published books for the Baptists. Cook's interest led him to become a Bible reader and missionary in 1828. His interest in the temperance movement led him to organize the first railway excursion on the Midland Counties Railway from Leicester to Loughborough, on July 5, 1841. Its success was followed by further excursions. Cook moved to

Leicester where he continued to print and publish books and to organize excursions to ever more distant places.

His son, John Mason Cook (1834–1899) became his partner in 1864, and, in 1865, they moved the office to London. The first tours to the USA followed in 1866. In 1872, Thomas made a tour round the world, to prepare the way for tourists. J M Cook became sole manager from 1878 after which Thomas, beset with oncoming blindness, withdrew from the concern. Under J M Cook, the company expanded enormously. He established the issuing of through tickets over Continental railways, and international hotel bookings. In 1884, the British government entrusted him with the conveyance of the Gordon Relief Expedition to Khartoum. He also organized the pilgrimages of Muslims from India to Mecca.

From 1948, control of Thomas Cook & Son passed to the British Transport Commission and its successors. On May 26, 1972, Thomas Cook & Son was sold for £22½ million to a consortium led by the Midland Bank.

Cooke, C J Bowen Born Orton Longueville, Peterborough, 1859; died 1920 aged 62. In 1875 became an apprentice at Crewe Works, LNER and, in 1878, a private pupil of F W Webb. He went to Rugby as assistant to the running superintendent of the southern division. All his early experience was on the 'running' side, yet his studies of design practice and workshop methods at home and overseas made him one of the foremost authorities of the day. He wrote a classic text 'British Locomotives', in 1893. His early work as chief mechanical engineer was distinguished by the successful introduction of high-degree superheating, particularly on the 'George the Fifth' class 4–4–0s; his appreciation of the mechanics of the locomotive led to his adoption of the four-cylinder system, with all cylinders driving on to the leading coupled-axle, thereby eliminating 'hammer blow'.

During the first world war, he turned the vast manufacturing capacity of Crewe Works on to special tasks of munition production. One of his locomotives, the four-cylinder 4–6–0 *Ralph Brocklebank* achieved the highest-recorded horsepower output of any British locomotive prior to grouping in 1923; 1,669 indicated hp on a run from Crewe to Carlisle in November 1913. Because of the burden of work during the war, Bowen suffered a breakdown in health in 1920, and died later that year, at the early age of 62.

Peter Cooper

Cooper, Peter Born New York, February 12, 1791; died New York April 4, 1883, aged 92. Inventor, philanthropist, and builder of the first American locomotive. At the age of 18, after no formal education, he was apprenticed to John Woodward, a New York coach builder. In 1828, after work in various activities, he and two partners established the Canton Ironworks at Baltimore. In 1830, he built *Tom Thumb* for the Baltimore & Ohio RR, the first load-hauling steam locomotive to be built in America. After 1836, he rapidly expanded his industrial interests until they embraced a wire works, rolling mill, glue factory, foundries, iron mines and electric telegraphs.

Crampton, Thomas Russell Born Broadstairs, Kent, August 6, 1816; died Westminster, April 19, 1888, aged 71. Civil and locomotive engineer. Educated privately and then trained in engineering, first under John Hague, then in 1839 under Marc Brunel. He later worked with Daniel Gooch (q.v.) on the Great Western Railway and with him designed the first GWR locomotives. In 1842, while with Gooch, he began work on his famous single driver design with its great driving wheels behind the firebox. He patented this design in 1843. In 1842, he left the GWR to work with Rénnie; in 1845, the first two Crampton engines were built for Belgium. Two were built for the London & North Western Railway, and one for the Dundee & Perth Railway in 1848. The largest British Crampton was the 6–2–0 *Liverpool* built for the LNWR in 1848. A total of 320 engines were built to Crampton's patent

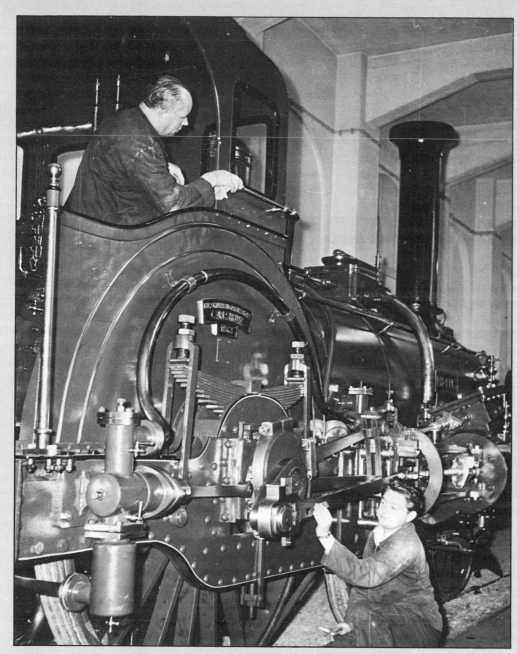

A German Crampton type locomotive, *Phoenix*, built in 1863.

— mostly in France, Germany and Belgium.

As a civil engineer, Crampton was responsible for several lines forming part of the London Chatham & Dover Railway and for others in Eastern Europe and Asia Minor. He became interested in the Channel tunnel project and invented a boring machine. This machine pulverized the chalk, mixed it with water, and sluice the solution out over the shaft.

Crampton laid the world's first international submarine cable across the Straits of Dover.

D

De Glehn, Alfred George Born Sydenham, Kent, 1848; died Mulhouse, Alsace, June 8, 1936, aged 88. One of the pioneers of steam locomotive compounding. As technical head of the Société Alsacienne, Belfort, he was responsible for the design and construction of the first four-cylinder compound locomotive, a 4–4–0 No 701, for the Nord Railway of France, in 1886. The two high-pressure cylinders outside drove the rear driving wheels and the two low-pressure inside cylinders drove the forward pair. The two pairs of driving wheels were uncoupled. In 1890 the Nord began the development of improved compound engines designed in conjunction with du Bousquet (q.v.) chief engineer and having the wheels coupled. The first batches of these were of the 4–4–0 type, but then came the very famous 'Atlantics' — design followed on the Paris-Orléans, in Egypt, India and elsewhere.

In 1903 the Great Western Railway of England ordered a similar engine and in 1905 two more. The De Glehn-du Bousquet system achieved its maximum size outside France in the great Pacifics built for the Bengal Nagpur Railway, India in 1928, but the Bréville and Collin Pacifics under the Nord Railway of France, and Chaficlon's work on the PO-Midi were all direct developments of the De Glehn system.

Diesel, Dr Rudolph Born Paris, March 1858; died North Sea, September 29–30, 1913, aged 55. Graduated at Munich Technical College in 1879 and, after a short period at the Sulzer works at Winterthur, Switzerland, became manager of the Paris works for manufacture of von Linde refrigerating machinery. From his student days, he was concerned with designing a prime mover with a higher thermal efficiency than a steam engine. This he achieved in 1893. The first reliable diesel engine was built in 1897 and was first applied to marine use in 1903. The first application to rail traction was in a Sulzer-Diesel locomotive built at Winterthur in 1913 for Germany. Dr Diesel disappeared from a steamer while on his way to Harwich to visit works at Ipswich.

Dr Rudolf Diesel

Dodge, Grenville Mellen Born Danvers, Mass, USA, April 12, 1831; died Council Bluffs, Iowa, January 3, 1916, aged 84. Civil engineer and politician. Graduated at Norwich University, Vermont, in 1851, and began on the Illinois Central RR. In 1853, he became chief assistant to Peter Dey on surveys for the Mississippi & Missouri RR from Davenport to Iowa City and Council Bluffs. Here Dodge made his permanent home. From 1855 to 1861 he built railroads in Iowa. During the Civil war he served in the Iowa Regiment.

In 1866, he was elected to Congress and became chief engineer of the Union Pacific RR. After the completion of the transcontinental line in 1869, he became chief engineer of the Texas & Pacific RR. When this failed in 1873, he joined Jay Gould and built nearly 14,500 km (9,000 miles) of line in the South West. In all Dodge's surveys totalled about 96,500 km (60,000 miles).

Dripps, Isaac L Born Belfast, April 14, 1810; died Altoona, Pennsylvania, December 28, 1892, aged 82. Locomotive engineer and inventor. Emigrated to Philadelphia with his parents as a child and was educated there. In 1826 he was apprenticed to Thomas Holloway, then the largest builder of steamboat engines in Philadelphia. In 1830 the company took on the Camden & Amboy Railroad in New Jersey and ordered a locomotive from Robert Stephenson & Co, Newcastle. This, the *John Bull,* arrived in sections in 1831. Dripps was given the task of assembling the *John Bull,* although he had never seen a locomotive before. In 1832 he added a pony truck and the first pilot or 'cow-catcher'; in 1833 he introduced the bonnet spark arrester.

After 22 years on the C & A, he became a partner in the Trenton Locomotive & Machine Works, New Jersey. From 1859 to 1870 he was superintendent of motive power and machinery on the Pittsburgh, Fort Wayne & Chicago RR. He was later appointed to the Pennsylvania RR.

E

Edmondson, Thomas Born Lancaster, June 30, 1792; died June 22, 1851, aged 58. Originator of the standard card railway ticket used throughout the world. He was a member of a Quaker family. Worked as a cabinet maker until 1836 when he obtained a post as clerk on the Newcastle & Carlisle Railway.

In 1837, he invented a machine for printing railway tickets on standard cards 57.5 × 30.5 mm (2½ × 1³/₁₆ in) and a press for stamping dates on the tickets. Almost identical date presses are still in use today. As the N & C was not interested in his inventions, he applied to the Manchester & Leeds Railway and was appointed to Manchester. Soon his system was in use throughout Britain and later throughout the world.

Eiffel, Alexandre Gustave Born Dijon, December 15, 1832; died Paris, December 28, 1923, aged 91. Eiffel is best known for his great tower in Paris built during 1887–1889. He designed many outstanding bridges on the French Railways. Studied at the Lycée Ste Barbe and the Central School of Arts and Crafts, Paris, until 1855. He developed his principle of bridge construction in wrought and cast iron, used in the great Sioule and Neuvial viaducts on the Orléans railway in 1868 to 1869. Among his most important works are the Garabit viaduct (1882), 122 m (400 ft) high, on the Midi railway of France, and the Tardes viaduct (1883) in central France 73.15 m (240 ft) high. By 1887 his bridges alone, in France, Portugal and Spain, totalled 38,000 tonnes of iron and steel works.

Engerth, Wilhelm Freiherr von Born Pless, Prussian Silesia, May 26, 1814; died Leesdorf near Baden, September 4, 1884, aged 70. Chief engineer, Austrian Southern Railway. He studied mechanical engineering at Vienna and in 1840 became assistant lecturer and in 1843 professor of machinery at Graz. In 1850 to 1852 he designed and built a locomotive named *Engerth* for working the Semmering Railway (opened in 1854). *Engerth* was one of the earliest articulated locomotives. Similar engines were built for Switzerland and France. From 1856 he was occupied in technical administration work. He was one of the judges at the Great Exhibition in London, 1851, and at Paris, 1855. In 1873 he supervised the building for the Great Exhibition in Vienna. In 1874 he was appointed to the Austrian House of Lords and later elevated to the Barony.

Eiffel's bridge over the Douro at Oporto, Portugal.

F

Fairbairn, Sir William Born Kelso, Roxburghshire, February 19, 1789, died Farnham, Surrey, August 18, 1874, aged 85. Designer and builder of bridges and general engineering, and manufacturer of locomotives. He was the son of a farm labourer and he had little formal education. In 1803, his family moved to a farm near Newcastle-on-Tyne and he obtained work at Percy Main Colliery. In 1804, he was apprenticed to a millwright near Newcastle. He studied literature and mathematics in his spare time and met George Stephenson in Newcastle. They became lifelong friends. After working in Newcastle, London and Dublin, he moved to Manchester in 1813. In 1817 he established an engineering works with John Lillie. By 1830 they employed 300 men. He bought out Lillie in 1832 and in 1846 the firm became William Fairbairn & Sons. From the early 1830s he built iron boats, stationary steam engines and boilers. The building of railway locomotives began in 1839 and from then until 1862 about 400 were built. His most famous productions were McConnell's Large Bloomers for the Southern Division of the London & North Western Railway.

From 1845 to 1848, he experimented with the design of wrought iron tubular bridges, subsequently erected by Robert Stephenson at Conway, Menai Strait and Montreal. By 1870 he had built nearly 1,000 bridges.

Favre, Louis Born Chène-Thonex, Canton Geneva, Switzerland, January 26, 1826; died inside St Gotthard tunnel, July 19, 1879, aged 53. Builder of St

Louis Favre

Gotthard tunnel. He started as a workman and later moved to Paris where he undertook public works with success. He tendered for the St Gotthard tunnel and was successful, basing his estimate on the use of dynamite rather than gunpowder and of a compressed air drill invented by his friend, Colladon. He undertook his part of the contract efficiently but was badly let down by the company and the Federal government. The attendant anxieties led to his breakdown and death from apoplexy inside the tunnel.

Sir Sandford Fleming

Fleming, Sir Sandford Born Kirkcaldy, Scotland, January 7, 1827; died Halifax, Nova Scotia, July 22, 1915, aged 88. Engineer of the Canadian Pacific Railway and other lines in Canada. He went to Canada in 1845 and worked on railway surveys with Casimir Gzowski, becoming chief engineer of the Ontario Simcoe & Huron Railway (later Northern Railway, finally Canadian National) from 1855 to 1863. In 1864, he was appointed chief railway engineer, Nova Scotia, and completed the line from Truro to Pictou in 1867. He then became chief engineer of the Intercolonial Railway which he completed in 1876, and in 1871 of the transcontinental railway. In 1872, he set out on his great expedition across Canada, locating the route through Yellowhead Pass and down the Thompson and Fraser valleys. This, however, was used by the later CNR and Canadian Northern lines. The Canadian Pacific used a more southerly route. He resigned from the CPR in 1880 when over 960 km (600 miles) were completed and returned to Scotland in retirement, though in 1883 he assisted in the survey through the Kicking Horse Pass.

From 1879 he worked on the laying of a Pacific cable between Vancouver and Australia. Completion in 1902 was his crowning success.

Fothergill-Cooke, Sir William Born near Ealing, Middlesex, 1806; died Farnham, Surrey, June 25, 1879, aged 73. Inventor of an electric telegraph system for railway signalling. In 1835 to 1836 while on leave from the Indian Army, he was shown a model demonstrating the principle of the electric telegraph. He resigned his commission and developed the idea in England. He published a pamphlet in 1836 which led to an experiment in a tunnel on the Liverpool & Manchester Railway. His work brought him into contact with Professor Charles Wheatstone (1802–1875) and in 1837 they took out a joint English patent. The success of the electric telegraph was proved on the Great Western Railway when it was instrumental in the arrest of a murderer at Paddington. In 1842 he published *Telegraphic Railways or the Single Way*. This publication was also translated into German, French and Italian and led to the introduction of the block system. With five others Cooke formed the Central Telegraph company in 1847. By the end of 1869 daily receipts exceeded £1,000.

Fowler, Sir John Born Sheffield, July 15, 1817; died Bournemouth, November 20, 1898, aged 81. Engineer of the Metropolitan Railway and the Forth Bridge. He was trained by J T Leather with whom he later worked on the Stockton & Hartlepool Railway where, in 1841, he was appointed engineer, general manager and locomotive superintendent. In 1844, he took up private practice in London. He designed the first railway bridge over the Thames in London, at Pimlico, completed in 1860. In this year he was appointed engineer of the Metropolitan Railway.

In 1875 he took Benjamin Baker (q.v.) into partnership. They were appointed joint engineers of the Forth Bridge, the greatest railway bridge in the world. (q.v. Arrol). The bridge was begun in 1883 and opened in 1890. Fowler received a baronetcy for his work in this project.

Fox, Sir Douglas Charles Born Derby March 11, 1810; died Blackheath, Kent, June 14, 1874, aged 64. Civil engineer and contractor. Articled to John Ericsson of Liverpool. Worked with Ericsson and Braithwaite on the *Novelty* entered in the Rainhill Trials on the Liverpool & Manchester Railway in 1829. In 1837 Robert Stephenson appointed him as an engineer on the London & Birmingham Railway. He later entered into partnership with the contractor Bramah (whose company later became Fox, Henderson

Garratt articulated locomotives at Salisbury, Rhodesia.

& Co) specializing in railway equipment, bridges, roofs, cranes, tanks and trackwork. They erected many large station roofs among which were those at Liverpool, Bradford, Paddington and Birmingham New Street. During 1850 – 1851 this team built the Crystal Palace for the Great Exhibition in Hyde Park. Later they dismantled the Crystal Palace and re-built it at Sydenham. He received a knighthood in 1851.

From 1857 he practised in London. In 1860, in collaboration with his two sons he pioneered narrow-gauge railways in India and in other parts of the world. He constructed hundreds of miles of railway all over the world.

Fox, Sir (Charles) Douglas Born Smethwick, Staffordshire, May 14, 1840; died Kensington, November 13, 1921, aged 81. Civil engineer and contractor, son of Sir Charles Fox (q.v.). Graduated from King's College, London, in 1858, he was articled to his father. In 1860 he and his brother (later Sir) Francis Fox were taken into partnership. The firm continued as Sir Charles Fox & Sons until the death of Sir Charles in 1874.

During this period they carried out extensive works on the London, Brighton & South Coast, London, Chatham & Dover and London & South Western lines around London.

In 1874 C D Fox became senior partner and the firm undertook many railway projects including the Mersey Tunnel; the Hawarden swing bridge, Cheshire; Liverpool Overhead Railway; the Great Central from Rugby to London; and various London tube railways, in addition to others abroad.

Fox was knighted in 1886, following completion of the Mersey Tunnel.

G

Garratt, Herbert William Born London June 8, 1864; died Richmond, Surrey, September 25, 1913, aged 49. Inventor of the Garratt articulated locomotive. He was apprenticed at the Bow works of the North London Railway from 1879 to 1882. After a period in Marine engineering, he went to the Central Argentine Railway in 1889. He became locomotive superintendent there in 1892. From 1900 he worked on railways in Cuba, Lagos, Peru and Australia. He returned to England in 1906. He devised a scheme for mounting heavy artillery on railway bogies which he discussed with Beyer, Peacock & Co, Manchester. This led to the design of an articulated locomotive. He patented the design in 1907.

The first two Garratt engines were 610 mm (2 ft) gauge 0-4-0 + 0-4-0 compounds for Tasmania. The first of these is now preserved in the National Railway Museum, York. Large numbers were built for railways of all gauges all over the world. Although the largest ever was an isolated unit built in 1932 for the USSR, this locomotive saw little service, and it was on the railways of Southern Africa that the Garratt had its most extensive and successful application.

Ghega, Karl Ritter von Born Venice, January 10, 1802; died Vienna March 14, 1860, aged 58. Engineer of the Semmering Railway, Austria. He graduated in mathematics at Padua University in 1819. After 17 years as engineer on street tramways and water supply works in Venice, he was appointed engineer on the Emperor Ferdinand's Nordbahn in

1836 – the first steam railway in Austria. He visited Belgium and England to study railways and in 1842 visited the USA on a study tour.

His greatest work was the Semmering Railway from Wiener Neustadt to Murzzuschlag begun in 1848 and opened in 1854. A large memorial to Ghega stands at Semmering station.

Giffard, Henri Born Paris, February 8, 1825; died Paris April 14, 1882 aged 57. Inventor of the injector. His career began in 1841 in the offices of the Paris–St Germain Railway. Shortly after this, he began to study ballooning to which he devoted much of his life. He is best known for the invention of the injector in 1859 for which he was awarded the Mechanics Prize of the Académie des Sciences. This enabled water to be injected into the boiler against the pressure of the steam, making feed pumps

Henri Giffard

unnecessary. The injector was first used on locomotives by Sharp, Stewart & Co of Manchester, England, in 1859. William Sellers (1824–1905) introduced the injector into the USA in 1860.

Gölsdorf, Dr Karl Born Vienna June 8, 1861, died Semmering, Austria, March 18, 1916, aged 54. One of Europe's most outstanding locomotive engineers. His father had been chief mechanical engineer of the Austrian Southern Railway from 1885 to 1907 (Died 1911). His son graduated with first class honours in Engineering at Vienna in 1884, joined the workshops of the Austrian State Railways, became chief of the erecting shop in 1889 and chief mechanical engineer in 1891.

Shortly afterwards, he was appointed chief of the Locomotive, Carriage and Wagon Section of the Austrian Railway Ministry. His first invention of international fame was his very simple and reliable starting apparatus for compound locomotives, which was used on many thousands of locomotives in Austria, Hungary, Russia, Italy, Germany, Greece, Turkey, Serbia, and also in America. The first of these was an Austrian 0–6–0 built in 1893. All his earlier compounds, including the very successful 2–8–0s for the Arlberg line in Austria, had two cylinders, but he later developed his four-cylinder version, to great advantage. His most famous class was the 2–6–4 express, originally designed for the Vienna-Prague service. His last was a huge 2–12–0 for the heavily-graded Tauern Line.

Gooch, Sir Daniel Born Bedlington, Northumberland, August 24, 1816; died Clewer Park, Berkshire, October 15, 1889, aged 73. The first locomotive superintendent and later chairman of the Great Western Railway and layer of the first trans-Atlantic cable. He was first employed at Tredegar Iron Works, South Wales. In 1834, he moved to the new Vulcan Foundry in Lancashire. After a few months, ill-health forced him to leave. After a year on marine engines at Dundee, he went to work at Newcastle, spending nine months at Robert Stephenson & Co.

In July 1837 he learned that Brunel required a locomotive superintendent on the Great Western Railway. Gooch applied and was appointed at the age of only 21. His loyal support for Brunel and the broad gauge was of immense value at a time when that policy was under severe criticism. With Brunel he planned the locomotive works at Swindon, and his

locomotives were without rivals at the time of the gauge controversy in 1844–46.

In 1864 after the death of Brunel he resigned and joined the Telegraph Construction Co. He chartered Brunel's great iron ship, *Great Eastern*, for the laying of the first Atlantic cable, completed in 1866.

In 1865, at a time of financial stress when he had been elected MP for the Cricklade Division of Wiltshire, he was invited to become chairman of the GWR. He guided the GWR to considerable success. In 1873, he laid the second Atlantic cable.

Gould, Jay Born Roxbury, N.Y., 1836; died New York, 1892, aged 56. One of the more important railroad magnates and financiers in the generation after the Civil War, Jay Gould was frequently a figure of controversy. In an age of unregulated industrial competition, his enemies denounced him as a 'pirate', while his friends spoke of him as a 'public benefactor'. In the late 1860s, in association with Daniel Drew and Jim Fisk, he won a lively contest with Commodore Cornelius Vanderbilt for the control of the Erie Railroad. Ejected from the Erie in 1872, he turned to western railroading, and in turn obtained major, or controlling interests in the Union Pacific, the Kansas Pacific, and the Missouri Pacific railroads. He also held substantial interests in the elevated railroads of New York City and the Western Union Telegraph Company. Gould was always more interested in the management and financial manipulation of existing railways than the construction of new lines. Shortly before his death Gould was reported to control half of the rail mileage in the American southwest.

Greathead, James Henry Born Grahamstown, Cape Colony, August 6, 1844; died Streatham, London, October 21, 1896, aged 52. Civil engineer and inventor of the Greathead tunnelling shield. He went to England in 1859 to complete his education and in 1864 began as a pupil of Peter W Barlow, followed in 1867 as assistant to W H Barlow and C B Baker (qq.v.) on the Midland Railway extension to London. In 1869 he worked with Barlow on the Tower subway under the Thames. For this he devised a boring shield forced forward by powerful screws as material was excavated in front of it.

From 1870 he practiced on his own account. After preparing several railway projects he patented further improve-

ments to his shield in 1884. In that year he was appointed engineer of what later became the City & South London Railway. This was opened in November 1890, the world's first electric underground railway.

With Sir Douglas Fox (q.v.) he was joint engineer of the Liverpool Overhead Railway (1893) and with W R Galbraith of the Waterloo & City Railway (1898). In collaboration with Fowler and Baker (qq.v.), he began work on the Central London Railway shortly before his death.

Greenly, Henry Born Birkenhead, June 3, 1876; died Heston, Middlesex, March 4, 1947, aged 70. Pioneer of miniature passenger-carrying railways. Like Baldwin (q.v.), he began as a jeweller. In 1897 he took up work as a draughtsman at the Neasden works of the Metropolitan Railway. From 1901 to 1906 he was assistant editor of the *Model Engineer*. He then became a consulting engineer specializing in model subjects and worked with W J Bassett-Lowke designing locomotives for miniature railways.

In 1922 he became engineer to the Ravenglass & Eskdale Railway which, under his guidance, was converted to 381 mm (15 in) gauge. He was also responsible for all civil engineering, design of locomotives and rolling stock, on the Romney, Hythe & Dymchurch Railway from its establishment in 1926 until 1930.

His books on railway modelling did much to establish the model railway hobby.

Gresley, Sir Herbert Nigel Born Edinburgh, June 19, 1876; died Hertford April 5, 1941, aged 64. Locomotive engineer, Great Northern and chief mechanical engineer London & North Eastern Railway. He was educated at Marlborough and in 1893 was apprenticed at the Crewe works of the London & North Western Railway, in 1897 moving to the Lancashire & Yorkshire Railway at Horwich works for two years. After various posts on the LYR, in 1905 he was appointed carriage and wagon superintendent on the Great Northern Railway at Doncaster. In 1907 he introduced articulated carriages, the first in Britain, using one bogie to support the ends of two coaches. On the retirement of H A Ivatt in 1911, Gresley became locomotive engineer.

He developed the three-cylinder locomotive, using a conjugated valve gear whereby only two sets of motions were needed to actuate the valves of three

Sir Nigel Gresley's observation car for the *Coronation* rebuilt 1966.

cylinders, derived from an invention by H Holcroft. His most famous engines were his Pacifics, of the 'A1', 'A3' & 'A4' classes and the Green Arrow type 2–6–2s. On July 3, 1938, his A4 class Pacific No 4468 *Mallard* achieved the world speed record for steam of 203 km/h (126 mph).

H

Hackworth, Timothy Born Wylam, Northumberland, December 22, 1786; died Shildon, Co Durham, July 7, 1850. Pioneer steam locomotive engineer. He was the son of a blacksmith at Wylam colliery where he began his training. In 1816 he moved to Walbottle colliery as foreman smith. In 1824 he was asked to supervize the newly opened works of Robert Stephenson & Co at Newcastle and he was responsible for building the first Stephenson locomotives. Declining

Timothy Hackworth

to take a share in the works, in 1825 he obtained employment on the Stockton & Darlington Railway as locomotive engineer and established his own workshops at Shildon. His *Royal George* of 1827 was the first six-coupled locomotive and the first in which the cylinders drove directly onto the wheels. In 1829 he built the 0–4–0 *Sans Pareil* which narrowly missed success in the Rainhill Trials on the Liverpool & Manchester Railway. In 1838 he introduced an improved 0–6–0 with inclined cylinders at the rear driving the front coupled wheels by long connecting rods. His locomotive, the 2–2–2 *Sans Pareil No 2* was built in 1849.

Haswell, John Born Lancefield near Glasgow, 1812; died Vienna, June 8, 1897, aged 85. Locomotive engineer and manager of the first locomotive works in Austria. Graduated at Glasgow in 1834 and then worked at William Fairbairn & Co, Manchester. He went to Vienna to erect locomotives for the Vienna Gloggnitzer Railway and was asked to remain as chief engineer. He began manufacture of some of the earliest locomotives built in Europe.

In 1851, he built the first European eight-coupled engine, for the Semmering Trials. His 0–8–0 of 1855 set a pattern for European heavy freight engines for many years. In 1861, he built one of the first four-cylinder locomotives. He remained head of the works until 1882.

Haupt, Herman Born Philadelphia, March 26, 1817; died Jersey City, NJ, February 14, 1905, aged 87. Civil engineer, author, inventor. After graduating at the US Military Academy in 1835, he worked as an assistant engineer on a railway survey from Norristown to Altentown, Pa, and later in Pennsylvania State service on railway surveys.

He began the study of bridge construction in 1840 and in 1847 became assistant engineer on the Pennsylvania RR, eventually becoming chief engineer. In 1855 he was appointed engineer of the Hoosac tunnel, Mass, 7.562 km (4.69 miles) long, completed after immense difficulties in 1875.

After several other major railroad construction jobs, he became general manager of the Northern Pacific Railroad in 1881 and saw its completion to the Pacific. From 1886 to 1888 he was president of the Dakota & Great Southern RR.

Hawkshaw, Sir John Born Leeds, 1811; died London June 2, 1891, aged 80. Civil engineer on the Lancashire & Yorkshire Railway, East London Railway, involved in projects such as the Severn Tunnel. He was trained on road construction in Yorkshire. Later he worked with Alexander Nimmo on the Manchester & Bolton Railway project. In 1832 he went to Venezuela as a mining engineer. He returned two years later. In 1836, after two years with Jesse Hartley and James Walker he became resident engineer on the Manchester & Bolton Railway, opened in 1838.

From 1845 he was chief engineer of the Manchester & Leeds Railway which became the Lancashire & Yorkshire in 1847. He built much of the system, with many long tunnels and high viaducts.

In 1850 he entered private practice in Westminster. Among the many outstanding and difficult works he carried out

Sir John Hawkshaw

were the adaptation of Marc Brunel's Thames Tunnel for the East London Railway, and the Severn Tunnel which he took over in 1879 and completed in 1887. With Sir James Brunlees (q.v.), he was joint engineer of the original Channel Tunnel project.

When he retired in 1888, he had been responsible for a greater number of major engineering works than any other 19th century engineer.

Hedley, William Born Newburn-on-Tyne July 13, 1779; died near Lanchester, Co Durham, January 9, 1843, aged 63. Inventor and mechanical engineer. At the early age of 21, he was appointed 'viewer' at Walbottle colliery near Newcastle, and later at Wylam colliery. He was one of the first engineers to insist that a locomotive with smooth wheels would obtain sufficient adhesion, without the use of a toothed wheel and rack. In 1813 he patented a smooth wheel and rail system. In 1811 he assisted Hackworth (q.v.) and Jonathan Foster in the construction of the first locomotive built

at Wylam. He built two more in 1814 and 1815. From 1824 his engineering activities were concerned mainly with collieries.

Helmholtz, Dr Richard von Born Königsberg, Prussia, September 28, 1852; died Munich September 10, 1934, aged 81. German locomotive engineer. He trained at the Borsig Locomotive works and at Stuttgart and Munich. In 1881 he entered the Krauss works (later Krauss-Maffei Locomotive Works) at Munich and in 1884 became chief of the drawing office, holding this position until his retirement in 1917. In 1884 he constructed the straight link modification of the Walschaert valve gear. In 1888 the first locomotive was built with the Krauss-Helmholtz combination truck in which the leading pony wheels form a bogie with the front coupled pair. He designed many varied types of locomotives built at the Krauss Works. In 1930 with Staby he published a history of the German steam locomotive, 1835 to 1889.

Hill, James Jerome Born near Guelph, Ontario, Canada, September 1838; died St Paul, Minnesota, USA, May 1916, aged 77. As a 17-year-old Canadian immigrant Hill quickly became involved in the frontier life of St Paul, Minnesota. After years of experience in freighting, river transportation, and the coal trade, Hill with Canadian banking friends purchased in 1878 the ailing St Paul and Pacific Railroad. Then, without the benefit of a land grant, his St Paul and Pacific line was extended northward to Winnipeg and westward into Montana. Under the corporate title of the Great Northern Railroad, and always in strong competition with the rival Canadian Pacific this road finally reached the Pacific in 1893.

Since Hill had insisted upon careful original construction and a conservative financial management, the Great Northern prospered while other US transcontinentals were facing receivership in the 1890s. Early in the twentieth century Hill struggled with E H Harriman for the control of the Chicago, Burlington & Quincy RR.

William Hedley's *Puffing Billy*

Huber-Stockar, Emil One of the pioneers of railway electrification in Switzerland, was a member of the management team of Maschinenfabrik Oerlikon from 1891. His researches showed that it was technically possible to equip main-line railways using high voltage alternating current, single phase and at low frequency. With the collaboration of another distinguished Swiss engineer, H Behn-Eschenburg, they extended their successful joint experiments to proposals for electrifying the Gotthard line. This was in 1904, but at that time the Swiss Federal Railways were not ready to take up what were then revolutionary proposals. But the new Alpine route through the Lötschberg Tunnel was under construction, and the responsible company, the Bern-Lötschberg-Simplon, adopted single-phase electric traction from the outset, exactly to Huber-Stockar's recommendation, at 15,000 volts ac 16⅔ cycles per second. The line was opened throughout in July 1913, but, before then, Huber-Stockar had been appointed chief engineer for electrification to the Swiss Federal Railways, using the same system.

His system was subsequently adopted as standard in Germany, Austria, and the Scandinavian countries. When Huber-Stockar died in 1939, it was said of him that few men had placed their technical skill to the service of their country with greater effect, and to the service of its people, and those of many other European nations. The present practice in Great Britain, France and elsewhere of using still higher voltages of single-phase alternating current for railway electrification all stems from the pioneer work of Huber-Stockar.

Hudson, George Born Howsham near York, March 10, 1800; died London December 14, 1871, aged 71. Railway promoter and financier. He was apprenticed to a draper in York. He later took a share in the business. In 1827, he received a bequest of £30,000 which he invested in North Midland Railway shares. He formed the York Banking Company in 1833, and rose to be Lord Mayor of York in 1837. At that time, he was appointed chairman of the York & North Midland Railway in which he owned 500 shares. He next assisted in establishing the lines from York to Darlington, Newcastle and Berwick. He became chairman of the Newcastle & Berwick in which he had subscribed five times as much as any other director.

In 1844 he helped to form the Midland Railway, with a capital of £5 million, and was elected chairman. By now he con-

George Hudson

trolled 1,635 km (1,016 miles) of railway, and he became known as the 'Railway King'. His acquaintance was sought by the aristocracy, even by the Prince Consort, despite his rough Yorkshire speech and uncultivated manners. From 1845 to 1859 he was Conservative Member of Parliament for Sunderland.

His financial dealings now became unscrupulous and following the discovery of several dishonest manipulations of railway affairs to his and his friends' profit, his fall was rapid.

Hughes, George Born Norfolk, October 1865, died Stamford, Lincolnshire, October 27, 1945, aged 80. Chief mechanical engineer of the Lancashire & Yorkshire and London, Midland & Scottish Railways. In 1882 he served a five-year premium apprenticeship at Crewe works, London & North Western Railway, under F W Webb (q.v.). He then moved to the Lancashire & Yorkshire Railway works at Horwich near Bolton, where he progressed through various jobs. In October 1895, he was transferred to the carriage and wagon works at Newton Heath near Manchester. In 1899 he returned to Horwich as works manager and principal assistant to the chief mechanical engineer, H A Hoy. On Hoy's resignation in 1904 Hughes was appointed his successor.

Hughes was one of the most progressive locomotive engineers of his time in Britain, and was, reputedly, among the earliest to use large boilers, super-heaters and long-travel, large-diameter piston valves. He re-designed his 4–6–0 in 1920.

At the amalgamation of the LYR and LNWR on January 1, 1922, Hughes became CME of both. A year later, on the formation of the LMS, Hughes was made CME of the entire system. His last locomotive design was the standard 2–6–0 of 1925. Hughes retired that year.

I

Ivatt, Henry Alfred Born Cambridgeshire, September 16, 1851; died Haywards Heath, Sussex, October 25, 1923, aged 72. Locomotive engineer, Great Southern & Western Railway, Ireland, and chief mechanical and locomotive engineer, Great Northern Railway. He was trained at Crewe works, London & North Western Railway, under Ramsbottom and Webb (qq.v.), after which he progressed through various positions on the LNWR. In October 1877 he moved to the Great Southern & Western Railway in Ireland and in 1886 succeeded J A F Aspinall as locomotive engineer at Inchicore, Dublin.

In 1895 he was offered the position of locomotive engineer on the Great Northern Railway at Doncaster and he began there in March 1896. His most outstanding locomotive designs were the first British Atlantic type in 1898 and its successor with large boiler and the first wide firebox in Britain.

Henry Ivatt's 4-4-2 *The Henry Oakley*, the first British Atlantic (1898).

J

Janney, Eli Hamilton Born London County, Virginia, November 12, 1831; died Alexandria, Va, June 16, 1912, aged 80. Inventor of the standard automatic coupler used throughout North America. In 1865, he became interested in the problem of coupling railroad cars automatically to end the numerous accidents with the link and pin couplers. Although he was not trained as a mechanical engineer, he designed and patented an automatic coupling in 1868. An improved version, patented in 1873, formed the basis of the present standard coupler. Its success led to the formation of the Janney Car Coupling Co which he controlled until the patent expired.

His automatic coupler was first adopted on the Pennsylvania RR, during the period 1874 to 1876, but was not made standard on American railroads until 1888.

Joy, David Born Leeds March 3, 1825; died Hampstead, March 14, 1903, aged 78. Locomotive and marine engineer and inventor of the Joy radial valve gear. He began his engineering career in the works of Fenton, Murray & Jackson, Leeds, and in 1843 joined the Railway Foundry, Leeds, then under the management of Shepherd and Todd; but the latter was in 1844 replaced by E B Wilson. There, as acting chief draughtsman, Joy was mainly responsible for the design of the famous *Jenny Lind* 2–2–2 express engine for the Brighton line. He left E B Wilson in 1850, and was successively locomotive superintendent of the Nottingham & Grantham, and then of the Oxford, Worcester and Wolverhampton Railways.

His famous diaries contain many vivid pictures of railway life at that time. In 1859 he returned to the Railway Foundry, Leeds, and became for a time involved in marine engineering.

Then in 1879 came his patent for the radial locomotive valve gear that bears his name. It was taken up by F W Webb (q.v.) and thereafter became standard for all Crewe locomotives (except the 4-cylinder 4–6–0 Claughtons) until 1923. It was also adopted by Aspinall (q.v.) on the Lancashire and Yorkshire Railway, and remained standard until 1920. The first locomotive to be so fitted was a 0–6–0 express goods, built at Crewe in 1880, and the last were a series of 0–8–4 tank engines built at Crewe in 1923.

Theodore Dehone Judah

Judah, Theodor Dehone Born Bridgeport, Connecticut, March 4, 1826; died New York City, November 2, 1863, aged 37. Engineer of the Central Pacific RR through the Sierra Nevada. After work as an engineer on several railroads in the eastern states, in 1854 he crossed to the Pacific coast as chief engineer of the Sacramento Valley RR. In 1856 he conceived the idea of a railway from California through the mountains and in 1869 he discovered a practical route. With Huntington and Stanford, he formed the Central Pacific Railroad Co and, after several visits to Washington, Judah secured the Federal Act of 1862 for the first transcontinental railway. During construction, disputes arose between Judah and Huntington's group and Judah was bought out in 1863. In crossing the Isthmus of Panama, he contracted typhoid and died in New York six years before the completion of his great transcontinental railway.

K

Kettering, Charles F Born Loudonville, Ohio, August 29, 1876; died Dayton, Ohio, November 25, 1958. Kettering with his son Eugene can well be described as the principal architect of modern diesel railway traction. After the formation of the Electro-Motive Engineering Corporation, in 1922, later to become General Motors, 'CF' became chief engineer. He was the inventor of the self-starter for cars and of knockless petrol. He next turned to the lightweight diesel engine.

His son, 'EW', designed his father's basic engine into the famous '567', which, in various combinations of cylinders, formed the power unit of the many thousands of diesel locomotives built by General Motors. The Ketterings insisted on absolutely *standard* components. No variations were permitted, and when certain railroads wanted variations of their own incorporated, the Ketterings refused to take their orders. A famous saying of 'CF', still treasured at General Motors, was: 'Never turn a problem to an expert; he'll be too educated to solve it!'

Kitson, James (senior) Born Leeds, October 27, 1807; died Leeds, June 30, 1885, aged 77. Founder of the locomotive builders, Kitsons, of Airedale Foundry, Leeds. A man of outstanding business ability who, in 1837, saw a future in railways and formed the firm of Todd, Kitson & Laird. They began to build locomotives in 1838. Their work included the famous 0–4–2s *Lion* and *Tiger* for the Liverpool & Manchester Railway.

In 1839, he established the Airedale Foundry and in 1840 began the long association with the North Midland Railway and its successor, the Midland. Overseas orders began in 1844 and, from then, many hundreds of engines were built for foreign railways.

He retired in 1876 and the business was continued by his two sons.

James Kitson

Krauss, Georg von Born Augsburg, December 25, 1826; died November 5, 1906, aged 79. Founder and general director of the Krauss Locomotive Works at Munich. He was trained at Augsburg Polytechnic and in 1847 entered the Maffei works at Munich. From 1849 he worked on the Bavarian

State Railways. In 1857 he was appointed chief locomotive superintendent on the Swiss North Eastern Railway.

In 1866 he founded Krauss & Co, locomotive builders, at Munich. In 1880 he opened a works at Linz in Austria. By 1904, this firm had built 5,220 locomotives 2,186 of which were exported.

L

Latrobe, Benjamin Henry Born Philadelphia, December 19, 1806; died Baltimore, Maryland, October 19, 1878, aged 71. Chief engineer, Baltimore & Ohio RR. Latrobe was the son of Benjamin Henry Latrobe (1764–1820), civil engineer and architect. He began his engineering career on the B&O in 1831. In 1832 he was given charge of the survey of a line from Baltimore to Washington. He designed the Thomas viaduct near Baltimore (the first stone railway viaduct in the USA) which was completed in 1835. From 1835 to 1836 he was chief engineer of the Baltimore & Port Deposit RR, returning to the B&O to carry the line through the mountains from Harper's Ferry to Cumberland. In 1842, he was appointed chief engineer of the B&O. In 1847, he built the extension to Wheeling, West Virginia, 322 km (200 miles) with 113 bridges and 11 tunnels. He then built the North West Virginia RR during the period 1851 to 1852. He retired in 1875.

List, Friedrich Born at Reutlingen, Württemberg in 1789; died Kufstein, 1847. 'Father' of the German railways. Was professor in various German universities but his liberal views were not to the liking of the reigning hierarchy and in 1825 he emigrated to the USA. There he built his first railway – the first in the world built by a German. His railway was built to transport coal from Tamaqua, Pennsylvania, to Port Clinton and was 34 km (21 miles) long. Its success inspired him to propose a plan for a complete system of railways in his homeland. His plans attracted considerable attention, and in 1832 President Andrew Jackson appointed him American Consul in Leipzig. In the following year, he published his plan for the German railway network. Although his proposals were staunchly backed by the Crown Prince of Prussia, afterwards King Friedrich Wilhelm IV, they were widely ridiculed, and progress was at first very difficult, particularly because, at that time, the

Friedrich List

numerous States had not yet been integrated into a uniform 'empire'. Early lines engineered by List were the Nuremberg-Fürth (6.4 km; 4 miles long, opened in 1835); the Leipzig-Alten (1837); the Berlin-Potsdam (1838), and the first German main line, Leipzig and Dresden 115 km (71¾ miles; including the first German tunnel). The main line was opened in 1839. Despite this, however, List reaped little except ingratitude from his contemporaries. Not until 80 years after his tragic suicide at Kufstein was a memorial raised to him at Leipzig, in 1927, in recognition of his great and far-seeing work.

Locke, Joseph Born Attercliffe near Sheffield, August 9, 1805; died Moffat, Dumfriesshire September 18, 1869, aged 64. Civil engineer. He was educated at Barnsley Grammar School and began his training at a colliery. In 1823 he was articled to George Stephenson (q.v.) at Newcastle, and later worked under him on the Liverpool & Manchester Railway. However, his discovery of errors in Stephenson's survey of the tunnel to Liverpool Lime Street station led to Locke's resignation in 1832 and he established his own business.

He built the Grand Junction (Birmingham to Warrington) 1835 to 1837; London to Southampton 1836 to 1840; Sheffield & Manchester (taken over from Vignoles, q.v.) 1838 to 1840; Lancaster & Preston Junction 1837 to 1840; Paris to Rouen 1841 to 1843; Rouen to Havre 1843; Barcelona to Mattaro, Spain, 1847 to 1848 and the Dutch Rhenish in 1856.

With his partner J E Errington who joined him in 1840, he built the Lancaster & Carlisle 1843 to 1846, Scottish Central 1845, parts of the East Lancashire 1846 to 1847, Caledonian (Carlisle

Joseph Locke

to Glasgow and Edinburgh) 1848, and other Scottish railways.

Locke's lines were noted for economy of construction and avoidance of tunnels.

Lomonossoff, Dr George Vladimir Born in Russia April 24, 1876; died Montreal, November 19, 1952, aged 76. Locomotive engineer; pioneer of diesel traction. He graduated at St Petersburg in 1898 and spent two years in the locomotive testing department of the Kharkov-Niclauf Railway. From 1901 he lectured in railway engineering at Kiev. From 1908 he was chief mechanical engineer of the Tashkent Railway. From 1911 to 1921 he was Professor of Railway Engineering and Economics at the St Petersburg Institute of Transport and also president of the Locomotive Research Bureau, chief mechanical engineer of the Nicolas Railway, assistant director-general of Russian Railways, member of Russia's Supreme Engineering Council, under secretary of transport and president of the Russian War Railway Mission to the USA. In this last position, he was responsible for the design and ordering of about 2,000 locomotives during the first world war.

He was an early advocate of diesel rail traction and, after some initial difficulties with unenlightened authorities, he was authorized to build three diesel locomotives. In 1925, he visited England and ordered a 1,200 hp diesel locomotive from Armstrong Whitworth.

Loree, Loenor Fresnel Born Fulton City, Illinois, 1858; died 1940. One of the greatest and most widely experienced of American railwaymen. After taking a civil engineering degree at Rutgers University, joined the Pennsylvania Railroad as an assistant in the Engineering Department, at the age of 19. In 1881 he joined the Mexican National Railway for surveying work on new lines, but in 1883 returned to the Pennsylvania. Between that year and 1889 he held various civil engineering appointments, but then transferred to the traffic side, becoming divisional superintendent of the Cleveland and Pittsburgh Division. In 1896 at the early age of 38 he was appointed general manager, and became fourth vice-president, in 1901. In the same year he became president of the Baltimore & Ohio, and then of the Chicago, Rock Island and Pacific. In 1907 he became President of the Delaware & Hudson, a post he was to retain for no less than 31 years. Although a relatively small railway, it was prosperous, and he came to exert a very strong influence in American railway affairs. Besides his own railway he held directorships with many others, and, during the first world war, worked in close co-operation with the USA government. He retired in 1938, at his 80th birthday.

Lott, Julius Born Vienna, March 25, 1836; died Vienna, March 24, 1883, aged 46. Engineer of the Arlberg Railway, Austria. In 1861, after studying in Göttingen and Vienna, he directed the construction of the Brenner Railway. From 1869 Lott worked on Hungarian railways until in 1875 he was appointed director of the Austrian State Railways.

In 1880 he was appointed engineer for the construction of the Arlberg Railway, including the Arlberg Tunnel, 10.25 km (6.37 miles) long and the Trisanna bridge with its span of 120 m (394 ft), 87.4 m (287 ft) high. He became ill and died during the construction. The railway was opened on September 20, 1884. His monument was erected at St Anton on completion of the Arlberg Railway.

M

Mackenzie, William Born Burnley, March 20, 1794; died October 19, 1851, aged 57. Railway contractor. He trained under Cargill and Telford on bridges and canals, and changed to railways about 1832, contracting for the tunnel to Lime Street Station, Liverpool. Other contracts followed on the Grand Junction, Glasgow, Paisley & Greenock, Midland and North Union railways.

In 1840 he began his connection with Thomas Brassey (q.v.) with whom he carried out much work on French railways under Matthew Locke (q.v.)

With John Stephenson he built all the railways from Lancaster to Edinburgh and Glasgow, the Scottish Central, Scottish Midland, part of the Chester & Holyhead, part of the North Staffordshire and the whole of the Trent Valley line.

His own contracts and those executed with Brassey and Stephenson totalled over £17 million. His early death resulted from overwork and exposure.

McNeill, William Gibbs Born Wilmington, North Carolina, October, 1801; died Brooklyn, New York, February 16, 1853, aged 51. One of the pioneer civil engineers on North American railways. He began his career in the army where he met George Washington Whistler (q.v.) who later married his sister.

He surveyed several of the canals and earliest railroads in North America, including the Baltimore & Ohio RR. On a visit to England to study railway construction with Jonathan Knight and Whistler in 1828, he met George Stephenson. Subsequently Knight and Whistler became joint engineers on several railway projects, including the Baltimore & Ohio, Baltimore & Susquehanna and several other important lines in New England and the south

Mallet, Anatole Born Carouge, near Geneva, 1837; died Nice, October 1919, aged 82. Locomotive engineer and inventor of the Mallet articulated locomotive. He was educated at the Central School of Arts and Manufactures, Paris, 1855–58 and in 1867, after various work, he became interested in compound

A Mallet 2-8-8-0 in Java

steam engines. The first compound locomotive to his design was a two-cylinder engine for the Biarritz Railway, France, in 1876. In 1884 he patented his four cylinder compound articulated locomotive with high pressure cylinders at the front of the fixed rear engine unit and low pressure cylinders at the front of the articulated front unit. It was first used on light railways in 1887. It reached its maximum development in the USA in the immense 2–10–10–2, built by ALCO for the Virginian Railway in 1918 with low-pressure cylinders 1,219 mm (48 in) diameter, the largest ever used on a locomotive.

Marsh, Sylvester Born White Mountain Village, New Hampshire, USA, September 30, 1803; died Concord, New Hampshire, December 30, 1884, aged 81. Builder of the first mountain rack railway. In 1855, after a variety of employments, he became interested in a cog railway to the summit of Mount Washington near his birthplace. With much difficulty, he at length obtained a concession and with financial assistance work began in 1866. The line was opened on July 3, 1869, and is still in operation. His ladder-type rack formed the basis of the later design by Riggenbach (q.v.).

Mason, William Born Mystic, Connecticut, September 2, 1808; died Taunton, Mass, May 21, 1883, aged 74. Inventor and locomotive builder. He began as a manufacturer of textile machinery and took up locomotive building in 1852. His 700th was completed after his death.

He claimed that he built locomotives 'for fun' and made no profit. His engines

were noted for good workmanship and handsome appearance. His work had a great influence on locomotive design and construction in the United States.

Meiggs, Henry Born Catskill, Green County, New York State, July 7, 1811; died near Lima, Peru, September 30, 1877, aged 66. Railway contractor and engineer. He was first a successful timber merchant in Boston and New York, where he made his first large fortune, only to lose it in the financial panic of 1837. After several other rises and falls, he moved to Chile and began constructing railways at great profit. In 1867 he moved to Peru and began the Oroya Railway from Lima to Oroya in the Andes, later known as the Central of Peru. In 1875 he suffered a paralyzing stroke and he died before the railway reached its summit but he had already worked out the entire route. This railway summit remains the world's highest.

He had an astute business sense and the ability to select the right men to work for him. He was the first big contractor in North or South America to treat the imported Chinese coolies as humans.

Millholland, James Born Baltimore, 1812; died 1875, aged 63. Locomotive engineer and pioneer of coal-burning fireboxes. He worked on locomotives from the age of 18 and in 1838 was appointed master mechanic on the Baltimore & Susquehanna Railroad. In 1855, while master mechanic on the Philadelphia & Reading RR, he designed a firebox for burning anthracite, and developed fireboxes for burning coal. In 1863 he built the first 0-12-0, *Pennsylvania*, at the Reading shops. He pioneered the use of feed-water heaters, superheaters and steel tyres. He retired in 1866.

Mitchell, Joseph Born Forres, Morayshire, November 3, 1803; died Inverness, November 26, 1883, aged 80. Civil engineer of the Highland Railway. He trained under Thomas Telford, and, on the death of his father, became responsible for Highland roads and bridges for 18 years. He also erected 40 churches in the Highlands and Islands.

In 1837 he surveyed the railway from Edinburgh to Glasgow via Bathgate and in 1844 the Scottish Central Railway. He surveyed the route of the Highland Railway from Perth to Inverness over the Grampians in 1845, but the Bill was defeated on grounds of impracticability.

Mitchell was the prime mover in the construction of the railway from Inverness to Nairn, Elgin and Keith where it joined the Great North of Scotland line from Aberdeen opened in 1855. In 1860, after laying out several Scottish lines, he began the survey of the Highland Railway from Forres to Dunkeld, 167 km (104 miles), opened throughout in 1861. In 1864 he surveyed the 'Skye' line, opened in 1870. He also surveyed the railway into Caithness but, following a stroke in 1862, he was forced to retire in 1867.

Modjeski, Ralph Born Cracow, Poland, January 27, 1861; died Los Angeles, June 26, 1940, aged 79. American bridge engineer. He decided to become an engineer but also studied music and became a fine pianist. Although his family moved to USA in 1876, he studied in Paris and graduated in engineering in 1885. On his return to the USA, he gradually became established as a bridge engineer and designed a total of over 50 bridges. Chief among these were the 104 m (340 ft) span steel arch carrying the Oregon Grand Trunk Railroad across the Crooked River Gorge at a height of 97.5 m (320 ft) (1911), the Metropolis bridge (1917) across the Ohio, Illinois, including a simple truss span of 219.5 m (720 ft); and the Benjamin Franklin suspension bridge over the Delaware River, Philadelphia (1921–1926) with a suspended span of 533 m (1,750 ft) – the longest in the world to carry trains. His last major work was the Bay Bridge, San Francisco.

Morgan, John Pierpont Born Hartford, Conn., USA, April 17, 1837; died Rome, March 31, 1913. The son of a successful international banker, Morgan was educated in America and Europe before joining his father's firm in London. He returned to New York in 1857, and soon was an agent for his father's bank. During the Civil War he engaged in foreign exchange, and later formed Drexel, Morgan & Co, which after 1895 was known as J P Morgan & Co. Well before the turn of the century Morgan was heading one of the most powerful banking houses in the world.

By the 1880s, he was increasingly interested in railroading, and in 1885 arbitrated a major dispute between New York Central and the Pennsylvania. During the 1890s he aided in the reorganization of several lines, especially the formation of the Southern Railway. In the struggle (1901–1904) between James Hill and E H Harriman, Morgan was a firm ally of Hill. By 1906 he and his banking partners controlled about 28,800 km (18,000 miles) of American railroads including the Erie, the Southern, and several other lines in the South.

Through his control of shares in many of the railroads in the USA, Morgan was able to bring influence to bear on the companies to agree upon more or less common rates for freight and passengers, and to avoid potentially ruinous cutthroat competition. He was succeeded as head of the banking empire by his son, John Pierpont Morgan Jnr.

Sir Richard Moon

Moon, Sir Richard From the mid-1850s director of the LNWR and the 'power behind the throne' of successive chairmen until 1861, when elected Chairman himself. Although many tales are told of his cold, ruthless personality, he was uprightness itself. Taking over at a time when many of the intrigues of early railway development were still rife, he specified that in future the general manager should be 'an intelligent executive officer – not an intriguing web-weaving protocoler'. He interviewed every chief officer personally on his appointment, with the invariable admonition: 'Remember, first, you are a gentleman; remember, next, that you are a North Western officer, and that whatever you promise you must perform . . .'. Promises meant above all the train movements set out in the timetables, and to Moon punctuality was akin to godliness. He had a superb grip on every facet of railway operations, and by his close attention to working expenses he increased the profits enormously. The profits were not dissipated in high dividends, grandiose stations, or other superficial ways but were ploughed back in enterprising improvements to the line such as modernized junction layouts, mechanised marshalling yards and improvements to the Crewe works. In the thirty years he was in command, from 1861 to 1891, the business trebled, and the dividend on ordinary shares was held steady at 6¼ to 7¼ per cent. In his time the London and North Western Railway rose to be the largest joint stock corporation in the world, and, without question, the most efficient transportation system.

Murray, Matthew Born near Newcastle-on-Tyne, 1765; died Leeds, February 20, 1826, aged 61. Inventor, mechanic and builder of the first commercially successful steam locomotives. He trained as a blacksmith and in 1795 he started a business in Leeds which later became Fenton, Murray & Jackson. He was one of the first engineers to improve the form of the steam engine, making its parts more accessible. In 1811 he was employed by John Blenkinsop to build four locomotives for the railway from his collieries at Middleton to Leeds. The engines were propelled by a toothed wheel engaging in a rack on the side on one rail. The engines ran for 20 years.

N

Nasmyth, James Born Edinburgh, August 19, 1808; died London, May 5, 1890, aged 81. Locomotive engineer, manufacturer and builder of the first steam hammer. After education in Edinburgh in 1829 he became assistant to Henry Maudslay (1771–1831) in London. In 1835 he established a business in Manchester which eventually became the Bridgewater Foundry at Patricroft. Here he built his first steam hammer in 1839. He patented the steam hammer in 1842. From about this time to 1850, he was joined by Holbrook Gaskell and the firm was known as Nasmyth Gaskell & Co. Nasmyth retired in 1857; Robert Wilson (1803–1882) joined and the firm then became Nasmyth Wilson & Co Ltd.

They built large numbers of locomotives including some of the early Norris type 4–2–0s for the Birmingham & Gloucester Railway (q.v. Norris), some Gooch broad-gauge engines for the Great Western in 1840 to 1842, and engines for India, New Zealand and elsewhere.

Norris, William Born Baltimore, Maryland, July 2, 1802; died Philadelphia, January 5, 1867, aged 64. Locomotive

Model of William Norris' *Austria*, built for an Austrian railway in 1843.

manufacturer. At the age of 30, he joined Stephen Long to form the American Steam Carriage Company and they built several early American locomotives. Norris then bought out Long and moved the works to Philadelphia where, with the *George Washington* of 1836 for the Philadelphia & Columbia Railroad, he established the design of 4–2–0, with the firebox behind the driving axle, for which he became famous. In 1837 he built 17 similar engines for the Birmingham & Gloucester Railway in England. By 1855, 100 Norris engines had been exported to various countries in addition to large orders for the USA.

Norris was not the best of engineers or businessmen and he was forced out of the company in 1844 by his brother, Richard. After two years in Austria he became engineer of the eastern division of the little Panama Railroad.

P

Paget, Sir Cecil W Born 1874; died 1933. Virtually the founder of modern British railway operating methods, C W Paget, was a son of Sir Ernest Paget, chairman of the Midland Railway. After an undistinguished school career at Harrow, he began an apprenticeship at Derby Locomotive works, in 1881. Probably because of his parentage, and an alertness of mind he was selected for various special tasks, including assignments on MR affairs in France and the USA and a spell at Cambridge University. In 1902 he was appointed works manager at Derby and in 1904 assistant locomotive superintendent. In 1907 under the gen-

eral managership of Guy Granet he was appointed to the new office of general superintendent, and began the complete and then revolutionary re-organization of the operating department of the Midland Railway. He formed the pattern of working for the LMSR after the grouping in 1923, and eventually of the nationalized British Railways. Another monumental achievement was his building up and command of the Railway Operating Division of the British Army in France in 1915–19, during which time the strength of the force increased from 3,000 to 20,000 men. For his services, he received the DSO in 1916, and the CMG in 1918. Soon after the war he resigned his post with the Midland Railway and went into industry. He succeeded his father in the baronetcy in 1923.

Peacock, Richard Born Swaledale, Yorkshire, April 9, 1820; died Gorton, Manchester, March 3, 1889, aged 68. Locomotive engineer and manufacturer. In 1834, after education at Leeds Grammar School, he was apprenticed at Fenton, Murray & Jackson, working on locomotives for the Liverpool & Manchester and Leeds & Selby Railways. In 1838, at the age of only 18, he became locomotive superintendent of the Leeds & Selby Railway, but, when this became part of the North Eastern in 1840 he moved to the Great Western. In 1841 he was appointed locomotive superintendent of the Sheffield & Manchester Railway on which he served for 14 years. He was responsible for the selection of the site for the works at Gorton, Manchester.

In 1854 he entered into partnership with Charles Beyer to form the firm of Beyer Peacock.

Pease, Edward Born Darlington, May 31, 1767; died Darlington, July 31, 1858, aged 91. The 'Father of Railways', friend of George Stephenson and promoter of the Stockton & Darlington Railway. He was a member of a staunch Quaker family. He began in the woollen industry. About 1817 he became interested in the problems of transport between the collieries of south Durham and Stockton-on-Tees. After investigating the possibility of a canal, he became acquainted with George Stephenson and decided to give all his support to a railway. He appointed George Stephenson as chief engineer and was responsible for launching him on his career in railways. In 1823 Pease, with George Stephenson and Thomas Richardson (1771–1853), founded the locomotive building firm of Robert Stephenson & Company, Newcastle. Edward Pease missed the opening of the Stockton & Darlington Railway on September 27, 1825, because of the tragic death of his son Isaac that day. However, he continued to guide the affairs of the railway to the end of his life.

Edward Pease

Peto, Sir Samuel Morton Born Woking, Surrey, August 4, 1809; died Tunbridge Wells, November 13, 1889, aged 80. Railway contractor and civil engineer. In 1823 he began an apprenticeship as a builder with his uncle, and later with his cousin Thomas Grissell succeeded to the business. Their works included part of the Great Western Railway, and erection of the Houses of Parliament.

With E L Betts (q.v.) he built the Great Northern loop line (1847) the Oxford, Worcester & Wolverhampton, and the GWR Oxford to Birmingham line. With Brassey (q.v.) he carried out extensive railway works in Australia and Canada. With Crampton (q.v.) he built the London, Chatham & Dover Railway.

In 1851 he was elected chairman of the Chester & Holyhead Railway until its amalgamation with the London & North Western in 1859.

Crest on a British Pullman coach

Pullman, George Mortimer Born Brocton, New York, March 3, 1831; died Chicago, October 19, 1897, aged 66. Founder of the Pullman Car Company. He began as a cabinet maker. In 1855 he moved to Chicago where in 1858 he rebuilt two coaches on the Chicago & Alton RR into sleeping cars. After some initial setbacks he and Ben Field built the first Pullman car, *Pioneer*, in 1865 and in 1867 they formed the Pullman Palace Car Company which grew to be the largest railroad car building firm in the world, with plants at Detroit, St Louis, Elmira, NY, Wilmington, Del., San Francisco and Chicago. Pullman introduced dining cars in 1868, chaircars in 1875 and vestibule cars in 1887.

R

Ramsbottom, John Born Todmorden, Yorkshire, September 11, 1814; died Alderley Edge, Cheshire, May 20, 1897, aged 82. Locomotive engineer. His early career was spent partly at Sharp, Roberts & Co, Manchester, and in 1842 he became locomotive superintendent of the Manchester & Birmingham Railway. When this became part of the newly formed London & North Western Railway in 1846 Ramsbottom became district superintendent of the North East Division. In 1856 he invented his famous safety valve and a displacement lubricator. The following year he succeeded

John Ramsbottom

Francis Trevithick as locomotive superintendent of the Northern Division with headquarters at Crewe, LNWR where, in 1858, he introduced the DX class 0–6–0 of which 942 were built, a British record. In 1860 following the invention of the device by one of his draughtsmen at Crewe, one John Bland, he installed the first water troughs, on the Chester & Holyhead section. In 1862 when McConnell retired from the post of locomotive superintendent at Wolverton, Ramsbottom became chief mechanical engineer of the LNWR. Perhaps his greatest achievement was the building and commissioning of the steel works at Crewe, in 1864, the first plant anywhere in the world to manufacture steel by the Bessemer process. From that time steel replaced wrought iron as the material for rails.

Rastrick, John Urpeth Born Morpeth, Northumberland, January 26, 1780; died Chertsey, Surrey, November 1, 1856, aged 76. Civil and mechanical engineer. He gained his early experience under his father and at the Ketley Ironworks in Shropshire, later going into partnership with John Hazeldine at Bridgnorth. In 1814 he patented a steam engine and experimented in steam traction on railways. He built the cast iron bridge over the Wye at Chepstow in 1815 to 1816.

His railway work began with the Stratford & Moreton Railway, 1822 to 1826. In 1829 he was one of the judges at the Rainhill Trials. He completed the Shutt End Colliery Railway in Staffordshire, working it with his engine *Agenoria* which now stands in the National Railway Museum at York. A similar engine, *Stourbridge Lion*, was the first to run in the USA. His greatest work was the London to Brighton railway opened in 1841.

He was also engineer of several other lines of the London, Brighton & South Coast Railway, the Bolton & Preston Railway, and the Grantham & Nottingham line. He retired in 1847.

Nikolaus Riggenbach

Riggenbach, Nikolaus Born Basle, Switzerland, May 21, 1817; died Olten, July 7, 1899, aged 82. Designer of the Riggenbach rack system. He was trained as a locomotive engineer and he drove the first train on the Zurich–Baden Railway, the first railway entirely located in Switzerland, on August 9, 1847. From 1855 he was locomotive engineer on the Swiss Central Railway at Olten.

He became interested in developing a rack railway and in 1863 he patented his ladder-type rack system. The first line, up the Rigi, was opened in 1871. His rack is also used on the Brünig and Bernese Oberland railways.

Rogers, Thomas Born Groton, Connecticut, March 16, 1792; died, New York, April 19, 1856, aged 64. One of the most famous early American locomotive manufacturers. After early training in carpentry, blacksmithing and pattern making, he formed a partnership with John Clark to make looms and to spin cotton. In 1832 he began making wheels for railroad cars and in 1837 built his first locomotive, named *Sandusky*. In 1844 his standard American 4-4-0 was produced, followed by his famous 2-6-0 of which great numbers were built.

S

Saxby, John Born Brighton, 1821; died at Hassocks, Sussex, 1913, aged 91. Signalling pioneer. He was at first employed as a carpenter in the locomotive department of the London Brighton & South Coast Railway at a time when much attention was being given to means of preventing railway accidents caused by faulty manipulation of points and the primitive forms of signal then in use. His own first patent of 1856, was for the simultaneous working of points and signals at a junction. It was not until others had postulated the great principle – that with one movement dependent on another, the new movement could not begin until the completion of any earlier movement, that his great development began, with a fresh patent in 1860. In 1862 his partnership with J S Farmer, also a Brighton Railway man, began. They established works at Kilburn, beside the London and North Western Railway, to which they became sole contractors, as they were also to the Brighton. The famous 'rocker and grid' interlocking frame was introduced in 1871, and more than anything else established Saxby's fame as a signal designer and manufacturer.

Schmidt, Wilhelm Born Wegeleben near Halberstadt, Saxony, February 18, 1858; died Bethel, near Bielefeld, Westphalia, February 16, 1924, aged 66. Pioneer of high degree superheating on steam locomotives. He was educated at Dresden Technical High School and in 1883 established a works in Brunswick where he built an engine to run on hot air and steam at a temperature of 350°C (662°F) at a pressure of 80 kg/cm^2 (1,138 psi) which led to the use of superheated steam. In 1891 he built an engine to work on superheated steam at 350°C. His first locomotive superheater was used on the Prussian State Railways in 1898. The fire-tube type appeared in 1901 and was first used in Belgium. Within two years it was in world wide use.

Séjourné, Paul Born Orléans, France, December 21, 1851; died Paris, January 15, 1939, aged 87. French civil engineer. He qualified as a bridge and road engineer in 1877 and carried out his first work on the Montauban à Castres line. From 1900 to 1928 he was chief civil engineer on the Paris, Lyon & Méditerranée Railway and during that time was responsible for some of the most difficult

mountain lines in France, including the Mont d'Or tunnel near Vallorbe, 6.097 km (3 miles 1,388 yd) and the Nice to Beil sur Roya. He published his great book *Grands Routes* in six volumes during the years 1913 to 1916.

Seguin, Marc Born Annonay, Ardèrche, France, April 20, 1786; died Annonay, February 24, 1875, aged 88. The pioneer of multi-tubular boilers. In 1825 he built a steamship with a fire-tube boiler. He patented a multitubular boiler in 1827 and in 1828 used this type of boiler on a locomotive. It used a forced draught from a fan driven by the tender wheels. This engine was the first to run on the Lyon & St Étienne Railway when it opened in 1829. It could haul 30 tonnes. Seguin obtained the concession for the railway which he surveyed in 1826. He published the first French study of railway engineering.

Marc Seguin

MARC SEGUIN   1786-1875

Shay, Ephraim Born Ohio, July 17, 1839; died Harbor Spring, Michigan, April 20, 1916, aged 76. Mechanical engineer and inventor of the Shay geared steam locomotive. The first was built in 1880. Large numbers were built by the Lima Locomotive works, Ohio, and they were used chiefly on logging lines. The two or three cylinder vertical engine was mounted on the right side of the boiler and drove the trucks by shafts, universal couplings and bevel gears. The last Shay was built for Western Maryland in 1945.

Siemens, Dr Ernst Werner von Born Lenthe near Hanover, December 13, 1816; died Berlin, December 6, 1892, aged 75. Builder of the first practical electric railway. He joined the Prussian artillery in 1834 and was commissioned in

Ernst Werner von Siemens

1839. He carried out numerous experiments in chemistry, physics and the use of electricity and in 1845 he invented a dial and printing telegraph instrument. While still in the artillery, he founded works in Berlin in 1847 for production of telegraph apparatus and in 1848 laid the first major underground telegraph line, from Berlin to Frankfurt-am-Main. Further developments in the telegraph followed. His first proposal for an electric railway was in 1867. At the Berlin Trades exhibition in 1879, he built and operated the pioneer line, 550 m (600 yd) long.

Sinclair, Robert Born London, July 1, 1817; died Florence, Italy, October, 1898, aged 81. Locomotive engineer, Great Eastern Railway. Educated at Charterhouse and then apprenticed with Scott, Sinclair & Co, Greenock; the Sinclair was his uncle, Robert. He then worked on the Liverpool & Manchester Railway at Edgehill, Liverpool, under Buddicom (q.v.) and in 1841 went with him to France, becoming manager of the works of the Paris & Rouen Railway at Les Chartereux near Rouen. In 1844 he was appointed locomotive superintendent of the Glasgow, Paisley & Greenock Railway. Then when this became part of the Caledonian in 1847, he became locomotive superintendent of the entire system.

In 1856 he succeeded J V Gooch as locomotive superintendent of the Eastern Counties Railway which, in 1862, became part of the Great Eastern Railway. Sinclair once more became responsible for the entire collection of locomotives. From 1857 he was engineer in chief, holding the dual office until he retired in 1866.

He designed engines for the Luxembourg Railway of Belgium, and for the East Indian Railway for which he was consulting engineer. He was one of the most progressive locomotive engineers of his time, adopting large bearing surfaces, structural rigidity, standardization of parts, injectors and steel axles and tyres, long before these were in general use. A notable experiment with roller bearings in the 1860s failed because of insufficiently developed materials. He was one of the founder members of the Institution of Mechanical Engineers, in 1847.

Stanier, Sir William Arthur, FRS Born Swindon, Wiltshire, May 27, 1876; died London, September 27, 1965, aged 89. Chief mechanical engineer, London, Midland & Scottish Railway. He was apprenticed at Swindon on the Great Western Railway under William Dean in 1892 and was transferred to the drawing office in 1897. He passed through various departments, becoming assistant locomotive works manager in 1906, works manager in 1920 and principal assistant to the chief mechanical engineer in 1922.

In 1932, he was appointed chief mechanical engineer of the LMSR with a mandate to 'scrap and build'. He was to provide the railway with a stud of new standard locomotives that, being capable of intensive utilization, would enable the traffic to be worked with a smaller total stock. Much of his work, particularly in boiler design, was based on his Great Western experience, but it was notably developed as time went on to include high degree superheating and maximum-power express-passenger Pacific engines. While the latter were achieving notable speed records, his Class '5' 4–6–0s and Class '8' 2–8–0s were proving among the most generally useful mixed traffic and freight classes ever to run in Great Britain.

Stephenson, George Born Wylam, Northumberland, June 9, 1781; died Tapton House near Chesterfield, August 12, 1848, aged 67. Mechanical engineer and inventor and the founder of the modern railway. He worked at local collieries and during his spare time, learnt to read and write and mended clocks and watches. His only son Robert (q.v.) was born in 1803 – three years later his wife died of tuberculosis. During this period

George Stephenson

his father became incapable of work and George had to support his parents.

In 1812 he was appointed enginewright at Killingworth Colliery where he invented a miner's safety lamp, first tested by him in the mine on October 21, 1815.

By this time, he was interested in steam traction on the railway and in 1814 he built his first locomotive *Blucher*. In 1819 he supervized the laying of the 12.9 km (8 mile) Hetton Colliery Railway, opened in 1822.

The Stockton & Darlington Railway Act was passed on April 19, 1821 (q.v. E Pease) and Stephenson was appointed engineer. He advised the use of malleable iron rails instead of cast iron and advocated use of locomotives. To manufacture the latter, Edward Pease and Thomas Richardson (1721–1853) joined him in establishing the works of Robert Stephenson & Company at Newcastle in 1823. The S & D opened in 1825.

Its success resulted in Stephenson's appointment as engineer of the Liverpool & Manchester Railway and the Manchester & Leeds. At the Rainhill trials on the L & M in 1829 the prize of

£500 was won by the *Rocket* built by George and Robert Stephenson. The railway was opened in 1830, and the Manchester & Leeds in 1839 to 1841.

Stephenson was also engineer to the Birmingham & Derby Junction, North Midland, York & North Midland, and Leicester & Swannington railways.

In 1854 he moved to Tapton House near Chesterfield to be near collieries and the Ambergate lime works which he had established. In 1847 the men who founded the Institution of Mechanical Engineers invited him to join and become the first president.

Stephenson, Robert Born near Newcastle-upon-Tyne, October 16, 1803; died London, October 12, 1859, aged nearly 56. Son of George Stephenson and one of the greatest of the early railway civil engineers. Educated at Bruce's Academy, Newcastle, from 1814 to 1819. Then apprenticed to Nicholas Wood at Killingworth colliery. In 1821 he assisted his father on the Stockton & Darlington Railway survey, and two years later took up management of the

newly established firm of Robert Stephenson & Company. In 1824 he went to Colombia in South America to superintend some mines. During his absence the works were managed by Hackworth (q.v.). In 1829, with his father, he built the *Rocket* which won the prize at the Rainhill trials. In 1833 he was appointed engineer of the London & Birmingham Railway, opened in 1838.

He is well remembered by his great bridges: the High Level bridge, Newcastle, (1846 to 1849); Royal Border bridge, Berwick, (1850); and the great tubular bridges at Conway (1847 to 1849), Menai Strait (1847 to 1850) and Montreal (1854 to 1859).

Through his achievements and sterling character he was a consultant on railway matters of world wide fame, and his standards of construction had a lasting influence. He was MP for Whitby, Yorkshire.

Stevens, John Born New York City, 1749; died Hoboken, New Jersey, March 6, 1838, aged 89. Pioneer of mechanical transport in the USA. He studied first law, then surveying and, by 1788, had become interested in the development of steam boats. In 1791 he designed two improved boilers and in 1803 patented a multitubular boiler. His *Phoenix* of 1809 was the world's first sea-going steam ship.

In 1810 he turned to railway development. In 1815 he obtained the first American railroad charter, for a railroad from the Delaware to the Rariton. He

Robert Stephenson

John Stevens

was granted another charter in 1823 for a railway from Philadelphia to Columbia, opened in 1834 under the title Pennsylvania Railroad. It subsequently became part of the later Pennsylvania system.

In 1825 he designed and built a steam locomotive to run on a circular track on his Hoboken estate. This was the first locomotive built in the USA; it was an experimental machine and not a load hauler, as was Peter Cooper's (q.v.) *Tom Thumb*.

Patrick Stirling

Stirling, Patrick Born Kilmarnock, June 29, 1820; died Doncaster, November 11, 1895, aged 75. Locomotive engineer, Glasgow & South Western and Great Northern Railways. From 1837 to 1845 he was apprenticed under his uncle at Dundee Foundries where, from 1839 to 1840, some engines were built for the Arbroath & Forfar Railway. After a period at the locomotive works of Neilson & Co, Glasgow, 1846 to 1851, and in marine engineering and other locomotive work, he was appointed locomotive superintendent at the Kilmarnock works of the Glasgow & South Western Railway. Here he built some outside-cylinder 2–2–2s which were the forerunners of his later '8 foot singles' on the Great Northern. He also adopted the domeless boiler which characterized all his locomotives.

In December 1866 he succeeded Archibald Sturrock as locomotive superintendent of the GNR at Doncaster, where, in 1870, he brought out the first of his famous 4–2–2 '8 foot singles'.

Stroudley, William Born Sandford, Oxford, March 6, 1833; died Paris, December 20, 1889, aged 56. Locomotive engineer, London, Brighton &

South Coast Railway. After a year at Swindon under Daniel Gooch (q.v.) in 1853, he moved to Peterborough to continue his training on the Great Northern Railway under Charles Sucré. In 1861 he was appointed manager of the Cowlairs works of the Edinburgh & Glasgow Railway and in 1865 became locomotive superintendent of the Highland Railways at Inverness. Because of financial difficulties he was not able to do much in the way of new engine designing, but he obtained authority for important improvements to Lochgorm works, Inverness.

In 1870 he was appointed locomotive superintendent on the LBSCR at Brighton. He equipped the railway with a stud of reliable, picturesque but small locomotives. His early death resulted from an attack of bronchitis while he was exhibiting one of his famous 'Gladstone' class 0–4–2s at the Paris Exhibition of 1889.

Stuart, Herbert Akroyd Born Yorkshire, January 28, 1864; died, Claremont, W. Australia, February 19, 1927, aged 63. Inventor of the compression ignition oil engine, later developed by Diesel (q.v.). He received his technical training at the City & Guilds of London and at his father, Charles', engineering works at Fenny Stratford. He later became manager of that works. He began his experiments with oil engines at Bletchley Iron works in 1886, leading to his discovery of compression ignition which he patented in 1890. The engines were manufactured by Richard Hornsley & Sons at Grantham. The idea was taken up in Germany and developed along different lines by Rudolph Diesel.

Sykes, Joseph Charles Born London, 1871; died London, January 5, 1931, aged 59. Signalling engineer, the son of W R Sykes (q.v.). He was trained under W Kirtley at the Battersea works of the London, Chatham & Dover Railway. In 1896 he joined his father in management of the Sykes signal works at London and Glasgow. He was a pioneer of electric signalling first on the LCDR and later on the Glasgow & South Western and the London Brighton & South Coast railways.

Sykes, William R Born in London, 1840; died Bickley, Kent, 1917. In 1862 a Mr Rudall, who had known Sykes in his early days, was appointed Electrical Superintendent of the London Chatham & Dover Railway. He needed an assistant

William R. Sykes

to look after clocks, watches and telegraph instruments, and Sykes got the job in 1863. He invented many devices for the safe working of trains, but it was his epoch-marking patent of February 23, 1875 of the 'Lock and Block' system that marked the turning point in his career. It was the first positive means of proving that trains had passed clear of a block section, and of ensuring that the signal for a following train to proceed could not be lowered until this proving was electrically and mechanically established. Use of the Sykes 'Lock and Block' system extended to several English railways, particularly those with heavy suburban traffic. Variations of it, to circumvent his patents, were developed elsewhere. In 1899 the business was turned into a limited company and the most important subsequent development was the electro-mechanical system of operation in which the points were operated mechanically by rodding, and the signals electrically, by small slide levers.

T

Thornton, Sir Henry W Born Indiana, USA, 1871; died 1933. Thornton graduated Bachelor of Science at Pennsylvania University in 1894, and then joined the Pennsylvania Railroad as a civil engineering assistant. He later transferred to the traffic side, and in 1911 was appointed general superintendent of the Long Island Railroad. In 1914, he came to England to be general manager of the Great Eastern Railway. During the first world war his exceptional abilities were utilized in France, where he became Inspector General of Transport, with the rank of Major-General. On the Great Eastern Railway, on the retirement of the chief engineer in the middle of the war, he took direct control of that department in addition to his other duties, with the title of general manager and engineer-in-chief. In 1919 he was created a Knight of the British Empire. In 1922 he returned to North America to take on the tremendous task of rationalizing the various bankrupt and subsidized constituents of the Canadian National Railways into a strong virile entity.

Trevithick, Richard Born Illogan, Cornwall, April 13, 1771; died Dartford, Kent, April, 22 1833, aged 62. Inventor of the high-pressure steam engine. His mathematical and mechanical ability were evident at an early age. On the expiry of James Watt's patent on steam engines in 1800, Trevithick built a double-acting high-pressure engine. He also built a steam carriage which, in 1801, was the first vehicle to convey passengers by steam power. He built a second in 1803 and in the same year built a locomotive which worked on a waggonway at Coalbrookdale, Shropshire. This was the first locomotive to run on rails. A second followed in 1804 while he was employed at Penydarren Ironworks in South Wales. This second pulled 10 tonnes of iron, 70 men and five extra wagons for 15 km (9½ miles) at 8 km/h (5 mph). His third locomotive was built at Gateshead by John Whinfield in 1805 and his fourth and last, named *Catch me who can*, was built in 1808 for demonstration on a circular track in London.

In 1807 he began a tunnel under the Thames at Rotherhithe but it had to be

Richard Trevithick

abandoned. The tunnel was later completed by Marc Brunel. Trevithick next built nine engines for mines in Peru and in 1817 went out to supervize their installation. He remained as engineer but, after ten years, was ruined in the war of independence. He was assisted home by Robert Stephenson (q.v.) and arrived in Britain in 1827. In 1832 he took out a patent for superheated steam, but he was never able to recover his fortunes and he died in debt.

Tyer, Edward Born Kennington, London, February 6, 1830; died Tunbridge Wells, December 25, 1912, aged 82. Signalling and telegraph engineer. As early as 1852 he patented an electrical signalling device operating on an engine but little is known as to its actual use. He also was a pioneer in telegraphic communication and instituted what became the postal telegraph service of London. He founded the firm of Tyer & Company Limited, and it is through the products of this firm that his name is so well remembered today. They manufactured one-wire and three-wire block instruments for ordinary block working; he invented a form of 'lock and block' in competition with that of W R Sykes (q.v.), and an early system of train description, to aid signalmen. His most famous and widely used invention was the electric tablet system for safety working single lines, of which the first version appeared in 1878. It was used in many parts of the world.

V

Cornelius Vanderbilt Born Stapleton, N.Y., 1794; died New York, 1877, aged 83. The young Vanderbilt left school at the age of eleven for the New York City waterfront, and successively ran a ferry, engaged in the coastal trade, operated Hudson River steamboats, and entered the competition for the transatlantic steamship traffic. At the age of 68, widely known as the 'Commodore' and worth $11,000,000, he left steamboating for railroading. After buying a railroad, he improved it, cut operating expenses by combining it with other lines, and endeavoured to increase its capacity to pay higher dividends. Vanderbilt failed in his attempt to control the Erie, losing out to Jay Gould, Jim Fisk and Daniel Drew. But in 1867 he gained control of the New York Central, and consolidated his several lines to form a through route from New York City to Buffalo. Acquir-

Cornelius Vanderbilt

ing other roads west of Buffalo, he soon had an efficient money-making railroad operating to Chicago and the midwest. The Commodore ran a good railroad, but hated to see any public control interfere with his operating methods. When he died in 1877, Vanderbilt was worth $100,000,000, and the New York Central System included 7,200 km (4,500 miles) of line.

Van Horne, Sir William Cornelius Born Will County, Illinois, February 3, 1843; died Montreal, September 11, 1915, aged 72. Railroad executive and the driving force behind the construction of the Canadian Pacific Railway. He began as a telegraph messenger boy at the age of 14, and used telegraphy as a stepping stone to railway service. He worked, in successively more responsible posts on the Michigan Central, the Chicago & Alton, the St Louis, Kansas City & Northern, and in 1874 at the age of 31 he became president and general manager of the Southern Minnesota. Then in 1879 he was appointed general superintendent and acting general manager of the Chicago, Milwaukee & St Paul, one of the lines controlled by the great tycoon J J Hill. The Canadian Pacific Railway, of which construction had so far advanced little, was then controlled by a syndicate of four, of whom Hill was one. He was anxious to carry the line to the south of Lake Superior, through the USA, and recommended Van Horne for

Sir William Cornelius Van Horne

the job of general manager thinking that he, an American, would fall in with Hill's ideas. But Van Horne came down solidly on the side of those who wanted an all-Canadian route, and between 1881 and 1885, in the face of appalling difficulties, carried the great imperial project through to completion. He was created a Knight Commander of the Order of St Michael and St George by Queen Victoria, in 1894, and accepted it proudly – an award given to an American *as an* American. He was president of the CPR from 1888 to 1889, and was chairman until 1910.

Vauclain, Samuel Matthews Born Philadelphia, May 18, 1856; died Rosemont, Pennsylvania, February 4, 1940, aged 83. Chairman of Baldwin Locomotive Works and inventor of the Vauclain system of locomotive compounding. He was trained in the Altoona shops of the Pennsylvania Railroad and at the age of 21 became a foreman in the frame shop. In 1887 he was appointed a superintendent in one of the shops of the Baldwin Locomotive Works and in 1890 he became superintendent of the entire plant. He became a member of the company of proprietors in 1896, became vice president of Baldwins in 1911, and president in 1919. In 1929 he was elected chairman.

In his 51 years with Baldwin he was responsible for many technical developments, producing his famous four cylinder compound design in 1889. In this system the piston rods of the high and low pressure cylinders on each side are connected to common crossheads, driving only two cranks. By 1907 over 200 such engines had been built. He also designed the first ten coupled heavy goods engine, in 1886, for Brazil; the first wagon top boiler, for the Denver & Rio Grande Railroad, and he built the first 2–8–2, or Mikado, in 1897, for Japan.

Vignoles, Charles Blacker Born Woodbrook, County Wexford, Ireland, May 31, 1793; died Hythe, Hampshire, November 17, 1875, aged 82. One of the leading early railway civil engineers. His early career was spent in the army until 1833. During this period he worked on surveys with the Rennies. With John Ericsson he patented a centre-rail incline railway in 1830, the forerunner of the Fell system.

The first railways to which he was appointed were the Wigan Branch and Preston & Wigan in 1831 and the Dublin & Kingstown, the first railway in Ireland, in 1832 to 1834. He began the Sheffield & Manchester, from which, in difficult circumstances he was dismissed. This railway was afterwards taken over by Locke (q.v.). He was also engaged on several continental lines; Paris – Versailles; German Union, and others in Germany. In 1837 he designed the flat-bottomed section rail named after him, similar to that invented in 1830 by R L Stevens in the USA.

His busiest period was from 1843 to 1860 when he was chief engineer to railways in England, Russia, Eastern and Central Europe and Brazil.

Von Borries, August Born Niederbecksen, Germany, January 27, 1852; died Meran, Austria, February 14, 1906, aged 54. Locomotive engineer. From 1875 to 1902 he was locomotive superintendent of the Prussian State Railways. In 1880 he built his first compound locomotives, and in 1884 introduced his well-known intercepting valve, which made starting automatic, with any adjustments needed from the driver.

W

Walker, Thomas Andrew Born 1828; died near Chepstow, Monmouthshire, November 25, 1889, aged 61. Civil engineer and contractor, builder of the Severn tunnel. From the age of 17 he was engaged on various railway surveys, later under Brassey (q.v.) on railways in England and on the Grand Trunk in Canada from 1852. He remained in Canada until 1861, then worked on railways in Russia, Egypt and Sweden. In association with Peto and Betts (qq.v.) he built the Metropolitan and Metropolitan District Railways in London, completed in 1871. For Hawkshaw (q.v.) he built the East London Railway, carrying it beneath the London Docks. His greatest work, and

the most difficult, again under Hawkshaw, was the construction of the Severn tunnel, from 1879 to 1887.

Egide Walschaert

Walschaert, Egide Born near Malines, Belgium, January 20, 1820; died St Lilles, Brussels, February 18, 1901, aged 81. Designer of the Walschaert valve gear used on steam locomotives. The family name was Walschaerts, but when Belgium because independent of Holland in 1830, the name was changed to Walschaert. He began as a mechanic on Belgian State Railways at Malines. In 1844 he became foreman of the Brussels Midi station and works. In that year he also invented his valve gear, but, because he was prohibited by Belgian Railways from receiving royalties, the valve gear was patented in his name by M Fischer, engineer of Belgian State Railways, in 1844. A similar gear was invented shortly afterwards by Professor Heusinger von Waldegg of Germany, but he recognized Walschaert's priority. The gear was first fitted to a Belgian 2–2–2 in 1848. Later the valve gear was used throughout the world. Walschaert retired in 1885. His death 16 years later passed almost unnoticed.

Webb, Francis William Born Tixall Rectory, Staffordshire, May 21, 1836; died Bournemouth, June 4, 1906, aged 70. Chief mechanical engineer, London & North Western Railway. He began as a pupil in the Crewe works, LNWR, in 1851, becoming chief draughtsman in 1859 and chief assistant to Ramsbottom (q.v.) in 1861. From 1866 to 1871 he was manager of the Bolton Iron & Steel Company.

When Ramsbottom retired in 1871, Webb was appointed chief mechanical engineer, and in 32 years of office proved the very epitome of a Victorian industrial autocracy. His management of the great works at Crewe was strict and stern, though scrupulously fair. He pursued the 'do it yourself' policy advocated by his chairman, Richard Moon (q.v.) to the utmost extent. Very few proprietary fittings were used on his locomotives, and he set up an important section of the works for manufacture of signalling equipment, in which he took out several patents. In locomotive construction he organized Crewe to heights of productivity unequalled elsewhere, combining with it superb standards of workmanship. His earlier locomotive designs, notably the 2–4–0 'Precedents' and the '17 inch', and '18 inch' 0–6–0 goods were extremely good and long lived; but in turning to compound expansion his passenger engines were less successful. His 0–8–0 compound mineral engines did many years of hard work.

Living in fear of a hereditary illness, a lonely austere bachelor, he was not an easy colleague, and the shortcomings of his compound passenger engines, although representing a very small proportion of his total activities, led to criticism of his work as a whole. He retired in 1903, at age 67, earlier than he would otherwise have intended. In Crewe however he is remembered as a munificent benefactor to the social amenities of the town.

Westinghouse, George Born Central Bridge, New York, October 1846: died New York, March 1914, aged 67. His early training was in his father's workshop in Schenectady, where agricultural machines and small steam engines were made. In 1863 he enlisted in the Union army, and fought in the Civil war, as an engineer-officer in the navy. In 1865 he returned to his father's works. His fame began with the introduction of compressed air braking on trains in 1868. This was quickly adopted on a number of American railroads. But, on his first visit to Europe in 1871, his first form of the brake had no more than a lukewarm reception. On the advice of an assistant editor of the English journal *Engineering*, he returned to America to work out details of the automatic air brake – in which the brake was applied on both sections if any part of a train broke away from that attached to the locomotive. Patents for this automatic air brake were taken out in December 1871. It is upon this that his fame rests, although he continued to introduce a great diversity of

George Westinghouse

products in companies specially founded to manufacture and market them; railway signalling, electric traction, electric street lighting, hydro-electric power generation inaugurated by the harnessing of the power of Niagara falls. At the zenith of his activities there were 104 companies, in which his products were involved.

Wheelwright, William Born Newburyport, Massachusetts, March 18, 1798; died London, September 26, 1873, aged 75. Promoter of railways in South America. After a varied career at sea and five years as US Consul at Guyaquil, in 1840 he established the Pacific Steam Navigation Company.

In 1844, he promoted the Panama Railway and in 1849 to 1852 he built the Caldera – Copiapó Railway (the first railway in Chile) and extended it to Tres Puntas, 2,012 m (6,600 ft) above sea level. He projected a Trans-Andean Railway of 1,600 km (nearly 1,000 miles) from Caldera to Rosario in Argentina. He began it in Argentina, opening the section from Rosario to Cordoba in 1870. He created the port of La Plata and completed a railway from there to Buenos Aires in 1872.

Whistler, George Washington Born Fort Wayne, Indiana, USA, May 19, 1800; died St Petersburg, Russia, April 7, 1849, aged 48. Civil engineer and pioneer of railways in the USA and in Russia. He began his career in the army, becoming a surveyor. In 1828, while engineer of the Baltimore & Ohio RR, he and W G McNeill visited England to study railway construction. On completion of the B&O in 1829, he undertook the Paterson & Hudson River RR, later part of the Erie system.

During this period he married McNeill's sister and in 1834 they had a son, James Abbot McNeill Whistler, who became the famous American artist.

After surveying various other railways in the USA, in 1842 Whistler was appointed by Czar Nicholas I as engineer of the Moscow – St Petersburg Railway. While in Russia he succumbed to an attack of cholera.

Whistler established the Russian gauge of 1.524 m (5 ft) – this was the standard gauge in the southern states of the USA in the 1840s.

Whitton, John Born Foulby near Wakefield, 1819; died Mittagong near Sydney, New South Wales, Australia, February 20, 1898, aged 79. Civil engineer of NSW railways. In 1835 he was articled to William Billington, an early railway engineer.

In 1856 he was appointed chief engineer of the NSW government railways. His first task was to convince the Government that the southward extension of the lines already built, to the state boundary at Albury, should be built for steam, rather than horse traction. This done, there came the problem of crossing the Blue Mountains. Again, strong opinion favoured road transport or tramways for horse traction on the mountain roads. Whitton argued for a railway. He put in two reversing zig-zags, one on each side of the mountain range, and the great Zig Zag near Lithgow was one of the most spectacular pieces of railway engineering in the world when it was completed in 1869. He built extensions to the NSW government railways in almost every possible direction from Sydney, increasing the route mileage to over 3,200 km (2,000 miles), by the time he retired in 1890. His crowning achievement was the crossing of the Hawkesbury River by a handsome 7-span lattice girder bridge, to complete the link between Sydney and Newcastle.

Winans, Ross Born Sussex County, New Jersey, USA, October 17, 1796; died Baltimore, Maryland, April 11, 1877, aged 80. Inventor, and builder of locomotives. In 1829 he visited England with Whistler (q.v.) to study railways and locomotives. He then became an engineer with Whistler on the Baltimore & Ohio RR, assisting Cooper (q.v.) with the *Tom Thumb* locomotive. From 1834 to 1859 he was in charge of the Mount Clare shops of the B & O, building an 0–8–0 in 1842 and the first of his 0–8–0 'Camels' with wide fireboxes for burning anthracite, in 1848. In all he built about 300 engines before he retired in 1860.

Above left: 'The Railway Station' (1862) by William Powell Frith (1819–1909) showing a bustling scene at Paddington Station, London, in the days of the 2133 mm (7 ft) gauge. (Royal Holloway College, Egham).

Above right: 'Rain, Steam and Speed, the Great Western Railway' (1844) by Joseph Mallard William Turner (1773–1851). Turner was the first great artist to find inspiration from the railway. (The National Gallery).

Below left: 'The old station of St Lazare, Paris' (1877) by Claude Monet (1840–1926). One of a series of ten paintings of the Gare Saint Lazare completed in 1877 when Monet, still impecunious and unknown, persuaded the station superintendent that 'Claude Monet, the painter' was a world-famous artist. Trains were stopped and started specially for Monet's benefit. (Chicago Art Institute).

Below right: 'Across the Continent; a railroad train speeding westward' (from the period 1860–1880) by Nathaniel Currier (1813–1888) and James Ives (1824–1895). The famous American partnership of Currier and Ives began in 1857 and lasted for some 25 years during which the artists produced about three lithographs every week.

RECORDS

Locomotive Pioneers

First steam locomotive engine to haul a load on rail was the one demonstrated by Richard Trevithick in 1804 over the Penydarren plateway in South Wales. It had a single horizontal cylinder and ran on unflanged wheels.

First steam locomotives commercially successful were of rack-and-pinion design with flanged wheels built by Matthew Murray in 1812 and used on the Middleton Colliery line, Leeds, England. First two were named *Salamanca* and *Prince Regent*.

Locomotion No 1 of the Stockton & Darlington Railway, in North-East England, built by George Stephenson in 1825, was the first to have its two pairs of wheels coupled by rods.

Nearby, at Shildon, the first six-coupled locomotive, Timothy Hackworth's *Royal George*, appeared in 1827.

The steam locomotive became established as a reliable form of motive power at the Rainhill trials – won by *Rocket* – on the Liverpool & Manchester, the world's first 'modern' style of railway, which was opened in 1830.

First successful steam line in the United States was the South Carolina Railroad, whose first locomotive, *The Best Friend of Charleston,* built in New York, hauled an inaugural train on Christmas Day 1830 and began regular traffic on January 15, 1831. However, five months later this engine suffered a boiler explosion and parts were salvaged for rebuilding into the *Phoenix*.

First locomotive to be built on the Continent of Europe, named *Olifant*, was constructed by Cockerill of Seraing, Belgium, for the Brussels–Malines line in 1835.

Biggest Wheels

Largest locomotive driving wheels ever were of 3.05 m (10 ft) diameter, fitted to three broad-gauge engines built in 1838 for the Great Western Railway in England, and named *Hurricane, Ajax* and *Mars*. None survived long and the largest on a successful type were the 2.75 mm (9 ft) driving wheels of eight broad-gauge Bristol & Exeter Railway 4–2–4T engines built in 1853–54.

Building Record

In December 1891, a six-coupled goods engine was erected by an efficient team at the Great Eastern works at Stratford, London, in less than ten working hours.

Biggest-Ever Steam

World's largest and heaviest steam locomotives were 25, dubbed 'Big Boys', built for the Union Pacific Railroad, USA, by the American Locomotive Company in 1941–44. With a 4–8–8–4 wheel arrangement, overall length was 40.481 m (132 ft 9¾ in) and they were 4.941 m (16 ft 2½ in) high and 3.353 m (11 ft) wide. Total weight, in working order and including tender, was around 410 tonnes.

Power Records

Most powerful steam – but rebuilt after a few years into two separate locomotives – was an experimental articulated six-cylinder 2–8–8–8–4 Mallet compound tank engine built in 1916 for the Virginian Railroad, by Baldwin of Philadelphia. It could exert a tractive effort of 75,500 kg.

An Erie Railroad 'banker', 2–8–8–8–2 *Matt H Shay*, attained 22 km/h (13.5 mph) with a train composed of 250 freight cars, each of which weighed 15,545 tonnes. The train stretched 2.6 km (1.6 miles).

Garratt Giants

Now the world's largest and most powerful steam locomotives in regular service are those of the Garratt articulated 4–8–2 + 2–8–4 type on East African Railways, delivered from Beyer Peacock, England, in 1955. Total weight is 256 tonnes and they produce a tractive effort of 33,300 kg (73,350 lb).

Largest and most powerful in Great Britain and Australia also were Garratts. A 2–8–0 + 0–8–2 built for the London & North Eastern Railway in 1925 weighed 181 tonnes. The 'AD60' class 4–8–4 + 4–8–4 Garratts on the New South Wales Government Railways were introduced into regular service in 1952 and weighed 269 tonnes.

Above: Union Pacific Railroad's steam locomotive No 4019, a 'Big Boy' with the 4-8-8-4 wheel arrangement and built in 1941 – the first of 25 of the type produced during 1941–44 for freight service.

Below: Locomotive No 389 is employed in passenger service in Rhodesia. This Garratt articulated 4-8-2 + 2-8-4 type is now one of the largest and most powerful steam locomotives in regular service.

Right: The first practical electric locomotive was built by Werner von Siemens (1816–92) for the Berlin Trades Exhibition of 1879. The locomotive operated for 4 months on a track of some 549 m (600 yd).

Electrical Pioneers

First electric railway resembling modern practice was a 550 m (600 yd) long, narrow-gauge line built by the German engineer, Werner von Siemens, for the Berlin Trades Exhibition in 1879. The 3 hp electric locomotive took current at 150 V from a centre third rail. The first public electric railway in the world, 2.5 km (1.5 miles) long and at Lichterfelde, near Berlin, followed two years later. The carriage seated 26 passengers and had a maximum speed of 48 km/h (30 mph).

First electric underground railway in the world was the City & South London, opened in 1890 with four-wheel locomotives.

Most-powerful electric

World's most powerful electric locomotive has been a Swiss Federal Railways experimental 1D2 + 2D1, built in 1939, developing 11,100 hp at 75 km/h (47 mph). Most powerful class is the Swiss 'Re6/6' Bo–Bo–Bo type, introduced in 1972, which produce 10,450 hp, weigh 122 tonnes and have a maximum speed of 140 km/h (87 mph).

Trans Siberian Electric

Longest electrified railway in the world extends 5,213 km (3,240 miles) from Moscow to Irkutsk, on the Trans Siberian Railway in Russia.

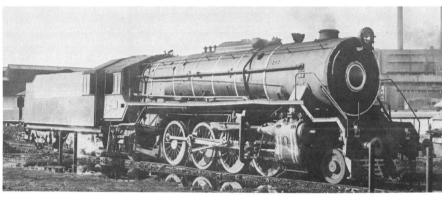

Above: Locomotive No 8982 of the Southern Railway of India at Basin Bridge shed, Madras. A fine example of the Indian 'WG' 2-8-2 class which was introduced in 1950.

Classes of Thousands

Most numerous class of steam locomotives in the British Commonwealth was the 2,450 Indian 'WG' 2–8–2s, introduced in 1950. World's most numerous probably was the Russian 'E' class 0–10–0 of 1912, eventually totalling around 14,000 engines.

In USA Pennsylvania RR class H6 2–8–0 was the most numerous and eventually totalled 2,226.

Right: The Stockton & Darlington Railway, which opened on September 27, 1825 was the first public railway to use steam power from the very beginning.

Below: The interior of one of the earliest Pullman cars. George Mortimer Pullman (1831–97) turned his entrepreneurial skills to the systematic development, provision and exploitation of first dining car and later sleeping car facilities in North America. He began by the conversion of two passenger coaches at a railway company's workshops in 1859. Pullman sleeping and dining cars stifled sporadic competition and were soon in common use throughout the USA.

Earliest Diesels

First diesel locomotive was an experimental direct-drive 1,000 hp Diesel-Klose-Sulzer unit of 1912. The following year came the first diesel railway vehicle in revenue service, an Atlas 75 hp diesel-electric railcar on the Mellersts–Södermanland Railway in Sweden. Five 200 hp diesel-electric railcars were built in 1941 by Sulzer in Switzerland for the Prussian & Saxon State Railways.

First diesel-electric shunters – or 'switchers' as they are called in the United States – were three 200 hp units built there by the General Electric Company in 1918. However, a GEC/Alco/Ingersoll 300 hp design of 1924 was the first considered a commercial success. Main-line diesels did not begin their revolution of USA motive power until 1934 on passenger trains, and about 1940 on freight.

First main line diesel locomotive was a 1,200 hp diesel-electric design by Lomonosoff, four of which were built for German State Railways in 1925. The same year eight long-distance diesel-electric railcars were placed in service by Canadian National Railways. In 1926, the Long Island Railroad was the first in the USA to operate a diesel-electric in main line traffic.

First experiment with diesel traction on British railways was in 1924 when a small German-built diesel-hydraulic locomotive was tested on the London & North Eastern Railway. Forerunner of diesel locomotives in regular shunting service appeared in 1933, when the London Midland & Scottish Railway converted a steam 0–6–0 tank engine using hydraulic transmission. The LMSR ordered the first prototype main line diesel locomotives, two of which were delivered by English Electric Company in 1948.

'Flying Hamburger'

First high-speed diesel train was the German streamlined 'Flying Hamburger', a twin-unit articulated railcar, which made trial trips in 1932 then next spring entered regular service between Berlin and Hamburg at an average speed of 124 km/h (77 mph). On tests it reached 199.5 km/h (124 mph).

Diesel-electric leaders

Most-powerful single-unit diesel-electric locomotive is the Union Pacific Railroad 'Centennial' type, rated at 6,600 hp, 47 of which were supplied by General Motors Corporation from 1969. Danish State Railways have the most powerful in Europe; they were introduced in 1972.

Gas-turbine locomotives

First gas-turbine locomotive was a 2,140 hp machine with electric transmission built by Brown Boveri & Company for the Swiss Federal Railways in 1941.

Largest gas-turbine-electric locomotives are the 8,500 hp double-units supplied to the Union Pacific Railroad by the General Electric Company, USA. They are 50.294 m (165 ft) long and weigh 414 tonnes.

Earliest Passenger Carriages

At first, railway passenger vehicles, pulled by horses, were adapted goods wagons or improvised 'wooden sheds on wheels'. An ordinary road horse carriage mounted on rail wheels began running on the Stockton & Darlington Railway in 1826.

For the opening of the Liverpool & Manchester Railway in 1830 first-class coaches were based on the well-established stage-coach design, but mounted on four-wheel railway-wagon chassis. Even on such main lines, the lowest-class carriages originally were open trucks.

First passenger car to make a regular scheduled run in the United States, horse-drawn, was on the Baltimore & Ohio Railroad, in 1829, but only two years later that line introduced bogie carriages.

Dining and Sleeping

Dining cars date back to early practice in North America – two, rebuilt from ordinary day coaches ran between Philadelphia and Baltimore from 1863 – and to George M Pullman's developments. Pullman cars equipped with kitchen and dining facilities, known as 'Palace cars', were introduced

in the USA in 1865: the first was named *Pioneer*. A 'Hotel car', a dining car convertible to a sleeping car at night, was introduced by Pullman on the Great Western Railway of Canada in 1867. A carriage with sleeping arrangements adapted from the seating had operated between Harrisburg and Chambersburg, USA, since 1857. Pullman's first sleeping car, converted from a day coach, ran from Bloomington to Chicago in 1859.

Electrically-lit Pullman

First train in Great Britain to be electrically lit throughout, in 1881, also was the country's first all-Pullman train, on the London Brighton & South Coast Railway. Gas lighting had been used since about 1860, this in turn having superseded earlier oil lamps.

Air Conditioning

First completely air-conditioned train in the United States was inaugurated between Washington and New York in 1931. First in Australia was a diesel-mechanical railcar which entered service in 1937 between Parkes and Broken Hill, in New South Wales.

World's Most Luxurious

South Africa claims the most luxurious train in the world, the *Blue Train*, which runs between Pretoria, Johannesburg and Cape Town. For the 26-hour journey accommodation is entirely in private rooms. A contender is the *Indian Pacific*, which crosses Australia from Perth to Sydney in 65 hours.

Mail by Rail

Mail was first carried by train on the Liverpool & Manchester Railway in 1830. First travelling post-office and mail-sorting carriage ran on the Grand Junction Railway in 1838.

Greatest Loads

A hydrocracker reactor weighing 560 tonnes, and 32 m (106 ft) tall, probably is the heaviest single item of freight ever to be carried by rail, from Birmingham, Alabama, to Toledo, Ohio, USA, in 1965.

Below: Australia's *Indian Pacific* closely rivals South Africa's *Blue Train* for the claim of the world's most luxurious train. After the necessary gauge conversions and track upgrading were completed in 1970, the fully air-conditioned *Indian Pacific* began service on the 3,968 km (2,461 mile) run between Sydney and Perth, across the Nullarbor Plain. Distance and arid desert combine to make riding the *Indian Pacific* feel like sailing on a passenger liner with many of the attractive features of shipboard life.

Heaviest and Longest

Extending about 6.5 km (4 miles) and weighing 43,000 tonnes), a freight train comprising 500 coal wagons hauled by three 3,600 hp diesel locomotives holds the record as the longest and heaviest ever noted. This freight train ran between Iager, Virginia, and Portsmouth, Ohio, in 1967.

Longest train ever assembled in Canada, of 250 loaded grain cars powered by seven diesel locomotives, about 4 km (2½ miles) overall, was tried by Canadian Pacific in 1974 from west of Moose Jaw, Saskatchewan, to Thunder Bay, Ontario, as part of experiments to increase capacity of the system.

Heaviest regular trains in the world run on the Hamersley Iron Railway, built in a remote corner of Western Australia in 1966. Up to five 3,600 hp diesel locomotives haul 186 loaded ore wagons having a gross weight of 24,000 tonnes.

World Speed Record

Fastest ever attained by a flanged rail vehicle is 410 km/h (255 mph) on August 14, 1974, by the Linear Induction Motor Test Vehicle of the United States Department of Transportation at its High Speed Ground Test Centre Track at Pueblo, Colorado. Jet engines provided the initial thrust to allow a speed of 400 km/h (250 mph) to be obtained on the first 4 km of the 9.9 km (6.2 mile) track.

Previous highest speed on rails elsewhere was by the French 'Aerotrain', powered by aircraft jet engines, which reached 378 km/h (235 mph) between Gomez-le-Chatel and Limours on December 4, 1967.

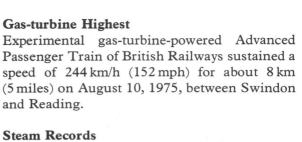

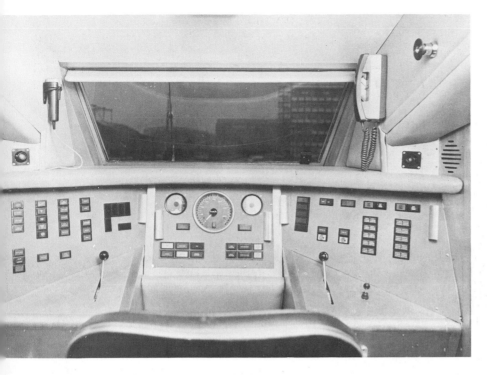

Above: An interior view of the APT-E's driving cab.

Far left: The heaviest regular service trains run on the Hamersley Iron Railway.

Below left: A prototype High Speed Train and the APT-E at Swindon.

Below right: Driver Joseph Duddington took the steam speed record at Stoke Bank on the footplate of LNER's A4 class No 4468 Mallard.

French Electric Records

On February 21, 1953, a Co–Co electric locomotive, No. 7121, of the French National Railways, hauling a three-coach test train between Dijon and Beaune averaged 240 km/h (149 mph) for 5 km (3 miles); speed rose to a maximum of 243 km/h (151 mph). This stood as a world record until March 28, 1955, when a locomotive of the same class, No. 7107, reached a speed of 330 km/h (205 mph) hauling a three-coach test train weighing 100 tons between Facture and Morcenx, on the Bordeaux-Hendaye line. On March 29 Bo–Bo locomotive 9004, during the same tests (for which the traction and overhead electrical equipment was specially modified), equalled this speed. Both locomotives travelled at more than 320 km/h (199 mph) for nearly 7 km (4 miles).

Fastest ever by Diesel

British Railways prototype High Speed Train holds the world record for diesel traction, having attained a speed of 230 km/h (143 mph) between Northallerton and Thirsk, in Yorkshire, on June 12, 1973. The previous record of 214 km/h (133 mph), was set in Germany over the Berlin-Hamburg line during speed trials on June 23, 1939.

Gas-turbine Highest

Experimental gas-turbine-powered Advanced Passenger Train of British Railways sustained a speed of 244 km/h (152 mph) for about 8 km (5 miles) on August 10, 1975, between Swindon and Reading.

Steam Records

World record for steam is claimed by London & North Eastern Railway 4–6–2 *Mallard* with the maximum speed of 202 km/h (126 mph) attained near Peterborough on July 3, 1938.

On the mainland of Europe, the highest authenticated speed with steam was a maximum of 200 km/h (124½ mph) by a German 4–6–4 locomotive, No 05.001, on an experimental run between Berlin and Hamburg in May 1935.

Speed in Germany

Also in Germany, a 15,000 V ac electric locomotive achieved 162 km/h (101 mph) in 1901. Two years later, two electric passenger railcars, on a test track near Berlin, reached 209 km/h (130 mph), which remained the authenticated record on rails until 1931, when it was exceeded on the German State Railway by a propeller-driven four-wheel coach. This maintained a maximum speed of 230 km/h (143 mph) for 10 km (6¼ miles) between Karstadt and Dergenthin.

American Claims

Though not internationally accepted, the Pennsylvania Railroad claimed that 4–4–2 steam engine No 7002 reached 205 km/h (127 mph) on the *Broadway Limited* as long ago as June 12, 1905. But 193 km/h (120 mph) was attained by the first American diesel-electric streamlined express, the M–10001 of the Union Pacific during a series of experimental runs in October 1934.

On July 23, 1966, a Budd passenger coach with two jet engines mounted on its roof reached 295 km/h (183½ mph) near Bryon on the New York Central.

World's Most Intensive High Speed

Japanese National Railways 'Hikari' super-expresses cover the 515 km (320 miles) between Tokyo and Osaka, on the New Tokaido line, in 3 hr 10 min including two intermediate stops – an overall average speed of 163 km/h (101 mph), with a maximum of 210 km/h (131 mph).

World's Longest Tunnels

Longest railway tunnel in the world is the second of the two Simplon bores, 19.823 km (12 miles 559 yd), opened in 1922 through the Alps between Switzerland and Italy. Next is the slightly shorter initial single-track Simplon Tunnel, of 1906, which is 19.803 km (12 miles 537 yd) long. In Italy the double-track Apennine Tunnel, on the Bologna-Florence route and opened in 1934, is 18.519 km (11 miles 892 yd) long.

Second longest to the Simplon bores is Japan's New Kanmon Tunnel, 18.700 km (11 miles 1,090 yd), completed in 1974 after nearly four year's work, for the Hakata extension of the Sanyo Shinkansen.

North of the Alps, longest tunnel is Lieråsen, 10.700 km (6 miles 1,142 yd), opened in 1973 to shorten the Oslo-Drammen line, in Norway.

Cascade is the longest tunnel in North America, 12.542 km (7 miles 1,396 yd), opened in 1929, the single-track bore having been built within three years to replace an earlier summit tunnel between Scenic and Berne, on the Great Northern Railway, USA. In Canada, the longest is the double-track Connaught Tunnel, 8.083 km (5 miles 39 yd), on the Canadian Pacific Railway.

Longest in the Southern Hemisphere is the single-track Rimutaka Tunnel, 8.798 km (5 miles 821 yd) and opened in 1955, between Wellington and Masterton in the North Island, New Zealand.

On British railways the longest is the Severn Tunnel, 7.011 km (4 miles 628 yd), which, when opened by the Great Western Railway in 1886, became the world's longest underwater tunnel.

Longest continuous tunnel – containing 24 stations – is on the London Underground system, from East Finchley to Morden via Bank, 27.842 km (17 miles 528 yd).

First tunnel to be used for passenger traffic was Tyler Hill 757 m (838 yd), on the Canterbury & Whitstable Railway in England, opened in 1830 and closed completely in 1952.

Top left: The summit of the standard 1,435 mm (4 ft 8½ in) gauge Moracocha Branch of the Central Railway of Peru at La Cima.

Top right: The train nears the Wolfort Tunnel on the Mount Pilatus Railway in Switzerland. Locher-Freuler devised the rack with horizontal teeth on each side to prevent any slipping and chose the 800 mm (2 ft 7½ in) gauge.

Left: The longest tunnel in Canada is the 8.083 km (5 mile 39 yd) double-track Connaught Tunnel in the Selkirks on the Canadian Pacific Railway.

Below: A trans-continental train crossing the world's longest straight stretch across Australia's Nullarbor Plain is shown here 320 km (200 miles) east of Kalgoorlie.

Bottom left: The south-east (English) portal of the Severn Tunnel, built over 14 years by the Great Western Railway to shorten the route between London and South Wales, is seen here at about the time of completion in 1886.

Highest Altitudes

Greatest altitude attained by a main-line railway is at La Cima, on the standard 1.435 m (4 ft 8½ in) gauge Peruvian Central, 4,818 m (15,806 ft) above Datum. A siding from near the summit to a mine reached 4,830 m (15,848 ft) but is now closed. Altogether, ten summits above 4,200 m (14,000 ft) are crossed by railways in Peru.

Outside South America, the highest summits are on two rack lines: at Pikes Peak, 4,302 m (14,110 ft), on the standard-gauge Manitou & Pikes Peak in the USA; and at Jungfraujoch, Switzerland, where the metre (3 ft 3⅜ in) gauge track climbs to 3,454 m (11,333 ft), though the upper section is in tunnel.

Steepest Gradients

Both the steepest funicular and the steepest rack railways in the world are in Switzerland. Between Piotta and Piora (Lake Ritom) – on a cable-worked incline built for transport of materials for hydro-electric schemes and later adapted for passengers – there is a maximum gradient of 1 in 1.15 (88 per cent). Over the steepest rack and pinion-assisted section, on the Pilatus Mountain Railway, there is a gradient of 1 in 2 (50 per cent).

Steepest incline worked by adhesion is the 1 in 11 (9 per cent) between Chedde and Servoz on the electrified metre-gauge Chamonix line of French National Railways.

Longest Straights

By far the longest stretch of straight track is on the Transcontinental Railway of the Commonwealth of Australia, extending 478 km (297 miles) across the Nullarbor Plain. Next in order comes the Junin and Mckenna stretch of the General San Martin Railway of Argentina, which is dead straight for 330 km (205 miles).

Longest and Loftiest Bridges

World's longest bridge by far was the Lucin Cut-Off, built in trestles across the Great Salt Lake, Utah, on the first American transcontinental line, which was nearly 19 km (12 miles) from end to end. During the 1950s, it was replaced by a rock-fill causeway through the shallow brine.

Left: Passengers in the open-air observation car of a Southern Pacific Railroad train approach the Great Salt Lake, just west of Ogden, Utah in 1876. The Lucin Cut-Off, the trestle bridge across the salt lake, was replaced by a broad embankment in 1959.

Present longest railway bridge (also used by road traffic) is the Huey P Long Bridge opened in 1935 across the Mississippi near New Orleans, USA, which, including approaches is 7.090 km (4 miles 705 yd) long. Eight river spans total 1,074 m (3,524 ft) with a central cantilever span of 241 m (790 ft), 41 m (135 ft) above the river.

Next longest, completed a year earlier, is the Lower Zambesi Bridge, in Mozambique, totalling 3.677 km (2 miles 500 yd), with 33 main steelwork spans each 7.9 m (26 ft) in length. The loftiest span is 8.2 m (27 ft) above high-water.

Africa's loftiest bridge, over the Zambesi River in Rhodesia, carries the railway 128 m (420 ft) above the water near Victoria Falls. It was built in 1904 and the single centre span measures 152 m (500 ft).

Mala Rijeka Bridge on the Belgrade to Bar line in Yugoslavia. The longest span of 151 m (495 ft) carries the railway 201 m (460 ft) above the river. It was completed in 1976, eclipsing the 132.5 m (435 ft) high Fades Viaduct in France.

Biggest Spans

Longest concrete arch is the Pfaffenberg–Zwenberg Bridge on the Tauern Railway in Austria, 120 m (394 ft) high and with a span of 200 m (660 ft). It was opened in 1971.

Largest cantilever span in the world is Quebec Bridge over the St Lawrence River, on Canadian National Railways and opened in 1917. Overall length is 987 m (3,238 ft) with a main span of 548.6 m (1,800 ft): the central suspended span of 205.740 m (675 ft) was the second to be built; the original collapsed into the river while being hoisted into position in September 1916.

British Notables

Oldest cantilever structure is the Forth Bridge, near Edinburgh in Scotland. Total length is 2,528 m (8,298 ft) and the two main spans, 521 m (1,710 ft), carry the double track 47.550 m (156 ft) above high water. More than 54,000 tonnes of steel were used during erection between 1882 and 1889.

Also in Eastern Scotland is the longest railway

Above: Locomotive No 60534, a 4-6-2 hauls the Edinburgh train across the Tay Bridge.

Left: Locomotive No 60919, class V2, leaves the north end of the Forth Bridge.

Below: The London & Greenwich Railway formed Britain's longest viaduct.

Right: Australia's Sydney Harbour Bridge.

bridge in Europe, 3.552 km (2 miles 364 yd), across the Tay Estuary at Dundee. Centre spans of the original Tay Bridge, opened in 1878 with 84 spans of iron trusses, were blown down in a gale the following year: reconstruction to a revised design was completed in 1887.

Britain's longest viaduct, of 878 brick arches and extending to 6 km (3 miles 1,300 yd), is on the first railway into the capital, the London & Greenwich, opened in 1836.

Biggest Steel Arches

Sydney Harbour Bridge, Australia, with a main span of 503 m (1,650 ft), is the largest steel-arch span in the world. Opened in 1932, Sydney Harbour Bridge now carries two tracks, as well as road and footways.

Hell Gate, which gave the Pennsylvania Railroad access to Long Island, New York, from 1917 is the largest steel-arch bridge in the USA. Its main span of 297.8 m (977 ft) carries four tracks 43 m (140 ft) above the water.

Largest in Sweden

Arsta Bridge, near Stockholm, built of concrete and steel in 1929, is the largest in Sweden. It is 722 m (790 yd) long and 28 m (91 ft) high, with a lifting span 27 m (89 ft) long.

Furthest North and South

Most northerly railway in the world was at Kings Bay, Spitsbergen, only 1,200 km (750 miles) from the North Pole. Of 889 mm (2 ft 11 in) gauge, it was 2.4 km (1.5 miles) long and connected coal mines with the harbour until finally closed in 1949.

Most southerly was a mineral line, also isolated, about 7 km (4.4 miles) long, from Punta Arenas to Loreto, in Chile.

RT HONE WE HUSKISSON.

Ul. Huskisson

Born in 1769. died at Eccles, near Manchester Sept. 15th and interred in St James's Cemetery. Liverpool, Sept. 24th 1830.

DISASTERS

Opening Day Fatality

Grand opening of the first British main-line railway, the Liverpool & Manchester, on September 15, 1830, was marred by a fatal accident to William Huskisson, Member of Parliament. He was standing alongside the train conveying principal guests at Parkside, where a stop was made for water. He was speaking to the Duke of Wellington, when the Stephensons' *Rocket* locomotive, passing on the other track, struck him down despite the warnings of the Duke.

'Best Friend' Explosion

Second fatal steam railway accident occurred on June 17, 1831, in the United States, on the South Carolina Railroad. At Charleston, the safety valve of the pioneer locomotive *Best Friend of Charleston* was unlawfully held down by its fireman and the boiler exploded, fatally injuring him.

First Major Disaster

Earliest major catastrophe was in France on May 8, 1842, when the main axle on the leading locomotive of a double-headed Versailles–Paris express broke without warning. Several coaches piled up on to the engines. Many passengers were unable to escape because compartment doors were locked – afterwards this practice ceased in France – and 53 people died in the fire that followed.

Earliest American Passenger Deaths

First passenger train accident in USA history recorded was on the Camden & Amboy main line between Spotswood and Hightstown, New Jersey, on November 9, 1833. A broken axle caused one carriage to overturn; two people died and 12 of the 24 occupants were seriously injured. One of the injured was C Vanderbilt, later a great railway 'king' in the USA.

Deadliest Disasters

Though more than 600 were reported killed when a troop train, filled largely with families of soldiers, plunged into a gorge near Guadalajara, Mexico, on January 18, 1915, probably the greatest disaster to a train in terms of casualties was near Modane, on the Mount Cenis Tunnel route in the Alpine region of south-eastern France on December 12, 1917. The train was heavily overloaded with soldiers returning home on Christmas leave and ran out of control on a steep gradient, finally derailing at a wooden bridge on a sharp curve, where the carriages piled-up and caught fire. The death figure was officially announced later as 543, but estimates placed the total much higher. In wartime Italy, on March 2, 1944, when two steam engines hauling a train stalled on the gradient through Armi Tunnel, near Balvano, almost all its passengers were suffocated by carbon dioxide and smoke. The figure for casualties has been variously documented as 426 to 569.

Britain's Worst

Another troop train, and again during the first world war, was involved in the most severe accident in terms of casualties that has occurred on British railways. On May 22, 1915, at Quintinshill, on the Caledonian Railway, two signalmen overlooked a passenger train standing in full view and accepted a troop train which collided with it at high speed; then an express on the opposite line ran into the wreckage. Gas-lit carriages of the troop train were destroyed by fire and an estimated 227 passengers and railwaymen were killed.

Tay Bridge Collapse

Bad design and construction of the 3.552 km (2 mile 364 yd) long Tay Bridge, in Scotland, led to collapse of the central spans as a train was crossing during a gale on the night of December 28, 1879. There were no survivors among the 78 passengers and staff.

Above left: Rt Hon William Huskisson, Member of Parliament for Liverpool, who was run over and fatally injured by the Stephensons' *Rocket* at Parkside near Newton le Willows on the opening day of the Liverpool & Manchester Railway in 1830.

Above: The funeral procession at Leith in May 1915 for the hundred soldiers killed in the troop train at Quintinshill near Gretna Green, Scotland.

Below: A Florida East Coast train passes the wreck of a 52-car freight train at Oak Hill. The wrecked train was derailed by deliberate sabotage.

Below right: The interior of one of the Royal Mail vans with its pigeon-hole racks – part of the travelling Post Office train which was ransacked by an armed gang in 1963.

New Zealand Flood Destruction

Christmastide collapse of a bridge caused by the forces of nature also produced the worst disaster in the history of New Zealand railways. On December 24, 1954, a volcanic eruption led to an abnormal flow of water in the usually shallow Wangaehu River at Tangiwai and tore away the central concrete piers of a bridge. A Wellington–Auckland express plunged into the flood and six coaches were swept away – one was found 4 km (2½ miles) down river – with a loss of 149 lives.

Argentine Calamity

A total of 236 passengers were killed and more than 400 injured in Argentine's worst accident, on February 1, 1970. The 'El Mixto' express of the General Mitre Railway, travelling at around 96 km/h (60 mph), ran into the rear of a local train which had come to a halt between Banavidez and General Pachedo stations. A contributing factor to signalling irregularities was that staff at Benavidez had been held-up at pistol point earlier in the day.

Animals on the Track

Even where railways are entirely fenced, straying animals are a potential danger. At San Nicola Varco, on the Salerno–Reggio di Calabria line in Italy, in fog early on the morning of November 9, 1967, the driver of 'Direttissimo 904' braked sharply when he observed a herd of cattle on the track ahead, his train became partially derailed and fouled the opposite track. The 'Rapido Conca d'Oro', approaching at high speed, collided first with the animals, then with Train 904. Twelve people lost their lives.

Crossing Collisions

In the USA level (grade) crossing collisions represent, in terms of total casualties, a more serious problem than all other railway accidents together. As elsewhere, the hazards have grown greater with faster trains and larger highway vehicles. 1,400 people were killed in 1973.

Buried Alive

While shunting at Lindal, in North-West England, on October 22, 1892, a Furness Railway 0–6–0 locomotive gradually subsided into iron-ore mines below, eventually sinking some 60 m (200 ft), beyond recovery. It remains interred there to this day.

Indian Raids

Hundreds of workers died before the completion, in 1869, of the spanning of America by rails – deaths not only from accidents and disease, but from incidents arising from the lawlessness that characterized the transient communities and – more horribly – at the hands of marauding bands of Indian warriors. During one of the many lurid raids, on August 6, 1867, near Plum Creek Station, 95 km (59 miles) east of North Platte, a band of Cheyennes wrecked, looted and burnt a freight train, killing seven Union Pacific Railroad employees and scalping another.

Malicious Wrecking

Railways are particularly vulnerable to sabotage, not only as an act of warfare, but as an aid to intended robbery; to prevent operation, as during a strike; to satisfy a grudge against them; or for mere curiosity or excitement, as by children. More than 200 people were killed when a troop train was derailed in Honan Province, China, on September 23, 1935. An infamous American example of train-wrecking was when someone interfered with track in the Nevada desert on August 12, 1939, and the Southern Pacific's crack 'City of San Francisco' demolished a bridge after leaving the track: 24 people died.

'Enterprise' Blown-up

Terrorists in Ireland detonated a bomb under the second coach of the Belfast–Dublin 'Enterprise' express near Scarva on February 6, 1976. The diesel-electric locomotive and six coaches were derailed but only one of the 200 passengers had to be detained in hospital.

An Irish locomotive was wrecked by explosives on August 16, 1973, after being ambushed by gunmen in South Armagh when hauling a Dublin–Belfast freight train. On November 8, 1975, armed men hijacked a Dublin–Belfast newspaper train and sent the locomotive northwards without crew. Running away at an estimated 110 km/h (70 mph), the newspaper train left the track on a speed-restricted curve at Portadown.

The Great Train Robbery

In what is known as 'The Great Train Robbery', nearly £3 million, mostly in used banknotes, was stolen when British Rail Post Office 'Up Special' from Aberdeen and Glasgow to London was halted by a faked signal and robbed near Cheddington at 03.15 on August 8, 1963. Some 120 mailbags were loaded by the armed gang into a lorry in the narrow public road below.

Film Wrecks

Crashes deliberately staged for film sequences, using real locomotives and rolling stock rather than models or stage devices, have provided spectacular scenes in feature films since 'The Wreck', produced by Vitagraph (USA) in 1914, in which two trains raced towards each other and collided, the explosion of the boiler of one engine adding to the horrifying effect.

CHRONOLOGY

Evidence of the earliest recognizable form of railways – with flanged wooden wheels running on plain wooden track – dates back to the 16th century, when they became a normal part of mining practice in Central Europe. During the early years of the following century mining railways were introduced into England from Germany; then industrial waggonways were built to convey minerals from pits to waterways. Iron rails appeared at Coalbrookdale in 1767. However, the full potential of railways was not realized until the 19th century, when they became general conveyors of goods and merchandise, and shortly afterwards of passengers.

May 21, 1801. Incorporation of the Surrey Iron Railway, the first public goods line in the world, sanctioned by British Parliament. Opened from Wandsworth to Croydon on July 26, 1803.

June 29, 1804. Oystermouth Railway (or Tramroad) Company incorporated, the first to convey fare-paying passengers, from March 25, 1807. The line, opened about April 1806 from Swansea to Oystermouth, in South Wales, was worked successively by horse, steam and electricity. Known for many years as the Swansea & Mumbles Railway and abandoned on January 5, 1960.

August 12, 1812. First commercial use of steam locomotives, on the Middleton Colliery Railway, Leeds, England, which dated back to 1758 and which had been relaid with John Blenkinsop's rack rail. Matthew Murray's steam engines were used. Rack operation ceased around 1835, but a section of the line is still working.

October 23, 1820. Patent granted to John Birkinshaw, of Bedlington Iron Works, under which rolled rails were introduced.

September 27, 1825. Ceremonial opening of Stockton & Darlington Railway, in North-East England. Stephenson's famous locomotive, *Locomotion*, was used at the opening for the conveyance of both passengers and goods, but, at first, steam was employed only for goods traffic.

September 7, 1827. First section of the first railway in the Austrian Empire opened, from Budweis (Česke Budejovice) to Trojanov, with animal traction.

October 1, 1828. Formal opening, with horse traction, of the St Etienne to Andrézieux Railway, the first in France. It was concessioned on February 26, 1823, and unofficially brought into service in May 1827. Passenger traffic began on March 1, 1832, and steam traction was introduced in 1844.

October 9, 1829. Carbondale–Honesdale Railway in the United States opened by the Delaware & Hudson Canal Company. Locomotive *Stourbridge Lion* had run trial trip on August 8 but was too heavy for the track and the line was worked for many years as a gravity coal railway.

May 24, 1830. First public railway in the USA, the Baltimore & Ohio Railroad, opened between Baltimore and Ellicott's Mills, Maryland, for regular passenger and freight traffic, with horse traction.

September 15, 1830. First public railway with all traffic operated by steam traction, the Liverpool & Manchester, formally opened.

January 15, 1831. First regular steam railway in the USA, the South Carolina Railroad, opened, with locomotive *Best Friend of Charleston*.

December 17, 1834. First railway in Ireland opened, Dublin to Kingstown (now Dun Laoghaire).

May 5, 1835. First Belgian railway opened, Brussels to Malines, with Stephenson locomotives *La Flèche* and *Stephenson*. Built and worked by Belgian Government as part of a planned national system, the first in the world to be designed as such.

August 24, 1835. First train entered Washington from Baltimore, witnessed by President Andrew Jackson.

December 7, 1835. First German railway, the Ludwigsbahn, opened from Nuremberg to Furth with Stephenson locomotive *Der Adler (The Eagle)*.

April 20, 1836. First narrow-gauge public railway in the world, the Festiniog, of 597 mm (1 ft 11½ in) gauge, opened for slate traffic in North Wales. Steam traction was introduced in 1863 and passenger traffic officially began in January 1865.

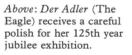

Above: *Der Adler* (The Eagle) receives a careful polish for her 125th year jubilee exhibition.

Left: A painting of the *Stourbridge Lion*. The locomotive was obtained from Foster, Rastrick & Company, Stourbridge, England.

Above right: George Stephenson's locomotive *Rocket* wins the competition at Rainhill Bridge, near Manchester on October 14, 1829.

Right: An engraving of Christ Church and Coal Staith near Leeds showing one of John Blenkinsop's rack locomotives.

July 21, 1836. First steam railway in Canada, the Champlain & St Lawrence Railroad, opened between Laprairie and St John with Stephenson-built locomotive *Dorchester*.

July 4, 1837. First British trunk railway, the Grand Junction, opened throughout.

January 6, 1838. First railway wholly in modern Austria opened from Vienna to Florisdorf, and Deutsch Wagram.

June 4, 1838. First section of Brunel's broad (2,133 mm or 7 ft) gauge Great Western Railway opened, from Paddington to Maidenhead.

September 24, 1839. First railway in Netherlands opened, from Amsterdam to Haarlem.

October 4, 1839. First railway in Italy opened, from Naples to Portici.

June 15, 1844. First railway in Switzerland opened, Basle to St Louis (St Ludwig).

July 15, 1846. First railway in Hungary opened, Pest to Vacz.

1846. Peak of the 'Railway Mania' in Great Britain, when 272 Acts were passed for new lines.

June 26, 1847. Oldest line in modern Denmark, the Copenhagen–Roskilde Railway, opened: the Altona–Kiel Railway, afterwards annexed with its territory by Prussia, had been running since 1844.

October 28, 1848. First railway in Spain opened, Barcelona to Mataro.

December 25, 1851. First railway in Chile opened – the first in South America.

April 18, 1853. First railway in India, the Great Indian Peninsula, opened from Bombay to Thana.

April 30, 1854. First railway in Brazil opened.

May 18, 1854. First public railway in Australia to carry passengers and goods, the Port Elliot & Goolwa, opened with horse traction.

September 1, 1854. Opening of first line in Norway, between Oslo (then Christiania) and Eidsvoll.

Above: The railway juggernaut of 1845.

Below: From the Mississippi basin the Union Pacific built westward, from Sacramento, the Central Pacific built east into the mountains. On May 10, 1869 Union Pacific and Central Pacific were formally joined at Promontory Point, Utah.

September 12, 1854. First steam-operated railway on the Australian continent, Flinders Street to Port Melbourne, opened.

October 28, 1856. Opening of first railway in Portugal, Lisbon to Carregado.

1856. Interlocking of signals and points patented by John Saxby.

December 1, 1856. Opening of first sections of Swedish State Railways, Gothenburg to Jonsered and Malmö to Lund.

August 30, 1857. First railway in Argentina opened, Parque to Floresta, with locomotive *La Portena*, built in Leeds, England.

1857. First steel rail made, by Robert Forester Mushet, and laid experimentally at Derby Station, Midland Railway, in England, on a line carrying heavy traffic (and remained in service until 1873). Steel rails came into general use a few years later.

September 1, 1859. George Mortimer Pullman's first sleeping car began service between Bloomington and Chicago.

June 26, 1860. First railway in South Africa, Durban to the Point (Natal), opened.

May 13, 1861. Opening of first railway in what is now Pakistan, from Karachi City to Kotri.

January 10, 1863. Section of first underground railway in the world opened, the Metropolitan Railway from Paddington to Farringdon Street.

December 1, 1863. Opening of first steam-operated railway in New Zealand, between Christchurch and Ferrymead.

1867. First recorded scheduled sleeping- and dining-car service in North America inaugurated by the Great Western Railway of Canada.

May 10, 1869. First USA transcontinental railway completed by connection of the Union Pacific and Central Pacific Railways at Promontory, Utah.

October 19, 1869. First railway in Roumania opened, Bucharest to Giurgiu.

September 18, 1871. First of the great Alpine tunnels, the Mont Cenis, opened.

June 12, 1872. Opening of first railway in Japan, Yokohama–Shinagawa; completed to Tokyo (then called Yedo or Jeddo) on October 14.

Above: American buffalo are shot down from a train.

Right: Interior of the sleeping-car train, *Australia*, showing the parlor car. The train was built in 1892.

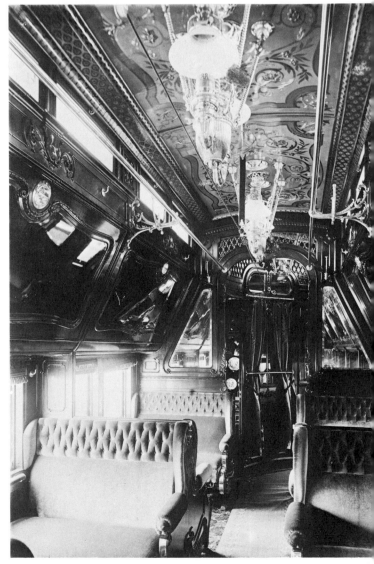

Below: A share certificate issued to stockholders by the Hull & Selby Railway Company.

June 1, 1874. Pullman cars introduced to Great Britain by the Midland Railway.

May 31 – September 30, 1879. Werner von Siemen's electric locomotive operated on passenger line in grounds of Berlin Trades Exhibition.

May 12, 1881. First public electric railway in the world opened at Lichterfelde, near Berlin.

September 15, 1884. First railway in Serbia opened, Belgrade to Nish.

November 7, 1885. Canadian Pacific Railway transcontinental line completed by joining of eastern and western sections at Craigellachie, British Columbia. Opened to traffic June 28, 1886.

December 18, 1890. City & South London, first underground electric line in the world, opened.

1895. First main-line electric service opened Baltimore & Ohio Rail Road.

January 25, 1906. First trial trips through the Simplon Tunnel, which was opened on June 1.

October 22, 1917. Opening of Trans-Australian Railway, owned by the Commonwealth, between Kalgoorlie and Port Augusta. The Trans-Australian Railway includes the longest straight stretch of track in the world, 528 km (328 miles) across the Nullarbor Plain.

May 1, 1928. World's longest non-stop run inaugurated by London & North Eastern Railway, between London and Edinburgh, 632 km (393 miles).

January 1, 1931. Turkestan–Siberia (Turksib) Railway opened, USSR.

March 19, 1932. First ordinary passenger train ran across Sydney Harbour Bridge, a local electric train.

October 14, 1936. Inauguration of Dover–Dunkirk train ferry service and through trains between London and Paris.

January 1, 1948. Nationalization of British railways.

November 8, 1956. Pneumatic-tyred trains introduced in regular service on Paris Métro.

June 2, 1957. Introduction of first stage of the Trans-Europ Express (TEE) services by self-contained diesel train sets, in standard red livery, evolved by collaboration between Belgian, French, West German, Italian, Luxembourg, Netherlands and Swiss railway authorities.

October 1, 1964. New high-speed Tokaido line, in Japan, equipped with the most modern devices, opened between Tokyo and Osaka.

January 16, 1969. Six-coach electric multiple-unit train of 'Metroliner' stock entered service on the Penn Central, USA, between New York and Washington, covering the 360 km (224 miles) in 179 min, with five intermediate stops. In March 1969 time was reduced to 150 minutes.

May 1969. First container shipped from Japan over the Trans-Siberian Railway arrived in England via the Zeebrugge–Harwich ferry, after a total journey of 12,222 km (7,596 miles).

Top far left: One of the first locomotives to work in China was the *Pioneer*.

Top near left: The world's longest non-stop run was the 643.2 km (399.7 mile) distance between London and Edinburgh introduced by LNER in May 1928. Gresley designed his corridor tender to permit crew change en route for this service.

Left: Turbotrains at work at Gare St Lazare, Paris.

Below left: An engineer checks the pneumatic rubber tyres on the Paris Metro. Pneumatic-tyred trains were introduced into regular service in November 1956.

Below: The Golden Spike ceremony near Kalgoorlie celebrated the opening of standard-gauge line between Sydney and Perth, Australia.

June 1, 1969. Weekly through sleeping car introduced between Togliattigrad, USSR, and Turin, Italy, covering the 4,000 km (2,485 miles) in 88 hours.

March 1, 1970. 'Indian Pacific' express inaugurated in Australia by opening of standard-gauge line between Sydney, New South Wales, and Perth, Western Australia.

May 1, 1971. National Railroad Passenger Corporation (Amtrak) assumed responsibility for long-distance passenger train services in USA.

May 6, 1974. British Railways inaugurated electric working over the whole 650 km (404 miles) west coast main line between London and Glasgow.

May 26, 1974. French Railways introduced a series of turbotrains between Bordeaux, Limoges and Lyon.

August 14, 1974. World rail speed record broken by research vehicle on standard-gauge US Department of Transportation's test track at Pueblo, attaining 410 km/h (255 mph).

July 14, 1976. 'Tanzam' line – the most important railway to be built in Africa for nearly fifty years – completed. It links the Zambian terminal of Kapiri Mposhi with the Tanzanian port of Dar es Salaam, over 1,859 km (1,155 miles).

FACTS AND FIGURES

WORLD RAILWAYS 1825-1977

The following table shows the development, in kilometres, of public main-line railways in most of the countries throughout the world, in twenty year periods. So far as possible, the progressive figures indicate the length within the *present* national boundaries. Light railways, tramways, and interurban electric lines are *excluded*. Nevertheless, the figures are not strictly comparable by reason of: (*a*) The difficulty in some cases of adjusting earlier lengths to present political boundaries, and (*b*) divergences in practice as to what constitute minor railways, light railways, and secondary lines.

Country	First line	1840	1860	Total length open in					
				1880	1900	1920	1940	1960	1975* *or latest figure
				Kilometres					
Albania	1947 Durres-Pekinj							105	203
Algeria	1860 Algiers-Blida			1,186	3,002	4,055	4,443	4,074	3,957
Angola	1928				364	1,241	2,342	2,884	3,061
Argentina	1857 Parque-Floresta			2,530	16,659	34,081	41,521	43,903	40,067
Australia									
National Railways	1879			105		2,792	3,542	3,625	3,595
NSW	1855 Sydney-Paramatta		113	1,367	8,071	9,883	9,830	9,756	
Queensland	1865 Ipswich-Grandchester			1,028	10,101	10,408	10,152	9,780	
S Australia	1856 North Terrace-Port Adelaide		90	912	3,755	4,115	4,076	3,884	
Tasmania	1871 Launceston-Deloraine			72	1,009	1,038	866	851	
Victoria	1854 Flinders St-Port Melbourne		137	1,929	6,782	7,659	6,904	6,658	
W Australia	1879 Geraldton-Northampton			53	5,696	7,051	6,630	6,163	
Austria	1838 Vienna-Wagram	278	1,036	3,573		7,033	7,161	6,588	6,174
Bangladesh	1862								2,874
Belgium	1835 Brussels-Malines	332	1,689	4,031		4,912	4,910	4,617	4,004
Benin	1912 Cotonou-Save				375	383	578	578	
Bolivia	1873					1,596	2,127	2,382	3,787
Brazil	1854		223	3,396		28,533	34,252	37,670	27,905
Bulgaria	1866 Varna-Kaspičan			539		2,598	3,213	3,335	4,045
Burma	1877			2,176		2,618	3,314	2,990	3,100
Cambodia	1930						319	386	649
Cameroun	1911 Bonaberi-Enkongoamba					378	504	504	1,104
Canada	1836 Laprairie-St John	26	3,324	11,577		63,382	68,502	70,858	71,953
Chile	1851 Caldera-Copiapo		438	1,781		8,202	8,610	7,744	8,097
China	1876 Shanghai-Woosung				2,346	11,189		31,382	35,000
Colombia	1874							3,589	3,088
Congo							410	575	515
Costa Rica	1890 Limon-Alajuela				303	654	654	655	655
Cuba	1837				1,921	3,934	5,163	5,733	5,053
Czechoslovakia	1839 Breclev-Ostrava	77	1,207	6,264	10,918	12,715	12,946	13,139	13,317
Denmark	1847 Copenhagen-Roskilde		109	1,537	3,014	4,842	4,915	4,300	4,001
East Africa	1897 Mombasa-Voi				678	3,016	4,830	5,546	6,039
Ecuador	1871			68	501	999	1,160	1,121	965
Egypt	1854 Alexandria-Kafr-el-Zayat		464	1,519	2,237	2,696	3,875	4,738	4,510
Ethiopia	1900				13	678	678	681	782
Fiji									644
Finland	1862 Helsinki-Hameenlinna			852	2,651	3,988	4,596	5,343	5,975
France	1832 St Etienne-Andrezieux	411	9,410	23,599	36,799	41,600	40,000	38,857	34,845
Germany	1835 Nüremburg-Fürth	539	11,558	32,515	51,958	57,698	59,139		
Germany West								30,761	28,771
Germany East								16,174	14,252
Ghana	1901 Sekondi-Tarkwa					483	787	948	953
Great Britain	1825 Stockton-Darlington	2,388	14,595	25,036	29,039	32,712	32,552	30,209	18,497
Greece	1869 Athens-Piraeus			10	1,045	2,419	2,664	2,569	2,521
Guatemala	1880				567	567	819	819	914
Guinea	1910 Konakry-Kouroussa					662	662	662	796
Honduras	1869						1,481	1,235	991
Hong Kong	1910					35	35	35	34
Hungary	1846 Budapest-Vác		1,006	2,731	6,056	7,685	7,852	8,006	7,610

Country	First line	1840	1860	1880	1900	1920	1940	1960	1975* *or latest figure
				Kilometres					
India (with Pakistan and Bangladesh)	1853 Howrah-Hooghly		1,349		39,835	59,119	66,234		
India (union only)	1854							56,670	60,508
Indonesia	1864 Semarang-Tanggung			406	3,584	5,783	6,709	6,097	7,891
Iran	1917					219	2,082	3,505	4,525
Iraq	1920					1,207	1,570	1,670	2,528
Ireland	1834 Dublin-Kingstown	23	2,195	3,815	5,123	5,540			
Republic	1834 Dublin-Kingstown					4,326	4,012	3,114	3,196
North	1839 Belfast-Lisburn					1,214	1,082	478	327
Israel	1891				87			420	902
Italy	1839 Naples-Portici	19	2,369	9,094	14,375	16,170	17,858	16,399	17,879
Ivory Coast	1912 Abidjan-Bouaké					316	806	1,173	1,173
Jamaica	1845 Kingstown-Angels		24	43	298	319	338	330	330
Japan	1872 Yokohama-Shimagawa			158	6,300	10,437	18,399	20,403	23,239
Jordan	1904 Damascus-Amman							365	552
Yugoslavia	1846 Seniilj-Celje		436	1,854	5,755	8,615	9,646	11,867	10,398
Korea	1899 Inchon-Noryanjin				35	1,873	4,318	2,977	5,448
								South Korea only	
Lebanon	1895				82	172	219	409	417
Liberia	1950							493	493
Luxembourg	1859 Sterpenich-Bettembourg		51	304	465	534	535	394	271
Malagasy	1904 Brickaville-Fanovana					369	858	858	884
Malawi	1907					208	465	465	566
Malaysia	1885				337	1,407	1,718	1,654	1,814
Mali	1904							645	640
Mauritania	1963 Nouadhibou-Tazadit								650
Mexico	1850		32	1,101	13,400	10,899	23,000	23,459	20,659
Mongolia	1938						43	1,397	1,425
Morocco	1911 Military lines					895	1,756	1,756	2,071
Mozambique	1887 Lourenço Marques-				428	745		2,675	4,161
Nepal	1927						76	103	101
Netherlands	1839 Amsterdam-Haarlem	18	340	1,854	2,765	3,407	3,180	3,103	2,825
New Zealand	1863 Christchurch-Ferrymead			1,902	3,658	4,852	5,449	5,369	4,797
Nicaragua	1881 Corinto-Chinandega			21	175	235	380	348	373
Nigeria	1901 Iddo-Ibadan					1,812	3,063	2,865	3,505
Norway	1854 Oslo-Eidsvoll		68	1,057	1,981	3,287	3,698	4,493	4,241
Pakistan	1861			1,067	5,076	8,111	10,704	11,333	5,465
									(Excluding Bangladesh)
Panama	1855 Aspinwall-Panama					180	369		581
Paraguay	1859 Asuncion-Paraguari			72	250	467	497	497	498
Peru	1851		103	2,026	2,796	3,602	2,770	2,662	2,295
Philippines	1892 Manila-Dagupan				195	1,243	1,352	1,119	1,168
Poland	1842 Zebrzydowice-Cracow					9,035		26,904	23,573
Portugal	1856 Lisbon-Carregado		68	1,236	2,396	3,287	3,567	3,602	3,600
Puerto Rico									96
Rhodesia	1897 Plumtree-Bulawayo				1,027	3,446	3,845	4,182	3,367
Roumania	1869 Bucharest-Giurgiu			1,382		3,588	11,360	10,981	10,994
Salvador	1882				56	283	623	604	1,031
Saudi Arabia	1949							573	612
Senegal	1855 Dakar-St Louis								1,034
Sierra Leone	1897 Freetown-Songo				89	544	501	501	84
South Africa	1860 Durban-Point		3	1,633	7,005	16,362	21,863	21,824	22,463
Spain	1848 Barcelona-Mataro		1,859	6,970	10,841	11,235	12,286	13,229	13,432
Sri Lanka	1865 Colombo-Ambepussa			221		1,170	1,530	1,446	1,534
Sudan	1896 Halfa-Kerma (military)				927	2,414	3,206	4,256	4,556
Swaziland	1964 Border-Kadake								224
Sweden	1856 Nora-Ervalla		526	5,876	11,304	14,869	16,610	15,219	11,933
Switzerland	1847 Zurich-Baden		1,052	2,499	3,599	5,737	5,222	5,118	4,691
Syria	1895				63	721	860	847	963
Taiwan	1891 Taipei-Keelung								1,001
Tanzania (not EAR)	1975								967
Thailand	1893 Bangkok-Pak Nam				264	2,247	3,130	3,494	3,765
Togo	1905 Lomé-Anecho					328	441	441	162
Tunisia	1876 Bonc-Guelma			192	875	2,028	2,089	1,952	2,257
Turkey	1856 Smyrna (Izmir)-Torbali		43		2,701	3,621	7,351	7,805	9,869
Uruguay	1872 Montevideo-St Lucia			431	1,654	2,628	2,908	3,031	2,987
USA	1831	4,535	49,288	150,100	311,187	406,941	374,978	354,050	337,560
USSR	1837 Leningrad-Pavlovsk	27	1,077	17,708	44,492	71,597	106,105	125,800	138,260
Venezuela	1877				528	649	966	1,072	244
Vietnam	1885				212	1,061	2,583	1,348	1,278
Zaire	1898				399	1,146	4,842	5,002	5,204
Zambia	1905							1,038	1,297

WORLD RAILWAYS TODAY

Country	Initials	Gauge mm	Length Km	Length Miles	Electrified Km	Electrified Miles	Electrified System	Loco-motives	Carriages	Freight vehicles
Albania	DH	1,435	203	125						
Algeria	SNCFA	1,435	2,657	1,651	299	186	3,000 V dc OH	253	419	9,800
		1,055	1,180	733				35	41	2,402
		1,000	120	74				2	3	181
Angola	CBF	1,067	2,904	1,805				253	241	3,820
		610	157	98						
Argentina	FA	1,676	23,235	14,438	159	99	550 V dc 3R;	1,246	3,361	39,049
		1,435	3,086	1,918			1,100 V dc OH	171	168	3,712
		1,000	13,461	8,365				846	1,287	19,560
		750	285	177				20	8	375
Australia		1,600	9,686	6,143	867	538	1,500 V dc OH	423	1,903	24,484
		1,435	15,209	9,451				742	2,220	24,420
		1,067	17,636	10,959				780	1,183	37,393
Austria	OBB	1,435	5,692	3,537	2,717	1,689	15 kV OH	1,194	3,876	35,696
		1,000	482	300				75	200	754
		760								
Bangladesh	BR	1,676	981	610				503	1,615	15,626
		1,000	1,893	1,176						
Belgium	SNCB	1,435	4,004	2,488	1,283	798	3,000 V dc OH	1,143	2,927	47,845
		1,000	221	137				5	334	182
Benin		1,000	578	360				22	32	346
Bolivia		1,000	3,735	2,321				163	268	1,927
		750	52	32				16		
Brazil	RFFSA	1,600	459	285	2,648	1,646	600, 750, 1,500			
		1,435	194	121			3,000 V dc OH			
		1,000	27,050	16,809				2,153	4,053	56,196
		760	202	126						
Bulgaria	BDZ	1,435	4,045	2,514	1,326	824	25 kV OH			
		760	245	152						
Burma	UBR	1,000	3,100	1,926				363	1,181	11,425
Cambodia	CFC	1,000	649	403				47	8	680
Cameroun	RPC	1,000	1,104	700				94	105	11,508
Canada	CN/CP	1,435	71,953	44,711	43	27	2,700 V dc OH			
		1,067	1,146	712				4,053	1,821	210,557
		914	178	111				21	30	420
Chile	FE	1,676	4,565	2,837	881	547	3,000 V dc OH			
		1,435	494	307				827	2,209	13,930
		1,067	447	278						
		1,000	5,434	3,377						
China		1,435 (most)	35,000 (about)	22,000	676	420	25 kV OH			
Colombia	FNC	914	3,088	1,919				176	338	5,625
Congo	CFCO	1,067	515	320				71	76	1,971
Costa Rica		1,067	655	410	124	77	15 kV OH	91	177	2,020
Cuba		1,435	5,053	3,140	145	90	1,200 V dc OH			
Czechoslovakia	CSD	1,524	101	63	2,039	1,267	1,500, 3,000 V dc,			
		1,435	13,039	8,102			25 kV OH	4,699	11,914	136,150
		1,000	177	110						
Denmark	DSB	1,435	4,001	2,500	99	61	1,500 V dc OH	445	1,873	9,428
East Africa	EAR	1,000	6,039	3,753				433	824	10,650
Ecuador	ENFE	1,067	965	600				46	74	499
		750								
Egypt	ER	1,435	4,510	2,820	26	16	1,500 V dc OH	643	1,752	17,705
Ethiopia	CFE	1,000	782	486				36	59	641
		950	306	190				24	24	565
		600	644	400				60		6,000
Fiji										
Finland	VR	1,524	5,975	3,713	571	355	25 kV OH	396	1,339	22,004

Country	Initials	Gauge mm	Length Km	Length Miles	Electrified Km	Electrified Miles	System	Loco-motives	Carriages	Freight vehicles
France	SNCF	1,435	36,060 ⎫	22,407 ⎫	9,557	5,940	600, 750, 800 V dc 3R	2,573	16,597	286,503
		1,000	785 ⎭	488 ⎭			1,500 V dc, 25 kV OH	18	63	368
Germany, West	DB	1,435	28,771	17,878	10,081	6,264	1,200 V dc 3R, 15 kV OH	5,982	18,802	287,365
Germany, East	DR	1,435	14,252	8,856	1,406	874	800 V dc 3R, 15, 25 kV OH			
Ghana	GR	1,067	953	592				178	253	3,862
Great Britain	BR	1,435	18,497	11,494	3,638	2,261	600, 660, 750, 1,200, 1,500 V dc, 3R, 4R, OH; 6.25, 25 kV OH	3,860	19,124	216,367
Greece	CH	1,435	1,560 ⎫	969 ⎫				193	632	10,334
		1,000	961 ⎭	597 ⎭						
Guatemala		914	914	568				118	198	2,285
Guinea		1,435	134 ⎫	83 ⎫				15	4	439
		1,000	662 ⎭	411 ⎭				30	36	500
Honduras		1,067	544	338				45	142	2,018
		914	447	278				24	26	729
Hong Kong	KCR	1,435	34	21				10	96	104
Hungary	MAV	1,435	7,610 ⎫	4,729 ⎫	1,296	806	1,000 V dc, 25 kV OH			
		760	329 ⎭	204 ⎭						
India	IR	1,676	30,274 ⎫	18,812 ⎫	4,448	2,782	1,500 V dc, 25 kV OH			
		1,000	2,551	1,585				9,698	33,367	397,924
		762	4,476 ⎭	2,781 ⎭						
		610								
Indonesia	UKA	1,067	7,246 ⎫	4,503 ⎫	77	48	1,500 V dc OH			
		750	540	336				925	2,564	21,982
		600	105 ⎭	65 ⎭						
Iran	RAI	1,676	92 ⎫	57 ⎫				315	342	7,998
		1,435	4,525 ⎭	2,812 ⎭						
Iraq	IRR	1,435	1,234 ⎫	767 ⎫				93	248	3,283
		1,000	1,294 ⎭	804 ⎭				98	366	6,111
Ireland	CIE/NIR	1,600	2,546 ⎫	1,582 ⎫				227	769	8,211
		914	650 ⎭	404 ⎭				250		3,360
Israel	IR	1,435	902	560				55	107	2,168
Italy	FS	1,435	17,879 ⎫	11,110 ⎫	9,632	5,985	3,000 V dc OH	3,576	13,433	168,184
		952	1,479 ⎭	919 ⎭				42	589	890
Ivory Coast	RAN	1,000	1,173	729				75	153	1,353
Jamaica		1,435	330	205				26	29	266
Japan	JNR	1,435 ⎫	23,239	14,440	13,773	8,538	600, 750, 1,500 V dc, 3R; OH; 20, 25 kV OH	4,485	36,870	124,300
		1,067 ⎭								
Jordan		1,050	552	343				17	8	369
Jugoslavia		1,435	9,353 ⎫	5,812 ⎫	2,309	1,335	3,000 V dc; 15, 25 kV OH	2,816	4,042	59,426
		ng	1,045 ⎭	649 ⎭						
Korea, S	KNR	1,435	5,448	3,385	348	216	25 kV OH	531	1,971	15,866
Lebanon		1,435	335 ⎫	208 ⎫				39		876
		1,050	82 ⎭	51 ⎭						
Liberia		1,435	348 ⎫	216 ⎫				34	5	742
		1,067	145 ⎭	90 ⎭				11		271
Luxembourg	CFL	1,435	271	168	137	85	25 kV OH	75	98	3,421
Malagasy	RNCFM	1,000	884	549				54	101	975
Malawi	MR	1,067	566	352				35	25	1,005
Malaysia	MR	1,000	1,814	1,127				156	373	6,370
Mali	CFM	1,000	640	398				25	31	308
Mauritania		1,435	650	404				37		1,084
Mexico	N de M	1,435	19,585 ⎫	12,170 ⎫				1,286	2,084	38,074
		914	1,074 ⎭	667 ⎭				26	89	1,232
Mongolia		1,524	1,425	885						
Morocco	ONCFM	1,435	2,071	1,287	708	440	3,000 V dc OH	176	312	8,697
Mozambique	CFM	1,067	4,014 ⎫	2,494 ⎫				318	223	8,511
		762	147 ⎭	91 ⎭						
Nepal		762	101	63				16	34	154
Netherlands	NS	1,435	2,825	1,755	1,713	1,062	1,500 V dc OH	599	1,909	17,002
New Zealand	NZR	1,067	4,797	2,981	99	61	1,500 V dc OH	593	557	29,450
Nicaragua		1,067	373	232				9	27	207
Nigeria	NRC	1,067	3,505	2,178				316	655	6,729
Norway	NSB	1,435	4,241	2,635	2,456	1,544	15 kV OH	247	1,104	8,673
Pakistan	PR	1,675	7,754 ⎫	4,818	290	181	25 kV OH	939	1,831	38,284
		1,000	444	276				36	126	1,018
		762	610 ⎭	379				41	114	464
Panama		1,524	190 ⎫	118				6	24	354
		914	391 ⎭	243				45	64	1,336
Paraguay		1,435	441 ⎫	274				21	15	206
		1,000	57 ⎭	35				4	3	30

Country	Initials	Gauge	Length		Electrified			Loco-motives	Carriages	Freight vehicles
		mm	Km	Miles	Km	Miles	System			
Peru	ENAFER	1,435	1,962	1,219				173	259	4,019
		914	333	207						
Philippines	PNR	1,067	1,168	726				78	246	1,900
Poland	PKB	1,435	23,573	14,648	5,638	3,503	600, 800, 3,000 V dc OH	4,466	8,421	189,500
Portugal	CP	1,676	2,833	1,760	432	269	1,500 V dc, 25 kV OH	290	641	6,830
		1,000	759	472				60	154	768
Puerto Rico		1,000	96	60				22		1,280
Rhodesia	RR	1,067	3,367	2,092				265	631	16,658
Roumania	CFR	1,435	10,403	6,464	1,926	1,196	25 kV OH			
		ng	591	367						
Salvador		914	1,031	641				54	62	1,247
Saudi-Arabia	SCR	1,435	612	380				26	21	1,024
Senegal		1,000	1,034	643				59	103	932
Sierra Leone		1,067	84	52				8		200
South Africa	SAR	1,065	21,723	13,498	4,800	2,982	3,000 V dc OH	4,337	9,363	171,009
		610	707	439						
Spain	RENFE	1,676	13,432	8,346	4,066	2,526	600, 1,200, 1,300, 1,500 V dc OH	1,242	3,937	44,859
		1,435	133	83				32	462	2,024
		1,000	3,257	1,843				364	1,358	9,217
Sri Lanka	SLR	1,676	1,395	867				163	1,009	3,895
		762	139	86				12	99	199
Sudan	SR	1,067	4,556	2,831				289	641	6,590
Swaziland	SR	1,067	224	139						693
Sweden	SJ	1,435	11,651	7,240	7,491	4,672	1,350, 1,500 V dc, 15 kV OH	1,660	2,278	49,652
		891	282	175						
Switzerland	SBB/CFF	1,435	3,518	2,186	5,062	3,145	Various dc, 15 kV OH	1,520	4,118	27,308
		1,000	1,183	735				124	1,098	3,370
Syria	CFS	1,435	963	560				56	148	1,242
Taiwan	TRA	1,067	825	513	In progress			302	1,265	7,172
		762	176	109						
Tanzania		1,067	1,860	1,156				102	100	2,100
Thailand	RSR	1,000	3,765	2,340				438	1,027	9,486
Togo	TR	1,000	162	101				18	68	450
Tunisia	SNCFT	1,435	536	333				100	191	5,755
		1,000	1,721	1,069						
Turkey	TCDD	1,435	9,869	6,132	196	122	25 kV OH	977	1,135	19,291
Uruguay	AFE	1,435	2,987	1,856				156	147	2,938
USA		1,435	337,560	209,756	2,328	1,446	650, 660, 700, 1,500 V dc, 3R, OH; 11 kV OH	26,516	6,135	1,168,500
USSR	SZD	1,524	135,324	84,089	38,923		3,000 V dc, 25 kV OH			
		1,435	73	45						
		1,000 600	2,963	1,841						
Venezuela	FNV	1,435	244	152						
Vietnam		1,000	1,278	794						
Zaire	SNCZ	1,067	3,919	2,435	858	533	25 kV OH	66	177	1,357
		1,000	126	78				350	568	8,400
		600	1,159	720						
Zambia	ZR	1,067	1,297	806				79	73	1,930

Key
ng = narrow gauge 3R = third rail 4R = fourth rail OH = overhead

WORLD FREIGHT TRANSPORT

Freight tonne-kilometres by rail

	1938	1948	1955	1960	1964	1969	1974
Albania	—	9	19	55	91	160	—
Algeria	857	1,132	1,462	1,675	959	1,375	1,531
Argentina	11,730	16,474	15,392	15,188	14,185	13,640	12,357
S Australia	572	795	1,123	1,217	1,265	1,348	1,753
W Australia	594	692	913	1,156	1,381	3,408	3,457
N S Wales	2,886	3,346	4,561	5,725	7,718	7,805	8,658
Victoria	968	1,915	2,072	2,114	3,329	3,341	7,011
Queensland	1,555	1,584	2,258	2,485	2,872	4,164	7,855
C'wealth Australia	57	180	274	399	1,452	1,994	2,200
Tasmania	112	107	157	169	191	196	277
Austria	—	5,117	7,711	7,802	8,346	9,061	11,319
Belgium	5,616	6,232	7,632	6,359	7,086	7,602	9,343
Brazil	4,032	4,726	5,623	7,791	8,555	11,570	18,249
Bulgaria	—	2,580	4,118	6,981	9,969	13,858	17,309
Burma	1,161	627	782	746	—	—	—
Canadian National	21,083	53,015	67,106	57,195	74,011	81,873	96,780
Chile	77	87	104	394	346	418	—
Czechoslovakia	8,239	11,563	31,702	43,904	51,352	53,195	61,567
Denmark	563	1,252	1,136	1,371	1,651	1,617	2,093
East Africa	875	1,459	2,020	1,934	3,071	3,859	4,297
Ethiopia	—	—	129	162	202	219	213
Finland	2,270	3,470	4,490	4,865	4,862	6,253	6,000
France	26,900	41,241	46,800	56,886	65,260	66,110	78,386
Germany East	—	12,398	25,222	32,860	39,113	39,468	49,168
Germany West	—	37,525	44,536	52,521	62,731	68,351	70,723
Gt Britain	24,991	35,063	34,916	30,496	28,100	23,034	21,633
Greece	219	112	268	291	459	587	902
Hungary	2,571	2,296	8,780	13,312	17,012	18,408	23,113
India	54,548	48,830	59,791	100,693	106,841	111,926	122,300
Iran	—	761	1,258	2,182	2,150	2,330	3,627
Ireland	—	513	494	345	350	548	603
Israel	—	—	122	205	323	463	418
Italy	11,137	9,851	14,213	14,767	15,555	18,035	18,145
Japan	2,396	—	44,919	53,592	58,880	61,482	57,778
Jugoslavia	3,318	—	11,576	13,895	18,604	17,691	25,081
Lebanon	—	18	24	36	49	45	78
Luxembourg	106	463	612	638	671	763	866
Malaya	200	172	241	431	587	735	785
Mexico	3,865	6,999	—	—	—	19,352	21,303
Morocco	419	1,077	1,500	1,727	1,965	2,615	3,025
Netherlands	—	2,541	3,432	3,409	3,977	3,433	3,370
New Zealand	714	1,537	1,694	1,897	2,416	2,750	3,638
Norway	804	1,153	1,059	1,062	1,227	1,898	2,048
Poland	20,429	19,304	48,221	66,547	79,059	95,025	125,156
Portugal	504	647	723	762	762	780	889
Rhodesia	—	3,280	5,806	7,615	8,759	7,301	6,623
Roumania	—	7,606	14,079	19,821	29,386	43,721	55,125
South Africa	13,827	25,487	23,284	28,400	37,455	49,219	60,599
Spain	3,674	5,530	6,998	5,123	8,359	9,071	12,670
Sri Lanka	178	253	270	302	321	326	338
Sweden	3,543	7,496	9,655	10,136	11,836	14,852	18,497
Switzerland	1,575	1,924	3,037	4,058	4,909	6,164	7,027
Syria	139	77	54	83	87	93	143
Taiwan	—	—	—	1,964	2,121	2,709	2,702
Thailand	206	536	649	1,146	2,083	1,979	2,296
Tunisia	409	381	382	480	431	1,317	1,426
Turkey	1,015	2,285	3,963	4,322	5,297	6,081	6,404
USA (Cl 1)	423,074	1,025,681	910,478	835,571	962,617	1,121,026	1,369,196
USSR	181,190	395,000	970,900	1,504,400	1,850,000	2,367,100	3,097,700
Zaire	—	—	1,445	1,243	1,022	1,807	—

GLOSSARY

Abutment supporting structure on each side of an arch or bridge.

Adhesion maintenance of contact between wheel and rail; the frictional grip of wheel to rail.

Adhesive weight the sum of driving wheel axle loads.

Air brake power braking system with compressed air as the operating medium.

Air conditioning equipment for, or process of, cleaning and controlling the temperature and humidity of the air in a vehicle or room.

Air cushion type of spring used in some modern carriage suspension systems with air as the operating medium.

Alternating current (ac) electric current which reverses its direction of flow at regular intervals.

Alternator a machine which converts mechanical energy to electrical energy and generates alternating current.

Anchor clamp fixed to the foot of the rail and bearing against the side of a sleeper for preventing rail creep.

Anti-slide/skid a device for detecting and automatically correcting wheel slide or skid during braking by a momentary reduction of braking force.

Anti-slip electrical circuit which detects driving wheel slip on diesel and electric locomotives. The difference in current taken by a particular traction motor when wheel slip occurs causes an illuminated warning to be given to the driver. In addi-

tion, an automatic reduction in engine power and/or partial application of the locomotive brakes may be effected.

Approach control arrangement whereby the clearing of a colour light signal from red to a 'proceed' aspect for a diverging line is delayed until the close approach of a train to ensure that a speed restriction over the facing points is observed.

Approach control automatic operation of lifting barrier level crossing, through treadles or track circuits, by approaching trains.

Arch a beam curved in a vertical plane for carrying loads over a bridge or viaduct.

Arch a fairly flat arch of firebrick or similar material, erected in a steam locomotive firebox below tube level, to promote efficient combustion of the fuel, reduce smoke emission and protect the flue tubes.

Arcing the luminous bridge which occurs when an electrical circuit carrying a large current is broken.

Armature the rotating part of a direct current electric motor or generator. Contains a number of coils, or windings which rotate in a magnetic field and are connected to the commutator.

Articulation the sharing of one bogie by adjacent ends of two vehicles.

Articulation steam locomotive having two sets of cylinders each driving an independent group of wheels supporting two sets of frames joined by a pivot or hinged joint.

Asynchronous an alternating current electric motor whose speed varies with load and has no fixed relation to the frequency of the supply.

ATC (Automatic Train Control) term covering various systems designed to assist the driver and provide against his mishandling or the misinterpretation of signals. Range from simple cab warning systems to fully automatic control.

ATO (Automatic Train Operation) system applied to some single purpose railways where the regulation of train working and train operation is undertaken automatically.

AWS (Automatic Warning System) British Rail's magnetic induction system for giving an audible indication of distant signal aspect to the driver. In the event of the signal being 'on', an automatic brake application is made unless the equipment is manually reset by the driver. A visual reminder is then displayed until passing the next set of magnets.

Axlebox box shaped casting of steel, bronze or cast iron, housing the axle bearing and its associated lubrication system. Working in vertical guides attached to the main frame, transmits the weight of the vehicle to the axle via the springs.

Back fire a malfunction in a mercury-arc rectifier when current is conducted in the wrong direction.

Back fire premature explosion in the cylinder, or explosion in the exhaust system, of an internal combustion engine.

Baggage car American term for luggage van.

Ballast material placed between the sleepers and formation of railway track to distribute the load of passing traffic, prevent lateral and longitudinal movement of the track, provide effective drainage and a convenient medium for maintaining level and gradient.

Ballast bed the layer of material spread over the formation on which the sleepers and track are laid.

Ballast materials crushed granite, whinstone, slag, limestone flints and ash are all materials in common use.

Banking assisting the working of a train, usually when ascending a gradient, by attaching one or more locomotives to the rear.

Baseplate a cast iron or steel plate which forms a bearing for the foot of flat-bottom rail. Spreads the load over a larger area of the sleeper than would be the case if the rail were placed directly on to it.

Battery-locomotive/railcar self-propelled electric vehicle which obtains electrical energy from storage batteries carried on the vehicle.

Bearings the bushing or metal block of anti-friction material which transmits the load via an oil film to a journal.

Bellows flexible ducting used for conveying cooling air to traction motors mounted on the bogie of an electric or diesel-electric locomotive.

Bellows flexible connection or corridor providing access from the end of one carriage to another.

Belt conveyor an endless belt running over rollers, used for carrying coal, gravel or similar loose material over considerable distances.

Belt transmission a means of transmitting power between two shafts some distance apart. The most usual types consist of endless flat or vee belts looped around pulleys attached to each shaft. The power transmitted depends upon the friction between belt and pulley.

Berne Gauge standard loading gauge for

main line railways on continent of Europe.

Berth bed in a sleeping carriage.

Bessemer a steel making process in which the excess carbon, manganese, silicon and phosphorous in the pig iron are slagged off by an air blast through the molten metal.

Bi-current locomotive designed to operate on two different electric current frequency systems.

Blade the movable portion of the switch rail, chamfered to fit closely against the stock rail, in a point or switch.

Blanketing the placing of a filter layer of sand between ballast and formation in areas where the presence of clay causes problems in maintaining good track condition.

Blast pipe (American, Exhaust Pipe) a vertical pipe usually of cast iron, bolted to the cylinder casting or saddle inside the smoke box in line with the chimney or smoke stack. Conveys the steam exhausted from the cylinders and products of combustion to the atmosphere inducing a partial vacuum in the smoke box and consequent 'pull' on the fire.

Block system space interval train working system whereby the line is divided into sections and only one train allowed to be in a section at a time.

Blowback flames entering the cab of a steam locomotive through the firehole as a result of the normal flow of hot gases from fire box to smoke box being reversed. May be caused by loss of smoke box vacuum, burst flue tube or superheater element.

Body shell basic body section of a vehicle without internal fittings.

Bogie (American, truck) independent short wheel base truck with four or six wheels, capable of pivoting about the centre at which it is attached to the underframe of long vehicles.

Boiler steam producing unit. Locomotive type consists essentially of a fire box surrounded by a water space in which the combustion of fuel takes place, and barrel containing the flue tubes surrounded by water.

Bolster transverse floating beam member of bogie suspension system supporting the weight of vehicle body.

Bolster wagon open freight vehicle fitted with one or more raised transverse beams on which the load is carried clear of the floor to facilitate loading and unloading.

Box car American term for van or covered freight vehicle.

Branch-line minor line acting as a feeder to main trunk lines.

Brush conductor, usually of carbon providing electrical contact with a sliding surface moving relative to it such as the commutator of a direct current machine.

Buffet car carriage equipped for serving light refreshments to passengers.

Bulk load freight in loose rather than packaged form.

Cable railway a system of train working by a cable connection to a stationary engine.

Caboose American term for brake or guard's van.

Cam reciprocating, oscillating or rotating body which imparts motion to another body known as a follower, with which it is in contact.

Camshaft a shaft which carried a series of cams for operating the inlet valves and exhaust valves of a diesel engine, contractors in some electric traction control gear systems.

Cant amount by which one rail of a curved track is raised above the other. Cant is 'positive' when the outer rail is higher than the inner rail and 'negative' when the inner rail is higher than the outer.

Cant deficiency the difference between the amount of cant provided and the amount of cant required to negotiate the curve at the maximum permitted speed without wheel flange to rail contact.

Cantrail longitudinal supporting member for carriage roof.

Car American term for a carriage or wagon.

Carriage passenger-carrying railway vehicle.

Catenary supporting cable for the contact or conductor wire of an overhead electrification system.

Caution indication given when a distant signal is in the 'on' or 'stop' position, advising the driver that at least one of the stop signals ahead is in the danger position.

CTC (Centralized Traffic Control) system developed for remote control, by coded electrical impulses on electro-magnetic stopper switches, of points and signals on single lines to eliminate need for signal boxes at crossing places. Now, since the introduction of electronic methods of code transmitting being applied to busy main lines.

Chair cast iron support for bull-head rail, affixed to a sleeper.

Check rail additional rail fixed to the

inside and parallel to the low rail on sharp curves to reduce wheel flange wear of the outer rail and the risk of the tyre climbing up and over the rail.

Chimney (American, Smoke stack) cast iron or fabricated steel pipe secured to the top of the smoke box, to convey the exhaust steam and products of combustion to the atmosphere.

Circuit breaker automatic switch for making and breaking an electrical circuit under normal or fault conditions.

Class of travel indication of the standards of comfort, facilities provided for passenger travel at different rates or fares for the same journey.

Clear signal fixed signal displaying a green, or proceed without restriction, aspect.

Clearance distance beyond stop signal protecting a junction, crossing or other area of confliction, from the fouling point. Allows for some degree of misjudgment in stopping at the signal without danger of collision.

Closed circuit TV television camera and receiver connected by cables to enable an operator to observe events occurring beyond visual limits.

Coasting running with power switched off or engine idling.

Cog wheel toothed wheel or pinion which engages with the rack laid between the running rails of a rack and pinion system mountain railway.

Coil one or more convolutions of bare on insulated wire which produce a magnetic force when subjected to an electrical current.

Collector shoe metal block in contact with conducted rail for collecting current from third rail electrification system.

Colour light signal fixed signal without arms displaying red, yellow or green aspects as required, sufficiently bright to be distinguished in daylight. Of two main types, 'multiple lens' and 'searchlight'.

Common carrier a transport organization which is not permitted to be selective in the freight accepted for conveyance. Required by law to carry, with very few exceptions, all traffic offered.

Common user freight vehicle in general use not confined to any particular traffic or route.

Commutator part of the armature of a direct current electrical machine upon which the brushes bear. Cylindrical assembly of copper segmented bars insulted from each other and connected to the coils of the armature winding.

Commuter holder of a railway season ticket. Term now generally applied to a person who travels by public or private transport daily between residence and place of work.

Communication cord chain or cord for pulling by a passenger to stop the train in an emergency. Connected to a valve in the braking system which when operated makes a partial application of the brake by venting the train pipe to atmosphere.

Compensation double-crank arrangement to nullify the effects of expansion and contraction of point rodding with changes in ambient temperature.

Composite coach/carriage vehicle with accommodation for more than one class of passenger.

Compression steam quantity of steam admitted to cylinder before completion of previous working stroke.

Compression stroke second piston stroke of four-stroke cycle diesel engine during which air charge in cylinder is compressed and heated by piston movement.

Compressor machine for raising the pressure of air above atmospheric. Provides compressed air for operation of brakes, auxiliaries and so on.

Concrete mixture of water, sand, stone and cement which hardens to a stone-like mass. Used as substitute for brick, stone, steel and other materials in many civil engineering applications.

Consist compostion or make up of a train.

Contactor remotely controlled switch used for frequently making and breaking electrical power circuits on load.

Continuous welded rail of any length greater than 60 metres (180 ft) formed from standard or short lengths of rail welded together.

Control focal point from which railway operations are directed on the basis of current information supplied from key points in the area of jurisdiction and adjacent area control centres.

COFC (American term) container on flat car.

Converter machine for converting electric power from alternating current to direct current or *vice versa.*

Conveyor equipment for moving sand, stone, coal, ore and other loose materials from point to point.

Core iron section around which is wound the coil of wire through which an electric current is passed to produce a magnetic force in an electro-magnet.

Couchette carriage with seats convertible into sleeping berths.

Coupling (American, Coupler) device for connecting vehicles together. Many types in common use, ranging from simple three link to automatic which may also provide electrical and air services connections.

Crank device for converting rotary to reciprocating motion or *vice versa.* Consists of an arm, one end of which is fixed to a shaft and the other free to rotate about the axis of the shaft.

Creep the tendency of rails to move gradually in the direction of traffic passing over them.

Cross-head solid or built up block of metal on slideways forming the connection between piston rod and connecting rod of a steam locomotive.

Crossing means by which a train on one line of track crosses another on same level.

Crossing loop additional line or loop on single line sections of railway to enable trains to cross or pass one another.

Crossover junction between two parallel railway tracks.

Current rate of flow of electricity round a circuit.

Curve classified as

1. *simple* – of one radius throughout
2. *compound* – two or more simple curves of similar flexure
3. *reverse* – a compound curve of contrary flexure.

Cut-off point in the piston-stroke at which the flow of steam to the cylinder is stopped.

Cycle series of events repeated in a regular sequence. Diesel engines operate on a two or four stroke cycle.

Damping reducing effects of shock loading or amplitude of vibrations.

Dead-end short section of running line terminating at buffer stops.

Dead head American term for non-fare paying passenger. Train crew on unbalanced working returning to home depot as passenger.

Dead-man's handle device for cutting off power and applying the brakes in the event of the driver becoming incapacitated whilst driving.

Dead section length of conductor in an electrified railway system which is not energised.

Dead weight static load or weight of stationary train.

Deck American term for cab floor or footplate.

Deflector plate protruding into firebox from firehole doorway to deflect secondary air flow downwards towards firebed.

Deflectors plates, usually affixed to the smoke box sides on a steam locomotive to induce an upward air flow and carry exhaust from chimney clear of the cab.

Demurrage penalty charge imposed on the trader for exceeding the time permitted for loading or discharging a freight vehicle.

Depreciation allowance made for loss in value due to age, decay, wear and tear.

Description system for advising the signalman of the classification and route of trains approaching his area of control. Possibly by coded bell signals or illuminated display.

Detector mechanical or electrical device for proving the correct operation of points before associated signals may be cleared.

Diagram display in diagrammatic form of trackwork and signals controlled by a signalbox. The display may provide illuminated indications of signal and point operation, train positions and descriptions.

Diesel compression ignition, internal combustion engine.

Direct current (dc) electrical current which flows in one direction continuously.

Direct drive direct mechanical connection between output end of prime mover and driving wheels of locomotive.

Disc brake braking mechanism utilizing friction pads applied by caliper action to a disc secured to vehicle axle or wheel centre.

Disc signal subsidiary signal for controlling shunting movements in a station area. Usually in the form of a white disc with red stripe capable of being rotated through 45°.

Divergence railway junction.

Dolly subsidiary signal.

Dome reservoir on top of the boiler barrel of a steam locomotive for collecting dry steam and housing the regulator or throttle valve.

Dome coach carriage with glass roofed upper section to facilitate scenic observation.

Double deck vehicle with two floors or levels.

Double end locomotive with a driving cab at both ends.

Double end type of marshalling yard with sorting sidings having inlet and outlet lines at either end.

Double head to attach a second locomotive to the front of a train.

Double slip curved switches making connections across both obtuse angles of a diamond crossing.

Down usually the line of track which carries trains in a direction away from the town or city in which the headquarters of the railway company are located.

Down grade American term for falling gradient – downhill.

Drawbar (American, Draft iron) device

for connecting locomotive to tender or to train.

Drive transmission of power.

Drop side type of open wagon where the vertical side is hinged horizontally and can be lowered to facilitate loading and unloading.

Dual control operated or controlled from two separate positions.

Dual gauge track able to accommodate vehicles of two different wheel gauges. Usually achieved by the laying of a third length of rail, one being common to both gauges.

Dump car American term for tipping body wagon.

Dynamic braking system of braking utilizing the braking characteristics of the engine compression, transmission or traction motors.

Dynamic loading load applied to track or structure by vehicle in motion passing over it.

Dynamo direct current electrical machine used for charging batteries and providing current for carriage lighting.

Dynamometer device for measuring the forces which tend to change the state of rest or uniform motion of a body.

Dynamometer car vehicle with equipment for measuring and recording draw-bar pull, horsepower, speed, and so on, of a locomotive under load.

Dwarf signal miniature subsidiary signal.

Earth electrical connection to complete a circuit.

Earthworks alterations to the land form to provide a near level track bed.

Eccentric disc, keyed to a shaft or axle whose centre does not coincide with that of the axle. It rotates inside a ring, known as an eccentric strap, to which is attached the eccentric rod, and imparts reciprocating motion to a link for operating the steam distribution valve to the cylinder.

Electric traction haulage of vehicles by electric-motor-driven unit utilizing electric power obtained from batteries or an external source via conductor wire or rail.

Embankment ridge of earth or rock to raise the natural ground level.

Emergency brakes application, with minimum delay, of maximum possible

braking power when stopping the train is of paramount importance.

Empty running American term for empty stock working; train conveying empty vehicles only.

End-loading design specification for forces applied to end of vehicle which must be withstood without permanent deformation.

End post vertical structural member or pillar supporting end section of vehicle body.

End-shocks shock loadings applied to the ends of vehicles due to impact, traction and braking forces.

Energy capacity for doing work.

Entrance – exit see *N X*.

Equalize to balance the load, pressure, contents, force, in different parts of a system. Compensated wheel springing.

European wagon pool agreement between some continental railway systems for pooling the use of wagons on international services to obtain maximum utilization under load.

Exchange movement of wagons between systems which may involve changing of wheel sets to suit different track gauge.

Exhaust steam emission of steam from the cylinder after completion of the working stroke.

Expansion of steam increase in volume of steam in the cylinder after the supply has been cut off. The ability to take maximum advantage of the expansive qualities of steam results in economies in the consumption of fuel and water.

Expansion gap space left between rail ends to allow for expansion.

Express fast train stopping at few intermediate stations.

Facing points switches which enable a choice of route to be taken in the direction of travel.

Fairing structure or cover to provide a smooth surface and reduce air resistance.

Fan group of sidings diverging or radiating from one line.

Feed supply with fuel or water, electrical current or other power source.

Field space around a magnet or a conductor carrying an electric current where magnetic lines of force may be detected.

Firebox part of a steam locomotive boiler where combustion of the fuel takes place.

Fireless locomotive (American, Steam storage locomotive) Steam locomotive of conventional design but with the steam producing boiler replaced by a reservoir charged with high-pressure steam from an external source.

Fireman (American, Stoker) member of the steam locomotive crew who feeds the firegrate with fuel.

Fishplates pieces of metal for joining rail lengths together. Fitted on either side of the web of adjacent rails and held together by fish bolts passing through holes in the fish plates and rail webs.

Fitted wagon freight vehicle equipped with remotely operated power brakes.

Fixed distant caution signal in the 'on' position which cannot be pulled 'off'.

Fixed signal semaphore, colour light or subsidiary signal in a fixed location.

Flag station at which trains only stop when specifically signalled to do so.

Flange projecting edge or rim on the periphery of a wheel or rail.

Flash method of electric resistance welding frequently employed for joining lengths of rail together.

Flat wagon freight vehicle with no structure above the level deck or floor.

Flat wheel flat area on wheel tread resulting from the wheel's locking and sliding along the rail during vehicle braking.

Flat rail flat area on head of rail caused by wheel slip or slide.

Flyover bridge carrying one route over another to avoid conflicting train movements.

Fly shunt method of speeding up shunting or sorting of wagons by giving them sufficient momentum to enable vehicle(s) to roll to desired position after uncoupling from locomotive.

Fly wheel wheel with a heavy rim which acts as an energy reservoir and is used to limit fluctuations in speed of an engine during each cycle.

Fog signal detonator placed on the rail which is exploded by pressure of wheel of vehicle passing over it to give audible warning to driver when observation of signals is obscured by fog.

Footplate (American, Deck) cab floor or operating platform of steam locomotive.

Force that which the locomotive is capable of exerting at the driving wheel treads. Frequently referred to as tractive effort, may be calculated for simple expansion steam locomotives from

$$T = \frac{N\ D^2}{2W} SP$$

where

T = tractive force; D = cylinder diameter; S = piston stroke; P = mean effective pressure on piston, usually taken as 75 per cent or 85 per cent of boiler working pressure; N = number of cylinders; W = diameter of driving wheels.

Formation surface of the ground on which the railway is constructed.
Formation make up of a train of vehicles.
Four-foot way space between running rails of standard gauge, 1,435 mm (4 ft 8½ in) track.
Frame foundation or chassis upon which steam locomotive is built. British practice to use deep, steel plate frames, substantially braced; American, open bar frames or cast steel bedplate incorporating cylinders and drag box.
Frame structure supporting point and signal operating levers in mechanical signal box.
Frequency number of times a second an alternating electric current reverses its direction of flow.
Friction force of resistance to relative motion.
Frog American term for common crossing which allows running rails to cross each other on the level at an angle of less than 90°.
Funicular cable operated way with ascending and descending vehicles counterbalanced for use in mountainous regions.

Gallery American term for upper deck of double-deck passenger vehicle.
Gallery American term for freight vehicles with two or three decks or floor levels.
Gallery American term for signal gantry.
Gangway passage between rows of seats or one giving access between vehicles.
Gantry structure supporting fixed signals.
Gap break in continuity of conductor rail.
Gas turbine rotary internal combustion machine driven by gas flow causing varied disc(s) mounted on common shaft to turn at high speed.
Gauge standard measure; the distance between running edges or inner faces of the rails of railway track.
Generator electrical machine which changes mechanical energy into electrical energy. Term generally applied to one which produces direct current.
Generator automatic oil fired steam producer fitted to diesel locomotives where there is a requirement for passenger vehicles to be steam heated.

Girder load carrying beam of metal or concrete construction which may be of solid, lattice, web or other construction.
Governor device for maintaining as closely as possible a constant engine crankshaft speed over long periods during which the load on the engine may vary.
Grade/gradient slope or inclination to the horizontal of a railway. Expressed in degrees from the horizontal, as a percentage, or unit rise or fall to the horizontal or slope length.
Graduate to perform in measured portions.
Gravity shunting wagon sorting or train marshalling undertaken on a falling gradient without the aid of a shunting locomotive or switcher.
Gross weight total weight of train including payload.
Ground signal low level fixed subsidiary signal.
Grouping amalgamation of the major railway companies in England, Scotland & Wales to form the LMS, LNE, GW and S railways on 1st January 1923.
Guard (American, Conductor) person in charge of a train.

Halt stopping place, without normal station facilities, for local train services.
Handbrake means of applying the brake blocks to the wheel treads without power assistance. Usually in the form of a screwed shaft with a running nut, attached to the brake gearing.
Hand signal method of communication by hand lamp, flag, movement or position of hand or arm.
Headroom clearance between the highest point of a railway vehicle and underside of an overhead structure.
Headstock main lateral end member of a carriage or wagon underframe to which the buffers and drawgear may be attached.
Headway interval between successive trains on same line.
Heating of trains usually effected by one of three methods:
1. steam-fed radiators
2. electric-resistance heaters
3. hot-air circulation from oil-fired combustion heaters.
Heating surface areas of locomotive

boiler exposed to heat on one side and available for water evaporation on other. Firebox and tube heating surfaces usually expressed separately.
Heel fixed end or pivot point of switch rail.
High-pressure steam boiler pressure in a compound locomotive, or above about 200 psi in a simple locomotive.
Home signal semaphore stop signal, located close to signal box controlling entrance to next block section, station or junction area. In complicated track lay outs there may also be outer and inner home signals.
Hopper freight vehicle with facility for discharging load through floor.
Horse power a unit of power equal to 75 kg metres per sec, 33,000 ft per lb per min, or 746 watts.
Hot box an overheated vehicle axlebox bearing resulting from breakdown of lubricating film between bearing and journal.
Hump yard marshalling yard with artificial mound or hump over which wagons are propelled and then gravitate to correct siding and position in the yard.
Hydraulic relating to the controlled flow of liquids.

Induction production of an electric current by change of magnetic field.
Injector device for forcing water into the boiler of a steam locomotive. Consists essentially of three cones, steam, combining and delivery. Steam at high velocity from the converging steam cone comes into contact with the cold feed water and resultant condensation causes a partial vacuum. The water is thus drawn into the converging combining cone at considerable speed. Completion of the condensation process there results in a solid jet of hot water flowing at high velocity into the diverging delivery cone. The velocity energy is then converted into sufficient pressure energy to lift the clack valve against boiler pressure and enter the boiler.
Injector device for feeding atomized fuel oil into cylinder or combustion chamber of a diesel engine.
Inspection car self propelled service vehicle used for inspecting track.
Insulate isolate an electrical conductor

by the inter-position of a non-conductor to restrict the current flow to a definite path.

Integral construction carriage construction where the body and underframe form one stress and load carrying structure.

Interchange point, or the exchange, of passengers or freight between trains or modes of transport.

Interfrigo International railway-owned company for refrigerated transport which allocates and controls a fleet of special vehicles throughout Europe.

Interlocking basic requirement of signalling installations. Ensures operation of points and signals are so interlocked that signals can only be cleared if points are correctly set and opposing signals are at danger. Also prevents setting up of conflicting movements. Three general methods of interlocking:
1. mechanical arrangement of locking tappets and dogs
2. electro-magnetic locks on the levers
3. electric relays and circuits.

International Union of Railways (UIC) a body founded in 1922 with the objective of standardization and improvement of railway equipment and operating methods.

Isolating process of separation by operation of valves, switches or circuit breakers. Particularly relevant to maintenance of overhead wire or third-rail conductors on electrified lines, when supply needs to be cut off from a section to ensure safe working conditions whilst trains are operating on adjacent lines or sections.

Jacket American term for outer covering of thin sheet steel over the lagging material of a locomotive boiler, cylinder or other insulated heat radiating surface.

Journal area of a shaft or axle supported by a bearing.

Journal log compiled by the guard of the make-up and events of train/movement.

Key wedge of hard wood or spring steel inserted between rail and chair to hold rail firmly in position at correct gauge.

Kinetic energy the energy of a moving body due to its mass and velocity.

Ladder American term for marshalling yard or siding layout where a series of points or switches follow each other giving leads off a straight line to one side.

Ladder term sometimes given to rack rail of mountain railway system.

L C L (Less than Car Load) American term for less than a full freight vehicle load or, sundries traffic.

Lease/Leave/Wayleave contract by which right of way is granted to pass over land for a specified period of time. Payment often based on amount of traffic carried over line or land.

Level crossing crossing of two railways, or a railway and road, on the same level.

Lifting barrier alternative to gates at a level crossing consisting of a pivoted boom which is manually, remotely or automatically raised or lowered across the roadway.

Light engine locomotive running without a train.

Lighting of carriages by axle driven dynamo, capable of generating when rotated in either direction. Also charges the batteries which supply lighting power when the train is stationary or running slowly.

Limit of shunt board marking the point beyond which vehicles must not pass during shunting operations.

Lining maintaining the correct track alignment.

Lining covering over rock or soil of a tunnel to prevent collapse.

Live rail electrical conductor for transmitting power to locomotives or train on third-rail electrified lines.

Load factor the ratio of actual train loading to maximum capacity.

Loading gauge the limiting dimensions of height and width of rolling stock and loads carried to ensure adequate clearance with lineside structures.

Local control arrangement whereby relay room, which normally automatically initiates operation of points and signals on command from remote power box can, in emergencies, be put under local control.

Local line line of track normally exclusively used by suburban or stopping passenger trains.

Lock and block signalling system in which signals can only be cleared when the preceding train has operated treadles on clearing the block section.

Locking bar long length of bar lying along the inside edge of running rails on the immediate approach to mechanically operated facing points. Connected to the point lock so that withdrawal of the bolt raises the bar into the flangeway and thus prevents movement of point blades whilst a train is passing.

Lodging turn period of duty which finishes at a depot other than that at which the person is based.

Long stroke piston stroke greater than 760 mm (26 in).

Long welded rail standard or short lengths of rail welded together to form a rail of up to 60 metres (180 ft) in length.

Longitudinals vehicle underframe structural members running lengthwise inside sole bars, from transoms or headstocks.

Loop additional running line with inlet and outlet controlled from one signal box.

Loop continuous circular connection between up and down lines at terminal station or yard enabling trains to reverse direction without releasing locomotive.

Loose coupled vehicles of a train loosely coupled together with three link couplings.

Low-pressure steam exhaust steam from high-pressure cylinders of compound locomotive or, boiler working pressure below about 200 psi in simple locomotive.

Lubricating oil viscous liquid introduced between moving surfaces to reduce friction.

Mail train express train including mail carrying vehicles which may have provision for letter sorting en route.

Main line primary trunk route or running line used by fastest or most important trains.

Main track American term for 'main line'.

Manganese rail rails made of steel containing more than 1 per cent of manganese making it appreciably tougher than ordinary steel.

Manifest list of wagons in a freight train.

Manual block operation of block system by manual means whereby signalmen in adjacent boxes communicate by block telegraph instruments and bells, with points and signals worked mechanically.

Marshalling yard area where wagons are sorted, assembled and marshalled into trains.

Mast slender tower structure used for supporting electric traction catenary, lighting fittings, cables and so on at a height.

Match wagon empty flat wagon coupled to vehicle carrying load which overhangs the headstock or, intermediate wagon used to enable vehicles with non-compatible draw gear to be coupled.

Mercury arc static device employing a mercury pool cathode for converting alternating to direct current.

Metro underground railway system for mass conveyance of short journey passengers.

Mineral wagon vehicle purpose designed for the conveyance of minerals, particularly coal, iron ore.

Mixed train consisting of both freight – and passenger – carrying vehicles.

Monocoque vehicle structure with underframe and body designed to form a single unit on aircraft construction principles.

Monorail railway system where the track consists of a single rail.

Motion movement; a moving mechanism; the valve gear of a steam locomotive.

Motor bogie bogie having driving wheels or motored axles.

Motor generator set electric motor and generator mechanically coupled for the purpose of converting direct current from one voltage to another.

Motorman driver of an electric tram, railcar or multiple-unit train.

Motor points points or switches remotely operated by an air or electric point motor.

Mountain railway specialized form of railway for ascending mountains.

Movable crossing track crossing having a swing-nose which presents a continuous running rail for the wheel tread. Eliminates the normal gap at crossing nose and permits use of high speed turnouts.

Multiple-aspect signalling (MAS) a system of colour light signalling, that could be provided either by multi-lens, or searchlight signals in which each signal unit can display more than two aspects.

Multi-system or voltage locomotive locomotive designed to operate on more than one electrical system.

Multiple track a section of railway track having more than just one up line and one down line.

Multiple unit two or more locomotives or powered vehicles coupled together, or in a train, operated by only one driver.

Narrow gauge railway track of less than the standard gauge.

Nominal rating full load output of machine capable of being sustained for continuous period of 12 hours without distress.

Normal usual position of points or signals before action initiated by signalman to allow a train movement.

Nose apex of vee of converging running rails in direction of travel over a crossing.

Nose-suspended motor traction motor mounted on bearings on axle being driven, with a 'nose' resiliantly fixed to a bogie cross member to prevent rotation round axle. Gear on axle is in constant mesh with pinion on armature shaft.

Notch intermediate position of electric traction power controller; indentation in manual signal box lever frame to hold lever in position.

N X Entrance – Exit system of signalling where operation of points and signals is initiated from track diagram by a switch adjacent to signal at entrance to route and push button at appropriate exit. Operation of intermediate points and signals and protection against conflicting moves is automatically carried out through circuit interlocking.

Observation car passenger-carrying vehicle, usually at rear of train, with windows and seating arranged to give maximum view of passing scenery.

Obtuse crossing track arrangement with one line crossing another on the level at an obtuse (more than 90° but less than 180°) angle.

Occupied term used to signify the presence of a train in a block section.

'Off' and 'on' terms applied to the aspect of signals, 'off' signifying clear or proceed, 'on' caution or stop.

One-hour rating 10 per cent above nominal rating which machine should be able to sustain for continuous period of up to one hour without distress.

Open line section of line where the normal position of signals is 'off'.

Open point type of switch or point which may be set with neither switch blade against a stock rail.

O S Sh D Organization for the collaboration of railways international organization of communist bloc countries for the development of road and rail traffic and exchange of information between member countries.

Out-of-gauge vehicle or load which exceeds the loading gauge limits.

Outer home signal stop signal farthest in rear of home signal controlled from same signal box.

Outer suburban passenger train serving the most outlying limits of a city.

Overhead catenary and contact wire of a suspended electrical distribution system.

Overlap distance (usually ¼ mile) beyond home signal which must be clear before signalman can accept a train from signal box in rear.

Over-ride take precedence over; manual control over a normally automatic operation.

Over-run travel beyond normal stopping point; length of line provided for specific purpose of accommodating a train failing to stop at correct place.

Over-speed trip mechanism for stopping a diesel engine in event of excessive crankshaft rotational speed.

Packing oil absorbing material used to assist the lubrication of an axle bearing.

Packing material placed in the gland to maintain a leak free joint when subjected to pressure.

Packing maintaining the correct level of sleepers by adjustments in the amount of ballast beneath.

Pallet portable platform for the transport or storage of loads.

Panel desk or board in power signal box on which operating switches for points and signals are mounted.

Pantograph link between overhead contact system and power circuit of an electric locomotive or multiple unit through which the power required is transmitted. Simplest form is spring loaded pivoted diamond frame with copper or carbon contact strip.

Parlor car American term for luxuriously fitted railway carriage.

Part load less than wagon load.

Parallel connection electrical conductors or circuits so connected that the sum of the currents in the individual conductors or circuits is equal to the total current supplied.

Passing loop short double line section of single line railway to allow trains to pass one another.

Path line on train-planning graph representing running of a particular train from point to point.

Pay load that part of the total weight of the train which is revenue earning; excluding weight of empty vehicles and locomotive.

Peak hour period of time when traffic levels are greatest.

Pedestal frame support for shelf on which block instruments are placed in signal box.

Pendular suspension carriage suspension system allowing body to tilt to counteract effects of cant deficiency on curves.

Percentage cut-off portion of the piston stroke or travel during which steam is admitted to the cylinder, expressed as a percentage of the total length of stroke.

Permissive block system whereby more than one train is permitted to enter a block section under caution.

Permissive signal controlling the enrance to a line on which permissive block working applies.

Pick-up electric current collector.

Pick-up freight train which stops at intermediate points to pick up or put off freight vehicles on an as required basis.

Piggyback system for conveying road vehicles on railway flat cars or wagons.

Pilot American term for cowcatcher.

Pilot additional locomotive coupled to the front of the train locomotive to provide assistance over a heavily graded section of line.

Piston valve inside or outside admission steam distribution valve with two piston heads spaced on a spindle and fitted with rings to maintain steam tightness.

Plate girder riveted or welded steel girder built up from vertical web plates with angles at their extremities forming compression and tension flanges.

Platelayer track maintenance man.

Play clearance, gap or freedom of movement between sliding surfaces.

Pneumatic operated by air pressure.

Point assembly of trackwork including a tapered movable rail by which a train is directed from one line to another.

Point heater electric or gas heater fitted to rail switches to prevent maloperation due to ice, frost or snow.

Point lock mandatory equipment on facing points of passenger-carrying lines. Usually consists of two slots in the stretcher bar connecting the two point blades, into either of which the lock bolt fits. The bolt is operated by a locking lever in the signal box and is also detected ensuring the relevant signal cannot be cleared unless the points are fully closed and securely locked.

Points man person who operates points manually.

Pole simple means of collecting electric current from an overhead wire, often used on street cars and low speed locomotives.

Pony truck two-wheeled pivoted truck to assist the guidance of a locomotive around curves.

Poppett valve independent inlet and exhaust valve operated by camshaft giving improved steam distribution and reduced back pressure compared with reciprocating valve gears.

Pool to share traffic, receipts, use of resources and so on.

Port aperture through which steam flows from steam chest to cylinder of a steam locomotive. Opened and closed by operation of the valve and valve gear.

Power signal box place where signals are controlled and routes set up by other than mechanical or manual means.

Power to weight ratio of power output of a locomotive to its total weight.

Preselector means of selecting or setting in advance of when required.

Primary suspension connecting system or mechanism between vehicle wheels and bogie or body frames or, in the absence of secondary suspension, between wheels and total load.

Private owner freight vehicle not owned by a railway company but permitted to run over its lines.

Private sidings siding or line connected with railway system but provided and maintained at expense of traders whose premises are exclusively served by it.

Privilege reduced rate travel ticket for employees of railway company.

Profile outline of vertical cross section of a shape or structure. Maintenance of correct wheel tread and flange profile within laid down limits is necessary to obtain good vehicle riding.

Programme machine means of regulating traffic working automatically on a single purpose railway by use of punched tape carrying train service details initiating operation of junction points.

Protection in case of obstruction of running line, protection is given by placing detonators on rails to give audible warning to drivers of approaching trains. The fitting of track circuit clips across a pair of rails puts automatic signals in rear to danger.

Prototype original or preliminary version of new product.

Proving electrical or mechanical means of checking correct operation of points or signals.

Pull-off operation of changing the aspect of a signal to proceed.

Pull-off amount by which overhead contact wire is displaced from track centre line by registration arm.

Pullman car railway carriage providing a high standard of comfort and service for which a supplementary fare must be paid.

Push–pull method of operating whereby the locomotive may be other than at the head of the train, although controlled from the head.

Race inner and outer parts of roller or ball bearing forming tracks on which rollers or balls run.

Rack rail rail with regular teeth or indentations with which a gear or cog wheel meshes on mountain railway systems.

Rack gear system used on mountain railways where gradient is too steep for smooth steel wheel on steel rail adhesion to be effective. Locomotive runs on normal rails but is propelled by prime mover driving one or more pinions or cogs which mesh with rack rail laid between running rails. Various systems in use employing vertical or horizontal pinions with single or double toothed racks.

Radial axle wheeled axle pivoted about a fixed radius.

Radial bolster swivelling bolster fitted to single bolster wagon to facilitate carrying of long loads by two such vehicles round curves.

Radio communication system of voice communication employing radio transmitting and receiving units.

Rail brake (American, Car retarder) longitudinal beams, parallel to rail, that when applied move inwards and grip the wheels of a wagon as it passes through. Used in mechanical marshalling yards.

Rail car self-propelled passenger carrying vehicle.

Rail head 1. outermost point reached by a railway

2. interchange point between rail and road transport

3. top portion of a rail on which the wheel tread bears.

Railroad American term for railway.

Rake collection of coupled vehicles.

Ram form of single acting piston where head subjected to pressure is of same diameter as rod. Used in hydraulic systems.

Rapid transit system for the high speed urban transport of passengers, often underground.

Rated output manufacturer's specification of performance of a machine.

Reception track line on which trains are received prior to marshalling or sorting.

Rectifier device for converting alternating electric current to direct current.

Reducing valve mechanism for reducing steam at boiler pressure to approximately 60 psi for carriage heating purposes.

Reefer American term for refrigerated wagon.

Refrigerated wagon freight vehicle equipped for keeping contents at below freezing temperature.

Refuge siding dead end siding entered through a trailing connection used for holding a train for others to pass.

Regenerative brake electrical braking system whereby the traction motors of direct current electric locomotives work as generators and feed electrical energy back into supply system.

Registration arm cantilever which gives contact wire an offset in relation to track centre line in overhead electrification system.

Regulator (American, Throttle) valve for controlling the flow of steam from boiler to steam chest of a steam locomotive.

RIC International Carriage and Van Union founded in 1921 and based in Switzerland.

RIV International Wagon Union founded 1921, based in Switzerland.

Relay remotely controlled electromagnetic switch for low electrical currents. Used to make and break circuits which in turn may operate power circuits, other relays and so forth.

Relay renew trackwork.

Repeater indicator in a signal box to advise the signalman of the correct operation of signals which are out of sight.

Repeater signal generally of the banner type consisting of a large glazed circular case containing a centre pivoted arm. Used to give an advanced indication of the aspect of a signal whose normal sighting is restricted by some permanent obstruction.

Re-railing equipment to facilitate the re-railing of derailed vehicles, includes high capacity rail mounted cranes and power operated jacks. A ramp, forming an inclined path to guide a derailed wheel back onto the rail is a frequently used item of equipment for dealing with minor derailments.

Resilient baseplate pad of resilient material such as rubber bonded cork, inserted between foot of flat bottom rail and sleeper or paved continuous track bed.

Resistance force, opposing motion; that which opposes the flow of current in an electric circuit, measured in ohms. Used to dissipate surplus electrical energy in form of heat.

Retarder equipment for regulating the speed of freight vehicles running down a hump in mechanized marshalling yards. Another name for rail brake.

Return crank and rod components of outside Walschaert valve gear which transmit motion from the crank pin to expansion link.

Reversing station point where train reverses direction of travel during course of journey. May be at normal dead-end or terminal station layout or on zig-zag section of steeply graded line.

Rheostat variable resistance for regulating the flow of electric current.

Rheostat braking electrical braking system whereby the traction motors work as generators, the resultant electrical energy being dissipated as heat in resistances.

Right of way precedence given to one train to proceed before another.

Rigid wheel base horizontal distance between the centres of the first and last axles held rigidly in alignment with each other; the coupled wheels of a steam locomotive.

Roller bearing hardened steel cylinders located in a cage which revolve in contact with inner and outer races.

Rolling stock carriages and wagons; railway vehicles.

Roomette single compartment in a sleeping car.

Roster duty list giving details of time of starting and work to be undertaken.

Rotor rotating part of an electrical (usually alternating current) machine.

Round house engine shed in which the locomotive stabling berths radiate from a turntable.

Route indicator multiple lamp panel attached to a junction signal to indicate which of a variety of possible routes has been set up. By illuminating the lamps in groups, figures or letters can be formed, eliminating the need for a multiplicity of signals.

Route setting power signalling system whereby operation of one lever controls a complete route from one stop signal to the next.

Route relay interlocking system of power signalling utilizing principle of route control of point and signals with electric circuit interlocking and operation by small thumb switches rather than levers.

Route release system whereby a route previously set up may be cancelled or reset after a certain time has elapsed (usually two minutes for main signals and half a minute for subsidiary). Sectional release enables the route set up to be cleared and reset in stages as the train proceeds without having to await clearance of the complete route.

Ruling gradient limiting gradient (and therefore train load) for traction and braking capacities.

Run-away train or vehicle running out of control.

Run-round facilities for, or operation of, changing the position of the locomotive from one end of the train to the other.

Running gear term generally applied to the wheels, axles, axleboxes, springs, frames of a railway vehicle.

Running light locomotive movement without a train attached.

Running line on which trains are run, not sidings.

Safe load maximum load which may be applied without undue risk.

Safety valve directly connected to the steam space of all boilers and set to operate automatically at a pre-determined pressure to release excess steam.

Saloon type of carriage with seats provided in open area rather than in separate compartments. The term also applied to special vehicles used by railway officers for inspection purposes.

Sand fine granular material carried in locomotive sand boxes from which it is fed by pipes to the rail ahead of the driving wheels to prevent them from slipping.

Scavenge to remove the products of combustion from an internal combustion engine cylinder by a regulated flow of air.

Scissor crossing junction between two parallel railway tracks enabling trains to cross over from one to the other in either direction.

Screening ballast operation of passing ballast over a sieve to eliminate small pieces and dirt.

Screw coupling one method of coupling railway vehicles tightly together. Consists of two links or shackles joined together by a screwed shaft with right and left handed threads and a lever for turning the screw.

Screw spike formal name for threaded rail spike.

Season ticket railway ticket giving any number of journeys over a specified route during period of validity.

Secondary winding output side of a transformer.

Semaphore type of fixed signal with a pivoted arm which can be raised or lowered as required. Of two general types, 'upper' and 'lower' quadrant. In both, the arm in a horizontal position denotes 'on', 'stop', or 'danger'.

Semi-conductor material used in electric traction rectifiers, whose electrical resistance depends on the direction of the applied voltage. Germanium and silicon are typical examples.

Semi-trailer trailer having wheels at rear only and supported by towing vehicle at front.

Series connection electrical conductors or circuits so connected that the same current flows in each conductor or circuit.

Series-parallel connection method of connecting traction motors whereby individual motors are connected in series to form groups and each group then connected in parallel.

Series motor direct current electrical machine with ideal traction characteristics. Produces a high torque when the vehicle is started and as the load increases the speed drops.

Service coach carriage used for railway departmental purposes, not in public use.

Service life expected working life of a component before replacement required.

Service track line on which servicing or maintenance operations are carried out or one giving access to area of such operations.

Servo control system whereby a small amount of effort is augmented to do a large amount of work.

Set out mark out track alignment and/or positions of switches and crossings with pegs prior to relaying operations.

Shock absorber telescopic hydraulic device for damping spring suspensions.

Shoe brake simple arrangement for applying a retarding or braking force to the periphery of a rotating drum or wheel, by pressure of a block of wood, metal or friction material against it.

Short circuit point of very low resistance in an electrical circuit usually, if accidental, resulting from insulation failure.

Short haul movement of freight traffic over a short distance.

Shoulder ballast laid against the ends of sleepers to prevent lateral movement of the track.

Shunt direct onto a minor track; marshal vehicles into a particular order.

Shuttle train which gives a frequent return service over a short route.

Side corridor passenger carrying vehicle with connecting corridor between compartments along one side.

Siding line used for temporary stabling or accommodation of vehicles or trains.

Signal means of controlling the movement of trains by warning or advising the driver of the occupational state of the line ahead or intention to divert to another route or line.

Signal box (American, Tower) building housing equipment for operation of points and signals in a particular area or section of route.

Silo American term for sand storage tower for filling locomotive sand boxes.

Single-line working system of operation whereby trains may be safely worked in either direction over a single line of railway. Maintenance of absolute block working ensured by each section of line having a unique staff or token which must be carried by every train passing over it. The single line working apparatus includes many staffs and tokens which are *unique* in that only one can be extracted from the apparatus at a time for each section.

Single-phase single alternating electric current. One phase of three-phase supply.

Six-footway area between parallel railway tracks.

Skew bridge spans obliquely and is therefore longer than the square gap.

Slab track rails laid on a continuous concrete or asphalt base instead of conventional sleepers and ballast, to minimize settlement and changes in alignment, thus reducing maintenance costs.

Sleeper steel, wood or precast concrete beam for holding the rails to correct gauge and distributing to the ballast the load imposed by passing trains.

Slide bar (American, Guide) steam locomotive piston crosshead guideway. The slide bar may be formed of one, two, three or four parallel bars in line with cylinder bore.

Slide valve outside admission distribution valve of inverted 'u' section held onto port face of steam chest by pressure of steam.

Slip 1. loss of adhesion between driving wheel and rail causing wheels to spin
2. short curved connecting line joining lines which cross one another on the level
3. driving member rotating at a higher speed than driven in a fluid coupling.

Slotted signal semaphore signal having home and distant arms on same post, but controlled from different signal boxes. To prevent operation of distant before home arm is cleared, balance weights and a slot bar are provided on the signal post.

Slow order written instruction given to train driver to reduce speed at a particular location, usually because of track condition.

Smalls less than wagon load or sundries traffic.

Smoke box extension to barrel at the front end of a locomotive boiler housing the main steam pipes to cylinders, blast pipe, blower ring and chimney. Other fittings may include superheater header, regulator, spark arrester.

Snifting valve designed to admit air into the steam circuit when the regulator is closed. Prevents creation of a vacuum by action of the piston, with resultant drawing of smoke box ash into the cylinders and burning of the superheater elements.

Snow fence solid fence structure erected on the line side in exposed areas to prevent snow drifts blocking the line.

Snow plough special vehicle propelled by, or attachment to, front of locomotive to remove snow from railway. The snow plough may be of simple wedge shape or rotary type.

Snow shed substantially built shed with sloping roof erected over the railway to provide a path for avalanches without blocking the line.

Solebar longitudinal main frame outer member of carriage or wagon underframe, usually of channel section.

Soleplate longitudinal main frame member of fabricated or built up carriage bogie, usually of standard rolled steel section or pressings. Also a plate inserted between the chairs and the sleeper at a pair of points to maintain the correct gauge and prevent any spreading of the gauge that might occur from the gradual enlargement of the spike holes in the wooden sleepers.

Spark arrester device, usually in the form of a mesh or baffle plate fitted in the smoke box to prevent the emission of live coals and sparks from the chimney or smoke stack.

Special train one not shown in the working time table or pre-planned.

Speedometer instrument giving a continuous indication of vehicle speed.

Spike square section heavy steel nail driven into wooden sleeper to affix flanged rail in position.

Spot American term – to marshall or shunt.

Stabling accommodating for a short period of time.

Staff wooden staff which must be carried by each train travelling on single line section of railway branch line to maintain absolute block working and prevent possibility of head-on collision.

Stagger interlacing of sleepers at switches and crossing or, making rail joints in one running rail not to coincide with those in other rail.

Stall to come to a stand under power. Occurs when train resistance exceeds tractive power.

Standard gauge most common distance between rails in a country.

Steam vapour of water resulting from the application of heat. The temperature at which the water boils is dependent upon the pressure to which it is subjected but steam produced remains in saturated form whilst in contact with water from which generated.

Stephenson valve gear or link motion for each valve there are two eccentrics fitted to the crank axle, which impart a reciprocating motion through eccentric rods to a slotted expansion link. The fore-gear eccentric rod is coupled to the top, and back gear to the bottom of the expansion link, which in turn is suspended by lifting links from the reversing shaft. In the slot of the expansion link is a die block which is connected to the valve spindle by an intermediate valve rod. Operation of the reversing gear in the cab lowers or raises the expansion link which, in turn, transfers the movement of fore or back gear eccentric rods to the valve. In the mid-gear position the link oscillates about the die block and imparts a reciprocating movement to the valve equal to twice the steam lap plus twice the steam lead. A feature of the Stephenson valve gear is that the steam lead is greatest at mid-gear and minimum at full forward or backward gear.

Stock car American term for vehicle used for the conveyance of cattle.

Streamlining special shaping of vehicles to minimize air resistance.

Stretcher bar connecting two switch blades to hold them in the correct position relative to the stock rails and gauge.

Stub American term for short dead end siding.

Stub axle short non-revolving axle which supports only one wheel.

Sub-station point in electricity distribution system where supply is converted or transformed to suit needs of user.

Sub-way underground passage to give access to platforms. American term for underground railway.

Supercharge supply air to the inlet valves of a diesel engine at above atmospheric pressure.

Superelevation see *Cant*.

Superheating increasing the temperature and volume of steam after leaving the boiler barrel by application of additional heat.

Survey map or drawing showing the layout of the ground and features or, the operation of determining a suitable route for a new railway.

Suspension connecting system, including springs, between vehicle wheel and body, designed to give best possible riding qualities by keeping unsprung weights to a minimum and reducing shock loadings on track.

Swing link metal bar pivoted at each end. Part of suspension system of many bogies and trucks.

Switch device for opening and closing an electrical circuit.

Switch American term for points.

Synchronous electric motor whose speed varies in direct proportion to the frequency of the supply.

Tachometer instrument giving a continuous indication of rotational speed of diesel engine crankshaft and so on.

Tamp to compact the ballast under sleepers by mechanical means. May be achieved by hand power tools or on-track self-propelled machines.

Tank locomotive one which carries its fuel and water supplies on its own main frames.

Tank wagon freight vehicle designed to carry liquids or gases in a tank like container.

Tap intermediate connection between the main connections of an electrical circuit or component.

Tariff list of charges.

Telecommunication means of communicating over long distances by telephone, telegraph, teleprinter or radio.

Teleprinter telegraph instrument for transmitting typewritten messages.

Tender locomotive one which carries its fuel and/or water supplies in a separate semi-permanently coupled vehicle.

Tender first tender locomotive running with tender leading in direction of travel.

Third rail non-running rail carrying electrical current to electric locomotive or train.

Three-phase simultaneous supply or use of three electrical currents of same voltage, each differing by a third in frequency cycle.

Three-way point or switch making connections to three alternative routes.

Throttle American term for regulator. Valve controlling flow of fuel to diesel engine.

Through travelling to destination without change of vehicle or line.

Ticket authority for train to enter single line section when next train over line will travel in same direction and require token. When issued with a ticket the driver must be shown the token.

Tie American term for sleeper.

Tipping wagon freight vehicle with facility for unloading contents by tilting body.

TOFC American term for a trailer on flat car.

Toe tip of switch rail at the end which fits against the stock rail.

Token authority for train to enter single

line section. Of different forms including wooden staff, electric staff, tablet, key token. Each unique and engraved with names of stations at each end of single line section to which they apply.

Tongue switch blade or rail.

Tower American term for signal box. Control centre of mechanized marshalling yard.

Trace graphical record of track alignment produced by recording instruments located in a vehicle travelling over the line.

Track circuit section of running line insulated from adjoining sections, into one end of which is fed a low-voltage electrical current with a relay connected across the rails at the other end. When the track section is unoccupied the relay is energised, but the wheel sets of a passing train produce a short circuit which leaves the relay without current. Consequent movement of the relay arm is used to make or break other electrical circuits connected to associated signalling equipment, including illuminated track diagrams, point and signal interlocking automatic colour-light signals.

Trail lamp lamp affixed to, or illuminated if an integral part of, the rear end of the last vehicle, to indicate the train is complete.

Trailing points switches which connect converging lines in direction of travel.

Train load full load conveyed by one train.

Train-pipe continuous air or vacuum brake pipe, with flexible connections between vehicles, through which operation of the train brake is controlled.

Tramway light railway or rails for tramcars.

Tramcar (American, Streetcar) electrically operated public service passenger vehicle on rails in the street.

TEE (Trans Europ Express) international European luxury express passenger services conveying only first class passengers at a supplementary fare.

Transformer device which by electromagnetic induction converts one voltage of alternating current to another.

Tranship transfer freight from one vehicle or mode of transport to another.

Transmission mechanical, hydraulic or electrical arrangement necessary with diesel traction to enable diesel engine to be run whilst locomotive is stationary and provide the necessary torque multiplication at starting. Mechanical transmission usually consists of clutch or fluid coupling, gearbox and final drive/reversing unit. Hydraulic transmissions include one or more torque convertors which may incorporate an automatic gearbox. Electric transmission consists of an alternator or generator directly coupled to the diesel engine which supplies electric current to one or more traction motors driving the locomotive wheels.

Trip means of release by knocking aside a catch.

Trolley pole mounted on roof of electric vehicle with wheel attached to outer end to pick up electric current from overhead contact wire.

Truck open railway wagon. American term for bogie on a locomotive or wagon.

Trunk main route or line of railway from which branch or feeder lines diverge.

Truss frame to carry a roof; bridge built up of members in tension or compression.

Tube railway underground railway running in a tunnel excavated by mining methods.

Turbine rotary machine consisting of one or more sets of blades attached to a shaft; driven by steam or gas flow in railway applications.

Turbo-charger turbine, driven by the flow of exhaust gases from a diesel engine, coupled to a rotary compressor which supplies air at above atmospheric pressure to the engine-inlet valves.

Turn of duty daily period of work.

Turnout simple lead consisting of one pair of switches and one crossing with intermediate closure rails.

Tyre (American, Tire) steel band forming the periphery of a wheel on which the flange and tread profile is formed.

UIC See International Union of Railways.

Ultrasonic testing non-destructive testing of components, particularly vehicle axles, by the injection of repetitive pulses of ultrasonic waves and interception of the returned echo.

Unbalanced working turn of duty or working which does not have provision for return to starting point or depot.

Underbridge underline bridge carrying the railway over a gap, road, river or whatever.

Underframe framework or structure which supports the body of a carriage or wagon.

Underground beneath the surface of the ground. Railway built below street level in large cities to avoid congestion.

Up line line over which trains normally travel towards the headquarters of the railway company concerned.

Up train one which travels on or in the direction of the up line.

Vacuum space from which air has been exhausted.

Vacuum brake braking system with atmospheric air pressure as operating medium.

Valve gear mechanism which controls the operation of the steam distribution valve in the steam chest of a locomotive cylinder.

Valve device for controlling the flow of a liquid or gas.

Van covered vehicle for conveyance of luggage, goods or use of guard.

Variable gauge vehicle or wheel set with facility for operating on more than one track gauge. Achieved by sliding wheel along axle and locking in appropriate position to suit required gauge.

Vestibule covered gangway giving access between vehicles.

Vigilance device ensures the continued vigilance or alertness of the driver by requiring him to make a positive action at frequent intervals. Failure to do so results in power being cut off and the brakes applied.

Voltage electromotive force (analogous to a pressure) measured in volts.

Waggon early type of horse drawn rail borne vehicle for conveyance of coal.

Wagon railway vehicle for the conveyance of goods.

Waist longitudinal line or structural member along carriage bodyside at window sill level. Widest part of vehicle body.

Walschaerts valve gear movement of the valve is obtained from two sources, a single eccentric or return crank and the piston crosshead. The eccentric rod is coupled to the bottom of the expansion link which pivots on trunnions at its centre. A die block slides in the link and is coupled to one end of the radius rod which is attached at the other end to the combination lever, above or below the valve spindle depending on whether inside or outside admission. Operation of the reversing gear causes the rear end of the radius rod, and therefore the die block in the expansion link to be raised or lowered, varying the cut-off and direction of locomotive travel. The lower end of the combination lever is attached to the crosshead via a union link and provides movement of the valve equal to twice the lap plus twice the lead. Unlike the Stephenson gear the lead is constant whatever the position of the reversing gear.

Water jacket space within internal combustion engine cylinder block and head in which cooling water is circulated.

Web vertical portion of rail section between foot and head.

Weighbridge weighing machine with a platform onto which a vehicle may be placed to be weighed.

Wheel arrangements a number of locomotive wheel arrangements are denoted by names, in addition to the Whyte classification or the number of axles, driven or otherwise. Names and classification are shown on page 160.

Wheel set pair of wheels secured to an axle.

Whistle steam or compressed air operated device giving a clear shrill sound. Used for giving audible warning of approach and coded messages from driver.

Whyte system of locomotive classification devised by F M Whyte based on locomotive wheel arrangement. Numerals are used to denote the number of wheels in each group, starting at the front end. Thus a tender locomotive with two-wheel leading truck, six coupled driving wheels and two-wheeled trailing truck would be 2–6–2. If a tank locomotive, the letter T is added after the last numeral, 2–6–2T.

Winding engine stationary engine driving a drum, usually located at top of steep incline. Used to haul up trains and control descending ones by means of cable or rope.

Wing rail continuous running rail forming the obtuse angle of a diamond crossing. Also running rail from switch heel towards nose which is then set to form check rail past nose of common crossing.

Working timetable timetable including all trains running over a particular route or area.

Wrong line working operation of trains over a line in the opposite direction to that which normally applies during periods of temporary blockage or maintenance of the normal line. Safety of working ensured by the introduction of a pilotman who must ride on the locomotive of all trains, or personally authorize the passage of a succession of trains in the same direction. Sometimes referred to as single line working.

Yard group of lines or sidings where auxiliary operations to train working are undertaken.

Y track tracks diverging to right and left from same point at equal radii. American term for reversing triangle.

INDEX

Page numbers in italics refer to illustrations.
Page numbers in bold type indicate major references in the text.

Acknowledgements

The publishers would like to thank the following individuals and organisations for their kind permission to reproduce the photographs in this book.

AFIP (Michel Bigot) 446–447 centre; American History Picture Library 52–53, 62 above left, 63 above and below, 158 above; Australian Information Service, London 91 above, 92–93 below, 94, 94–95 above and below, 95 above and below, 202 centre, 234, 234–235 above and below, 273, 278, 280–281, 347 above, 447; Barnaby's Picture Library 241 above; R Bastin 188, 344 below, 346 below; J C Beckett 224–225, 278–279 above; F J Bellwood 132 below left and below right, 133 centre and below, 143 below, 144 above; Berne – Lötschberg – Simplon – Bahn 186, 187 centre, 189 above left and above right, 221 centre; P S A Berridge 78 above, 215 below; The Bettman Archive 52 below left and below right, 61, 415 above, 425 left, 429 below, 444 below, 445 below right; British Railways Board 14 below, 19, 126 above, 135 below, 136–137, 137, 164 above, 190–191, 207, 209 above left, 221 above, 270–271 below, 272–273 above, 330–331 above and below, 434–435, 435 above, 436 below; Yves Broncard 27 below left, 201 below; Elmer E Burruss 343 below left; Camera Press Ltd 270–271 above, 440–441 below, (Almasy/Vauthey) 446–447 below; Canadian National Railways 354 below left, 355; Canadian Pacific 66–67, 68, 68–69, 69 below left, 110 below, 122–123 above, 143 above left, 138–139, 139 below, 147 centre, 219 below, 225, 230, 231 above, 260 below, 263 below, 264 centre right, 264–265, 390 above left, 409 above, 426 left, 436 centre; Kenneth Cantlie 79 below, 388 above centre; J Allan Cash Ltd 197 below; Central Electricity Generating Board 295 below; Chicago Transit Authority 304–305; J A Coiley 117 above, 124–125 above, 124 below, 142–143, 304 above left, 305 left, 336 centre, 340 below, 352–353 below; Colourview Picture Library 13 below right, 14 above, 46 above left, 49 below, 50, 83 above left, 87 below, 91 below left, 109 above right, 111 above, 114 above, 119, 126 below right, 131 below, 146 centre, 147 below, 164 below, 214 above right and below, 219 above, 223 centre, 232 below right, 254–255 above and below, 256, 286 above, 291, 319 below left, 321 below, 339, 345 above left, 346 above left, 348 above, 397 below, (Dr Ian C Allen) 290–291 below, (Sir Peter Allen) 294 below, 314 above, (W J V Anderson) 24, (Derek Cross) 316 left, (M V E Dunn Collection) 158 below, (J M Jarvis) 150 above left and above right, 177, 182 below, 187 below, 203, (D P Morgan) 410 above, (H Nave) 111 below, (R C Riley) 396 above, (E S Russell) 334–335 above, (Brian Stephenson) 342 below left, (R Watson) 345 above right, (C M Whitehouse) 36–37, 37 above and below, 38 below left, 47 above and below right, 79 above right, 80 above, 319 below right, 430–431 below; (Patrick B Whitehouse) 38 above, 46 above right, 78 below, 87 above, 88–89, 89 above, 122–123 below, 146 above, 183, 214 above left and centre, 315 above, 318 below, 319 above, 349 below, 351 above right and centre, 354 above, 357 above, (Patrick B Whitehouse Collection) 15 below left and right, 134 above right, 167 above, 171 below right, 175 below, 227 above right, 287 below, 346–347; Thomas Cook Ltd 406 left; C P Cooper 325; Cooper Bridgeman Library 9 above right and below, 10, 11 above and below, 13 above and below left, 15 above, 21 above, 101 below, 328 below, 432–433; Coras Iompair Eireann 46 below; J R Day 300 below, 304 centre left and below left; Deutsche Bundesbahn 33 below, 129 below, 240 below left; EMI Elstree Studios Ltd 376, 376–377 above, 377 above and below; Mary Evans Picture Library 23 above and below, 29 above right, 91 below right, 103 below, 106–107 below, 130 below, 130–131, 169 below, 185 above, 190 below, 329 centre, 331 above and centre, 332 below, 400 above, 406 right, (Illustrated London News) 143 centre right; Falmer/Bruce Coleman Ltd 428 below; Brian Fawcett 73 centre, 75 below, 147 above right, 174, 313 above and below; M H Finch 72 below right; FPG 200–201, 201 above, (Bill Patterson) 332 above right; Fujiphotos 223 below, 380 above; C J Gammell 2–3, 4–5, 71 above, 76, 77 above, below and centre, 85 above right, 86 below, 87 centre, 88, 89 below, 121 above, 176 above, 238 above, 238–239, 239 below right, 248 left, 250–251, 255 above left, 312 below, 324, 329 above, 347 below, 348 below, 349 above, 356 above, 357 centre, 358–359, 376–377 below; Victor Goldberg 16–17 below, 69 above right, 113 above left, 231 below left and below right, 247 centre above, 249 above, 314 below, 335 above, 341 centre, 354 below right; Victor Goldberg Collection 109 above left and below, (Photo M Holford) 128 below, 140 above left; S Gooders (Guildhall Library) 268–269 above; John Gorman Collection 16 above; R Griffen 358 below left, 408; Victor Hand 25 below, 44 above, 64 above, 81 above, 84, 105 below, 113 centre, 118 above, 120 above, 180 above, 194–195 above, 196, 200, 213 below, 217 below, 247 below, 276–277 above and below, 417; Helsinki Rapid Transit Authority 303 above; Ken Hoole 445 below left; Angelo Hornak 18 above; John Huntley 362 left and right, 363 above and below, 364–365 below, 370–371; Alan Hutchison Library 86 above, 278–279 below; Illustrated London News 315 below; Imperial War Museum 380–381, 381 above and below, 384–385 above, below and centre, 385, 386 above and centre, 386–387, 387 above, 388 above and below, 389 above, above centre, below centre and below, 390 below, 390–391, 392, 393 above and below right, 396 below, 397 above; Government of India Tourist Office 114–115, 139 above, 142, 143 above right, 143 centre left, Interfoto 238 below, 431 above; Italian State Railways 283, 318 centre, 322 below; Japan Information Centre 83 below, 226 below, 242, 242–243, 243 below and centre left; J M Jarvis 69 above left and below right; D Jenkinson 105 centre below, 116–117 centre, 125, 144 below, 145 above and below, 240 below right, 341 above, 353 below; Keystone Press Agency 243 above left and centre right, 301 below, 394 above and below, 395, 396–397, 402 above, 407 left, 442–443; Kobal Collection 372 above; Leicester County Museum 12 above and below; Loco Pulser 282–283; London Transport 297 above and below, 299; Mansell Collection 53 below, 56 centre, 444 above; L G Marshall 42–43 below, 44 below, 79 above left, 85 above left, 118 below left, 122 above, 173 below right, 274 below, 295 above right, 329 below; Melbourne Underground Rail Loop Authority 308 above, 309 above; Merseyside County Museums 100; Metro Helsinki 303 below, 311; Metropolitana Milanese 303 centre; Middleton Railway Trust 443 below; Ken Mills 70, 71 below and centre, 72 above left, 74 above and below, 75 above left and above right, 120 below, 122 below, 134–135, 146 below, 182–183, 216, 224 below right, 253 below, 288 above and below, 290 above, 294–295, 327 above, 436 above; J G Moore Collection 399 left, 402 below, 415 below, 418, 422 above, 423 right, 424 left, 439 below; Montreal Urban Community Transit Commission 306 above left; Andrew Morland 14 centre, 133 above; Moscow Metropolitan Railway 338 above; Murray 293 above; Museum of British Transport (Cooper Bridgeman) 438 below; National Coal Board 208, (J G Moore Collection) 268–269 below; National Film Archives, Stills Library 364 above and below, 365 above left, above right and below, 366 above left, above right and below, 366–367, 367 above, 368 above right and above left, 369 above left, above right, below left, below right and centre, 370 above left and above right, 371 above left and above right, 372 below, 373 above left and above right, 374 above left, above right and below, 375 above and below; National Gallery (Cooper Bridgeman) 429 above; National Railway Museum 106–107 above, 108 above right, 109 above, 108–109, 126 below left, 127 below left, 135 above, 140 above right, 268 below right, 380 below, 400 below, 405 centre, 414 below, 416 right, (Wagon-Lits) 140 below left and below right, 232 above and centre, 233, Netherlands Railways 42–43 above and centre, 327 below, 351 above left; Department of Railways, New South Wales 90 below left and below right; Public Transport Commission of New South Wales 308–309; New Zealand Railways 96–97 above and below, 97 below right, 98 above, 98–99 below, 99 above, 110 above, 112, 120–121, 216–217, 222 above left, 227 below, 279, 340 above, 354 centre; L A Nixon 6–7, 18 below, 178–179, 179, 191 above left and above right, 251 below, 343 above, below right and centre, 431 below, 352–353 above, 353 above, 358 above left, 359 above and below; O S Nock 256–257, 257 above left, 258 below, 258–259; Nordisk Pressefoto 49 above; Ed Novak 171 centre, 247 centre below; Novosti Press Agency 40 above right, 245 below; Photri 54–55 above, 60–61 below, 62 below, 126 centre, 140–141, 184 below, 249 below, 253 centre left, 260–261, 262–263 above, 271 below, 282 above left, (Santa Fe Railway) 274–275 above and below; Pilatus Railway, Lucerne, Switzerland 316 right, 317 above and centre, 322 above, 323 above and below, 437 above; K P Plant 272 above; Popperfoto 244, 326–327, 332 above left 336 below, 374–375, 393 below left, 440–441 above, 441 right, 446; F L Pugh 72 above right, 73–74 below, 284, 285 above, 286 below, 289, 292 above, 292–293 below, 344 above, 360 centre, 361 above; Radio Times Hulton Picture Library 16–17 above, 17, 30 below, 54 above right and below, 56 above, 57, 90 above, 134 above left, 184 above, 202 left, 227 above left, 232 below left, 296, 364–365 above, 390 above right, 391 below right; Rapho Agence de Presse 237; Rex Features 129 above left and above right, 356 below, 435 below; Rhaetian Railway, Switzerland 218–219 below; G R Roberts 93 below, 97 above right, 217 above, 281 below, 285 below, 337 below right, 437 centre; Peter Roberts 20; D Rodgers 357 below left, 358 above right and below right; Ronan Picture Library 53 above, 54–55 below, 60–61 above, 158–159 above, 165 above, 379 below, 399 right, 410 below, 437 below, 443 above; Royal Holloway College (Cooper Bridgeman) 428 above; Santa Fe Railway Co 59 above and below right, 62 above right, 64 below, 65, 108 above left, 175 above, 206–207, 210–211, 213 above; SATOUR 228 above and below, 229 below; Schweizerische Wagons – und – Aufzugefabric Schlieren, Zurich 147 above left, 302 above; The Director, Science Museum, London 8, 9 above left, 150–151, 151 above left and above right, 158–159 below, 159 below, 164 centre above and centre below, 167 below, 168–169, 171 below left, 172 above, below and centre, 172–173, 173 below left, 184–185, 187 above, 206, 398 below, 403 left, 404, 405 above left and below, 407 right, 412 below left and below right, 413, 419, 420 right, 422 right, 423 left, 424 right, 425 left, 442, (Michael Holford) 148–149, 154 below left and below right, 414 above, 420 left, 421 right, 440 above left; SNCF 1, 26, 26–27, 113 below, 197 above, 211 above left and right, 218–219 below, 220 above, 255 below, 262–263, 272–273 below, 282 above right, 301 above, 341 below, (Denihal) 236–237 below, 268 below left, (Dewolf) 236–237 above, (Lambert) 116–117 below, (Mazo) 281 above; Société Nationale des Chemins de Fer Belges, Brussels 401, 426 right; Spectrum Colour Library 336 above, 346 above right; Brian Stephenson 25 above, 27 below right, 32 below left and below right, 32–33, 35 above left and above right, 36 above and below, 40 above left, 43, 44–45, 45 above, 47 below left, 48 above and below, 50–51 above and below, 51, 199 below, 224 above, 241 below; Allan Stewart 350 below; Stockcolour International 297 centre; Suddeutscher Verlag 28, 29 above left and below, 30 above, 31 above, above left, above right and below, 72 below left, 73 above, 130 above, 131 above, 218, 239 below left, 312 above, 367 below, 382 above, 382–383 above and below, 383, 388 centre below, 392–393; Swiss National Tourist Office 190 above, 222 above right, 223 above, 317 below, 320 below, 350 above, 409 below, 421 centre; Swiss Locomotive and Machine Works, Winterthur, Switzerland 403 right; R E B Switer 84–85, 360 below; RTZ Photographic Library 287 above, (Hammersley Iron Pty Ltd) 266, 434; John Topham Picture Library (Fotogram/Cabaud) 21 centre, 22; Toronto Transit Commission 306–307; P N Trotter 18–19, 113 above right, 118–119 below, 121 below, 127 below right, 136 below right, 185 below, 209 below, 210 above left and above right, 211 below, 212, 212–213, 220 below, 222 below, 232–233, 271 above, 298 above and below, 326, 342 below right, 345 below, 357 below right, 361 below, 412 above, 420 left, 438 above; Tramweg – Stichting, Holland 351 below; R R Tweetsie 352; Ullstein GMBH 416 left; Union Pacific 54 above left, 55, 56 below, 430–431 above, 432; USIS 102 below, 445 above; US National Archives 378 above and below; J T Van Riemsdijk 159 above, 162 above, below and centre, 165 centre, 168 above, 169 above, 170 above left, above right, below and centre, 171 above left and above right, 178, 180 below left and below right, 181 above left, below left and above right, 182 above, 446–447 above; La Vie du Rail 101 above, 116, 128 above, 236, (J N Westwood) 244–245, 245 above; Patrick Watters 215 above, 333 above left, above right and below, 334, 335 below left, 337 above and below left, 338–339; Wengernalp – Jungfrau – Bahn, Switzerland 318 above, 320 above; Western Americana Picture Library 58, 59 below left, 60 above, 379 above; Westinghouse Brake and Signal Co Ltd 427; J N Westwood 33 above, 34, 35 below, 38 below right, 39 above and below, 40 below, 41 above and below, 42, 82 above and below, 83 above right, 92 below, 92–93 above, 93 above, 174–175, 181 below right, 202 below, 209 centre, 221 below, 226 above, 258 above, 330, 335 below right, 439 above; J S Whiteley 124–125 below, 176–177, 321 above; Weiner Stadtwerke 302 below; William R Wilson 270, Peter Winding 194–195 below, 195, 202–203; J S Winkeley 209 above right, 224 below left; Ian Yearsley 274 above, 277.